Biographies and Burial Sites
of
Free Will Baptist Ministers

VOLUME TWO

Compiled
by

Dr. Alton E. Loveless

Copyright 2018
By
Dr. Alton E. Loveless

ISBN **978-1985669949** Soft cover

VOLUME TWO

To order additional copies of this book, contact:

FWB Publications
Alton.loveless@prodigy.net

Or

WWW.Amazon.Com

Published by
FWB Publications

Cover photo:
Large tall tombstone is of famous preacher Elias Hutchins in Stafford cemetery, New Hampshire.
Small one in front of his is Marilla Marks Hutchings. First wife of David Marks.

Table of Contents

Volume Two
This Volume Contains 1394 Locations
List Of States Continues

Editors Remarks

This edition has 1394 burial locations covering New Mexico to Wisconsin from one of the oldest denominations in the United States and covers a vast range of ministers who set the pace for growth and change where they were. In the north this movement were abolitionist and active in the Underground Railroad and began training schools to teach the freeman as they came from the south after the Civil War. They were stronger than the southern groups in establishing colleges and active in government. But every territory had its own story to tell. This book will share these messages.

This edition will include additional women ministers or missionaries from every area of the country and abroad.

I have found the history of every minister fascinating. I know you will also.

This book represents the National Association, Randall Movement that united with the Northern Baptists in 1911, the Stone, John-Thomas, John Wheeler Assn's, North Carolina Original Free Will Baptists and unidentifiable affiliations.

Many of the photos are poor quality, but it was all I had. Likewise, I do not have photos or tombstones for many of them. The information about these ministers were all that was available to me or found in archives. I made every effort to include those from which they would be remembered. Some I had no information, but research had shown they were of our denomination. Others were with the National Association but left and I included their contribution to the movement.

There were some that somewhere, sometime, someone within these movements contributed to what we are today. It was not my purpose to promote any single group, but to let history present its own case. Likewise, the length of the column of the person does not denote the lesser or greater value of the person.

There are many words not spelled correctly, but were taken from the text of the history or book written about the person. E.g. Freewill, Free Baptist, Free Communion Baptists, Free Will Baptists, etc.. In different periods clergy were addressed as Elder, Rev., Dr. etc. I have made every effort to make it reliable, grammatically correct, but errors still reflect the time.

The sources used for accumulating these hundreds of men and women; were found in graveyard records, county histories, church records, genealogies, biographies, Google research, valuable denomination resource materials such as: Cyclopedia of Free Baptists, pub. 1889 by Burgess and Ward. The Native Ministry of New Hampshire, published by Rev. N. F. Carter, 1906 and reprinted by FWB Publications, 2014. There is no way I could remember all of the resources used. But it is the product of hundreds of hours and the help of others to put these two volumes together.

Please advise me at alton.loveless@prodigy.net to help me make the corrections for future editions.

We have a story to tell. Let us do it while we can.

Dr. Alton E. Loveless

New Mexico

Lester C. Pinson
Birth:
Mar. 14, 1917
Death:
Jul. 7, 1963
Burial:
Carlsbad Cemetery, Carlsbad,
Eddy County,New Mexico,
Plot: Division F

New York

Asa G Abbott
Birth:
Sep. 11, 1803
Death:
Feb. 11, 1877
German, N. Y.
Burial:
Westview Cemetery
German Four Corners,
Chenango County, New York

Abbott, Rev. A. G., a native of Pennsylvania. He entered the ministry with the Methodists at an early age, but later moved to Chenango Co., N. Y., and spent the last twenty years of his ministry with the Free Baptists of the McDonough. M. His faith in God survived many afflictions. He was an earnest, thoughtful preacher..

John J Allen
Birth:
1822
Death:
May 26, 1899
Burial:
Old Depauville Cemetery
Depauville
Jefferson County,
New York

He was educated at Whitestown Seminary and Biblical School. He began to preach in 1849 and was ordained in September 1853. He baptized about 300 converts during his ministry in the area where he had served so long. For 20 years he served as the clerk and treasurer of the Jefferson Quarterly Meeting.

Adon Aldrich
Birth:
Jul. 22, 1795
Uxbridge
Worcester County,
Massachusetts
Death:
Jul. 20, 1853
Ashford
Cattaraugus County,
New York
Burial:
Bond Cemetery
Springville
Cattaraugus County,
New York

He was a minister in the Ontario quarterly meeting in New York State. In 1827 went to Chenango County, where he preached and established the Norwich and New Berlin churches.

Albert A. Armstrong
Birth:
1848
Cuba, Allegany County, New York
Death:
1937
Great Valley,
Cattaraugus County,
New York
Burial:
Willoughby Cemetery,
Great Valley,
Cattaraugus County, New York

Albert was educated at the Pike Seminary in Tenbroeck, New York. He received his license to preach in the Free Will Baptist Church in 1869. The year after his conversion, he was ordained by the Cattaraugus Quarterly Meeting June 11, 1878. Except for a few years in Pennsylvania around

1900, his ministry was continued in Western New York State.

As A Well-Spent Day Brings Happy Sleep, So A Life Well Used Brings Happy Death.

Dr George Harvey Ball
Birth:
Dec. 7, 1819
Sherbrooke, Canada
Death:
Feb. 20, 1907
Burial:
Forest Lawn Cemetery
Buffalo
Erie County, New York
Plot: Section 3

Ball, who was the son of William and Marcy (Harvey) Ball, had his early days in Massachusetts. In 1836 they removed to Ohio, where, while making a home in the wilderness for the family, his used the time to study systematically the evenings until ten o'clock, under the guidance of his mother, and when twenty years of age commenced teaching. During that winter Rev. Ransom Dunn, holding meetings in the schoolhouse, said to him, "Do you think it reasonable and right to serve God?" "Yes," he replied. "And you aim to be a reasonable man do you not?" "Most certainly." "Then you will serve God of course," said the preacher, and passed on. The appeal to reason

prevailed, where other appeals had failed. After about two years at Farmington Academy, he spent two years more at Grand River Institute, and preached occasionally in the vicinity, receiving license to preach from the Ashtabula Q.M. in 1843. The next year he went to Ontario, Can., to teach, but was kept constantly at preaching for more than a year, and enjoyed several revivals. He then attended the Biblical School at Whitestown, graduating in 1847. The following year he was married to Maria L. Bensly and entered upon a three years' pastorate at Chester, O. A part of this time he was principal of Geauga Seminary, and numbered James A. Garfield among his pupils. In 1851 he went to Buffalo, N. Y., to plant a church. After four years he settled with the Roger Williams church, Providence, R. I., but soon returned to Buffalo to save the interest there. In 1870 he became New York editor of *The Morning Star,* and the next year editor of the *Baptist Union.* In 1877 he returned to Buffalo Where he still remains pastor of a flourishing church planted by himself. Bro. Ball has always been a diligent student and an indefatigable worker. He received the degree of Doctor of Divinity from Bates College, Me. He has published several small books of merit, and wrote extensively for the religious and secular press. As a preacher he is argumentative, pungent and direct; as a pastor, sympathetic and helpful. He had a wide influence in the denomination, having served as Trustee of Storer College from its foundation, and of Hillsdale College also, except one term; and being now a member of the Foreign Mission and Conference

Boards. In 1886 he visited the General Baptists of England, for the General Conference. His daughter Julia was a graduate of Packer College, Brooklyn, N. Y.,. and Ella J., since completed the Classical Course at Hillsdale College, and for some eight years was lady-principal of Pike Seminary, N. Y.

Rev Laban Eli Bates
Birth:
Jul. 10, 1820
Ellisburg
Jefferson County
New York
Death:
Aug. 14, 1896
Fabius
Onondaga County
New York
Burial:
Fabius Evergreen Cemetery
Fabius
Onondaga County
New York

Rev. Laban Eli Bates, son of Liberty and Mary (Russell) Bates, was born July 10, 1820. He was led to Christ in 1838, began to preach in 1844, and was ordained in 1849.

He first united with the Congregational church in Norway, NY, but was soon baptized and has since taught and practiced baptism by immersion. He engaged in evangelistic work with success, and later ministered to the West Camden church eleven years, and the Florence and Redfield church five years. In 1871, he united with the Free Baptists, and has been pastor at Fabius five years at Potter four years, Cowlesville three years, and at Marilla, six years, the last four begin devoted exclusively to the Marilla church. In these fields his labors have been blessed of God.

Bro. Bates has always taken advanced positions on all moral questions. As an abolitionist, he voted for Birney, with the "third party"; and in temperance work he is a staunch prohibitionist.

Feb. 19, 1849, he married Caroline D. Bronson, who passed to rest May 30, 1868. Their oldest son, since deceased, graduated from Cornell University; Charles P. practices law at Sioux Falls, Dak; Carrie is a missionary in New York City, and the four other daughters have engaged in teaching.

Sept. 19, 1874, he married Anne S. Dudley of Kingsfield, Maine.

Velorus Beebe

Birth:
Sep. 10, 1810
Cuba, Allegany County,
New York
Death:
May 28, 1879
Friendship,
Allegany County, New York
Burial:
Richburg Cemetery,
Richburg, Allegany County,
New York

He commenced preaching at 18 years of age in Yates County. Travelling as an evangelist he held meetings in many places in Ohio and Michigan. After this he ministered to the church in Bradford, New York, fourteen years; in E. Troy, Pennsylvania, two years; in Veteran, New York, two years, and Wert and Boliver fourteen years. Revivals, some

quite extensive in these places. He represented the New York and Pennsylvania Y.M.in the General Conferences of 1847 and 1850.

Rev Justus L Bingham

Birth:
1819
Death:
Jan. 21, 1853
Summerhill
Cayuga County
New York, USA
Burial:
Indian Mound Cemetery
Moravia
Cayuga County
New York

Rev. Justus L. Bingham, was suddenly killed at Summer Hill, N.Y., about 1853. He was ordained by the Jefferson Quarterly Meeting, in 1845, and labored in that vicinity for a time, and later in the south part of the state.

A native NY Freewill Baptist minister, ordained in 1845. He died young from an accident.

Rev Elijah F. Bliven

Birth:
Jun. 30, 1815
Death:
Sep. 11, 1894
Burial:
Rogersville Forest Lawn Cemetery
Dansville
Steuben County
New York
Plot: SD 13

Ordained in 1848 by the Methodist Episcopal church, and united with the Free Baptists in 1873. He worked in revivals and building of several churches.

What is your life? You are a mist that appears for a little while and then vanishes" (James 4:14b).

Rev Charles Bowles

Birth:
1761
Boston
Suffolk County
Massachusetts
Death:
Mar. 16, 1843
Malone
Franklin County
New York
Burial:
Constable Cemetery
Constable
Franklin County
New York

Located through Northern New York Tombstone Transcriptions.

Erected to the memory of Rev. Charles BOWLES. A Soldier of the Revolution and for more than 40 years a successful Minister of one Gospel in the Freewill Baptist Connection. He departed this life in Malone, March 16, 1843, AE 82 Y'rs.

Elder Bowles was the founding pastor of a number of Baptist churches in Vermont. His biography can be read on line.

John W. Lewis, The Life,Labors, and Travels of Elder Charles Bowles, of the Free Will Baptist Denomination, (Watertown MA, 1852). submitted by Rev. John Burbank, clerk of the First Baptist Church of Starksboro VT

Daniel Brown

Birth:
unknown
Death:

Aug. 5, 1882
Dayton, N. Y.
Burial:
Parklawn Cemetery
Wesley, Cattaraugus County,
New York

At the age of twenty-one he professed religion, and united with the Hamburg, N. Y., church. Soon after his marriage to Miss Fanny Perham, in 1841, he moved to Boston, N. Y., and in 1848 to Dayton. He was ordained in 1860. His ministry was confined to the Cattaraugus and Erie Q. M's and was characterized by earnestness, fidelity and self-sacrifice. Aged 69 years 19 days

Nathaniel Brown

Birth:
Apr. 7, 1765,
Warren
Litchfield County,
Connecticut
Death:
Sep. 2, 1844
Bethany Center,
Genesee County,
New York
Burial:
West Bethany Cemetery,
West Bethany,
Genesee County,
New York,
Plot: New Section

He was ordained by the Stratford Association June 27, 1802 and after six years of successful ministry moved in 1808 to Bethany, New York where he purchased a large tract of land and build a sawmill and grist mill. He organized the Bethany Church, the first Free Will Baptist Church west of the Genesee river and remained its pastor until his death for a period of 30 years. Besides this work in New York, he assisted in the organization of the Ohio yearly meeting. He was a prominent member of the first Gen. Conference and did much to shape the policy for its future years. Nathaniel was a Revolutionary War veteran. He Enlisted in the Strafford, Orange County, Vermont.

Rev Adam B. Bullock

Birth:
Jul. 9, 1806, USA
Death:
Apr. 14, 1848
Montgomery County
New York
Burial:
Morris Family Burial Ground
Ames
Montgomery County
New York

Rev. Adam B. Bullock, died aged 41 years. He was converted sixteen years before, attended Hamilton Theological Seminary, spent some time in teaching, and was ordained in 1841.
He labored with the Canajoharie and Ames churches, saw many additions, and was much respected. His gentleness of spirit endeared him to the people. His loss was deeply felt.

Rev Benjamin Bundy

Birth:
1796
Connecticut
Death:
Aug. 25, 1870
Burial:
River View Cemetery
Willisville
St. Lawrence County, New York

He was a native of Conn, d. in W. Parishville, NY, aged 74 years. He was converted in Randolph, VT, and at age 25, mar. Miss Betsey Kibber. He soon began to preach, and was ordained by Elders Kimball and Hall, in Bershire, VT.
Inscription:
Age 74

William C Byer

Birth:
1814
Eaton
Madison County, New York
Death:
Oct. 30, 1868
Fabius
Onondaga County, New York
Burial:
Fabius Evergreen Cemetery
Fabius, Onondaga County,
New York

Rev. Byer, Sr., was a native of Eaton, NY. While attending school in Clinton (NY) he became acquainted with Miss Samantha Ward, who became his wife and helper through life. Her influence was instrumental in leading him to Christ.He was ordained in 1842 to the Freewill Baptist ministry, and labored in Union Yearly Meeting until about 1856, when he became connected with the Burlington Flats Church. He held many protracted meetings and baptized, during his ministry, about five hundred converts. As a preacher he was warm-hearted and earnest. He never feared to rebuke sin, yet was kind and benevolent.The son, William C., Jr., also became a Free Baptist minister. He mar. Inez K. Smith Oct. 18, 1876. He was educated at Whitestown Seminary and received ordination in 1883, taking charge of the North Scriba FB church, where he continued some years. He enjoyed the esteem of his people.

Elder Chester Chaffee
Birth:
Oct. 7, 1791
Death:
Sep. 5, 1876
Arcade, N. Y.
Burial:
Arcade Rural Cemetery
Arcade, Wyoming County,
New York

Chaffee, a native of Grafton, Vt., died at age 85 years. In 1816 he moved to Boston, N. Y., where he served the church as deacon. After fourteen years he moved to Arcade, receiving ordination in 1832, and was connected with the China, Hume and Elton churches. He was a reliable man, faithfulto the trusts committed to him. Parents: David Chaffee (1765–1835) and Anna Johnson (1771–1827)1st Spouse: Abigail _ (1793–1827)2nd Spouse: Mrs. Lydia Jackson (?-1869)

Daniel Chase
Birth:
Unknown
Death:
Mar. 2, 1850
Mount Pleasant, NY
Burial:
West Windsor Cemetery
West Windsor
Broome County, New York

Rev. Daniel Chase, born about 1771-72, and died at age 79 years.He began his ministry about 1800, Elder Randall assisting in his ordination. He labored in New Hampshire and Vermont, and in 1816, removed to Jackson, Pennsylvania, being, it is thought, the first minister of the denomination to settle in that state. He rendered faithful service in Susquehanna and Wayne Counties, Pennsylvania, and in Broome County, New York. He represented the Gibson Q.M. Pennsylvania at the organization of the Susquahanna Yearly Meeting.

Elbridge Gerry Cilley
Birth:
Feb. 19, 1821
Danbury
Merrimack County
New Hampshire
Death:
Dec. 26, 1901
Bolton
Warren County
New York
Burial:
Cilley - Pratt
Warren County
New York, USA

Elbridge Cilley, aged about eighty years, a resident of Bolton, died Saturday, at the home of his son-in-law, Lawrence Pratt. Mr. Cilley was twice married. His first wife was Miss Sylvia Phelps (1825-69); his second. Mrs. Nancy Hill Bidwell (1830-). He Is survived by three sons and one daughter, Frank, Fremont and Stephen Cilley and Mrs. Lawrence Pratt, all of Bolton. Deceased is also survived by four step-daughters, Mrs. Jane Ann Turner, Mrs. Alexander Pratt. Mrs. Samuel Harrington and Miss Belle Bidwell, The funeral was held Saturday at the Lamb school house.
Grave unmarked
  Parents:

Stephen Cilley (1798 - 1861)
Cyrene King Cilley (1801 - 1863)
Spouse:
Nancy H. Hill Cilley (1830 - 1895)
Children:
Benjamin Cilley (1846 - 1917)*
Frank P. Cilley (1853 - 1908)*
Fremont Cilley (1857 - 1937)*
Adeline Cilley Pratt (1859 - 1943)*
Sibling:
Elbridge Gerry Cilley (1821 - 1901)
Serena K Cilley Pratt (1832 - 1860)*

Ardon Cobb
Birth:
1802
New York
Death:
Aug. 10, 1868
Burial:
Overackers Cemetery
Middlesex,
Yates County,
New York

He became a minister after a conversion in 1833, ordained 1840. His labors were with the Danville, Middlesex, North Potter, Sparta, Italy, Scottsburg and Jerusalem churches. He was earnest and active in the work. The Middlesex church especially was blessed under his efforts. His devotion found expression in the frequent inquiry, "How can I render the most efficient service to Christ?".-

Isaiah Bangs Coleman
Birth:
Mar. 7, 1809
Stephentown
Rensselaer County,
New York
Death:
Mar. 14, 1883
West Stephentown
Rensselaer County,
New York
Burial:
Hillside Cemetery
Stephentown,
Rensselaer County,
New York

Coleman died of paralysis at his home age 74 years. He was converted when but a boy, and baptized by Rev. John Allen. His facilities for education were limited, but his studious habits and thirst for knowledge soon prepared him to serve as a teacher for ten years; an advantage to himself, as well as others. May 1, 1834, he married Miss Ann V. Dunham, his companion through life. May 10 of the same year he was licensed to preach, and March 25, 1835, was ordained. He labored with the old Stephentown and Sand Lake churches until Jan. 6, 1844, when he became pastor of the West Stephentown church, then having fifty-eight members. He remained its pastor thirty-nine years, and left it at his death a flourishing church of 180 members, a living testimony to the faithful service rendered. Of those who united with his own church, he baptized 225, besides many who went to other churches. It is said that he married over fourteen hundred couples. Few ministers have attended more funerals than he. His charities were generous and frequent. He was a strong advocate of temperance and all virtues. His modest, unassuming spirit, together with home duties, confined his helpful influence to narrower limits, though he served as delegate to the General Conference a number of times. On March 3 he told his wife he had had a shock, and could be with her but a short time. In less than an hour his power of speech was gone, and in a few days a vast multitude gathered around his bed, attesting the high esteem in which he was held by the community.He was a teacher, storekeeper, postmaster and minister of the Church he helped found.

Ashel J Cooley
Birth:
July 6, 1826.
Death:
Sep. 25, 1905
Point Peninsula
Jefferson County, N. Y.
Burial:
Woodlawn Cemetery
Elmira
Chemung County, New York

He was married in September, 1846, to Miss Rachel Leonard, and in January,1865, was baptized, uniting with the Three-Mile Bay church, of which his wife was a member. He was ordained June 7, 1874, by the Jefferson Q. M., and was pastor of the Three-Mile Bay church a brief period. He has since served as city missionary at Ithaca, N. Y., in 1880, and as pastor at Dryden, 1881-83; at Stephentown Center, 1883-85, and for a time at Hadley. Died at 82 yrs, 10 mos, 3days Utica, NY

Rev Oliver L. Cooper
Birth:
Oct. 10, 1846
New York
Death:
1933
Burial:
Riverview Cemetery
Oxford
Chenango County
New York

Served in the military, and afterward, ordained to the ministry March 13, 1881. He was a pastor in German, Willet, and East McDonough churches.
In 1871, he was married to Carrie Blanchard. They had the following children:

Amos Daniels
Birth:
Aug. 23, 1787
Hartford,
Hartford County,

Connecticut
Death:
Apr. 29, 1873
Burial:
Vestal Park Cemetery,
Vestal,
Broome County, New York

He worked with the Methodists as a licensed preacher, but because of his views on baptism they did not ordain him, and he united with the Free Baptists, receiving ordination at the Owego Q.M. in 1822. He was pastor of the Virgil and Dryden church twenty-five years, reorganized the Dryden church and was its pastor twelve years; organized the Fabius church and was its pastor several years and was also pastor at Jackson, East Troy and other points. He labored extensively in the Susquehanna Yearly Meeting as an evangelist, witnessing many revivals during his ministry. His ministry was over 51 years, and full of usefulness.

Freeman Darte
Birth:
1804
Death:
Jan. 22, 1883
Yorkshire,
Cattaraugus County, New York
Burial:
Delevan Cemetery,
Delevan,
Cattaraugus County, New York

He lived in the Cattaraugus, Yorkshire, area, and farmed to support his family. Freeman was a member, clerk, and then preacher of The First Free Will Baptist Church of East Randolph, NY. He consecrated his life to Christ in 1832, was licensed to preach about 1837 and ordained about 1842, in the Freewill Baptist Church. He was a faithful minister, laboring with good acceptance in many churches of the Erie and Cattaraugus Q.M.'s.

Ira Day
Birth:
Oct. 6, 1818
Burlington, New York

Death:
Jul. 29, 1883
Fabius, New York
Burial:
Willet Cemetery
Willet, Cortland County,
New York

He was converted when thirteen years of age, and joined the Free Baptists soon after moving to Willet, in 1856. He soon began to preach, and ultimately became pastor of the Willet church. Three years before at his death he settled with the Fabius church, which was blessed under his labors. He was a devoted Christian, giving his service and his wealth to the Lord. A gift of $500 to the Norwich church is worthy of special notice. The Central Association, of which he was a trustee, honored him with resolutions of esteem. Spouse: Susannah Whitmore Day (1818 - 1880).

Inscription:
For we know if our earthly house of this tabernacle were dissolved, we have a   building of God an house not made with hands, eternal in the   heavens.
2 Corinthians 5:1

Zebulon Dean
Birth:
1779
New York
Death:
Dec. 4, 1883
Yates County, New York
Burial:
Evergreen Cemetery, Dresden,

Yates County, New York
Zebulon settled early in Yates Co., and was ordained a Free Will Baptist minister in 1813, probably in Benton church. It's influence and interest extended over a territory of forty miles in diameter along the western shores of Lake Seneca. He pastored that church and at Barrington in 1829, a church he helped organize in 1819. His ministry was in the surrounding towns and villages In 1819, he with Samuel WIRE, then a licensed preacher, heard that David Marks, a boy preacher of fifteen, was in need of spiritual consolation at Junius, so they went thirty miles and encouraged David and baptized him July 11. Marks was soon afterwards associated in revival meetings with Rev. Dean, who had helped him. In 1829, Rev. Dean attended the third General Conference, at Spafford, N.Y.

Behold I Come Quickly And Every Eye Shall See Me!

Rev Jacob Decker
Birth:
1808
Death:
Jan. 12, 1865
Buena Vista, N. Y
Burial:
Baker Farm Cemetery
Canisteo
Steuben County
New York

He was a native of Spencer, N. Y., and experienced religion at Urbana in 1830. He soon began to preach and was ordained in 1835. He spent most of his ministerial life as an itinerant in southwestern New York and northern Pennsylvania, where he saw much of God's power in the quickening of professors and in the conversion of sinners. He was a man of an excellent spirit.

Manoah Delling
Birth:
1782
New Hampshire
Death:
Jul. 30, 1851
Wayne County, New York
Burial:
Zurich Cemetery
Arcadia
Wayne County, New York

Manoah was a Baptist minister who eventually settled in Lyons, NY
Ordained in New York soon after 1820, and labored there in the Free Baptist church.

Oscar Hanning Denney
Birth:
Jul. 10, 1860
Gallia County, Ohio
Death:
Jan. 7, 1945
Canandaigua
Ontario County, New York
Burial:
Borden-Elk Creek Cemetery
Borden
Steuben County, New York

He was born near Rio Grande, Ohio and was converted in 1869 after which he pursued studies at Rio Grande college and for a season at Hillsdale in Michigan. He received his license to preach in 1879 and was ordained on December 17, 1882. He pastored a number of churches in Ohio before moving to the state of New York where several revivals attended his labors. He also assisted in the organizing of four churches.

Amasa Dodge
Birth:
1768
New London County, Connecticut
Death:
Aug. 13, 1850
Lewis County, New York
Burial:
West Lowville Rural Cemetery
West Lowville
Lewis County, New York

He was ordained that Lowville, New York, April 4, 1818. He was an exhorter rather than a sermonizer; a true man, devoted to the cause of the Master, yet conservative; and when the Free Communion Baptists united with the Free Will Baptist, he, almost alone opposed the union, yet his integrity was never questioned.

Asa Dodge
Birth:
Apr. 14, 1799
Ludlow, Hampden County, Massachusetts
Death:
Aug. 2, 1877
New York
Burial:
Nanticoke Valley Cemetery
Union Center, Broome County, New York

Rev. Asa Dodge was the son of Asa and Sarah Dodge--one of four sons who were Freewill Baptists ministers [Edward E., Gurley, Calvin and Asa] In 1806, this family settled in New Concord

(now Lisbon) N.H. At age 13 yrs, with his brother Edward E, he conducted meetings in which several were converted. He was baptized by Rev. J. Quinby and united with Sugar Hill Church. He attended Morse Academy in Hanover four years, when his family moved to NY. He then entered upon the active life of the ministry. He was licensed by Owego Quarterly Meeting in 1821, and ordained the next year. The first Free Baptist meeting in Troy, NY was held by him in 1822. The Owega QM owes much to him for its prosperity, where most of his ministry was spent. His influence was felt in other QM's as well. He was a successful minister and many souls were converted through his agency.

He occupied a prominent position in the denomination, having represented the Susquehanna, NY Yearly Meeting (YM) in the General Conference of 1829 and several times later. The last ten years of his life was laid aside by infirmities, but he rejoiced in the assurance of a bright home above.

Jacob Hilton Durkee
Birth:
Apr. 30, 1847
Yarmouth
Nova Scotia, Canada
Death:
1925
Monroe County, New York
Burial:
Riverside Cemetery
Rochester
Monroe County, New York
Plot: Sect. M.

Rev. Durkee, was born of Free Baptist parents in Yarmouth Co. Nova Scotia. April 30, 1847. He was converted when about nineteen years of age, and soon entered the New Hampton Institution, N.H., graduating in 1871. Subsequently, he studied about a year in the theological department of Bates College [Maine]. He was ordained a Free Baptist minister at Meredith, N.H., Sept. 28, 1871; a properous pastorate at that place followed. Later he gathered the Free Baptist church of Halifax, N.S., which secured a house of worship under his labors. After supplying the New Market, N.H,, church for a season he went to New York in 1877, where his four years labor at Phoenix and three at Pike resulted in strengthening these churches. He also aided in organizing the Bliss church. In 1884, under direction of the Central Ass'n., he opened a mission at Batavia (NY) which is growing into permanence. Brother Durkee has occupied a prominent position in the Central Association, serving as its corresponding secretary and on its board of trustees.

Rev George Elliot
Birth:
Mar. 1, 1757
Voluntown
New London County
Connecticut, USA
Death:
Mar. 30, 1817
Ames
Montgomery County
New York
Burial:

Ames Cemetery
Ames
Montgomery County, New York
Plot: Section 1

Rev. George Elliott was ordained Feb. 6, 1794, at the organization of the [Freewill Bapt] church in Florida, N.Y. of which he became pastor. He moved with the church to Bowman's Creek, now Ames, and remained its pastor until his death in 1817.

He was born in Pomfred, Conn, had been a teacher, and was wounded while in the Revolutionary army. His life was saved by the careful nursing of his betrothed, Miss Percy Kimball, who became his wife.

He was a tall, strong, man, intellectual, affectionate, unblamable, and, as a pastor, more than usually watchful. Hence, he had many warm friends, and exerted a very great influence for good.

Rev Silvester R. Evans
Birth:
Jul. 9, 1818
Livonia
Livingston County, New York
Death:
May 18, 1890
Burial:
Sugartown Cemetery

Sugartown
Cattaraugus County,
New York

John Farley
Birth:
1777
New Hampshire
Death:
Dec. 12, 1858
Prospect, Oneida County,
New York
Burial:
Prospect Cemetery,
Prospect, Oneida County,
New York

He was converted at the age of fifteen and at twenty-four commenced preaching with the Open Communion Baptists at Richfield, N.Y. For twelve years he journeyed through the wilderness preaching two or three times a day, and his labors were blessed in the conversion of many souls." He died at the advanced age of 81 years.

Rev William Fuller
Birth:
1843
Death:
1908
Burial:
Garfield Cemetery
Stephentown
Rensselaer County, New York

Veteran of the Civil War Pastor 1876 - 1880 Free Baptist Church in Stephentown. Husband of Elizabeth Jane Sampson Fuller.

James Salmon Gardner
Birth:
Jun. 24, 1822
New York
Death:
Apr. 23, 1881
Whitestown,
Oneida County, New York
Burial:
Grandview Cemetery,
Whitesboro,
Oneida County, New York

Prof. James Salmon Gardner graduated from Whitestown Seminary, N.Y. in 1846, and Hamilton College, Clinton, N.Y, in the class of 1849. In his studies he won the honors for superior scholarship and the degree of Doctor of Philosophy was bestowed by his Alma Mater in 1863. While in school he began teaching and in 1853 he became principal of Whitestown Seminary, a position which he held until his death. While head of the school, he devoted much attention to the successful pursuit of special studies in the sciences, and was interested in every movement for the advancement of education. The year of his graduation, 1849, he married Elizabeth E. PHILLIPS, sister of the Rev. Jeremiah Phillips, the missionary to India.

Levi Geer Gardner
Birth:
1804
Massachusetts
Death:
Apr. 13, 1861
Burial:
Grandview Cemetery
Whitesboro
Oneida County New York

His father served in the Revolution under Gen. Gates. In 1806 the family moved from Worthington, Mass., where Levi was born, to Plymouth, NY. Soon after this they with others united in forming a Free Baptist church under the labors of Elder Campbell. He was baptized by Eld. C. Easterbrooks and soon began to preach, receiving ordination in July 1825. Following the custom of that period, he went forth as an itinerant, preaching much on weekdays, as well as the Sabbath. He had great success in his extended work to the western part of the state and even into Canada. He baptized about 500 converts, nine churches were organized by his assistance, and his counsels were helpful to many, as he encouraged them to higher attainments and to more devoted living.

Squire D. Gardner
Birth:
Feb. 1, 1808
Death:
May 18, 1864
Burial:
Grandview Cemetery,
Whitesboro,
Oneida County, New York

Squire D. was a brother of Rev. Levi Geer Gardner. His father did service in the Revolution under General Gates. He was an ordained Free Will Baptist minister, began preaching in 1841, at the Sherburne church, and was ordained about 1844. He was for seven years pastor of the church in Columbus, where many members were added and a house of worship erected. He was with the Plainfield church four years and saw refreshing seasons, and his labors with the Prospect church were greatly blessed. He was a judicious pastor, an instructive preacher, a candid and prudent councilor, and stood among his brethren in the front rank in the great moral conflict.

Truman Gillett
Birth:
Jul. 23, 1779
Schuyler
Herkimer County, New York
Death:
Feb. 8, 1850
Burial:
Seventh Township Cemetery
Camden
Oneida County, New York

He was converted at 18 years of age. In 1809 he commenced preaching among the Methodists and after six years joined the Free Baptists in Russia, New York receiving his ordination on October 15, 1818. He labored much and had many conversions in Fairfield, Poland, and Oswego County, New York as well as in Canada..

Rev Hiram Gilman
Birth:
1810
Vermont
Death:
Jan. 23, 1868
New York
Burial:
North Byron Cemetery
Byron
Genesee County
New York

Rev. Hiram GILMAN, a native of Vermont, moved to New York in early life; was converted about 1831, and ordained by the Monroe Quarterly Meeting at Byron in 1834. The thirty-four years of his ministry were spent with the Ogden, Byron, Royalton, Ridgeway, Oakfield, Alabama, Claredon, Parma, and Middlebury churches.

In all these fields he was successful as the scores, if not hundreds, of converts testify.

He was stricken with apoplexy while in the pulpit at Ogden, whither he had gone from Parma to supply, and died aged 58 years. Nobly he accomplished life's great work, and died on the battle-field. An ordained minister for 34 yrs to several churches in his area. He was a successful worker. He on two census' showed he was a FWB clergyman...I believe he was a man of intregity, as records attest.

David Greene
Birth:
Oct. 1, 1807
Hoosick,
New York
Death:
Aug. 7, 1882
Fairport, New York
Burial:
Ouleout Cemetery
North Franklin
Delaware County,
New York

In his early life he was a resident of Delaware County and with his wife in 1836 joined the Franklin church that had been recently organized. Two years later he was chosen Deacon and in 1842 was ordained as it's pastor, a relationship he continued for 18 years adding to the church by baptisms.

Rev Ansel Griffith
Birth:
Feb. 10, 1804
Herkimer County
New York
Death:
May 15, 1892
Clymer
Chautauqua County
New York
Burial:
Town Line Cemetery
Cassadaga
Chautauqua County
New York

Rev. Ansel Griffith, was ordained June 24, 1832, age 28yrs. A Freewill Baptist minister for 60 years. He was converted five years before, and preached while teaching and while a student at Hamilton, N.Y. He engaged with success in revival work before ordination, and afterward ministered in the Schroeppel, Scriba, and Phoenix churches.

In 1846, after being laid aside by disease for a year, he continued his work at Clayton, Theresa, Lyme, Three-Mile Bay, Harrisburgh, and Turin. He was pastor of the Townline Baptist Church for many years. He was a successful minister and baptized over two hundred converts. His spouse was Nancy S.Griffith in 1850 census and forward. (The 1870 census, listed spouse as "Sophia" which was probably Nancy's middle name, as "Nancy" was spouse in 1880.) Year of their marriage is unk at this time.

Inscription:
"Blessed are the dead which die in the Lord"

Waiting and watching within the gate.

Rev Susan Cilley Griffin

Birth:
Feb. 28, 1851
Boston
Houghton County,Michigan
Death:
Jan. 5, 1927
New York
Burial:
Keuka Park Cemetery
Jerusalem
Yates County,New York

Rev. Susan "Libbie" (Cilley) Griffin was the daughter of E. G. Cilley. She was the 2nd wife of Rev. Dr. Zebina Flavious Griffin. They were married Jackson, Michigan February 28, 1881. She was a Free Baptist Missionary to India 1873-1909, a teacher, and studied one year at Woman's Medical College at New York, and then entered again upon her course of study at Hillsdale. She did effective work organizing women to raise mission's funds for India.

Rev Zebina Flavious Griffin

Birth:
Nov. 14, 1844
Byron
Ogle County,Illinois
Death:
Feb. 11, 1938
Keuka Park
Yates County,New York
Burial:
Keuka Park Cemetery
Jerusalem
Yates County,New York

Rev. Dr. Zebina Flavious Griffin was the son of Rev. Jacob and Emmaline (Wade) Griffin. Mary Gertrude (Harwood) Griffin was his 1st wife. They were married July 20, 1865 and she died November 18, 1879. Rev. Susan "Libbie" (Cilley) Griffin was his 2nd wife. They were married February 28, 1881 and she died January 5, 1927. He was graduated from Hillsdale College, Mich. 1881, where his first wife, Mary Harwood, died in 1879; He and 2nd wife Libbie Cilley, served missionaries to India; he also had a successful pastorate at Gilbert's Mills, NY.

Alma Harriet (Goulton) Bond Griffin was his 3rd wife. They were married in 1934 when he was 85 years old. He was a minister in the Baptist Church and a missionary to India 1883-1909.

C. E. Hallock

Birth:
July 31, 1847
Constantia, New York
Death:
May 6, 1895
Burial:
Constantia Center Cemetery
Constantia Center
Oswego County, New York

He experienced religion in 1869 and was ordained June 2, 1878 after which he served the Constantia church as pastor. He was actively connected with the temperance work for 18 years.

Ely Hannibal

Birth:
Mar. 18, 1780
Fairfield,
Fairfield County, Connecticut
Death:
Aug. 28, 1876
Clarkson,
Monroe County, New York
Burial:
Garland Cemetery, Clarkson,
Monroe County, New York,
Plot: 1 - 8

Freewill Baptist pioneer minister in New York. Rev. Ely was converted Aug. 1806, and two yrs after, he joined a Baptist church; and removing to Yates (later Clarkson), NY, in 1811, he assisted in organizing the church in Sweden. In 1820 he joined a Free Baptist church that was organized in Clarkson; and the church had a council to ordain him on June 12, 1824. A revival immediately began, and fifty were converted. He preached in the surrounding towns and soon became a leader among the people in the rude dwellings of those times, in the big schoolhouses, and in the church, then uncommon, he preached with great earnestness the free gospel of Jesus Christ. There was scarcely a church organized w/o his aid, or a minister ordained without his counsel. He was not a scholar in any modern sense, but was at once popular and successful.

Death Is The Crown Jewel For The Christian.

—Rev. Joseph Hallenbeck died at his residence in Corning, Dec. 20, aged fifty-nine years. He had been a resident for about thirty five years. He was a native of Scoharie Co. He was by trade a stone mason, and followed that vocation till disabled by illness. He was enterprising, and built several brick buildings for business purposes, all of which he sold except that leased to C. W. Smith. As a contractor, he was faithful to his obligations, and as an employer he was kind, considerate and honorable. He was highly esteemed by those with whom he had business dealings or relations, and maintained a reputation for honesty, and the sure fulfillment of his word. He was for many years a zealous Christian, and a preacher, first of the Free Methodist, and after that of the Free Baptist Church. He was the pastor of the Free Baptist Church in Corning, and owned the meeting house, which a year ago at much expense, the most of it his own, he fitted up so that it could be used for Gospel Temperance meetings; and he was always enthusiastic on the subject of Temperance, or of religion. He preached every winter in some remote and sparsely settled locality, and his whole compensation for a score of years for these services would not pay for the expenses of his horse and conveyance. He thus labored on Handy Creek, in Southport, "Kelly town," in Caton, and Curtis Hollow, in Campbell. Successful revivals there and in Knoxville, in this town, repeatedly occurred under his preaching, and he claimed that the converts "held out" well in all of his fields of labor. In his early life he was for some years a sailor. He had no educational advantages but that did not deter him from preaching as he had opportunity; and no inclemency of the weather, roughness of the roads, or fatigue of the service after laboring at his trade, for a week, prevent I him from preaching at his appointments. His funeral was largely attended on Sunday afternoon at the Free Baptist Church.

Joseph Hallenbeck

Birth:
1820
Death:
Dec. 20, 1878
Burial:
Hope Cemetery
Corning
Steuben County
New York

Rev. Joseph Hallenbeck died at his residence in Corning, N.Y., Dec. 20, 1878, age 59 years. He had lived there thirty-five years and with Elder Rollins, organized the Corning Church. His preaching was with fervor, and evidenced familiarity with the Bible.

Luther Hanson

Birth:
1820
Death:
1894
Burial:
Glenview Cemetery
Pulteney
Steuben County, New York,

He was licensed in 1845 and attended Whitestown Seminary between the years of 1846-47. His ordination took place June, 1849. His pastorates were in Maine and New York and he had several revivals under his labors. Besides his preaching, he was engaged for several years in teaching. In 1853 he was a delegate to the General Conference.

Isaac Hill

Birth:
1783
Death:
1840
Burial:
West Hill Cemetery
Hornby
Steuben County, New York

He was converted in his youth and ordained on February 22, 1838 and died at the age of 57 years. He was earnest and pointed in preaching, gentleman in manner, and much respected.

Rev James Wightman Hills

Birth:
Oct. 1, 1816
Fabius
Onondaga County
New York, USA
Death:
May 5, 1898
New York
Burial:
Quaker Basin Cemetery
DeRuyter
Madison County
New York

Rev. James Wightman HILLS, granadson of Elder Jno. HILLS of the Six Principle Baptists and older brother of Rev. O.C. HILLS, was born at Fabius, NY, Oct 1, 1816. He was educated at Fabius' Academy, De Ruyter Institute and Whitestown Seminary, all in NY., and received license to preach in 1836, and was ordained by the Spafford Quarterly Meeting (QM) Sept. 8, 1844. His pastorates have been Willet, Sherburne, Virgil, and dryden, Willet (again), and Union Center, NY; Jackson and West Lennox, PA; Summer Hill, Philadelphia, Depauville, Holmsville, and Oxford, NY; East Troy and sullivan, PA, Caroline and Dryden, NY, Warren Center, Windham and Belle Vernon, PA; South Plymouth, Prospect, and Grant, NY.

The years of his long ministry have been filled with active service, some of the time two or more churches being under his care. He has engaged in many revivals and organized seven churches. In the time of the war he labored in the South under the Christian Commission.

He was for several years clerk and treasurer of the Susquehanna Yearly Meeting, and has twice served as delegate to the General Conference.

He was married to Miss Clarissa Quivey in 1847, and two years after her death to Miss Rebecca A. Randall in 1862. Both were of Cincinnatus, NY, the latter a teacher in the academy at that place.

Charles H Hoag

Birth:
March 25, 1835
Ridgeway, New York
Death:
Dec. 16, 1904
Burial:
Evergreen Cemetery
Pine Plains
Dutchess County, New York

He turned to God when he was 18 years of age and married Mrs. Minerva Power on December 25, 1858. He received his license to preach in 1876 and was ordained on December 11, 1880. His ministry it was in the Genesee Yearly Meeting most all of his ministry. --Pine Plains Register, 23 Dec 1904.

To Live is Christ To Die is Gain.

Isaac J Hoag
Birth:
Mar. 11, 1819
Chatham, New York
Death:
Mar. 22, 1891
New York
Burial:
Union Cemetery
North Creek
Warren County, New York

Converted at age 15 and became acquainted with the Free Baptists and united with them at West Stephentown. He received license to preach from the Rensselaer Quarterly Meeting in 1846 and supplied two churches for two years in that area. He was ordained on September 10, 1848 where he served pastorates in New York and Massachusetts. He assisted in organizing four churches and baptized nearly 400 converts.

Ephraim Chapelle Hodge
Birth:
Jan. 17, 1876
New York, USA

Death:
Mar. 22, 1941
Jefferson County, New York
Burial:
Adams Rural Cemetery
Adams
Jefferson County, New York

He was ordained at Oneonta Plains in September, 1850 and preached in the churches of the Otsego Quarterly Meeting having ministered the West Onenota church 20 years and for shorter periods other churches in the area. He was held in high esteem by the people of whom he lived around so long. He baptized about 500 converts.

Rev George R Holt
Birth:
Apr. 26, 1844
Lykens
Crawford County
Ohio
Death:
Aug. 18, 1931
Hilton
Monroe County
New York
Burial:
Parma Union Cemetery
Parma
Monroe County
New York
Plot: Sec. 9, West Div, Lot 7

His parents were Martin W. and Salley L (Black) HOLT. He was

educated at Hillsdale College, Mich., in the college and theological departments. Devoting his life to God in September, 1854, he received license to preach in 1865, and was ordained Feb. 24, 1868. While pursuing his studies at Hillsdale, he had the pastoral care of the Cook's Prairie church three years and of the Pittsford church three years and of the Pittsford church two years. He has since done substantial work as pastor of the Rome and Cambridge churches seven years, and of the Jackson church eight years. He has conducted several series of revival meetings, organized one church and baptized 209 converts. For six years he served on the executive board of the Home Mission Society, and he was a trustee of Hillsdale College. He was a representative of the Michigan Yearly Meeting in the General Conference. He was married July, 1868, to Marilla Waller. In 1888 he became pastor at North Parma, NY, After his wife, Marilla, died he married Annette M Woodruff, abt 1897.

He was a Corporal in Co. D, 12th Wisconsin Inf.Enlisted Sept 1861, W.Bend, WI, and Disch'd, Dec. 13, 1864. (He is listed in the Parmar Union Cemetery list of Veterans.)

Solomon Howe
Birth:
Nov. 4, 1786
Hillsborough County,
New Hampshire
Death:
May 9, 1859
Smyrna
Chenango County, New York
Burial:
Cincinnatus Cemetery
Cincinnatus
Cortland County, New York

He was converted in 1804, licensed in 1812 and ordained in New Hampshire in 1819. He labored in New Hampshire and Vermont until 1826, when he moved to New York and became one of the honored fathers of the Union Quarterly Meeting. He spent many years in the MacDonough

Quarter Meeting and from 1845 to 1850 was in the Nelson Quarterly Meeting.

Daniel Huling

Birth:
May 5, 1797
Washington County,
Rhode Island
Death:
Jan. 8, 1853
French Creek,
Chautauqua County,
New York
Burial:
Cutting Cemetery
Cutting
Chautauqua County, New York

He was converted in 1817 and ordained in 1847.

Robert Hunt

Birth:
Nov. 25, 1792
Schoharie County, New York
Death:
Dec. 7, 1872
Utica
Oneida County, New York
Burial:
Forest Hill Cemetery
Utica
Oneida County, New York
Plot: 30B-1 (Lot 1285)

He was a younger brother of William Hunt and received ordination among the Free Communion Baptists of New York about 1835. He was a man of considerable education, progressive in his tendencies and a good pastor.

Rogers Ide

Birth:
May, 1788
Vermont,
Death:
Jun. 2, 1863
Spafford
Onondaga County, New York
Burial:
Borodino Cemetery
Borodino, Onondaga County,
New York

Ide fought in the War of 1812, and co-founded the Free Will Baptist Church in Spafford, NY. In 1831 he began preaching, and by 1836 was ordained. Shortly thereafter, he traveled to the southern part of Indiana, where he preached against the sins of slavery, even when slave owners had a reward on his head.

Chester H Jackson

Birth:
Oct. 21, 1834
Death:
Dec. 9, 1912
Burial:
Alger Cemetery
Hume
Allegany County,
New York

He was converted in 1849; was a student at Pike Seminary, New York in 1860-61, and received ordination June 7, 1863. He went from Pike, New York to Michigan where he ministered to the Dover Church while pursuing theological studies at Hillsdale College.

Daniel Jackson

Birth:
Apr. 12, 1804
Death:
Dec. 9, 1890
Burial:
Varysburg Cemetery, Varysburg,
Wyoming County, New York

A leading Free Will Baptist minister in New England who was born in Madison, New Hampshire. He received his early religious impressions from Rev. John Colby, and was converted under the labors of Rev. Jonathan Woodman in 1818. He was ordained at East Ossipee, New Hampshire on Sept. 14, 1826. His pastorates were: E. Ossipee (five years), Wheelock, VT (two yrs), Topsham (four yrs), Meredith Village, N.H., Lewiston Falls, ME, Charleston, Mass, Topsham, ME, Saco, South Berwick, Lyndon Centre, VT. and Gardiner City, ME. After 1854, he traveled in the South, and returning, became pastor at Wells, ME. In these pastorates he was successful. At Topsham as a result of one revival ninety-six were baptized. He was active in the general denominational work, having served in the General Conferences of 1827, 1841, and 1880, the centennial meeting.

He was married to Miss Mary P. Kenneson, Sept. 20, 1827, and after her death, to Miss Hannah B. Fernald in 1853, and again bereaved, to Mrs. Clara Hewes, in 1857, with whom, after a long life of usefulness he is passing the remaining years at Varysburgh, N.Y. He wrote An Autobiography of 214 pages in 1859.

Nelson A Jackson
Birth:
Dec. 28, 1811
Arcade, N. Y
Death:
Aug. 30, 1871
New Hudson, N. Y
Burial:
Arcade Rural Cemetery
Arcade, Wyoming County,
New York

Jackson was born of Quaker ancestry died at aged 59 years. He was converted under the labors of Elder H. Jenkins when nineteen years of age, and licensed to preach five years later. After spending some time in study, he was ordained in his native town June 6, 1841. His pastorates were with the Varysburgh, Arcade,

Elton, Yorkshire, Ashford, and Humphrey and Great Valley churches. But one testimony was borne of him: that he was an earnest, loving, Christian minister. His quiet manner helped to develop thoughtful, abiding piety.

Calvin Jenkins
Birth:
Jan. 18, 1798
Stoddard, Cheshire,
New Hampshire
Death:
Jan. 31, 1882
Burial:
St. Lawrence County,
New York

Nathaniel Ketchum
Birth:
Unknown
Death:
Jan. 11, 1838
Burial:
Pike Cemetery
Pike
Wyoming County,
New York

He was ordained in 1813 and labored in New York. In 1816 he joined the Bethany Quarterly Meeting and leader in the Erie Quarterly Meeting which was sustained by a very strong revival under his labors.

George Washington Knapp
Birth:
Sep. 23, 1842
Cameron
Steuben County
New York
Death:
Jun. 20, 1892
New York
Burial:
South Hill Cemetery
Cameron
Steuben County
New York

Rev. George W. Knapp, was the son of William and Eliza J. (Osborn) KNAPP. He professed faith in 1851, and received license to preach in 1862, and ordained a Freewill Baptist minister in 1866. He pastored in Meredith Centre, and Contoocook, NH; Granville NY; and Aurora and Kenesaw, Neb. He was blessed in his ministry with over one hundred conversions in one year. In 1883, he was elected delegate to the General Conference. He was educated in Hillsdale College, Mich, and Bates Theological School in Lewiston, Maine. In Sept. 1865, he married Caroline [Carrie] Dennis.

Rev Stephen Krum
Birth:
1807
Death:
Feb. 13, 1903
Burial:
Snyder Hill Cemetery
Dryden
Tompkins County
New York,

Pastor of the Snyder Hill Free Will Baptist Church
Husband of Almira Coon
Parents: Mathew Krum & Margaret VanDermark

Rev John M. Langworthy
Birth:
Mar. 6, 1831
New York
Death:
Aug. 17, 1896
New York
Burial:
New Forest Cemetery
Utica
Oneida County
New York

An ordained FWB minister and pastor. His father, Nathan, was also active in the church as was his bro, Nathan, Jr.

James Letts
Birth:
Unknown
Death:
Dec. 9, 1864
Burial:
Pleasant Lawn Cemetery
Paris, Oswego County, New York

Letts, a native of Ulster, N. Y., was converted in 1850 and united with the Paris church at its organization. He acted as colporteur and agent of the American Tract Society three years, during which time he also held revival services and was connected with the Parish, Lyndon, and Angelica churches. Early in 1858 he held services with the Burns church; many were added and he became its pastor. He was ordained March 3, 1861, and in 1863 returned to the Oswego Q. M., and took charge of the Parish, Redfield, and Constantia churches, holding revivals with them and with the Osceola church the following winter. He was an active, persevering, and successful minister, and died of fever at 40 years of age. The minutes of the national Association of the Randall movement of Free Will Baptists said his death was 1864.

Waiting and watching within the gate.

W. A. Lighthall
Birth:
Aug. 22, 1813
Fort Ann,
Washington County, New York
Death:
Jul. 8, 1865
Burial:
Pike Cemetery,
Pike,
Wyoming County, New York

In May 1832, he moved to Weathersfield, and in September became totally blind. But this providence brought to him spiritual light. He was baptized in 1835 and licensed to preach in October, 1837.
Immediately commenced to preach at Middlebury, and in four years the church increased greatly in strength and numbers. At Attica he labored with good success three years. Having thus given proof of his call to the ministry, he was ordained a Freewill Baptist minister at Varysburgh in May, 1845. His later labors were with the churches in Weathersfield, Hamburg, Cowlesville, Ellington, Chautaqua, and Pomfret, besides itinerant preaching. His mind was vigorous and clear; his memory, quickened by loss of sight; was retentive, and his powers were devoted fully to his work

Rev Aaron B. Loomis
Birth:
Sep. 13, 1837
Lexington
Greene County
New York
Death:
Jun. 27, 1927
New York
Burial:
Forest Park Cemetery
Camden
Oneida County
New York

An ordined Freewill Baptist minister in NY, after he had served NY military in the Civil War. He was a dedicated minister.

Horatio N. Loring
Birth:
1806
Death:
1847
Burial:
Forest Hill Cemetery
UticaOneida County
New York

He was ordained in Rhode Island in 1825. He was one of the four young man, under 30 years of age, who sat in the first General Conference with Rev. Zalmon Tobey. He was delegate to the fourth General Conference in 1830, and Sec. of the sixth General Conference at Meredith, New Hampshire in 1832. He was pastor of the Broad St. Baptist Church.

Source: Forest Hill burial list carried in the *Utica Morning Herald and Daily Gazette*, May 30 1882.

Rev Arad Losee
Birth:
Jan. 11, 1821
Corinth
Saratoga County
New York
Death:
Mar. 23, 1897
Burial:
Sherman Cemetery
Sherman
Chautauqua County
New York

Rev. Arad Loosee (sic), of Sherman, NY, son of John and Lucy (Ellis) Loosee was brought into the Lord's service in 1834, studied at Edon Academy, Erie Co., and began to preach in 1849. He was ordained in June 1853, by a council from the French Creek Q.M., Rev. B. McKoon, preaching the sermon. His ministry was in western NY, and Penn, his pastorates being Lake Pleasant, Waterford, Rockdale, Salem, Greenwood, Spring Creek, Bloomfield, Greenfield and Northeast, PA, and Charlotte, Sherman, Collins, South Harmony, and Clymer and

Harmonny NY, frequently having the care of two churches at a time. He has baptized about four hundred converts, and served the Yearly Meeting as delegate to the General Conference.

John H. Loveless
Birth:
1809
Death:
Aug. 22, 1871
Johnsburgh, N. Y.
Burial:
Lynwood Church Cemetery
Hadley, Saratoga County,
New York

Loveless died at age 61 years. He was born in Poultney, Vt., and when seventeen years of age united with the Free Communion Baptists in Hadley, N. Y. The following year he began to preach and, being ordained in 1842, continued his labor at Hadley with unremitting ardor. He also labored in Poestenkill, N. Y., and six years in the Monroe Q. M., returning to his former home for the closing years of service. He was an amiable, modest pastor, faithful in precept and example, and his ministry was crowned with success.

Daniel Lyon
Birth:
Unknown
Death:

Sep. 23, 1842
Walworth, New York
Burial:
Walworth Center Cemetery
Wayne County, New York

He died at age 47. In 1824 he was ordained and became pastor of the Walworth Church having been a member since its organization in 1816. He was a successful preacher, a wise counselor, a father to his church. More than 300 converts were baptized by him and his death was greatly lamented.

Enoch Mack
Birth:
Jan. 30, 1806
Connecticut
Death:
Feb. 20, 1881
Catskill
Greene County, New York
Burial:
Catskill Village Cemetery
Catskill
Greene County, New York

Rev. Enoch Mack, M.D., born in Connecticut, in his childhood with his family moved to Susquehanna Co. PA, and here, after graduating in medicine he practiced his profession. After a time, he turned toward the ministry and became interested in temperance and anti-slavery causes. In 1833, he went on horseback to Philadelphia, where, with Garrison, Whittier, and others, he signed the Declaration of Sentiments, put forth by the Anti-Slavery Society. He was attracted to the Free

Baptists because of their anti-slavery sentiments, and became an early contributor to the "Morning Star". At the suggestion of Editor William Burr, he was called to Dover. NH, in 1835, and ordained pastor of the first Free Baptist church there. Subsequently, he resigned the pastorate to serve as agent of the Foreign Mission Board, and was also corresponding secretary of the Foreign and Home Mission Societies. During these years and later, he was a frequent correspondent and an editorial contributor of the "Star," and his vigorous pen did much to awaken an interest in missionary work and in the other great moral and Christian enterprises of the day. About 1849, he went to New York City, where he was appointed city missionary for the northern portion of the city. In this capacity he served with earnestness and devotion nineteen years. His last years were spent with his son at Catskill Station in Columbia County.His devoted labors for those causes that would save men from intemperance, give freedom to the bondmen, rescue the heathen millions from idolatry, and lift up the degraded in our great cities, evince the breadth of his sympathies and give him a high place among the benefactors of our race. He was married to Phebe L. Roberts, and they were on 1850 census together, along with Narcissa, a daughter, age 17.On the 1860 census, Enoch stated he was a 'retired minister.'

William Mack

Birth:
1798
Lyme
New London County, Connecticut
Death:
1877
Steuben County, New York
Burial:
Mack Cemetery
Steuben County, New York

He was an active preacher for forty-five years. His labors were mostly in northern Pennsylvania and southern New York, where his ministry was abundantly blessed in the salvation of souls. He assisted in organizing most of the churches of the Tuscarora quarterly meeting. He was the son of Samuel and Mary Mack, Husband of Eliza Kimball. Mack Cemetery is a family cemetery that contains six graves and is located on Mack Road.

Benjamin McKoon

Birth:
Sep. 2, 1799
Death:
Nov. 16, 1880
Columbia, N. Y.,
Burial:
Millers Mills Cemetery
Millers Mills,
Herkimer County,
New York

Rev. Benjamin, a brother of Rev. D. W. McKoon, died aged 81 years. At the age of seventeen, he obeyed the call to a Christian life and was baptized by Rev. Wm. Hunt. He was ordained at Unadilla Forks in 1823, and for fifty-seven years, he preached the gospel with zeal and earnestness, and often with great power. His early labors were in the Chemung Valley and adjacent country. Afterwards for sixteen years he labored in central New York and in Oswego and Jefferson counties, his efforts being crowned with very marked success. Then, after years of successful ministry in western New York, he moved from Ellington to Hillsdale to educate his children. Returning in 1861, he preached at Columbia, German Flatts, Oxford and Holmesville, and, six years later, took up pastoral work in Chautauqua and Cattaraugus Counties, and continued it until health would no longer permit.

He had baptized about eight hundred converts, and the last three years of life were largely spent in visiting former fields of labor, confirming the saints. Christ and his cross were themes he loved to dwell upon, and the atonement was to him the pivotal point on which rested the great work of the soul's salvation. He was a delegate to the General Conference of 1847 from the Holland Purchase Y. M. His son, Prof. Bela P. McKoon, of Hillsdale College, Whitestown Seminary, and later of Cornell University, in these institutions rendered efficient service as an educator.

Daniel W McKoon

Birth:
Jun. 6, 1811
Herkimer County, New York
Death:
Jan. 4, 1871
Sugartown
Cattaraugus County, New York
Burial:
Sugartown Cemetery
Sugartown
Cattaraugus County, New York

Rev. Daniel William McKoon, a native of Columbia, N.Y., was baptized by Rev. Wm. Hunt when eighteen year of age. He was licensed to preach in 1838 and ordained Feb. 9, 1840 in Free

Baptist Church. He commenced immediately a six-years' pastorate with the Newport and Poland church, sixty being added to the church by baptism and lasting good resulted. In 1847 he was prostrated by disease, which so affected the mind that on recovery he found it necessary to study the alphabet again and regain his former knowledge step by step. After this, twenty years of usefulness remained to him, which were spent in the Cattaraugus and Chautauqua Quarterly Meetings, his last pastorate being with the Ashford church. He died at Orlean aged 59 years. Brother McKoon was a warm-hearted Christian, earnest in every good work and faithful to duty. As a preacher he was systematic and pathetic. In his early ministry he rendered efficient service in securing friends and funds for Whitestown Seminary at a time when both were needed. He represented the Central N.Y. Yearly Meeting in the General Conference of 1844. His son, Newton C. McKoon of Ellicottsville, N.Y., was for many years clerk of the Cattaraugus Q.M., and commissioner of schools for Cattaraugus County.

Newton C McKoon
Birth:
Dec. 17, 1835
Herkimer
Herkimer County, New York
Death:
Aug. 27, 1906
Humphrey
Cattaraugus County,
New York
Burial:
Sugartown Cemetery
Sugartown
Cattaraugus County,
New York

His parents were Rev. Daniel W. McKoon and Jane T. (Young) McKoon.There is an enlistment for him in the Civil War Muster, of 1862, Great Valley, NY. He became a Free Baptist minister and was a leader in the Humphrey Free Bapt Church, where his father

ministered. He was also clerk of the Yearly meeting for many years, and was Commissioner of schools.He married Ann Crary (1845-1914), in 1865 per 1900 census.

Rev Melville Corner Miner
Birth:
Jan. 18, 1857
Death:
Feb. 17, 1923
Burial:
West Oneonta Cemetery
Oneonta
Otsego County
New York, Plot: BR-05

Rev. Dr. Miner was ordained to preach Dec. 16, 1883, and held pastorates in Indiana and Osseo, Michigan. Supporting himself as teacher and pastor he has attended Ridgeville College, Indiana, and Hillsdale College, Theology Dept. 1885-1888. Ordained Freewill Baptist minister; DD probably conferred by Hillsdale College in Mich, late 1880's.
He married Anna R. Root, May 25, 1873.

Robert Edward Nesbitt
Birth:
Nov. 19, 1854
Hamlin, NY
Death:
Oct. 12, 1893
Burial:
Blossom Cemetery
Hamlin
Monroe County
New York

Born in Hamlin, NY. Son of James and Isabella "Gabe" (Edgeworth) Nesbit, who came to the United States from Co Cavan, Ireland in 1850. Married Emma Stuart of Hamlin on Nov. 29, 1882. Father of: Stuart James (1885-1959), William Henry Francis (1887-1964), who became Secretary General of General Electric in Canada, and Nellie Mae (Walter) Blodgett (1890-1965).
Attended Brockport Normal School and taught in the Hamlin School district. Went to Seminary at Hillsdale College (Michigan) and then returned to become a well-known temperance minister in the Free Will Baptist Church. Served as minister at Walker, Scriba, and Hilton, NY churches.
Was also well known as a carpenter. Died in Hamlin, NY at age 39. Was originally buried at High Street Cemetery in Brockport, NY. Body moved to Blossom Cemetery when his wife Emma died in 1907.

Rev Samuel Newell
Birth: 1788
Barnstead,
New York
Death: Sep. 6, 1880
Lawrence
Nassau County
New York
Burial:
Mound Hill Cemetery
Nicholville
St. Lawrence County
New York, Plot: 290-7A

He served in the Legislature from Woodstock and was converted in 1831, at Johnstown, Canada, where he began to preach with the Methodists. In 1837 he settled in Lawrence, NY where he joined the Free Baptists. His ministry was mostly confined to the Lawrence, Hopkinton and Dickinson churches. He was a logical and instructive preacher, and a most exemplary christian; and even after he had passed his fourscore years, he was listened to with interest.
An ordained Free Baptist minister, died aged 91 yrs. Spouse was Polly Erwin.

Asahel Nichols
Birth:
1851
Ames, New York
Death:
unknown
Burial:
Ames Cemetery
Ames
Montgomery County,
New York

He joined the church in his native town, Chesterfield, Massachusetts, in 1840. He later taught two terms at Geauga Seminary, Ohio and graduated from the theological department of Oberlin College, Oberlin, Ohio in 1846. He returned then to preach in Maine and New York.

John Nicholson
Birth:
Mar. 21, 1793
Connecticut
Death:
Apr. 7, 1863
Burial:
Steere Cemetery
East McDonough,
Chenango County,
New York

Nicholson was a native of Stonington, Conn., was converted and united with the McDonough, N. Y., church in 1813. He was ordained at the session of the Q. M. held at Plymouth, N. Y., in June, 1833, and continued with the McDonough church, except two years with the Second Otselic and three with the German, 1854-59, until his death, which occurred at the advanced age of 70 years. his wife was the Roby Steere (1798 - 1840).

William Nutting
Birth:
Nov. 6, 1794
Death:
Jan. 25, 1872
Parish, N. Y,
Burial:
Nutting Cemetery
West Monroe, Oswego County,
New York

At the age of twenty-five, after many conflicts, he consecrated himself to the Master's service. His ministry, for nearly forty-five years, was mostly with the churches of the Oswego Q. M. He was an eccentric, zealous man, useful in the work of the Lord. At his death one son was state senator in Virginia and another district attorney of Oswego County, New York.

Thomas Parker
Birth:
1794
Foster, R.I.
Death:
Aug. 4, 1865
Perrinton (Fairport), N. Y.,
Burial:
Elmwood Cemetery
Perrinton,
Monroe County, New York

He was converted under the labors of Rev. J. Fowler and joined the Walworth church. At the age of twenty-eight he commenced preaching in Penfield, and soon a church was organized there. He was ordained in 1828 and remained pastor of the church twenty-eight years. He also preached in Ontario, Webster, Macedon and Perrinton. For some years before his death he did not have the care of a church, but preached as opportunity presented. During his ministry he baptized over five hundred converts, married 500 couples and attended more than one thousand funerals. His joy was in the Lord, both in life and at its close.

Rev Washington Parker
Birth:
Aug. 7, 1829
Chautauqua County
New York
Death:
Jun. 19, 1901
Burial:
Sherman Cemetery ,Sherman
Chautauqua County,New York

His parents were George and Myra (Gardinier) PARKER. He Married Sarah L. Goodrich in 1852, and ordained a Free Baptist minister June 7, 1868.
He pastored twelve years with Waterford and Lake Pleasant churches in Pennsylvania. He also served Wellsburg and Bloomfield churches in PA. He then was with the church at Sherman, NY. In all these pastorates his work was successful and blessed.

A. P. Phinney
Birth:
Apr. 8, 1828
Reading, New York
Death:
Nov. 7, 1897
Burial:
Pleasant Lawn Cemetery
Parish
Oswego County, New York
He experienced religion in 1857 in Allegheny County. The same year he was licensed to preach and supplied churches near his home for about three years where his labors were blessed. He moved to Oswego County in 1864 and was ordained on June 10, 1867 under

the ministry of the First Parish Church which was greatly strengthened and the Second Parish Church was organized. In 1870 became the pastor of the Hastings church.

Rev Thomas Pratt
Birth:
1747
Madison County
New York
Death:
1822
Rushford
Allegany County
New York
Burial:
First Burying Ground Cemetery
Rushford
Allegany County
New York

Rev. Thomas Pratt, a native of Middlebury, Massachusetts, moved to Rushford, NY in 1812, where he remained until his death at the age of 73 years. He was converted in 1822, he was united with the Rushford & Lyndon churches & soon felt called to preach. He was ordained about 1836*, having been licensed some years before, and some of the time had care of several churches. he was a man of power, outspoken & positive & represented his Yearly Meeting in the General Conference of Freewill Baptist" *Ordained, Nov. 18, 1834.
A History of Rushford, shows that they had a semi- centennial celebration in 1859, in which " Rev. Thomas L Pratt, delivered an introductory speech, which was highly praised by all there."[the author stated it was a shame it couldn't have been preserved.}

To Live is Christ To Die is Gain.

Thomas L Pratt
Birth:
May 6, 1794
Madison County
New York
Death:
Jun. 9, 1873
Rushford
Allegany County,
New York
Burial:
Rushford Cemetery
Rushford
Allegany County,
New York

Rev. Thomas L. Pratt, was a pioneer minister in Allegany Co. NY. He was ordained Nov. 18, 1834, and ministered to churches in that area until he died.

Rev Levi C. Preston
Birth:
Nov. 10, 1829
Death:
Aug. 8, 1878
Caroline Center
Tompkins County
New York
Burial:
Caroline Centre Cemetery
Caroline Center
Tompkins County
New York

He was ordained in 1858, and after four years' active work, failing health compelled him to change his work and residence. He moved to Centralia, Kan., where he exerted an influence by his modesty, charity and general benevolence. Nearing the end of life with consumption, he returned to New York to die. For the purpose of educating his children he made his home at Hillsdale, Mich., several years

Charles Putnam
Birth:
Unknown
Death:
Feb. 1, 1878
Byron, N. Y.
Burial:
West Bethany Cemetery
West Bethany, Genesee County,
New York

Putnam was a native of Bethany, died at aged 55 years. After graduating from Union College in 1848, he engaged in teaching at Varysburgh, N. Y. He was converted under the labors of Rev. M. H. Abbey, and after a few months was ordained. After teaching and preaching at Cowlesville, when Pike Seminary was purchased he became its principal, and served the church as pastor. Here his labors were severe and exhaustive, but crowned with generouis results. Most of his labors were in western New York, his last pastorate being at Byron. He was an excellent minister, in preaching logical, instructive and inspiring, and frequent revivals were enjoyed.

"I See Heaven Open And Jesus On The Right Hand Of God."

Rev Thomas R Reed
Birth:
Oct. 13, 1830
Lowville
Lewis County,New York
Death:
Mar. 23, 1894
Burial:
Seventh-Day Baptists Settlement
Cemetery
Watson
Lewis County, New York

Rev. Thomas R. Reed, of Petrie's Corners, N.Y., is son of William and Chloe (Wetmore) Reed. He was brought to Christ in 1850 and, three years later, was married to Martha A. Robinson. He received license to preach in 1865, and was ordained in 1868 by the Seventh Day Baptist church of Watson, of which he has continued pastor. Some ten years since he began also to minister to the New Bremen and Watson church, which about 1865 became connected with the Jefferson Quarterly Meeting, of the St. Lawrence Yearly Meeting.

Richard Richardson
Birth:
Jan. 14, 1799
Leek
Staffordshire, England
Death:
Jun. 10, 1872
Varysburg
Wyoming County, New York
Burial:
Cowlesville Cemetery
Cowlesville
Wyoming County, New York

He was a student at the Montpelier and Bates College. He was converted in 1876 and was licensed on June 28, 1885, and ordained July 10, 1887. He also was a student at Cobbett divinity school. He married Elizabeth about 1822 and after her death, he married Sally Munger about 1845

Edson M. Roel
Birth:
December 28, 1858
Dummerston,
Vermont
Death:
1939
Burial:
Morningside Cemetery
Hartford
Washington County,
New York

On March 1, 1882, he was married to Etta L. Payne. Having given himself to God in the work of the gospel ministry, he was licensed in 1879, and ordained in 1884. He is held pastors in Vermont and New York.

Rev D M Lafayette Rollin
Birth:
Aug. 12, 1804
Franklin County
Maine
Death:
1895
Maine
Burial:
Maple Wood Cemetery
Boston
Erie County
New York

He was the son of Samuel Rollin and Susan (Lawrence) Rollin. (Some genealogies give his first name as De Marquis Lafayette). His land records show "D.M. Lafayette Rollin." On August 29, 1837, he married Miss Mary Carey, in Boston, NY. She was the eldest daughter of the Hon. Truman Carey of Boston. There are four children recorded in censuses: Mary; Delia; Carey; and Emma.
Rev. D.M.L. Rollin, was taught early in life to love books. He received his formal training at Farmington Seminary, under the Principal of the Seminary, Nathaniel Green, A.M. In 1825, his views and feelings changed, and he publicly professed the Christian religion and united with the Free Baptist Church.
In 1829, he was ordained by a council called by the church. He turned his attention to the study of theology and began upon a successful work in the Wayne Quarterly Meeting which soon became the Ohio and Pennsylvania Yearly Meeting subsequently, he labored in western New York. In this state he held pastorates with many of the strongest churches and exerted an extended influence for good during many years. For fourteen years he held the pastorate of the Byron church, and preached for four years at Clarendon, Orleans Co. NY. He received very little remuneration for his services, believing, "freely you have received; freely give."
He represented the Holland Purchase Y.M., in the General Conferences of 1833, 1835, and 1844, the Ohio and Pennsylvania Y.M. in that of 1841, and the Genesee Y.M. in 1853.
He had a sixty-six year ministry and died loved and esteemed, at 91 years of age.

David Valoy Ross
Birth:
1831
Death:
September 6, 1878
Burial:
Forest Lawn Cemetery
Buffalo
Erie County, New York

When five years of age with his parents he moved from Pennsylvania to Clermont, Ohio. In 1861 he entered the Civil War and received an Hon. discharge at the end of three years. He began preaching with the Methodists, but joined the Free Baptists in 1876 and was ordained by the Miami Quarterly Meeting in Ohio the January before his death. His many qualities endeared him to all.

Benjamin Rowland
Birth:
Unknown
Death:
Aug. 3, 1872
Sherburne, N.Y.,
Burial:
Christ Church Cemetery
Sherburne, Chenango County,
New York

Rowland, a native of Lyme, Conn., died at age 88 years. Having moved to Burlington, N. Y., he was converted in 1812, three years after his marriage to Miss Seraph Sweetser, and almost immediately began to preach. The next year he was ordained, entering at once upon a seven years' pastorate with the Burlington and Exeter churches. In 1821 he took charge of the Sherburne church, just organized, and remained with it seventeen years, preaching also to other churches. The churches at Oneonta, Plainfield, Brookfield, Holmesville, Oxford, Lebanon, Smyrna, German Flats, and Columbus were also recipients of his labors, some of them for years. He labored extensively as an evangelist, at one period for seven consecutive years continually in revivals. In 1854 he went to Binghamton, remaining there ten years, and preaching to the Apalachin, Warren, Windham, and Vestal churches. After this he made his home in Sherburne. He was a man of arduous labors. His name was a household word over a large section of country. His baptisms numbered over eight hundred. His preaching was descriptive and hortative. He seemed to embrace the truth with the heart more than the head. He "was an advocate of temperance, a lover of education and missions. His ministry was a ministry of love.

Rev Samuel Newell
Birth:
1788
Barnstead, New York
Death:
Sep. 6, 1880
Lawrence
Nassau County, New York
Burial:
Mound Hill Cemetery
Nicholville, St. Lawrence County

New York
Plot: 290-7

He served in the Legislature from Woodstock and was converted in 1831, at Johnstown, Canada, where he began to preach with the Methodists. In 1837 he settled in Lawrence, NY where he joined the Free Baptists. An ordained Free Baptist minister, died aged 91 yrs. Spouse was Polly Erwin. His ministry was mostly confined to the Lawrence, Hopkinton and Dickinson churches. He was a logical and instructive preacher, and a most exemplary Christian; and even after he had passed his fourscore years, he was listened to with interest.

Rev George J Scobey
Birth:
Aug. 22, 1854
Buffalo
Erie County, New York
Death:
1934
Iowa
Burial:
Hillside Cemetery
Stephentown
Rensselaer County, New York

Rev. George J. SCOBEY, son of Geo. V. and F.E. (French) SCOBEY, was born at Buffalo N.Y. Aug. 22, 1853(sic). He yielded his heart to God in Feb. 1876, received license in 1880 and was ordained June 10, 1883.

James Sharp
Birth:
Unknown
Death:
May, 18, 1874
Fairport, N. Y.
Burial:
Mount Hope Cemetery
Rochester, Monroe County, New York

A native of Massachusetts, he died at age 76 years. He was converted in youth, his early labors being with the Methodists, much of the time in Canada. The latter part of

life he was connected with the Free Baptists in western New York as a pioneer Freewill Baptist minister in Monroe County. Possessing a vigorous intellect, some culture, strong willpower and persistence, with a personal address imposing for a colored person, he had influence with the abolitionist leaders, especially with Gerritt Smith, and took great interest in the progress of their work. The visions of his earlier years were realized in the emancipation of his race (being Black) and in the gift of the elective franchise. He ceased not to thank God for the privilege of labor in this cause and for the results attained.

Rev George H Siver
Birth:
Jan. 6, 1814
Herkimer County, New York
Death:
Sep. 15, 1891
Burial:
Garrison Cemetery, Pitcairn
St. Lawrence County, New York

Rev. George H. Siver, was born in Herkimer County, N.Y., and married Eliza Ostrander, Sept. 22, 1834. He served for many years as a licensed preacher in connection with the Diana church of the Jefferson Quarterly Meeting (N.Y.) and about 1870 received ordination, his subsequent ministry being with the Pitcairn church

Cyrus Steere
Birth:
Jun. 3, 1801
Glocester
Providence County,
Rhode Island
Death:
Feb. 26, 1878
East McDonough
Chenango County, New York
Burial:
Steere Cemetery
East McDonough
Chenango County, New York

First pastor of the Free Will Baptist Church, erected in 1831 in East McDonough. Organized churches of the same denomination at German Hollow in 1844 and in Oxford in 1848. Steere, was a native of Burrillville, R. I., began his ministerial labors when twenty-six years of age, and was ordained at East McDonough, N. Y., Aug. 26, 1829. He was a pioneer in the vicinity and assisted in building up and organizing many churches. His labors were chiefly in the McDonough Q. M., and were greatly blessed. He died at aged 76 years

George B Southwick
Birth:
November 22, 1863
Humphrey Ctr., New York

Death:
1923
Burial:
Cherry Creek Central Cemetery
Cherry Creek
Chautauqua County, New York
Plot: 252

He graduated from Pike Seminary, New York in 1885 and student at Bates College and Cobb Divinity School. He received his license to preach in April 1885 pastoring thereafter in New York and Maine.

Thomas A. Stevens
Birth:
April 11, 1837
Death:
1912 Burial:
Keuka Park Cemetery
Jerusalem
Yates County, New York

Ordained to preach 1868 in Plymouth, Vt. Where he ministered in that state, then to N.Y. ending with Keuka College, 1891-1901 where he died and was buried. He was a delegate to the General Conference in 1870.He was also an ordnance office in the army for three years.

Anna Matteson Stone
Birth:
Aug. 26, 1813
Burlington
Otsego County, New York
Death:
Apr. 26, 1895
Oxford
Chenango County, New York
Burial:
Riverview Cemetery

Oxford
Chenango County, New York

Her parents were John D and Philura Williams Matteson her mother being a descendant Roger Williams. She was married Joshua B Stone Feb 5 1840 and several years after his death on Dec 22 1869 to Lewis B Anderson. She received a good education and in early engaged in teaching. She was when eighteen years of age and after few years with the Baptists united with the Free Baptists in Columbus, NY. She received license to preach about 1839 and for years engaged actively in ministerial work. While pastor she exchanged with other ministers for the administration of the ordinances. Though successful as a pastor her chief labors were as an evangelist. Her work was mostly in Madison, Chenango, and Cortland counties, NY though extending also as far as Pennsylvania and Rhode Island. Sometimes alone sometimes with other ministers she called sinners to repentance. The conversions under her labors numbering several hundreds. Her voice was clear and full not boisterous. Her manner in the pulpit was deliberate and dignified, her style hortatory yet with method and her appeals often thrilling.

Rev Freeborn W Straight
Birth:
1806
Washington County
New York

Death:
Dec. 23, 1878
Monroe County
New York
Burial:
Beach Ridge Cemetery
Brockport
Monroe County
New York
Plot: B.R. II 165

Soon after his birth in 1806, with his father, William Straight, moved to Walworth, Wayne Co. NY. When about twenty-one years of age he was converted under the labors of Eld. Lyon and united with the Walworth Free Baptist church. In about a year he was licensed to preach and soon after, with Elder Marks [David], he went to Ontario, Can., where they traveled and labored with great success. Marks, returning, he remained in Canada and supplied the Woodstock and London churches, forty miles apart, and preached at intervening points. More than a hundred were converted during the winter, and he was sent to New York for ordination in March 1828. He remained in Canada several years and churches were formed which grew to become the Ontario Yearly Meeting. Returning to New York, he was inactive for a time. In 1841, he took up the work and a year later he assisted Brother Bathrick at Conneaut, Ohio, and Bro. Dunn at Mecca, many being converted at each place. He was pastor at Conneaut two years, assisted in a great revival in Pennfield, N.Y., and settled as pastor of the church at Fairport for eight years. In the winter of 1851-52 he assisted Bro. Bathrick again at Saco, ME, and more than four hundred were converted in the congregation, the revival being one of unusual power and extending also to other congregations and towns. He seemed almost inspired in his labors here. A part of the following winter was spent in revival work in Saco. After a year at Brockport, he settled at Manchester, N.H., where he remained for three years, and eighty were converted

the first winter. After one year at Boston, MA, and two at Saco ME he went to Conneaut OH in 1861, and two years later to Jackson, Mich. He remained there nine years, reorganizing the church and carrying it through many difficulties. He then made his home in Lansing, intending to rest, but could not. He gathered fragments of several churches together at Grand Ledge, encouraged them to build their beautiful brick church, and by his visits aided the churches at Reading, Cambridge, Paw Paw, Bath, Macon, Delta and Leslie. Then in 1877, visiting the scene of his early labors in Ontario, he took charge of two churches in Zorra, and worked with the zeal and ardor of his youth until his sudden death, Dec. 23, 1878. Brother Straight was a man of large and commanding form, and of robust health, rather diffident unless aroused by some exigency, pre-eminently social and companionable. His intellect was of a high order, quick, discriminating and logical. He was several times a member of the General Conference. He died at the post of duty near where he preached his first sermon fifty-one years before, and was buried at Brockport, N.Y., near the scenes of his early ministry

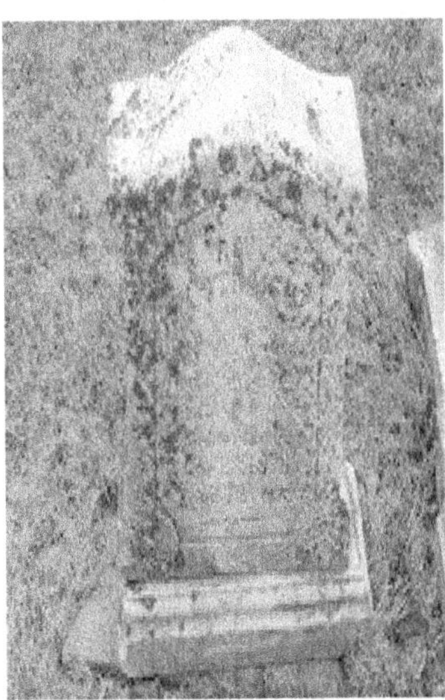

Ezra P Tallman
Birth:
May 31, 1814
Death:
Aug. 21, 1867
Burial:
Elmwood Cemetery
Perrinton, Monroe County,
New York

Tallman was a native of Galway, N. Y., united with the Penfield church in his twenty-third year, and was ordained when twenty-eight. He became pastor of the Perrinton (Fairport) church, formed at the time of his ordination, and remained with it four years. He then spent nearly three years at the Biblical School at Whitestown, and afterwards was pastor of the Middleville and Norway, Byron, Penfield, and Elba and Alabama churches successively. After caring for his father, Deacon Tallman, in his last sickness, he preached occasionally, and died aged 53 years. He was highly esteemed by his brethren, and his preaching was well adapted to develop spirituality and to establish gospel principles among the people.

William Taylor
Birth:
Mar. 20, 1823
Ontario,
Canada
Death:
Apr. 4, 1877
Italy
Yates County,
New York
Burial:
Italy-Naples Cemetery
Italy
Yates County,
New York

He married Elizabeth Bodine in 1844 and Mary Morse in 1850 and had 10 children. He came to God in 1841 and was ordained in 1858. His labors were in Ontario, Canada, Western New York and Michigan. He aided in building several meeting houses and baptized several hundred converts in represented the St. Joseph's yearly meeting in the General Conference of 1883.

Charles Luther Vail
Birth:
Oct. 21, 1806
Long Island, New York
Death:
Dec. 23, 1887
Windsor, New York
Burial:
West Windsor Cemetery
West Windsor
Broome County, New York

He was 20 at his conversion and joined the church in West Windsor. Here he was ordained on November 3, 1840. His pastorates were West Windsor, New York, South Killingsly Connecticut and Franklin, Oxford, Virgil and Dryden, New York. He continued in active service until 73 years of age.

Freeman VanAmburgh
Birth:
May 1, 1793
Fishkill,
Dutchess County,
New York
Death:
Aug. 3, 1871
Bath, Steuben County, New York
Burial:
Mount Washington Cemetery
Urbana, Steuben County,
New York

Rev. Freeman VanAmburgh, is listed in names of deceased ministers in the "Register of Freewill Baptists", as having "d. Aug. 3, 1871, age 78 yrs, at Bath, N.Y."He was in the War of 1812, proven as his wife, Anna, filed a widow's pension on his service in Capt. Ellis Co., N.Y. Mil., #URS orig 44506.Rev. VanAmburgh settled a few years after his military service at Bath, where he remained for most of life. He was converted in 1824 along with others under the labors of Rev. Z. Dean, and later was organized into a Freewill Baptist church. He was ordained on Sept. 4, 1836, and continued a faithful laborer until strength and life failed.

William Van Tuyl
Birth:
Unknown
Death:
Feb. 21, 1829
Burial:
Raplee Family Cemetery
Milo
Yates County, New York
Early Free Will Baptist preacher.

Elder Alverdo Wait
Birth:
Mar. 23, 1805
Death:
Aug. 13, 1849
Burial:
Lower Cincinnatus Cemetery
Cincinnatus
Cortland County
New York,

He began preaching in 1844, and ordained by Freewill Bapt. McDonough Quarterly Meeting June 3, 1848. Elder/Rev. Alverdo WAIT, was an ordained Freewill Baptist minister, who ministered in his short lifetime in Cortland Co. He was interested in benevolent work, was active yet unassuming, and labored with the Cincinnatus and Cortlandville FWB churches until his death.

Orrin Wynant Waldron
Birth:
Jul. 13, 1859
North Creek,
Warren County, New York

Death:
1910
Burial:
Ames Cemetery, Ames,
Montgomery County,
New York

He consecrated his life to God in 1878, and was educated at Hillsdale College, Michigan, in the college and theological departments, receiving honors from his literary society for excellence in oratory. While in college he supplied the churches at Scipio, Litchfield and Hadley's Corners, and afterwards became pastor of the church at Marion, Ohio, receiving ordination Oct. 12, 1884 in the Free Will Baptist. After a successful pastorate of three years he entered upon the work with the church at Saco, Me. He has baptized about thirty converts and assisted in revival work. Aug. 5, 1884, he was married to Mary E. Phillips.

Rev Russell Way
Birth:
1780
Death:
Jul. 23, 1848
Burial:
Collinsville Cemetery
Turin
Lewis County
New York

Rev. Russell Way died aged 69 years. He was converted when about twenty years of age. In 1815 he was ordained.
In his early ministry he gathered the Turin church. And remained its pastor to the end of a long and honored life. He was a ready speaker, an efficient and judicious pastor, a safe counselor and an ardent friend of the benevolent enterprises of the denomination.

Inscription:
age 68 years

Hiram Whitcher
Birth:
Mar. 18, 1809
Danville, Caledonia County,
Vermont
Death:
Jun. 7, 1896
Sweden Center,
Monroe County, New York
Burial:
Lakeview Cemetery,
Brockport,
Monroe County, New York,
Plot: A-111-1

The family moved to Sweden, NY in 1815. Here in 1823, Hiram was converted and uniting with the Union Free Baptist Church of Sweden and Ogden. He received from it a license to preach in 1829. During the summer he was chiefly engaged in study and attended the Middlebury academy. In the spring, he assisted Elder T. Parker in a glorious revival at Penfield and soon joined the church there, after which he was ordained May 30, 1830, by a council of the Bethany Quarterly Meeting. In 1831, he went into Chautauqua County and held revivals in many places and also in Cataraugua County. Many converts were baptized, among them Miss Lavina Crawford and Miss H. Baldwin later to become missionaries, and also Dr. Kingsley, later a bishop of the M.E. church. He held meetings in Ohio, Michigan, and Pennsylvania. In 1834 he settled at Springville and entered the academy, preaching also in the vicinity. In 1840, he with others served as a committee from the General Conference to arrange a union with the Free Communion Baptists. He preached also at Clinton, Poland, Unadilla Forks, and Whitestown, NY. From 1845 to 1854, he labored in Rochester, NY. From there he went to Concord, NH under direction of the Home Mission Society. The following twenty years were spent in Maine, at Booth Bay, Bath, Augusta, Phillips, Falmouth, Saccarappa and elsewhere. After fifty years of active service he accepted a home provided by his brother, C.J. Whitcher, and moved to Brockport, NY, from which place he has rendered service to several churches. During his ministry, Bro. Whitcher has been engaged in many revivals, and has baptized 680 converts.

William Whitfield
Birth:
December 27, 1811
London, England
Death:
1891
Burial:
Pierpont Hill Cemetery
Pierpont
St. Lawrence County, New York

He was converted in September 1830 receiving license eight years later and ordination on June 14, 1841. He assisted in organizing the Pierpoint and several other churches. And with the exception of two years in the Jefferson Quarterly Meeting, he has resided at Pierpoint ministering to the people. For 16 years he was clerk of the town and has been for 37 years clerk of the St. Lawrence Yearly Meeting. Among its churches he is had wide influence. He joined in marriage 387 couples. In 1831 he was married to Diantha M. Axtell.

Edwin E. Whittemore
Birth:
Nov. 26, 1850
Oneida County, New York
Death:
1932
Burial:
Prospect Cemetery
Prospect
Oneida County, New York

He married Ellen M. Myers, August 1, 1876. He was educated at Whitestown Seminary, and was principal of the Prospect School six years. He was appointed as village clerk at Prospect. After a religious awakening he turned to God in March 1873, and after serving one year as a licentiate, was ordained by the Whitestown (NY) Quarterly Meeting. He held pastorates at Prospect, Grant and Unadilla Forks and has supplied elsewhere.

Philip Wight
Birth:
Aug. 26, 1793
New Hampshire
Death:
Mar. 11, 1853
Hornby
Steuben County
New York
Burial:
Beaver Dams Cemetery
Beaver Dams
Schuyler County, New York

"Rev. Phillip Wight, a native of New Hampshire, died in Hornby, N.Y., March 11, 1853, aged 60 years. He commenced preaching with the Free Baptists when thirty years of age, and after gathering the Milan church, was ordained as an evangelist in 1826.
In 1836 he removed to New York. He was a faithful advocate of the reforms of the day, and his labors were blessed."--from the "Free Baptist Cyclopedia, pub. 1889, by Burgess and Ward.
His parents were Daniel and Hannah (Lyon) WIGHT, his father being of Revolution War fame. Rev. Wight married Dorcus Hibbard, about 1810, the daughter of John and Sarah Hibbard, of Mass. They had several children, which names are shown on 1850 NY census.

John Wilcox
Birth:
1776
Death:
Feb. 19, 1863
Burial:
Bemis Cemetery
Antwerp
Jefferson County
New York

A Free Baptist minister ordained after June 1796. Died at 86 years, 11 months & 29 days. Husband of Mary Wilcox.
Military Service:
WAR OF 1812 Ballengers Reg., NY Militia.

Rev John Wilcox
Birth:
Nov. 12, 1760
Westerly
Washington County
Rhode Island
Death:
Jul., 1835
Allegany County
New York
Burial:
Wheeler Cemetery
Wirt
Allegany County
New York

He went from RI to Petersburg, NY, where he united with the church at its organization, June 18, 1796. He was subsequently ordained.

Rev Noah D Wilkins
Birth:
Jun., 1806
New York, USA
Death:
Apr. 21, 1871
New York
Burial:

North Afton Cemetery
Afton
Chenango County
New York

An ordained Free Baptist minister from NY, whose name appears in the General Conf. Minutes, in a list of their ministers who had died in 1871.

Joseph Wilson

Birth:
July 8,.1808
German Flats, N. Y.
Death:
Nov. 12, 1878
Gilbert's Mills, N. Y.
Burial:
Gilbert Mills Cemetery
Pennellville, Oswego County,
New York

His spiritual life began in 1835, and he soon received license to preach. In 1840 he was ordained. He was pastor at Granby four years, at German Flats six years, witnessing a gracious outpouring of the spirit, at Gilbert's Mills six years, and also preached in Hastings, Constantia, West Monroe, Parish and other places.He preached a full gospel and was abundant in labors of love. Aug. 29, 1829, he married Ruth Thomas, of German Flats. Benjamin Randall was a great-uncle of Mrs. Wilson.

Amos Wing

Birth:
Nov. 29, 1796
Saratoga County, New York
Death:
Jun. 29, 1879
Oneonta, N.Y
Burial:
Oneonta Plains Cemetery
Oneonta, Otsego County,

New York, Plot: Old Section Son of John and Sylvia Wing. He was Free Baptist clergyman for 45 years in the Freewill Baptist denomination in various places. History of Second Freewill Baptist, Oneonta, shows that he founded it, and pastored it. He was married on Nov. 12, 1820, to Chloe Lyon, b. 26 June, 1801, and d. 25 April 1823. In 1822 he married a second time to Lucinda R. Newman, b. 26 June 1801, and died 1887. Rev. Amos Wing, died at age 82 years. He was born in Saratoga County, but when young moved to Burlington, where he was baptized by Elder William Hunt. He soon began to preach and spent the remainder of his long life in the ministry, being connected many years with the Oneonta church of the Otsego Quarterly Meeting. He was a good man and God blessed his labors

Joseph Wood

Birth:
1809
Death:
May 3, 1878
Naples, N. Y.
Burial:
Burns Cemetery
Burns, Allegany County, New York

For nearly thirty years he was devoted to the work of the ministry. He preached for some twelve churches in western New York, and in nearly every instance good results were manifest. He was a man of excellent judgment and a good minister. The Genesee Y. M. made him a member of the General Conference at Fairport in 1877. His only son fell at Gettysburg.

Inscription:
Age 69 Years
(Civil War Vet)

Ray Woodmansee

Birth:
1794
Death:
Dec. 13, 1875
South New Berlin, N. Y.
Burial:
Riverside Cemetery
South New Berlin,

Chenango County, New York Woodmansee died at age 81 years. He was son of Joseph Woodmansee, of Richmond, R. I., and received ordination with the Reformed Methodists in 1836. In 1845 he moved to New Berlin, N. Y., and soon joined the Holmesville Free Baptist church and was their pastor several years. With the infirmities of age he retired from the pulpit, but gave the influence of his sweet-spirited life to the cause. He loved every cause that honored God and promoted religion.

Death Is The Entry To Life Evermore

Dyer Woodworth

Birth:
Jan. 26, 1798
New York
Death:
Feb. 2, 1859
Burial:
West Hill Cemetery
Hornby
Steuben County, New York

After joining the Calvinistic Baptists when 22 years of age and studying three years in Madison University in preparation for the ministry, he became a Free Baptists in 1840 and was ordained the following year. He was pastor of the Free Baptist Church at Addison, New York for nine years. While living he gave for benevolent purposes about $4000 and he perpetuated his influence by the bequeathing $8000 to the Free Baptist Foreign Mission Societies and the American Bible Society. In his pulpit ministrations he was clear, argumentative and impressive.

William W Young

Birth:
Sep. 22, 1813
Parma
Monroe County, New York
Death:
Oct. 5, 1884
Morganville
Genesee County,
New York
Burial:
Morganville Cemetery
Stafford
Genesee County,
New York

He was converted in youth and uniting with the Clarkson church, soon began to preach. About 1836, Elders D.(David) Marks, J. N. Hinckley and E. Hannibal, ordained him.

His labors were mostly with the churches of the Monroe and Rochester Quarterly Meetings. His sermons were plain and instructive, and many embraced redemption through his instrumentality.

His parents were Eli Montgomery Young and Temperance Palmer.

He married Hester Ann Knapp, 22 June 1837, in Knapps Corner, NY. at age 23.

North Carolina

John William Alford

Birth:
Oct. 3, 1881
Death:
Dec. 5, 1960
Burial:
Kenly Cemetery,
Kenly, Johnston County,
North Carolina

A recognized and respected pastor in eastern North Carolina. Even at age 75 he was driving 100 miles to pastor. He was a brother in law to Mrs. Alice Lupton who was an early leader in the women's movement in North Carolina and on the national level. Records show that he was a member of foreign missions board in the late 50s.

William Edmond Anderson

Birth:
Dec. 9, 1872

North Carolina,
Death:
Feb. 9, 1958
Morehead City
Carteret County
North Carolina
Burial:
Woodlawn Memorial Park
Durham
Durham County
North Carolina

Listed as ordained Free Will Baptist minister in 1916 Western Conference Minutes of Orig. FWB when convened at Johnston Co. NC. His address was "Durham, NC." Age: 85.

Joseph Garfield Ange

Birth:
Dec. 19, 1922
Martin County, North Carolina
Death:
Jul. 16, 2011
Raleigh, Wake County,
North Carolina
Burial:
Win, Washington County,
North Carolina

Ange pastored Free Will Baptist churches in Tennessee, Michigan, and North Carolina. From 1960 to 1976, he served on the Foreign Mission Board for Free Will Baptists. In 1971, Dr. Ange was awarded an Honorary Doctorate from Bob Jones University. In 1972 he became the director of

Religious Activities and the Campus Pastor at Free Will Baptist Bible College in Nashville, TN. Dr. Ange was elected the first full-time President of Southeastern Free Will Baptist College in 1983. He oversaw the construction and occupation of the new campus in 1987. As long as his health permitted, Dr. Ange was a devoted member of Landmark Free Will Baptist Church, where he served as an Adult Sunday School teacher and Senior Saints pastor for 10 years.

Dr. Gerald Porter Ballard
Birth:
Oct. 16, 1936
North Carolina
Death:
Mar. 24, 2014
Shell Point Village
Lee County,
Florida
Burial:
Cremation

The youngest son of Baptist minister Reverend Loy Everett Ballard and Gertrude Oakley Ballard, Jerry grew up immersed in a strong and deep belief in God. As his faith in God grew, so did his passion to reach out to others in the name of Jesus to empower their lives not only with the gospel but also with provisions for their daily lives. Graduating high school in Ayden, NC, Jerry went on to earn degrees from East Carolina University, Columbia Bible College, and Syracuse University.

When Jerry was little, his family moved from town to town because his father was a circuit minister, so Jerry created his own world complete with close friends. He was fond of telling us how he had a group of imaginary friends. One boy was Chinese, one black African and a third from India. Their favorite game? Shooting marbles. These imaginary friends and those games provided the appreciation for all cultures around the world and laid the foundation for his greatest challenge in life: spear-heading the international relief and development arm of the National Association of Evangelicals known as World Relief Corporation from 1978-1991.

Jerry loved and ultimately mastered the power of words—in writing, teaching, and in international negotiation. His first official reporting assignment scooped the landmark case that resulted in passing the law requiring school busses to have side-panel stop signs and flashing red lights, making it illegal for vehicles to pass a stopped school bus while children loaded or unloaded. Of the articles he wrote during the 1950s, he was especially proud of having interviewed a young upcoming actor in 1956 by the name of Andy Griffith.

Jerry and Winnie were long acquainted because of their shared denomination. They finally officially met and started dating when they were teenagers. They married in August 1958 and left eastern North Carolina for Columbia, SC to attend Columbia Bible College. Upon graduation, Jerry and Winnie moved to Nashville, TN to join the Free Will Baptist Foreign Missions Board. Soon their family grew—Kim was born in 1963 and Keri was born in 1967.

Since high school, Jerry wrote prolifically for newspapers, communication as well as marketing and advertising, and several books, winning numerous awards. For Free Will Baptist Foreign Missions Board he created Heartbeat magazine, films and film strips linking the church with missions worldwide. When World Vision International invited him to join their headquarters in Monrovia, CA, he pioneered comm-unication through television and magazine writing and editing as well as raised funds with such innovative projects as the Love Loaf, created by Bobb Biehl.

The Ballard's moved back to the east coast where Jerry taught in a newly formed Master's Program Commun-ications Department with radio, recording and television studios at Columbia Bible College, now Columbia International University in S.C. Jerry began fielding so many marketing and advertising projects that he opened Jerry Ballard Associates in Atlanta hiring Merriana Branan straight out of art school while Winnie ran the office. Jerry took on as partner his long-time friend and award-winning artist Kent Puckett whose wife Pat took over the billing and finance department for Winnie. Kent and Jerry excelled with highly creative and successful campaigns for Christian and secular organizations with such clients as the Stephen Olford Ministries, Bill Gaither Trio, and Chic-fil-A.

In 1977, Dr. Everett Graffam retired as CEO of World Relief Commission (now World Relief Corporation), and Jerry, having been a Board member, was invited to become CEO, providing for people at risk worldwide primarily working through established, national churches and missionaries, including CMA. In the early 1980s, Jerry appointed Grady Mangham from CMA as vice President in charge of refugee resettlement during the war in Cambodia, Vietnam, and Laos setting up a model program for receiving the "boat people" in nations of first asylum and resettling them in participating countries. The writings he produced during this time were the most brilliant, succinct insights into the human condition and call to meet the needs of people everywhere in the name of Jesus.

After Jerry retired from World Relief he continued to work for the causes he loved by consulting with Christian Children's Fund, the Heifer Project, and Feed the Children. He and Don Miltner teamed up for some projects and to write materials for fund raising for a Christian school in Cary, NC before retiring with Winnie to Shell Point in 2006.

Loy Everett Ballard

Birth:
Mar. 20, 1899
Buncombe County,
North Carolina
Death:
Nov. 19, 1978
Greenville, Pitt County,
North Carolina
Burial:
Greenwood Cemetery,
Greenville, Pitt County,
North Carolina

He was born in the mountains of Western North Carolina where he spent the majority of his years as a Free Will Baptist ministers within the bounds of the North Carolina State Convention where he served more than 50 years. Not only was his leadership shown as a pastor to the local church, but was very active in organizing the Free Will Baptist League within his area. He also played an active role in establishing and promoting Craigmont Assembly serving 10 years as co-manager with his wife. For 22 years he was Field Sec. of the state Sunday school convention he also served the Free Will Baptist orphanage at Middlesex as director of religious work. He attended Mars Hill College and the Free Will Baptist Seminary in Ayden.

He served pastorates throughout North Carolina as well as holding the state and national offices in the denomination as listed. He was known as an avid collector of memorabilia and gave his valuable historical materials about Free Will Baptists to the Free Will Baptist Historical Collection at Mount Olive College. He also wrote for many of Free Will Baptist denominational publications encouraging the gathering of materials about Free Will Baptist history.

He was the father of Dr Gerald Porter Ballard who held many roles in the national convention and also was director of World Relief of the National Association of Evangelicals.

John Henry Ballard

Birth:
Oct. 23, 1844
Yancey County, North Carolina
Death:
Jul. 8, 1934 Walnut,
Madison County,
North Carolina
Burial:
Ballard Cemetery,
Buncombe County,
North Carolina

Rev. John H. Ballard was an ordained Free Will Baptist minister, being ordained after 1865. He was converted in Oct. 1862, but served in the Union Army for NC, until it ended. Afterward, the Association wanted him to be ordained and he was reluctant because he had limited education. He preached for over fifty years, and had a fruitful ministry. He was a friend of the Temperance movement and all benevolent causes. The French Broad Association, of which he was affiliated, wrote a tribute they published to honor him and his long life of usefulness in the gospel ministry.

Willis W Ballard
Birth:
1868
Death:
1924
Burial:
Ballard Cemetery,
Barnardsville,
Buncombe County,
North Carolina

James Moses Barfield
Birth:
Oct. 13, 1838
Greene County,
North Carolina
Death:
Sep. 3, 1918

Burial:
Ayden Cemetery, Ayden,
Pitt County, North Carolina

Co-Author of the Barfield and Harrison History of North Carolina Free Will Baptists. He served as a Confederate soldier under the command of Capt. Byrd and in the battalion commanded by Maj. Harding of Greenville. He was licensed to preach the gospel in the year 1867 and was ordained soon after to the full work of the ministry. He was devoted to the Free Will Baptist Denomination and did all in his power to advance their doctrine which he felt was the doctrine of the Bible. It is said that he was not a brilliant speaker, nor great orator and word painter. He was one of the earliest ministers interested in a publication for the denomination which was first published in the town of Fremont, but later moved to Elm City in Wilson County. Later the conferences in North Carolina, with the exception of one, took the matter under their consideration and Elder R. H. Hearn was elected editor and ran the paper in new Bern for several years. Later a Elder Barfield became editor and publisher and soon the office was moved to Ayden by the stockholders in 1897. Elder Barfield was also a pioneer in the work of the Seminary which was started shortly after he moved to Ayden while publishing the *Free Will Baptists,* the state publication.

Jesse Parrott Barrow
Birth:
Oct. 26, 1898
Greene County, North Carolina
Death:
Mar. 11, 1990
Nashville, Davidson County,
Tennessee
Burial:
Hull Road Church Cemetery,
Greene County,
North Carolina

Rev. Jesse P. was student at the Free Will Baptist Seminary, Ayden, NC, per his 1917 WW I Draft Registration. In 1920, he was employed in Chicago, perhaps where he met Anna, his future wife. He possibly studied at a College in Nashville, where they were living in 1945-46, per old minutes which stated Nashville as their residence. In the 1949 Nashville City Directory, he and Anna were still in Nashville, with "Free Will Bible College." The 1958 Nashville City Directory showed him employed as Teacher at FWBBC, and Anna as Librarian there. Records show Rev. J. P. Barrow as having served on National FWB Church Boards and committees. He was honored as a leader and minister among the church.

Nigel Bruce Barrow

Birth:
October 23, 1911
Greene County,
North Carolina
Death:
March 8, 2004
Greene County,
North Carolina
Burial:
Hull Road Church Cemetery,
Greene County,
North Carolina

Well-known Free Will Baptist minister in North Carolina and the National Convention in the 50's and 60's, he attended Moody Bible Institute and Northwestern Theological Seminary in Chicago and later attended the graduate school at Texas A&M University. He was ordained to the ministry in 1931 at the Hull Road Original Free Will Baptist Church. He was faithful to his ministry over seven decades and during this period pastored over 30 churches, principally in Eastern North Carolina. He served as the Assistant Superintendent of the Children's Home at Middlesex and was a founding member of the Board of Trustees of Mount Olive College. He managed the denomination's publishing house in Ayden during the 1960s. His family established the Barrow Family Endowment at Mount Olive College endowing professor-ship in the Department of Religion

Rev J A Blalock

Birth:
Mar. 22, 1869
Death:
Oct. 7, 1960
Burial:
Greenwood Cemetery
Dunn
Harnett County
North Carolina

An ordained minister of the Free Will Baptist church, whose name is in list of ministers in 1903, Conference, in Harnett Co. N.C. when meeting at the Hodges Chapel Church.

Thomas Elijah Beaman

Birth:
Jan. 6, 1899
North Carolina
Death:
Dec. 7, 1961
Goldsboro,
Wayne County,
North Carolina
Burial:
Willow Dale Cemetery,
Goldsboro,
Wayne County,
North Carolina

Jesse R Bennett

Birth:
Jul. 1, 1902
Death:
Jan. 17, 1964
Burial:
New Bern Memorial Cemetery,
Trent Woods,
Craven County,
North Carolina,
Plot: Section A

Rev Edward Dee Bissette

Birth:
Feb. 1, 1890
Nash County, North Carolina,
Death:
Apr. 9, 1970
Nash County
North Carolina
Burial:
Bailey Cemetery
Bailey,Nash County
North Carolina

Rev Edward Dee Bissette; son of Kennon and Etta Bailey Bissette
Rev. Dee Bissette," is listed in a roll of ordained Free Will Baptist ministers in 1935 Minutes of the Western

Conference of Free Will Baptist, which included Nash, Wilson, and other counties.
Rev. Dee Bissette, is also shown in several obits in Wilson Co. *Daily Times*, as having conducted funerals for Free Will Baptist persons at the White Oak FWB Church, Wilson County, in the 1940's and on up through the 1960's.

Andrew Jackson Bordeaux
Birth:
May 17, 1840
New Hanover County
North Carolina, USA
Death:
Aug. 1, 1916
Bladen County
North Carolina
Burial:
Haw Bluff Baptist Church
Cemetery
Kelly
Bladen County
North Carolina

An active minister in the early history of the Free Will Baptist church, and his name appearing in old church records. Son of Rebecca Holly and James Bordeaux.
Enlisted in Company A, North Carolina Co. A 1st Heavy Artillery Company on 15 May 1862.Promoted to Full Corporal on 08 Aug 1863.

Clarence F. Bowen
Birth:
January 5, 1912
Death:
January 22, 1984
Wayne County, North Carolina
Burial:
Stoney Creek, Stoney Creek,
Wayne County, North Carolina

He was a well-known pastor, writer, and denominational leader for the FWB League. He was a past president of the North Carolina state convention and had been honored as Minister Of The Year by the convention. He was a graduate of Campbell and Wake Forest universities. He received his Master's degree at George Peabody College For Teachers in Nashville, Tennessee. He was the pastor of the Pleasant Hill, First Free Will Baptist Church of Wilson, and Stony Creek Free Will Baptist Churches in N.C. He also had served as pastor of the East Nashville Free Will Baptist Church in Nashville, Tennessee. He was an honorary life member of the North Carolina Free Will Baptist Foreign Mission Board and had for many years been a writer for the Free Will Baptist Church Literature Program. Delois Loveless the authors wife was converted under his ministry.

William G. Boykin
Birth:
Oct. 10, 1900
Death:
Mar. 1, 1974
Burial:
Raines Cross RoadsCemetery
Princeton
Johnston County,
North Carolina

An ordained Free Will Baptist minister, whose name appears in early NC records, minutes, etc.

Levi Braxton
Birth:
Nov. 7, 1886
Death:
Oct. 15, 1964
Burial:
Hollywood Cemetery
Farmville
Pitt County,
North Carolina

Early North Carolina FWB minister.

Charles Brown
Birth:
Unknown
Death:
Feb. 22, 1998
Goldsboro,
Wayne County,
North Carolina
Burial:
Evergreen Memorial
Cemetery,
Goldsboro,
Wayne,
North Carolina

He had a fruitful ministry of 42 years out of his life of 75. He organized seven churches in three states which included North Carolina, South Carolina and Virginia. His most noted work was the Collingswood Free Will Baptist Church in Portsmouth, Virginia where he pastored 13 years. He also started two other churches in the Tidewater Virginia area. The Great Bridge and Faith Free Will Baptist churches.

Noah D. Brown
Birth:
July 8, 1918
Death:
February 8, 1988
Burial:
Mount Moriah Cemetery,
Garner,
Wake County, North Carolina

Seldon D. Bullard
Birth:
Unknown
Death:
Sep. 26,
Myrtle Beach,
Horry County,
South Carolina
Burial:
Guilford Memorial Park,
Greensboro,
Guilford County,
North Carolina

He was a native of Carthage, North Carolina, but moved to Myrtle Beach, South Carolina in 1970 and organized the First Free Will Baptist Church. He had served pastorates in Darlington, South Carolina; Louisa, Kentucky; Bristol, Tennessee; Glennville, Georgia; Leadington, Missouri; and Morehead city, North Carolina. He received his theological training at Columbia Bible College. He was an active denominational leader serving on the General Board of the National Association of Free Will Baptists, Superintendent of the Kentucky Children's Orphanage in Louisa, Kentucky, and on the National Publications Board.

Tommy Lynn Burch, Jr
Birth:
unknown
Death:
Oct. 26, 2012
Bryson City, Swain County,
North Carolina
Burial:
Cornerstone Wesleyan
Church Cemetery,
Bryson City, Swain County,
North Carolina

A native of Tennessee, Tommy spent over 30 years of his life in Graham and Swain Counties. He was a Minister and Pastored Churches in Elizabethton TN at Moore's Chapel Freewill Baptist Church and in Bryson City at Sawmill Hill Freewill Baptist Church. He graduated from The Freewill Baptist Bible College) with a B.S. degree in Pastoral Administration and also an E.T.T.A. Teaching diploma. He also worked for Swain County West Elementary School for 12 years.

J. W. Byrd
Birth:
Aug. 30, 1867
Death:
Sep. 7, 1917
Burial:
Saint Mary's Grove Original
Free Will BC Cemetery,
Benson, Johnston County,
North Carolina

Rev Ruffin Bryant Carroll
Birth:
Oct. 10, 1864
North Carolina
Death:
Sep. 24, 1940
Bailey
Nash County
North Carolina
Burial:
Rock Springs Free Will Baptist
Church Cemetery
Bailey
Nash County, North Carolina

An ordained Free Will Baptist minister/pastor.

J F Casey
Birth:
Sep. 30, 1872
Death:
Dec. 31, 1918
Burial:
Willow Dale Cemetery,
Goldsboro
Wayne County, North Carolina

Mance R. Cason
Birth:
unknown
Death:
Jun. 22, 2016
Morehead City
Carteret County
North Carolina
Burial:
Gethsemane Memorial Park
Morehead City
Carteret County
North Carolina

Dr. Mance R. Cason, 88, of Morehead City, NC passed away at his home. A funeral service was held at First Free Will Baptist Church in Morehead City with Rev. Rick Cason and Rev. Reuben Cason officiating. Dr. Cason was a pastor for over 68 years; for 20 of those years he served at First Free Will Baptist Church in Morehead City.

Rev James W Chatham
Birth:
Jan., 1849
Alexander County
North Carolina
Death:
1925
Morganton
Burke County
North Carolina
Burial:
Broughton Hospital Cemetery
Morganton
Burke County
North Carolina
Plot: r26 g8

James W Chatham is the son of Joseph Maxwell Chatham and Martha Artela Underwood. He was reared in Alexander County, NC and is a brother to Sarah Jane, Mary E, Rachel Amanda and Joseph Elisha Maxwell Chatham.

Named in Woolsey's Hist. as a minister in the Freewill Baptist, who were in the John Wheeler Association organized in 1881, in Washington, Co. VA. (Washington Co. and NC's Sullivan Co. were next to each other, in NC's eastern part, next to VA. This Association was an outgrowth of the Toe River Association in Sullivan Co. TN.

According to online family trees James is said to have had a traumatic brain injury and to have served as a clergyman. He was admitted to the asylum after 1910.

Floyd B. Cherry
Birth:
April 15, 1916
Dothan, Alabama
Death:
February 24, 2005
North Carolina
Burial:
Selma Memorial Gardens,
Selma,
Johnston County,
North Carolina

He was an educator, minister, and writer in the Free Will Baptist denomination. Dr.

Cherry, was a native of Alabama and was a minister for 65 years beginning at the age of 16. He was ordained a Free Will Baptist minister in Dothan, Alabama on July 16, 1933. He pastored churches in Alabama, Florida, Georgia and North Carolina. He attended Zion Bible School in Georgia; the University of Florida where he received a Bachelor's Degree in Bible Study; and Thomas Edison college, where he received his Master's in Bible Study. He earned his Doctor's Degree from Bob Jones University in Greenville, South Carolina in 1975. He came to pastor the Pine Level Free Will Baptist Church in North Carolina where he was the founder of the Carolina Bible Institute that still continues to this day. He wrote three books and also several pamphlets..

Cadmus Hunter Coates
Birth:
Apr. 16, 1899
Death:
Aug. 13, 1968
Burial:
Lakeside Memorial Gardens
Angier
Harnett County
North Carolina

He was an Original Free Will Baptist minister active in the formation of the North Carolina State Association of Orig. FWB.

W. Ruffin Coats
Birth:
Dec. 2, 1866
Death:
Sep. 11, 1950
Burial:
Saint Mary's Grove Original Free Will Baptist church Cemetery
Benson, Johnston County, North Carolina

Richard Ray Cordell
Birth:
Aug. 28, 1935
Cincinnati, Ohio,
Death:
Jul. 28, 2011
Goldsboro, North Carolina
Burial:
Evergreen Memorial Cemetery,
Goldsboro,
Wayne County,
North Carolina

He served his Lord in ministry for over 54 years and had also served his country in the United States Army. Pastor Cordell was a graduate of the Free Will Baptist College in Nashville, Tennessee, where he received a Bachelor of Science degree in Pastoral Studies. His three pastorates included three states: Indiana, Tennessee, and Alabama. After retiring in Guin, Alabama, Rev. Cordell served for three years as the promotional director for the Alabama Free Will Baptist State Association. He later came to Goldsboro to serve as the Outreach Pastor for Faith Free Will Baptist Church. His greatest joy in life was door-knocking, leading someone to the Lord and asking people to come and visit the church.

Louis N Coscia
Birth:
1926
Death:
May 23, 2010
Burial:
West Memorial Park,
Weaverville,
Buncombe County,
North Carolina

A native of Memphis, Tenn., Rev. Coscia was a Free Will Baptist Missionary serving for 28 years in Brazil. Louis was a running and jogging enthusiast and a gardener. He especially enjoyed growing pansies and is known by many in his area as the "pansy man." He enjoyed reading and writing poetry and had a wonderful sense of humor. A celebration of Rev. Coscia's life was held with Rev. Danny Gasperson officiating.

Clyde W. Cox
Birth:
Mar. 26, 1920
Rowan County, North Carolina
Death:
Unknown
Wilson, Wilson County,
North Carolina
Burial:
Selma Memorial Gardens,
Selma, Johnston County,
North Carolina,

Rev. Cox dedicated his life to the Lord. Throughout his ministry, he was a pastor at 15 churches beginning in 1952 and ending in 2003 at Spring Hill Church in Goldsboro, N.C. He conducted 274 revivals. He also taught music school in churches throughout North Carolina. He sang, played piano, wrote music and songs and directed music for several revivals. Rev. Cox touched many people's lives over the last 52 years as a dedicated messenger of God. He also served in WWII in the US Navy on the USS Birmingham in the Pacific.

**As The Rain From Heaven Refreshes The Parched Ground,
So Death Provides The Saint To Partake Of The Refreshing Of The Soul In The Presence Of Jesus.**

Rev M E Cox
Birth:
May 20, 1927
Bath
Beaufort County
North Carolina
Death:
Jul. 7, 2016
North Carolina
Burial:
Oakdale Cemetery
Washington
Beaufort County
North Carolina

He was born in Bath where he graduated from high school May 10, 1944. He was a World War II Veteran. Rev. Cox spent most of his life in the ministry of Original Free Will Baptist. He served in several capacities including 18 years as moderator of the Piedmont Conference and in several churches as pastor and was originally ordained in July 1956. He was the author of the book "From the Plow to the Pulpit."

John S. Craft
Birth:
1942
North Carolina
Death:
1980
Burial:
Ayden Cemetery, Ayden,
Pitt County, North Carolina

He was a Free Will Baptist missionary serving in Brazil from 1968-1973.

**Today is not a day of distress
But a day of delight.**

Elder Parrot Creech
Birth:
Sep. 12, 1832
Death:
Jan. 6, 1874
Burial:

Saint Mary's Grove Original Free Will Baptist Cemetery, Benson, Johnston County, North Carolina

Elder Creech was founder of St. Mary's Grove Original Free Will Baptists Church.

John Linward Crocker, Sr
Birth:
Apr. 1, 1931
Death:
Dec. 12, 2010
Burial:
Branch Chapel Free Will Baptist Church, Smithfield, Johnston County, North Carolina

Funeral services at Branch Chapel Free Will Baptist Church with the Rev. Terry Dennis and Mr. Luby Tyner officiating. Burial was with military honors.

Elder Moses LaFlaver Cummings
Birth:
Jun. 2, 1876
Canada
Death:
Dec. 26, 1963
Raleigh

Wake County
North Carolina
Burial:
Marsh Swamp Church Cemetery
Wilson
Wilson County
North Carolina

Son of Richard Cummings and Cordelia Pickens. FindaGrave contributor Winnie shared that "he was an ordained minister in the Free Will Baptist church, shown in 1935 Minutes' list of ministers in the Western Conference".

Inscription:
Traveling Evangelist and Home Missionary
Known as "Blackie of the North Woods"

Rev William Alonzo Dail
Birth:
Aug. 22, 1876
Pitt County
North Carolina
Death:
Jan. 1, 1956
Pitt County
North Carolina
Burial:
Reedy Branch Baptist Church

Cemetery
Winterville
Pitt County, North Carolina

Rev. William A. Dail was the son of Thomas Dail and Sarah (Cannon) DAIL. He died at aged 79 yrs, having lived most of his life in the Winterville area. He was an ordained Free Will Baptist minister. He served several churches as pastor in counties in northeastern North Carolina, before failing health caused him to retire about ten years prior to his death. He married Hattie L. Barber.

The deacons of Reedy Branch Free Will Baptist Church served as pallbearers, and members of the FWB Central Conference were honorary bearers.

Frank Davenport
Birth:
1923
Death:
1997
Goldsboro,

Wayne County, North Carolina
Burial:
Wayne Memorial Park,
Goldsboro,
Wayne County,
North Carolina

He was a Church builder organizing 12 churches in North Carolina where he spent most of his ministry. He also helped start four Christian schools. All were in North Carolina. His longest pastorate was a 20 year tenure at the Faith Free Will Baptist church in Goldsboro, one of the 12 churches he organized. His ministry spanned 45 years in North Carolina and Kentucky. He was a native of Pitt County, North Carolina. He was ordained to preach in 1952 at age 29. As a leader he was elected to numerous positions in North Carolina and on the national level. He served six years on the national Home Mission Board and on the national Executive Committee. He Served The North Carolina State Home Missions, and the Bible Bookstore Board. He was also manager of Jubilee, Inc. and as Treasurer of the Free Will Baptist Superannuation Assn.

James Robert Davidson
Birth:
May 28, 1898
Death:
Jan. 9, 1972
Burial:
New Bern Memorial Cemetery,
Trent Woods,
Craven County,
North Carolina,
Plot: Section G

Davison is remembered as a long-time crusader for Christian education. Davison made the Board Of Education's report at the 1939 session of the national Association at Bryan, Texas with the proposition of beginning a national Bible college. He at the 1942 meeting in Columbus, Mississippi during his report for that the board was authorized by the convention to open the school in Nashville, Tennessee on September 15, 1942. The first building purchased by the college still bears the name of the man who labored for the college's promotion for so many years. He served on the Board of Trustees of the college in 1943 until 1964. During this 21 year tenure, he served as chairman, vice chairman, and secretary of the board. He also served the as Business Manager during 1942-1944 and again in 1946-1947 He served the National Association as an Assistant Moderator from 1938-1944. At the 1940 for meeting he was elected as Moderator, a post he held until 1946.

Rev James E Davis
Birth:
Dec. 5, 1918
Death:
Apr. 26, 2006
Burial:
Ashelawn Gardens of Memory

Asheville
Buncombe County
North Carolina

Rev J.E. Davis' name was in roll of ordained ministers in the 1935 Western Conference Minutes.

Benjamin Bardin Deans
Birth:
Mar. 18, 1866
Death:
Jun. 17, 1934
Burial:
Joseph J. Bissette Cemetery,
Nash County,North Carolina

Garrett Deweese
Birth:
1772
Botetourt County,
Virginia
Death:
Nov. 28, 1839
Buncombe County,
North Carolina
Burial:
Big Ivy Cemetery,
Barnardsville,
Buncombe County,
North Carolina

He was the son of Henry Deweese and Elizabeth (Hughes) Deweese, both bn PA. (per Family Trees).

He married Susannah Palmer about 1795 in Buncombe, NC. They had nine children.

He was an early Baptist preacher, but became of the free will type, and worked in North Carolina and East Tennessee region with Revs Moses Peterson and John Wheeler. At first they were members of the French Broad Association of Baptists. This Association became divided over the Calvinistic and the Arminian question. The Arminian group led by Rev. Garrett Dewese, was "free will" but practiced close communion. Although the Reverends Peterson and Wheeler agreed with Deweese on the question of the free moral agency of man and they both invited all Christians to the Communion, they agreed to meet with prayer, and settle the questions between them regarding communion. They did that became known as the "Free Will Baptist." Pioneers from other parts of North Carolina and Virginia settled here, which were of this persuasion, and six small churches were formed, in five counties, in two states, and separated by mountains. These old preachers carried out their "calling" in very difficult circumstances and hardships.

A little later, Rev. Wm. Bonaparte WOOLSEY, joined in and formed the Toe River Association of Free Will Bapt. churches which during his lifetime, grew tremendously.

Not many records exists of Rev. Deweese's detailed ministry, but the records do show he was a faithful man and a leader in his time for his Free Will Baptist church to help serve the spiritual needs of these scattered people.

His son, Levi, also became a minister.

Where he is buried is not exactly known, as I have found no records that show where he was interred. Rev. Garrett Dewesse, and first wife, Susanna Palmer Deweese, lived in Buncombe and died there...she in 1815-16, and he in 1839, and his Will was proved in January, 1840, Buncombe Co. NC.

I've been told there are no "Deweese" family buried in Big Ivy Cemetery; it is recorded that Deweese preached at that Baptist church, and may have pastored it.

God Will Not Let Death Win

Levi Deweese
Birth:
Sep. 2, 1810
North Carolina
Death:
May 25, 1902
North Carolina
Burial:
Gabriels Creek Baptist Church, Cemetery,
Mars Hill, Madison County, North Carolina

Rev. Levi Deweese was the son of Rev. Garrett and Susannah (Palmer) Deweese..In the Census of 1850, Levi was listed as a head of household in Buncombe Co, NC. .A pioneer Free Will Baptist preacher in North Carolina and East Tennessee..

Sigbee Bryant Dilda
Birth:
Jan. 8, 1936
Death:
Sep. 11, 2002
Greenville
Pitt County, North Carolina
Burial:
Queen Anne Cemetery
Fountain
Pitt County, North Carolina

Rev Sigbee Dilda, former pastor of Pamplico FWB Church, NAFWB General Board member from South Carolina for many years, and long time soldier of the Cross went to be with the Lord on September 11th. Brother Sigbee had recently resigned from Pamplico FWB Church and moved to Hookerton,NC because of ill health. His wife, Mary, had taught for many years at Maranatha Christian School (First FWB Church, Florence) and is now continuing her labors at Mt. Calvary Christian School; where she lives close to son, Bryant. Daughter, Susanna, is married to Rev Carroll Bazen,Pastor of Grace FWB Church in Lake City, SC.Many things stand out about Brother Sigbee. He was a long time Pastor Glenwood FWB Church (Arkansas) 1965-67; Pamplico FWB Church (SC) 1967-1970; Ruth's Chapel FWB Church (NC) 1970-1980; Great Bridge

FWB Church (Virginia) 1980-1983; Tabernacle FWB Church (NC) 1983-89; Lebanon FWB Church (SC) 1989-1990; Pamplico FWB Church (SC) 1990-2002. He believed what he believed and was willing to stand for that belief (A sentiment echoed by all of the speakers at his funeral service). He knew how to have fun but he also knew when to stand firm.And he was a faithful soul winner and soldier for the Lord.

Rev Burrell Thomas Dixon
Birth:
May 5, 1870
Death:
Feb. 16, 1951
Burial:
Pineview Cemetery
South Rocky Mount
Edgecombe County
North Carolina
Plot: PV: 46:0:86

Ordained Free Will Bapt. minister/pastor in NC. Name on roll of Western Conference minutes in 1935.

Robert Jefferson Durham
Birth:
Mar. 23, 1927
Wayne County, North Carolina
Death:
Sep. 9, 2012

Rocky Mount, Nash County, North Carolina
Burial:
Rocky Mount Memorial Park, Rocky Mount
Nash County, North Carolina

He was born in Wayne County to the late Jeff and Pearl Harris Durham. He lived with his parents and helped them run their farm until 1945, when he was drafted into the Army. After being stationed in France and completing his service he returned home and worked as a Deputy Sheriff in Greene County.

He later became Associate Sales Manager with the Western and Southern Life Insurance Company where he worked for eleven years, which moved him to Rocky Mount in 1954; during which time he answered the call to preach. He attended the Evangelical Baptist College and graduated from the William Carter Bible College. In 1960, he founded and organized Grace Free Baptist Church with eleven charter members. Prior to his retirement he saw the church attendance grow to over 500, and in 1976 the church founded Grace Christian School. He had a passion for soul winning and preaching God's word and was honored to see ten of the church members be ordained and begin full-time work for God. Reverend Durham was speaker on the Grace Baptist Hour on WECE radio for 20 years. He served two terms as local moderator and six years as state moderator of the Palmer Association of Free Baptist Churches. After retirement, he held numerous revivals, was interim pastor for several area Baptist churches and continued being a faithful working member of Grace Free Baptist Church. He was survived by his devoted loving wife of 63 years, Gladys Speight Durham.

Nathan Earl Eason
Birth:
Nov. 2, 1932
Greene County, North Carolina
Death:
Apr. 4, 2008
Rocky Mount
Nash County, North Carolina
Burial:
Queen Anne Cemetery
Fountain
Pitt County, North Carolina

Nathan Eason married Mary Agnes Dilda on May 24, 1952 in Greenville, Pitt Co., and NC. His parents were James C Eason (1893 - 1975) and Ora Mae Moore Eason (1899 - 1970). He had been the pastor of Grace Free Will Baptist Church in Greenville.

Lonne R. Ennis
Birth:
1895
Death:
1977
Goldsboro,
Wayne County,
North Carolina
Burial:
Willow Dale Cemetery,
Goldsboro,
Wayne County,
North Carolina

Denominational leader, pastor, educator, and conference speaker. He pioneered for a educational program which was greatly needed in our denomination. The Lord equipped to deal with the keen mind and thorough education he acquired abilities that few men among us possessed.. At a time when we needed an educational vision, and someone who could implement that vision, brother Ennis conducted Bible institutes across our denomination. He built an interest in education which finally resulted in Free Will Baptist Bible College being established in Nashville, Tennessee. He stepped into a world of national prominence among Free Will Baptists in 1940 when he preached the opening sermon in the fourth annual session in Paintsville, Kentucky. His sermon *Rivers Of Living Waters* was considered a masterpiece. He was elected as the first executive Sec. of the restless, newly organized denomi-nation in 1940. He served in that position until 1943. He traveled thousands of miles promoting denomination outreach during which time he. Pastored three churches at the same time and in addition to his extensive travels. He was summons to Nashville, Tennessee in 1944 where he was appointed president of the Free Will Baptist Bible College serving from 1944 until 1947. His training had been secured from Moody Bible Institute and his diplomatic skills required as an Executive Sec. had been soundly tested for the job. He led the college in purchasing the Sword building in 1945, the same year that the college yearbook, *The Lumen* was dedicated to him. He taught a variety of courses while at the college including English, Sunday School and Church Administration, Bible and others. Ennis remained a guiding voice in his native North Carolina because of his great spiritual strength and wisdom.. He was pastoring two churches at his death at age 81. One of the buildings at Free Will Baptist Bible College is named for him.

Nor pain, nor death can enter there.

James A. Evans
Birth:
November 10, 1905
Death:
October 25, 1999
Lucama, Wilson County,
North Carolina
Burial:
Lucas Cemetery, Lucama,
Wilson County,
North Carolina

He was a early Free Will Baptist preacher from Wayne County in eastern North Carolina. He attended Eureka College in Ayden, North Carolina, and was a graduate of the Pastor's Institute of Duke University. In 1994 he received the first honorary Doctor Of Divinity degree given by Mount Olive College. He was an ordained minister for 74 years and served churches in North Carolina, Texas, and Florida. He was selected the outstanding Free Will Baptist Minister of the Year by the North Carolina Association OFWB in 1972. He was the first full-time employee of Mount Olive College where he began in 1954 serving as the Director Of Public Relations. From 1940-1949 he served as the Superintendent of the Children's Home in Middlesex. He was the co-founder of the Free Will Baptist Church Finance Association in 1940 and the first Chairman of

Craigmont Assembly of the Original Free Will Baptist Conference Center in 1945.

W. B. Everett
Birth:
1877
Death:
1948
Craven County, North Carolina
Burial:
Cedar Grove Cemetery,
New Bern,
Craven County,
North Carolina

Early leader and minister in the eastern area of North Carolina.

James W Everton
Birth:
Nov. 2, 1923
Death:
Mar. 4, 1971
Burial:
East Duplin Memorial Gardens,
Beulaville,
Duplin County, North Carolina

Free Will Baptist preacher and WWII veteran.
Inscription:
GM3 USNR WWII

Elder George W. Ferrell
Birth:
Nov. 11, 1871
Wilson, North Carolina
Death:
Aug. 17, 1942
Wilson, North Carolina
Burial:
Stony Hill Free Will Baptist Church Cemetery
Nash County
North Carolina

George is the son of Jacob M. Ferrell and Mary Della Lancaster. He married Martha Bryant. Ordained Free Will Baptist minister, listed in minutes of the 1935 Western Conference of Orig. FWB. Active minister and pastor as long as physically able...he was included in the 'retired minister' list at the 1935 session.

William M Ferrell
Birth:
Oct. 25, 1886
Johnston County,
North Carolina
Death:
Nov. 6, 1937
Durham,
Durham County,
North Carolina
Burial:
Bethel Original
Freewill Baptist Church

Cemetery,
Four Oaks, Johnston County,
North Carolina

Rev Zalph P. Ferrell
Birth:
Feb. 13, 1857
Death:
May 11, 1940
Burial:
Shady Grove Free Will Baptist Church Cemetery
Durham
Durham County
North Carolina

His first name was Zalpheus; He used initials, Rev. Z.P.Ferrell. An ordained Free Will Baptist minister/pastor. His name was in list of ministers in Minutes of the 49th Session of the Western Conference, convened in 1935.

John Eugene Floyd
Birth:
Jan. 17, 1906
Caldwell County,
North Carolina
Death:
Nov. 21, 1996
Charlotte
Mecklenburg County
North Carolina
Burial:
Hillcrest Gardens
Mount Holly
Gaston County
North Carolina

Rev. John Floyd, 90, of Mt. Holly, a retired Free Will Baptist pastor, evangelist and church planter. He was converted on July 10, 1927 and was ordained in 1946. He overcame tuberculosis at the age of 24, but still refuse to preach. He struggled to accept the call to preach for 15 years because of his fear and an inability to read and his lack of formal education. Six years later at age 30 after over hearing a doctor tell his wife that he would die of pneumonia, he finally accepted the call. He pastored the First Free Will Baptist Church, Marion, North Carolina in 1946 leading the church to grow from 29 members to 412. He pastored several other churches in the 50s and 60s including the Sea Level and Cedar Island Free Will Baptist churches, and the Calvary Free Will Baptist Church in Jacksonville. At the age of 66 he began pastoring the Adawolfe Free Will Baptist Church in Virginia. The church grew from 60 in Sunday school and added 130 members while baptizing 100 members and had four men call to preach and they paid for a new parsonage. He was known as a man of prayer and prayed that 100 men would enter the ministry through his preaching. Some 132 men did answer the call to preach including his son, a son-in-law, two grandsons and a nephew. Also, through his ministry Miss Volena Wilson went to India as a missionary. He preached in 37 states, Canada, Mexico, Puerto Rico and Jerusalem. He organized 15 churches and preached revivals in 100 churches where he witnessed more than 23,000 professions of faith in response to his 7500 sermons which he preached. He also had a continuing the radio ministry for 30 years.

Elder Frederick Asa Fonville

Birth:
Mar. 6, 1770
Alamance County,
North Carolina
Death:
Apr. 21, 1835
Alamance County,
North Carolina
Burial:
Fonville Family Cemetery
Alamance County,
North Carolina

A pioneer Free Will Baptist minister, along with others, who ministered in the remnant left of the Philadelphia Association, in 1832. He was a worthy and faithful man, of good reputation, who stood on his convictions. Beloved son of Stephen Fonville and Lucy Kibble. He was the husband of Rebecca Oliver, whom he married Jan 29, 1790. Their son was William Washington Fonville. After her death in 1793, he married Mary Polly Averett on Dec 12, 1793. Their children were Nathan Fonville; Hannah Fonville; Edna Fonville; John Averett Fonville; Sallie Fonville; and James Roney Fonville. After Mary died in 1816, he married Charity Graham on May 30, 1816 in Orange, North Carolina. Their children were Mary Fonville; Frederick W Fonville; Asa Graham Fonville; Francis Fonville; and Brice Frederick Fonville.
Spouses: Mary Polly Everette Fonville (1775 - 1816). Rebecca Oliver Fonville (1777 -93),
Charity Graham Fonville (1789 - 1858).

William M Fulcher, Jr
Birth:
May 6, 1933
Bridgeton,
Craven County,
North Carolina
Death:
Mar. 23, 2004
New Bern,
Craven County,
North Carolina
Burial:
Dixon Cemetery, Aurora,
Beaufort County,
North Carolina

Bill graduated from the Bridgeton High School in 1952 and thereafter, played baseball for the New Bears. He was drafted into the United States Army in 1953 and served in Korea and Japan. He was trained in radio communication. In 1955 he was honorably discharged from the Army and enrolled in Free Will Baptist Bible College in Nashville Tennessee, to prepare for the Ministry.

He graduated in 1959 with a BA degree. While in school he married Linda Barks in 1957 and during their marriage life they had five children. He pastored the Bethany Free Will Baptist Church in Winterville, North Carolina during 1959-1960. It was at the end of 1960 that he was commissioned as a foreign missionary for the International Mission Board Of Free Will Baptists. He attended the Spanish language Institute in San Jose, Costa Rica during 1961. From 1961 to 1969 he served in Uruguay, South America and from 1971 through 1979 served in Panama, Central America. He returned to the pastorate in 1979 and served the Bethel Free Will Baptist Church in S. Roxana, Illinois. He served there until 1981 when He was hired by the National Home Mission Board to serve the Spanish-speaking people in Houston, Texas. In 1988 through 1992 he was employed by the Southeastern Free Will Baptist College in Wendell, North Carolina as the Promotional Director. Afterwards he pastored the Faith Free Will Baptist Church in Carrollton, Virginia from 1992 to 2000, and then the Faith Free Will Baptist Church in Maysville, North Carolina from 2000 until 2004 where he was serving when he died.

Houston Owen Ganey

Birth:
Nov. 17, 1931
Death:
Mar. 23, 2003
Nashville, Davidson County, Tennessee
Burial:
Richmond Memorial Park, Rockingham, Richmond County, North Carolina

Brother Ganey was a well-respected minister, evangelist and pastor. He was always an encourager to all who knew him. The native North Carolinian was living in Nashville at the time of his death.

Owen B. Garriss

Birth:
Nov. 12, 1850
Death:
Sep. 11, 1929
Burial:
Garriss Cemetery (Watha) Pender County, North Carolina
Son of Rufus & Sophia J. Garriss. His name was listed in 1903 Harnett Co. NC Free Will Baptist roll of ministers.

Rev Henry Hood Goff

Birth:
1874
Death:
1950
Burial:
Hodges Chapel Cemetery
Benson, Johnston County
North Carolina

His name was in a list of minister's names in 1903 in the Free Will Baptist Minutes of Cape Fear Conference, when it met at Hodges Chapel Church, Harnett Co. NC.

Inscription:
Ordained 1898

Raymond Albert Gaskins

Birth:
Jul. 1, 1921
North Carolina
Death:
Nov. 22, 2010
Ayden, Pitt County
North Carolina
Burial:
Ayden Cemetery,
Ayden, Pitt County,
North Carolina

He graduated as salutatorian of his 1938 Ayden High School class, lettering in football and boxing. In 1943 he completed a three-year Coppersmith apprenticeship from the Norfolk Navy Yard and entered the U.S. Navy, serving as a quartermaster in World War II. He returned to Ayden after the war, attending Banking School at UNC-Chapel Hill, while employed with Planter's Bank and Trust Co. Raymond became a minister in 1957, after completing studies at The Free Will Baptist Bible College in Nashville, Tenn. He served as pastor of Liberty Free Will Baptist Church in Ayden from 1958-2004. He met Beatrice Loftin Gaskins in 1946, marrying her in 1947. She preceded him in death after 57 years of marriage.

If You Spend All Your Time Worrying About Dying, Living Isn't Going To Be Much Fun.

Rev Earl Glenn
Birth:
Jan. 6, 1925
Durham
Durham County
North Carolina
Death:
Sep. 24, 2013
Wayne County
North Carolina
Burial:
Wayne Memorial Park
Goldsboro
Wayne CountyNorth Carolina

The Rev. Earl Hollis Glenn, 88, Kitty Askins Hospice Center. Funeral services at Stoney Creek Original Free Will Baptist Church. The Rev. Johnny Sullivan and the Rev. Barry Williamson officiated. Rev. Glenn was a native of Durham, N.C., the son of Edward D. Glenn and Coy Inez Glenn.

Louis H Green
Birth:
Sep. 26, 1940
Death:
Feb. 18, 1986
Burial:
Sweet Hope Freewill Baptist Church Cemetery,
Pitt County, North Carolina

Jesse Christopher Griffin, Sr
Birth:
June 22, 1879
Nash County,
North Carolina
Death:
1968
North Carolina
Burial:
Cedar Grove Cemetery,
New Bern,
Craven County,
North Carolina

Well-known Free Will Baptist minister, pastor, writer and denominational leader. He was the author of an early Free Will Baptist *Minister's Handbook.* He was ordained to the ministry on June 10, 1910 just before his thirty-first birthday. He attended Eureka College and the Free Will Baptist Seminary at Ayden, North Carolina from 1912 until 1914. During his 57 years of ministry he pastored 28 churches, conducting numerous revivals, funerals, performing marriage rites, and won scores of people to Christ in a ministry that led from the eastern seashore to the mountains of North Carolina and extensive work in many other states. He united with the Free Will Baptist denomination at the White Oak Hill church in Nash County in 1905. He was manager of the Free Will Baptist Press 1914-16. His column "Notes and Quotes" appeared in the *Free Will Baptist* for 25 years. He was moderator of the Eastern conference of North Carolina Free Will Baptists 1919-1923. He was a member and served as secretary to the Free Will Baptist Orphanage Board between 1923-28..

He was Vice President of the North Carolina State Association 1931-36. President of the North Carolina State Association 1940-42. Field Sec. North Carolina State Association 1942-45. Publicity Director of the General Conference 1929. Statistician of the General Conference-Eastern General 1933-35.

Chairman of the Treatises Committee of the National Association 1935. Member of the Revision Committee of the Treatise 1940.

Chairman of the Board Of Publications and Literature 1942. Re-elected for five years in 1943. He was a member of the General Board of the National Association and a member of the Executive Committee. He did evangelistic meetings in South Carolina, and Florida, Alabama, Mississippi, Texas, Tennessee and North Carolina. He was the author of many booklets and a book entitled, *The One Foundation*. He was married twice and had a total of 15 children.

Rev Milford H. Hales
Birth:
1898
North Carolina
Death:
1976
North Carolina
Burial:
Mount Zion FWB Church
Cemetery
Wilson County,
North Carolina

An ordained minister in the 1935 Minutes of the Old Western Conference of the Free Will Baptist.

Rev James J. Hall
Birth:
Nov. 3, 1849
England
Death:
Jul. 9, 1921
Harlem
Columbia County, Georgia
Burial:
Cross Creek Cemetery #3
Fayetteville
Cumberland County
North Carolina
Burial:
Cross Creek Cemetery #3
Fayetteville
Cumberland County
North Carolina

Rev. J. J. Hall, son of S.E. and Eliza (Combs) Hall, was born in London, Eng. He was educated at Spurgeon's College, London, and in 1870 married Angelina Bartlett.

Coming to this country, he was ordained July 9, 1871, and became pastor of the churches at East Farnham, Quebec, and Enosburgh Falls, VT, serving them three years. After a pastorate of two years (1874-76) at Waterloo, IA, he was pastor of the Pine Street church, Manchester, NH, 1879-80; at Auburn, ME, 1880-86; and at Minneapolis, Minn, 1886-88.

Additions to these churches were received during these years. Brother Hall aided in establishing the Ocean Park Association, Maine, was secretary and treasurer of the Maine Central Yearly Meeting, was six years on the Maine Home Mission Board, and for a time president of the Western Association.

John Hall, Jr
Birth:
Unknown
Death:
Mar. 11, 1992
Reidsville,
Rockingham County,
North Carolina
Burial:
Evergreen Memory Gardens,
Reidsville,
Rockingham County,
North Carolina

He organized a Free Will Baptist Church in Readsville in 1977 as a home mission's project. He served as moderator of the Maryland State Association and editor of the Maryland Newsletter. He had been a schoolteacher, principal and administrator. He attended Free Will Baptist Bible College, Maryland Bible Institute, Covington Theological Seminary and Elkton Bible College.

David Wells Hansley
Birth:
Dec. 21, 1909
Folkstone,
Onslow Co. N.C.
Death:
Apr. 24, 1989
Burial:
Dalys Chapel
Free Will Baptist Church
Cemetery,
Liddell
Lenoir County,
North Carolina

He was an active leader as Chairman of the Board of Directors that led in the creation of the Mount Olive College in North Carolina, a role he held from 1953 to 1963, but continued on the board until 1970. He was a member of the Board of Directors for the Free Will Baptist Press, Ayden, N.C., Chairman of Board of Superannuation and League Board of the National

Association. He was a grandson of Jesse Heath an early FWB preacher. He became a minister in 1930 at the age of 21 and served 37 churches in 15 N.C. counties from 1931-1988.

Rev Charlie Jackson Harris, Sr
Birth:
1870
North Carolina
Death:
1943
Pitt County
North Carolina
Burial:
Greenwood Cemetery
Greenville
Pitt County,North Carolina

He was the first Field Secretary for the North Carolina State Convention when it was organized in 1913.

Rev William Harris
Birth:
May, 1810
Death:
Nov. 30, 1893
Burial:
Pleasant Grove Free Will Baptist Church Cemetery
Dunn
Harnett County
North Carolina

Eld. Wm. Harris' ministry dates back to the infancy of the Cape Fear Conference [ed. abt 1850]. Eld. Harris was a man of very much energy in the calling wherewith he was called. In the beginning of his ministerial labors he was a very successful ingatherer to the conference...His manner of preaching was very plain and stately. Though uneducated, his familiarity with the word of God was hardly excelled. Like many others, he was actuainted with sorrow, tribulations and disappoint-ments. We believe that his last days were his happiest ones.He attended the annual conference held with the church at Shady Grove, in Sampson county, 1893. He went home from the conference and immediately he was taken sick with pneumonia and died in the latter part of the year, 1893. "Blessed are the dead which die in the Lord."--from Minutes of Cape Fear Conference

Inscription:
He died as he lived trusting in God

Bobby E. Harrell
Birth:
Jul. 1, 1933
Death:
unknown
Burial:
Dalys Chapel Free Will Baptist Church Cemetery,
Liddell, Lenoir County,
North Carolina

Thaddeus F. Harrison
Birth:
March 8, 1878
Washington County
North Carolina
Death:
October 24, 1897
Ayden, Pitt County,
North Carolina
Burial:
Ayden Cemetery,
Ayden, Pitt County,
North Carolina

His family gave him all the advantages of an education that they possibly could in his early life.. In 1884 he went to Plymouth High School, then to the Academy at Pantego to study under Prof. A. L. Johnson for 10 months. From there he went to the Carolina Institute to study under Prof. Rightsell. And from there to Chapel Hill after which he returned home and taught school. Sometime before his last schooling he united with the Disciples church. Not long after he commenced exhorting and speaking in public and soon became dissatisfied and united with the Free Will Baptist at Union Chapel in January of

1894 and was ordained in the same year. He and his twin brother (Theodore) published two books and pamphlets, one containing 10 sermons and the other was on feet washing.. Later he wrote two more pamphlets, one was 100 facts on baptism and another on feet washing. In the spring of 1896 Elder Harrison decided to write a history of the Free Will Baptist of North Carolina. Thus he became a co-author of the *History of North Carolina Free Will Baptist* with J.M. Barfield.

Edward David Hathaway, Sr
Birth:
Jul. 28, 1849
Belvoir
Pitt County,
North Carolina,
Death:
Feb. 2, 1919
Greenville
Pitt County,
North Carolina
Burial:
Hathaway Family Cemetery
Belvoir
Pitt County,
North Carolina

Elder Rufus K. Hearn
Birth:
Oct. 20, 1819
Pitt County,North Carolina
Death:
Mar. 3, 1894
Pitt County
North Carolina
Burial:
Gum Swamp Freewill Baptist
Church Cemetery
Greenville
Pitt County
North Carolina

He was a leading minister in the mid-1800 until his death in the NC Free Will Baptist movement. Also, was a pastor of Gum Swamp and other churches, but remained a member of Gum Swamp until his death.
He wrote about the early movement and was an editor of the first paper in North Carolinia. He is remembered here. Son of Howell Hearn & Sarah Elmina Randolph.

He Is The Beginning And The End

Jeremiah Heath
Birth:
Oct. 4, 1793
North Carolin
Death:
Feb. 22, 1867
Cove City
Craven County, North Carolina
Burial:
Heath Family Cemetery
Craven County, North Carolina

An early Free Will Baptist minister in a remnant of churches in 1832 from the Philadelphia Association. Rev. Jeremiah HEATH's name is found among historical records with early FWB minister's names who contended for, and remained influential in sustaining the Orig. Free Will Baptist church in its early formation and growth, especially the old Bethel Conference, when it could have been merged. He was a leader, with others, during this time who carried forward the FWB cause. Jeremiah was a prominent surveyor in the early formation of the area, to which land records attest; also, he was a Free Will Baptist minister. He organized the Core Creek FWB Church, and also pastored the FWB church at New Bern, NC, and probably others. He raised several children who became worthy citizens. Rev. Jesse Heath's name is known as a prominent leader in the area. (Family papers are held in Joyner Library, East Carolina University, Greenville, N.C. -- Index is online). Parents: Rigdon and Elizabeth (Jackson) HEATH. Spouse: Clemmie Holland Jones (NC mar rec'ds)

Inscription:
Organized Core Creek Free Will Baptist Church 1865.

John David Hill
Birth:
Sep. 30, 1924
North Carolina
Death:
Nov. 10, 2008
North Carolina
Burial:
Bethel Original
Freewill Baptist Church
Cemetery,
Four Oaks, Johnston County,
North Carolina

Milton Aaron Hollifield, Sr
Birth:
Apr. 19, 1926
Mitchell County,
North Carolina
Death:
Jul. 14, 2014
Swannanoa
Buncombe County,
North Carolina
Burial:
Old Fort City Cemetery
Old Fort
McDowell County,
North Carolina

He was the son of the late George and Annie Baucombe Hollifield. For over 60 years, Rev. Hollifield was a caring and dedicated Free Will Baptist Minister having served in McDowell, Haywood and Buncombe Counties and in Wayne, MI. and was active in the work of several committees and boards of the National Association of the Free Will Baptist. Pastor Hollifield organized and was a promotional representative for the Free Will Baptist Blue Ridge Association in Western North Carolina. He was a member and care pastor of Rocky Pass Free Will Baptist Church in Marion. He fulfilled his passion for evangelism through his involvement in conducting revivals in

numerous states and other countries.
Rev. Hollifield was passionate about visiting hospitals, nursing homes and the homebound. He was a charter member of the board of Directors of the Swannanoa Valley Medical Center. An autobiography was published about his life entitled "Why Me Lord".Revs. Milton Hollifield, Jr., Steve Lytle and Alan Sailors officiated.

The Will Of The One Who Understands

G W Homes
Birth:
unknown
Death:
unknown
Burial:
Maple Springs Baptist Church
Cemetery
Louisburg
Franklin County
North Carolina
Plot: Plot # 37

Rev. G. W. Homes' name is in list of ordained Free Will Baptist ministers, in the Western Conference minutes, when in 49th Session convened in 1935.

Elder Curtis Daniel Howell, Sr
Birth:
Jan. 4, 1836
Goldsboro
Wayne County
North Carolina
Death:
Apr. 9, 1921
Wayne County
North Carolina
Burial:
Deans Cemetery
Goldsboro
Wayne County
North Carolina

Father: Morris Howell. Mother: Mary Polly Deans Howell. Eld. Curtis D. Howell, was a native of NC, born near, and dying near Goldsboro.

He served in the Civil War until its close in 1865. He professed religion soon after returning home and joined the M.E. Church. About 1894, he withdrew and joined the Free Will Baptist at Stony Hill Church in Wayne County.

He was faithful to his charge as a minister. It seemed his mission was to build up weak churches.

He was twice married: first, to Miss Sophia Deans, Feb. 6, 1868; to this union.

In Sept. 1912, he was married to Miss Josephine West, who died a few days after

Elder Howell. An ordained Free Will Baptist minister/leader in the Western Conference in NC He was a good man, and has gone to his final reward."-- taken from 1921 Minutes of the 35th Session of the Western Conference, when convened at Holly Springs Church, Johnston Co. NC.

Elder W. M. Howell
Birth:
Dec. 1, 1866
Death:
Aug. 13, 1929
Burial:
Pike Cemetery ,Pikeville
Wayne CountyNorth Carolina

Rev. W. M. Howell, was the son of Robert B. Howell, and Zilphia Howell. He married Ora Pannell Dec. 9, 1914, Wayne Co. NC. He was an ordained Free Will Baptist minister/pastor in the Western Conference of Original FWB churches, which included Wayne County. His name appears in leadership positions in old Conference Minutes (1916) as being moderator of the Conference, and again re-elected the next session. Unknown are the churches he pastored and other fields of labor in which he worked. He was a leader and an asset to his church and the area in which he ministered.

The will of the One who understands.

Danny H Howell
Birth:
Oct. 19, 1946
Death:
Sep. 4, 1993
Burial:
Fairview Cemetery
La Grange
Lenoir County, North Carolina
While working in the church gymnasium, he climbed a ladder and had a fall which caused his death at age 46. He was called to preach in 1977 and was ordained to the ministry in 1981 pastoring two

North Carolina churches; Morehead City and the Goshen church in Mt. Holly. He attended Free Will Baptist Bible College and Lenore Community College, North Carolina and received his Doctor of Ministries from Bethany Theological Seminary, Dothan, Alabama.

Clint Hardrick Holt

Birth:
Mar. 31, 1915
North Carolina
Death:
Dec. 19, 2009
Johnston County, North Carolina
Burial:
Selma Memorial Gardens, Selma,
Johnston County, North Carolina

Holt retired from the NC Dept. of Transportation and was a Free Will Baptist Minister for most of his adult life. He lived in Hendersonville before moving to Smithfield in the early 1980's.

Rev Eugene A. W. Husketh

Birth:
Aug. 7, 1857
Death:
May 1, 1931
Burial:
Lewis Augustus Wilson Cemetery
New Light
Wake County, North Carolina

An ordained Free Will Baptist minister whose name was shown in a minister's list of church conference minutes in 1920. Parents shown as William Husketh & Maria Wilson (both b Granville Co.

Billy Gray Jackson

Birth:
Jul. 27, 1934
Wilson, Wilson County, North Carolina
Death:
Mar. 2, 1997
Chapel Hill, Madison County, North Carolina
Burial:
Onslow Memorial Park, Jacksonville, Onslow County, North Carolina

Billy was the pastor of the Cardinal Village Free Will Baptist Church that grew from 30 to a total of 350. He had a high Sunday of 525 on Easter one year. He was truly a man who cared for the people of his church and the entire community. His church loved him so much that they paid for his resting place and for the headstones for he and his wife. His son, Kevin, follows his father in the ministry.

Robert Copps Jackson

Birth:
November 19, 1865
Sampson County, North Carolina,
Death:
June 21, 1908
North Carolina
Burial:
Roberts Grove
Free Will Baptist Church, Dunn
Sampson County, North Carolina

As a young man he joined a Missionary Baptist Church where he was a very faithful member, but in July of 1887 he severed his relationship with this church and united with the Free Will Baptist Church at Shady Grove where he held his membership for several years until he organized a new Free Will Baptist Church near his home. He was licensed to the ministry on August 1, 1891 and the next year in 1892 he was ordained to the ministry. He served for 17 years as a preacher of the gospel of Christ his ministry took him beyond his own state into South Carolina and even as far north as Ohio in his evangelistic work. He was active in the Cape Fear Conference, establishing several Churches of the Free Will Baptist faith.

Roy H Jackson

Birth:
Jun. 20, 1901

Death:
Aug. 31, 1991
Burial:
Pleasant Grove Free Will
Baptist Church Cemetery,
Dunn, Harnett County,
North Carolina

Rev Hannibal Washington Jernigan, Sr
Birth:
Sep. 11, 1849
Mingo
Sampson County,
North Carolina
Death:
Jan. 22, 1942
Dunn
Harnett County, North
Carolina
Burial:
Stoney Run Pentecostal FWB
Church
Sampson County, North
Carolina

In a list of ministers in Minutes of 1903 Cape Fear Conference, which met at Hodges Chapel Church, Harnett Co. NC.

Rev Isaac W Jernigan
Birth:
Dec. 15, 1898
Death:
Aug. 31, 1968
Burial:
Spring Hope Memorial
Gardens
Spring Hope
Nash Count, North Carolina
A Free Will Baptist minister, who ministered in Bailey, and other churches in Nash Co. and was pastor at Rose Bud, Wilson, in 1935-36.

Walter L. Jernigan
Birth:
Mar. 21, 1900
Bladen County, North Carolina
Death:
Nov. 19, 1962
Bladenboro,
Bladen County, North Carolina
Burial:
Lewis Cemetery, Bladenboro,
Bladen County, North Carolina

An ordained Free Will Baptist minister and pastor.

Milton Lee Johnson
Birth:
Aug. 19, 1915
Johnston Co., North Carolina
Death:
February 11 1969
Middlesex
Nash Co., North Carolina
Burial:
Marsh Swamp Church
Cemetery,
Wilson, North Carolina

He was a well-known pastor and did a remarkable work throughoutthe denomination. He was Business Manager of Mount Olive Junior College between 1956-61 He served as the Superintendent of the Free Will Baptist orphanage in Middlesex a total of six years before a heart attack took his life.

Rev Calvin B Jones
Birth:
Sep. 1, 1873
Augusta
Richmond County
Georgia
Death:
Dec. 19, 1957
Winston-Salem
Forsyth County
North Carolina
Burial:
Evergreen Cemetery
Winston-Salem
Forsyth County
North Carolina

Name in a roll of ministers from Old Central Conference and its districts.

Rev James Read Jones
Birth:
Nov. 29, 1840
Death:
Jul. 21, 1925
Burial:
New Garden Friends Cemetery
Greensboro
Guilford County
North Carolina

Rev. J.R. Jones, of Cape Fear Conference was present at the 1916 Western Conf. which met in Johnston Co. NC, Oct. 1916.

Daniel Andrew Jordan, Jr
Birth:
Dec. 7, 1924
Death:
Jan. 26, 2016
Burial:
Evergreen Memorial Park
Wilson
Wilson County
North Carolina

Daniel Andrew Jordan, Jr., 91, of Mooresville passed away and The Rev. Rudy Owens will officiated.

Alan Clinton Joyner
Birth:
Oct. 8, 1963
Wilson County, North Carolina
Death:
Oct. 24, 2011
Burial:
Queen Anne Cemetery
Fountain
Pitt County, North Carolina

Son of Llewellyn Brann Joyner and the late Clinton Hubert Joyner, he was a graduate of Wilson Christian Academy. He attended Atlantic Christian College (Barton College) and graduated from Mount Olive College in 2005. He was ordained as an minister in the Original Free Baptist denomination. He served as pastor of the Free Union OFWB Church for eight years where his funeral was held on October 28, 2011, with The Rev. Kelley Smith and The Rev. Dr. David Hines officiating.

Rev George Joyner
Birth:
Oct. 16, 1823
Pitt County, North Carolina
Death:
Sep. 12, 1885
Kinston
Lenoir County, North Carolina
Burial:
Hollywood Cemetery,
Farmville
Pitt County, North Carolina

Reverend George Joyner was the son of J. and C. Joyner and husband of Louisa A. Blount Joyner.   Rev. George Joyner, a native of this county, died at his home in Kinston on last Thursday. His remains were brought to Marlboro on Friday for interment. He was a most excellent and devout man and his death is much regretted.

Rev Grover Cleveland Joyner
Birth:
1893
Death:
1966
Burial:
Sunset Memorial Park
Smithfield
Johnston County
North Carolina

An ordained Free Will Baptist minister.

Charles Edward Keith
Birth:
Jun. 15, 1922
Dickenson County, Virginia
Death:
Mar. 9, 2008,
Sanford,

Lee County, North Carolina
Burial:
Markham Memorial Gardens, Durham,Durham County, North Carolina

A Free Will Baptist minister serving churches in North and South Carolina. Father of N.C. Promotional Director Billy Keith.

Eld. Robert C. Kennedy
Birth:
1881
Death:
1954
Burial:
Whaley Cemetery, Duplin, County, North Carolina

His son was Rev. Rashie Kennedy (1911 - 2012) who lived to be 100 years of age. He was in the first graduating class of Free Will Baptist Bible College, Nashville, Tennessee in 1942. His ministry among Free Will Baptists is well recorded not only here but in heaven.

Rashie Kennedy, Sr
Birth:
Jul. 15, 1911
Duplin County, North Carolina
Death:

Jun. 19, 2012
Beulaville,
Duplin County,
North Carolina
Burial:
East Duplin Memorial Gardens,
Beulaville, Duplin County, North Carolina

Converted at age 11, Kennedy was licensed to preach in 1940 and ordained in 1941. His 70-year ministry was marked by a passion for prayer and evangelism. Reverend Kennedy sold his North Carolina home in 1942 and relocated to Nashville, Tn. , with his wife and two children to attend FWBBC. He was 31 at the time, three years older than the college president, Dr. L.C. Johnson. While a student at FWBBC, Kennedy organized and pastored Sylvan Park Free Will Baptist Church in West Nashville. He graduated in 1945 and later pastored in North Carolina, Texas, Florida, and Louisiana. His denominational service included eight years on the Free Will Baptist International Missions Board, six years on the Home Missions Board, two years as Texas Executive Secretary, two years on the Oklahoma Bible College (now Hillsdale FWB College) Board and other district and state boards in North Carolina and

Texas. He and Myrtle Kennedy were married 63 years. He started a writing career at age 90 by embracing Internet technology and creating a website that featured many of his articles and sermons.

Needham Sanders Lancaster
Birth:
May 5, 1884
Wayne County,
North Carolina
Death:
Nov. 16, 1928
Onslow County,
North Carolina
Burial:
Pate Cemetery
Stoney Creek,Wayne County, North Carolina

Ordained a minister, 4th Sun. Aug. 1915, of the Orig. Free Will Baptist Church.

Rev James Merritt Langdon
Birth:
Feb. 10, 1863
Johnston County
North Carolina
Death
Oct. 12, 1910
Johnston County,
North Carolina
Burial:
Benson City Cemetery
Benson, Johnston County,
North Carolina,

An ordained Freewill Bapt. minister, whose name was in a list of ministers in the 1903 E. Conference, meeting in Harnett Co. NC. "He was ordained in 1900 and preached at the Benson Free Will Baptist Church till his death in 1910.Parents Merritt Langdon and Margaret I Stephenson were married on December 31st 1856.

Rev Lunda Lee
Birth:
Jun. 24, 1854
Death:
Oct. 20, 1917
Burial:
Lee Cemetery
Sampson County
North Carolina

His name is in a list of ordained ministers in Minutes of 1903 Cape Fear Conference, which met at Hodges Chapel Church, Harnett Co. NC.

John W Lucas
Birth:
Oct. 23, 1857
Death:
Jun. 14, 1925
Burial:
Pleasant Grove Free Will Baptist Church Cemetery
Dunn,
Harnett County North Carolina

Reverend J. W. Lucas, a graduate of Wake Forest, was born Averysboro, N. C. in 1850, and was ordained in 1872. For over a quarter of a century, he served as a Free Will Baptist minister and as an educator in East Tennessee. Most of this time he was affiliated with the Union Association. He served as principal of high schools at Parrotsville, Midway, and elsewhere. He succeeded Brother Woolsey as pastor of the Woolsey College Church. His work at the college both as teacher and as pastor was outstanding in quality.
He was in attendance at the General Conference at Harper's Ferry, West Virginia, 1901 and again along with Dr. T. H. Woolsey at Hillsdale, Michigan in 1904.--from One Hundred Years of Paul Woolsey's Free Will Baptist Family, pub. 1949.

Malachi Daniel Lucas
Birth:
Mar. 12, 1884
Wilson County,
North Carolina
Death:
Jun. 14, 1909
Wilson County,
North Carolina
Burial:
Lucas Cemetery,
Lucama,
Wilson County,
North Carolina

Patrick Thomas Lucas
Birth:
Sep. 8, 1854
North Carolina
Death:
Jul. 2, 1912
Wilson County, North Carolina
Burial:
Lucas Cemetery, Lucama,
Wilson County,
North Carolina

Alice Voliva Lupton
Birth:
Oct. 13, 1875

Death:
Jan. 24, 1962
Burial:
Cedar Grove Cemetery,
New Bern,
Craven County,
North Carolina

She was one of the earliest organizers for women within the denomination. She organized the first "lady's aid society" in the St. Mary's church in the historic city of New Bern. In May of 1927, a state women's convention was organized in Goldsboro, North Carolina where Mrs. Lupton became the first president of the statewide organization. The 1928 session met at the Eureka College at Ayden, where the work was departmentalized with directors for missions, Christian education, Superannuation, stewardship and youth training. In 1935, a national auxiliary convention was organized at Black Jack church, near Greenville. The North Carolina convention affiliated with it and Mrs. Lupton became it's first president and the North Carolina women joined with others in working toward a Bible college and a foreign missions program. From the earliest days of the women's movement Alice Lupton was always seen at the forefront. She was a author and columnist writing for the *Free Will Baptists* for many years a woman's column. She freely wrote programs for the women's movement and also was the author of one book, *Footprints Of Jesus* which was widely used by women's auxiliaries and ministers and in pre-Easter observations.

William Howard Lupton, Sr

Birth:
Mar. 5, 1851
Lowland
Pamlico County, North Carolina
Death:
Aug. 19, 1888
Lowland
Pamlico County, North Carolina
Burial:
Mercer Cemetery
Lowland
Pamlico County, North Carolina

Spouse: Ellenor Susan Johnson Ireland (1854 - 1938). Children: Charles B. Lupton (1877 - 1953), William Howard Lupton (1878 - 1962) and Alice Lupton Mayo (1889 - 1978).

Note: He was buried in the back of the cemetery near the woods with a wooden marker. Time and weather deteriorated the marker.

Rev Thomas Calvin Marks

Birth:
Jun. 28, 1873
Stanly County
North Carolina
Death:
Jul. 18, 1941
Durham
Durham County
North Carolina
Burial:
Woodlawn Memorial Park
Durham,Durham County
North Carolina

Rev, T.C. Marks, was an ordained Free Will Baptist minister that served churches in the area where he lived. His name was in the Minutes of the 49th Session of the Western Conference of FWB in 1935.Married to Alice Rebecca Lockamy around 1895. Son of James Marks and Mary Rickford Marks.

William Royster Martin

Birth: unknown, USA
Death: unknown
North Carolina
Burial:
Micro Memorial Gardens Cemetery
Johnston County
North Carolina

Reverend William Royster Martin Micro-, age 68, pastor of Holly Springs Free Will Baptist Church on Kenly was a retired fertilizer and chemical dealer and a US Navy veteran of WW II. He was a former member and chairman of the Johnston County Board of Education. He was a member of Kenly Masonic Lodge # 257, a member of the Scottish Rite, and was a Shriner. Rev. Martin was also a member of the Western Conference Board of Ordination of Original Free

Will Baptist Churches and a member of Micro Free Will Baptist Church.

The Rev. Clyde Cox and Rev. Dewey Boling will officiated

Thomas Hillman Matthews

Birth:
Oct. 9, 1830
Nash County, North Carolina
Death:
Sep. 7, 1918
Nash County, North Carolina
Burial:
Thomas H. Matthews
Cemetery,
Nash County, North Carolina

Thomas was a Free Will Baptist Minister and served in the Civil War as a Private in the Civil War during 1861-1865, Confederate Regiment State Origin: North Carolina

Harry Edward Mintz

Birth:
7 Sep 1932
North Carolina
Death:
6 Oct 2017
Loudon, Loudon County, Tennessee
Burial:
Garrett-Hillcrest Memorial Park
Waynesville, Haywood County, North Carolina

He preached and pastored for sixty years at various churches. Preceded in death by wife, Edith Mintz; parents, Robert and Mae Mintz.

William Moses Monk

Birth:
Jul. 1, 1877
Sampson County, North Carolina
Death:
Oct. 30, 1959
Bell Arthur,
Pitt County, North Carolina
Burial:
Arthur Chapel
FWB Church Cemetery,
Bell Arthur, Pitt County,
North Carolina

Monk was the founding pastor of Arthur Chapel Free Will Baptist Church.

Alfred Moore

Birth:
May 28, 1813
Death:
Aug. 28, 1870
Lenoir County,
North Carolina
Burial:
Moore Family Cemetery
Hugo,
Lenoir County,
North Carolina

Rev. Alfred Moore was a Free Will Baptist minister for 38 years. He was 59 yrs when he died, leaving his widow and children to mourn his passing. His ministerial work was with the remnant of his church which labored to spread the word after severe hardships. He remained with the part of the dissenting Free Will Baptists who declined to merge with a Disciples coalition in about 1832. His name appears in other records and books. The churches he pastored, are not known, but he remained a faithful minister until death. Several of his children are buried in this cemetery.

Elder J. W. Moore

Birth:
Sep. 22, 1845
North Carolina
Death:
Jan. 27, 1932
North Carolina
Burial:
Bethel Original Freewill
Baptist Church Cemetery,
Four Oaks,
Johnston County,, North Carolina

Parents: Henry Moore (1821 - 1884) - Culia Ann Beasley Moore (1832 - 1917)
Spouse: Mary E Lee Moore (1860 - 1923)*
Children: George Edward Moore (1869 - 1931)- Norsissa Moore Faircloth (1872 - 1928)- Ida Moore McLamb (1874 -

1947)- John Ira Moore (1876 - 1962)- James Henry Moore (1878 - 1944)- Lonnie D Moore (1881 - 1954)-Jesse B Moore (1882 - 1959)- Willie Allen Moore (1893 - 1964)- Joseph Randle Moore (1894 - 1969)- Dora Mae Moore Blackman (1896 - 1959)- Allie Hawkins Moore Martin (1900 - 1984).

Siblings:
John Wesley Moore (1845 - 1932)
James H Moore (1845 - 1931)
Britta Ann Moore Stanley (1848 - 1920).

J. H. Moore
Birth:
Sep. 11, 1874
Death:
Nov. 6, 1950
Burial:
Sweet Hope Freewill Baptist Church Cemetery,
Pitt County, North Carolina

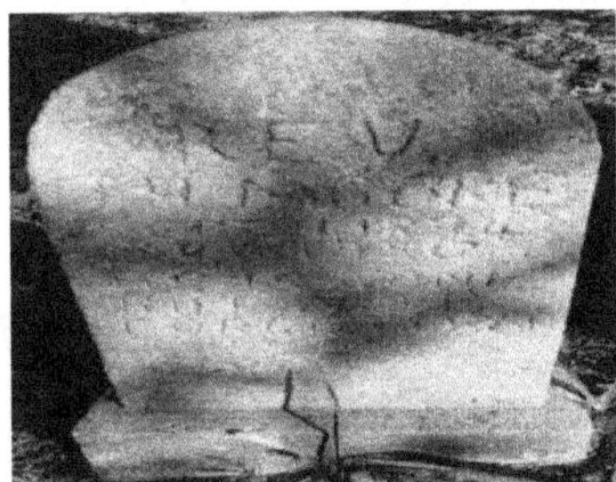

James Moore
Birth:
March 20, 1793
Edgecombe Co.
North Carolina
Death:
1882
Greene Cty, North Carolina
Burial:
Free Union Church Cemetery,
Greene Cty, North Carolina

He moved from Edgecombe County to Greene County at a very young age and joined the Grimsley Free Will Baptist Church. He accepted the call to preach and was licensed in January 1825 and ordained in February 1827.

He became a very active preacher taking care of many churches in the area. In 1850 he started a church in Greene County that will he named Free Union. It became a flourishing church and he remained a member of the church until his departure in July 1882. Elder Moore served for 53 years as a faithful Minister. Elder J.M. Barfield heard him preach his last sermon which was a funeral service. He was so feeble that two man sat behind him ready to catch him should he began to fall. He had to be ushered in and out of the church building. His funeral was preached by brother Barfield who used the 13th and 14th chapters of the book of Revelation.

John Moore
Birth:
Jun. 1, 1832
Death:
Dec. 13, 1889
Burial:
Hodges Chapel Free Will Baptist Cemetery,
Harnett County,
North Carolina
Eld. John Moore was a native of Harnett County, N. C., where he was converted and began to hold prayer-meetings, and was ordained to preach the Gospel, Oct. 13. 1874. He served the remainder of his life in the Master's cause and to Christianize this part of God's moral vineyard.

Rev Thomas Moore
Birth:
Dec. 22, 1826
Death:
Aug. 13, 1898
Burial:
Elaney Woods Cemetery
Snow Hill
Greene County
North Carolina

There is old Minutes of the NC Orig. Free Will Baptist Gen. Conf., held at Kit Swamp Meeting House, Craven Co. NC, in 1854, with a list of ministers, and one is Rev. Thomas Moore.

Edward C Morris
Birth:
Aug. 16, 1891
Death:
Oct. 21, 1976
Burial:
Woodlawn Memorial Park,
Durham,
Durham County,
North Carolina,
Plot: Section 5,
Lock 12, Lot 15

He moved to Georgia from North Carolina in 1942 to pastor the Glennville and

Ebenezer churches in Glennville which at the time were half-time churches. He was the first full-time promotional director in the state of Georgia beginning in 1947 serving through 1961. He worked to unite the state of Georgia. He started printing and sending out a monthly paper which was named *Promotional Bulletin* which is still in use today by the state of Georgia. He was known as a leader, promotional director, editor and publisher, and had an interested in the state youth camp program. During his time the work in Georgia grew and even land given to the state in 1948 for the youth camp. Many new churches were formed, joining the state association which had begun in 1937. By 1953 the state of Georgia had 127 churches. Even though the state Association was relatively young at the time. The Chattahoochee Association, was the oldest Association being organized in 1842 and was the first to have all of its churches participating in the state work. After his resignation in 1961 Rev. Morris returned to North Carolina.

J R Morris, Jr
Birth:
Feb. 15, 1881
North Carolina
Death:
Oct. 24, 1921
North Carolina
Burial:
Branch Chapel Free Will
Baptist Church
Smithfield
Johnston County,
North Carolina

A minister in the Original Free will Baptist Western Conference.

James Clayton Moye
Birth:
Jul. 19, 1890
Greene County, North Carolina
Death:
May 21, 1961

Wilson, North Carolina
Burial:
Snow Hill Cemetery,
Snow Hill,
Greene County,
North Carolina

He attended Ayden Seminary and the Whitsett Institute afterwards, serving Free Will Baptist churches as pastor in. Pitt, Green and Lenoir counties, but had to retire in 1949 because of failing health. He served in the North Carolina General Assembly as the Representative from Greene County for three terms, 1929, 1931 and 1933. He was Mayor of Snow Hill for six years and served on the Snow Hill School Board. He was also on the Board of Directors of the Free Will Baptist Children's Home in Middlesex. He was a former moderator of the North Carolina Free Will Baptist Convention and was a benefactor of the Free Will Baptist College in Mt. Olive. J. C. Moye Library was named in his honor. He was an extensive farmer and also operated a Chevrolet dealership in the Snow Hill for 27 years.

> *If the Spirit of him that raised up Jesus from the dead dwell in you, he that raised up Christ from the dead shall also quicken your mortal bodies by his Spirit that dwelleth in you.*
> *Romans 8:11*

Richard Evans McKeel
Birth:
Jan. 31, 1948
Death:
Dec. 21, 2015
Burial:
Evans Cemetery
Pine Level
Johnston County
North Carolina

Rev. Richard E. McKeel, 67, of Selma, went home to be with his Heavenly Father following a brief illness. Born in Johnston County, he was the youngest of ten children born to Roby and Elizabeth Evans McKeel. Richard was a graduate of Princeton High School and Carolina Bible Institute and also served his country in the US Army during the Vietnam War. He has been a Free Will Baptist Minister since 1992, the last 15 years at Stevens Chapel Original Free Will Baptist Church near Benson. Richard was a devoted

husband and Christian as well as a loving father and grandfather.

Rev Walter Brown Nobles
Birth:
May 3, 1866
Pitt County, North Carolina
Death:
Jul. 8, 1960
Greenville
Pitt County, North Carolina
Burial:
Winterville Cemetery
Winterville
Pitt County, North Carolina

In list of NC minister's name in 1950.

Elder Isaac H Pipkin
Birth:
Feb. 28, 1835
Death:
Aug. 4, 1917
Burial:
Core Point Free Will Baptist Church Cemetery
Core Point
Beaufort County, North Carolina

A minister in the early work of Free Will Baptists in North Carolina.

Inscription:
"I have fought a good fight, I have finished my course, I have kept the faith."

Addie H Outlaw
Birth:
Aug. 15, 1871
Death:
Nov. 27, 1942
Burial:
Suncrest Cemetery,
Monroe,
Union County,
North Carolina

Clarence H Overman, Jr
Birth:
Oct. 31, 1930
Death:
May 23, 2012
Pikeville, Wayne County, North Carolina
Burial:
Pikeville Cemetery Pikeville, Wayne County, North Carolina

At the age of fourteen, C.H. joined Union Grove Free Will Baptist Church, where his lifelong career with the Free Will Baptist denomination began. In 1952, he was ordained into the ministry and spent sixty years serving as a Free Will Baptist minister.

He graduated from Atlantic Christian College in 1957 with a degree in Religion and has held numerous pastorates in eastern North Carolina. The Rev. Overman was most recently a member of Rose Hill OFWB Church. C.H. also taught in the public school system for 20 years and was a member of the Ayden Rotary Club for 31 years. Throughout the years he has served as pastor of 12 churches and served on various boards and committees. He served as editor of FWB press for more the 16 years, and general secretary of the OFWB Convention for more than five years.

Elder Henry Parker
Birth:
Sep. 28, 1840
Death:
Nov. 14, 1887
Burial:
Gum Swamp Freewill Baptist Church Cemetery
Greenville
Pitt County, North Carolina

Wondering if he was descendant of Eld. Wm. Parker or Eld. Joseph Parker, early FWB ministers in this area? No grave maker found by contributor

Joseph Parker
Birth:
1711
Death:
1798
Burial:
Parker Family Cemetery
Windsor
Bertie County
North Carolina

Son of James Parker. Brother of Rueben. Probably kin the early Rev. Joseph Parker, FWB preacher of that time.

Joseph Parker
Birth:
1705
Death:
1791 Wheat Swamp,
Lenoir County,
North Carolina
Burial:
Private burial ground on Cajah Barfied place,
Lenoir County,
North Carolina

He was one of the earliest founders and preachers in the Free Will Baptists is North Carolina. The Historical Commission of the North Carolina Original Free Will Baptist erected a highway sign there in 1966.

Today is not a day of demotion, But a day of crowning.

The marker in at the church started by Joseph Parker at about 1760 and remained a Free Will Baptist Church until 1843 when it was lost to the Disciples of Christ.

Joseph Parker is buried on a private plot near this church.

Rev Bryant Hanley Pate
Birth:
Oct. 17, 1879
Wake County,
North Carolina
Death:
Jun. 27, 1959
Raleigh
Wake County,
North Carolina

Burial:
Montlawn Memorial Park
Raleigh
Wake County, North Carolina

Rev. B.H. Pate, was a minister in the Free Will Baptist Church, where his name is enumerated in a list of ordained ministers of the Free Will Baptist Western Conference Minutes held in Johnson Co., 1916. In the proceedings, Rev. B.H. Pate was elected Financial officer of the Seminary for the Conference. Married his wife Hettie in Wilson County, NC. He was the son of Rev. Thomas J.D. Pate and Anna Hollard.
Inscription:
TOGETHER FOREVER

Rev Thomas JD Pate
Birth:
Aug. 13, 1848
Death:
1903
Burial:
Apex Cemetery
Apex
Wake County
North Carolina

Thomas Jefferson Pate, was the son of Bryant Handley Pate and his wife Zilphia. He was pastor of Rock Springs Freewill Baptist Church on Olive Chapel Road at the crossroads near the Ed Clark homeplace near Apex, North Carolina. [He married Susan Ann HOLLAND, 17 August 1864]. He is brother to Zilphia Pate who married second Enos J. Holland.

--- from Holland Family Genealogy.

Christopher Lafayette "C.L." Patrick
Birth:
Aug. 17, 1911
Death:
Dec. 9, 1996
Burial:
Snow Hill Cemetery,
Snow Hill,
Greene County,
North Carolina,

Thomas E. Peden
Birth:
Sep. 13, 1832
Huntington Township,
Gallia County, Ohio
Death:
Feb. 3, 1913
Ayden, Pitt County,
North Carolina
Burial:
Ayden Cemetery,
Ayden, Pitt County,
North Carolina

Ordained Free Will Baptist minister, church planter, college president and a faithful man to his calling. He was ordained May 8, 1859 in Syracuse, Meigs Co. OH, by Elders G. Goler and Ira. Z. Haning. He was still in college at the time but was teaching school and preaching to a congregation in the vicinity of Syracuse. He enlisted in Co. I, Ohio 173rd Infantry, 16 Sep 1864 and mustered out 26 Jun 1865, at Nashville, TN (Official Records of the State of Ohio). He was active in the Ohio Yearly meeting, and pastored The Harrisburg Free Will Baptist Church. He served as Associate pastor of Rio Grande Church, Ohio, while connected with the Rio Grande College faculty during the 1870/1880's. He also served on the council when the Gilboa FWB Church Ohio, was organized. He was aware that Free Will Baptists in the north were taking steps toward a union with another denomination, and that there were FWB churches in the South not affiliated with the northern churches, and he envisioned a possible union of these southern branches of FWB into a national organization. He announced through the "Free Will Baptist" that a Gen. Conf. would convene in Nashville, TN. Oct. 7, 1896. Subsequent meetings were held, and Dr. Peden was a leading advocate of this organization hoping to bring a union of North and South, and avert any move toward a merger of the Northern FWB with another denomination. His dream was not realized, but did succeed in drawing FWB in the South closer together. He was called from Ohio to the Seminary in Ayden, NC, beginning in 1899 (from his diary). He held the principalship until 1910, when he retired because of "age and declining health." Prof. Peden became head of the Theological Dept. when it was started. His tenure as head set the tone of the institution to provide a basic liberal arts education as well as theological training for a number of ministers who would render valuable services. He was well-liked, and esteemed by his peers, and honored for his service in the early beginning of the school. Rev. Robert F. Pittman, a graduate of the Seminary and a member of the faculty, conducted Prof. Peden's funeral.

Rev Hiram Gooding Paul

Birth:
Jan. 5, 1816
Death:
Jul. 8, 1865
Burial:
Cedar Grove Cemetery
New Bern
Craven County
North Carolina

His name is in a list of ministers and Elders belonging to OFWB conference. Taken from Minutes of NC Original Free Will Baptist Gen'l Conference held at Kit Swamp Meeting House, Craven Co. NC on the 9, 10,and 11th of Nov, 1854.

Moses Washington Peterson

Birth:
Apr. 14, 1794
North Carolina
Death:
Aug. 1, 1879
Burial:
Peterson Hill Cemetery,
Burnsville,
Yancey County,
North Carolina

A spiritual leader and guide in an early time in our history serving mainly in Western North Carolina.

Edgar T. Phillips

Birth:
Mar. 26, 1857
North Carolina
Death:
Dec. 27, 1945
North Carolina
Burial:
Ayden Cemetery,
Ayden, Pitt County,
North Carolina

Cedric Dixon Pierce, Jr

Birth:
Unknown
Wayne County, North Carolina
Death:
Oct. 23, 2012
Greenville
Pitt County, North Carolina
Burial:
Wayne Memorial Park
Goldsboro, Wayne County,
North Carolina

Pauline Pinyan

Birth:
unknown
Death:
Apr. 27, 2010
Kernersville, Forsyth County
North Carolina
Burial:
Eastlawn Gardens of
Memory,
Kernersville,
Forsyth County,
North Carolina

She was an ordained minister of the North Carolina State Association.

Robert F. Pittman
Birth:
Nov. 8, 1883
Jerome, Bladen County,
North Carolina
Death
Jul. 15, 1938
Ayden,
Pitt County, North Carolina
Burial:
Ayden Cemetery,Ayden,
Pitt County,North Carolina

An ordained Free Will Baptist minister and educator. He taught at Mt. Olive College, NC. He also pastored churches at Sweetgum Grove, Bethany, and Ayden, which erected an imposing stone at his death showing their admiration and esteem for his work among them.

Matthew C. Prescott
Birth:
1873
Death:
1943
Pamlico County, North
Carolina
Burial:
Sand Hill Cemetery
Reelsboro, Pamlico County
North Carolina

Free Will Baptist minister in eastern North Carolina.

Francis Radford
Birth:
December 1, 1929,
Davidson County,
North Carolina
Death:
Dec. 1, 2009
North Carolina
Burial:
Radford Cemetery
Madison County
North Carolina

Frances was valedictorian of her graduating class at Beech Glen High School when she was 16 years old in 1941. When Frances was a young girl, she went to a secret prayer place beneath a limb of an old fallen chestnut tree and fully surrendered her life to God. This full surrender meant giving up the plans to become a lawyer, and when she was 17 years old she became the first lady licensed to preach the gospel in the Free Will Baptist Churches in her area. Frances had a unique way of preaching the gospel by reaching the heights, depths and sweetness using illustrations in a way that made it a vivid, memorable message.

Something you never forgot. It was so plain that the young could understand and so intense that the old were impressed and motivated. During her 60 plus years of active ministry, she served as pastor of several different churches in North Carolina and Tennessee and held revivals in many parts of the United States and Mexico. She was a member of Terry's Fork Free Will Baptist.

Today is
not
a day of
demotion,
But a
day
of
crowning.

William Burkette Raper
Birth:
Sep. 10, 1927
Black Creek
Wilson County, North Carolina
Death:
Aug. 1, 2011
Mount Olive
Wayne County, North Carolina
Burial:
Friendship Free Will Baptist
Church Cemetery
Jones County, North Carolina

After the death of his father in 1936, Burkette entered the Free Will Baptist orphanage in Middlesex, North Carolina, where he lived until graduation from Middlesex High School in 1944.

He entered the ministry in the Free Will Baptist denomination in 1946 and was ordained by the Western Conference in North Carolina. He served as the pastor of the Oak Grove, Stony Hill, Memorial Chapel of the Free Will Baptist Children's Home in Nash County; Arapahoe in Pamlico County, Friendship in Jones County, Howell Swamp and Hull Road in Greene County. All were in North Carolina. He earned a Bachelor of Arts in Liberal Arts in 1947 from Duke University and a Master of Divinity in 1952 from the Duke Divinity School. He served as the Promotional Director of the Original Free Will Baptist State Convention between 1953 and 1954. On August 2, 1954 he became the president of Mount Olive College, Mount Olive, North Carolina while it was still a two year liberal arts college. At that time he was only age 26, which was the youngest college president in the United States and when he retired as president in January of 1995 he held the distinction of being the current longest tenured president in the nation. During his 40 years as president he guided the development of the college from a two-year junior college to an accredited four-year senior college. In 1960 Atlantic Christian College awarded him an honorary Doctorate of Laws degree. In 1962, he earned a Master of Science in Higher Education from Florida State University. After retirement he served as the college's Director of Planned Giving for 10 years, making his tenure at the college a total of 50 years of service. Prior to his death, he held the distinction of being the longest tenured living ordained minister in the North Carolina Original FWB convention. Altogether, his ministry to his denomination led him to complete 65 years of service to God and mankind.

Archie W. Ratliff
Birth:
Nov. 29, 1949
Sneedville,
Hancock County, Tennessee
Death:
Dec. 17, 2012
Houston, Harris County, Texas
Burial:
Pinelawn Memorial Park,
Kinston, Lenoir County,
North Carolina

Senior Pastor of Bethel Free Will Baptist Church and Bethel Christian Academy in Kinston, NC, passed away at M.D. Anderson Cancer Center in Houston, Texas. Following graduation from Free Will Baptist Bible College in Nashville, Tn. Ratliff was ordained in 1972 in Glennville, Georgia, where he served five years as pastor of Glennville Free Will Baptist Church. He served as Moderator of the South Georgia Association from 1974 – 1976. and then Peace Free Will Baptist Church, Indianapolis, IN. He served as Moderator of the Indiana State Association for seven of his 14-year tenure there. Archie served as Senior Pastor of Bethel Free Will Baptist Church twenty-two years. Pastor Ratliff battled and defeated esophageal cancer in 2009; however, the radiation and chemotherapy treatments caused him to develop leukemia. Pastor Ratliff was a great respected leader in the Free Will Baptist Denomination. He served 12 years (1996 – 2008) on the Welch College Board of Trustees, including several years as vice chairman. And was very involved with Free Will Baptist International Missions. Pastor Ratliff guided Bethel Church to be globally involved in spreading the Gospel.

Willie E Renfrow
Birth:
Sep. 11, 1914
North Carolina
Death:
Oct. 23, 1970
North Carolina
Burial:
Branch Chapel Free Will
Baptist Church
Smithfield
Johnston County,
North Carolina

Rev. Willie E. and Sallie Hare Renfrow set up a Renfrow Family Endowment Scholarship for the Christian Ministry.

William Walter Reynolds
Birth:
Oct. 25, 1926
Columbia, Tyrrell County,
North Carolina
Death:
Dec. 22, 2009
Greenville,
Pitt County,
North Carolina
Burial:
Hollywood Cemetery,
Farmville,
Pitt County
North Carolina

A veteran of WWII (United States Army), he was ordained to the ministry of the Original Free Will Baptists (Albermarle Conference) on July 30, 1949. He graduated from Free Will Baptist Bible College in Nashville, TN, in 1951. He pastored churches in Tennessee and in North Carolina retiring in 2001.

Mary Ellen Rice
Birth:
Unknown
Death:
Nov. 20, 2015
Morehead City
Carteret County
North Carolina
Burial:
Bayview Cemetery
Morehead City
Carteret County
North Carolina

Mary Ellen Rice served for over 30 years at Beaufort Christian Academy, both as teacher and principal. Before that, she worked with the Child Evangelist Fellowship. She was also her church's first foreign missionary who served in Brazil on the field for seven years. She was always a godly lady and active in her church where she taught her junior class until her illness.

She is survived by her nieces and nephews and their families; Karen Hutton, Rhonda Sullivan, Roy F. Rice Jr., Jennifer Styron, John Rice, Greg Rice, Ruth D. Simpson, Leisha Mace, Kelly Sharpe, John Sharpe, Sandra Green, Janet Confer, Albert McElmon Jr. and R. L Rice; two sisters-in- law, Hyacinth Rice and Barabara "Bobbi- Ann" Rice Goodwin; her companion, Brancie Steele; and friends, Sarah Steele, Yvonne Humphrey and Douglas Elliott. Lastly, she is survived by the love of her life, Jon A. Swecker, her godson.

She was preceded in death by her parents, Bonnie McCoy Rice and Sarah B. Rice; three brothers, Roy Fields Rice, Robert "Mousey" Rice and Gregory Rice; two sisters, Marie McElmon and Burnette Sharpe; two brothers-in-law, Joe Sharpe and Al McElmon; and two nephews, Danny Rice and Joseph Sharpe.

Her funeral service was held at the First Free Will Baptist Church in Morehead City with the Rev. Jerry Johnson officiating.

Gabriel Pinkney Rice
Birth:
Aug. 10, 1854
Marshall, North Carolina
Death:
Jan. 20, 1923
Asheville
Buncombe County,
North Carolina
Burial:
West Memorial Park
Weaverville
Buncombe County,
North Carolina

He was converted in 1875 and received his ordination on December 14, 1878. His ministry was in the vicinity of

Eastern Tennessee, much of it having been spent in evangelistic work; he baptized about 1100 converts. He was the son of Isaac   Rachel Elizabeth Arrowroot Rice .

Roy Lee Rikard, Sr
Birth:
May 27, 1909
Caldwell County,
North Carolina
Death:
Mar. 14, 2008
Gastonia,
Gaston County,
North Carolina
Burial:
Gaston Memorial Park,
Gastonia,
Gaston County,
North Carolina

He was founder of Cramerton Free Will Baptist Church and a Bible Institute.

Fred A. Rivenbark, Sr
Birth:
unknown
Duplin County, North Carolina
Death:
Aug. 23, 2000
Durham,
Durham County,
North Carolina
Burial:
Woodlawn Memorial Park,
Durham,
Durham County, North
Carolina

He was a resident of Durham for 52 years. Rev. Rivenbark was born in Duplin County, N.C., and was a native of Mount Olive. The Rev. Rivenbark pastored Sherron Acres Free Will Baptist Church, prior to retiring from full-time ministry, and served on staff there as assistant pastor for 25 years. He also pastored Oak Grove Free Will Baptist Church in Durham, St. Paul Free Will Baptist Church, Elizabeth City, N.C., First Free Will Baptist Church, Wilson, N.C., Fairmont Park Free Will Baptist Church, Norfolk, Virginia Beach Free Will Baptist Church, and Stoney Creek Free Will Baptist Church, Goldsboro. In addition to pastoring seven churches, Mr. Rivenbark preached in hundreds of revival meetings.

Moses Duckworth Roberts
Birth:
May 13, 1869
Madison County
North Carolina, USA

Death:
Apr. 4, 1949
Buncombe County
North Carolina
Burial:
Union Chapel Church
Cemetery
Weaverville
Buncombe County
North Carolina

An ordained Original Free Will Baptist minister, whose death was noted in the Minutes of the Western Conference, the next session after his death.
Son of John Roberts and Mary Reece

Oscar Patrick "Pate" Rose
Birth:
Aug. 2, 1860
Johnston County
North Carolina
Death:
Feb. 27, 1938
Selma
Johnston County
North Carolina
Burial:
Snipes-Pearce Cemetery
Princeton
Johnston County
North Carolina

Rev. O.P. Rose was an ordained minister serving in Johnson and surrounding counties. His name is listed in the roll of ministers in the 35th session of the Western Conference, meeting at Holly Springs, Johnson Co., Oct. 13, 1921.

Rev John Alfred Rouse

Birth:
Jan. 31, 1861
Duplin County
North Carolina
Death:
Mar. 7, 1947
Wilmington
New Hanover County
North Carolina
Burial:
Clay Hill Cemetery
Rose Hill
Duplin County, North Carolina

Listed in 1903 Cape Fear Conference, meeting at Hodges Chapel church, Harnett Co. NC.

Rev Joseph Kindred Ruffin

Birth:
Apr. 29, 1861
Death:
Feb. 5, 1939
Burial:
Rock Springs Free Will Baptist
Church Cemetery
Bailey
Nash County
North Carolina
Name in list of ordained Free Will Bapt. ministers, 1935 Association minutes. Son of John Davis Ruffin and Mary Ann Mercer.

Rev Joseph Salmon

Birth:
1842
Death:
Mar. 23, 1914
Burial:
Cross Creek Cemetery #1
Fayetteville
Cumberland County
North Carolina,

Rev. Joseph Salmon's name is in a list of 1903 ministers of the E. Conf. meeting in Harnett Co., at Hodges Chapel Church, NC. Also, there are marriages in county performed by, Rev. Joseph Salmon, Bapt. minister. Company B, 36th North Carolina Infantry, Confederate States Of America.

John Ephriam Sawyer

Birth:
Jan. 26, 1886
Death:
May 15, 1962
Arlington, Virginia
Burial:
Ayden Cemetery, Ayden,
Pitt County, North Carolina

He studied at Ayden Seminary after which he received his ministerial credentials. Later, he was principal at Ayden Seminary and taught at the Seminary for eight years until he was 76 years of age. He believed in a strong academic program coupled with a strong biblical foundation. He was a fluent speaker who took his the ministry seriously.

William Riley Sawyer

Birth:
Jul. 20, 1884
Merritt, Pamlico County,
North Carolina
Death:
Oct. 17, 1922
Pamlico County, North
Carolina
Burial:
Trent Free Will Baptist Church
Cemetery
Pamlico County, North
Carolina

He was affiliated most of his life with the Trenton Free Will Baptist Church, Merritt, Pamlico County North Carolina. He was associated with the Free Will Baptist Press as early as 1874 as an agent, and was on the Board of Directors from at least 1895 until 1900. He became president of the company in 1901 and continued until 1912. He was the father of John E. Sawyer.

Rev David Robert Stafford
Birth:
Jan. 11, 1844
Death:
Sep. 27, 1914
Burial:
Antioch United Methodist
Church Cemetery
Strickland Crossroads
Johnston County
North Carolina

His name appears in roll of ministers in 1903 Minutes of the Free Will Baptist church, when it convened at Hodges Chapel church, Harnett Co. NC. He also was enlisted in the CSA NC 20th Reg. Co. H; entered Pvt, Final rank: Sgt.

Rev Spartan D Scalf
Birth:
Oct. 10, 1862
Greenville
Greenville County
South Carolina
Death:
Aug. 24, 1920
Durham
Durham County
North Carolina
Burial:
Maplewood Cemetery
Durham
Durham County
North Carolina

Eld. S.D. Scalf, age 60 years of the Eastern Conference, spirit took its flight from earth to glory, Aug. 24, 1920. He was a resident of Durham, NC. And a member of Mineral Springs Free Will Baptist Church. He was a pious, good and faithful member as well as a preacher. Son of Henry & Rebecca Jones Scalf.

He died of paralysis living only 22 hrs. from onset.

The funeral was preached by Rev. T. C. Marks in the presence of a large crowd, after which this body was placed in the Durham Cemetery to await the resurrection.

Rev Carlee Elizabeth Smith Stallard
Birth:
Nov. 20, 1927
Wise County
Virginia
Death:
Unknown
Burial:
Mount Gur Cemetery
Kernersville
Forsyth County
North Carolina

Her name is in the Original FreeWill Baptist Directory of Ordained NC Ministers, showing she was a member of Piedmont Conference, and serving Piedmont Church House of Prayer. Wife of Lee Hardrick Stallard, 1920-1986.

Adam Scott
Birth:
Jan. 23, 1917
Texas County,
Missouri
Death:
Mar. 26, 2004
North Carolina
Burial:
Knollwood Cemetery, Clayton,
Johnston County,
North Carolina

He was a Free Will Baptist minister and part of a large relationship consisting of ministers with names of Scott, Smith, and Vandivort that had ministries across the FWB denomination.

Rev Ervin Daniel Sluder
Birth:
Oct. 22, 1887
Buncombe County
North Carolina
Death:
Apr. 18, 1970
Weaverville
Buncombe County
North Carolina
Burial:
Mountain View FW Baptist
Church Cemetery, Leicester
Buncombe County
North Carolina

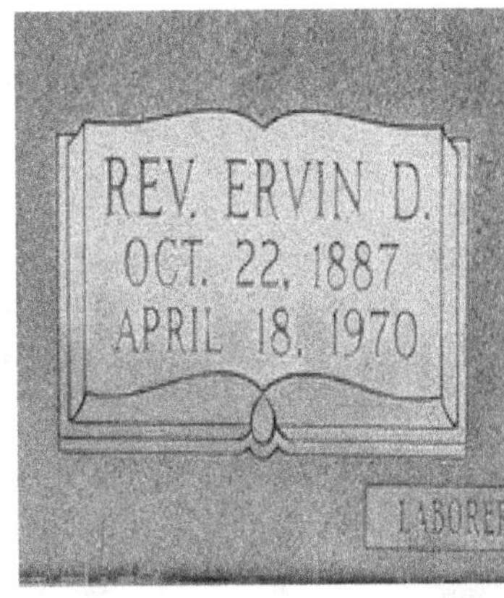

Parents:
John Sluder (1845 - 1915) -
Malinda Minerva Black Sluder
(1852 - 1938),
Spouse:
Hester DeWeese Sluder (1888 -
1961).

Samra Smith
Birth:
Jul. 31, 1891
Death:
Nov. 25, 1923
North Carolina, USA
Burial:
Mount Olive Baptist Church
Cemetery
Mount Olive
Stokes County, North Carolina

Rev. Samra Smith (a North Carolina native) had merged his publication, the Biblical Beacon, into the New Morning Star published by S. L. Morris of Texas and whose publication was representing the Co-operative General Association with the news of the new movement. He became one of the early presidents of Tecumseh College and pastor of the Tecumseh Church. Smith also taught Chemistry and Biology at the college and his wife Pearl Smith taught Preparatory Work. He served as Moderator of the Co-operative General Association

LTC David Leonard Spears
Birth:
Nov. 24, 1960
Vicenza,Veneto, Italy
Death:
Dec. 25, 2011
Sanford, Lee County,
North Carolina
Burial:
Jonesboro Cemetery,
Sanford, Lee County,
North Carolina

Free Will Baptist minister and Chaplain. Chaplain (LTC) David Leonard Spears, 51, of Sanford, died at his residence.

David was a member of the Kendale Acres Free Will Baptist Church.

The funeral at Kendale Acres Free Will Baptist Church with Rev. Richard Barnes and CH (CPT) Ken Lewis officiating.

R. B. Spencer
Birth:
Mar. 2, 1886
Pamlico County,
North Carolina
Death:
Jan. 25, 1954
Pitt County, North Carolina
Burial:
Ayden Cemetery, Ayden,
Pitt County, North Carolina

A minister and educator. He was educated in Whitsett Institute and the University of North Carolina. He taught for a number of years. In 1932 he was ordained to the gospel Ministry. He was elected to the position of Editor of "The Free Will Baptist" in 1936, which position he held until September 1953. He was a member of Little Creek Free Will Baptist Church. Funeral services were held at the Free Will Baptist Church by the Rev. R. N. Hinnant, of Micro, assisted by the Rev. Bruce Barrow of Snow Hill, and the Rev. Charles Craddock of Ayden.

Rev David Robert Stafford
Birth:
Jan. 11, 1844
Death:
Sep. 27, 1914
Burial:
Antioch United Methodist
Church Cemetery
Strickland Crossroads
Johnston County
North Carolina

His name appears in roll of ministers in 1903 Minutes of the Free Will Baptist church, when it convened at Hodges Chapel church, Harnett Co. NC. He also was enlisted in the CSA NC 20th Reg. Co. H; entered Pvt, Final rank: Sgt.

Rev Thomas Walter Stancil
Birth:
Jul. 3, 1880
Wilson, North Carolina
Death:
Jul. 14, 1959
Woodard Herring Hospital
Wilson, Wilson Co., NC
Burial:
Piney Grove Church Cemetery
Nash County, North Carolina

An ordained Free Will Baptist minister in the Western Conference of FWB, listed in 1916 conference minutes.

Chester V. Stanley
Birth:
1912
North Carolina
Death:
1968
North Carolina
Burial:
Bethel Original Freewill
Baptist Church Cemetery, Four
Oaks,
Johnston County, North
Carolina

James Dallas Stepps
Birth:
Nov. 2, 1940
Pitt County, North Carolina
Death:
Sep. 2, 2013
Duffield
Scott County, Virginia
Burial:
Pinewood Memorial Park
Greenville
Pitt County,
North Carolina,

Rev. James "Dallas" Stepps, 72, a native of Pitt County, was a graduate of Hookerton High School and attended FWB Bible College in Nashville, TN. He pastored in TN, SC, NC and in FL for 30 years, and for 15 years served as the NC Advancement Representative for Harvest FWB Child Care Ministries in Duffield, VA. He was a member of Unity FWB Church.

Rev James Lawrence Strickland
Birth:
Apr. 19, 1843
Death:
Dec. 5, 1929
Burial:
Flood Chapel FWB Church
Cemetery
Floods Chapel
Nash County,
North Carolina

Rev. J.L. Strickland, was an ordained Free Will Bapt. minister. James is the son of Hariett Strickland. He married Sallie C. Robinson, daughter of Joe and Edna Roberson.

U.S. Civil War Enlisted in Company A, North Carolina 47th Infantry Regiment on 11 Apr 1862. Mustered out on 09 Apr 1865 at Appomattox Court House, VA.

Simon Hill Styron, Jr

Birth:
Mar., 1891
Sealevel
Carteret County, North Carolina
Death:
Dec. 17, 1939
Pine Level,Johnston County, North Carolina
Burial:
Oliver Cemetery
Johnston County,
North Carolina

Early Free Will Baptist minister serving in North Carolina. He was married to Ida Oliver.his parents were Simon Hill Styron (1851 - 1933) Nancy Lupton Styron and his son was Simon Daniel Styron (1925 - 1990).

Thomas O. Terry, Jr

Birth:
1921
Death:
2009
Craven County,
North Carolina
Burial:
Greenleaf
Memorial Park,
New Bern,
Craven County
North Carolina

He was a Free Will Baptist minister in eastern North Carolina.

Rev Duffy Toler

Birth:
Oct. 4, 1881
Death:
Sep. 6, 1955
Burial:
Oakdale Cemetery
Washington
Beaufort County
North Carolina

An active ordained minister in the Free Will Baptist church. His name appears in many old church records, serving on boards, committees, and as pastor

John Samuel Thompson

Birth:
Jul. 25, 1860
Death:
Dec. 11, 1938
Burial:
Woodlawn Memorial Park
Durham
Durham County
North Carolina

Listed in roll of Free Will Bapt. ordained ministers in Minutes of 49th Session of Western Conference, which convened in 1935, and then his death reported as the year before in the 1939th Session. He was active minister,pastor and serving until his death.

Herbert Turner Tripp

Birth:
Sep. 2, 1909
Death:
Oct. 17, 1981
Burial:
Juniper Chapel FWB Church Cemetery
Vanceboro
Craven County
North Carolina

Listed with names of organizers of NC State Association of FWB, from Vanceboro.

Inscription:
Gone to be with his Lord
Granddaddy Herbert

Benjamin Wesley Tippett

Birth:
Feb. 15, 1856
Johnston, North Carolina
Death:
May 8, 1922
Little River;Zehulsa, Wake
Burial:
Harris Daniel Cemetery
Middlesex
Nash County
North Carolina

Rev. B.B. Tippett, was an ordained minister in the Original Free Will Baptist church, and was active in the Western Conference of Free Will Baptist churches. His name is among ordained ministers in the Thirteenth session Minutes for said conference, held in 1916, and in earlier church records. Besides as pastor of churches, he held positions on boards and committees in the Conference, and lived a useful life.

Benjamin is the son of William Tippett and Elizabeth Hinton. He married Mary Jane Daniel, daughter of Harris Daniel and Mourning Jane Tisdale about 1879.

A. A. Tyson
Birth:
Nov. 28, 1838
Death:
Apr. 27, 1914
Burial:
Pineview Cemetery
South Rocky Mount
Edgecombe County,
North Carolina

This info is from a 1937 cemetery survey compiled by the Historical Records Survey of North Carolina and located in the Family Records Collection of the State Archives. It appears here exactly as written in that document.

Father, into thy hands I commend my spirit."

Luke 23:46

Rev. James Turnage
Birth:
Jun. 10, 1821
Death:
Nov. 2, 1882
Burial:
Hodges Chapel Cemetery
Benson
Johnston County
North Carolina

A Free Will Baptist minister, listed as being one of the original ministers of churches from 1855-1901, in Cape Fear Conferance.

Rev A. B. Utley
Birth:
Sep. 25, 1859
Death:
Oct. 8, 1938
Burial:
Collins Grove Baptist Church
Cemetery
Holly Springs
Wake County
North Carolina

He was an ordained Free Will Bapt. minister, listed in the 1935 minutes of the Western Conference. He was an active minister and pastor.

Jacob Utley
Birth:
Nov. 6, 1803
Raleigh
Wake County, North Carolina
Death:
Mar. 28, 1888
Thomasville
Davidson County,
North Carolina
Burial:
Gods Acre, Thomasville
Davidson County,
North Carolina

Rev. Jacob Utley, was an early pioneer Free Will Baptist minister in NC, whose name appears as one of the several ministers who helped sustain the scattered churches after 1832. On Sept. 1, 1887, he came to the orphanage as a home for aged ministers. No others were ever received as the plan was abandoned.

Spouse: Aplis Wallace Utley (1810 - 1888).

Inscription:
Native of Wake County, for many years a missionary pastor in North Carolina.

Elder Jesse Vause
Birth:
Dec., 1799
Death:
Jun. 29, 1854
Burial:
Vause Family Cemetery,
Lenoir County,
North Carolina

One of the very early Free Will Baptist preachers in North Carolina.

Rev Alonzo A. Wells
Birth:
Sep. 9, 1896
Death:
Jul. 1, 1939
Burial:
Raines Cross Roads Cemetery
Princeton
Johnston County
North Carolina

An ordained Free Will Baptist minister, listed in the minutes of the 49th Session of the Western Conference, NC, convened in 1935.

Robert West
Birth:
1947
Death:
2009
Burial:
Hills of Neuse Memorial Gardens,
Smithfield,
Johnston County,
North Carolina

Free Will Baptist pastor and missionary to the Ivory Coast, Africa.

Pamela "Pam" Stanley West
Birth:
Feb. 7, 1949
Johnston County
North Carolina
Death:
Oct. 9, 2016
Four Oaks,
Johnston County
North Carolina
Burial:
Hills of Neuse Memory Gardens
Smithfield,
Johnston County
North Carolina

Pamela "Pam" S. West, was born to the late Thomas Milford and Ada Pearl Hall Lassiter Stanley. She was a secretary with Rose & Graham Funeral Home in Four Oaks and the former Minshew Funeral Home. She and her husband served as missionaries to Ivory Coast West Africa for 21 years. She was a member of Unity Free Will Baptist Church in Smithfield.

Rev Luke Wetherington
Birth:
1890
Death:
1944
Burial:
Cedar Grove Cemetery
New Bern
Craven County, North Carolina

An ordained Free Will Baptist minister in Craven Co. Amazon sells a book of his life, "A Chosen Vessel- Luke Herbert Wetherington.

Lee Whaley
Birth:
1914
Death:
1988
North Carolina
Burial:
Pinelawn
Memorial Park,
Kinston, Lenoir County,
North Carolina

He was a Free Will Baptist pastor serving in various pastorates and was a home missionary to Alaska.

John Wheeler
Birth:
Jan. 1, 1800
North Carolina
Death:
Aug. 15, 1871
Yancey County,
North Carolina
Burial:
Silvers Cemetery,
Pensacola,
Yancey County,
North Carolina

He was a early minister and leader whose legacy spreads across a four state area consisting of N.C., TN., Va. West Va.

Elder Jonas Hardie Whitley
Birth:
Dec. 5, 1875
North Carolina
Death:
Jul. 7, 1941
North Carolina
Burial:
Rock Springs
Free Will Baptist
Church Cemetery
Bailey
Nash County
North Carolina

An ordained Free Will Bapt. minister, useful in service of his church.

Rev Phillip Carl Wiggs
Birth:
Oct. 29, 1907
Death:
Apr. 8, 1974
Burial:
Queen Anne Cemetery
Fountain
Pitt County
North Carolina,

Ordained Free Will Baptist minister whose name appears in church records and obits of funerals he has conducted.

I Am Come That You May Have Life Abundantly

Nestus VanDelon Wiggs
Birth:
Mar. 23, 1889
Pine Level,Johnson Co., N.C
Death:
Jan. 13, 1941
Burial:
Cedar Grove Cemetery,
New Bern, Craven County,
North Carolina

He was a member of the Eastern Conference. In 1912 he entered the Free Will Baptists Seminary in Ayden for his Theological study while serving churches in the eastern part of N.C. He was active in revival work and other activities of the Denomination. He served as moderator of the Union Meeting and was a member of the Church Extension Board of the State Convention of N.C. for several years. His funeral was conducted by D.W. Alexander, J.L. Hodges and J.C. Griffin.

Daniel Anderson Windham
Birth:
Nov. 7, 1887
Wilson County
North Carolina
Death:
Jun. 17, 1961
Greenville,Pitt County
North Carolina
Burial:
Greenwood Cemetery
Greenville
Pitt County, North Carolina

A North Carolina minister who was the Son of William Edward Windham and Sarah Elizabeth (Rasberry) Wind-ham.

Missionary Emma Ruth _Bennett_ Willey
Birth:
Dec. 19, 1935
Death:
Dec. 13, 1972
Panama City,
Panama, Panama
Burial:
New Bern Memorial Cemetery,Trent Woods,
Craven County,
North Carolina,Plot:Section A

Served as a missionary in Panama for Free Will Baptist missions. She served as a missionary in the interior as well as the capital Panama city. She died in the Gorgus hospital in Panama City and was returned to New Bern for her burial. She was the wife of Thomas Willey, Junior.

**Missionary
Zadie Volena Wilson**
Birth:
Mar. 11, 1918
Rutherford County,
North Carolina
Death:
Mar. 30, 2001
McDowell County,
North Carolina
Burial:
McDowell Memorial Park,
Marion
McDowell County,
North Carolina

A missionary to India for many years. She later worked for the Presbyterian Journal until her retirement. During her retirement, she continued to be faithful in ministry visiting the hospitals, nursing homes and shut-ins. She also continued to promote the missionary endeavor in India through her many speaking engagements in churches.

Marcellus A. Woodard
Birth:
September 6, 1879
Greene County, North Carolina
Death:
1957
Pitt County, North Carolina
Burial:
Reedy Branch Baptist Church,
Winterville,
Pitt County, North Carolina

An early Free Will Baptist preacher who in 1903 at the age of 24 was licensed to preach the gospel at Howell Swamp Free Will Baptist Church, Greene County, North Carolina. He prepared for the ministry at the Free Will Baptist Seminary, in Ayden and began his early ministry in the Midway Association in South Georgia in 1909. He married the daughter of W.A. McDonald, a pioneer Free Will Baptist minister in South Georgia. His ministry existed in South Georgia and North Florida until the fall of 1921, when he returned to his native state becoming the pastor of the church in Davis, North Carolina. For 53 years he was a faithful minister the gospel with 32 of those years as a member of the Central conference of North Carolina..

T. E. Woody
Birth:
Apr. 4, 1876
Death:
Dec. 10, 1967
Yancey County,
North Carolina
Burial:
Will Young Cemetery,
Yancey County,
North Carolina
A Free Will Baptist minister who was active in the organization of the N C State Association of Orig. FWB. Free Will Baptist preacher in western North Carolina.

Rev James William Wooten
Birth:
Jul. 2, 1922
Death:
Jan. 30, 1987
Burial:
Mount Harmony Baptist
Church
Matthews
Mecklenburg County
North Carolina

North Dakota

Avery Clark
Birth:
Oct. 17, 1818
Springfield,
Hampden County,
Massachusetts
Death:
Sep. 3, 1863
Dickey County,
North Dakota
Burial:
Whitestone Hill
State Historic Site,
Merricourt,
Dickey County,North Dakota

Rev. Avery Clark moved to Iowa from his native Mass. in 1846, and began preaching about 1853. He was ordained a Freewill Baptist minister in May 1856 at Delaware Clayton Q.M., Iowa. He was a strong man, positive in his convictions and at Pres. Lincoln's Emancipation Proclamation, he said, "Now I can go." He acted as a "chaplain" in ministering to his regiment, and fell in battle far from home. Enlisted Sept. 22, 1862. Sixth Iowa Cavalry Mustered Sept. 22, 1862. Killed in action Sept. 3, 1863, White Stone Hill, Dakota.

Benjamin Rackliff
Birth:
Jun. 3, 1819
Montville, Maine
Death:
Sep. 10, 1892
Burial:
Prairie Home Cemetery
Gilby,Grand Forks County,
North Dakota

He was ordained in 1858 and was pastor of the church at Wesley, Maine for eight years. He held several local offices and was a representative in the Maine Legislature. He later was a pastor of the Diamond Bluff church, Wisconsin, but much of his ministry was in itinerant work for short periods preaching in a weak churches.

I Am Come That You May Have Life Abundant

Ohio

Walter Abrams
Birth:
1894
Death:
1979
Burial:
Lagrange Cemetery,
Ironton,
Lawrence County, Ohio

Rev Barton Davis Addis
Birth:
Jun. 2, 1866
Ohio
Death:
Oct. 3, 1916
Jamestown
Chautauqua County
New York
Burial:
Memorial Burial Park
Wheelersburg
Scioto County, Ohio

Portsmouth Daily Times
Portsmouth, Ohio
Saturday, 5 October 1916

REV. BARTON D. ADDIS
John P. Addis, of Harrisonville, former superintendent of the county infirmary, Wednesday afternoon received a telegram announcing the death of his brother, the Rev. Barton D. Addis, who had been living in Hyde Town, Pa. When relatives here last heard from Rev. Addis, he was enjoying splendid health. He was 50 years old last August and is survived by his wife and four children. His body left Hyde Town Thursday morning and will arrive here some time Friday.

Rev. Addis was a splendid minister and the news of his death will be learned of here with genuine sorrow. He was well known throughout Scioto County.

Portsmouth Daily Times
Portsmouth, Ohio
Saturday, 7 October 1916

FUNERAL NOTICE FOR REV. BARTON D. ADDIS
The funeral services of the late Rev. Barton D. Addis, who died in Jamestown, N.Y., will be conducted Sunday morning from the Glendale Church near Harrisonville. The body arrived here Friday and was conveyed to the home of the dead man's brother, John P. Addis of Harrisonville.

Portsmouth Daily Times
Portsmouth, Ohio
Monday, 16 October 1916

REV. BARTON D. ADDIS
Relative to the recent and sudden death of the late Rev. Barton D. Addis, a brother of John P. Addis, of Harrisonvile, the Titusville, Pa., Herald recently said: The many friends of Rev. B.D. Addis of this city and Hydetown were shocked to learn of his death in the W.C.A. hospital at Jamestown, N.Y., following an operation for gallstones performed earlier in the day.
Rev. Mr. Addis served the Hydetown M.E. Church the past year and at the Erie conference held two weeks ago in Clarion, he was assigned by Bishop Franklin Hamilton to the church at Sinclairville, N.Y., a thriving village about twelve miles north of Jamestown. He

went to Sinclairville with his son, George Addis, in his automobile last Saturday. He preached both morning and evening Sunday and was taken ill soon after the evening service.

Being no better on Monday morning, the attending physician advised that he be taken to the Jamestown hospital and submit to an operation for gallstones. He was taken to the hospital on Monday afternoon and the operation was performed Tuesday morning.

Mrs. Addis was notified of her husband's serious illness on Monday evening and she went to Jamestown on the early New York Central train Tuesday, arriving at the hospital at 11 a.m., while Mr. Addis was still on the operating table. He rallied after the operation and knew his wife, but he gradually failed int he afternoon and passed away at 10 p.m.

Rev. Barton D. Addis had been a minister of the gospel for the past eighteen years and was 50 years, 4 months and 1 day of age. He was well known in Crawford County, where he had served numerous charges and during the past year, while in charge of the Hydetown pastorate had become acquainted with many residents of Titusville and vicinity. He was active in the tabernacle meetings held in this city last spring and conducted a series of evangelistic meetings in the Hydetown church following those services.

He leaves besides his wife, Mrs. Mary A. Addis, four children, George F., Wilbur J., Adra A. and Paul B. Addis, all of Hydetown, the eldest being a conductor on the Titusville traction line. He also has two brothers, John P. Addis, of Harrisonville, O., and George C. Addis, of Waterloo, O., and three sisters, Mrs. Millie Massie and the Misses Huttie and Bertha Addis, of Waterloo, O. He was a member of the Masonic Lodge at Pierpont, Ohio, and of the Hydetown I.O.O.F. Lodge.

Schuyler Aldrich
Birth:
Apr. 26, 1822
Ontario, Canada
Death:
Sep. 20, 1904
Buffalo, Erie County, New York
Burial:
Evergreen Cemetery, Pierpont, Ashtabula County, Ohio

He was brought to Christ in 1839, and studied at Oberlin College, Ohio receiving his ordination May 23, 1847. His ministry was with the Mecca, Henrietta. Pittsfield, and Macedonia churches, Ohio, and with the Buffalo, Bethany, Phoenix, Elmira, and Poland churches, N. Y. Several revivals resulted from his labors, and about 200 converts were baptized by him. About 1880, he made his home in Buffalo, N. Y. His devotion to the cause of education is evidenced by a gift of ten thousand dollars to Hillsdale College, to be used in endowing a theological professorship.

Jonas Allen
Birth:
Royalton, Mass.
Death:
Sept. 29, 1864
Madison, Ohio
Burial:
Dock Road Cemetery
Madison, Lake County, Ohio

Allen died aged 86 years. He was baptized by Elder Alva Buzzell, in 1809. At the close of the war of 1812 he began to preach, having his first revival in Charleston, Vt., where a church was organized, and he was ordained in 1824. Soon after churches were organized at East Charleston and at Brighton as a result of his labors. About 1837 he moved to Madison, 0hio, where he continued to preach until more than threescore and ten. He was devoted to every good work, enjoying the work of the ministry and awaiting in confidence for the rest prepared.

James Thornton Arthur
Birth:
Apr. 22, 1853
Pinkerman
Scioto County, Ohio
Death:
Oct. 14, 1925
Scioto County, Ohio
Burial:
Harrison Furnace Cemetery
Minford
Scioto County, Ohio

He was ordained on August 20, 1887 and spent several months in evangelistic work in the Little Scioto Quarterly Meeting in Ohio and then also in the Kentucky Yearly Meeting. At one time he pastored the Harrison church which is at Minford Ohio.

Leonard Ashley
Birth:
Jan. 19, 1792
Deerfield
Franklin County
Massachusetts
Death:
Jan. 31, 1873
Rockaway
Seneca County
Ohio
Burial:
Steuben Cemetery
Steuben
Huron County, Ohio

Aged 81 Years 12 D
From the Biographical Record of the Counties of Huron and Lorain, Ohio. Chicago, J.H. Beers & Co. 1894 (305-306)
Leonard Ashley learned shoemaking under his father, and worked at the trade during his life in Massachusetts. His mother died about the year 1799, and the youth then went to reside with an elder brother, Luther. After some years he wished to see the world outside of his native State, and migrated to Canada, where, in 1815, he married Sally McDougal, who was born in 1794, in Nova Scotia, for whose father young Ashley worked; and while living on Yonge street, and near Toronto, in the Province of Ontario, the following named children were born: Thomas, who died in infancy; James, who, in 1824, accompanied his mother to Ohio, where he married, became a Free-will Baptist preacher, and thence moved to Michigan, where he died, leaving twelve children ; Stewart B., late a resident of Steuben, Ohio, who died October 30, 1893, and is buried in Greenfield cemetery; Sally, who first married David Skeeles, and subsequently Dean Keefer (she is now a widow, residing at Columbus, Kans.); and John, a Free-will Baptist preacher, of Hillsdale, Mich., who was a fellow schoolmate of James A. Garfield. After the family joined the father in Greenfield township, in 1824, there were born Luther, a resident of Bellevue, Mich.; William, of Knoxville, Iowa; Allen T., the subject of this sketch; Joseph B., of Oberlin, Ohio; Mary, wife of Judge G. W. Lewis, of Medina, Ohio; Henry, a resident of San Francisco, Cal.; and Daniel, who went to California in 1862 and died there.
In 1822 Leonard Ashley left Canada for Huron County, Ohio, and worked on farms and at his trade here for two years. In 1824 his wife and children arrived, and all found a home with Alden Pierce, a brother-in-law, who then occupied what is known as the "Sturges Farm" in Greenfield Township. The father was known as a good farmer and a good shoemaker, and was a very active man until his death, which occurred in 1873. At that time he was on a visit to his son John at Rockaway, Seneca Co., Ohio, from which place his remains were returned to Huron County for interment in the Greenfield cemetery. His wife, who died March 19, 1863, was interred in Steuben cemetery. Leonard Ashley was a Whig until the organization of the Repub-licans, when he became a stanch supporter of the new party. In religious matters he and his wife were members of the Free-will Baptist Church."

Rev Lewis A Atkinson
Birth:
Apr. 24, 1821
Virginia
Death:
Sep. 18, 1882
Jackson County, Ohio
Burial:
Fairmount Cemetery
Jackson
Jackson County, Ohio

He was a minister of the Gospel. He served as a Captain in Co G 91st OVI in Civil War. Spouse: Amanda Long Atkinson (1832 - 1913).
Children:
Charles Andrew Atkinson (1852 - 1925), Eliza Long Atkinson Strider (1856 - 1937), Mary Atkinson (1858 - 1859), Caroline Bundy Atkinson Jones (1866 - 1945).

Hobart C. Ashby
Birth:
Nov. 8, 1925
Virginia
Death:
Jan. 16, 1998
Dayton,
Montgomery County, Ohio
Burial:
Miami Valley Memory Gardens,
Centerville,
Montgomery County, Ohio

He was ordained a Free Will Baptist minister in 1956. He began his pastoral duties in 1957 at the Fairborn Free Will Baptist Church where he served three years and in 1961, the Virginia born minister, became the pastor of the First Dayton Free Will Baptist Church, where he served for 33 years. Some 30 men answered the call to the ministry under his ministry. He retired from the church in 1994.

He was a member of the Board of Directors of the Ohio State Association of Free Will Baptists for 22 years. Twice he was moderator of the Ohio State Association. He served six years on the national Home Missions Board. And preached at the national convention in Anaheim, California in 1980. He served in the U.S. Navy during WWII aboard the USS Crux in both the Atlantic and Pacific theaters.

George Washington Baker
Birth:
Oct. 22, 1803
Litchfield Corners,
Kennebec County, Maine
Death:
Oct. 11, 1881
Marion, Marion County, Ohio
Burial:
Marion Cemetery,
Marion, Marion County, Ohio

One of the "Fathers" of the denomination in Ohio. He came from Litchfield, Maine, with his parents in 1822, and settled in Marion, Ohio until his death. He was converted under the labors of Rev. David Dudley and united with the Marion Free Will Baptist Church in 1827.
He received license to preach, though with the firm resolve that he would never be ordained. However, when his labors were crowned with success and he found himself surrounded by many converts who were pressing him to baptize them, he could refuse no longer, and in 1834, was ordained. He was pastor of churches, but he delighted in, and greatly preferred revival work. He was deeply spiritual, affectionate in manner, and a good singer. He was sustained by a large body and a strong constitution. He preached to all classes throughout the region. It is estimated that no less than 3,000 persons became professed Christians under his ministry, and 2,500 of these he baptized. Of these, some twenty-six entered the ministry. He continued to preach until the fall of 1880. During his long ministry, he took a prominent place in the general state and denominational work.
His last sermon was preached August 28, 1881, at a reunion of the pastors and members of the Centreburgh church, one of the first he gathered.

Rev Alvin Bacon
Birth:
Unknown
Death:
Dec. 5, 1818
Burial:
Rochester Station Cemetery
Rochester
Lorain County
Ohio, USA

Inscription:
Aged 27yrs 5mos 27dys

Clifford H. Ball
Birth:
Unknown
Death:
Feb. 22, 2007
Kansas City,
Wyandotte County,
Kansas
Burial:
Forest Lawn Memorial
Gardens,
Columbus,
Franklin County, Ohio

Clifford died in Kansas City but was the former pastor at Trinity Free Will Baptist Church and Welch Avenue Free Will Baptist Churches in Columbus, Ohio. He was the current pastor of the Bethel Free Will Baptist Church in Kansas City at his death.

Mance Ball
Birth:
1901,
Death:
1967
Scioto County, Ohio
Burial:
South Webster
Cemetery,
South Webster,
Scioto County, Ohio

Early Free Will Baptist minister in southern Ohio

Vernie Bare
Birth:
Oct. 22, 1926
Death:
Dec. 1, 2006
Burial
Ohio Western Reserve
National Cemetery,
Rittman,
Medina County, Ohio, Plot:
Section 20 Plot 189

Pastor of the Rock of Ages FWB Church.

Peter Barnhart
Birth:
Sep. 22, 1897
Death:
Aug. 8, 1993
Burial:
Lawrence Furnace Cemetery,
Lawrence Furnace,
Lawrence County, Ohio
Free Will Baptist preacher in

the early days in southern Ohio.

While We In The Dust And The Shadows Wait

Selah Barrett
Birth:
1790
Stafford,
Tolland County,
Connecticut
Death: there my

Jul. 12, 1860
Rutland,
Meigs County, Ohio
Burial:
Miles Cemetery,
Rutland,
Meigs County, Ohio

Barrett was baptized by Elder Alva Buzzell at Strafford, Vermont. in 1812. Five years later he moved to Rutland, Ohio, where he was one of the early Free Baptists. He was licensed in 1837 and ordained at Cheshire in 1849. His ministerial labors were with the churches of the Meigs Quarterly Meeting of which he was clerk as early as 1835, and with several in the Athens Q.M.

Selah Hibbard Barrett
Birth:
Feb. 24, 1822
Rutland, Meigs County, Ohio
Sep. 1, 1883
Rutland, Meigs County, Ohio
Burial:
Miles Cemetery,
Rutland, Meigs County, Ohio

Deprived of the advantages of the schools because of ill health, he devoted perseveringly to study at home and gained a knowledge of the branches usually taught in college and afterwards completed courses in law and medicine. He experienced forgiveness of sins in 1838, received license to preach in

1845, and was ordained in 1856 by the Meigs Q. M., his ministry being spent within its bounds. He devoted much time to literary labor, having been a frequent correspondent of the *Morning Star* and other periodicals nearly forty years, and prepared several pamphlets and books, among them *"Memoirs of Eminent Preachers of the Freewill Baptist Denomination,"* and a Autobiography of about 400 pages.

Daniel E. Bates
Birth:
Feb. 2, 1927
Norton, Wise County, Virginia
Death:
Aug. 16, 2010
Ohio
Burial:
Oak Grove Memorial Park, Lexington, Richland County, Ohio

Pastor of the Blooming Grove Free Will Baptist Church.

Samuel D. Bates
Birth:
Oct. 13, 1828
Oneida County, New York
Death:
Sep. 17, 1886
Marion,
Marion County, Ohio
Burial:
Marion Cemetery, Marion, Marion County, Ohio,
Plot: Sharpless Sect. S43 L1

Samuel D. Bates, D.D, in the fall of 1834 moved to Ohio, and settled in Trumbull Co. Samuel was reared on a farm but received his education at Geauga Seminary, which became a part of Hillsdale College, Michigan. He began to teach school when he was 19 years old and in 1848-49 taught the school at which James A. Garfield, afterwards President of the United States, was a pupil. Garfield was three years Mr. Bates' junior, and was persuaded to attend Geauga, from which a friendship existed until President Garfield's tragic death. Of Mr. Bates, Garfield once said, *"To him I owe more than to any other living man for what I am today."* He continued to teach until he entered the ministry of the Free Will Baptist Church in 1851. The first six years were spent in Trumbull Co. Ohio. In 1857 he came to Marion to accept the charge of the FWB church in that city. He remained pastor of the local church without interruption until 1876, and during his ministry of 19 years built up a strong congregation. When he came to Marion, the Free Will Baptist worshipped in the old church located on Mt. Vernon Avenue, but through his energy and executive ability the church on East Center Street was built at a cost of $16,000, more than half of which was donated outside of the society. He also was connected with the erection of five other church edifices in the county. He organized the Grand Prairie Free Baptist Church, and was its pastor for nine years. He organized the Claridon Free Will Baptist Church during the winter of 1870-71, and assisted in building the first church of that denomination in the township. He was pastor of the Claridon Church for 15 years, ministering to the wants of his people until a few months prior to his death. Mr. Bates was zealous in the cause of education as well as religion. He was a trustee of Hillsdale College for 15 years. In 1872 he was elected president of Ridgeville (Indiana) College and so continued up to the time of his death. In June 1884, Ohio Central College, at Iberia, in recognition of his thorough learning and earnest work in behalf of education, conferred upon him the degree of Doctor of Divinity. (Marion County, Ohio, 1907 History, Biography)

Warner Beebe

Birth:
Feb. 1, 1808
Death:
Oct. 5, 1851
Burial:
Beebe Town Cemetery,
Beebetown,
Medina County, Ohio

He was born Canandaigua, Ontario, NY. By 1825, he was in Liverpool, Ohio, where he united with the Free Will Baptist Church. He was ordained to the gospel ministry in 1835. In 1850, he represented the Ohio Northern Yearly Meeting in the General Conference.

Ben Bird

Birth:
Sep. 1, 1907
Death:
May 11, 1990
Burial:
White Gravel Cemetery,
Minford,
Scioto County, Ohio

Brother Bird's ministry was in the southern part of Ohio.

James Andrew Blair

Birth:
Oct. 10, 1928
Kentucky
Jun. 25, 2004
Crossville,
Cumberland County,
Tennessee
Burial:
Miami Memorial Park
Cemetery,
Covington, Miami County, Ohio

He was a retired minister, a member of Williams Road Freewill Baptist Church and attended Crossville First Freewill Baptist. He pastored for more than 30 years in the Ohio area and was the founder of Troy Freewill Baptist Church in Troy, OH. He truly loved taking care of his people in the church. He was also a U.S. Army veteran, having served our country during Korea.

Rev Payton Blackburn

Birth:
Feb. 21, 1924
Lawrence County, Kentucky
Death:
Oct. 3, 1991
Columbus
Franklin County, Ohio
Burial:
Obetz Cemetery,
Obetz
Franklin County, Ohio

Blackburn, died at age 67, member and former pastor of

the Hillview Freewill Baptist Church and Brice Road Freewill Baptist Church. Retired from David Davies Packing in Columbus, Ohio after 20 years. Veteran of WW II. Payton was married to Edna (Gullett) daughters, Carol Willadean (Homer) Brickey, Betty Jean (Clyde) Endicott; sons, Cecil Payton, Rev Bobby Joe.

Orvil Blake
Birth:
Apr. 8, 1824
Death:
Aug. 12, 1877
Burial:
Westlawn Cemetery
Mantua,
Portage County, Ohio
Plot: Sect A, row 07

Blake, a native of Cornwall, Conn., married in 1850, and two years later moved to Mantua, Ohio, where he lived, labored, and died. His conversion and early labors were with the larger Baptist body, but as they refused him ordination because of his Free Baptist views, he found a home with the latter. He assisted in gathering several churches, and, besides his pastoral work at Mantua, preached also at Brimfield, Troy, Maple Grove, Hiram Rapids and Chester. He was a grand man, loved by all, and his death, at the age of 53 years, was a great loss to the Yearly Meeting. He had lectured on various topics, was correspondent of several journals, and had represented his county in the State Legislature.

John Leonard Blount, Sr
Birth:
Jul. 18, 1930 Ohio
Death:
Apr. 10, 2006
Wilmington,
Clinton County,
Ohio
Burial:
Morrow Cemetery Morrow,
Warren County,
Ohio

Blount was the pastor of Beech Grove Church of God that later became the Beech Grove Free Will Baptist Church. He served as pastor from 1988-2006. The last year Rev. Allen Kinard assisted him in his duties.

Marvin Booth
Birth:
Unknown
Death:
Feb. 17, 2000
Columbus, Ohio
Burial:
Obetz Cemetery,
Obetz, Franklin County, Ohio,
Plot: Sect 23, lot 91, spc 1

He founded in 1966 the Friendly FWB church in Columbus and pastored it for 25 years. At the time of his death he was pastor of the Reese Community Church. A noted leader and respected minister. He was 65 at his death.

Charles R. Bowman
Birth:
Jun. 25, 1924
Ramsey,
Nelson County, Virginia
Death:
Apr. 7, 2008
Columbus,
Franklin County, Ohio
Burial:
Alton Cemetery,
Alton, Franklin County, Ohio

He served our country in the United States Army during the Second World War, and had lived in Columbus, Ohio since 1952. He attended Moody Bible Institute and Liberty University. Rev. Bowman was gloriously saved on March 16, 1952 at Old Memorial Hall in Columbus, Ohio, and began preaching in 1953 and would preach everywhere the doors were opened. Many people accepted Christ as their personal Savior under his ministry. He pastored the Westside FWB Church for 35 years, and faithfully served this church and congregation through 1987. He also pastored in Key West, FL for ten years.

While We In The Dust And The Shadows Wait

Rev James Darmin Boyd
Birth:
Nov. 17, 1944
Logan, Logan County
West Virginia
Death:
Dec. 14, 2015
Mount Sterling
Madison County
Ohio
Burial:
Sunset Cemetery
Galloway
Franklin County, Ohio

He was a retired banker and served our country and protected our freedom by serving with the U.S. Navy as a Naval Hospital Corpsman with the U.S. Marine Corps. He was an ordained minister and a member of the Westside Freewill Baptist Church. His favorite saying was, "I preach the gospel for a living and work at a bank to support it." While living in Columbus, OH he served his community as a past president of the Hilltop Kiwanis and past President of the Hilltop Business Association. He served in numerous leadership positions with the Central Ohio Council of the Boy Scouts of America.

Rev Daniel Brackett
Birth:
Oct. 4, 1803
Berwick
York County
Maine
Death:
Dec. 22, 1836
Burial:
Old Ricker Family Cemetery
Locust Corner
Clermont County,
Ohio

He was ordained a Free Will Baptist minister in 1829. He was residing in Houlton, and a council travelled over a hundred miles through the wilderness to ordain him. He labored in Maine, then journeyed to Ohio for his health and died of consumption at age 33.

Rev Hiram Brooks
Birth:
Apr. 23, 1810
Schoharie County, New York
Death:
Sep. 11, 1846
Ann Arbor
Washtenaw County, Michigan
Burial:
Bennetts Corners Cemetery
Brunswick
Medina County, Ohio,

Hiram Brooks was born 23 Apr 1810 in Schoharie County, New York, USA to James and Lydia (Bennett) Brooks. Hiram must have initially come west with his family as evidenced by the following:
A Society of Free Will Baptists was organized in Bennett's Corners as early as 1828 with Hiram Brooks acting as lay minister." (From: Brunswick: Our Hometown A history of the community and its families)

The first school house was a log structure, erected in 1828, and located at the township corner-stone. Hiram Brooks was the first teacher, receiving $13.00 per month for his services, and boarding at home." (From the History of Medina County, page 593).
It would appear that Hiram must have returned to the east to receive his theological training (possibly at either New Hampton Institute or Parsonsfield Seminary—not confirmed which one yet).
Hiram married Sarah Jane Hackett (daughter of Moulton and Mary (Ward) Hackett) 4 Dec 1839 in North Providence, Rhode Island, USA.
That same year Smithville Seminary was founded by the Rhode Island Association of Free Baptists. At the time, the Free Baptists already had two academies, one in New Hampshire (the New Hampton Institute), the other in Maine (Parsonsfield Seminary), and Rhode Island desired to have one of their own. Reverend Hiram Brooks was asked to start the school, and raised $20,000, all of which he put toward buildings. Sadly, the entire commitment of these monies to brick and mortar rather than an endowment fund may have caused financial difficulties for the institution, as it was unable to support itself through tuition revenue.
According to the History of Medina County, "One of the best saw-mills ever in Brunswick was built in the northeast part in 1843 by Hiram Brooks". "Hiram Brooks operated the mill until his death, which occurred some three years after its erection."
"This young man was a fine scholar, a graduate of one of

the Eastern theological colleges, and often preached in cabins and schoolhouses in those early years. He had great resolution and superior courage."

The following notice of his death is from the: Free Baptist Cyclopedia, Historical and Biographical: The Rise of the Freewill Baptist Connection and of Those General and Open Communion Baptists Which, Merging Together, Form One People, Their Doctrines, Polity, Publications, Schools and Missions, with Brief Biographies of Ministers and Others Identified with the Growth and Strength of the Denomination - 1889 By Rev G A Burgess and Rev J T Ward.

Brooks, Rev. Hiram, died near Ann Arbor, Michigan, 11 Sep 1846, aged 36 years. His early labors were in Rhode Island where he assisted in raising funds for the school at North Scituate. He moved from La Grange, Lorain, Ohio to Michigan and was ordained but a little while before his death. He was well prepared for the ministry, and high hopes were entertained of his usefulness.

From records we believe that his son George H Brooks was born in New Jersey and daughters Sarah and Lucinda Jenny were born in Ohio. We also know that Sarah Jane, daughters Sarah F and Lucinda Jenny died in Lowell, Massachusetts. It is unknown whether his son, George H Brooks, died elsewhere or in Lowell, Massachusetts. No death record has been found.

Aged 36y; ordained Freewill Baptist minister with great promise; sad he had to leave so soon.

Homer S. Brooks

Birth:
Feb. 9, 1926
Harrogate,
Claiborne County,
Tennessee
Death:
Feb. 11, 2003
Springfield,
Clark County, Ohio
Burial:
Ferncliff Cemetery,
Springfield,
Clark County, Ohio

Rev. Brooks was in the ministry for 54 years. He pastored the South Charleston Church for 35 years. In addition, he pastored the Sunset Church in Springfield for 18 years. For much of his ministry, while he pastored, he would preach 26 weeks of revivals for other churches. He was well known as an evangelist across the region. Brother Homer also was active in denominational roles, holding offices in the Little Miami Conference.

Rev Elias P. Brown

Birth:
Apr. 17, 1792
Strafford
Orange County, Vermont
Death:
Aug. 29, 1867
Ohio
Burial:
Cleveland Street Cemetery
Amherst
Lorain County, Ohio

Rev. Elias P. Brown, a native of Strafford, VT, died in Amherst, OH, aged 75 years. He was converted in youth, and joined the Free Baptists in Bethany, NY, where his labors were blessed. Later he moved to Lorain County, O., where he was ordained Nov. 10, 1836, and continued to preach until called to his reward. His birth is recorded in VT Vital Records and gives his father's name, and his mother, "Mary." Census' show his spouse as Mabel Brown. She is bur. in this cemetery

Morgan Hillman Brown

Birth:
Feb. 16, 1901
Death:
Mar. 8, 1986
Burial:
Vernon Cemetery,
Lyra,
Scioto County, Ohio

William Brundige

Birth: 1741
New York
Death: Nov. 12, 1825
Ohio
Burial:
Wyatt Cemetery
Waldo
Marion County, Ohio

William BRUNDIGE was born in the vicinity of Rye, New York. He was the son of Joseph BRUNDIGE and Elizabeth JENNINGS Brundige.

On 29 October 1761 at Rye, New York, William Brundige married Anna PURDY.

William Brundige served in the Revolutionary War while living in New York.

Through the years, he was a Baptist minister in New York, Virginia, and Ohio. William Brundige and Anna Purdy Brundige were among the first settlers of Waldo, Marion County, Ohio.William Brundige died as reached the age of 84 years.

William Brundige (1741 - 1825) and his wife Anna Purdy Brundige (1743 - 1823) are buried in historic Wyatt Cemetery near Waldo, Marion County, Ohio. Their children:

Anna Brundige Wyatt (1762 - 1838)*

Nathaniel Brundige (1771 - 1825)*

Sarah Nancy Brundige Tarboss (1773 - 1845)*

Thomas Brundige (1778 - 1844)*

John Brundige (1788 - 1850)*

Paul Russell Calvert
Birth:
Sep. 26, 1932
Yellow Springs,
Greene County, Ohio,
Death:
Mar. 11, 2010
Springfield,
Clark County, Ohio,
Burial:
Garlough Cemetery,
Pitchin,Clark County, Ohio,

Rev. Calvert was a member of the Beatty Freewill Baptist Church and was an avid fisherman. He was bi-vocational and was retired form Navistar.

Albert N Carmine
Birth:
1879
Death:
1964
Burial:
Green Camp Cemetery
Green Camp
Marion County Ohio

He was on the 37th session program in 1907 Central Ohio Yearly Meeting at the west Mansfield FWB Church. He led in the Young People's Meeting as president.

Hamilton James Carr
Birth:
1810
New York
Death:
Apr. 8, 1887
Jackson, Jackson County, Ohio
Burial:
Fairmount Cemetery, Jackson, Jackson County, Ohio

He was the son of Walter Moore Carr. His first wife Rebecca Conaway died in 1845 in Alexander Twp., Ohio. After his wife and father died, he married Ziare and they moved to Jackson, Ohio, where he was a Free Will Baptist preacher until his death. He was pastor of several churches in the Ohio River Y. M. The first two years of his ministry he baptized over 200 persons. He organized many churches and aided in the ordination. of several ministers. He was one of the trustees and an earnest supporter of Rio Grande College. He represented Ohio at the 1880 Centennial Conference in New Hampshire and is pictured in the photo of those over the age of 70 at this meeting. He is in the front row right with Bible in his hand. He was active in his denomination. Mr. Carr was an anti-slavery man and a Republican.

During Morgan's raid in Ohio he lost property and subjected to ill-treatment from the rebels.

Emil Carl Cartee
Birth;
23 Jun 1937
Portsmouth, Scioto County, Ohio
Death:
9 Jan 2018
Portsmouth, Scioto County, Ohio
Burial Vernon Cemetery Lyra, Scioto County, Ohio

WHEELERSBURG   Emil   Carl

Cartee, 80, of Wheelersburg, passed away at SOMC ER in Portsmouth, OH. Emil was born in Portsmouth to the late Forrest Wallace and Susie L. Dutiel Cartee. He retired from Ironton Iron as a Grinder. He was also a pastor at Dogwood Ridge Freewill Baptist Church and he was a US Army veteran of the Vietnam War. In addition to his parents he was preceded in death by his wife Betty Jean Sizemore Cartee, October 2, 2014 whom he married September 12, 1960 in Wheelersburg; a son, Read More Dennis Cartee; a brother, Gary Cartee; three sisters, Faye Cartee, Lorrena Henry and Wilma Gifford and a great grandson, Bo Cartee. Emil is survived by a son, Rick Cartee; a daughter, Rebecca (Mark) Stapleton; a brother, Harold Cartee; daughter-in-law, Carol Cartee; three sisters, Hazel Blackburn, Phyllis Micucci and Mary Brannigan; six grandchildren, Nathan, Nicholas, Ashlee, Chelsee, Ashton, and Hank; three great grandchildren, Daxton, Ashlyn and Remington.

Funeral services at Harrison-Pyles Funeral Home in Wheelersburg with Pastor Dan King officiating.

John Casebolt
Birth:
1872
Death:
1959
Scioto County, Ohio
Burial
Bennett Cemetery,
Minford,
Scioto County, Ohio

A Righteous Child Has Great Joy.

Forrest L. Chamberlin
Birth:
Feb. 23, 1922
Scioto County, Ohio
Death:
Jun. 8, 2012
Portsmouth, Scioto County, Ohio
Burial:
Vernon Cemetery,
Lyra, Scioto County, Ohio

Brother Chamberlin was one of the most respected ministers in southern Ohio. He was a retired barber and Free Will Baptist Minister ordained in 1947. He was the pastor of the Porter, Harrison, Long Run and Germany Hollow Free Will Baptist churches. However, his ministry extended beyond the local level and served on the Board of Directors for the Ohio State Association of Free Will Baptists for a number of years. He was active on various other committees and boards. He was a veteran of the United States Army serving during World War II in Germany and Austria as a radio operator with the 13th armored division.

Clarence O Clark
Birth: 1855
Death: 1943
Burial:
Calvary Baptist Cemetery, Rio Grande,

Gallia County, Ohio
He was a very active minister, pastor, leader and professor at Rio Grande College before and after the merger with the Northern Baptist.

Uriah Chabot
Birth:
Feb. 6, 1816
Greene, Ohio
Death
Aug. 18, 1897
Burial:
Powellsville Cemetery
Powellsville
Scioto County,
Ohio

Rev Uriah Chabot was pastor in the early 1880s at "The Free Will Baptist "Church of Powellsville, Ohio. This church was originally organized on Aug 16, 1841, as nondenominational and it was the first church in Powellsville. In the early 1930's, it was organized as a Free Will Baptist Church. In 1884, Rev. Uriah Chabot was pastor at the Chaffin Mills FWB Church. Uriah Chabot was active in his community, not only as pastor, but in other areas as well. When the small Methodist Episcopal Church in Powellsville, was dropped out of circuit, Rev. Uriah Chabot and Rev. Patrick Henry held a union meeting with them and it gave that church new life.

He married Luvina Hudson on 29 Sep 1841 in Scioto Co. and they had six children one of which was Dr. G. W. Shabot. He was converted the same year of his marriage and received license to preach in 1854 and was ordained in 1874 after which he became minister to many churches in the little Scioto and Pine Creek Quarterly Meetings.

Listed as a minister in the 1858 FWB Register from the Green Church.

Rufus B. Clark
Birth: Nov. 23, 1819
Conneaut,
Ashtabula County, Ohio
Death: Nov. 25, 1889
Conneaut
Ashtabula County, Ohio
Burial:
City Cemetery, Conneaut,
Ashtabula County, Ohio

Rufus was converted in 1830 and attended Geauga Seminary, and was ordained in 1843. For sixteen years he was pastor of the church in his native town, and he since ministered to the Lenox, Cherry Valley, Burgh Hill, New Lyme, Greenburg and Colebrook, Ohio; Sheffield and Wellsburg, Pennsylvania; Warren, Illinois, and Fon du Lac and Winneconne Wisconsin churches. He was actively identified with the anti-slavery movement. He was a life member of the Home and Foreign Mission Societies. He wrote sketches of the early history of Conneaut and other towns in northern Ohio. He delivered many lectures on various topics and a contributor to the religious and secular press. Rev. Clark wrote a *"Early History of South Ridge"*, about Ashtabula Co, in 1880.

Sam Crabtree
Birth:
Apr. 17, 1917
Otway, Scioto County, Ohio
Death:
Feb. 4, 1997
McDermott, Scioto County, Ohio
Burial:
Scioto Burial Park,
McDermott,
Scioto County,
Ohio

Bi-Vocational minister retired from the Empire-Detroit steel Corporation where he was stationary engineer. He was also a Free Will Baptist Minister for 47 years pastoring churches in the area.

Phillip E. Crabtree
Birth:
May 5, 1912
Death:
Jan. 14, 1994
Burial:
South Webster Cemetery
South Webster
Scioto County, Ohio

Phillip E. Crabtree, 81, of Oak Hill Branch Road, South Webster, died at a Columbus hospital. The son of the late John A. and Viola Lute Crabtree, he was a miner in a clay mine, a member of the Eifort Free Will Baptist Church, and a Free Will Baptist minister for 54 years. He is survived by his wife Mallie Green Crabtree, who he married Oct. 31, 1932. He has a son who is a home missionary in New Brunswick, Canada.

William Ershel Curfman
Birth:
Aug. 8, 1920
Ohio
Death:
Feb. 7, 2000
Gallipolis, Gallia County, Ohio
Burial:
Gravel Hill Cemetery,
Cheshire,
Gallia County, Ohio

Ordained October 6, 1951 by the Freewill Baptist Church. He pastored the following Freewill Baptist Churches: Kelly's Creek and Spring Hollow, West Virginia, Mt. Olive, Bidwell, Ohio, Coalton, Ohio, Old Kyger, Ohio. and Centerpoint, Ohio., where he was a member. Retired Blacksmith, Kaiser-Aluminum Plant, Ravenswood, W.Va. WW II Marine Veteran, serving when Pearl Harbor, Hawaii, was attacked in 1941. Life member Middleport DAV 53. he was a lifelong member of the Meigs County Free Will Baptist Association and a member of the General Board for the Ohio Association of Free

Will Baptists.

Elial Curtis
Birth:
Connecticut
Death:
September 19, 1848
New Haven, Ohio
Burial:
Guinea Corners Cemetery
Huron County, Ohio

He was a native of Connecticut and in his early life moved to New York then later to Ohio. He was ordained in 1837 and died at New Haven. He was a judicious brother, safe in Counsel, careful in deportment, highly esteemed by a large circle of Christian friends.

Rev John Andrew Daniels
Birth:
Sep. 20, 1928
Death:
Dec. 10, 2016
Burial:
Obetz Cemetery
Obetz

Franklin County, Ohio
Reverend John Andrew Daniels age 88 passed away peacefully at home. John was born to his parents, the late John H. and Roseanna Daniels in Patrick, Kentucky. He followed the call to minister for over 67 years. Retired from White Westinghouse Corp.
A member of The Mechanicsburg Freewill Baptist Church. Preceded in death by his wife of 54 years. Pastor Jesse Walters officiating.

Budd L. Darst
Birth:
1900
Gallia County, Ohio
Death:
1993
Gallia County, Ohio
Burial:
Gravel Hill Cemetery,
Cheshire,
Gallia County, Ohio

Herbert C. Davis
Birth:
Mar. 21, 1934
Johnson County, Kentucky
Death:
Sep. 3, 2012
Fairborn, Greene County, Ohio
Burial:
Byron Cemetery, Fairborn,
Greene County,
Ohio

He was born in Johnson Co., Kentucky, the son of the late James Herbert and Alka (Sadler) Davis. Herb was employed with General Motors as a tool and die maker, retiring in 1982; and was a minister for over 50 years at many churches. One of Herb's hobbies was woodworking and enjoyed playing the violin and singing while Anna played the piano with him.

John Merrill Davis
Birth:
Nov. 16, 1846
Harrisonville,
Meigs County,
Ohio
Death:
Nov. 11, 1920
Raccoon Township,
Gallia County, Ohio
Burial:
Calvary Baptist Cemetery,
Rio Grande,
Gallia County, Ohio

His childhood education was in the public schools of Scipio Township. He joined the Free Will Baptist denomination in 1860 and in 1863 served the Government as an army teamster during the Civil War. Between March and September of 1865 he served in active duty with the 188th Ohio Volunteer Infantry. He entered Ohio University in 1868 and graduated in 1873. He was ordained in 1872. In 1874, he became President of Ridgeville College in Indiana and pastor of the Free Will Baptist church there. In 1876 He received his M.A. from Ohio University and in 1878 took over Wilkesville Academy in Ohio 15 miles from Rio Grande College where he joined the college staff a year later.

In 1887 he became the third president of Rio Grande College at the age of 41.He served Rio Grande College for 40 years and 24 of those as President. He resigned as president in 1911, but remained on the faculty until 1919, also returning to ministerial duties. The University of Wooster conferred upon him the Ph.D. Degree. Ohio University conferred upon him the honorary degree of Doctor of Divinity. He served as President of the Southeastern Ohio Teacher's Association. President of the Ohio Free Communion Baptist Association. Delegate to several Free Baptist General Conferences between 1883 and 1904. Delegate to the Federal Council of Churches of Christ in Americas. He played an active role in the merger between Free Baptist and the Northern Baptist in 1911.

Alfred Franklin Delawder
Birth:
Jun. 4, 1878
Death:
Jun. 17, 1963,
Jackson County,
Ohio
Burial:
Glen Roy Cemetery,
Glen Roy,
Jackson County,
Ohio

Early Free Will Baptist pastor

in southern Ohio.

Rev Roy Tommy Depreist
Birth:
Sep. 29, 1931
Center Station
Lawrence County, Ohio
Death:
Jun. 4, 2014
Columbus
Franklin County, Ohio
Burial: Obetz Cemetery
Obetz, Franklin County, Ohio

Roy C. "Tommy" Depriest, to Floyd and Nora Depriest who preceded him in death.

Roy trusted Christ as his Savior at a young age when his mother took him to Mount Calvary Baptist Church. He often spoke how he was baptized in the creek near that church. In 1953, Roy announced that God had called him to preach the gospel and was ordained as a Free Will Baptist minister and very faithful to that call till major issues caused he and his first wife to divorce.

Roy served in the US Navy during the Korean War. Following that, he returned to southern Ohio and got a job as a Safety Supervisor at Marquette Cement Company.

He enjoyed reminiscing about a revival in 1958 when he, Calvin Evans, his cousin Eddie Depriest and another minister preached revival services at the Mt. Calvary FWBC near his birthplace. During those

revival days, more than 150 people were won to Christ and baptized.

Roy liked to tell and show pictures of a special baptism service when they broke through 3 inches of ice and planned to baptize 29 people in the Ohio River. More were saved at the River and joined were also baptized. He testified that about 5,000 people were present!

After 25 years of service, Roy retired as Director of Manufacturing from Stewart and Warner in Chicago, IL. Roy and Doris faithfully attended Immanuel Lutheran Church (Crystal Lake, IL) for many years. In 1993, they returned to Ohio and were active members at a local Lutheran Church. Roy served that Church as a Deacon and Board Member.

In 2002, they returned to their Free Will Baptist roots and on March 2, 2003, they became members at Heritage FWBC..

Doth God Favour Thee? Fear Not, Though The World Frown Upon Thee.

Thomas Dimm
Birth:
1810
Pennsylvania
Death:
Jul. 10, 1886
Huron County, Ohio
Burial:
Guinea Corners Cemetery
Huron County,
Ohio

A native of Pennsylvania, moved to Ohio in 1834, and united with the Free Baptist Church in Huron, Ohio in 1841.

He was ordained in 1844, and for several years labored in the Lake Erie Quarterly Meeting and subsequently with the Seneca, Huron and Lorain Quarterly Meetings. The last years of his life he was afflicted with blindness, but maintain his integrity and his love for Christ and the denomination he had served.

Eusebius M Dodge
Birth:
May 22, 1806
Lyme
New London County,
Connecticut
Death:
Jan. 2, 1852
New Lyme
Ashtabula County, Ohio
Burial:
Dodgeville Cemetery
New Lyme,
Ashtabula County, Ohio

An ordained Freewill Baptist minister from Ohio who was faithful in his service. Rev. Dodge, was the son of Eld. Eusebius and Anna (Merchant) Dodge--family records state that his father was also a Baptist clergyman, as well as Justice of the Peace. Eusebius M. married Hannah H. Hall, Oct. 15, 1826.His parents and extended families moved to Ohio where Rev. Eusebius was ordained as an evangelist, Oct. 15, 1837. He labored with poor churches and in destitute places, and saw many souls converted.He was a man of uncommon power, with great faith and perseverance and love for people. He baptized about a thousand persons.He died at an early age of 45 years. He moved from Conn., in 1811, along with ninety persons from Conn., (per local records), through great privations and hardships on the trip in the wilderness and terrain, to Ohio, where he and his family established themselves in the new country. He bought 1,200 acres of land, and became a representative citizen, taking part in community affairs, and business, where they lived. He owned a mercantile business at one time, hauling supplies from Pittsburg by oxen.

Eusebius served in the 1812 Spanish Amer. War, and his father, Jeremiah, served in the American Revolution (DAR records).

He married Anna Merchant, 02 Feb. 1794, Lyme Co. CT., (CT mar. records). They raised ten children, many bur. in this cemetery. Three sons, John, Calvin, and Hiram L; daughters,

And with unfaltering lip and heart, I call the Saviour mine.

Cyrus Dudley
Birth:
Unknown
Death:
Mar. 3, 1871
Blanchester,
Ohio
Burial:
West Woodville Cemetery
Warren County,
Ohio

His parents were Peter DUDLEY and Ruby (Soule) DUDLEY. He married Frances Teetor, 1819. They had three children: Hannah, Colmbus J., and Amelia E. There were several "Dudley" families from Maine who migrated to Ohio and began the town, "Maineville," because so many from Maine had come. Rev. Cyrus Dudley, a native of Maine, died at the age of 70 years. When quite young he became a member of the Maineville Freewill Baptist Ohio church. He was married and settled in West Woodville, where he resided until his death. In 1835 he commenced his ministerial duties and until near the close of life was active in the work. He was a man of much power in the pulpit, and successful as an evangelist.

David Dudley
Birth: Jul. 16, 1791
Mt Vernon, Maine
Death: May 29, 1867
Waldo, OH
Burial:
Wyatt Cemetery,
Waldo, Marion County, Ohio

He was an early Free Will Baptist Minister, first found in the Ohio records at Rutland, Ohio. He attended the General Conference at Mainsville, Ohio, where he later pastored. However, most of his ministry

was to be found in Marion County, Ohio, where many of his churches still exist. He had a powerful influence during his early days in Ohio, but for a while he ministered in Iowa where his first wife died. He returns back to Ohio and here married Lovinah Wyatt. He was the 2nd husband of Lovinah Brundige Wyatt, widow of Samuel Wyatt.
Source: "Ohio, the cross road of our nation", Vol IV, No. IV.

Moses Dudley
Birth:
1755 Maine
Death:
Nov. 24, 1842
Maineville, Warren County, Ohio
Burial:
Maineville Cemetery, Maineville, Warren County, Ohio

In 1815, Moses Dudley, with his family, moved from Maine and settled in Maineville. Dudley built the first frame house in the village. The Maineville Free-Will Baptist Church was organized by Elder Moses Dudley, Henry Greely and others as early as 1822 or 1823. It was called Salt Spring Church. For a number of years they worshiped in a schoolhouse east of Maineville, and not far from the Maineville Graveyard. About 1830, they built the present brick building. Elder Moses Dudley

was the first pastor of this church.

Thomas Dudley
Birth:
Apr. 18, 1783
Mount Vernon, Kennebec County, Maine
Death:
Aug. 7, 1860
Pagetown, Morrow County, Ohio
Burial:
Crossroads Cemetery, Albany,Athens County, Ohio

He was the brother of Rev. Moses Dudley, who moved to Ohio and died in Warren, Ohio, and buried in Maineville Cem. At the age of eighteen he joined the church in Mt. Vernon, ME where he was ordained about 1813. In 1836, he moved to Pittsfield ME, where he remained until his removal to Ohio, about 1853, or seven years before his death.

Charles Thomas Dutton
Birth:
Jan. 15, 1927
Dickerson County, Virginia
Death:
Jan. 12, 2004
Marion,
Marion County, Ohio
Burial:
Grand Prairie Cemetery,
Brush Ridge,
Marion County, Ohio

He was a longtime Free Will Baptist Minister serving in the northern Ohio Association.

"As the image on the seal is

stamped upon the wax, so the thoughts of the heart are printed upon the actions."

Jimmy R Dutton
Birth:
Jul. 20, 1940
Clintwood VA.
Death:
Aug. 22, 2014
Burial:
Grand Prairie Cemetery
Brush Ridge
Marion County, Ohio

He was born to the late Ervie and Keturia (Fletcher) Dutton. He was preceded in death by his first wife, June (Taylor) Dutton; survived by his second wife, Mildred (Becky) Holt Dutton.
Jimmy retired in 2002 after working for Khempco Building Supply.
Jimmy loved the Lord and preached the gospel for many years leading people to Christ, living life to it's fullest always putting God first. He enjoyed his bluegrass music. He started playing fiddle at age 16. He could play many instruments, but his favorite was the mandolin and fiddle. He had a bluegrass gospel program called HYMNTIME that aired on the local TV station in Marion for almost 20 years. He has played music in his own bands; The Dutton Brothers, Kentucky Grass and New Gospel Ship. He has played with Red Allen, Kenny Baker, and Lillie Mae and the Dixie Gospel Aires. He also enjoyed photography especially stills like flowers and collecting cameras. Pastor Grover Caudill officiated assisted by Rev. Freddie Dutton.

Donald Enos Ellis
Birth:
Mar. 20, 1931
McDermott, Scioto County, Ohio
Death:
Mar. 4, 2013
Portsmouth, Scioto County, Ohio
Burial:
Rush Township
Scioto County, Ohio

He was born a son of the late Charles and Lula Mae Kennard Ellis. Don was a retired mechanic from Dayton Walther Corp, Pastor of Stoney Run Free Will Baptist Church, and a U.S. Navy Veteran. Funeral services were conducted at the Stoney Run Freewill Baptist Church with Craddock Frye and Roger Clark officiating.

Burial followed where military graveside rites were performed by the William A. Baker and James Irwin Posts of the American Legion. (Portsmouth Daily Times, March 6, 2013)

John Elswick
Birth:
1891
Death:

1947
Scioto County, Ohio
Burial:
Buckeye Cemetery,
Ohio Furnace,
Scioto County, Ohio

John William Elswick
Birth:
Jul. 27, 1938
Lawrence County, Kentucky
Death:
Jul. 26, 2006
Columbus, Franklin County,
Ohio
Burial:
Graham Chapel Cemetery,
Athens County, Ohio

He was the son of the late Fred and Malissia Ellen Boggs Elswick. He was a 1957 graduate of Shade High School. He was retired from Ohio University after 31 years. He was also a minister for the past 38 years. He was recently the pastor of the Carpenter Baptist Church and Poplar Ridge Free Will Baptist Church. He was a member of Grahams Chapel Church. He was involved with the World Christian Outreach Ministry with Rev. Dr. David T. Rahamut.

Quentin U. England
Birth:
Unknown
Death:
Mar. 30, 2000
Burial:
Obetz Cemetery, Obetz,
Franklin County, Ohio,
Plot: Sect 25, lot 34, spc 1

He was active in the early organization of the Ohio Free Will Baptist Association. He was a member of the Franklin Conference where most of his ministry was.

Floyd J. Estep
Birth:
Jan. 6, 1911
Paintsville,
Johnson County, Kentucky
Death:
Feb. 6, 2009
Portsmouth,
Scioto County, Ohio
Burial:
Evergreen Union Cemetery,
Waverly Pike County, Ohio

He was a member of the Wakefield Free Will Baptist Church, a retired N W Railroad employee, an active Free Will Baptist Clergyman, former pastor of seven Free Will Baptist Churches, Member of Lucasville, Ohio. Life Certificate in Scioto Ministerial Conference of Free Will Baptist and Veteran of WWII.

Calvin Evans
Birth:
Mar. 30, 1930
Death:
Jan. 11, 2006
Tampa,
Hillsborough County,
Florida
Burial:
Highland Memorial Gardens,
South Point,
Lawrence County, Ohio

He was nationally known for founding the Evangelistic Outreach Inc. 48 years ago with a $250 love offering. It grew to spread the word through the Internet, a weekly television show and a daily radio show in numerous markets in the tri-state and throughout the Midwest. He was well-known for his revivals, one of which lasted 13 weeks. Evans started the Spring Jubilee which is held every spring at the Scioto County Fairgrounds. He had worldwide crusades in decade in Jamaica, Uganda and Haiti. He had extended ministries in many countries in the Caribbean. He had thousands to complete correspondence courses in his outreach efforts. Evans, 75, had just entered his fifth decade as an evangelist. He preached his first sermon in 1956 and pastored in churches in Ohio and Kentucky. He was ordained by the Free Will Baptist Denomination and had preached in the national convention in 1974 in Wichita, Kansas to 5000.

Fred C Evans
Birth:
Aug. 7, 1926
Blaine, Kentucky
Death:
Nov. 26, 2001
Burial:
Galena Cemetery,
Galena,
Delaware County, Ohio

Rev. Evans was the second pastor of the Welch Avenue Free Will Baptist Church in Columbus, Ohio. He served as Pastor from January 1958 through March 1961 when he left to serve for many years at the Pleasant View Free Will Baptist Church. Afterwards, he began the Greenleaf Road Free Will Baptist Church, which today is called the Southwest Free Will Baptist Church. At the time of his passing, he was 75 years of age and had completed

over 52 years in the ministry. He was pastor of the Faith Harvest Church in Marysville, Ohio at the time of his departure. The funeral services were conducted by Rev. Paul Thompson and the Rev. Glenn Derifield. He was also a veteran of the US Navy serving during WW II.

Vernal Lee Fairchild
Birth:
Jun. 14, 1928
Blaze, Morgan County,
Kentucky
Death:
Sep. 1, 2011
Xenia, Greene County, Ohio
Burial:
Valley View Memorial
Gardens,
Xenia, Greene County,,Ohio

Rev. Fairchild was a graduate of Bethany Bible College where he received his Bachelor of Ministry degree. He also graduated from ITT Technical Institute. He was the Retired Pastor of Fellowship Tabernacle in Xenia; formerly Pastor of Sunset Freewill Baptist Church in Springfield and served as a chaplain with Greene Memorial Hospital. He began his ministry as Director of Xenia Rescue Mission and retired from Wright Patterson Air Force Base.

Edmund Burke Fairfield
Birth:
Aug. 7, 1821
Virginia
Death:
Nov. 17, 1904
Oberlin, Lorain County, Ohio
Burial:
Westwood Cemetery
Oberlin, Lorain County, Ohio
Plot: O-10

Rev. Dr. Edmund Burke Fairfield Theologian, Educator, Politician and Author. Rev. Fairfield was born in Parkersburg, Virginia which at present is Parkersburg, West Virginia. He was a graduate of Oberlin College in 1842. Studied theology for three years while teaching school after graduation. Received an honorary LL.D. degree from Madison University (now Colgate University), a D.D. degree from Indiana University and the Sacrae Theologiae Doctor (Doctor of Sacred Theology) from Denison University. After two years of ministry he then accepted the Presidency of Michigan Central College (later known as Hillsdale College) in 1848. He held the position for twenty-one years. His political ambitions also came into play from the years 1857-1861. During this time he was elected to the Michigan Senate (1857-1858) and as the 12th Lieutenant-Governor of Michigan (1859-1861). Rev. Fairfield's reputation began to grow after his powerful speech on the Prohibition of Slavery in the Territories. It has been said that 50,000 copies of the speech were published and distributed. In 1864, after a ten month tour in Europe, Rev. Fairfield started a series of lectures which ran through fifteen states. In the anti-slavery and war campaign he took a prominent part in Michigan, Ohio and Indiana. He was later elected the second Chancellor of the University of Nebraska in 1876. He held this position for six years. The last term of administration was one of the most heated times in the history of the university. Rev. Fairfield was a Fundamentalist Christian and strongly opposed the teaching of Darwinism. On his faculty were three young professors who were attempting to bring Modernism to the young university. Some accounts say Rev. Fairfield was later forced to leave his position. In actuality, he and all the other professors resigned in 1882. After his resignation he again assumed pastoral duties until 1889. At this time he accepted the position of United States consul at Lyons, France having been appointed by President Benjamin Harrison. He held the position for four years. The Rev. Dr. Edmund Burke Fairfield retired from active public life to Oberlin, Ohio in 1900.

His Parents were Micaiah Fairfield (1786 - 1858) & Hannah W. Fairfield (1787

Raymond Lewis Fife

Birth:
Apr. 29, 1937
Meigs County
Ohio
Death:
Nov. 2, 1993
Point Pleasant
Mason County, West Virginia
Burial:
Gravel Hill Cemetery
Cheshire, Gallia County, Ohio

Minister in SE Ohio. Parents: Albert Raymond Fife and Anna Myrtle Ward. Wife: Anita Ann Scott

Anthony Franklin

Birth:
Feb. 11, 1968
Delaware
Delaware County, Ohio
Death:
Dec. 15, 2014
Chesterville
Morrow County, Ohio
Burial:
Maple Grove Cemetery
Chesterville
Morrow County, Ohio

He was born, the son of Paul I. and Ida Christeen (VanHoose) Franklin, in Delaware, Ohio. Tony grew up in Ashley and graduated from Buckeye Valley High School in the class of 1986, where he enjoyed playing football and basketball. On August 10, 1991, Tony married Jerri I. McDaniel in Lewis Center, Ohio. Together they shared 23 wonderful years of marriage.

Tony he enjoyed working for Delaware Hayes High School where he was a teacher's aid in the multiple handicap classroom. He also enjoyed sharing God's word as a preacher at the North Woodbury Freewill Baptist Church.

Tony had a strong faith in the Lord and loved going to church and various church related activities such as camps and plays.

Two years before his passing, Tony was diagnosed with stage 4 colon cancer. That is where his faith and trust was really put to the test. With all of the struggles he had, he never complained and always kept a smile on his face because he knew God had him under His wings and was taking care of him.

Rev Hersey Kingston Freeman

Birth:
Dec. 19, 1877

Putnam County
West Virginia
Death:
Aug. 7, 1968
Galion
Crawford County
Ohio
Burial:
Rivercliff Cemetery
Mount Gilead
Morrow County
Ohio
Plot: Sec 24

Parents:
John Fletcher Freeman (1844 - 1897)- Delaney Arbaugh Freeman (1857 - 1929)
Spouse: Lillie Minerva Gow Freeman (1888 - 1973)
Children: Carl Wellington Freeman (1912 - 2010)*

Inscription:
Rev.Hersey K. Freeman

Kenneth Lee Frisbee, Sr
Birth:
Dec. 25, 1928
Marion, N.C.
Death:
Oct. 21, 2017
Burial:
Hillside Memorial Park
Akron
Summit County
Ohio,

Pastor Kenneth Lee Frisbee, Sr., faithfully served the Lord Jesus Christ from age 19 until his passing at 88.. He was born to parents, Roy and Mae (Maney) Frisbee.

He is survived by his loving family: wife, Betty; sons, Kenneth Lee Frisbee Jr. (Nancy) of Marion, N.C. and Dennis Wayne Frisbee (Lois) of Brimfield, Ohio; brothers, Cecil, Bruce, and Bobby; sisters, Ruby (deceased), Ruth, Betty Jo, and Sandra; seven grandchildren, Kenny III (Laura) and Todd (Lesley) of California, Megan and John of Marion, N.C., Sheila (David) of Green, Roy (Kerri) and David (Kelly) of Tallmadge; and fourteen great-grandchildren; He also leaves his church family which he pastored for 57 years, friends who fondly remember his love and concern for them all.

Isaac Fullerton, Sr
Birth:
Feb. 15, 1809
Greenbrier County,
West Virginia
Death:
Nov. 11, 1886
Scioto County, Ohio
Burial:
Butler & Martin Cemetery,
Minford, Scioto County Ohio

He moved with his parents while still young and settled in Scioto Co., Porter Township, Ohio. He and his sons entered the War in 1861...Rev. Isaac was a Capt. in 59th OH. Rev. Rufus Cheney was the first preacher of the denomination to preach in Scioto Co., in 1816, and he organized the Porter Free Will Baptist Church Sept. 6, 1817, in a schoolhouse on Ward's Run. Rev. Fullerton received license to preach in 1834, and was ordained to the gospel ministry in November 1836. He farmed to provide for his growing family, and most of his long ministry (about 52 yrs) was spent with the FWB churches of Little Scioto Quarterly Meeting, where he had been closely identified with all its work, organizing the FWB church in Wheelersburg, May 17, 1851, and was first pastor of the Sciotoville Church. He attended the General Conference at Marion (1886) as a delegate from the Ohio and Kentucky Y.M. (Info from Ohio records, family genealogy, and Hist. of Ohio, 1884, chap 17, in archives).

Rev Samuel Fulton
Birth:
Aug. 10, 1856
Gallia County
Ohio
Death:
Mar. 23, 1912
Springfield Township
Gallia County
Ohio
Burial:
Gravel Hill Cemetery
Cheshire

Gallia County, Ohio

Rev. Samuel Fulton, a well-known and highly esteemed F. B. minister, died at his home in Bidwell Sunday evening, after long and brave struggle with asthma and lung trouble.

He had been living at Brunswick, O., and the last few years where he was engaged in the ministry, but was compelled on account of failing health to give up regular pastoral work several months ago. Realizing his time on earth was short he expressed a desire to spend his last days near relatives and friends, and with his family moved to Bidwell only a few weeks ago.

The last sad rights were held at the Campaign Church. Conducted by Rev. J. M. Davis of Rio Grande, Samuel Fulton, son of Samuel and Nancy Malaby Fulton, being 55 years, seven months and 14 days old. He suffered a lingering sickness, after being ill since August 1911. He was fully conscience of his condition and said many times he was coming to what lies ahead of us all.

He was united in marriage March 28, 1876 to Elizabeth Shuler. To this union six children were born. The oldest to precede him, and four survive him as follows: one son Wm. Fulton, of Morral, Ohio, Mrs. Hugh Quinn, of Huntington, W. Va., Mrs. Leo Barry, of Morral Ohio, and Miss Petal at home, and with their sorrowing mother mourn his departure. He also leaves three brothers, Royal of Kansas, W.J. of Rio Grande, and J. of Gallipolis, and one sister Mrs. Mary E. Pierce, of Iowa.

Inscription:
FULTON

REV
SAMUEL FULTON
1856 - 1912
ELIZABETH FULTON
1855 - 1948

SWEETLY RESTING

Rev. Samuel Fulton was a brother of Rev. W. J. Fulton, also a Free Baptist minister.

William J Fulton
Birth:
1847
Death:
1927
Burial:
Calvary Baptist Cemetery,
Rio Grande, Gallia County,
Ohio

Rev. Dr. Wm. Fulton pastored Calvary FWB Church for 40 years, and was teacher in Rio Grande College. He was one of the most popular and respected ministers in Southeast Ohio and especially after the death of Rev. Ira Haning. He died at 80 yrs.

Millard Green
Birth:
1917
Death:
2001
Burial:
Burbank Cemetery, Burbank
Wayne County, Ohio

He was pastor of the Creston church for many years in northern Ohio.

Death Is The Crown Jewel For The Christian.

Rev Cornelia Evangeline White Gow
Birth:
Nov. 4, 1860
Scioto County
Ohio
Death:
Aug. 28, 1950
Parkersburg
Wood County, West Virginia
Burial:
Radnor Cemetery
Radnor
Delaware County
Ohio

Retired Minister, of Pomeroy Pike, Belpre, Ohio. Daughter of Horace & Mary Eliza (Pinkerman) White, Cornelia was married to Rev. David William Gow on February 18, 1879. They were the parents of three children: Rev. Ruda Marion, William Purvis, and Lillian Minerva.

Rev David William Gow
Birth:
Aug. 7, 1859

Scioto County, Ohio
Death:
Jul. 12, 1938
Lima
Allen County
Ohio
Burial:
Radnor Cemetery
Radnor
Delaware County, Ohio

Baptist Minister, of North Pearl Street, Spencerville, Ohio. At the time of his death he was the oldest active minister in point of service in the state. His last charges were at Needmore and Neptune.

He was the son of William Purves Gow, a native of Scotland, and Mary Ann Brown, of Scioto County, Ohio. He was converted at the age of 14 years. At the age of 19 he began work in the ministry. February 18, 1879, he was united in marriage to Cornelia E. White of Scioto County. To this union were born two sons, Ruda M. and William P. Gow, and one daughter, Lillie M, the wife of Rev. H. K. Freeman.

Rev. Gow spent his entire life in the ministry. He was a fearless and tireless preacher of the word. He held pastorates in the states of Michigan, Pennsylvania, Indiana and Ohio, his native state. He has more years of service to his credit than any Baptist preacher in the state of Ohio.

With his passion for souls and seeing the need of laborers he was always encouraging young ministers to preach the word. He has made and baptized thousands of converts. In his earlier life he was very popular in giving patriotic addresses. His last public address was given at the union services held at the Spencerville Federated church, on Good Friday, 1928.

During his last illness, even while at the hospital, he would ask people who called to see him if they knew the Lord. He was a good husband and a very affectionate father and a kind and friendly neighbor.

He was survived by wife Cornelia (also a minister), two sons, a daughter, ten grandchildren, and twelve great-grandchildren.
Spouse:
Cornelia Evangeline White Gow (1860 - 1950)
Children:
Ruda Marion Gow (1880 - 1969)*
Lillie Minerva Gow Freeman (1888 - 1973)

Rev Ruda Marion Gow
Birth:
Feb. 11, 1880
Scioto County, Ohio
Death:
Dec. 10, 1969
Scioto County
Ohio
Burial:
Iberia Cemetery
Iberia
Morrow County
Ohio

Born in David William Gow and Cornelia Evangeline White. He married Mable Diantha McCartney on February 27, 1901. To this union were born 7 children, Ellen Lilly Gow, Dorothy Otho Gow, Merle Densmore Gow, Paul David Gow, Ruth Gow, Carl Kenneth Gow, and Glenn Ruda Gow. He was a Baptist minister for many years, serving in churches in Michigan and Illinois and at the Fite Memorial Baptist Church in Marion. He had also been employed as a railroad worker.

Delbert Glendon Gould
Birth:
Sep. 28, 1908
Tom Corwin,
Jackson County, Ohio
Death:
Jan. 18, 1958
Columbus, Franklin County, Ohio
Burial:
Forest Lawn Memorial Gardens,
Columbus, Franklin County, Ohio

He was converted in the Methodist Church at Glenroy, Ohio. Later he became a member of the Wellston Free Will Baptist Church. He went to Columbus where he united with the Free Will Baptist Church on South Parsons Avenue, which later became the Gibbard Free Will Baptist Church. He was called into the ministry and was licensed in 1949 and ordained in 1950. He served the Rosedale Church and then was chosen as the first pastor of Welch Avenue Free Will Baptist Church in February, 1952 which was started by the Gibbard Ave. church. While pastor of this church he had a massive heart attack on the parking lot of the White Cross hospital where he was going to his doctor. He died at death 49 years. This church continues today as the Heritage Free Will Baptist Church as a large church and multiple staff.

Rev Olen L Gould
Birth:
Oct. 9, 1915
Ohio
Death:
Jul. 1, 1989
Ohio
Burial:
Forest Lawn Memorial
Gardens
Columbus
Franklin County
Ohio

He was the son of Grover C. and

Pearl H. (Vititoe) GOULD, both b. Ohio. He was married to Grayce E. Widdefield, and they made their home in Columbus. He worked as a machinist early in their marriage for some time. He became a Free Will Baptist minister at an early age, and was affiliated with the Eastern General Association of Free Will Baptists in the mid-1930. His name appears in the old 1936 Minutes of the Ass'n when it met in Glennville, GA: "Ohio Sunday schools, by Rev. Olen Gould, Wellston, OH, where he had collected offerings for Sun. Schools. Possibly a colleague was Rev. I. B. May, who also attended from Ohio that year.

His older brother, Rev. Delbert G GOULD, is also bur. in this cemetery.

James W. Hall
Birth:
May 28, 1909
Death:
Sep. 25, 1941
Burial:
Butler-Martin Cemetery,
Minford,
Scioto County, Ohio.

Ira Z. Haning
Birth:
June 1825
Death:
Sep. 27, 1878
Burial:
Calvary Baptist Cemetery,
Rio Grande, Gallia County,
Ohio

Haning was born in Alexander, Ohio.. His parents were first Methodists and later Freewill Baptists, and were faithful in giving religious instruction to their twelve children. Ira was converted in 1843 and joined the church in Lodi, where the family then resided. He studied two years in the University of Ohio at Athens. He also engaged in teaching, and preached at various places acceptably. He received license in February, 1846, and two years later was ordained at Lodi by Rev's Job Kittle, D. C. Tapping, and S. S. Branch. The churches of the Athens Q. M., then recently formed, needed pastoral care, and he itinerated among them all for several years.. He influenced Deacon Nehemiah Atwood to give $50,000 to start Rio Grande College in southern Ohio which still exist as a popular college.

Joseph Franklyn Harness
Birth: Mar. 25, 1916
Greene County, Ohio
Death:
Nov. 20, 1995
Portsmouth,
Scioto County, Ohio
Burial:
Lucasville Cemetery,
Lucasville, Scioto County, Ohio

He attended Rio Grande College where he played basketball and received his education. His pastorates were mainly in the Porter Conference in southern Ohio. He was a member of the General Board of The Ohio Association Of Free Will Baptist. He also served as the moderator of the state convention on a number of occasions. His voice was readly heard and respected.

Henry Lee Hawkins
Birth:
May 24, 191

Kentucky
Death:
May 9, 1993
Wheelersburg,
Scioto County, Ohio
Burial:
Memorial Burial Park,
Wheelersburg,
Scioto County, Ohio

Reverend Henry Lee Hawkins was the pastor of several Free Will Baptist churches in southern Ohio, the last of which was Porter Free Will Baptist. He also built many homes and churches in the area and was a skilled craftsman who made many beautiful clocks and pieces of furniture in his later years. He was a strong leader for many years within the Scoio Yearly conference.

Dave A. Hayes
Birth:
Aug. 22, 1889
Lawrence County, Kentucky
Death:
Aug. 28, 1968
Columbus,
Franklin County, Ohio
Burial:
Forest Lawn Memorial Gardens, Columbus,
Franklin County, Ohio

Retired from Columbus First Freewill Baptist Church in 1964. In the ministry for 50 years. Elected honorary pastor in 1963 Columbus First Freewill Baptist Church.

Today is not a day of defeat

Herbert J Henson
Birth:
1912
Death:
April 1, 1987
Burial:
Woodlawn Cemetery,
Ada, Hardin County, Ohio

Luther Hecox
Birth:
Dec. 28, 1795
Whitestown,
N. Y.
Death:
Sep. 1, 1878
Meigs County,
Ohio
Burial:
Brick Cemetery,
Meigs County,
Ohio

Hecox was the son of Truman and Sarah Hasford Hecox. His parents settled in Meigs County, Ohio, where he married in 1817 and early became one of the active Free Baptists. After serving as a licentiate several years, he was ordained in 1850, and continued in the work of the Lord in that vicinity until the infirmities of age compelled him to desist. He was a consistent Christian, pathetic and earnest in preaching. Luther was 81 years old when he died. He was the husband of Matilda Dean and the father of

Truman.

Abraham Hemmerly
Birth:
Patterson, Jackson Twp.,
Hardin County, Ohio
1846
Death:
King, Washington
1917
Burial:
Jackson Center Cemetery
Kirby, Wyandot County
Ohio

Occupation: Baptist Minister
Event: Graduated 1894 Marion
High School, Marion, Ohio

Kendal F. Higgins
Birth:
March 18, 1813
Cayuga County, New York
Death:
May 8, 1887
Union County, Ohio
Burial:
Oakdale Cemetery
Marysville
Union County, Ohio

He was one of the fathers of the Free Baptist ministry in central Ohio. He experienced religion at the age of 12. He moved to Ohio in early life and felt it an imperative duty to enter the ministry. His ordination took place on April 6, 1845, with Elders G. W. Baker, and Arron Hatch and G. H. Moon serving on the Council.

For over 40 years he was an earnest and successful preacher. He had the care of the churches in central and southern Ohio and Indiana. He had an excellent natural ability and was a strong reasoner, and his sermons were clear and strong presentations of gospel truth.

Rev Horace G. Hill
Birth:
1853
Death:
1904
Burial:
Waldren Hill Cemetery
Idaho, Pike County, Ohio

An ordained Free Will Baptist minister from Ohio. Worked in several states.

Jacob Hisey
Birth:
Jul. 30, 1816
Death:
Dec. 26, 1847
Waynesville,
Ohio
Burial:
Miami Cemetery
Corwin
Warren County,

Ohio

He was converted in 1836, licensed by the Miami Quarterly Meeting in 1843 and spent some time at the Biblical School at Whitestown, New York.

Rev John Hisey
Birth:
Apr. 27, 1821
Death:
Unknown
Burial:
Miami Cemetery
Corwin
Warren County
Ohio

Son of Jacob Hisey, Sr., and Amelia HISEY. Affiliated with the Freewill Bapt. church in Warren Co., and preached in the vicinity. His father, though not a minister, was a faithful, liberal, and exemplary Christian in the FWB church there.

Rev Donald Wayne Hix
Birth:
Feb. 14, 1943
Grove City
Franklin County
Ohio
Death:
Jun. 12, 2017
Urbana
Champaign County
Ohio
Burial:
Jenkins Chapel Cemetery
Urbana
Champaign County
Ohio

Rev. Donald W. Hix, 74, of Woodstock, Ohio went home to be with the Lord in Mercy Memorial Hospital, Urbana.

He was born the son of Henry and Edna (Ward) Hix. Rev. Don was ordained in June 1966. In March of 1973, he was called to pastor in his home church, Woodstock Free Will Baptist Church, where he pastored 26 years of his 50 years of pastoral service. He is currently the pastor at the Redeemer Free Will Baptist Church in London (Somerford). He retired from Honda in 2004. Don cherished his wife, adored his children and grandchildren, and led his family by modeling Christ's marriage to the church. There was no better example of how to lead a family than Don Hix. Don enjoyed doing yard work and could often be found mowing the yard, planting flowers, or weeding the garden. Donald was survived by his wife of 56 years, Dorothy Hix; Tamara (Dwayne) Brewer, Tracie (Dale) House and Amy (London)Rogan; grandchildren, Dawn, Drake, DeAndra, Destanee, Chelsie, Halie, Tabitha and Jaxon; great grandchildren, Desirae, Dristian, Jocelyn, Zayden, Kailynn and Kane, sister, Linda (Rev. Jim) Blankenship as well as several nieces and nephews. He was preceded in death by his parents, siblings, Russell "Bud", Carl, Robert and Mildred.

Woodstock Free Will Baptist Church, 332 W. Bennett St., Woodstock, Ohio. A Celebration of Life service was held at the church with Pastor Mike Mounts officiating.

William Hooper
Birth:
Dec. 2, 1818
Death:
Mar. 21, 1877
Burial:
Miles Cemetery
Rutland, Meigs County, Ohio

Rev. William Hooper, M. D. was a native of New Jersey, was converted at Alexander, Ohio, where he was soon licensed to preach, and ordained a few years later. He labored as an itinerant minister in Athens, Meigs, Gallia, Lawrence and Scioto Counties twelve years, and gathered one or two churches. He then turned his attention to medicine, graduating from the Starling Medical College at Columbus in 1857, and devoted but little time to ministerial duties. He died at age 58 years.

Elder Jonathan Hoyt
Birth:
Apr. 19, 1772
Litchfield
Litchfield County,Connecticut
Death:
Apr. 12, 1840
Scioto County,Ohio
Burial:
Turner Cemetery
Scioto County,Ohio

Spouse: Peggy Taylor Hoyt, Marriage: Abt 1794 - Litchfield, Connecticut.

Rev Sardine P. Humphrey
Birth:
Feb. 2, 1862
Rutland
Meigs County
Ohio
Death:
1934
Ohio
Burial:
Woodlawn Cemetery
Toledo
Lucas County
Ohio

Rev. Sardine P. Humphrey, son of William G. and Sarah B. (Cook) He was educated at Rio Grande College, and was principal of the Middleport High School. In 1884, he received license to preach, and Jan. 1, 1886, he was ordained by Rev. W. J. Fulton, and others. For a time had charge of the church at Camaam.(OH).

Cyrus Cordon Inman
Birth:
Jan 21, 1839
Spencer, Ohio
Death:
1917
Burial:
Spencer Cemetery,
Spencer
Medina County,
Ohio

A worthy and esteemed minister of the Freewill Baptist church in Randall's movement. He attended Hillsdale FWB College in Hillsdale, MI, and organized and pastored churches. He was married to Clemma C. Smith. He was the son of Deacon Stephen Inman, b. 1808 NY, and prob. charter members of that Spencer church. He was for a few years pastor of churches in the Oceana Q. M., Mich. He was ordained in 1869, and not long after returned to Ohio and took charge of the Spencer church, and was pastor of the Beebetown church in the Cleveland Q. M. Cyrus also served in the Civil War from Ohio, Ohio 124th Inf. Regiment, Co. B, as Cpl, then promoted to Sgt. Mustered out 1865.

John Jeffrey
Birth:
Unknown
Death:
Ohio
Burial:
Resthaven Memory Gardens
Avon
Lorain County,
Ohio

He was an early Free Will Baptist minister in northern Ohio that began the Vincent FWB church. He was a missionary, pastor and known servant.

John Robert Kemper
Birth:
1875
Death:
1957
Scioto County, Ohio
Burial:
Vernon Cemetery,
Lyra, Scioto County, Ohio,

Early pastor in Southern Ohio. Pastor of Union Free Will Baptist church for many years.

Marcus Kilbourn
Birth:
1790
Vermont
Death:
Nov. 28, 1836
Delaware County
Ohio
Burial:
Wyatt Cemetery
Waldo
Marion County, Ohio

Rev. Marcus Kilborn a native of Connecticut, experienced religion in Alexandria, NY, in 1816, and ordained in Ohio in 1820.

That same year he organized the First Free Baptist church in Indiana, the Bryant's Creek (later Randall) church. He also labored in southwestern Ohio, making his home at Maineville. He assisted in organizing the Miami Quarterly Meeting, and the Ohio Yearly Meeting. He was a faithful pioneer minister, and died triumphantly in 1837. Ohio marriage records show he married Mary Price, 11 June 1818, Scioto, OH, by Rev. Rufus Cheney. [a companion in the ministry].

It was said of him that he was a pious man, and built up churches. He often traveled on foot, leaving wife and babies at home, and not having much of the world's goods. His wife passed on before he did.

Inscription:
Aged 41 Years

Howard Kimble
Birth:
Unknown
Death:
Unknown
Lawrence County, Ohio

Burial:
Oakland Chapel Cemetery,
Kitts Hill,
Lawrence County, Ohio

A well-known minister in southern Ohio and northeast Kentucky remembered for pastoring Brush Creek in Ky. and the Union Church near Wheelersburg, Ohio. He was a member of the Ohio Board of Directors.

Jobe Kittle
Birth:
Apr. 28, 1805
Death:
Mar. 26, 1877
Scioto County, Ohio
Burial:
Old Wheelersburg Cemetery
Wheelersburg
Scioto County, Ohio

He had been a member of the Porter church 44 years. Receiving ordination to the ministry in 1841, at the hands of Rev. J. M. Shurtliff and others. He labored faithfully for the cause of Christ in the Little Scioto Quarterly Meeting.

George W Lawrence
Birth:
Jun. 2, 1854
Dover
Kent, England
Death:
Jul. 26, 1932
Geneva
Ashtabula County
Ohio
Burial:
Cherry Valley Cemetery
Cherry Valley
Ashtabula County, Ohio

He was brought to America by his parents when a year old, and lived on a farm till nine, had the benefit of the district school three months in the year. He came to Hillsdale in 1874 and took the A. B. degree in 1880. He spend the next year in special study at Normal, Illinois. He was rhen the Principal of the Academy at Pierpoint, Ohio, for two years, but moved to Kansas in 1883. In the following spring he became Principal of the High school at Jellico, Tennessee, and held the position until May 18, 1888, when he was shot down by a drunken hireling for his temperance principles. The next nine years were spent in Illinois, Michigan, and Iowa seeking to recover his shattered health, but in 1897, by solicitation of Rev. and Mrs.

A.A. Myers, he went to Cumberland Gap, Tennessee, where he was an Instructor in Mathematic in Lincoln Memorial University.

While at Hillsdale he was identified with the Theological Society, and his loyalty and that of his brother were the founders of the Lawrence Prize beginning in the spring of 1879. George Lawrence was the brother of Richard M. Lawrence, and Alfred Hogbin and they were children of John & Mary Hogbin. George & Richard changed their last name when they attended college in Hillsdale, Michigan. Death Age: 78 years 1 month 24 days. Spouse's Name: Angelia A. Lawrence.

Even Death Is Not To Be Feared By One Who Has Lived Wisely.

Claudis Lewis
Birth: Jul. 8, 1922
Johnson County, Kentucky

Death:
Sep. 28, 2003
Franklin. Ohio
Burial:
Springboro Cemetery,
Springboro,
Warren County,
Ohio

Lewis was a World War II veteran of the United States Army and was an escort to Gen. George S. Patton and General Dwight D. Eisenhower. He was a member of the Franklin Free Will Baptist Church. His funeral was held at the Franklin Church with the Rev. Dencil Owsley officiating with full military honors.

James Littlejohn
Birth:
Sep. 8, 1820
Ohio
Death:
Nov. 27, 1884
Wheelersburg, Scioto County
Ohio
Burial:
Old Wheelersburg Cemetery
Wheelersburg
Scioto County, Ohio

James Littlejohn was the son of John & Lucy Littlejohn and the husband of Cynthia Smith md October 12, 1843 Scioto Co., Oh. They were the parents of three children.

His name appears in the FWB Register 1858 as a minister from the Green FWB church.

Rev Edgar N Long
Birth:
1885
Death:
1959
Burial:
City View Cemetery
Salem
Marion County
Oregon, USA
Plot: Sec. U

He was on the 37th session program in 1907at the west Mansfield FWB Church. He preached on Wednesday and address on the Subject, What Free-will Baptist stand for after George Barnard had spoken on What Regular Baptist Stand for. E. N. Long addressed, Is union of Free-will Baptists with regular Baptist Desirable?

Charles Lykins
Birth:
Aug. 7, 1907
Death:
Mar. 5, 1978
Ohio
Burial:
South Webster Cemetery,
South Webster,
Scioto County,
Ohio

Minister in southern Ohio.

Bobby J Lyons
Birth:
Mar. 13, 1940
Death:
Oct. 13, 2007

Burial:
Plattsburg Cemetery,
Plattsburg, Clark County, Ohio

He was a member of the Eastside Free Will Baptist church and a Korean veteran.

David Marks
Birth:
Nov. 14, 1805
Shandaken,
Ulster
County, New York
Death:
Dec. 15, 1845
Oberlin, Lorain County, Ohio
Burial::
Westwood Cemetery,
Oberlin, Lorain County, Ohio,
Plot: Sect. F, Lot 5

Rev. Marks, as a child, felt impressed that God was calling him to a great work and began preaching at age 15 years. He traveled all over New England preaching to large crowds wanting to hear "the boy preacher." At 13 yrs of age, he walked over 368 miles from his home in New York to Providence, Rhode Island to attend Brown University where he had free tuition, but no further assistance towards room and board could be rendered; with sad heart, he walked back home. He had a thirst for knowledge and immediately began to study and read while walking or riding horse-back to another preaching appointment in his itinerant ministry. He found he was in sentiment with the teaching of 'Free Will, free grace and free salvation' and united with the Free Will Baptists in July 1819. He became a leader in that church and in the 1831 General Conference, was appointed Agent of the newly established Book Concern, a publishing house, which position he held for four years, leading it to solid footing financially.

He also was an ardent promoter of Home and Foreign Missions and Education societies. He held pastorates in New Hampshire, Rhode Island, New York, and organized a church in Rochester, New York, and had an iterant ministry all over New England, Upper Canada, and into Ohio. He kept a journal and a "Narrative" of his work and ministry which was printed in 1831, at the insistence of others. After his death, his wife, Marilla, edited *"Memoirs of David Marks"* which was published by the FWB Printing Establishment in 1846; William Burr, Printer. He went to Oberlin College in Ohio, a place of abolitionist creativity and thought, he having carried the same sentiments in his church and life. He had spoken, written and labored to see slavery abolished. He was without a doubt, one of the most esteemed ministers of his day in his church and in the public's eye. It was while in Oberlin with his wife, that his health failed even more. His great desire to preach even in his weakened condition was so great that he requested that "I be carried to the meeting house to give one more talk for God before I die." This they did, even though it was thought he would die before he finished, but he lived a few weeks longer. Dr. Charles G. Finney of Oberlin preached his funeral. Finney said of Mark's "There is none greater among Free Will Baptists."

His wife published his memoirs entitled, "The Life of David Marks."

His sister Elizabeth was the first woman to graduate from Oberlin as a lady minister. He had a brother and nephew who went on to Kansas and began the FWB work there. They are listed under the Kansas section herein.

Herman Marcum
Birth:
Apr. 3, 1933
Wayne County,
West Virginia
Death:
Feb. 7, 2012
Orlando, FL
Burial:
Union Cemetery,
Columbus,
Franklin County, Ohio

He was pastor of the Philadelphia Free Will Baptist Church before his retirement to Florida. For 20 years he raised money locally by coordinating walk-a-thons and rock-a-thons, used for donating fruit baskets to nursing homes in the Columbus area. Rev. Marcum was a member of Faith Freewill Baptist Church in Orlando, FL.

Marvin Dale Markin
Birth:
Aug. 14, 1937
Vinton County,
Ohio
Death:
Jun. 3, 2010
Athens, Athens County, Ohio
Burial:
Harkins Chapel Cemetery,
Bolins Mills,
Vinton County,Ohio

Free Will Baptist pastor is southeast Ohio and active in his district and state associations. He had been a minister for 53 years with 22 years at Black Oak FWB.

Amos P. Marmon
Birth:
Unknown
Death:
Nov. 28, 1879
Burial:
Marmon Valley Cemetery
East Liberty,
Logan County, Ohio

Amos Marmon's parents were Edmund Marmon, 1786-1831, and Sarah (Stanton) Marmon, 1788--.He married Cynthia Ann Outland, (1830-1903). Amos P. Marmon, was born in Marmon Valley, Ohio and died near his native place. He was converted under the ministry of Rev. O.E. Baker and united with the East Liberty church in 1853. He proved himself a useful member, and was ordained June 3, 1872. His sermons were thoughtful and carefully prepared, and being

deeply emotional, his words touched many hearts.
He was age 53 years, 3 months and 14 days at his death.

James W Martin
Birth:
Jul. 11, 1829
Guernsey County, Ohio
Death:
Oct. 28, 1899
Athens County, Ohio
Burial:
Crossroads Cemetery
Albany, Athens County, Ohio

Rev. James W. Martin, was the son of James H. and Tracy (Triplett) MARTIN, and was married to Jane Gibson, April 15, 1852. To them were born three children. He was educated at the Albany Academy and the Ohio University; was converted in 1860 and ordained May 23, 1868. He has held the pastorates of several churches in the Ohio River Yearly Meeting to which his ministry has been spent conducting revivals, baptizing a large number of converts and organizing one church. He has been influential in the local denominational gatherings, and has served as trustee of Rio Grande College and of the Ohio State Association, as president

of the board of Atwood Institute, and several times as a delegate to the General Conference.

Eugene Martin
Birth:
1910
Death:
Unknown
Scioto County, Ohio
Burial:
Bennett Cemetery,
Minford, Scioto County, Ohio

Moses Walter Martin
Birth:
Apr. 10, 1887
Scioto County, Ohio
Death:
Dec. 18, 1964
Portsmouth,
Scioto County, Ohio
Burial:
Old Wheelersburg Cemetery
Scioto County, Ohio

Moses and his family moved to Portsmouth where he was employed as a street car conductor on the Portsmouth to Sciotoville run. In 1921 the family moved back to Dogwood Ridge in Wheelersburg where he farmed. Later he moved and was employed as a locomotive fireman and engineer at the local Wheeling Steel plant in New Boston. He worked for the steel mill until he retired at the age of 70 (1957). Moses was an ordained Free Will Baptist minister and served several churches in the Scioto County area.

Chester A. Masters
Birth:
Dec. 9, 1928
Lewis Couny, Kentucky
Death:
Jun. 12, 2012
Mansfield, Richland County, Ohio
Burial:
Franklin Cemetery, Mansfield, Richland County, Ohio

He was a bi-vocational Free Will Baptist minister who retired from the Empire Detroit Steel. He was a veteran of the United States Army. At the cemetery he was given full military honors by the Richland County Joint Veterans Burial Detail.

Virgil Ouinton Masters

Birth:
Oct. 10, 1926
Lewis County
Kentucky
Death:
Dec. 23, 2014
Burial:
Springmill Cemetery
Mansfield
Richland County, Ohio

Virgil Q. Masters, 88, was the son of Ora and Celia (Zornes) Masters. A faithful, pleasant, generous man, Virgil served as a Corporal in the Army from 1942 until 1952, serving in Korea and Japan. He retired from Stone Container where he was a Teamster Local #40 truck driver. A member of Dean Road Freewill Baptist Church, Virgil served as assistant Pastor for 8 years and Pastor for 32 years.
Funeral services was conducted by Rev. Clifford Earl Tackett and Pastor Randy Nichols. Military services conducted by the Richland County Joint Veterans Burial Detail.

Irey Berdell May
Birth:
Mar. 24, 1899
Pennsylvania
Death:
Dec. 15, 1970
Brecksville
Cuyahoga County
Ohio

Burial:
Grandview Cemetery
Salem
Columbiana County, Ohio

He was also a minister and represented Ohio Yearly Meeting in the 1936 Eastern General Association of Free Will Baptists, when in session in Glennville, GA. Per 1940 census had a wife Annabel age 24 and a son Robert L age 2 in house - living in Salem Ohio.

Isaac May
Birth:
Oct. 5, 1796

Strafford,
Orange County,
Vermont
Death:
Dec. 8, 1874
Clyde
Sandusky County, Ohio
Burial:
Ellsworth Cemetery
Clyde
Sandusky County, Ohio

He was the son of Harvey May Joanne (Wedge); husband of (1) Racheal McMillen, (2) Nancy McMillen. approx 16 children between the two marriages. He was converted at age 18 and united with the Christian denomination. Later he joined the York church in Ohio and was ordained by the Huron

Quarterly Meeting in 1831. For some time he labored as an itinerant: after which he settled at Townsend, and organized a church and remained with it the remainder of his life.

Rev Lovell J May
Birth:
May 2, 1929
Death:
Nov. 27, 2017
Burial:
Obetz Cemetery
Obetz
Franklin County, Ohio
Reverend Lovell J. May, age 88, Retired pastor with Canaan Land Free Will Baptist Church. Pastored for several CCU and Hilltop Community Church. Member of UAW Local 969. U.S. Army Veteran. Served in Army and Navy Reserve and National Guard.
Preceded in death by twin brother, Lowell, brother, George Jr., sisters, Vivian Eicher, Joyce Holbrook, Elsie Saxour.
Survived by wife of 71 years, Wanda May; children, Steven May, Sharon (Michael) Adams, and Ronald (Cindy) May; grandchildren, Todd, Tami, Tara, Jennifer, Joseph, Justin, Jim, Makenna, Elana, and Ethan; 14 great-grandchildren; 3 great-great-grandchildren; many nieces, nephews, other relatives and friends.

Arthur "Pete" Maynard
Birth:
Jul. 14, 1939
Beauty,
Martin County, Kentucky
Feb. 21, 2002
Washington Court House
Fayette County,
Ohio

Burial:
New Holland Cemetery,
New Holland,
Pickaway County, Ohio
He was founder of the Woodlawn Free Will Baptist Church in Washington Courthouse. He served his country in the United States Navy during the Vietnam era, and as a bi-vocational minister. He was employed as a corrections officer with Ohio Dept. of Corrections in Pickaway County.

Rev Robert Lee Maynard
Birth:
Mar. 10, 1938
Beauty
Martin County, Kentucky
Death:
Aug. 12, 2014
Columbus
Franklin County, Ohio
Burial:
New Holland Cemetery
New Holland
Pickaway County, Ohio

Bob was a Free Will Baptist Minister and a member of the Capital City Conference of Free Will Baptists and faithful member and minister of the Heritage Free Will Baptist Church of Columbus, OH.

Billy O. McCarty
Birth:

Aug. 7, 1926
Salyersville,
Magoffin County, Kentucky
Death:
Jan. 8, 2008
Springfield,
Clark County, Ohio
Burial:
South Vienna Cemetery,
South Vienna,
Clark County, Ohio

He ministered in Free Will Baptist churches in Urbana, West Jefferson, Youngstown, Ohio; California and Georgia during his long ministry. He was actively involved with the Family Life Ministries of Tennessee. He was a man of patient compassion and a wise counselor.

Rev Sturgell McCarty
Birth:
Jan. 29, 1923
Magoffin County
Kentucky
Death:
Apr. 19, 2016
Springfield
Clark County
,Ohio
Burial:
Maple Grove Cemetery
Mechanicsburg
Champaign County,
Ohio

Age-93 at the time of his passing.
Besides his parents, he was

preceded in death by his wife and mother of his 2 daughters, Recie Deloris (Miller) McCarty, brothers: Chatham, Herchell, Willard, Reverend Billy O. and Reverend Cecil McCarty.

He served 1 year in the 3c's, and the US Army during WW 11, in the European Theater. Became an ordained Freewill Baptist Minister in 1953, serving several churches in the Clark, Champaign, and Franklin Counties along with several other denominations in the area.

The Dead In Christ Shall Rise

William McCarty
Birth:
Sep. 16, 1938
Death:
Feb. 2, 1984
Lawrence County, Ohio
Burial:
Aid Cemetery,
Aid, Lawrence County, Ohio

He pastored the Fox Hollow and Symes Valley FWB churches in Lawrence Co., Ohio.

Alva McDaniel, Sr
Birth:
1907
Death:

Unknown
Scioto County,
Ohio
Burial:
White Gravel Cemetery,
Minford,
Scioto County,
Ohio

Robert Lee Meade
Birth: Jul. 11, 1930
Portsmouth,
Scioto County, Ohio
Death:
Mar. 23, 2001
Springfield,
Clark County, Ohio
Burial:
Ferncliff Cemetery,
Springfield,
Clark County, Ohio

He was ordained as minister in 1954 and was State Evangelist for four years. He served as pastor in six different churches from 1956 to 1993: The Shumway Freewill Baptist Church, Houston Hollow Freewill Baptist Church, The Fairborn Church, Turkey Creek Freewill Baptist Church, Belmont Freewill Baptist Church, and twenty-two years at the Forest Valley Freewill Baptist Church, where he was a member.

Redford Meadows
Birth:
Feb. 12, 1925
Wittensville, Ky
Death:
Apr. 6, 2007
Ironton, Ohio
Burial:
Rose Hill Burial Park and Mausoleum, Ashland,
Boyd County, Kentucky, Plot:F

Meadows was a Free Will Baptist Minister for more than 50 years and pastored churches in Michigan, Ohio and Kentucky.
His more recent ministry was at the Union Free Will Baptist Church near Wheelersburg, Ohio

Russell Milam
Birth: 1882
Death:
1967
Scioto County, Ohio
Burial:
Bennett Cemetery,
Minford,
Scioto County, Ohio

Early leader in the district, state, and national programs of the Free Will Baptists. His name appears on a regular basis as a representive from Ohio on the national General Board. He was the publicity chairman when the nation convention met in Huntington, WVA.

Bert Miller
Birth:
Feb.21, 1913
Death:
Apr. 5, 2001
Burial:
Obetz Cemetery,
Obetz,
Franklin County,
Ohio

Ordained a Minister in 1935 and instrumental in starting many Freewill Baptist Churches. In 1968 he founded and pastored Lockbourne Freewill Baptist Church in Lockbourne, Ohio. In 1992 Rev. Miller oversaw the building of the new church on Rohr Rd. where he continued to pastor until his death. Past President for 16 years of TWU Local #208. Retired from COTA after 35 years..

Troy Miller

Birth:
Sep. 11, 1942
Wonder, Floyd County,
Kentucky
Death:
Aug. 18, 2012
Jackson, Jackson County, Ohio
Burial:
Franklin Valley Cemetery,
Wellston, Jackson County,
Ohio

Troy Miller was born in the hills of eastern Kentucky 30 minutes from the Prestonsburg area. His family moved to West Virginia and Clyde, Ohio before settling in Jackson, Ohio. It was here that he met and married his high school sweetheart, Janice Forshey, in 1958. Together they had 3 sons and 1 daughter: Bob, Julie, Brian, and Jamie. At the approximate age of 25, Troy accepted Christ as his Savior and soon felt the call to go into the ministry. He would go on to pastor the Coalton Free Will Baptist church on three separate occasions, the Glenroy FWB church (both in Jackson county), and would re-open the Bethesda Chapel FWB church in Pike county after it had closed its doors several years earlier. During this time he held many revivals, performed hundreds of weddings and funerals and became well known throughout the community. He continued in the ministry until April of 2012 by serving as clergy member for Four Winds Nursing Home in Jackson. In 1995, Troy was diagnosed with kidney cancer and underwent surgery to completely remove one kidney and a portion of the other. He remained cancer free until 2008, when he was diagnosed once again with kidney cancer, this time

terminal. Troy Miller passed away in Kingston, Ohio in Ross County at the home of his youngest son.

Troy was formerly employed at Pillsbury in Wellston. He enjoyed visiting and ministering to the residents at Heartland and Four Winds Nursing Homes, as well as ministering to others through his weekly radio broadcasts.

Gerald G. Moore
Birth:
Mar. 9, 1931
Clintwood, Dickenson
County,
Virginia
Death:
Jul. 9, 2009
Sandusky County, Ohio,
Burial:
McPherson Cemetery,
Clyde,
Sandusky County, Ohio,

Member of the First Freewill Baptist Church in Clyde, Ohio. He served his country in the Air Force during the Korean War. Mr. Moore was a bi-vocational minister had also worked 34 years at the Whirlpool Corp in Clyde.

Rev Milo Moore
Birth:
Jan. 8, 1887
Carterville
Williamson County
Illinois
Death:
Mar. 30, 1974
Gallipolis
Gallia County, Ohio
Burial:
Mound Hill Cemetery
Gallipolis
Gallia County

Ohio
He pastored the Bryan First FWB church in Texas in 1926.

Tommy Moore
Birth:
Sep. 19, 1928
Adams, Lawrence County, Kentucky
Death:
Sep. 23, 1967
Burial:
Yatesville Cemetery, Louisa, Lawrence County, Kentucky

He was the third pastor of the Welch Avenue Free Will Baptist Church in Columbus, Ohio.

Horace Morse
Birth:
Sep. 19, 1795
Worthington
Hampshire County,
Massachusetts
Death:
Nov. 24, 1854
Williamsfield
Ashtabula County, Ohio
Burial:
Richmond Center Cemetery
Richmond Center
Ashtabula County, Ohio

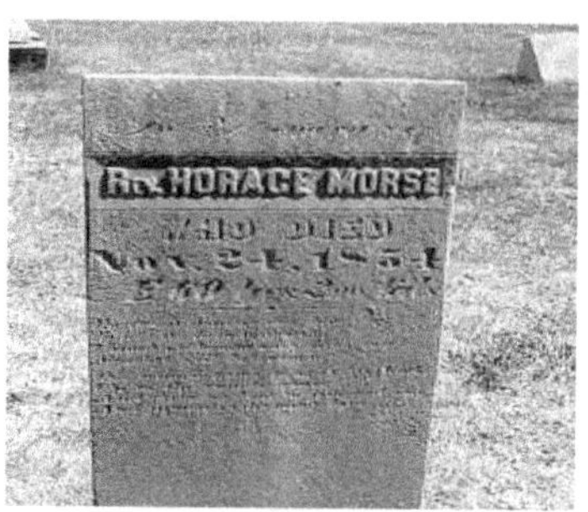

He moved to northern Ohio in 1810 where for several years he was engaged in teaching school. In 1818 he married Lydia, a daughter of Judge S. Stanton. He was converted in the revival which led to the formation of the Williamsfield church, of which he was one of the original members, and he immediately began preaching. He was active in the formation of the Wayne Quarterly Meeting and for some years was a leading minister in the Crawford and Ashtabula Quarterly Meetings.
Inscription:
Rev. HORACE MORSE
WHO DIED Nov. 24, 1854
60 yrs. 2 mos. 6 days (rest of script not legible from photo)

Kevin Willard Morris
Birth:
Sep. 13, 1978
Mansfield, Richland County, Ohio
Death:
Nov. 21, 2008
Plymouth,
Richland County, Ohio
Burial:
Greenlawn Cemetery,
Plymouth,
Richland County, Ohio

He preached the Gospel for 12 years, serving as pastor at Paradise Free Will Baptist Church two years. He graduated from Pioneer Career and Technical Center where he received the Byron Carmean Award-an award granted to non-traditional students and received his Associate's Degree in Early Childhood Education at The Ohio State University. At the age of 11, he underwent a heart transplant, a very special gift allowing him to spend 19 more years with his family and friends.

William Moses
Birth:
Unknown
Death:
Oct. 26, 1879
Cincinnati, Ohio
Burial:
Spring Grove Cemetery
Cincinnati,
Hamilton County, Ohio
Plot: Garden LN, Section 14, Lot 0, Space 262

Moses was a native of Connecticut and one of the early New York ministers, having been ordained in 1814. In 1832 he was connected with the Betheny Q. M., and after that time, until 1857, with the churches of the Genesee Q. M. Here he preached and labored faithfully. After this he spent about twenty years in Ripon, Wis., and, a year before his death, went to live with his children in Cincinnati. His wife, with whom he had lived sixty-two years

Albanus Avery Moulton
Birth:
Mar. 23, 1848
Massachusetts
Death:
Jun. 22, 1888
Colorado
Burial:
Calvary Baptist Cemetery,
Rio Grande,
Gallia County,Ohio

He took the freshman year of his college course at Bates College, the sophomore year at Hillsdale College, and the junior and senior years at Yale College, where he took honors and graduated in 1871. He then completed a course in mathematics and civil engineering in the University of Michigan, and worked for a time at railroad surveying. He was made professor of mathematics at Rio Grande College at its opening in 1876. Three years later he was made president. He discharged the duties of this position for six years with the highest degree of ability, zeal and success. In 1887, it was manifest he could not serve the college longer. His last three years were spent in Colorado, where he worked some at teaching and surveying. His noble Christian spirit made its impression on his schoolmates even, and was felt still more by the young people under his care at Rio Grande. In this influence to shape its opening years, the college was greatly favored.

Albanus K Moulton
Birth:
Sep. 26, 1810
Hatley, Quebec, Canada
Death:
Jun. 19, 1873
Linndale,
Cuyahoga County, Ohio
Burial:
Woodland Cemetery,
Cleveland,
Cuyahoga County, Ohio,
Plot: Section 40 Lot 84

Like others of the family he was early converted to Christ, and an accident, partially disqualifying him for manual labor, was the occasion of more schooling than was usually enjoyed by boys in his circumstances. While hesitating to devote himself to the ministry, he providentially found himself in 1837 at Mecca, Ohio, at the August session of the Ashtabula Quarterly Meeting, at which Ransom Dunn was ordained. Brother Moulton's position was understood; and the ordination services, with special prayer for him and special exhortation and persuasion by Rev's Wire, Miller and Dunn, resulted in suspending his journey to the South. A congregation was formed from which other preachers were intentionally detained, and thus he was almost compelled to preach his first sermon. From this time he labored faithfully. In October he received license and the next August was ordained by the Geauga Quarterly Meeting at Burton.. Many souls were converted and two or three churches organized. under Brother Moulton's labors in the Geauga Quarterly Meeting the next few years. In 1841 he settled with the Washington Street church, Dover, N. H., where an extensive revival was enjoyed, and a house of worship commenced which was completed the year after he left. Early in 1843 he commenced a successful pastorate in Portland, Me., the church being greatly strengthened. The church in Roxbury, Mass., secured his services in 1848, and the outlook became more encouraging than in any previous field but the church in Lowell was in great need and he soon began with them a useful pastorate, during which they erected a house of worship. But in these years of earnest labor his nervous system became debilitated and he retired to the prairies of Iowa, where with returning health he preached some and edited a weekly paper. In 1860 he returned to active work and labored effectually at Great Falls, New Hampshire., Auburn, Maine, Concord, New Hampshire, and Cleveland, Ohio. His death was instantaneous, resulting from a fall from a bridge at Linndale, a suburb of Cleveland.

Rev Carl Muncy

Birth:
Oct. 27, 1953
Wayne County, West Virginia
Death:
Mar. 2, 2016
Jackson
Jackson County, Ohio
Burial:
Salem Cemetery
Jackson County
Ohio

Carl was a loving father, grandpa, and preacher. He loved his family and they will miss him dearly. He was a preacher, Sunday school teacher, and he had a monthly appointment at Edgewood Manor where he sang and read scriptures to the residents. Burial with Pastor Burley Muncy officiating.

James R Music, Sr

Birth:
Dec. 22, 1926
Meally,
Johnson County, Kentucky
Death:
Nov. 10, 2008
Ohio
Burial:
Kingwood Memorial Park,
Lewis Center,
Delaware County, Ohio,

He ministered in several Free Will Baptist churches including Columbus First FWB and Lockbourne FWB.

Homer Nelson

Birth:
1912
Sciotodale,
Scioto County
Ohio
Death:
Apr. 27, 1985,
Portsmouth
Scioto County, Ohio
Burial:
South Webster Cemetery,
South Webster,
Scioto County, Ohio

He was a active Free Will Baptist pastor and denominational leader. He retired after 50 years' service and was a member of the Union Free Will Baptist Church. He was the former pastor of the Germany Hollow, Garden City, Sciotodale, Powellsville, Tick Ridge and the Union churches. He also had been the State Evangelist for the Ohio Free Will Baptist Convention and was the clerk for the Ohio State Association for a number of years. He served as the editor of the *Ambassador Magazine* from 1962 to 1972. His abilities and activities in the denomination are well recorded.

William "Junior" Naves, Jr

Birth:
Apr. 23, 1926
Limestone County, Alabama
Death:
Jul. 22, 2013
Holland
Lucas County, Ohio
Burial:
Ottawa Hills Memorial Park
Ottawa Hills
Lucas County, Ohio

William "Junior" Naves, Jr. was the son of William and Sarah (Scroggins) Naves, Sr. He married in Athens, Alabama on December 11, 1948. A WWII Navy Veteran, Junior was the Pastor of the Liberty Free Will Baptist Church for over 30 years, as well as a freight handler for Interstate Motor Freight for over 22 years. Published in Toledo Blade on July 23, 2013.

Clarence J. Newman
Birth:
Sep. 30, 1925
Huntington, Cabell County,
West Virginia
Death:
May 18, 2002
Ohio
Burial:
Forest Grove Cemetery.
Plain City.
Madison County.Ohio

Rev. Newman was converted at the age of 12, called to preach in 1957, ordained to the ministry in 1958. His ministry spread over 45 years, with most of it spent in the state of Ohio and with 10 years in Arizona. He was best remembered for his pastorates at the West Jefferson and Marysville Free Will Baptist Churches in Ohio. He served as moderator of the Ohio State Association and as its Promotional Sec. He was a powerful preacher with a distinctive voice conducting revivals in 16 states. He noted his best revival was at the FWB Church in Cleveland in the 1960s, where 75 were saved in one week. During World War II he served in the Merchant Marines. He was a classic car collector and was the 1969 Grand National winner with his 1969 Mustang convertible. He was known for taking small churches and building them into a renewable health.

Rev George S Oiler
Birth:
Mar. 11, 1902
Ewington
Gallia County, Ohio
Death:
Mar. 26, 1983
Pomeroy
Meigs County, Ohio
Burial:
Gravel Hill Cemetery
Cheshire
Gallia County, Ohio

The Rev. George S. Oiler, 81, Racine, died at Veterans Memorial Hospital.
He was born son of the late Andrew J. and Mary Hutchinson Oiler. He was also preceded in death by his first wife, Georgie Frazier Oiler, three brothers and a sister.
At the time of his death, the Mr. Oiler was the minister of the Syracuse Church of God. He had been a minister for 59 years serving several churches over that period. He also had been the owner and operator of coal mines in both Meigs and Gallia Counties for 30 years. He was a member of the West Virginia and Ohio Ministerial Associations.
Surviving are his wife, Virginia L. Gibbs Oiler, Racine; a daughter, Mrs. Ithamer (Mona Lee) Neal, Middleport; a son, Gene Oiler, Middleport; two grand-daughters, Janet Russell, Pomeroy, and Lisa Oiler, Middleport; a grandson, Eric Oiler, Middleport; a great-grandson, Ryan Russell, Pomeroy; a stepdaughter, Karen Lyons, Racine; two stepsons, Mike Nease, Pomeroy, and Mitch Nease, Racine; four step-granddaughters, Melanie and Amber Lyons, Racine, and Cassie and Jennifer Nease, Pomeroy; two sisters, Clara Short, Florida, and Lenora Jenkins, Syracuse; a brother, Marion Oiler, Little Hocking, and several nieces and nephews. *Pomeroy Times-Sentinel* March 27, 1983. (Bio by: Robert V Darst)

Inscription:
OILER
MINISTER
FATHER
GEORGE S.
1902 - 1983

Rev Harold Owens
Birth:
Mar. 25, 1944
Carter Co., Kentucky
Death:
Nov. 18, 2016
Mansfield, Ohio
Burial:
Mount Hope Cemetery
Shiloh
Richland County, Ohio

Harold was born to Art and Tina (Stone) Owens. Harold enjoyed preaching and was a member of Dean Road Freewill Baptist Church. He enjoyed playing guitar and singing and spending time outside with his family and friends. He worked at Voisard for 35 years where he retired.
Funeral Services with Brother Earl Tackett officiating.

Isaac Tirrell Packard

Birth:
May 3, 1826
Cummington
Hampshire County,
Massachusetts
Death:
May 21, 1849
Licking County, Ohio
Burial:
Old Fredonia Cemetery
Licking County,
Ohio

Isaac was the son of Theophillus and Esther Packard, born in Mass. When about seven years his father removed to Ohio, where he became an honored resident. His mother died when he was eight yrs of age, missing his best friend and counsellor. He went, after this, to live with a responsible family in Licking Co., where he remained several years. He came under the preaching of Rev. Geo. W. Baker, and at about sixteen years of age he began attending the Granville Academy. Afterward, he entered upon the business of teaching. In 1844, he spent about nine months in KY in this employment, when he was prevented by an attack of fever, implicating his lungs. After a few weeks recuperating, he returned to Ohio to his family and friends. He united with the Freewill Baptists at Liberty, was baptized by Rev. Goodwin Evans, a FWB minister. He soon felt impressed to enter the work of the Christian ministry. He received license by the First FWB church in Liberty, Licking Co., April 11, 1846. He received public ordination in May 28, 1848.He rode horseback through the western counties of the State, preaching from place to place, then spent the winter teaching and filling in regular preaching appointments. Again, he entered a course of study in Granville College in early 1848, but constant preaching and studies began to prey upon his feeble bodily powers and his health became much impaired. His disease was such that he knew his time was short. He made disposition of his books to his family, chose President Bailey, of Granville College to preach his funeral. He requested that he be buried beside his mother and sister--- and on May 21, 1849, with his devoted sister and a minister by his bedside, he passed peacefully to the other world. It is written, that "those who knew him best, esteemed him most. He was a young man of uncommon promise. He was mild, modest, and affable in all the intercourse of life, and was greatly endeared to many hearts."

Seth Parker

Birth:
Jul. 7, 1802
New York
Death:
Oct. 19, 1868
New York
Burial:
Steuben Cemetery
Steuben, Huron County, Ohio

Parker was a native of New York and moved to Ohio in 1820. He was converted in 1828, ordained in 1839, and continued with the churches of the Huron Q. M. until his death in Greenfield, Ohio Oct. 19, 1868, aged 66 years. He was twice a delegate to the General Conference, was corporator of the Printing Establishment from 1835 to 1847, and associate judge of the Court of Common Pleas from 1851 to 1858. He read much and was well informed on general topics. He was a faithful minister.

Asa Pierce

Birth:
1809
Berkshire
Berkshire County,
assachusetts
Death:
Jun. 1, 1900
Centerburg, Knox County, Ohio
Burial:
Centerburg Cemetery
Centerburg, Knox County, Ohio

Pierce, Rev. Asa, son of Orange and Ruth (Heath) Pierce. In 1812 his parents went to Ohio and located in Delaware County. In 1843 he was converted, and in 1846 was ordained by Rev's G. W. and O. E. Baker. His first pastorate was the Second Centerburg Free Will Baptist church, since which time he has preached for a number of churches in central Ohio and in Indiana. Many precious revivals have blessed his ministry and resulted in the organization by him of several churches. In 1830 he was married to Margaret Debold. Four children blessed this union. In 1852 he was married to Catherine Myers

James Jasper Perry
Birth:
Feb. 12, 1884
Martin County,
Kentucky
Death:
Aug. 29, 1928
Lyra, Scioto County, Ohio
Burial:
Vernon Cemetery,
Lyra, Scioto County, Ohio

A Free Will Baptist Minister.

Edwin Pimlott
Birth: April 10, 1853
Smethwick, England
Death: May 9, 1890
Burial:
Ferncliff Cemetery
Springfield
Clark County, Ohio
Plot: Section I lot 77

His father, Rev. Frank Pimlott, whose two sons became ministers were associated in England with the Primitive Methodist. Edwin was converted in 1868, educated at Hillsdale College, Michigan, and ordained on December 28, 1879. He became the pastor of the Breech Grove church, Ohio and about 1883 entered upon the pastor of the church in East Kendall, New York. He was engaging revival work baptized 30 converts.

Bill Pitts
Birth:
Sep. 10, 1931
Death:
Feb. 26, 2003
Columbus,
Franklin County, Ohio
Burial:
Harrison Township Cemetery,
South Bloomfield,
Pickaway County, Ohio

Rev. Pitts was the founder and longtime pastor of the Greater Columbus Free Will Baptist Church. He was in the ministry for 41 years.

Arnold J Pollard
Birth:
1931
Death:
1985
Burial:
Putnam Chapel Cemetery
Vinton County, Ohio

He was a retired US Air Force Korea and Vietnam veteran and Free Will Baptist minister pastoring the Puritan church for a number of years.

James Thompson Pollock
Birth:
1834
Death:
Apr. 29, 1917
Ohio
Burial:
Woodland Cemetery and
Arboretum
Dayton
Montgomery County, Ohio

POLLOCK, Rev. J. T. (may be the one on list?) 1834-1917, OH. He was m. to Elizabeth A. Andrews, 12 June 1867, OH; Children: Frances (Fannie), 1868, OH; Margaret R, 11 March 1870, Osborn, Greene Co. OH; infant son: C. Freddie, 07 Jan-1872; Melville, b. 14 Mar. 1876, Tiffin, Seneca, OH. James Thompson POLLOCK, served as Chap. in Civil War, Indiana 96th Inf. Drew pension in 1897 until he d. 1917.

R. P. Porter
Birth:
1821
Death:
1883
Burial:
Mount Tabor Cemetery,
Huntington Township,
Gallia County, Ohio

The Harrisburg Freewill Baptist Church was organized April 4, 1862 with Porter being one of the organizing ministers. He was later a it's pastor.

Raymond Sebastian Powers
Birth: Mar. 6, 1921
Virginia
Death:
Oct. 23, 1982
Norwalk, Huron County, Ohio
Burial:
Mount Hope Cemetery
Shiloh
Richland County, Ohio

He died from an apparent heart attack at the Crestview-Edison in football game in Milan, Ohio. He moved to Mansfield, Ohio in 1955 and then to Shiloh in 1962. He had been a clerk at the Empire-Detroit Steel Company since 1955. He was a Past Master of the Shiloh Masonic Lodge number 542 and Past Patron of the Shiloh Eastern Star number 322. He held the Knights Templar degree. He was ordained to the ministry in 1949 for the Free Will Baptist denomin-tion. He served with the United States Army Air Force from 1940 to 1945. Services were held at the Wesley Evangelical church in Shiloh by the Rev. Carlos Allen Junior of the Clear Creek Church of Christ, Ashland.

Cecil William Price
Birth:
Mar. 27, 1927
Gallia County, Ohio
Death:
Jan. 6, 1991
Jackson, Ohio
Burial:
Gravel Hill Cemetery,
Cheshire, Gallia County, Ohio

He was a US Navy and Army World War II veteran who retired from the Ohio Valley Electric Corporation at Kyger Creek. He was a member of the Old Kyger Free Will Baptist Church near Cheshire. He was also a Free Will Baptist preacher.

Pemberton Randall
Birth:
Oct. 6, 1807
Lebanon
New London County,
Connecticut
Death:
Jan. 4, 1891
Minneapolis
Hennepin County, Minnesota
Burial:
Spring Grove Cemetery
Medina
Medina County, Ohio
Plot: section 2 lot 97

Medina County Gazette-January 9, 1891: Pemberton Randall - in his book entitled *"The Wonderful Tent"*, Rev. D. A. Randall, D. D., is written, and from which we learn that "Rev. Pemberton Randall was one of seven children born to James Randall and his wife, Joanna Pemberton Randall. The parents were able to bestow upon their children little less than those born with good blood and Christian influences. The Randall's originated in bonnie Scotland, in this stirring annual of which County the family name is not obscure. The Pemberton's sprang from sturdy English stock, possessed of both ability and nobility. Joanna was a direct descendent of Ebenezer Pemberton, D. D., one of the early distinguished pastors of Old South Church, Boston. Both father and mother were native New Englanders. Rev. Pembleton Randall departed this life at the home of his daughter, with whom he and his wife were living. Mrs. Sarah) A. R. (Randall) McGeah, in Minneapolis, Minnesota, at about eight o'clock on Sunday morning, January 4, 1891, being a little past 84 years of age. He was born in Lebanon, Connecticut. In early life, in fact in the autumn of 1826, he and his brother, Rev. Austin Randall, D. D., embraced the Christian religion in a revival meeting held by Rev. David Marks, a Free Will Baptist revivalist who came to a neighboring church and began a series of meetings. In addition to attending the meetings for some three weeks, he and his brothers, alone or in concert, engaged daily in Scripture readings, praying or in meditation. Both made a public profession of religion and on the day before Christmas, by Elder Haskell, pastor of the local church, baptized into Canandaigua

Lake. Pemberton adopted the doctrine of the revivalist, and in due time became a cultivated and conscientious minister of the Free Will Church.

Soon after his conversion he removed to Ohio, and after receiving a common school education, he pursued a classical course for two years in Geauga Seminary.

In 1840 he was ordained by Elders Cyrus Coltrim and Warmer Beebe. His labors was with churches in northern Ohio. He has an able preacher, his sermons being clear, logical and strong arguments in favor of the religion of Christ. Young ministers have always considered it a great privilege to listen to his preaching, and although over 80 years of age his mental powers were clear and strong, and the Free Will Baptist Quarterly Meetings were often blessed with his presence and counsel. In February 1834 he was joined in marriage to Maria T. Beebe, who died in February, 1839, and in 1840 he was married to Sarah C. Foster. He was the father of 10 children; five of whom and his wife survived him.

He was regarded as one of the strongest intellectual scriptural preachers of the denomination, and of which he was a worthy and honored member.

His membership was transferred from Spencer, Ohio, to the Free Will Baptist church of Minneapolis, Minnesota, where his wife is also a member. He was able to converse intelligently to the last, and died trusting in Jesus for the life of one which he has entered in the immortality of the glory world.

His remains in Medina, Ohio on Wednesday morning was, accompanied by his wife and son in law, Mr. J. A. McGeagh, and the funeral services were Thursday afternoon at 2 PM, in Medina in the Baptist church, conducted by Rev. G. H. Damon and assisted by resident and other ministers of other denominations.

Earl E. Rankin
Birth:
Sep. 14, 1897
Olive Hill,
Carter County,
Kentucky
Death:
Jan., 1970
Portsmouth,
Scioto County Ohio
Burial:
Salisbury Cemetery
Stockdale,
Pike County,
Ohio

He was a bi-vocational Minister and a Free Will Baptist pastor who resided in Scioto County, Ohio for 40 years. As a Free Will Baptist pastor he served the Sciotodale, Bloom, Antioch and Owl Creek churches; Sciotodale Baptist and the Fallen Timber Christian church. He was a retired Detroit Steel Corp. He was a member of the Scioto Valley Ministerial Association.

John Robert Reese
Birth:
May 11, 1921
Death:
Jun. 18, 1993
Ohio
Burial:
Buffalo Cemetery
Buffalo
Guernsey County, Ohio

Churches Pastored: Hickory Grove Baptist Church, Oak Hill, Ohio; Germany Hollow Free Will Baptist, Wheelersburg, Ohio; Buckeye Free Will Baptist Church, Jackson, Ohio; Coalton Free Will Baptist Church, Coalton, Ohio; Buffalo Free Will Baptist Church, Buffalo, Ohio. As well as being an evangelist for several years.

David Lyman Rice
Birth:
May 1, 1820, Green, Ohio
Death:
Nov. 19, 1886
Burial:
Westwood Cemetery
Oberlin
Lorain County, Ohio
Plot: H-001-03A

His father resided for a while in Québec but shortly after settled in Ohio before 1820. David was converted in 1834 and baptized the following March by Reverent Ransom Dunn.

His education was obtained at Geauga Seminary. He was licensed by the Green church in 1843 and ordained by the Ashtabula Quarterly Meeting at Lenox on May 17, 1846. After a pastoring a number of churches, he entered another work as an agent for Hillsdale College in 1855. He continued this work until 1876 traveling among the churches conducting revivals and instructing the people as to the needs of the college and its importance to the denomination. In all he gathered more than $50,000 for the endowment of the college and at the same time turning the footsteps of many young men and women toward classic calls and higher life. In 1877 he became pastor of the church at Pierpoint, Ohio and then in 1884 the Burgh church. He is buried in the same Cemetery as the famous Charles Finney and Free Will Baptist leader David Marks.

Melford William Riddlebarger
Birth:
Oct. 10, 1906
Scioto County, Ohio
Death:
Nov. 27, 2003
Portsmouth,
Scioto County, Ohio
Burial:
Memorial Burial Park,
Wheelersburg,
Scioto County,
Ohio

He pastored in southern Ohio and was popular among the churches in the area.

Russell Homer Risner
Birth:
Mar. 20, 1934
Death:
Sep. 23, 1987
Burial:
Preston Cemetery,
Alger,
Hardin County,
Ohio

James Richard Roby
Birth:
Jul. 1, 1977
Bellefontaine, Logan County, Ohio
Death:
Aug. 14, 2011
Bellefontaine, Logan County,, Ohio
Burial:
Greenwood Cemetery
De Graff, Logan County, Ohio

Rev. James Richard Roby, 57, of De Graff, was a son of Richard Wilbur Roby of De Graff and the late Shirley Joanne Vaughn Roby. On September 23, 1977, he married Debra Diane Kendall in Bellefontaine.
He was a 1972 graduate of Riverside High School and a graduate of Urbana College. He was the Pastor at the De Graff Freewill Baptist Church.

Rev Ferrell M. Rood
Birth:
Jun. 13, 1937
Huntington
Cabell County, West Virginia
Death:
Dec. 4, 2015
Chillicothe
Ross County, Ohio
Burial
Oak Grove Cemetery
Zaleski, Vinton County, Ohio

Pastor Ferrell M. Rood, age 78 of Zaleski, passed away at the Adena Regional Medical Center in Chillicothe, Ohio. He was born in Huntington, W.Va. to the late Perry U. Rood and Lillie A. Shaver Rood. Ferrell was a 1955 graduate of Wellston High School. He was the Pastor of the Zaleski Free Will Baptist Church for 20 years, as well as being a self-employed contractor. Ferrell was an avid West Virginia Mountaineer fan, who enjoyed reading and spending time with his family. Funeral Home in Wellston with Brother Mark A. Rood, Jr. officiating.

M. Kenneth Rose

Birth:
Feb. 4, 1932
Emerson, Lewis County,
Kentucky
Death:
May 17, 2010
Mansfield, Richland County,
Ohio
Burial:
Franklin Cemetery, Mansfield,
Richland County, Ohio

Rev David Valoy Ross

Birth:
Sep. 1, 1842
Pennsylvania
Death:
Sep. 6, 1878
Ohio
Burial:
West Woodville Cemetery
Warren County, Ohio

Rev. David V. Ross, was born to William Ross and Amanda Pratt Ross, in Penn. When five years of age with his parents he moved from Pennsylvania to Clermont, OH. In 1861, he entered U.S. military service, and received honorable discharge at end of three years. He began preaching for the Methodists, but joined the Free Baptist in 1876 and was ordained by the Miami Quarterly Meeting the January before his death.

Samuel S Schnell

Birth:
Apr. 22, 1854
Liverpool, Ohio
Death: May 2, 1936
Burial:
Beebe Town Cemetery
Beebetown
Medina County, Ohio
Being converted in 1875, he entered Hillsdale College in 1877 taking the classical course and later at the theological. On September 24, 1883 he was ordained by the Genesee Quarterly Meeting, Michigan, and has since served the churches of Millington and Leslie, Michigan and Lenox, Ohio.

Rev Miranda Searl

Birth:
Mar. 14, 1808
Steuben County
New York
Death:
Dec. 19, 1891
Wheelersburg
Scioto County
Ohio
Burial:
South Webster Cemetery
South Webster
Scioto County
Ohio

Rev. Searl was converted in 1834, received license in 1837, and was ordained in April 1843, his connection being with the United Brethren.

In 1857, he united with the Freewill Baptists and has since ministered to the Hamilton, Union, Porter, Madison, Wheelersburg, and Sciotoville churches of the Little Scioto Quarterly Meeting, Ohio. He has baptized about fifty converts. Rev. Miranda Searl, of Iron Furnace, OH, was the son of Nathaniel and Rebecca (White) SEARL.
He was married to Mary Coburn, Jan. 22, 1829.

Rev Jacob Harrell See

Birth:
Aug. 8, 1893
Lawrence County
Kentucky
Death:
Nov. 8, 1967
Portsmouth
Scioto County
Ohio
Burial:
Memorial Burial Park
Wheelersburg
Scioto County
Ohio

Son of William V. and Nancy Jane Kirk See. Married first to Rhoda Frances Meek, who predeceased him. His second wife was Della Mae Barker.

He was a Freewill Baptist minister and was retired from Norfolk and Western Railroad as an air inspector and car repairman.

An ordained FWB minister in Ohio, and in the formation of Ohio's State Association, his name appearing with other minister's names who were present.

Rev. Isaac Seitz
Birth:
Aug. 2, 1828
Seneca County,Ohio
Death:
1890
Burial:
Greenlawn Cemetery
Tiffin
Seneca County, Ohio
Plot: Sect C, row
Plot 6, grv 23

Rev. Isaac Seitz was converted in 1866 and united with the Methodist church and in 1875 was licensed as a local preacher. In his studies he changed his doctrinal belief on the question of baptism and other doctrines; and in 1877, he changed his church relations, uniting with the Bloom Free Baptist church. In May 1878, he was ordained by the Seneca and Huron Quarterly Meetings (QM). He has had care of churches in the Marion, and Richland and Licking Q.M's, and organized one church. He has written an interesting book containing an account of his own experiences; a reply to Ingersoll, and a statement of his doctrinal views as gathered

from the word of God. He pastored also the church as Rome, OH.
Note: 1st Sgt Co G 164 OVI

Louis E. Shannon
Birth: 1855
Death: 1924
Burial:
Pleasant Union Cemetery
Old Fort
Seneca County
Ohio
Plot: sec 7 lot 49

William J. Sheppard
Birth:
1881
Death:
1945
Scioto County, Ohio
Burial:
Vernon Cemetery,
Lyra,
Scioto County, Ohio

Early pastor and Ohio leader in the newly formed Free Will Baptists State re-organization.

Warren Simpkins
Birth:
Sep. 5, 1948
Paintsville, Kentucky
Death:
Mar. 15, 2010
Commercial Point
Pickaway County, Ohio
Burial:
Beckett Cemetery
Commercial Point
Pickaway County, Ohio

He was the assistant pastor at the Mt. Sterling Free Will Baptist Church where he also taught the Young Adult Sunday School and was the head of the Youth Olympics for the Trinity Conference. He was active in the Courthouse Manor Nursing Home services and sang in the Lighthouse Singers Quartet.

Rev Jesse C "Jessie" Sizemore
Birth:
Nov. 4, 1888
Death:

Mar. 11, 1954
Burial:
Puckett Cemetery
Pedro
Lawrence County, Ohio

Father: James Sizemore b: 01 MAY 1848 & Mother: Sarah Henry b: MAR 1852
He was a minister in the Free Wlll Baptist, and was elected assistant moderator of the Ohio State Association in 1939. Other information concerning his ministry is unavailable. Spouse: Hattie Delawder Sizemore (1891 - 1968).

Jacob Shonkwiler
Birth:
May 1, 1805
Scioto County, Ohio
Death:
Dec. 18, 1882
Lucasville
Scioto County, Ohio
Burial:
Owl Creek Cemetery,
Beaver, Pike County, Ohio

He was one of the earliest Free Will Baptist ministers in southern Ohio and especially in Scioto County. He was a minister and farmer in this County as well as Pike County, Ohio.
Married twice and had five children by each wife. In August of 1841, he was ordained a Free Will Baptist. He was the pastor of the Hamilton Free Will Baptist Church in 1884, which had been organized in 1881 and a church building was erected that same year. The first pastor of this congregation was Isaac Fullerton. Jacob preached in southern Ohio and in Maysville, Kentucky area. He was a rabid abolitionist and became engaged in the abolition movement. Tradition says that he and his cousin the Rev. Isaac Fullerton, helped slaves escape from Kentucky into Ohio then into Canada.

James A. Shonkwiler
Birth:
Oct. 7, 1877
Pike County Ohio
Death:
October 21, 1955
Hilliard,
Franklin County, Ohio
Burial:
Owl Creek Cemetery
Pike County, Ohio

He was one of the older of the Free Will Baptist ministers in southern Ohio and was a member of the Owl Creek church which still exists.

Carl R. Sizemore
Birth:
July 17, 1917
Death:
2009
Burial:
Puckett Cemetery, Pedro,
Lawrence County, Ohio

Rev. Carl R. Sizemore, 91, of Pedro, Lawrence County, Ohio native was the son of the late Rev, Jesse C. and Hattie Delawder Sizemore. Mr. Sizemore attended Pedro Schools, was a U.S. Army WWII Veteran and a former coal miner for over 40 years with Collins Mining Company. He was a member of Symmes Valley Freewill Baptist Church in Aid, Ohio.

Denver Earl Smith
Birth:
Apr. 8, 1920
Death:
Feb. 14, 1992
Burial:
South Webster Cemetery,
South Webster,
Scioto County, Ohio

Rev Troy W. Smith, Jr
Birth:
Apr. 22, 1944
Death: Apr. 1, 2015
Ohio
Burial:
Fairview Cemetery
Mount Vernon
Knox County, Ohio

Rev. Troy W. Smith, Jr., age 70, of Nebo, went home to be with the Lord Wednesday, April 1, 2015 at Memorial Campus – Mission Hospital. Rev. Smith was born April 22, 1944 and was a son of the late Troy Weaver Smith, Sr. and Annie Jackson Smith. He was a very loving, meek and happy person.. He had grit, and was a hard worker. His family will remember him as a wonderful husband, father, grandfather and great grandfather, brother, brother-in-law and friend to many. He was a great mentor to his children and friends. He pastored numerous churches for 42 years in MI, VA, NC and TN. He proudly served his country in the US Army 82nd Airborne.
Surviving Rev. Smith is his wife of 50 years, Bobbie Jean Smith, of the home; Rodney Smith, son

and wife Melinda of Nebo; Michelle Smith Scoles, daughter and husband Keith of Nebo; two brothers, Jackson Smith and wife Shirley of Candler and Roy Smith and wife Sue also of Candler; three sisters, Claudine Reese and husband Jimmy of Weaverville, Peggy Smith Warren of Leicester and Debbie Brittain and husband Gene of Mills River; nine grandchildren, two great granddaughters and a brother-in-law, Lamar Crisp and wife Sharon of Bostic.

A funeral service was held Saturday, April 4, 2015 at 3:30 pm at Fairview Free Will Baptist church with Revs. Elisha Fish, Ted Reynolds, Terry McDaniel and Scott Hollifield officiating.

Ted B Sowards

Birth:
1905
Death:
1989
Burial:
Friendship Cemetery,
Friendship,
Scioto County,
Ohio

Crate D. Sparks

Birth:
Dec. 18, 1934
Culver,
Elliott County,
Kentucky
Death:
Mar. 16, 2012 Mount
Vernon,
Knox County,
Ohio

Burial:
Fairview Freewill Baptist
Church Cemetery,
Mount Vernon,
Knox County, Ohio

He began preaching the gospel in 1968. A lifelong servant of God, he founded the Ashley now Victory Freewill Baptist Church. He served the Blooming Grove Freewill Baptist Church, Pleasant Hill Freewill Baptist Church, and founded the Fairview Freewill Baptist Church, where he pastored until 2008. In 1993 he retired from Sunray Stove Company in Delaware, after 33 years of service. A US Navy Veteran, he came to Galena at the age of 18, moved to Mt. Vernon in 1993 and onto Delaware in 2011 to be near his family. Services were held with military honors.

**To Live is Christ
To Die is Gain.**

Delmar C Sparks

Birth:
Nov. 7, 1927
Death:
Aug. 17, 2002
Estes Park,
Larimer County,
Colorado
Burial:
Blendon Central Cemetery,
Westerville,
Franklin County,
Ohio

He was founder of the Westerville Free Will Baptist Church where he served for 31 years. Besides being an outstanding pastor he was a very active denominational leader. He represented the state of Ohio on the General Board of the National Association from 1984-2002. He was also honored to speak at the national convention in 1989 in Tampa, Florida. As a local pastor he served on many district ordaining council's, mission board and moderator. On the state level he served as the moderator of the state Association, served on the State General Board and Executive Board. His early ministry was among the Enterprise Baptist churches before his leaving to organize the Westerville church in 1959. He was a marvelous mentor and fellow servant.

Asa Stearns
Birth:
Feb. 3, 1782
Death:
Sept. 7, 1851
Mercer County, Ohio
Burial:
Elm Grove Cemetery
Saint Marys
Auglaize County, Ohio

Sophia Higley was married to Asa Stearns, a Free Will Baptist preacher, finally settled in Mercer County, Ohio, where they both died. They had four children, Rufus, Amos, Louise, and Joel. Rufus became a doctor and is buried in the same Cemetery with his mother and father. He was connected with the Meigs Quarterly Meeting in South East Ohio in its early years and saw the fruits of his labor they are because many of the churches and influence still exist. An interesting note appears in the history of Athens County Ohio about how the early ministers were supported. "In the Ames Township area secured to the services of Elder Asa Stearns a pioneer Free Will Baptist preacher to preach for them once a month during the year, to be paid with three barrels of whiskey. Rev. Stearns had an arrangement with Ebenezer Currier, at Athens, to take the whiskey and allow him there for $24 be credited him toward the farm he had bought from Judge Currier. The contract was faithfully carried out on all hands, Elder Stearns visiting the congregation every third Saturday and Sunday of each month during the year at the end of which he received a salary of whiskey and made the transfer he did as agreed to Judge Currier."

Eli Stedman
Birth:
Aug. 17, 1777
Tunbridge,
Orange County, Vermont
Death:
Mar. 28, 1845
Rutland, Meigs County, Ohio
Burial:
Miles Cemetery, Rutland,
Meigs County, Ohio

He came to Ohio in 1804, locating in Belpre, Washington County, but removed to Leading Creek in 1805. He was a preacher of the Free Will Baptist denomination. Elihu Stedman was the youngest child of Eli Stedman and wife. He married Adaline Elliott, daughter of Simeon Elliott, Esq., and a sister of Rev. Madison Elliott, at one time principal of the Chester Academy. Elihu Stedman lived in Middleport many years, but moved to Iowa. Eli started the Old Kyger Free Will Baptist Church in 1805 which is the oldest church in Ohio of this denomination which still exists.

Hertis Stone
Birth:
Jul. 30, 1932
Olive Hill,
Carter County, Kentucky
Death:
Sep. 16, 1998
Mansfield, Richland County,
Ohio
Burial:
Mansfield Cemetery,
Mansfield,
Richland, Ohio

Although he was a Kentuckian he spent the majority of his adult life in Ohio, where he retired from the General Motors CPC plant.

Brother Stone was pastor of the Wyandotte Free Will Baptist Church of Mansfield for over 20 years. He was the evangelists for the Northern Ohio Free Will Baptist Conference and was a member of the Cuyahoga-Lorain Free Will Baptists Executive conference board. He also pastored churches in Amherst, Ohio; Huntington, Indiana;

Buckeye Lake and Fitchville, Ohio Free Will Baptist churches

J. A. Sutton
Birth:
1847
Symmes Township
Hamilton County, Ohio
Death:
1921
LaRue, Ohio
Burial:
LaRue Cemetery, La Rue
Marion County, Ohio

Rev. Jeremiah Augustus Sutton, LaRue's grand old man, was found dead in bed by his wife. Sunday morning. Death being caused from heart failure. He had been in his usual health Saturday and was to deliver the sermon at the funeral of Mrs. Milton Anderson, near DeCliff, Sunday afternoon. On the desk in Rev, and Mrs. Sutton's room was the obituary, funeral text and notes on the sermon to be used. The service was conducted by Rev. F. E. Hawes, pastor of Fite Memorial Baptist church, of Marion, who used the text chosen by Rev. Mr. Sutton. Rev. Mr. Sutton was perhaps the most widely known minister in the county and to know him was to win a friend in the truest sense of the word. He had long been called the "marrying and burying parson," having delivered 2,089 funeral sermons and performing 746 marriage services. Rev. Mr. Sutton was ordained to the ministry October 24, 1874. He came to Marion County in 1879 accepting the pastorate in Green Camp Baptist church. This position he held until April 8, 1890 when he was appointed chaplain to the Ohio State penitentiary, which position he filled for about two years. During his pastorate in the institution, Rev. Mr. Sutton organized what was known as the Ohio Penitentiary Sunday-school and through his association had eighty-four conversions. In 1894 Rev. Mr. Sutton moved to LaRue, where he served twelve consecutive years as pastor of the Free Will Baptist church. With the exception of a short time passed as pastor of a charge in West Mansfield, he passed the remainder of his life in LaRue. Rev. Mr. Sutton was twice married, the first wife being Miss Mollie Cox, who died November 28, 1869. March 22, 1883, he was married to Mrs. Helen Kniffin..

Rev. Mr. Sutton had held all the offices in the church and a large number of offices in the township and village. He had been a notary public for the past thirty-one years, and at the time of his death was clerk of Montgomery Township. At one time he was editor of the LaRue News.

Rev Lawson C. Swaim
Birth:
Apr. 16, 1846
Scioto County
Ohio
Death:
Nov. 7, 1900
Burial:
Buchtel Cemetery
Buchtel
Athens County, Ohio

Rev. Lawson C. Swaim, son of George W. Swaim, was born in Scioto Co. Ohio. He was converted at the age of twenty-three years and began preaching soon after, but was not ordained until 1878. The most of his time has been devoted to evangelist labor and several hundred persons have been converted under his preaching and baptized by him. He has organized four churches and was pastor at Madison and Scioto. In March, 1866, He was married to Feemelia Woodruff.

Brighton N Tanner
Birth:
1852
Chester, Ohio
Death:
Apr. 1, 1932
Burial:
Lake View Cemetery
Cleveland
Cuyahoga County,
Ohio
Plot: Section 42 Lot 782-0

He was educated at Geauga, Ohio. In 1885 he consecrated his life to God and May 20, 1888 was licensed to preach by the Geauga and Portage Quarterly Meeting.

Paul Elden Taylor
Birth:
Aug. 18, 1921
Cheshire,
Gallia County, Ohio
Death:
Dec. 20, 2004
Rutland, Meigs County, Ohio
Burial:
Gravel Hill Cemetery,
Cheshire, Gallia County, Ohio

Rev. Taylor served as pastor to the Rutland Freewill Baptist Church for 30 years and he shared his ministry for 12 years in Utah. During World War II he served four years in the U.S. Army in the Philippines as a foot soldier.

Rev Merlin Eldridge Teets
Birth:
Jan. 25, 1920
Braxton, West Virginia
Death:
March 6, 1993
Columbus, Franklin Co., Ohio
Burial:
Glen Rest Memorial Estate
Reynoldsburg
Franklin County, Ohio
Plot: Section B

He was raised in a Christian home, the fourth of five children born to Cleova and Leota (Helmick) Teets of Braxton County, West Virginia. In 1942 he met Ida Stout at a cottage prayer meeting. They were married June 9, 1943. Shortly after he enlisted in the army for the duration of the war plus six months. He was sent to France.

The year 1949 a revival was held at Eureka Methodist Church where they attended with his family during his years at home. Shortly after they were saved, they moved back to Cabin Creek, West Virginia where he went to work in the coal mines. During that time, he met and joined a group of men who formed a quartet. They traveled to various churches to minister through song.. During those years he was feeling a strong call from God to preach. In 1949 he surrendered to that call.

He did trial preaching in many area churches and denominations. After studying the doctrines of many churches, he came to believe the tenets of the Free Will Baptist Association most closely mirrored his understanding of the scriptures. He was ordained by the Free Will Baptist Association. Although he was an ordained FWB preacher, he never turned down an opportunity to share the unfiltered gospel of Christ in any church, regardless of their denomination. His preaching ministry spanned six states and some 15 denominations.

In addition to his pastorates, he had a vibrant and effective evangelistic and radio ministry. He did a live half-hour program on WMPO Middleport, Ohio every Sunday afternoon. While he was the Ohio state Evangelist he had a weekly program in Jackson, Ohio. During good weather he would set up his big tent and hold tent revivals wherever he felt a call, and had an opportunity to go. He pastored the following churches: Mt. Union FWB Church, The Plains, FWB Church Silver Run FWB Church, Zaleski FWB Church, Woodland Chapel FWB (twice) First FWB Church (formerly Belmont Baptist Church, Puritan FWB Church, and the Wellston FWB Church. After retiring helped with the revitalization of a number of churches. He had a great love and burden for people and worked in churches until he became physically unable to serve. He held the following known positions during his ministry: Promotional Secretary for State of Ohio, Ohio State Evangelist, and was the third Editor of "The Ambassador," a denominational state publication. He was a featured speaker at the 47th annual Ohio State Association. Most of his record books were lost, but in an old one that was found, a compilation of this record showed that for August 1953 through August 1963 (nine years, he preached 2,185 sermons, held 83 revivals, and saw 812 people give their life to Christ. These numbers do not include those in the unfound record books, nor include the marriages or funerals that he preached, or the number of baptisms he conducted.

His ministry spanned over 44 years. He wrote, "I feel God has called me to preach His word, and woe is me if I preach not this gospel." He had the God-given ability to present God's word in an effective, compelling manner. He was privileged to start two churches and assist in starting three others, all of which are still thriving churches. He also had a deep appreciation and love for the young ministers who had received the call to preach and mentored many. Jim Eberts preached his funeral. His message was "Who Will Carry the Torch?"

Rev James C. Thacker
Birth
unknown
Fishtrap, Kentucky,
Death
19 Jan 2018
Burial
Kingwood Memorial Park
Lewis Center,
Delaware County,
Ohio

Rev. James C. Thacker, age 94, of Columbus, passed away peacefully at home. Born in Fishtrap, Kentucky, WWII veteran, and 27 year employee of White-Westinghouse where he gave his life to the Lord on April 18, 1961. He was a dedicated servant of Columbus First Freewill Baptist Church for half a century. Preceded in death by his wife Mary Magdalene, his son James Michael, his parents and his siblings. Survived by daughter-in-law, Sandra Thacker; beloved nieces and nephews, Glen (Debbie) Mullins, Bobby (Mike) Goodfleisch, Sarah Kerwood; granddaughters, Karen hobor and Nikki (Lance) Golden; five great-grandchildren and three great-great-grandchildren. his funeral service was held at The First FWB Church of Columbus with Rev. Edwin Hayes officiating

Clyde Thompson, Jr
Birth:
Mar. 28, 1939
Grahn, Carter County,
Kentucky
Death:
May 2, 2012
Mansfield, Richland County,
Ohio
Burial:
Mound Cemetery, Piketon,
Pike County, Ohio

He was a veteran of the United States Army and had retired from Wickes Lumber Company after driving a truck for over 30 years. He was a Free Will Baptist minister having pastored churches in Ohio and Indiana. He was a member of the Dean Road Free Will Baptist Church in Mansfield, Ohio.

Rev Robert Barry Thompson
Birth:
Nov. 18, 1944
Logan County
West Virginia
Death:
Jan. 30, 2015
Cheshire
Gallia County, Ohio
Burial:
Gravel Hill Cemetery
Cheshire
Gallia County, Ohio

He was son of the late Okey and Inez Thompson, and was the youngest of twelve children.
Bob was the Pastor of Old Kyger Freewill Baptist Church. He worked as a meat cutter in the D.C., Maryland and Beckley, WV area, and retired as the meat manager of Save-A-Lot in Pomeroy, Ohio. He loved preaching, serving, and doing work for the Lord since 1980. He pastored several churches in West Virginia, Tempa Baptist, Kilsyth FWB, and Odd FWB. Bob enjoyed vacationing at the beach, riding his motorcycle, fishing, and loved reading and talking about eagles. He served in the U.S. Navy during the Vietnam Era. Bob was married to Opal in Upper Marlboro, Maryland on August 26, 1966.

Samuel Titus
Birth:
1796
Northumberland County
Pennsylvania
Death:
Feb. 18, 1859
Harrison Furnace, Scioto
County, Ohio
Burial:
Titus Cemetery
Minford, Scioto County, Ohio

He married 15 Jul 1816 Ontario Co, New York, Clarrisa Coryell. Son of:
Tetus Titus 1755-1765 Montgomery Co, NY who died in 1825 at Scioto Co, Ohio. His mother was Polly Johnson B: Unknown who died in 1819 at Madison Twps., Scioto Co, Ohio 1884). He was the first pastor of the Harrison FWB church of Minford, Ohio.

Miles Lee Trout
Birth:
Sep. 17, 1922
Gallipolis
Gallia County
Ohio
Death:
Sep. 8, 2013
Cheshire
Gallia County,Ohio
Burial:
Ohio Valley Memory Gardens
Gallipolis
Gallia County, Ohio

He was a retired supervisor of the Columbus Southern Power Co. He also was the pastor of several Free Will Baptists churches, and was a member of the Silver Memorial FWB church, the Gallia County Ministerial Association, and the Gallia Quarterly Conference. He was a World War II veteran having served in the U.S. Army Air Corp. Son of James W. and Nell Board Trout. He was married to Ada E. Saunders Trout and second to Helen A. Shuler Trout.

Alvin Trusty
Birth:
1918
Death:
1955
Burial:
Preston Cemetery, Alger,
Hardin County, Ohio
Plot: Section 2 (East), row 18

Live For Eternity God Esteems And Calls

Charles Alexander Twining
Birth:
May 23, 1821
Hunterdon County
New Jersey
Death:
Dec. 21, 1903
Kipton
Lorain County
Ohio
Burial:
Camden Cemetery
Kipton, Lorain County, Ohio

Charles Alexander Twining, one of the most prosperous and wealthy of the prominent farmers of Henrietta Township.
Samuel Twining, father of subject, was born Feb. 22, 1796, in Hunterdon County, N. J., and moved his family to Broome County, N. Y., in 1823, where he died April 10, 1831. On September 23, 1815, he married Elizabeth Stout, who died October 17, 1882. Her people were wealthy, but on the death of her parents she lost all that she became heiress to. Samuel was a farmer, miller, cloth dresser and distiller; and at the time of his death owned fifty acres of land near Binghamton, N. Y. He left five children, a mother-in-law and sister-in-law for our subject to

assist in providing for, and, although the latter was but ten years old when his father died, he was the '"main spoke in the wheel."

Charles A. Twining, whose name opens this sketch, received but a limited education at the subscription schools of the place of his nativity. On October 18, 1842, he was married. by Squire Jesse Richards, to Miss Nellie Schermerhorn, and for about seven years thereafter they continued to reside in Broome county, N. Y. In 1840 they came to Lorain County, Ohio, and Mr. Twining, having saved some five hundred dollars from his earnings, bought a small piece of land in Pittsfield Township, Lorain County, where he resided three years. At the end of this time he sold out to his three brothers and returned to Broome County, N. Y., where he bought the old home farm formerly owned by his father. After residing here three years he sold out, returned to Ohio, and bought a farm in Camden Township, Lorain County. Sold this farm and bought in Russia Township; sold this and bought a farm in Henrietta Township, which he still owns. In 1888 he built a comfortable modern dwelling, situated in Henrietta Township. and his property has increased from time to time till he now owns 720 acres of prime farm land, divided into seven farms, with good buildings. He has owned farms in Brownhelm and West Henrietta, and in Erie County, in Florence Township; three farms in West Clarksfield, Huron County, Brighton Township, Lorain County, and Wakeman, Huron County, and resided on all of these except the one in Wakeman. He has given his daughter Sarah Ann a good farm in Camden Township, and has settled his six living sons on good farms, and has also dealt quite extensively in livestock.

Eleven children were born to Mr. and Mrs. Twining,

The entire family are members of the Freewill Baptist Church, except Perry, who is a member of the Methodist Church, and all brought up in the path of Christian rectitude, which they have in no instance deviated from. The sons have never used liquor or tobacco in any form. Mr. Twining in his political affiliations has always been a staunch Democrat, and has served his county to the best of his ability, and held offices of trust. Mr. Twining formerly belonged to the Methodist Church, where he was class-leader and superintendent of Sabbath schools for a number of years, and also held an exhorter's license. In 1866 Mr. Twining spent one year with his family in Ocean county, N.J., stopping at a pleasure resort in Point Pleasant.

(Source: Commemorative Biographical Record of the Counties of Huron and Lorain, Ohio, Chicago, Beers and Co., 1894.)

Death is the crown jewel for the Christian.

F. A. Twining
Birth:
Jun. 30, 1866
Florence
Erie County
Ohio
Death:
Jan. 7, 1945
Hiram
Portage County
Ohio
Burial:
Camden Cemetery
Kipton
Lorain County
Ohio
Plot: Section A - 44D West

Information from Ohio Death Cert. Occupation, retired minister.
Parents: Charles Alexander Twining (1821 - 1903) Nellie Schermerhorn Twining (1824 - 1907) Spouse:
Carrie M Hardy Twining (1873 - 1961)

REV. F. A. TWINING

Rev. F. A. Twining, 79, a former pastor of Fite Memorial Baptist church, died in his home at Hiram, O., yesterday. He died as the result of a stroke of paralysis. He had suffered previous strokes.

A native of Oberlin, he held Baptist pastorates at Coshocton, Canton, Green Camp and Marion. He was pastor at Green Camp from April, 1905 to October, 1907. In 1913 he served the Fite Memorial congregation when the organization was yet in the form of a mission Sunday school, then again for two years when it was an established church, about 15 years ago.

The widow, Mrs. F. A. Twining, survives. A daughter, Mrs. Ruth Whitcomb is a librarian at Hiram college, Hiram, O., and a son, Arthur, some time ago located in Iowa. Three grandchildren survive also, one of whom, a grandson, is in service.

William Tracy Twining
Birth:
Sep. 4, 1847
New York
Death:
Sep. 22, 1936
Henrietta
Lorain County
Ohio
Burial:
Camden Cemetery
Kipton
Lorain County,Ohio

William was a retired Farmer. Son of Alex Twining.
His Death Certificate lists him as Married to Clara Twining.
W. T. Twining. The Twining family has been represented in Lorain County for nearly sixty-five years. W. T. Twining is now living practically retired in Henrietta Township but for many years was engaged in the vigorous prosecution of his business as a general farmer, dairyman and stockman. The name is one that has always been associated with honorable citizenship and a substantial influence in behalf of community welfare.
A native of New York State, W. T. Twining was born September 4, 1847, a son of Charles A. and Nellie (Schermerhorn) Twining. The Twining family is of old American ancestry, and the first of the name was William Twining who came from England and settled on the Atlantic coast soon after 1630. Grandfather Samuel Twining was born February 22, 1796, and followed the business of farmer and miller, making his home in Broome County, New York. In that county he was married in 1813 to Elizabeth Stout.
Charles A. Twining was born in New York State April 23, 1821 and died December 21, 1903. His wife was born in the same state October 8, 1824, and died in 1907. Charles A. Twining, so long known as one of the most successful men of Lorain County, started life with absolutely nothing, and for a number of years had to support not only his sisters but his mother and stepfather. At the time of his death his estate included over 500 acres of land. He first came to Ohio in 1849, but it was in 1852 that he made permanent settlement in Lorain County. He brought to this county $500 and with that as capital purchased his first land in Pittsfield Township. Later he bought a farm in Camden Township and still later in Henrietta Township, in which locality he lived until his death. He became a prominent stock raiser and also dealt extensively in lands, and at one time owned eight different farms. Charles A. and Nellie Twining were married in 1842 and of their eight children seven are still living: Sarah Ann, widow of LeGrand Gibson, and living at Clarksfield. Ohio; W. T.; Gertrude Elizabeth, now deceased; Alvah F. of Henrietta Township; Floyd Odell of Henrietta Township; Virgil Leroy, who has gained success in the hotel business and is now owner of four different hotels and lives at Maumee. Ohio: Perry Eugene, a farmer in Maryland; and Fred A., who is a minister of the Regular Baptist Church, at Coshocton, Ohio. The parents were members of the Free Will Baptist Church, and the father was a democrat in politics.
W. T. Twining gained his early education in the public schools. He worked for his father on the farm until gaining his majority, and was then married to Miss Drucilla Ann Bulkley. They have lived together and worked out their destinies for almost a half a century. Mrs. Twining was a daughter of Jeremiah and Mary Ann (Vincent) Bulkley. Her father was born in New York State September 12, 1824, and died October 20, 1908, and her mother was born in Canada August 8, 1825, and died December 7, 1905. The Bulkley family came to Lorain County in pioneer times and the grandfather and father of Mrs. Twining cleared up a large acreage of land in this section. The Vincent's were also early settlers in Henrietta Township. From "A Standard History of Lorain County "by Geo Frederick Wright.

(1854 - 1923)*
Floyd Odell Twining (1856 - 1939)*
Virgil L Twining (1859 - 1941)*
Fred A Twining (1866 - 1945)*

Benjamin Tufts
Birth:
Feb. 12, 1777
Maine
Death:
Aug. 27, 1849
Maineville
Warren County, Ohio
Burial:
Maineville Cemetery
Maineville
Warren County, Ohio

He was converted in 1802 and became connected with the church in Phillips, Maine where he was ordained in 1822. The same year he moved to Ohio where he united with the Maineville Free Will Baptist Church, Hamilton County, and continued to preach as opportunity presented going as far west as Indiana.

Francis Tufts
Birth:
Feb., 1743
Medford, Mass.
Death:
Oct. 2, 1833
Warren County, Ohio
Burial:
Maineville Cemetery,
Maineville,
Warren County, Ohio, Plot:
Sec.E

Tufts was a true pioneer. He was born in Medford, Mass., but as Maine and Mass. were one large area, he moved from Medford, MA to Farmington, Maine, and was an early contributor to area.

He served Maine in the Revolutionary War, enlisting in 1775-1777, in Lincoln Co. Maine. He finally received a pension shortly before his death. Where and when he was ordained was associated with the Farmington Q.M., when it was dealing with Rev. Edward Lock on the subject of open communion before 1800, and the votes came out yeas for Rev. Tufts to have open communion. Rev. Moses Dudley (of Maine) had moved to Ohio from Maine, served in the ministry and meetings in this area. They are both buried in this cemetery. (Maineville history states that in 1850 this

name was adopted because so many citizens had migrated there from Maine). When Samuel Knowlton, a kinsman friend was removing there, Rev. Francis Tufts (at 87 yrs of age) decided to ride horseback the one-thousand-mile trip with them to get there. They started Sept. 1, 1831, and arrived Oct 13, 1831, went through nine states, stopping only for "the Sabbath" to worship. Rev. Tufts was always invited to preach which he ably did. It was reported he had a retentive memory--well versed in Old and New Testaments that he could quote entire chapters or suitable portions of scripture. Rev. Tufts was in near perfect physical conditions, but two years later, he passed away.

"The Story of His Predecessors and Descendants" by Marion Thomas Whitney, pub. 1995, states that Josiah Tufts (1780-1841), who mar. Jane (Greely) Tufts, was his son. Jane was dau. Of Seth Greely (1737-1825) who came to Maineville in 1815.

John F. Tufts
Birth:
Oct. 7, 1829
Barrington
Strafford County, New Hampshire
Death:
May 13, 1873
Warren County, Ohio
Burial:
Maineville Cemetery
Maineville, Warren County, Ohio

His service was among the churches of the Miami Quarterly Meeting. He received license to preach the gospel about 1846 when connected with the Rossbourgh for church and was ordained about three years later. He spent some time at the biblical school in Whitestown, New York. He was a prominent man and much loved in the Miami Quarterly Meeting where he had long service and, noble, and Christian example causing him to be liked by others. He also spent a few years in Iowa. He represented the Ohio Yearly Meeting in the General Conference in 1850.

Clyde Marshall VanHoose
Birth:
Feb. 20, 1933
Johnson County, Kentucky
Death:
Aug. 22, 2011
Burial:
Big Darby Cemetery,
Plain City,
Madison County, Ohio

Employed by Columbus Auto Parts and was the assistant pastor of the North Woodbury Freewill Baptist Church. He was a U.S. Army veteran (1953 to 1955) during the Korean Conflict.

Clovis Vanover
Birth:
Oct. 9, 1933
Laredo, West Virginia
Death:
Columbus, Franklin County, Ohio
Burial:
Mifflin Cemetery,
Gahanna, Franklin County, Ohio

He was the founder and Chairman of the C.W. Vanover Evangelistic Association and a member of the Williams Road FWB Church. He as a State-Wide Evangelist for Ohio Free Will Baptists. He was widely used and well liked.

Rev Kenneth Walker
Birth:
Sep. 18, 1928
Portsmouth, Ohio
Death:
Aug. 20, 2015
Wheelersburg, Ohio
Burial:
Sunset Memorial Gardens
Franklin Furnace
Scioto County, Ohio

Rev. Kenneth Mason Walker, 86, at Best Care Nursing and Rehab Center in Wheelersburg from compl-ications related to cancer. He was born the son of the late Wilburn W. and Dora Frances Arthur Walker. He served in the U.S. Air Force during the Korean Conflict, He was a graduate of Welch College in Nashville and also served as the chairman of its Board of Trustees for 12 years. He established and pastored several Free Will Baptist churches throughout his career, including churches in Washington, D.C., Tulsa, OK, Mobile, AL, Ashland, KY and Deerfield Beach, FL.
His wife, Emma Louise Walker, to whom he was married 68 years; one son, James Stanley Walker, Ph.D; two grandchildren, Dailey and Danner Walker all of Nashville, TN and one brother Walter (Nan) Walker of Waynesville, OH.
A Celebration of Life at the Union Free Will Baptist Church in Wheelersburg with Pastor Chris Oiler, Reverends Dan Widdig and Randy Skaggs officiating.

Rev Francis M. Watkins
Birth: Jul. 18, 1857
Ohio
Death:
Aug. 17, 1927
Burial:
Nye Cemetery
Chauncey
Athens County, Ohio

Ordained Free Baptist minister; son of Wm. T. and Elmira L (Beaman) Watkins. He was ordained in Salem, Ind. Jan. 6, 1889 and pastored the church there, where he prospered in that work
Inscription:
PVT 119th INF. 50 DIV.
WORLD WAR I VETERAN

Charles H. Webb
Birth: Mar. 29, 1926
Auxier,
Floyd County, Kentucky
Death:
Mar. 15, 1976
Springdale,
Washington County, Arkansas
Burial:
Woodlawn Cemetery,

Ada, Hardin County, Ohio Rev. Charles H. Webb, 49 died at of an apparent heart attack in Springdale Hospital, Springdale, Ark. He was an army veteran of World War II, former pastor of the High Street Freewill Baptist, Rt. 2, Ada, a retired factory worker and member of the High Street Freewill Baptist Church.

Eugene Webb

Birth:
Nov. 5, 1931
Bonanza, Kentucky
Death:
Dec. 10, 2010
Dola, Hardin County, Ohio
Burial:
Dola Cemetery, Dola,
Hardin County, Ohio

Free Will Baptist Minister in western Ohio. He and his wife, Carolyn Yoxsimer Gene was born again on Oct. 12. 1959, in a Freewill Baptist Church and in 1969 he was ordained to preach in the Freewill Baptist Organiza-tion. He served as a pastor and assistant pastor. He was a member of the White Oaks Road Freewill Baptist Church, in Marion.

Webb, worked as house parents at the FWB Home for Children in Greeneville, Tn. for three years and later served as a Field Representative for the home in Ohio for three additional years. He served his country in the Korean Conflict from 1951-1953 as a member of the U.S. Army 2nd Division.

Harrison Webb

Birth:
May 4, 1927
Lawrence County,
Ohio
Death:
Nov. 28, 2007
Ashland, Boyd County,
Kentucky
Burial:
Community Missionary Baptist
Church Cemetery,
Lawrence County, Ohio

The Lawrence County, Ohio native, the son of the late Simeon and Hazel May Fetters Webb. He is survived by his wife, Maxine Faye Littlejohn Webb, whom he married August 18, 1951.Mr. Webb attended Spring Branch Schools. He was a U.S. Army Korean War Veteran serving from 1948-1952 and received a Bronze Star. He was an iron pourer at the Dayton Malleable Iron Company for 27 years, retiring in 1989. He was a member of Symmes Valley Freewill Baptist Church and was a former pastor at several local churches. He lived in this area all his life.

Simeon J Weed

Birth:
1854
Death:
1927
Burial:
Calvary Baptist Cemetery,
Rio Grande,
Gallia County,
Ohio

Minister, leader, professor at Rio Grande College in Ohio before and after the merger with the Northern Baptists.

John Wheeler

Birth:
Sep. 6, 1787
Rehoboth
Bristol County, Massachusetts
Death:
Aug. 4, 1879
Greenwich
Huron County, Ohio
Burial:
Steuben Cemetery
Steuben
Huron County, Ohio

In 1805 he married Miss Mary Franklin and moved to Richmond, New York. After serving in the Army of the war of 1812 he was converted and in 1818 moved to Greenfield, Ohio where he began to preach, gathered a church and received ordination in September 1825. After the church was put up on a good basis he resigned the pastorate and labored in that region of the country becoming a circuit preacher helping to found several Free Will Baptist Churches. He had two marriages to the following ladies: Huldah Gregory Wheeler   Mary Franklin Wheeler

Inscription:
Rev. John Wheeler
Died Aug 4, 1879
Aged 90 years 11 months

Billy Joe White
Birth:
May 8, 1941
Logan,
Logan County,
West Virginia
Death:
Aug. 11, 2009
Sullivan,
Ashland County, Ohio
Burial:
Southview Cemetery,
Sullivan,
Ashland County,
Ohio

Billy Joe worked at the Ford Motor Co. in Brook Park for many years, retiring as a general foreman. A man of faith, Billy Joe had served as the pastor of the Free Will Baptist Church in Wellington since 1985. He enjoyed farming.

Philander E. Whittier
Birth:
Aug. 8, 1834
Death:
Oct. 2, 1871
Ohio
Burial:
Cheshire Cemetery
Delaware
Delaware County,
Ohio

Rev. Philander Ellis WHITTIER,

was the son of John and Loerza Whittier. He was converted in early life, and after various journeying's [lived in Wisconsin], he married in 1863, in Farmington, ME to Mary Parker Tuffs, and soon settled in Ohio. He was licensed to preach by the Richland and Licking Quarterly Meeting in May 1877, and devoted himself to the work of the ministry with good acceptance, but the end of his labors came soon after.

David Widdig
Birth:
Mar. 17, 1906
Springs,
Sciotoville,
Scioto County, Ohio
Death:
Nov. 16, 1993
Huntington, Cabell
County,West Virginia
Burial:
Memorial Burial Park,
Wheelersburg,
Scioto County,
Ohio

He was a retired electrician employed by the Goodyear Atomic Corporation and was a Free Will Baptist Minister for more than 50 years pastoring four churches.

Marion Wilburn
Birth:
1891
Death:
1951
Scioto County, Ohio
Burial:
South Webster Cemetery,
South Webster,
Scioto County, Ohio

Alvin Gardner Wilder
Birth:
Nov. 22, 1828
Chesterfield
Hampshire County,
Massachusetts
Death:
Aug. 27, 1875
Berea, Cuyahoga County, Ohio
Burial:
Beebe Town Cemetery
Beebetown, Medina County,
Ohio

Wilder died at aged 46 years. The family moved to Ohio in 1833 and ten years later Brother Wilder was converted, uniting with the Hinckley church. He was ordained Oct. 5, 1856, by a council from the Medina Q. M. His labors were chiefly with the Hinckley, Royalton, Rockport, Liverpool, and Henrietta churches, and in most of them there remained living evidences of the fruit of his labors.

Charlie Wiley
Birth:
Nov. 29, 1929
Stirrat, Logan County,
West Virginia
Death:
Dec. 8, 2010
Columbus,
Franklin County,
Ohio
Burial:
Glen Rest Memorial Estate,
Reynoldsburg,

Franklin County, Ohio

Allen Williams, Jr
Birth:
Jan. 9, 1929
Scioto County, Ohio
Death:
Mar. 26, 1996,
Ashland,
Boyd County, Kentucky
Burial:
Clapboard Cemetery,
Franklin Furnace,
Scioto County,
Ohio

He was a son of Allen Williams, Sr and Hazel Ruth Chamberlain. He was a former employee of the Williams Manufacturing Company with 25 years of service. He retired as an employee of Martin Marietta and was a Korean War veteran. He was ordained as a minister in the June, 1957 and served as a pastor of the Pine Creek, Union, Mount Hope and Germany Hollow churches.

Paul Eugene Williams
Birth:
Dec. 8, 1957
Portsmouth,
Scioto County,
Ohio
Death:
Jul. 26, 2010
Portsmouth
Scioto County, Ohio
Burial:
Bennett Cemetery,
Minford,
Scioto County,

Ohio
He was the pastor at Frederick Free Will Baptist Church. Along with Frederick Free Will Baptist Church, he served as pastor at Swauger Valley Free Will, Bloom Free Will, Tick Ridge Free Will and Harvest Chapel Church in Sciotoville. He was a bookkeeper for E.E. Blair Construction Co. in Wheelersburg, and had worked as a bookkeeper for Colonial Florists, Reynolds Bordan and Chapman Accountants in Portsmouth, and the Nancy Rae Supermarket in Wheelersburg. He was a graduate of Minford High School in the class of 1976, and he was very active in the ministry and work of the Free Will Baptist Denomination.

Joe M. Wireman
Birth:
Sep. 10, 1927
Magoffin County,
Kentucky
Death:
Burial:
Fairmont Cemetery,
Uniopolis,
Auglaize County, Ohio

The Rev. Wireman retired from Boilermakers Local 85 in 1990. He was a member of the Cridersville Church, where he was pastor in previous years and continued to minister throughout his life. He has been a faithful and active member of the church for 58 years.

Leslie Wireman
Birth:
Nov. 14, 1932
Death:
Jan. 22, 2007
Alger, Hardin County, Ohio
Burial:
Preston Cemetery, Alger,
Hardin County, Ohio

Floyd I. Wolfenbarger
Birth:
Feb. 16, 1949
Springfield,
Clark County, Ohio
Death:
May 22, 1985
Little Rock,
Pulaski County, Arkansas
Burial:
Vale Cemetery, Springfield,
Clark County, Ohio

A Free Will Baptist minister, writer and denominational leader. He attended Free Will Baptist Bible College, Oklahoma Bible College, Ohio State University and Cedarville College. Called to preach at age 12 and ordained to the ministry at age 20. He pastored in Oklahoma, Ohio and Arkansas. He was moderator of the Ohio State Association of Free Will Baptists for four years and served eight years as Ohio's General Board Member to the National Association of Free Will Baptists. Six of those years he was a member of the Executive Committee. He wrote articles printed in the *Contact* and *Ambassador Magazines*. A respected leader and minister by his peers.

Andrew Workman
Birth:
Jul. 25
Wayne County,
West Virginia,
Death:
Jun. 21
Portsmouth, Scioto County,
Ohio
Burial:
Evergreen Union Cemetery
Waverly,
Pike County
Ohio

Rev. Workman was known throughout the tri-state area of Ohio, Kentucky, and West Virginia as a Free Will Baptist evangelist and preacher. He was short in stature but tall in evangelism.

Death is the crown jewel for the Christian.

Nathaniel Wyatt
Birth:
Jan. 5, 1762
New York
Death:
Aug. 18, 1824
Norton
Delaware County
Ohio
Burial:
Wyatt Cemetery
Waldo
Marion County,Ohio

He was the son of Nathaniel Wyatt and Temperance Hubbell Wyatt.As a young man, Nathaniel Wyatt served in the Revolutionary War, in the New York Militia.

Nathaniel WYATT married Anna BRUNDIGE on October 1, 1786, in Ulster County, New York. Nathaniel and Anna Brundige WYATT started their married life in New York. From there, they migrated to Virginia. From Virginia, they settled briefly in Pickaway County, Ohio, and then settled in what was known as Marlborough Township, Delaware County, Ohio.

The Wyatt and Brundige families became known as the very first settlers in this area, upon their arrival there in February 1806.

Upon his homestead property, Nathaniel WYATT built, owned, and operated Wyatt's Tavern & Hotel, which was a two-story brick building that served an important role in the history of this area of Ohio. Wyatt's Tavern & Hotel was located near the historic Military Road.

Wyatt's Tavern & Hotel was located within the protective stockade fort walls of historic Fort Morrow, all located on Nathaniel Wyatt's homestead property. Fort Morrow had a vital role in the military history of Ohio during the War of 1812 time period.

In addition to Wyatt's Tavern & Hotel, Nathaniel WYATT owned and operated an important mill business for many years in this area of Ohio. He is also noted in Marion County history books as serving as Justice of the Peace.

From his homestead, Nathaniel WYATT donated the land for the Wyatt Family Cemetery, which is the oldest cemetery in Marion County, Ohio. This cemetery is located near the original site of Wyatt's Tavern & Hotel and the historic site of Fort Morrow.

Historically known as "Wyatt's Graveyard", the Wyatt Family Cemetery is situated on a beautiful knoll about 30 feet high on the west bank of the Olentangy River. Past veterans from the Revolutionary War, the War of 1812, and the Civil War are buried there, along with many of earliest settlers from Marion County and Delaware County, Ohio.

Nathaniel WYATT died on his homestead. The DELAWARE PATRON newspaper published in Delaware, Delaware County, Ohio, carried the news of his death in their weekly issue printed on 19 August 1824, in the following words:

"DIED ~ At Norton, last evening, Nathaniel WYATT, Esquire, an AGED and RESPECTABLE citizen."

Nathaniel Wyatt's estate sale was held later that fall on 5 November 1824 at his residence located in Marlborough Township.

In the 21 October 1824 edition of the DELAWARE PATRON newspaper, an advertisement proclaiming the news of his estate auction was advertised in this way:

"NATHANIEL WYATT's ESTATE ~ The personal property of said estate will be sold at public auction at the house of Nathaniel WYATT, deceased, in Marlborough Township, on the 5th day of November next (Year: 1824). Sale to commence at 10 o'clock on said day. Terms of sale made known at day of sale."

Nathaniel WYATT (1762 - 1824) was buried in historic Wyatt Cemetery in August 1824 where he rests today with many members of the Wyatt and Brundige families who played such a vital part in the early history and

settlement of Delaware County and Marion County, Ohio.

Rev Samuel Wyatt
Birth:
Oct. 8, 1796
Death:
Aug. 25, 1842
Burial:
Wyatt Cemetery
Waldo
Marion County
Ohio

A Freewill Baptist minister, ordained 1827, mentored by Rev. David Dudley, and affiliated with the Mt. Pleasant church.

Rev John W. Wynn
Birth:
1857
Death:
1929
South Dakota
Burial:
Camden Cemetery
Kipton
Lorain County
Ohio
Plot: Section A - 31 West

News Topic: WYNN, JOHN W.
Topic Details: Died In S. Dakota, Buried In Kipton; Brief Obituary. Date: June 27, 1929.
Source: Oberlin News
Page: 1, Col: 6

He was on the 37th session program in 1907 Central Ohio Yearly Meeting at the west Mansfield FWB Church. He preached on Friday evening on Missions.

Gilbert Lafayette Yeley
Birth:
Nov. 2, 1868
Death:
Mar. 1, 1951
Scioto County,
Ohio
Burial:

Turner Cemetery
Scioto County,
Ohio

He was an early Free Will Baptist preacher in southern Ohio and represents a name that had many other notable Free Will Baptists.

He was farmer and filled pulpits as a Free Will Baptist minister. He was a member of Bloom FWB church. He married Mary Henning in 1890. His sister Miss Bessie Yeley was a missionary.

Bessie N. Yeley
Birth:
Nov. 26, 1895
Death:
Jan. 23, 1969
Wheelersburg,
Scioto County, Ohio
Burial:
Memorial Burial Park,
Wheelersburg,
Scioto County, Ohio

She was ordained by the Porter Conference of Free Will Baptists. In 1936, at the age of 40, Bessie entered Venezuela as a missionary. In subsequent years Bessie served in Cuba under Free Will Baptist Foreign Missions. She also served under the Home Mission Board in Arizona and Texas along the Mexican border, and later in Miami to Cuban refugees. She was ordained by the Porter Conference.

John Sowers Yeley
Birth:
Feb. 11, 1874
Slocum,
Scioto County,
Ohio
Death:
Dec. 26, 1936
Scioto County,
Ohio
Burial:
Vernon Cemetery, Lyra,
Scioto County, Ohio

Rev. Yeley began his career as a minister of the gospel at age 31 and continued in the service of Free Will Baptists for 25 years. He was a brother to missionary Bessie Yeley, who at the time of his death was serving as a missionary in Venezuela but later in Panama and Cuba. Many notable Free Will Baptists came from the Yeley family in the future years.

Benjamin Franklin Zell
Birth:
August 7, 1833
Warren County, Ohio
Death:
1916
Burial:
Miami Cemetery
Corwin
Warren County,

Ohio

He was educated at Mainville Academy and Lebanon normal school. He was ordained in 1862 by Elder Cyrus Dudley, John Hisey and F. Myers. In 1856 he was married to Jane M. Phillips. In 1863 he moved to Salem, Indiana and took charge of the Salem, Ridgeville, and Bear Creek churches. The following year he returned to Ohio and assumed the pastorates of the East Liberty, Union, York, Green, and Newton churches. With these churches he labored 14 years. During that time he baptized over 600 persons.. He was on the 37th session program in 1907 Central Ohio Yearly Meeting at the west Mansfield FWB Church. He led in the Y M Covenant meeting.

Zell, Rev. B. F., son of John and Mary (Tyson) Zell, was born in Warren County, O., Aug. 7, 1833. He was educated at Mainville Academy and Lebanon Normal School. He was ordained in 1862 by Elder Cyrus Dudley, John Hisey and F. Myers. In 1856 he was married to Jane M. Phillips, and has three children. In 1863 he moved to Salem, Ind., and took charge of the Salem, Ridgeville, and Bear Creek churches. The following year he returned to Ohio, and assumed the pastorate of the East Liberty, Union, York and Newton churches. With these churches he labored fourteen years. During that time he baptized and received into the churches over six hundred persons. Three new meeting-houses were built, and one church was organized. Since then he has preached for the La Rue, Green Camp, Pleasant Grove, and Grand Prairie churches. He has served the Ohio, and the Ohio Central Y. M's as clerk, and has been three times a delegate to the General Conference. He is at present pastor of the La Rue and Grand Prairie churches.

Oklahoma

Eldie Clifton Able
Birth:
Aug. 28, 1937
Coweta,
Wagoner County, Oklahoma
Death:
Jan. 5, 2010
Tulsa,
Tulsa County, Oklahoma
Burial:
Vernon Cemetery, Coweta,
Wagoner County, Oklahoma

A retired machinist, Eldie was an active minister who enjoyed mowing, painting cement figurines, horses, reading Westerns and especially his grandchildren.

Maxi Lee Adair
Birth:
Jan. 10, 1940
El Paso,
El Paso County, Texas
Death:
Aug. 6, 2012
Muskogee, Muskogee County, Oklahoma
Burial:
Greenhill Cemetery Muskogee, Muskogee County, Oklahoma

Maxi graduated from Tahlequah High School in 1959. In 1960, he joined the United States Army and received an honorable discharged in 1963. He worked for Acme Engineering beginning in 1965 until his retirement in 2002. Maxi gave his life to God on March 14, 1969 and surrendered to preach New Year's Eve 1974. He pastored the Grovania Free Will Baptist Church, Fort Gibson Free Will Baptist Church, Hitchita Free Will Baptist Church, and the First Free Will Baptist Church in Muskogee.

Rev Casey J Adams
Birth
9 Dec 1918
Oklahoma
Death
1 Dec 1991
Oklahoma
Burial
Welty Cemetery
Welty, Okfuskee County, Oklahoma

Rev. Casey J. Adames was the son of F. M. Adams, b. ca 1881, TX, and Dora Helen ADAMS. b ca 1884, MO. When he was ordained is not known. His name is in a roll of ministers for the OK State Ass'n of Free Will Baptist Minutes, Oct. 1982. He was listed as living at Welty, OK, and his church was Bristow.
Gravesite Details PFC US ARMY WW II

Rev Delbert Akin
Birth:
Nov. 22, 1927
Pottawatomie County
Oklahoma
Death:
Nov. 16, 2014
Midwest City
Oklahoma County
Oklahoma
Burial:
Resthaven Memorial Park
Shawnee
Pottawatomie County
Oklahoma

James Delbert Akin, 86, was born to Daniel and Anna Akin in Maud, OK.

He began this ministry at the First FWB church in Tecumseh, Ok on June 10, 1951. He has pastored the following FWB Churches all of which are in Oklahoma: Tecumseh Church, 1951-1956; Ada First, 1956-1963; Norman First, 1963-1967; Spencer Road, 1967-1968; Ada First, 1968-1977; Ardmore First, 1977-1980; Westgate, Shawnee, as a missionary for First OK Association 1980-1989; Tecumseh 1989-1991; Wolf Church 1991-1993; Choctaw 1993-2004; Senior Adult Pastor at Harrah FWB Church 2004 to his death.

Akin has been active in serving his denomination while serving as a Pastor. He was Oklahoma Executive Secretary 1953-1955 on a part-time basis, a member of the State Mission Board 1955-1975, member of the National Home Mission Board 1974-1985, and a member of the Hillsdale College Board of Trustees, 1975-1985. He was on the faculty of Hillsdale College for a number of years, 1965-1989, teaching English and Speech and was Director of the Ministerial Intern Program. He was a member of the Ministers Quartet for 43 years, and United Commercial Travelers 1960-present where he served as International Secretary Treasurer for a number of years.

His service was held at Hillsdale Free Will Baptist College in Moore.

Elder William Charles Austin
Birth:
Jun., 1864
Savannah,
Hardin County, Tennessee
Death:1933
Shawnee, Pottawatomie County,
Oklahoma
Burial:
Fairview Cemetery,
Shawnee, Pottawatomie County,
Oklahoma

He was an ordained Free Will Baptist preacher, but research is needed to obtain the date he was ordained. His name is in old church records as having preached several years before statehood in 1907. He was a prominent preacher and able debater in the central part of Oklahoma, and western Arkansas. He was an acceptable orator, and a great preacher. Many were converted under his ministry, and it is unknown just how many churches he organized, but he did a good work. He was editor of a church paper, *The Pruning Hook.*

Starks Washington Baldwin
Birth:
Jun. 23, 1865
Tawamba County, Mississippi
Death:
Jan. 27, 1920
Wister,Le Flore County,
Oklahoma
Burial:
Ellis Chapel Cemetery,
Wister,Le Flore County,
Oklahoma

Rev John Henry Ballard, Sr
Birth:
May 22, 1935
Stratford
Garvin County
Oklahoma
Death:
Jun. 24, 2013
Norman
Cleveland County
Oklahoma
Burial:
McGee Cemetery
Stratford
Garvin County
Oklahoma

John was born OK to Leslie and Lucy (Ernest) Ballard. He was raised and attended school in Stratford, graduating about 1953. John married Margaret Thompson on April 15, 1954 in Stratford. He continued his education at Hillsdale Freewill Baptist College in Moore. They made their home in the area in 1973. John was a minister and pastored many churches.

He was pastor and a member of the Lexington Free Will Baptist Church at the time of his death. He preached his last sermon a week or so before his death.

He enjoyed fishing, mowing, eating, attending and singing at revivals, and spending time with his family.

Jerry Cleo Banks
Birth:
Aug. 3, 1948
Tulsa,
Tulsa County, Oklahoma
Death:
Jan. 6, 2005
Oklahoma
Burial:
Moore Cemetery,
Moore,
Cleveland County
Oklahoma

Jerry served as a missionary in Japan for 19 years and a pastor in Colquitt, Georgia, and Cushing, Oklahoma. He was also an instructor at Hillsdale FWB College as is his wife Dr. Janice Banks. He also was serving as pastor of Kingsview FWB Church, So. OKC, when he was tragically killed in an auto accident

Larry Nolen Barnhardt
Birth
14 Feb 1940
Helena,
Phillips County,
Arkansas
Death
28 Dec 2012
Tulsa, Tulsa County,
Oklahoma
Burial
Fort Gibson National Cemetery
Fort Gibson, Muskogee County,
Oklahoma,
Plot Sec. 24, Site 597

Larry Nolen Barnhardt, 62, to Nolen Edward and Ruby Evelyn (Gasaway) Barnhardt. He was both a mechanic and plumber.

Alford Barnhill
Birth:
Jan. 19, 1810
Tennessee
Death:
Mar. 3, 1899
Arpelar, Pittsburg County,
Oklahoma
Burial:
White Chimney Cemetery,
Stuart,
Pittsburg County Oklahoma

He was ordained as Free Will Baptist preacher, but unknown when and where. He came into Indian Territory, in what is now Oklahoma, where these pioneer ministers preached and organized churches for the settlers. When several churches were organized, they met at Nubbin Ridge school house, near Spiro, Choctaw Nation, Sept. 1, 1894, and formed the Territorial Association of Free Will Baptists. Eld. A. Barnhill, was elected the first moderator, Eld. O.J. Taylor, Ass't Moderator, and Eld. I.W. Graham, clerk. Eld. A. Barnhill's name appears in old Territorial marriage records of those he performed.

John Barnes
Birth:
Jul. 19, 1917
Cherokee County, Oklahoma
Death:
Dec. 3, 2014
Muskogee
Muskogee County, Oklahoma
Burial:
White Oak Cemetery
Qualls, Cherokee County
Oklahoma

John Barnes, 97, of Gore, was a Free Will Baptist minister per church records. And was bi-vocational working in construction.

Rev Pleasant A Barton, Jr
Birth:
Jan. 5, 1940
Sulphur, Oklahoma
Death:
Mar. 4, 2010
Burial:
Oaklawn Cemetery
Sulphur, Murray County,
Oklahoma

Rev. Pleasant A. Barton, Jr., our beloved Husband, Daddy and Papa passed away on Thursday, March 4, 2010, surrounded by his family as he crossed over into Heaven's Gates. He exemplified the true definition of a Champion and valiant warrior, as he fought Parkinson's disease for the last fifteen years of his life.

Junior was born to P. A. (Buck) Barton and Goldie Bulla Barton. He and his high school sweetheart, Lawana Sue Fisher, were married November 2, 1957, at Gainesville, Texas. Junior and Sue graduated from Sulphur High School in 1958.

For over 24 years, he had been a faithful employee of the Oklahoma Vending Company. He had served in the Oklahoma National Guard and the 4002 Army Reserve Service Unit. The most important thing in his life was to know and serve his personal Savior, Jesus Christ. Of Free Will Baptist faith, he had served as pastor of several churches around the Ardmore area. Prior to recently moving to Ardmore.

John E. Bean
Birth:
1876
Texas
Death:
May, 1961
Edmond,
Oklahoma County, Oklahoma
Burial:
Sunny Lane Cemetery, Del City,
Oklahoma County, Oklahoma

He was an ordained Free Will Baptist minister. His brother, Will L. Bean, was also a preacher. In Oklahoma during the 1920's through 1950's. Rev. Bean was very active, and known as an outstanding evangelist. He was chosen to preach in the 1932 and 1934 Oklahoma FWB State Associations. He authored the book, *"What Would the World Be Without the Bible,"* a book that defends the Biblical record in various aspects of its historical statements. He is also author of a number of poems based on Bible subjects, and being a natural elocutionist, he often recited from memory upon request.

Leonard Bean
Birth:
1898
Death:
1996
Burial:
Wetumka Cemetery
Wetumka
Hughes County
Oklahoma

An ordained Free Will Bapt. minister and pastor. He pastored churches in Hughes County, and surrounding areas.

Rev Dalton D. Beene
Birth
4 Sep 1914
Death
10 Oct 2000
Burial
Bixby Cemetery
Bixby, Tulsa County,
Oklahoma

Eugene Benson
Birth:
Feb. 3, 1933
Death:
Aug. 27, 2004
Fort Smith
Sebastian County
Arkansas
Burial:
Howe Cemetery
Howe
Le Flore County
Oklahoma

Minister and pastor for many years. Korean War Navy Veteran.

Ransom "Rance" Bess
Birth:
Apr. 22, 1844
Grenada,
Grenada County, Mississippi
Death:
Aug. 5, 1932
Pontotoc County, Oklahoma
Burial:
Egypt Cemetery, Ada,
Pontotoc County, Oklahoma
Early pioneer minister of the Chickasaw Nation (Pontotoc Co. OK). He was well-liked and esteemed and ministered to many. Civil War Veteran Pvt. Co. F, 18th TX Ochiltree's Inf. CSA

Paskel Dale Bevan
Birth:
Apr. 15, 1946
Death:
Sep. 3, 2010
Burial:
Friends Church Cemetery,
Cromwell,
Seminole County Oklahoma

Paskel was the owner and operator of Seminole Sheet Metal for many years. He was also a longtime minister of the Friends Free Will Baptist Church of Seminole County. Paskel also enjoyed reading his Bible and helping build missionary churches.

Rev Roy Melvin Bingham
Birth:
Dec. 21, 1900
Drynob
Laclede County, Missouri
Death:
Nov. 15, 1971
Tulsa
Tulsa County, Oklahoma
Burial:
Rose Hill Memorial Park , Tulsa
Tulsa County, Oklahoma
Plot: Section Memories (16) L-678
#3

He was the son of William and Clara Bell (Ferguson) BINGHAM and married Opal Gregory, on Sept. 16, 1917, in Laclede Co. MO. He and his wife had three children. His family was in Missouri in the 1920 census, but before 1930, they had moved to the Tulsa area, he as a bi-vocational minister, and was working as a "steel worker" to support his family.
Family history reports he began preaching at age 16; after he moved to Oklahoma, he pastored churches, held revivals, and was established by reputation and work, so that they sent him as a delegate from the Cooperative Association of Free Will Baptist from OK, to the organizational meeting of the National Association of the FWB, at Cofer's Chapel Church, Nashville, TN. in 1935.
He was active, productive, and was loved and respected among his brethren.

W. M. Bingham
Birth:
Feb. 26, 1871
Death:
Mar. 11, 1947
Burial:
Sub-Station Cemetery,
Freedom Hill,
Creek County, Oklahoma

Kenneth Brandon
Birth:
Sep. 6, 1921,
Death:
Jan. 29, 2008
Talihina, Le Flore County,
Oklahoma
Burial:
Macedonia Cemetery,
Pocola,
Le Flore County, Oklahoma

Rev. Brandon was a veteran of World War II, where he served in the Marine Corps, receiving a Purple Heart for wounds received during the Bougainville Island campaign. He started and pastored many Freewill Baptist Churches in his lifetime. He never had much in the way of material wealth; he gave everything he had to the less fortunate.

If You Spend All Your Time Worrying About Dying, Living Isn't Going To Be Much Fun.

Rev Joe Blair
Birth:
Nov. 26, 1934
Purcell
McClain County,
Oklahoma
Death:
Jul. 25, 1998
Oklahoma City
Oklahoma County
Oklahoma
Burial:
Willow View Cemetery
Cleveland County,
Oklahoma

The Rev. Joe Blair answered the call to preach at age fifteen, and began pastoring at age sixteen. He invested 50 years of ministry in Okla. and Calif. Free Will Baptist churches. He organized one church in Calif. and pastored four. He pastored seven OK churches. His final pastorate at Southwest FWB Church, OK, lasted 20 yrs.
The congregation voted him Pastor Emeritus title. The church had planned an Aug. 30th celebration to honor his 50 years in the ministry.
Joe stayed active in district, state, and national works. He served 16 yrs. as moderator of Oklahoma District First Oklahoma Association.
Funeral services were conducted by Revs. Wade T. Jernigan, and Jack Richey.

Addie Fay Green Bookout
Birth:
Sep. 4, 1911
Drumright
Creek County
Oklahoma
Death:
May 28, 1991
Blackwell
Kay County
Oklahoma
Burial:
Blackwell Cemetery
Blackwell
Kay County
Oklahoma

Born to Russell & Mabel Green.Lived in Drumright,Ok-- Wellington, Ks & Blackwell, Ok, Member Free Will Baptist Church.Life time Bible Teacher. Mother of B.WayneBookout-- Jackie D. Bookout & Sharon F. (Bookout) Steelmon.. Spouse:
Lester Dee Bookout (1909 - 1996)

William "Bill" Bratcher
Birth:
Oct. 16, 1916
Garvin County, Oklahoma
Death:
Mar. 31, 2012
Oklahoma
Burial:
McGee Cemetery, Stratford,
Garvin County, Oklahoma

The Ada Newspaper: April 3, 2012 Stratford —Mr. Bratcher was ordained in the Free Will Baptist church in the late 1940's, in Pontotoc Co. OK. He preached and ministered to churches throughout the area.

Ernest E. Bristow
Birth:
Aug. 31, 1894
Tecumseh,
Pottawatomie County, Oklahoma
Death:
Nov. 26, 1941
Asher, Pottawatomie County,
Oklahoma
Burial:
Wanette Cemetery, Wanette,
Pottawatomie County, Oklahoma

After he finished college, he taught school in many small oil towns in south central Okla. He was also an ordained minister, and music instructor, and often led the singing in many churches. He taught "singing schools" in communities all over that area. Related to teaching school, his name is found in the old 1920's Ada Weekly newspaper with items such as, "E.E. Bristow, Stratford, teacher, for 8 terms; then "Prof. Bristow with his able corps of teachers attended teachers meeting Thursday, Friday and Saturday." He had left Oklahoma to find work in California due to hardships following dustbowl. He worked one day there, had a heart attack and returned to Oklahoma where he died a few months later. In the book, *"History of Oklahoma Free Will Baptist State Association, 100 Years, 1908-2008"*, pub. 2008, it records that in 1926, "Eld. E. E. Bristow, was Rep. from Center to the State Ass'n of FWB, and in the 1932 annual state Association, he was elected clerk of that organization.

You Are Home At Last!

Rev Joseph H. Brown
Birth:
1853
Illinois
Death:
1924
Burial:
Fairlawn Cemetery
Oklahoma City
Oklahoma County, Oklahoma

Rev. J.H. Brown, is named in an early list of ministers, who was in the early organization of the Territorial Association of Free Will Baptist churches, in 1894, near Spiro, OK."

Rev Johnny Dean Bullard, Sr
Birth
10 Feb 1936
Beggs, Okmulgee County, Oklahoma
Death
12 Sep 2017
Ardmore, Carter County, Oklahoma
Burial
Fort Gibson National Cemetery
Fort Gibson,
Muskogee County, Oklahoma
Plot Sec. 23A, Site 40

Johnny Dean Bullard Sr., in the Ardmore Veterans Center in Ardmore, Oklahoma. Johnny was born the son of Earl and Ethel Marie (Schultzy) Bullard. He served in the United States Army from 1955 to 1958. He and Mary were married at Muskogee, Oklahoma on March 2 1957. He was ordained as a Free Will Baptist minister in 1970 and served churches in Tulsa, Cushing Rock Chapel, Missouri, Harmony, Missouri, Warren Read More Arkansas and helped establish the Hew Hope Free Will Baptist Church in Lone Grove, Oklahoma.

He was a bee keeper, enjoyed hunting, gardening and especially enjoyed working with the youth in church. Services in the New Hope Free Will Baptist Church at Lone Grove, Oklahoma.

Rev William David Burgess
Birth
27 Sep 1948
Poteau,
Le Flore County, Oklahoma,
Death
3 Oct 2017
Muskogee,
Muskogee County, Oklahoma,
Burial
Vaughn Memorial Cemetery
Gilmore,
Le Flore County, Oklahoma,

William David Burgess, 69, of Poteau, OK in Muskogee, OK. Bill was born to Chester Sylvester & Wana Sue (Chester) Burgess. Bill was a Free Will Baptist Pastor, a handyman, maintenance man & case manager. He had a Master's Degree and was a veteran of the US Navy. He married Naoma Fostine Scroggins on May 24, 1975. Bill enjoyed many things which include riding motorcycles on nice days with his wife and sons. He loved spending time with his grandchildren. Playing his guitar and singing were his favorites. He enjoyed skiing in Tahoe with his family; little things like grilling, watching his fireplace gleaming on cold winter days. Bill once said if you didn't pay me to preach; I'd pay you to let me. Bill loved to preach; loved going to church; and most of all Bill loved the Lord. He was preceded in death by his dad;

grandson, William David Burgess III, sister in law, Laura M. Burgess, & many other family members.

Survivors include his wife of 42 years, Fostine of the home; sons & daughters in law, William David II & Bobbie Burgess, Nathan Lee & Casandra Burgess, Titus Ray & Tia Burgess; mother, Wana Sue Burgess Dobbins all of Poteau, OK; brothers, Chester Dale Burgess of Oakland, CA; sister & brother in law, Deborah Sue (Burgess) & Larry G. Wilson of Reno, NV; grandchildren, Nathan Lee Burgess II, Hailey Alexis Burgess, Charity Naomi (Lynn) Burgess, Tristen, Chyenne & Brayden Wade Burgess, Ashley & Jose Rivera of Poteau; great granddaughter, Kaydence Rayne Rivera; other relatives, loved ones and friends. Services at Evans Chapel of Memories, Poteau, OK with Rev. Jim Cook officiating.

Rev Connie Dearl Cariker
Birth:
Nov. 15, 1935
Hoyt
Haskell County, Oklahoma
Death:
Feb. 21, 2016
Jenks
Tulsa County, Oklahoma
Burial:
Hoyt Cemetery
Hoyt
Haskell County, Oklahoma

Connie Dearl Cariker passed from this life on February 21, 2016, at his home in Jenks, Oklahoma. Connie Was born, the third of sixteen children, to Champ Clark Cariker and Joy Myree (Cleveland) Cariker at Hoyt, Oklahoma. He grew up in the Hoyt area and attended school at Hoyt School, Stigler High School, and Oklahoma Bible College.

Connie married Wanda Glo Gideon, on November 2, 1954, in Hoyt, Oklahoma. They moved to West Texas, where he worked in the West Texas Oil Fields. Upon moving to Tulsa, Oklahoma in 1956, He worked at Sunray DX Refinery. During his time at DX, Connie answered God's Call to preach. Soon after, in January of 1962, he became the full time pastor of the West Tulsa Free Will Baptist Church. He remained at the church as pastor for 21 years, during which time he served on the National Free Will Baptist Sunday School Board. In February of 1983, Connie took a position with the National Home Mission Department of the National Association of Free Will Baptists in Nashville, Tennessee, where he pioneered church growth and evangelism programs, and conducted church growth and evangelism conferences across the U.S. In January of 1986 Connie took the position of Executive Director of Oklahoma Free Will Baptists in Moore, Oklahoma. He left this position in 1994 to return to the pastorate of West Tulsa Free Will Baptist Church. He pastored there until his retirement from full time ministry in January, 2004. During his early retirement he remained active in ministry by preaching many revival services across the denomination.

Connie was an avid sports fan, especially of the St. Louis Cardinals. He loved people and loved to share the Gospel of Jesus Christ. He was an encourager to all and loved by many.

Services at West Tulsa Free Will Baptist Church, Tulsa, OK. Rev. Russell Payne and Rev. Dennis Cariker officiated

Edna Hunt Buckelew
Birth:
1909
Death:
1985
Burial:
McGee Cemetery,
Stratford,
Garvin County, Oklahoma

She was a Free Will Baptist minister in the early part of Center Association, OK.

Robert William Carter
Birth:
Apr. 30, 1916
Ola, Yell County, Arkansas
Death:
Sep. 5, 2001
Broken Arrow,
Tulsa County, Oklahoma
Burial:
Park Grove Cemetery,
Broken Arrow,
Tulsa County, Oklahoma

A Free Will Baptist minister, Rev. Carter was licensed in 1957 and ordained in 1958. He pastored churches in California, Arkansas, Missouri and Oklahoma.

Max Campbell
Birth:
Nov. 6, 1929
Wichita
Sedgwick County
Kansas
Death:
Mar. 29, 2017
Sperry
Tulsa County
Oklahoma
Burial:
Floral Haven Memorial Gardens
Broken Arrow
Tulsa County
Oklahoma

He was the long time pastor of the Dawson FWB Church in Tulsa. He loved music, wrote songs and played as variety of instruments. Max Campbell, 87, passed away in Sperry, Oklahoma.

Rev James Amos Caskey
Birth
10 Nov 1853
Liberty,
DeKalb County,
Tennessee
Death
22 Jul 1930
Box, Cleveland County,
Oklahoma

**Burial
Box Cemetery
Cleveland County,
Oklahoma**

**Rev. James A. Caskey's name appears in a list of ministers in 1917 Minutes of the Cooperative General Association of Free Will Baptists, when convened at Tecumseh, OK.
Unknown when and where he was ordained, but he apparently was active as his name shows up in these old records.**

James Nathaniel Caton

Birth:
Oct. 14, 1862
Cooper County, Missouri
Death:
May 18, 1953
Ada, Pontotoc County, Oklahoma
Burial:
Oakman Cemetery,
Oakman,
Pontotoc County,
Oklahoma

Old Brother" Caton, as he is known to his innumerable friends, was born in Missouri where he grew to young manhood, and remembered back as he tells of the time when the "Bluecoats," part of Custer's army, passed through his town on their way to the badlands of South Dakota. He left his home state of Missouri in 1886 for Texas. He was a farmer, made a few crops in Texas, moved to Oakland, Indian Territory, and made a crop, then back to Texas and in 1895, he moved to a place near Allen and lived in Pontotoc County. Definitely an Ada pioneer. Rev. Caton, a Free Will Baptist preacher since 1902, has probably married and buried as many people in the county as any other preacher. Even at 85, he still performed these ministerial duties. He has pastored at nearly every small community in the northern part of the county. His first pastorate was at Sikes school, where Atwood now stands. Other places where he

pastored are Black Rock, Happyland, Cedar Grove, Yeager, Center, Culley west of Sasakwa, Pecan Grove, Stedman, McCalls Chapel, and Big Springs south of Wewoka. He was pastor of the Oakman church, his home community, for 19 years. At age 84, he was recalled as pastor with an assistant to take his place if he was unable to appear. Preaching in the "good old way," Caton would have four or five churches at the same time preaching in them only about once a month. He would arrive on Saturday in the community where he was pastor and hold one service that day, another on Sunday morning, another Sunday evening. During the summer session, he would hold revival meetings from two to five weeks long in each community he pastored.

Marion L. Caton

Birth:
Aug. 12, 1898
Pontotoc County, Oklahoma
Death:
Sep., 1965
Oklahoma City,
Oklahoma County, Oklahoma
Burial:
Arlington Memory Gardens,
Oklahoma City,
Oklahoma County,
Oklahoma

He grew up around Oakman, Pontotoc Co. Oklahoma attending schools there. He was an ordained Free Will Baptist minister and pastor.

James Cearley

Birth:
Jul. 26, 1921
Death:
Sep. 19, 1996
Burial:
Tecumseh Cemetery, Tecumseh,
Pottawatomie County Oklahoma

He was a Free Will Baptist minister and a member of the US Navy during WW II.

James B. Chism

Birth:
May 12, 1925
Tupelo, Mississippi
Death:
Sep. 9, 2007
Tulsa, Oklahoma
Burial:
Floral Haven Memorial Gardens,
Broken Arrow,
Tulsa County, Oklahoma,
Plot: Sermon on the Mount
Garden

He grew up in East Tupelo where he played football and the clarinet in the band. After graduation he became a medic in the United States Army during World War II. After his discharge he married Imogene Martin on October 15, 1946. They both graduated from

Bob Jones University in Greenville, S. C. where he earned a Master's Degree in Church History in 1952. He became the Minister of the Horse Branch Free Will Baptist Church in Turbeville, South Carolina. Later the First Free Will Baptist Church in Newport News, Virginia. In 1967 he moved his family to Tulsa to become the pastor of the New Home Free Will Baptist Church where he was pastor until 1988 where he retired.

He founded the greater Tulsa the senior's organization OASIS and was very active on the Oklahoma State Mission Board starting churches across the state. They served over six decades in the ministry.

Claude C. Chisum
Birth:
Mar. 25, 1894
Texas
Death:
Jun. 6, 1962
Hughes County, Oklahoma
Burial:
Non Cemetery,
Non, Hughes County,
Oklahoma

He served in the Infantry WW I, where he was exposed to mustard gas which caused him health problems thereafter. He lived in the Non community where he served the FWB church as a deacon for many years. He then was ordained as a minister of the gospel and pastored churches in the area, among them; Crossroads, Calvin, and others, and preached wherever he was needed. He attended the Quarterly and State Association meetings.

William M. Coggins
Birth:
April 27, 1848
Texas
Death:
1946
Oklahoma
Burial:
McGee Cemetery,
Stratford,Garvin County,
Oklahoma

W. M. Coggins came to Indian Territory, probably after 1900, from Wise Co. Texas, upon request by a letter from Eld. Tom J. Townsend, an early arriver to the Indian Territory, asking him to come and help form some four churches into an association and preach for them.

By 1904, he was preaching in the area churches from which the Center Association was formed in 1893 of Chickasaw Nation. He was elected to be moderator of this Center Association in 1906, following Rev. Mark Harris's move to Arkansas. He continued in this position for years, in most every session until his late retirement. He was pastor of several churches throughout the years, that included Blanchard in McClain Co., and his name appears in many old church records as having preached or pastored there.

He was the elected delegate by this group to represent them in the Southwestern Association of Free Will Baptists, which met Nov. 1906

at Decatur, Texas. He was always in the forefront of leadership in the support of the Tecumseh FWB College which had been started in 1917. At the August 1946 session, it was reported that "our old beloved moderator has passed away;" then it was voted "for the Association to place a monument at his grave."

Judge James Thomas Colleps
Birth
29 Oct 1852
Naples, Scott County,
Illinois
Death
19 Jan 1928
Alex, Grady County, Oklahoma
Burial
Alex Cemetery
Alex, Grady County, Oklahoma
Plot Sec. 2S

Tribune, Alex, Grady Co., OK, January 27, 1927: "Another Pioneer Citizen Passes to His Reward - One by one the old settlers who hewed this great state into its present civilization, are passing off the state of action and to their reward beyond this vale of tears. Last Wednesday afternoon one of these old pioneers was laid to rest at Alex, after a long life in which he did his part in leaving to the present generation and those to follow a grand heritage; a country flowing with wealth and rich in traditions such as no other state can boast. J. T. Colleps was born at Naples, Illinois, Oct. 29, 1853. At the age of 20 he was united in marriage to Miss Rosanna Turner. To this union were born six sons and one daughter, three of whom, Charles I. of Beaumont, Texas, Ben H. of Waxahatchie, Texas, and Mrs. W. A. Hearron of Trousdale, Okla., survive him. Soon after his marriage they moved to western Texas, where he was a cowboy and ranch boss for many years, and later moved to Denton, Texas. He came to Oklahoma when this country was the Indian Territory, where he had since made his home. He was a citizen of this section of the state when Alex was born and had been connected with the law enforcement department of the town and county in some capacity up to the time of his death. He was converted at an early age, and for many years was a Methodist preacher. Later he became a Free Will Baptist, in which faith he died. Judge Colleps, as he was commonly called, being a Justice of Peace , perhaps performed more marriage ceremonies than any justice in the county, scarcely a week passing that he was not called upon to minister in this capacity. He was small of statue but noted for his bravery. He went to his grave carrying bullets received in an encounter with a bandit near Alex several years ago. After the death of his first wife, he was married in 1892 to Mrs. Caroline Smith at Grandbury, Texas and soon after returned to Oklahoma. Seldom a day passed that he was not upon the street to greet his friends with a smile, and while he had not been well of late, he would make his regular trips to town until stricken with paralysis on Saturday, and passed away early Wednesday morning, Jan. 28, 1928. The funeral services were held at the Methodist Church Wednesday afternoon at 3:3 o'clock, conducted by the pastor, Rev. H. P. Robertson, in the presence of a large number of relatives and friends and his body laid to rest in the Morris cemetery southeast of Alex. He is survived by his aged wife, two sons, one daughter and several grand-children.

J.T. Colleps was credited with helping to begin the Hawkins Free Will Bapt. Church, north of Alex, and preached there as early as 1908. He possibly knew the Grady Co. Sheriff, DeArthur Wilson, also affiliated there. Old church records are source.

Note: He was Will Hearon's Father-in-Law and Grandfather of Clarence Hearon.

If You Spend All Your Time Worrying About Dying, Living Isn't Going To Be Much Fun.

Albert Lee Collier
Birth:
Jul. 25, 1918
Death:
Mar. 19, 2008
Burial:
Highland Cemetery,
Okemah,
Okfuskee County,
Oklahoma

He spent the majority of his life in and around the Okemah area. At the time of his death Albert was a member of the Okemah Free Will Baptist Church. He was ordained as a deacon in the Schoolton Free Will Baptist Church west of Okemah, April 10, 1949, and was ordained as a Free Will Baptist minister on May 20, 1951. He received a certificate of award from the Oklahoma Bible College on May 15, 1961. He helped organize Schoolton Free Will Baptist Church. He preached his second sermon after the organization of the church that Saturday on Schoolton corner. He preached his third sermon at Pleasant Oak School. His first pastorate was at the Schoolton Free Will Baptist Church. He also pastored Free Will Baptist Churches at Hannah, Sunnylane in Del City, Wewoka, Prague, Henryetta, Calvin, and Faith Free Will Baptist Church in Holdenville. He built or remodeled every place he pastored. He built an educational wing a new sanctuary at Sunnylane, a completely new facility at Wewoka, remodeled the facility at Prague and totally remodeled the Henryetta church. Brother Collier was instrumental in founding of the Okemah Free Will Baptist Church and labored in the construction of the facility under the pastorate of Brother Frank Young. The north wing of the church was dedicated in his honor. He served on the Oklahoma State Church Training Board, Oklahoma State Mission Board, and moderator of many associations while serving on several district boards. He celebrated 50 years of ministry on December 30, 2001. Records show that during his ministry he preached 170 funerals, 24 weddings, 56 revivals.

James Kemper "Jim" Combs
Birth
13 Jan 1938
Crab Orchard, Raleigh
County,
West Virginia
Death
7 Fe
b 2017
Moore,
Cleveland County,
Oklahoma
Burial
Moore Cemetery Moore,
Cleveland County,
Oklahoma
Plot Phase II, Sec D

James Kemper Combs, 79, was born in their family home In Crab Orchard, WV, and passed from this life on to glory at at his home in Moore, Oklahoma. James (Jim) was born the third of fifteen children, to Rev. William Cecil Combs and Norma Elizabeth (Ball) Combs, in Crab Orchard, West Virginia. He grew up in the Crab Orchard area and after high school joined the United States Navy and served on the USS Everglades. While on ship, at 19, he determined to read more surrender his life to Christ and later to the ministry.

Jim enrolled at Welch College (FWBBC) in Nashville, Tennessee, and while there accepted the call of God to a ministry with International Free Will Baptist Missions. In college, Jim met Shirley Alberta Roberts, a preacher's daughter from Oklahoma who was also a mission's candidate. They married and left for Brazil in 1964, and left Brazil from their last residence there in 2008.

This was an especially blessed time in his life as they raised their three Brazilian born children who helped in the ministry. In Brazil he was a church planter, mentor, spiritual shepherd, and friend to many. He was a professor at seminaries, member of the Brazil FWB Field Council and also served as their treasurer and director. He led the Brazilian church to found the Lar Nova Vida Children's Home, in Araras. In Brazil he used his great love for sports (soccer!), fishing, hunting, and chess to meet folks and make friends. His used his gifts through "Friendship Evangelism." He loved the people God had given him.

In the United States he served churches in Tennessee, Ohio, and OK. He served at Randall University (Hillsdale), and American Christian College in OK. He was chaplain at Lexington State Prison, in OK. One of his favorite jobs was working with handicapped students on school buses in Franklin, Ohio and in Moore, OK. He was an avid reader and received his Master's Degree from Tulsa University, in OK. He entertained his friends and family with his spontaneous songs and jokes about every subject. He was also a member of the Moore Community JOY CHOIR.

Jim was preceded in death by his parents, Rev. William Cecil Combs and Norma Elizabeth (Ball) Combs and three siblings: Sharon R. Combs, John C. Combs, and Mark D. Combs, Sr. Also by his sisters-in-law Charlotte Berry Combs and Lisa Belcher Combs Martin, and his brothers-in-law Donald Ray Basham, and Kenneth L. Bibb.

Jim is survived by his wife of 53 years, Shirley Roberts Combs of the home; and three children: his son Kemper Jonathan Combs of Moore, Oklahoma. His daughter Cindy Weinette and son-in-law Will Anderson of Moore, OK.; his daughter and son-in-law Tania Marita and Rodrigo Ferreira of OKC; his foster son and wife, Rev. Marco Antonio Pena and wife Claudiana and children. The proud grandfather of six; Jonathan Kemper, Julia Marita, and David William De Aquino of Moore, OK; and Daniel, Bianca, and Isabela Ferreira of Oklahoma City; foster grandchildren, Vitoria, Jesse, Suzana, and Ana Carolina, of Brazil.

His surviving sisters and their spouses are: Nancy and Rev. Ed Cook of Ashland, KY; Betty Basham of Jumping Branch, WV; Norma Bibb of Fredericksburg, TX; Mary and Wayne Sisk of Sophia, WV; and Judy and Rev. Jim Puckett of Norman, OK. He is also survived by six brothers and their spouses: Billy and Jackie Combs of Seymour, TN; Rev. Bob Combs of Jumping Branch, WV; David Combs of Coal City, WV; Donnie Combs of Rainsville, AL; Greg and Vicki Combs of Donaldsonville, GA; and Scott and Carla Combs of Brandywine, WV. In addition, he has a host of nieces and nephews.

A funeral service was held at the Randall University (Hillside College), Moore, OK.

Leonard Crowder
Birth:
Apr. 12, 1917
Death:
Nov. 19, 2009
Barling,
Sebastian County,
Arkansas,
Burial:
Stigler Cemetery,
Stigler, Haskell County,
Oklahoma,

He was a Free Will Baptist Minister and a member of the Bethlehem Free Will Baptist Church of Van Buren, Arkansas.. He served in many churches in the area over the years but served as Pastor of the Walnut Street Free Will Baptist Church for over 30 years. He served in the Civil Conservation Corp and was an active member of the Ministerial Alliance of Fort Smith for many years.

Marvin P Dalton
Birth:
Mar. 9, 1906
Arkansas
Death:
Nov. 28, 1987
Tulsa County, Oklahoma
Burial:
Floral Haven Memorial Gardens,
Broken Arrow,
Tulsa County, Oklahoma

Well-known gospel song writer who was the son of William Henry Dalton and Effie (Thomas) Dalton. who were both Free Will Baptist preachers in Arkansas and Oklahoma. Marvin, a noted and published song writer, with *"Looking for a City"*, *"When Jesus Passed By"*, and *"O' What a Saviour"* being the most popular of his songs. He attend Free Will Baptist Bible College in the late 40's. He directed music at the First Free Will Baptist Church in Tulsa under John West, but at the time of his passing was a member of the Assembly of God which had been the denomination of his wife.

Stephen Andrew Dame
Birth:
Feb. 9, 1847
Jasper, Marion County,
Tennessee
Death
Apr. 3, 1927
Burial:
Center Cemetery, Center,
Pontotoc County, Oklahoma,
Plot: Dame Family
(near entrance)

As a young boy, Stephen brought food and supplies to his older brother who was fighting in the Civil War. They moved from Jasper to Randolph County, Arkansas, in about 1878 or 1880. They lived in a tiny community known both as Water Valley and DeMun. Here, they built a log cabin. and farmed in Randolph County. Stephen was called to preach the Gospel at a young age. He could not read or write, but his wife could. She would read him passages from the Bible and he learned to read it. The Bible was the only thing he ever learned to read. He was a Freewill Baptist preacher. A man of great stature, Stephen stood 6'4" and was very slim. The obituary in the Ada Evening News (Ada, OK), read:"Rev. S. A. Dame, aged 82, died Sunday at 1 o'clock at his home at Center. Funeral services were set for this afternoon. Internment in Center cemetery. "Mr. Dame was a pioneer Freewill Baptist minister who had spent many years of his life in this country, doing his part in reclaiming it and making it a better place for later comers. He was highly respected by all who knew him."

William David "Voss" Dame
Birth:
Dec. 31, 1881
Death:
Jul. 23, 1957
Burial:
Center Cemetery, Center,
Pontotoc County, Oklahoma

George S Davidson
Birth:
Jan. 17, 1890
Sunset, Texas
Death:
Oct. 4, 1966
Muskogee, Ok
Burial:
Greenlawn Cemetery
Checotah
McIntosh County,Oklahoma

Davidson was a veteran of World War One and a retired Free Will Baptist minister and U.S. Naval Ammunition Depot employee at McAlester. Funeral services with Rev. McCage officiating.

William Edward Dearmore

Birth:
May 25, 1881
Charleston, Arkansas
Death:
Dec. 12, 1945
Wanette,
Pottawatomie County, Oklahoma
Burial:
Wanette Cemetery, Wanette,
Pottawatomie County, Oklahoma

Rev. William Edward Dearmore was active in the first session of the Texas State Association of Free Will Baptists, which met at Bradley, Texas, October 8-9, 1915. We glean from the minutes of that meeting, written in Dearmore's own beautiful handwriting, several pieces of information about him. He was chosen to preach the "introductory sermon" at the meeting. The introductory sermon was the initial sermon preached at meetings in those days. They were what we today might call a keynote sermon or keynote address. This was a very distinct honor and indicates something of the high esteem in which Dearmore was held by his fellow Texas ministers. He was until the association could be organized, and then was elected permanent clerk. In addition, he was elected treasurer. Furthermore, he was appointed to serve with J. J. Tatum and C. C. Wheeler on a committee to draft a constitution for the fledgling association.

With numerous other ministers present, and with him being appointed and/or elected to so many positions of great responsibility at the first session of the association, we learn something of the abilities with which he was gifted. At the time Dearmore lived in Boyd, Texas. Boyd is on State Highway 114 seven miles south of Decatur in southern Wise County.

At the second session of the Texas State Association, held in January of 1917, Dearmore was not present. He had made, or was preparing to make, a move to Oklahoma to be involved in the first year of operation of Tecumseh College. It seems that he took on more and larger responsibilities of ministry in Oklahoma. In addition to his years of service to Tecumseh College, where he served on the teaching faculty, he served a number of churches as pastor in Oklahoma, such as the Box Church and the Wolf Church. He served as moderator of the Oklahoma State Association a number of years: 1932, 1936-1939. He was also the owner of an insurance agency.

In 1935 he served as a delegate to the organizational meeting of the National Association of Free Will Baptists in Nashville, Tennessee. He was active in several sessions of the National Association thereafter. The Oklahoma State Association paid tribute to him in 1945 as a pioneer Free Will Baptist minister.

He was married to Ada Ann Baze on December 28, 1900, and they had seven children: William Henry (April 21, 1902 - April 29, 1909; Ethel Idel (October 30, 1903 - July 2, 2975; Grace Lilly, January 11, 1910-December 6, 1992; James, August 30, 1914 - September 26, 1914; Floydette E. April 3, 1917 - September 26, 2002; Joy Yvonne, August 9, 1921 - January 1985; and Mildred Marie, July 4, 1923 - August 15, 1925).

His wife Ada was a teacher at Tecumseh College and served briefly as president of the school. She died on November 23, 1936, in Wanette. His World War II draft registration lists his wife as Mrs. Nora Dearmore. Apparently he had remarried after the death of Ada. His tombstone indicates that he was a Mason.

Austin R. Deaton, Sr

Birth:
Sep. 1, 1903
Death:
Sep. 17, 1967
Burial:
Rosedale Cemetery
Ada
Pontotoc County
Oklahoma, USA
Plot: N-112-7-4

Othel Thomas Dixon

Birth:
Jun. 20, 1919
Hector, Pope County, Arkansas
Death:
Oct. 27, 2007
Claremore,
Rogers County, Oklahoma
Burial:
Greenlawn Cemetery, Checotah,
McIntosh County, Oklahoma

He was the first Dixon to achieve outstanding All Star Basketball Player status. He graduated from Checotah High School in 1940. He moved to Oklahoma City working as a clerk at the Veterans Administration.

O.T. moved to Enid where he went to work at Vance Air Force Base as Personnel Director for the Army Air Corp. He was discharged from the Army Air Corp. in San Antonio, Texas.

They moved to Arkansas where he attended John Brown University and then College of the Ozarks where he obtained a degree in Education in 1952.

He pastored several Free Will Baptist Churches and built new buildings for the churches. He was ordained in May 1948 having served as pastor and evangelist for 59 years. Throughout his preaching career, he held many revivals throughout the United States. In the 1950's he published a book of sermons called, *Meetin' Time In The Ozarks*. He began a radio ministry while pastoring churches in Arkansas and Missouri. New buildings of worship were built during his pastorate at Charleston and Russellville, Arkansas, Mountain Grove and Springfield Missouri, and Norman, Oklahoma.

In the late 1960's he obtained a Masters Degree in Counseling from Oklahoma City University. In 1976 he became the chaplain of the Oklahoma City Dept. of Corrections where he developed the Chaplaincy Program. He was a son of Rev. Thomas H. Dixon.

To Live is Christ To Die is Gain.

Thomas H Dixon
Birth:
Jun. 21, 1887
Hector,
Pope County, Arkansas
Death:
Feb. 14, 1973
Muskogee,
Muskogee County,
Oklahoma
Burial:
Greenlawn Cemetery,
Checotah,
McIntosh County, Oklahoma

A prominent Free Will Baptist preacher and church organizer, During his long tenure as pastor, Rev Dixon established several Free Will Baptist churches. He organized the Hitchita Free Will Baptist church in 1932 and served as pastor until 1937. In 1939 he organized the First Free Will Baptist Church in Checotah and served as pastor 11 years. He organized the Harmony Free Will Baptist Church at Hilltop and was its pastor at the time of his death. He pastored churches in both Arkansas and Oklahoma and served as state moderator for both Arkansas and Oklahoma.

Jerry D. Dudley
Birth:
Oct. 2, 1927
Oklahoma
Death:
Jan. 2, 1988
Garvin County,
Oklahoma
Burial:
McGee Cemetery,
Stratford,
Garvin County,
Oklahoma

Jerry was a WW II Navy veteran. He was raised by pious parents and early in life he became a Christian, and then entered the ministry. He entered ministerial studies at Nashville, Tennessee at Free Will Baptist Bible College in the late 1940's/1950's. His parents moved to California and Jerry and Bea began a pastorate at First FWB Church in Bakersfield, California. He pastored Tulare, CA where he saw the church grow and add members. He started a church in Oregon, and later was elected as Exec. Secretary of California FWB, where he helped edit *"The Voice"* the state paper. He accepted a pastorate in Oklahoma City, at Southern Oaks, where he built an additional facility. After several years, he entered the pastorate in Stratford FWB Church and at Choctaw. He was always active in his denomination's work, holding positions in the district, as well as state and national. Sadly, one daughter, Kaye, and her husband, John, who were on their itinerary for a mission assignment to Brazil, were killed in a tragic auto accident.

D. B. Duniphin
Birth:
Feb. 22, 1858
Arkansas
Death:
Aug. 8, 1927
McClain County,
Oklahoma
Burial:
Fairview Cemetery
Tuttle, Grady County,
Oklahoma
Plot: Blk D, Lot 117

His parents were Burrel S. Duniphin and Nancy Jane "Annie" Gilmore. He married 1st: Mary Elizabeth STOVER, and they had several children. She died in 1900, and he married, 2) Mrs. Nannie J. Welsh Aug. 29, 1900, in Garvin Co. OK (from Kinard Files, on Indian Terr. marriages, Garvin Co, OK).When he entered the ministry is not known; but there is a record of The Southwestern Convention meeting at Tecumseh College, Dec. 26-30, 1917, recorded in G.W. Million's book, "History of Free Will Baptist," pub. 1958, that "at 7 o'clock, Rev. I.W. Yandell and Rev. D.B. Duniphin, preached uplifting discourses..."

Rev Elmer Dye, Jr
Birth
10 Oct 1921
Death
7 Mar 1990
Burial
Dale Cemetery
Dale, Pottawatomie County,
Oklahoma
Spouse Reba P Dye, 1924–1995
Children
Elmer Edwards Dye,1944–2016

His name in a minister's list of 1981 OK State Association, address was Harrah, OK.

Lewis Allen Edwards
Birth:
Dec. 11, 1842
Quincy
Adams County
Illinois
Death:
Jun. 20, 1918
Skiatook
Osage County
Oklahoma
Burial:
Ridgelawn Cemetery
Collinsville
Tulsa County, Oklahoma
Lewis enlisted in the Kansas 10th Volunteer Infantry Company "E" on July 23, 1861 and received an honorable discharged Aug 18, 1864. He married Nancy Jane Fredrick in Bourbon Co., KS on Apr 27, 1865. He moved his family to Elkins, AR in 1895 and in 1909

they came by covered wagons and settled in Skiatook, OK. (Info taken from book titled: Gateway to the Osage Nation)

Rev. Lewis A. Edwards. He consecrated his life to God in 1867; in 1878 he received license and Aug. 18, 1884, he was ordained in Pleasant Valley, Greenwood, KS. He has had pastoral charge of three churches, and been blessed of the Lord in his ministerial labors. He has served as clerk of the Row Valley Quarterly Meeting (QM) (KS) and the Kansas Southern Yearly Meeting.

Rev Arlie Barton Epperson
Birth:
Jul. 26, 1878
Bradley County
Tennessee
Death:
May 30, 1963
Burial:
Tecumseh Cemetery
Tecumseh
Pottawatomie County
Oklahoma

His parents were Thomas and Barthola Epperson, born Tenn. They removed to Oklahoma to the Shawnee and Tecumseh areas where they farmed. Arley Barton Epperson married Mattie Elizabeth Collins. He registered for both WW I and WW II Wars.

He was a minister, and was active in the Free Will Baptist church. Also, when the Tecumseh College was established by the Free Will Baptists, he was part of the faculty. In 1920, he and his wife lived in the Seminole area where they appeared in the census:

Reverend Danny Lee Farmer
Birth
June 28, 1934
Checotah, OK
Death
January 15, 2018

Dan was born to Ulmont and Ruth Virginia (Bankston) Farmer. Most of his early life was spent in and around Checotah, with a few years in California. On July 17, 1952, not long after high school graduation, he married his brown-eyed beauty, Joyce Wood, whom he had first met in 2nd grade and then later again as a high school student. Dan surrendered to the ministry at the age of 16 and wasted no time beginning to preach the Gospel. He pastored his first church at 18 years.

After marrying, Dan & Joyce moved to Siloam Springs, Arkansas where they attended John Brown University. He earned his Master's at Southern Nazarene University. Their early marriage was spent pastoring, but in 1963 God moved the family to Oklahoma City where Dan began teaching at what is now Randall University. Dan loved teaching and impacted the lives of many. He returned to the pastorate in 1972, and pastored the First Free Will Baptist Church of Moore for thirty-six years. Upon retirement, he joined Windwood Free Will Baptist Church where he served as the Education and Administration Minister with Bro. Tom Drake as his pastor. He loved his new church and they embraced Dan and Joyce. The First Free Will Baptist and Windwood families are truly that…family.

Dan and Joyce were married 65 years, 5 months, 4 weeks, and 1 day. He was preceded in death by his parents, his sister, Pauline, and his brother, Jerry. He is survived by the love of his life, Joyce, their 4 children and their families: Sharon Compton, Ginger and husband Lefty Martin, Danna and husband Kim Cobble, and Tim and wife Suzy FarmerWe praise God for who Dan was and know his godly legacy will live on in all of us who knew him, who learned from him, and who were ministered to by him.

Dan's homegoing celebration service was at Randall University, Moore, OK.

Cecil R. Fassio

Birth:
Jan. 18, 1927
Wilburton,
Latimer County, Oklahoma
Death:
Dec. 6, 2008

Hartshorne,
Pittsburg County, Oklahoma
Burial:
Springhill Cemetery,
Le Flore County, Oklahoma

He began his ministry in the 1950's and later became a Free Will Baptist ordained minister in 1966. He pastored various churches in Oklahoma and at Bell Gardens, California and in 1972 returned to Oklahoma to the Wilburton Free Will Baptist Church. He later made home in Stonewall, where he pastored the FWB church from 1979 to 1983. He moved to Hartshorne and be began pastoring the Hartshorne FWB Church until 1994, and later the Pittsburg FWB until 2001.They owned and operated the Little Rascals Day Care for more than 23 years.

Ward W Fellabaum

Birth:
Jun. 21, 1916
Death:
Feb. 21, 2001
Burial:
Tamaha Cemetery
Tamaha,
Haskell County,
Oklahoma

Today is not a day of defeat

James Anderson Fergueson

Birth:
May 15, 1916
Olney, Texas
Death:
Mar. 28, 2011
Ardmore,
Carter County, Oklahoma
Burial:
Hall Cemetery,
Antlers,
Pushmataha County,
Oklahoma

Fergueson, known as J. A., died at the age of 94. J.A. married Velma Ella Ford on December 28, 1940, in Stephenville, Texas. He lived in this area since 1962, was a rancher, and raised dairy and beef cattle. J. A. also enjoyed hunting coyotes and wolves. He served his country as an artillery soldier in World War II, where he shot the big guns. He was a Free Will Baptist preacher and pastored the

Mt. Zion, Pleasant View, Hall and the Free Will Baptist Church of Antlers.

William G Fields
Birth:
May 2, 1870
Cedar County, Missouri
Death:
Nov. 25, 1943
Seminole,
Seminole County, Oklahoma
Burial:
Tecumseh Cemetery, Tecumseh,
Pottawatomie County,
Oklahoma,
Plot: A2B8-R12-20

Rev. Fields was listed as an ordained Free Will Baptist minister in the Roll of Ministers in the old Center Association (Pontotoc Co) Minutes, as early as 1915, pastoring a church at Woodland. His name appears frequently in their records after 1917, preaching, pastoring and serving on boards and committees. In the 1919 Minutes, this is recorded, "Rev. W.G. Fields was elected delegate to the Co-Operative General Association which meets at Nashville, Tennessee." In his ministerial report of 1924, "travelled 1,430 miles; preached 106 sermons; conversions witnessed: 100; baptized 9; married two couples; conducted two funerals; receipts, $170.00." He was living at Wanette, Pottawatomie, Oklahoma in the 1930 census and gave his occupation as teaching. He also pastored a church at Trousdale.

Sadie E Fincher
Birth:
Jul. 10, 1894
Indian Territory, Oklahoma.
Death:
Apr. 18, 1987
Burial:
Fairlawn Cemetery
Cushing
Payne County
Oklahoma,
Plot: Blk 10

Rev. Sadie Fincher, a pastor of the Olive Free Will Baptist Church and Silver City Free Will Baptist Church, She was 92 and born in Indian Territory, Oklahoma.

Jesse Augustus Fox
Birth:
May, 1861
Pike County, Arkansas
Death:
Aug. 8, 1932
Asher, Pottawatomie County,
Oklahoma
Burial:
Vista Cemetery,
Asher, Pottawatomie County,
Oklahoma

Between1910-1920, he came to Antlers, Pushmataha Co., Oklahoma where he and his wife, Savanna, were enumerated in 1920. In the southeastern Oklahoma marriage records, at Darwin, his name was listed as a "Free Will Baptist minister" who performed marriages there. Nothing is known where he was ordained, or of his ministerial labors.

**Let other's seek a home below,
Which flames devour,
or waves o'er flow
Be mine a happier lot to own
A mansion in glory,
my own new home.**

James Albert Franklin
Birth:
Sep. 29, 1910
Crawford County,
Arkansas
Death:
Aug. 23, 2003
Ada,
Pontotoc County,
Oklahoma
Burial:
Fairlawn Cemetery,
Cushing,
Payne County,
Oklahoma,
Plot: Blk 9

Rev. Franklin was an ordained minister of the Free Will Baptist Church for well over 60 years, pastoring churches in Arkansas, Oklahoma, and California. He was still active up until his death, supplying pulpits for pastors as needed.

Claud Freeman, Jr
Birth:
Oct. 10, 1926
Stratford, Garvin County,
Oklahoma
Death:
Aug. 2, 198 6
Ada, Pontotoc County, Oklahoma
Burial:
McGee Cemetery,
Stratford, Garvin County
Oklahoma

As a bi-vocational minister, he had pastored many area churches. He had retired from the Stratford Fire Department. He married Bernadean Ballard on Jun 15, 1945 in Stratford.

Howard Joe Gage
Birth:
Aug. 24, 1914
Death:
Aug. 24, 2005
Oklahoma
Burial:
Graham Memorial Cemetery,
Pryor,
Mayes County, Oklahoma

An ordained Free Will Baptist minister, pastor, missionary, and evangelist. Country Missionary Work and taking the Good News here and to different Countries.
As a missionary he served some time as a builder in the Ivory Coast, West Africa. He was also a member of the arm services achieving the rank of T Sgt U S Army World War Ii.

Jake W. Gage
Birth:
Feb. 5, 1891
Madison County, Arkansas
Death:
Mar., 1984
Pryor,
Mayes County, Oklahoma
Burial:
Fairview Cemetery, Pryor,
Mayes County, Oklahoma

In 1932, Jake was visiting an old-time preacher, Rev. George Washington Benton, on his farm, and was led to become a Christian. He began at once to witness to his friends, not intending to become a minister, but when a dear friend, Bob McClendon, died whom he had led to Christ, he was asked to preach his funeral. Jake's first revival was at the Paris School House by Spavinaw Creek. He said he really didn't know anything about the Bible, but the people didn't either, and his love and compassion must have shown through to them as there were 33 conversions. In 1936, Jake left his son, Howard, to help care for the farm and his wife, Callie and children, and walked to Arkansas for a series of revivals. At Kingston there were 105 conversions, and baptized 65 of them. A pool hall, whiskey store, and a beer joint closed. Five hundred persons attended the baptizing that followed the meeting. He also held revivals in the court houses of Berryville, and Eureka Springs. After eight weeks of revival, he had walked 300 miles and was carrying his offerings of $18.00, tied in a handkerchief. He built and pastored the Cole Free Will Baptist

Church for eight years. Other pastorates were Lowery, for eight years, where he built a church; First FWB Church in Pryor for six years, resigning to go into full time evangelistic work. He preached revivals in 125 different churches in Oklahoma, Arkansas, Missouri, California, New Mexico, and Idaho.

Richard Henry Gallant
Birth:
May 22, 1945
Death:
Jan. 30, 1994
Arizona
Burial:
Oakland Cemetery,
Poteau,
Le Flore County, Oklahoma,
Plot: Section L

He was born in Boston, Massachusetts, but came to the state of Oklahoma. He pastored for a time the Poteau Free Will Baptist Church then became a staff member for the Hillsdale Free Will Baptist College in Moore, Oklahoma. He ran for the Senate in the state of Oklahoma but did not achieve his goal. He moved to the state of Arizona and developed Valley fever while there and died.

Shelby Van Greeson
Birth:
Dec. 30, 1933
Oklahoma,
Death:
Jun. 8, 2008
Oklahoma City,
Oklahoma County, Oklahoma
Burial:
Sunny Lane Cemetery,
Del City,
Oklahoma County, Oklahoma

He attended Oklahoma City schools, and Hillsdale College, and completed his Master's in Theology. He was also retired from the US Post Office. His last pastorate was First FWB Church in Oklahoma City.

Alva Preston Gumm
Birth:
Nov. 25, 1923
Oklahoma
Death:
Feb. 13, 2008
Oklahoma
Burial:
McMillan Cemetery
McMillan
Marshall County, Oklahoma

Honored as a minister and servant to his fellowman. His name was in a list of ministers in the Freewill Bapt. State Association Minutes, 1982, as pastor of Murray Hill.He graduated Durant HS, and attended Southeastern State Teacher College in Durant before departing to work on the railroad. He was inducted into the U.S. Army and served in Algeria and India before being discharged as a Master Sergeant in 1946.

Upon returning home, Alva married Lucille Cox on Nov. 14, 1947, in Ashdown, AR. He continued to attend college and graduated from Southeastern State College in 1959.

Mr. Gumm would later become the full-time preacher at Murray Hill Free Will Baptist Church, east of Colbert. He also served as Chaplain of the Oklahoma State Senate for a week in March 2007, as part of a celebration of his four decades in serving the ministry. Senators unanimously passed a resolution in his honor of his service to the Lord and his congregation. From his military service, to four decades in the pulpit, he helped a countless number of people.

He also worked for the Katy Railroad for nearly 50 years. He held various positions on the RR and at the hospital.

Ernie E Hale
Birth:
Nov. 20, 1944
Death:
May 3, 2001
Burial:
Wann Cemetery

Oologah
Rogers County
Oklahoma

Pastor.
Parents: Johnie Eli Hale
(1924 - 2008)

Johnie Eli Hale
Birth:
Nov. 4, 1924
Theodosia,
Ozark County,
Missouri
Death:
Jun. 23, 2008
Burial:
Wann Cemetery,Oologah,
Rogers County, Oklahoma

He pastored three churches in Oklahoma, five in Arkansas and two in California. He organized the church in Mountain Home, Arkansas and also served under the State Mission Boards in Arkansas and California starting the churches in Ash Flat, Arkansas. and Anderson, California. He preached revivals in Oklahoma, Missouri, Arkansas, Michigan, and to supplement his income while he worked as a tile setter and had his own business in Mountain Home, Ark.

John R. "J.R." Hall
Birth:
Dec. 8, 1927
Pottawatomie County,
Oklahoma,
Death:
Oct. 18, 2004
Blanchard,
McClain County, Oklahoma
Burial:
Lexington Cemetery,
Lexington,
Cleveland County,
Oklahoma, Plot: SW

He was an ordained minister of the Free Will Baptist Church. He had preached over fifty years, and always was successful. He served in the U.S. Navy with honor. They lived in California and Oklahoma where he pastored churches and he died while pastor at First Free Will Baptist Church, Blanchard, Oklahoma, where he had completed twenty years.

Lonnie Hall
Birth:
Oct. 18, 1912
Hercules,
Taney County, Missouri
Death:
Dec. 2, 2003 Sapulpa,
Creek County,
Oklahoma,
Burial:
Green Hill Memorial
Gardens Cemetery, Sapulpa,
Creek County, Oklahoma

He preached at churches in Oklahoma and Texas.

Rev Clyde Arthur Hamar
Birth:
Sep. 5, 1906
Putnam
Dewey County
Oklahoma

Death:
Sep. 12, 1992
Enid
Garfield Countym Oklahoma
Burial:
Mound Valley Cemetery
Thomas
Custer County Oklahoma
Plot: 184-3-4

Ordained minister/pastor of Free Will Baptist churches. Pastored at Weatherford, OK when it was a mission; did other useful work.

Ralph Clayton Hampton, Sr
Birth:
Mar. 3, 1915
Oklahoma
Death:
Dec. 29, 1986
Pottawatomie County, Oklahoma
Burial:
Resthaven
Memorial Park, Shawnee,
Pottawatomie County, Oklahoma

He was an Minister for Free Will Baptist all his life. Three of his sons all became ministers and professors. Ralph Clayton Jr, Charles Edgar, James A, Larry Don. FWB Ministers. Ralph, Jr, and Charles Edgar, became college professors. Larry was editor at Thomas Nelson, Randall House Publications, and ACE publications.

George Washington Hanks, Jr
Birth:
Nov. 23, 1872
Texas
Death:
Mar. 16, 1958
Keller, Carter Co., Oklahoma
Burial:
Keller Cemetery,
Carter County, Oklahoma

Inscription: Married Aug. 2, 1911

Ernest Harrison
Birth:
May 4, 1920
Henrietta, Oklahoma
Death:
Sep. 10, 1985
Henrietta, Oklahoma
Burial:
Henryetta Cemetery, Henryetta,
Okmulgee County, Oklahoma

He pastored churches in Oklahoma at Weleeka, Henrietta, McAlester, Allen, and other places. He held positions in his local District Associations wherever he lived, and was elected to the Clerk position of the State Sunday School Board. He was elected as Ass't moderator of the State Association in 1970. He was always actively engaged in the work of the ministry and church. While at Weleeka, he was burned badly in an accidental fire on his job, and it was doubtful for a while he would survive. He recovered and went right back to his ministry, serving faithfully until his death. He had a brother, Harold, who became a noted minister, and he also left a son, Ernest, Jr., who is a successful pastor and administrator.

Rev Arty Hearod
Birth:
Jun. 18, 1940
Gerty
Hughes County
Oklahoma
Death:
Jan. 23, 2016
Holdenville

Hughes County
Oklahoma
Burial:
Hearod Family Cemetery
Holdenville
Hughes County
Oklahoma
Plot: On their home place

The Rev. Arty Hearod, 75, of Holdenville, was the son of Joe Arty Hearod & Stella (Miller) Hearod. He was brought up and attended schools in Gerty, and was a 1958 graduate of Gerty High School. He moved with his family to California, where they lived a few years and worked on various farms. He returned to Holdenville and worked several years on the Ramsey Ranch, moved to Choctaw for a few years and in 1969 moved back to Holdenville, his home for the past 46 years. He married Marguerite Hicks on Dec. 17, 1971, in Sand Springs. They lived in Holdenville, where he drove a school bus and worked for the R.H. Ramsey Lumber Company from 1971 until the store closed in the 1980s. One week following their wedding, he became pastor of Lone Grove Free Will Baptist Church in Scipio, their shared calling until his wife preceded him in death on Jan. 13, 2016. He was a leader in establishing the Kiamichi Free Will Baptist Association. He loved visiting with church family. His favorite things were farming and gardening, and he loved cows. His greatest love was his grandchildren. He was preceded in death by his wife, Marguerite; his

parents, Joe and Stella Hearod; one son, Paul Hearod; granddaughter Koby Fiero; grandson, Cliff Rogers; parents-in-law, Oscar and Opal Hicks, and nephew, Wayne Hearod. Funeral services were at Lone Grove FWB Church in Scipio with the Rev. Jim Lawrence officiating.

Elder William H. Hearron
Birth:
1882
Death:
1957
Burial:
Dibble Cemetery,
Dibble County,
Oklahoma

An early FWB minister. Great leader.

J. Arthur Hearron
Birth:
1905
Death:
1968
Burial:

Dibble Cemetery,
Dibble,
McClain County,
Oklahoma

A good preacher and singer. He was the son of Eld and Mrs. W.H. Hearron.

Rev James P. Henderson
Birth
15 Oct 1828
Lewis County, Kentucky
Death
28 Apr 1909
Oklahoma
Burial
Ingalls Cemetery
Ingalls, Payne County,
Oklahoma,

Rev. James Porter Henderson, was son of James and Jane (Thompson) Henderson.
He was married to Elizabeth R. Pell on 10 Nov. 1854, in Lewis Co. KY. She was the daughter of Richard O. Pell, b. 1787, VA, and Rebecca (Bonham) Pell, b. 1795, b. Lewis Co. KY.
James and Elizabeth had seven children, all b. KY:
Rev. Henderson was licensed to preach in 1863 and ordained by the Little Scioto Q.M., Ohio. He was pastor of five churches, and spent over ten years preaching on the Kansas prairies resulting in conversions and organization of several churches."

Rev Jess M. Henson
Birth
16 Apr 1905
Arkansas,
Death
17 Oct 1989
Sallisaw, Sequoyah County,
Oklahoma
Burial
Arpelar Cemetery
Arpelar, Pittsburg County,
Oklahoma,

Father of Helen [Johnson], Olene [Kelley], Leola Fay [McKnight] and Rev. J. D. Henson.
Ordained Free Will Baptist minister, whose name appeared in 1962 OK State Association Minutes, showing his church as Tannehill, McAlester, Route 6. Remembered here.

Rev Barb Eldridge Hickman
Birth
22 Jul 1891
Stigler, Haskell County, Oklahoma
Death
24 Feb 1966
Stigler, Haskell County, Oklahoma,
Burial
Stigler Cemetery
Stigler, Haskell County,
Oklahoma,

Honored here for his ministry as an ordained Free Will Baptist minister in the eastern OK churches. Rest in peace.

Robert Dean Hidde
Birth:
Oct. 23, 1950
Fort Smith
Sebastian County, Arkansas
Death:
Mar. 15, 2013
Tulsa
Tulsa County, Oklahoma
Burial:
Memorial Park Cemetery
Tulsa
Tulsa County, Oklahoma

Bob Hidde was born to Robert and Nadine Hidde in Ft. Smith, Arkansas. He graduated from Tulsa Central High School in 1968 and went on to obtain his Doctorate in Sacred Theology at Princeton University in Princeton, New Jersey. On July 3, 1969, he married Vicki Reynolds. They welcomed a daughter Leah, on August 6, 1971.Bob answered God's call to ministry and began preaching at the age of 15. He served as a Free Will Baptist pastor for over 40 years. Churches he served included First Free Will Baptist in Tulsa, West Tulsa Free Will Baptist in Tulsa, Madison Avenue Free Will Baptist in Tulsa, Rose Hill Free Will Baptist in Monticello, Ark, Ballews Chapel Free Will Baptist in Grubbs, Ark, and most currently, Northside Free Will Baptist in Broken Arrow. He believed in being prepared for ministry at a moment's notice. Pastor Hidde was in ministry as the on-call chaplain for Ninde Funeral Home for 25 years, ministering to thousands of Tulsa families and beyond. Since 1999, he was the Managing Trustee for Memorial Park Cemetery. He served as the Moderator for the Tulsa Free Will Baptist Association

and sat on the Credential Boards. He was the past President for the Oklahoma Personnel Consultants. He was also a member of the Tulsa Men's Club, the Tulsa Summit Club and the University of Arkansas Alumni Association. Along with his wife, Vicki, he owned and worked in their career development business, Resume Source, Inc., helping thousands of people and companies around the United States.

Rev Robert Luther Hidde
Birth:
Jun. 22, 1910
Death:
Jan. 25, 1999
Burial:
Memorial Park Cemetery
Tulsa
Tulsa County, Oklahoma

Ordained Free Will Baptist minister/pastor. Listed in State Association of 1982 roll of ministers.

Herbert Curtis Hogue
Birth:
Apr. 16, 1931
Roff
Pontotoc County, Oklahoma
Death:
Mar. 17, 2013
Oakman
Pontotoc County, Oklahoma
Burial:
Francis Cedar Grove Cemetery
Francis
Pontotoc County, Oklahoma

Curtis Hogue, 81, of Ada, at his home. He attended Steedman and Byng grade school and graduated from Byng High School. He attended Hillsdale Bible College in Moore. Mr. Hogue pastored Free Will Baptist Churches for many years. He operated a Christian Bookstore for 10 years and formerly owned and operated Yard Ornaments, Etc. Mr. Hogue was a longtime active member of the First Free Will Baptist Church in Ada where he taught Sunday School Class for over 50 years.

Henry S Huckeby

Birth:
May 8, 1858
Arkansas
Death:
Jan. 26, 1913
Garvin County, Oklahoma
Burial:
McGee Cemetery,
Stratford,
Garvin County
, Oklahoma,
Plot: Sect 3, Row 13

He was the son of George and Lucinda Huckeby, and was in Chickasaw Nation in the 1900 census with wife, Annice who he married 27 Apr. 1879 in Madison Co. AR. In the 1900-1901 Center Ass'n Minutes it is recorded "Rev. H.S. Huckeby as pastor at Summers Chapel" Maxwell, (Pontotoc Co) OK.

He was in a list of preacher's names the association accepted as ordained ministers after examination, and issued them a Certificate of Ordination showing they had recently come into the area.

In the 1902 session, he was elected to preach and then was elected to be Moderator. In 1908, he is credited with organizing the Non, FWB church, Hughes Co. OK, that produced so many FWB preachers just after statehood.

James D. Huling

Birth:
May 17, 1827
South New Berlin
Chenango County, New York
Death:
Nov. 6, 1900
Kingfisher County, Oklahoma
Burial:
Oak Grove Cemetery
Dove, Kingfisher County,
Oklahoma

Rev. J. D. Huling, whose parents were Daniel and Lydia (Burlingame) Huling, was born in Willett, Broome Co., N.Y., May 17, 1827. In September 1852, he was married to Mary W. Moore.

In 1870 he was ordained, and labored from 1870 to 1875 in connection with Rev. J. B. Fast in evangelistic work in the Cherokee Co. Quarterly Meeting.. In 1877 he organized the Caney church and with Brother Fast they organized the Montgomery Q.M., and also the church in Nevada, Kansas. Increasing infirmities prevented his holding a pastorate, but he still preached as opportunity offered and strength permitted.

Inscription:
"J. D. HULING,
CO.I., 15 ILL. INF."

Retes Hunsucker

Birth:
Feb. 22, 1928
Hoyt, Oklahoma
Death:
Sep. 23, 2002
Stillwater
Payne County,Oklahoma
Burial:
Fairlawn Cemetery
Stillwater
Payne County,Oklahoma
Plot: Blk-P2, Lot 6

He was born to Hiramm and Sammie Sallie (Busbee) Hunsucker. He married Lola Joyce Jones Dec. 30, 1947. After she died, he married Elsie Elvina (Bearry) Turner Sept. 2, 1989, in Eureka Springs, Ark.

He attended schools in the country area and worked on his parents' farm. He was one of 12 children. After completing six years of school, he was self-educated. He served two years in the Marine Corps. during the Korean War.

An ordained Free Will Baptist minister. His name in 1962 Minutes showed him with Silver City Church, near Tulsa. He preached for more than 30 years and pastored in four Freewill Baptist Churches. He was also a sewing machine salesman and sold storm shelters. He was a member of Highland Park Freewill Baptist Church.

Inscription:
Buried: 09/29/2002

Marion Leander "M.L." Hunt

Birth:
Feb. 26, 1859
Indiana
Death:
Apr. 23, 1938
Pontotoc County,
Oakman Cemetery
Oakman
Pontotoc County,Oklahoma

Son of John C. Hunt and Samantha S. (Round) HUNT. He married Ruth Harriet (Crump) Dec. 24, 1883, in Scott Co. AR. The moved to Indian Territory after 1890. Although not a minister, he was a deacon and a long-time member of the Free Will Baptist Center Association (Pontotoc Co. OK), and served as its first permanant clerk for many years.

His careful recordings were the basis for a concise history of its proceedings that was published in 1981, with Rev. Jimmy R. Nichols, Chairman of the committee, which history is dedicated to "M.L. Hunt, because of his dedication and service to this association." He also was one of the first Pontotoc County Commissioners.

Phillip "Phil" Iker
Birth:
Aug. 12, 1949
Allen
Pontotoc County,Oklahoma,
Death:
Jun. 29, 2012
Calvin
Hughes County,Oklahoma
Burial:
Calvin Cemetery
Calvin
Hughes County,Oklahoma

Listed in roll of OK Free Will Baptist state ministers in the 1982 State Association Minutes. He was pastor at Stuart at that time.
He served in Vietnam and also as mayor of Calvin. He was retired from the Army.

George M. Isham
Birth:
Sep. 9, 1848
Tennessee
Death:
Nov. 10, 1938
Henryetta,
Okmulgee County,
Oklahoma
Burial:
Oakman Cemetery,
Oakman,
Pontotoc County, Oklahoma

He became a minister and joined the Free Will Baptist where he was found in Chickasaw Nation (Pontotoc Co. OK) by 1900. During the next several years he was active in the old Center Association, and his name appears in the Minutes of its meetings. He was elected its moderator in the 1900 session at Oakman Church. In this 1900 account, he was listed as pastor of Egypt Church, and Union Arbor at Midland, west of Ada. In 1902, he was pastor of four churches...one each Sunday. (This was frequently done then to supply the churches part of the time with a minister).These four churches were: Egypt, Summers Chapel, Union, and Union Arbor. His address was Ada, Indian Territory. In 1903, he was pastor of Oakman church. He was frequently called upon to preach at these meetings. He moved to Stephens Co, and 1920 census, he was a widower at age 67; by 1930.

Clarence Albert Jarrett
Birth:
Sep. 13, 1925
Missouri
Death:
Sep. 14, 2008
McAlester,
Pittsburg County, Oklahoma
Burial:
Tannehill Cemetery,
McAlester,
Pittsburg County, Oklahoma

He joined the U.S. Navy and served during WWII in the Aleutian Island Campaign. Albert worked as an auto mechanic and painting contractor. He built and pastored Crowder Free Will Baptist Church, North McAlester Free Will Baptist Church and Fellowship Free Will Baptist Church in McAlester. He assisted with building other churches and was an active member of the Gaines Creek Free Will Baptist Association. He was a member of the American Legion and served as chaplain for the Harrison Powers Post #79 of McAlester for many years. He was a member of Canadian Shores Free Will Baptist Church.

Earl Jenson
Birth:
Jun. 18, 1911
Pittsburg County, Oklahoma
Death:
Feb. 21, 1985
McAlester,
Pittsburg County, Oklahoma
Burial:
Indianola Cemetery,
Indianola, Pittsburg County,
Oklahoma

He was serving as pastor of the Lone Oak Free Will Baptist Church at the time of his death. He was ordained as a Free Will Baptist Minister Aug. 14, 1943 and pastored churches in Oklahoma, California and Missouri.

Wade T. Jernigan
Birth:
Sep. 25, 1927
Bladenboro,
Bladen County,
North Carolina
Death:
May 15, 2006
Tulsa,
Tulsa County, Oklahoma,
Burial:
Willow View Cemetery,
Cleveland County,
Oklahoma

The ministry of the well-known Free Will Baptist preacher and educator spanned more than 60 years. His education included an English Bible diploma, a bachelor of science of arts, a master's degree and doctorate in Theology. Five colleges and universities have conferred honorary degrees upon him. He was 17 when he announced his call to preach on March 25, 1945, at his home church, Oak Grove Church in Bladenboro, N. C. He was licensed to preach the following Sunday and preached his first sermon April 8, 1945, at Oak Grove Church. He has conducted more than 800 revivals, pastored 14 churches including the First Free Will Baptist Church in Miami, and served four churches as interim pastor. He was involved in church pioneering and was instrumental in starting 25 churches. He was referred to across the United States as "Mr. Free Will Baptist." He helped start Oklahoma Bible College (now Hillsdale Free Will Baptist College), and was a member of the Christian Education Board. Most recently, he served as a Professor of Homiletics and in Public Relations with the office of Institutional Advancement at Hillsdale Free Will Baptist College. Jernigan's bold style and gift for doctrinal preaching made him a popular conference and revival speaker. He was a leader wherever he served: Moderator of the Oklahoma State Association, Executive Secretary of the California State Association, Chairman of the national Home Missions Board, member of the Commission on Theological Liberalism, Home Missionary to Idaho, member of both the national General Board and Executive Committee. Wade was a member of the five-man committee that recommended starting in 1958 what is now Hillsdale FWB College. However, his signature work in education came during a nine-year span (1969-1978) when he served as president of California Christian College in Fresno. A prolific writer, Jernigan produced four books, including his best-known work published in 1975, *The Unsealed Book, an Amillennial commentary on the Book of Revelation.* He also wrote 60 songs, poetry, and numerous articles.

Rev B T Kirby
Birth
12 May 1904
Death
Feb 1985
Burial
Resthaven Gardens Cemetery
Oklahoma City,
Cleveland County,
Oklahoma
Plot Garden of the Holy Family -
Section 27

Ordained Free Will Baptist minister and pastored in Okla. City at one church for 40-plus years. His name is in many old church Minutes and records.

Live For Eternity God Esteems And Calls

Scott Jones
Birth:
Aug. 8, 1910
Death:
Jan. 15, 1976
Burial:
Francis Cedar Grove Cemetery,
Francis,
Pontotoc County, Oklahoma

William Chapman "Bud" Jones
Birth:
Feb. 3, 1856
Death:
Sep. 5, 1944
Burial:
Rosedale Cemetery,
Ada, Pontotoc County, Oklahoma,
Plot: West-26-5-5

A minister and son-in-law of Rev. Ransom Bess.

George Earl Judd
Birth:
Mar. 9, 1915
Death:
Feb. 21, 1989
Burial:
Sub-Station Cemetery,
Freedom, HillCreek County,
Oklahoma

He served as a PVT. in the U.S. Army during World War Two.

Myrl Floyd Kellett

Birth:
Jan. 18, 1926
Antlers
Pushmataha County
Oklahoma, USA
Death:
Jan. 25, 2015
Lawton
Comanche County, Oklahoma
Burial:
Sunset Memorial Gardens
Lawton
Comanche County, Oklahoma

He became a Christian in February 1956 at Trinity Baptist Church, Lawton. He and Wanda became members of the First Free Will Baptist Church on April 20, 1958. He served as Sunday School Superintendent and in various other capacities. In July 1960 he and a small band of Christians organized and established the Brockland Free Will Baptist Church, Lawton. On September 8, 1962 he was licensed to preach the Gospel in the Dibble Association of Free Will Baptist, then on September 7, 1963 he was ordained as a Free Will Baptist Minister. In May 1965 he became the Pastor of the First Free Will Baptist Church and was pastor until 1970. During this Pastoral work there was a new sanctuary built. He evangelized all over Kansas, Arkansas, Texas and Oklahoma. He was also the Associate Pastor at Brockland Free Will Baptist Church from April 1975 through August 1977. Again in February 1979 he became the Pastor of the First Free Will Baptist Church and was there for 34 years. He was blessed to see his vision with the completion of the educational facility built. Over the years there have been many saved, many baptized and those who surrendered to preach the Gospel. He counted it a privilege to be a servant of the Lord Jesus Christ. He was involved in all phases of the Free Will Baptist work. He served in different capacities in the Hopewell No. 2 Association of Free Will Baptist and in the Dibble Association of Free Will Baptist.

Richard P. Kennedy

Birth:
Oct. 10, 1949
Richmond,
Contra Costa County, California
Death:
Aug. 10, 2012
Owasso,
Tulsa County, Oklahoma
Burial:
Graceland Memorial
Park Cemetery, Owasso,
Tulsa County, Oklahoma

Dr. Kennedy served in the ministry of Jesus Christ for 30 years. His formal education began at California Christian College in Fresno, California, where he received his Bachelor of Science Degree. He continued his education at Golden Gate Baptist Seminary in Mill Valley, California, where he began his Master of Divinity Studies.

He then attended Liberty University in Lynchburg, Virginia, and completed his Masters and his Doctor of Ministry at Fuller Theological Seminary in Pasadena, California. Always venturesome, Dr. Kennedy began two churches; Temple Church, Greenville, North Carolina, and Northside Church, Stockton, California. Both grew at record rates and continue to impact people's lives around the world. He was Co-Pastor at Big Valley Grace Community Church in Modesto, California, for seven years and ended his career as head pastor of Los Gatos Christian

He supported the work of the Free Will Baptist in the State of Oklahoma and the National Free Will Baptist as well.

Church, Los Gatos, California. Dr. Kennedy also served as an adjunct professor for Oklahoma Wesleyan University and Hillsdale Free Will Baptist College.

Bob L. Ketchum

Birth:
Jul. 30, 1936
Liberty,
Tulsa County, Oklahoma
Death:
Feb. 28, 2010
Tulsa,
Tulsa County, Oklahoma
Burial:
Bixby Cemetery, Bixby,
Tulsa County, Oklahoma

Bob received and accepted the call to the ministry during his teenage years, preaching his first sermon in May 1953 at Shahan. Shortly after ordination in 1955, he was asked to preach two Sundays each month at Duck Creek Church and twice monthly at Hitchita Free Will Baptist Church. His pastorates included Okmulgee, Cushing, and Shady Grove in Tennessee, Central in Tulsa, Owasso and Grace North of Indian Springs, Broken Arrow. He served the Lord as founder, then pastor of Grace for 25 years. During his years of pastoring, he served the Free Will Baptist denomination in various positions. For several years he was a member of the Board of Trustees of Free Will Baptist College in Nashville, TN, his alma mater. He was selected to preach at the Free Will Baptist National Convention at Macon, Georgia in 1973. He also was privileged to serve the

Oklahoma Free Will Baptists on several boards and committees during these years and two as the state moderator.

William O. "Bill" Ketchum
Birth:
Unknown
Death:
Jul. 15, 2004
Oklahoma
Burial:
Prairie Gardens Cemetery,
Liberty,
Tulsa County, Oklahoma

The Rev. Bill Ketchum, 86, of Bixby, an ordained Free Will Baptist minister for many years. He pastored churches and was used extensively as an evangelist. (Sapulpa Herald)

John Dudley Kimbrough
Birth:
Nov. 17, 1880
Alabama
Death:
Jan. 3, 1958
Oklahoma
Burial:
Allen Cemetery,
Allen, Pontotoc County,
Oklahoma

John D. Kimbrough was an ordained Free Will Baptist minister, where and when he was ordained is unknown, but probably as a very young man. He was one of those who preached and ministered in Indian Territorial days (before 1907) and afterward. No record is available that tells the number that he baptized, churches organized, weddings or funerals that he was

the officiant, but he is acknowledged by descendants of those who knew him that he was well-loved, engaged in his work and did a great service for his Master. His name and picture in the book, *"History of the First Hundred Years 1908-2008,"* show his name is still honored today for his labors. In the *"Annuals of Red Oak*, pg 153, his name is listed with a few other ministers that preached at the Norris FWB church, even back to 1890's.

Richard G. Lane
Birth:
Feb. 28, 1896
Texas
Death:
Jun. 16, 1959
Arkansas
Burial:
Little Cemetery, Little,
Seminole County, Oklahoma

He was a Free Will Baptist minister and pastor from Sulphur, Oklahoma. Much of his ministry was in central Arkansas at the Pleasant Grove Free Will Baptist Church in Greenbrier and later he organized the First Free Will Baptist Church in Conway. His daughter, Jean, was the wife of J. Reford Wilson who became the National Director for Foreign Missions in Nashville Tennessee for the National Association of Free Will Baptists.

He was the authors pastor when he was a boy. Mom Lane impacted me dearly. Their son-in-law, J.Reford Wilson conducted our marriage. A godly couple to whom I owe my early Bible instruction. They were a great indian couple from Oklahoms who ministered in my church many years in Arkansas. "Mom" Lane taught me in SS to tithe 4 years before I was saved. She taught me to trust in God fully.

Jimmy D Layne
Birth
unknown
Death
May 2014
Burial
Elmwood Cemetery Bennett
Addition
Wagoner,
Wagoner County
Oklahoma,

Harry L. Lee
Birth:
Feb. 11, 1914
Death:
Nov. 19, 1996
Burial:
Arpelar Cemetery
Arpelar, Pittsburg County,
Oklahoma

Ordained Free Will Baptist minister/pastor. He pastored churches in his locality, while also being bi-vocational, and helping others. He was a quiet, mild-mannered man, who was esteemed by all who knew him.

What Shall Be The End Of All Covetous Persons?

—Eternal damnation."

John Alvin Lee
Birth:
Sep., 1862
Illinois
Death:
Jun. 4, 1951
Pontotoc County, Oklahoma
Burial:
Francis Cedar Grove Cemetery,
Francis,
Pontotoc County, Oklahoma

John moved to Oklahoma in 1887. Elder Lee was ordained a Free Will Baptist minister in 1894. His name appears often in old church records, having served as pastor of several churches, and moderator of the Center Association in 1900. He preached, performed weddings, conducted funerals, and was active in revival work.

William E Lindsey
Birth:
1873
Death:
Jul. 24, 1945
Burial:
Oak Park Cemetery, Chandler,
Lincoln County, Oklahoma,
Plot: Section 9, Lot 69

He was a FWB pastor in the early years.

John W. Lunsford
Birth:
Apr. 21, 1850
Tennessee
Death:
May 17, 1928
Oklahoma
Burial:
West Hill Cemetery,
Roff, Pontotoc County, Oklahoma

John was a Free Will Baptist minister in the old Center Ass'n, (Pontotoc Co)of churches where he is shown to have pastored various churches. In 1912, he was pastor at Shady Grove, Dolberg, Pontotoc Co. He had a brother, W.G. Lunsford, also a minister listed in the names of a committee in a 1902 meeting, of this same Center Association.

John Thomas Lynch
Birth: Oct. 10, 1866
Crockett
Houston County
Texas, USA
Death: Jan. 15, 1941
Burial:
Mount Zion Cemetery
Thackerville
Love County
Oklahoma, USA
Plot: Section C, Plot 36

Parents:
Samuel Lynch (1824 - 1867)
Mary A Hallmark Lynch (1839 - 1918)
Spouse:
Nannie K Blue Lynch (1878 - 1966)*
Sibling:
Samuel Stegal Lynch (1864 - 1880)
John Thomas Lynch (1866 – 1941

Marvin Kenneth Mann
Birth:
Sep. 19, 1928
Briartown
Muskogee County, Oklahoma
Death:
Jul. 14, 2013
Tulsa
Tulsa County, Oklahoma
Burial:
Greenlawn Cemetery
Checotah
McIntosh County, Oklahoma

His life was service to his Lord and Savior Jesus Christ, to love on his family and serve with his church family. He enjoyed golf and raising cattle. He was preceded in death by his parents, Rev. LW and Lula Belle Mann. He honorably served our nation in the United States Army and was proud to be a veteran. Along with his brother Bill, he started Ace Fence Company in November 1953 in which he operated until his retirement in 1990. He and a brother planted churches and denominational associations and in the early days preached revivals together. They labored together. He was ordained as a preacher of the gospel on

September 11, 1960 in Broken Arrow, OK. The fruit from the churches planted and many souls led to Christ will only be fully known in Heaven. After years of pastorates, he cherished being the moderator of the Arkansas Valley Association of Free Will Baptist as well as serving in the General Board of the Oklahoma Association of Free Will Baptist. He preached his last sermon one week before his home-going. He was thrilled to see his grandsons continue his passion of church-planting in Texas and Illinois.

David T. Mansker
Birth:
Jun. 4, 1847
Johnson County, Arkansas
Death:
Mar. 6, 1929
Paden, Okfuskee County,
Oklahoma
Burial:
Lambdin, Prague,
Lincoln County,
Oklahoma

His great-grandfather was George Mansker, born about 1747 in Germany; his grandfather was William Mansker, born about 1774 in Pennsylvania; and his father was John R. Mansker, born in Tennessee. During the 1830s, the Manskers moved from Tennessee to Arkansas. By 1834, Thomas Mansker's father and mother were married in Lawrence County, Arkansas, one of the first counties to be settled in the state. By at least 1836, they had moved into Johnson County, Arkansas, where Tom was born on the 4th of June 1847. When he was 17, and at the point of enlistment, all the males of his family were already active in military service except for his youngest brother. Tom Mansker enlisted into the 7th Missouri Cavalry of the Confederate States of America. Tom was assigned to Captain Nathan Horn's Company, Lieutenant Colonel C. H. Nichol's Regiment of Colonel Sidney D. Jackman's Brigade under General Sterling Price. The Manskers came into Indian Territory probably after September 1891 to an area opened up to White settlement. Sometime between 1900 and 1910, David Thomas Mansker received his call and appointment to the ministry, a calling he pursued to the end of his life. Sometime between 1910 and 1920, Tom Mansker and his wife Martha Jane moved to Ontario, Malheur County, Oregon. However, before another two years had passed, they were back in Oklahoma, but this time in Paden, Okfuskee County, Oklahoma. In the obituary of Martha it read, "They lived and bore the trials and hardships of the early life of Oklahoma. She was converted about the age of 27 and ever afterwards lived a beautiful devoted Christian life, her companion being a minister of the gospel of the Free Will Baptist Church. "Reverend McElvaney officiated. Published in The Prague Record, Thursday, November 17, 1921. Seven and a half years after her death, the Rev. Mansker died in Paden, and was buried beside Martha Jane. After the funeral, Elder Epperson wrote these words about his friend and colleague: David Thomas Mansker "came nearer being loved by everybody than any man I ever knew. He had been preaching some forty years, after having come to Oklahoma in an early day. He was as faithful to his church as he was to his family. You can't say too much for him as a man or as a minister—he was the best pastor I think I ever saw. To make it plain, it will take all eternity to tell about Brother Mansker. We know where to find him. Oh, I could say so much, but he will tell us all about it over there." ("Obituary for Elder David Thomas Mansker", published in The Free Will Baptist Gem, April 1929, p. 12)On his next birthday, he would have been 82 years old. The funeral was held in the Free Will Baptist Church in Paden. Several preachers were in attendance and had a part in the funeral. The services were conducted by Elder A. B. Epperson. Reverend McElvany, of Prague, a life-long friend of Tom's, talked at the gravesite.

Inscription:
Co. C. Mo. Cav. CSA

Freedom Prospers When Religion Is Vibrant And The Rule Of Law Under God Is Acknowledged

Leona Mae Churchill Mayfield
Birth:
May 15, 1882
Kansas
Death:
May 20, 1948
Lincoln County,
Oklahoma
Burial:
Iowa Chapel Cemetery
Lincoln County,
Oklahoma

Parents:Menzo Churchill (1843 - 1922)-Sarah Violetta Clarke Churchill (1853 - 1933). Spouse: Rufus Mayfield (1879 - 1960).Children: Orial C. Mayfield (1905 - 1975), Rex V Mayfield (1911 - 1993), Otis Clyde Mayfield (1919 - 1987).

Early Oklahoma lady preacher.

Lester James Maynard
Birth:
Mar. 3, 1915
Death:
Jun. 27, 2002
Burial:
Blanchard Cemetery,
Blanchard,
McClain County,
Oklahoma

He was a minister over 50 years.

Alvis Lee McAffrey
Birth:
Sep. 23, 1914
McGee, Garvin County,
Oklahoma
Death:
Nov. 9, 1994
Madill, Marshall County,
Oklahoma
Burial:

Woodberry Forest Cemetery,
Madill,
Marshall County,
Oklahoma

He was ordained a Free Will Baptist minister when a young man, and then pastored churches throughout the area, among them were Stratford, Gaar Corner, and a long pastorate at First Free Will Baptist Church in Sulphur; Non FWB, and Memorial at Sulphur. He was a minister for over 50 years. He served on boards for his association and was active in the Oklahoma State Association of FWB.

Rev Lonnie Eugene McAlister
Birth
24 Sep 1927
Death
4 Jan 2017
Oklahoma
Burial
Lexington Cemetery Lexington,
Cleveland County, Oklahoma

OKLAHOMA CITY
McAlister, Reverend Lonnie Eugene, 89, minister and carpenter, died Jan. 4. Services 10 a.m. Wednesday, Southern Oaks Freewill Baptist Church (John M. Ireland, Moore).
Published in The Oklahoman, Oklahoma City, Oklahoma, Sunday, January 8, 2017, Page 19A.
Lonnie Eugene McAlister, 89 was born in Asher, Oklahoma to Roy and Ida Ruth (Paddack) McAlister. Lonnie pastored many churches in California and Oklahoma. He enjoyed gospel music and had a wonderful tenor voice. Lonnie also was a 3rd degree Mason. He was a generous person and liked to garden. In his younger-years he enjoyed cooking and having company come over. He was known for his Mexican cuisine, especially his enchiladas. Most of all he loved his family; he loved his daughters-in-law as his own, and loved spending time with his kids and grandkids.
Lonnie is survived by his wife of 69

years, Mary Fern (Rolen) McAlister; 2 sons, Philip Duane McAlister and wife Andrea of Nicoma Park and David Rolen McAlister and wife Priscilla of Shalimar,
Funeral Services was held at Southern Oaks Free Will Baptist Church Oklahoma City, Ok.

Rev Robert Lee McAlvain
Birth
21 Jan 1878
Caston,
Le Flore County,
Oklahoma
Death
1969
Berryville,
Carroll County, Arkansas
Burial
Kennedy Cemetery
Kennady
Le Flore County,
Oklahoma

Son of Polk McAlvain and Mary Choate McAlvain.
He travelled many miles as Freewill Baptist Evangelist and started many a Freewill Baptist church in his lifetime.
He was orginally buried at Berryville, Arkansas, but his remains were moved to Kennedy as this had been his wish expressed while he lived.
Rev. R.L. McAlvain's name is in the Dec. 1917, Minutes of the Cooperative General Association of FWB, when it met at Tecumseh, OK. He was active and faithful in the ministry.

Furman Archie McCage
Birth:
Nov. 22, 1907
Stigler, Haskell County,
Oklahoma
Death:
Dec. 29, 1972
Oklahoma City, Oklahoma County,
Oklahoma
Burial:
Stigler Cemetery, Stigler,
Haskell County, Oklahoma

Ordained Free Will Baptist minister/pastor in Oklahoma and California where he held various positions in the denomination.

Freedom Prospers When Religion Is Vibrant And The Rule Of Law Under God Is Acknowledged

Rev Millard "Preach" McGuire
Birth:
Jul. 19, 1931
Kellyville
Creek County
Oklahoma
Death:
Mar. 19, 2015
Kellyville
Creek County
Oklahoma
Burial:
Sunrise Cemetery
Kellyville
Creek County
Oklahoma

Millard "Preach" McGuire, 83 years, 8 months, and 3 days, went to be with the Lord at his home in Kellyville.

Reverend McGuire was preceded in death by his parents, Clint and Willie McGuire; his brothers, Marvin "Winks" Eugene McGuire and Melvin Verlin McGuire; and his eldest son, Darrell Eugene McGuire.

Joshua E. "J.E." McGee
Birth:
Sep. 20, 1857
Fayette County, Alabama
Death:
Jan. 21, 1923
Oklahoma,
Burial:
Garwin Cemetery, Antlers,
Pushmataha County, Oklahoma

Eld. J.E. McGee was a pioneer Free Will Baptist minister in the Indian Territory and after statehood until his death. He was a great evangelist who did a great work in the Choctaw Nation. In 1885, he began a work at CullaChaha, near Cameron, and was one of the founders of the Old Territorial Association organized at Nubbin Ridge, near Spiro, Oklahoma, in 1894. The boundaries were from 18 miles west of Tahlequah, to the Arkansas line at Fort Smith and south to Antlers. Later, the growth produced two associ-ations, and one carried the name, Roberts-McGee, after two of the founding fathers.

Dottis McGehee
Birth:
Jan. 29, 1881
Thackerville,Love County,
Oklahoma
Death:
Sep. 26, 1939
Pontotoc County,
Oklahoma
Burial:
Oakman Cemetery,
Oakman,
Pontotoc County,
Oklahoma

Rev. McGehee was ordained a Free Will Baptist minister in 1927 (per old minutes) of the Center Association where he chiefly labored.

Cecil E. McKenzie
Birth:
Aug. 14, 1902
Death:
Apr. 19, 1976
Burial:
Holdenville Cemetery,
Holdenville,
Hughes County,
Oklahoma

Martin M McKee
Birth:
Oct. 1, 1889
Nelson, Choctaw County
Oklahoma
Death:
Nov. 14, 1947
Paris, Lamar County, Texas
Burial:
Soper Cemetery, Soper,
Choctaw County,
Oklahoma

He was an ordained Free Will Baptist minister, who preached, pastored, baptized and performed weddings all over southeastern Okla. in the 1920-1940's. He was active in Associational meetings, often writing an article about it for a church publication. His name appears in old records of the church. In 1929, he was elected Moderator of the Oklahoma State Ass'n of FWB. We know he was a beloved and faithful minister. He died in a Paris, TX hospital.

Raymond Henry McMillen
Birth
10 Mar 1913
Death
22 Dec 2003
Burial

Wann Cemetery
Oologah, Rogers County,
Oklahoma

Throughout the 1960s, Raymond McMillan was an impassioned preacher (of that old-time religion) for Vera's Free Will Baptist Church.

His name appears in list of ordained Free Will Baptist ministers in OK, in 1962. He is remembered here for his work and ministry.

Rev John Metcalf
Birth:
Jun. 4, 1957
Death:
Feb. 28, 1984
Burial:
Ridgelawn Cemetery
Collinsville
Tulsa County
Oklahoma

A Free Will Bapt. missionary-appointee to South America., when he and wife, M. Kaye, were killed in a tragic car accident in Tenn. A great loss. Spouse: Melinda Kay Dudley Metcalf (1958 - 1984)

Rev Carroll Dean Milner
Birth
9 Aug 1940
Atwood, Hughes County,
Oklahoma
Death
22 Sep 2016
Oklahoma City,
Oklahoma County, Oklahoma
Burial
Hillside Cemetery
Purcell,
McClain County,
Oklahoma

Carroll Dean Milner died in Oklahoma City, Oklahoma at the age of 76 years 1 month 13 days. Carroll was the middle child of 5 children, born August 9, 1940 in Atwood, Oklahoma to William Joel and Essie Pearl (Desheilde) Milner. He graduated from Fox Public School in 1958. He was inducted into the United States Army on February 4, 1961. He proudly served and honorably discharge on November 9, 1965. On March 30, 1965, he married Frances Kay McClain in Wichita Falls, Texas.

Carroll was a Pastor and ministered for 43 years at 3 different churches. He was the Pastor at Country Side Freewill Baptist in Velma, Oklahoma for 17 years, at Center Freewill Baptist in Ada for 10 years, and then the Purcell Freewill Baptist for 10 years, retiring in 2013. During his ministry, he performed 78 marriages, and numerous funerals. Carroll also served the City of Purcell as the head of the Chamber of Commerce for 12 years. He was the builder of many creations such as a 40 foot train, parody ½ scale plane made of wood. Oil derricks, restored Herald Hauler and was featured on "Is This A Great State". Carroll loved to camp and travel, and always enjoyed staying at the lake house at Little Glasses. His families, both biological and church, were the light of his life.

l Rev Allen Alford Moore
Birth:
Jul. 5, 1929
Carter County
Oklahoma
Death:
Mar. 18, 2016
Seminole
Seminole County
Oklahoma
Burial:
Berwyn Cemetery
Gene Autry
Carter County, Oklahoma

Rev. Allen Alford Moore, age 86 years, went to be with his Lord and Savior in Seminole, OK. Born to the late Leonard Allen Moore and Minnie Lee Huckaby Moore. He attended Berwyn School. He married Vivian Ella Brown on August 15, 1947. He was a member of the United States Marine Corp serving his country honorably in the Korean Conflict. He was an Ordained Pastor for the Free Will Baptist Denomination on May 21, 1955. Serving the Lord was his daily passion. He pastored seven churches in Texas and Oklahoma. He was a member of the Free Will Baptist National Association, Free Will Baptist District Mission Board, and the Free Will Baptist Texas State Executive Board. Rev. Moore served as a minister for over 61 years. He loved spending time with his family. Seeing his grandchildren in church on Sunday's brought much joy to his life. He was known for his loving spirit and his wisdom he offered to those around him.

Funeral service was held at the Stout-Phillips Funeral Home Chapel in Wewoka. Rev. George Fergueson, Rev. Allen Wood, and Leonard Moore officiated.

The will of the One who understands.

Edward E Morris
Birth:
Jun. 8, 1897
Arkansas
Death:
Feb., 1987
Oklahoma City
Oklahoma County, Oklahoma
Burial:
Memorial Park Cemetery,
Ada, Pontotoc County, Oklahoma

E. E. Morris, was born in Arkansas, but soon was living in Oklahoma. He served in the U.S. Army in WWI. He was an ordained Free Will Baptist minister and pastored churches in Oklahoma and California for many years pastoring the Ada First FWB for several years in the 1930-40's, then the Capitol Hill FWB Church, in Oklahoma City, where it grew and he carried on a weekly radio program. He was used as an evangelist frequently. He served on State Boards and also in local Districts. He served a term as the moderator of the National Association in its early days. He was a promoter of the denominational enterprises. He pastored in California where his wife, died in 1957. He later served as California State Promotional Director. He pastored other churches at Tulare and Arvin, California. He was known for his strong positions on issues he believed in and was a leader in those things. He was a "hands on" pastor, frequently using a carpenter's tools to get a job finished.

J C Morgan
Birth:
May 6, 1931
Death:
Aug. 23, 2013
Burial:
Bixby Cemetery
Bixby
Tulsa County, Oklahoma

Shortly after High school, J. C. married the love of his life, Lila Fay James in Bixby Oklahoma. In those early years J.C. worked as a welder for Yuba Heat Transfer and McNamara Tank in Tulsa.

J.C. was led to Christ by Reverend Ray Gwartney at the Bixby Free Will Baptist Church. He became an ordained minister in December of 1961. Shortly thereafter he accepted his first pastorate at Pensacola Free Will Baptist church near Grand Lake. Under his guidance and Lila Faye's support, the church grew and thrived. In the early 1960's the family moved to Oklahoma City where he and Lila Faye managed the Free Will Baptist Bible book store. J.C. attended the Hillsdale Free Will Baptist Bible College at night during this time, and honed his preaching style at numerous small churches throughout Oklahoma. The Lord led J.C. to Pastor Churches in Chickasha and Lawnwood Free Will Baptist church in Tulsa, where he retired. After his retirement in the mid 1990's, J.C. and Lila Faye returned to their hometown of Bixby where they continued to serve in local churches. All in all he preached over 4,000 sermons, and hundreds of baptisms, funerals and weddings. He always challenged young people to trust God and live the Christian life. In retirement, he served as an interim pastor at Lewis Avenue Free Will Baptist church. In the past few years he has served in various roles, including the senior's ministry at the Bixby Free Will Baptist church.

Rev W. E. Mullendore
Birth:
Sep. 5, 1912
Death:
Oct. 24, 1999
Burial:
Resthaven Memorial Park
Shawnee
Pottawatomie County
Oklahoma

An ordained FWB Minister and pastor.

B C Munkus
Birth:
Nov. 20, 1876
Ellis County, Texas
Death:
Sep. 15, 1952
Norman, Cleveland County, Oklahoma
Burial:
Moore Cemetery, Moore, Cleveland County, Oklahoma

He left home at an early age, and moved to the Oklahoma Indian Territory before 1900. He was a Free Will Baptist minister & evangelist and was active in the early years of the Oklahoma FWB State Association.

The Statistics On Death Have Not Changed. One Out Of One Person Dies.

Rev James Edward Murray
Birth
12 Nov 1933
Konawa,
Seminole County,
Oklahoma
Death
25 Nov 2016 Oklahoma City, Oklahoma County, Oklahoma
Burial
Resurrection Memorial Cemetery
Oklahoma City, Oklahoma County, Oklahoma
Plot Sec. 1, Blk. 39, Lot 3, Sp. 3

Reverend James Edward Murray, 83, of Oklahoma City, in OKC, OK, after a long life committed to serving the spiritual needs of his congregation. He is now reunited with Marie, his bride and soulmate for 60 years.

James was born to James Washington "Wash" and Stella Steed Murray. He was preceded in death by his brother, Bob; sisters, Mildred and Wilma; and his granddaughter, Kelly Beth Cosby of Overland Park, Read More Kansas.

James attended school in Vanoss. James and Marie were married in 1951 in the Garr Corner Free Will Baptist Church, near Stratford OK, where Marie's father pastored. James was ordained as a Free Will Baptist minister on August 15,

1954. James and Marie first resided in Ada, OK and pastored the Cedar Grove FWB church before relocating to Clinton, OK in 1956 to start the Clinton Free Will Baptist Church. They continued their ministry in Free Will Baptist Churches in Seminole (1958-59) and Henryetta (1959-62), and then moved to Oklahoma City to accept the pastorate of the Northwest Free Will Baptist Church (1962-83). James' ministry flourished in Oklahoma City where he had the opportunity to serve a large and committed congregation consisting of both new and mature believers. After a successful twenty-year ministry, James and Marie moved to Ada, OK where they continued their ministry at Wilson Free Will Baptist Church (1983-96). James and Marie returned to Oklahoma City and then pastored the Yukon Free Will Baptist Church until 2008. In later years, James was a successful insurance executive while pastoring churches part-time.

James was a leader in the National Association of Free Will Baptist, serving in a variety of local, state and national roles, including as Chairman, Oklahoma State Mission Board (1958-63); Chairman, Hillsdale FWB College Board (1965-69); National Foreign Mission Board (1970-82); Chairman, National Foreign Mission Board (1977-82); Moderator, Oklahoma State Association of FWB (1976-80). James was most fond of his role mentoring an outstanding group of young Free Will Baptist ministers, who remained dear to him throughout his ministry.

Rev Clifford C. Myers

Birth:
May 27, 1930
Williams
Le Flore County
Oklahoma
Death:
Mar. 12, 2014
Pocola
Le Flore County,
Oklahoma
Burial:
Greenhill Cemetery
Cameron
Le Flore County,
Oklahoma

He was the founding pastor of Pocola Heights Free Will Baptist Church in 1971 where he served as pastor until his death, having been a minister for 57 years, a retired truck driver, and a baseball coach. Born to Andrew Jackson and Nora Isabel (Byrd) Myers.

Rev Clifford Garlan Myers

Birth:
Jun. 22, 1904
Cabaniss
Pittsburg County
Oklahoma
Death:
Jan. 17, 1992
McAlester
Pittsburg County
Oklahoma
Burial:
Hugh Low Cemetery
Pittsburg County
Oklahoma

Clifford Garlen Myers was the son of Miles Travis and Claudia Sarah Swilling Myers.

He was an ordained Free Will Baptist Minister and pastored churches in Pittsburg Co. and in eastern Oklahoma, Lone Grove and others. He attended state meetings and raised a nice family.

John Columbus Newby

Birth:
Oct. 30, 1884
Arkansas
Death:
Aug. 12, 1957
Le Flore County, Oklahoma
Burial:
Ellis Chapel Cemetery, Wister,
Le Flore County, Oklahoma

Newby, known affectionately as "Clum" Newby, was an ordained Free Will Baptist minister. When he came from Arkansas to Indian Territory he soon found and worked with others of like faith, such as Eld. J.M. Roberts, who in 1894, gathered some of them together to form a Territorial Association. An old Latimer Co. record, *"Annals of Red Oak"*, page 153, we find his name among the earliest ministers, alone with Wilson Yandell, Rouche Allen, Mr. West, Clum (Columbus) Newby, Jack Shipman and Elzie Yandell, who preached at Norris Church (outside Red Oak) as early as 1890. We find his name in old minutes, where he preached and organized churches all over eastern Oklahoma. He was in the group of ministers who helped form the State Association of FWB, in 1908, at Holdenville, (Hughes Co) Oklahoma.

Dennis H O'Donnell

Birth:
Oct. 17, 1907
Death:
Sep. 3, 1991
Burial:
Little Cemetery, Little,
Seminole County, Oklahoma

A Free Will Baptist minister and pastor.(Bro. to Rev. E. A. O'Dnnell).

To Live is Christ
To Die is Gain.

Emris Allen O'Donnell

Birth:
Feb. 9, 1900
St. Clair County, Alabama
Death:
Mar., 1979
Holdenville,
Hughes County, Oklahoma
Burial:
Fairlawn Cemetery, Chickasha,
Grady County, Oklahoma,
Plot: Blk 5 Lt 14 Sp 8 SE/4

He was an ordained minister of the Free Will Baptists. He pastored FWB churches in Oklahoma where he was involved in their ministries, serving in various positions, and was editor of a state church paper, *"The Gospel Truth"* at one time. He had a great singing and speaking voice, and a pleasant personality. He was a WW I veteran.

James Montgomery Pannell

Birth:
Jun. 3, 1856
Tishomingo County, Mississippi
Death:
Jul. 16, 1909
Pontotoc County, Oklahoma
Burial:
Maxwell Cemetery, Oil Center,
Pontotoc County, Oklahoma

Parents were Bartlet Pannell Cecilla. Married to Nancy Melvina Burgess 6 April 1877. An ordained minister in the Free Will Baptist Center Association, Pontotoc/Garvin counties. His death is recorded in its old Minutes. Nancy Ann Melvina Burgess Pannell (1857 - 1941).

Rev Daniel Webster Parker

Birth
22 Oct 1932
Creek County,
Oklahoma
Death
13 Apr 2016
Tulsa,
Tulsa County,
Oklahoma,
Burial
Highland Cemetery
Oilton,
Creek County,
klahoma

Daniel Webster Parker, age 83 a longtime minister and educator of Oilton, in Tulsa with his family by his side.

Funeral services at the First Free Will Baptist Church, Oilton, OklahomaParents of Dr. Daniel Webster Parker, were Ben and Georgia (Culpepper) Parker. He was 83. Dr. Parker grew up in the Silver City area, and graduated in 1950 from Oilton High School. Following high school, he received an AA degree from OSU. His education was interrupted during the Korean War, where he served in the U.S. Air Force. Following his military service, he received a BS degree from OU and later a BA from Free Will Baptist Bible College, an MA from Northern University, and EdD from the University of Idaho.

Dr. Parker married Juanita Lomenick in 1952. He was ordained as a Free Will Baptist minister in 1959, and pastored churches in Oklahoma, Texas, Idaho and Washington State. In between pastorates, Dr. Parker and his wife, Juanita, taught at Kayenta, Arizona Navajo Reservation for the Bureau of Indian Affairs. He also served as Dean of Men for Wisconsin University at River Falls, Wisconsin; and became President of California Free Will Baptist Bible College in Fresno. He later taught briefly at Rogers State College and Hillsdale Free Will Baptist College. One of his last teaching ministries was as the Superintendent of Schools in Oilton, Oklahoma where he served for 7 years. During his retirement years, Dr. Parker was involved in the Oilton Free Will Baptist Church in various ministries. He was also an active member of Oilton Senior Citizens and wrote grants for several needed projects. He was recognized as an effective spiritual counselor, and as one who provided wise personal and educational advice in addition to sound spiritual counsel.

Isaac Newton Pate

Birth:
Dec. 22, 1870
Pike County, Arkansas
Death:
Jun. 22, 1951
Antlers, Pushmataha County,
Oklahoma
Burial:
Antlers City Cemetery,
Antlers, Pushmataha County,
Oklahoma

Pate was a pioneer Free Will Baptist preacher in Oklahoma.

Rev Donald William Payne

Birth
12 Mar 1930
Death
28 Apr 2008
Tulsa,
Tulsa County,
Oklahoma
Burial
Memorial Park Cemetery
Tulsa, Tulsa County, Oklahoma
Inscription
AD3 US NAVY

Past president of Hillsdale College, and minister.

Rev Berton Perry

Birth
7 Sep 1937
Prague, Lincoln County, Oklahoma
Death
13 Feb 2015
Broken Arrow, Tulsa County,
Oklahoma
Burial
Bixby Cemetery
Bixby, Tulsa County,
Oklahoma,

Berton Perry was born to Bert M. Perry & Eva (Edmonds) Perry. He went to be with his Lord on He was preceded in death by his parents and 2 sisters; Alene Smith & Irma Smith.

Rev. B. Perry, was a pastor, preacher, and FWB State Missions Director for some time besides other offices he held during his ministry. He was always involved in 'the work of the Lord.' .

He Is The Beginning And The End

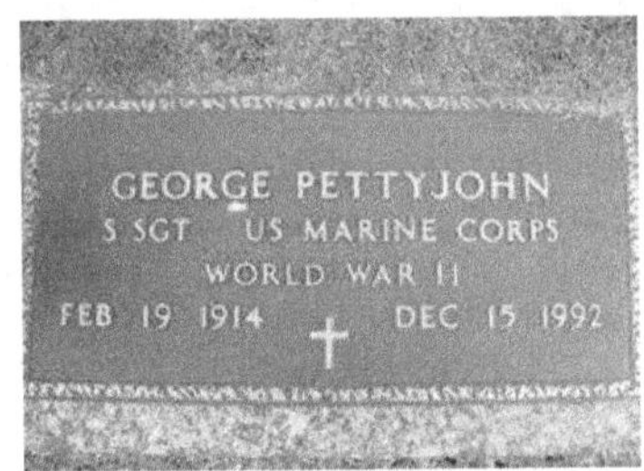

Rev George Pettyjohn
Birth:
Feb. 19, 1914
Death:
Dec. 15, 1992
Burial:
Resthaven Gardens Cemetery
Oklahoma City
Cleveland County
Oklahoma

Ordained Free Will Bapt. minister, serving churches in Okla. County and others. He also sang with feeling.

He served as a SSgt US Marine Corps in the S. Pacific, Guam, Guadalcanal islands, which time he was pinned down. They had to fight their way out. He lived to come home, then surrendered to preach the gospel, which he did for years.

David Leroy Poynor
Birth:
Jul. 3, 1820
Death:
Nov. 12, 1903
Burial:
Shahan Cemetery
Broken Arrow
Wagoner County, Oklahoma

A leader in the early beginnings in NW AR/MO for his church and association of churches. Raised a large family.

Johnny H. Priest
Birth:
Dec. 30, 1920 Non, Hughes County,
Oklahoma
Death:
Dec. 16, 1988
Boise City,
Cimarron County, Oklahoma
Burial:
McGee Cemetery,
Stratford,
Garvin County, Oklahoma

He entered WWII military service and served his country. He announced his call to preach in the Free Will Baptist Church of Non and began to preach in area churches. He began a Free Will Baptist Church in the panhandle of Oklahoma at Boise City.

Rev J. R. Proctor
Birth:
Aug. 26, 1924
Death:
Jul. 20, 2003
Burial:
Graceland Memorial Park
Rogers County, Oklahoma

Ordained Free Will Bapt. minister/pastor.

Rev Susie Loggains Pruitt
Birth:
Feb. 17, 1895
Arkansas
Death:
Sep. 3, 1987
Tulsa,
Tulsa County,
Oklahoma
Burial:
Park Grove Cemetery,
Broken Arrow
Tulsa County,
Oklahoma
Plot: Section I, Block 17, Lot 2, Space 3

Susie was the daughter of Charlie Loggains and was born in Arkansas. She married John Robert Pruitt in Carroll County, Arkansas on Dec. 24, 1913 and was the first ordained female minister in the Freewill Baptist Church in that area.. She died at Tulsa, Oklahoma at the age of 92.

Rev Eli Pults
Birth
15 May 1851
Tennessee,
Death
20 Dec 1924
Pottawatomie County, Oklahoma
Burial
Tecumseh Cemetery
Tecumseh,
Pottawatomie County,
Oklahoma

Rev. Eli Pults was born in Tenn. May 15, 1851. His mother died when he was only six weeks old. When he was two years old his father moved to Texas County, Missouri. His father died when he was only ten years old.

Bro. Pults was married while in Tex County; was converted at the age of twenty-one, and was called to the ministry at about the age of twenty-two.

Bro. Pults moved to Pottawatomie County, Oklahoma in September, 1894 and has spent the most of thirty years here in the interest of the Free Will Baptist; and we must say that with all the hard things that could come against one with every wind of doctrine, he never faltered: his record may be equaled, but hardly excelled.

He was pastoring one church when he departed this life December 20, 1924. He was 73 years, 6 months and 5 days old.

He leaves six children, four girls and two boys, and a host of friends to mourn his loss,.

Funeral Services were conducted by Bro. Fleet. His text was 2nd Tim. 7 and 8 verses of the 4th chapter and truly it was appropriate. "I have faught a good fight, I have finished my course. I have kept the faith. Henceforth there is paid up for me a crown of rightousness, which the Lord, the rightousness judge shall give me in the day: and not to me only, but unto all them also that love his appearing."

His body was laid in the Shawnee Mission Cemetary beside his companion who had made life's journey with him. Children will miss him, grandchildren will miss him, friends will miss him,

churches will miss him; but we know where to find him.

Rev. Pults founded the Free Will Baptist Church in Earlsboro.

An ordained Freewill Baptist minister, pastoring at "North View church, Shawnee, OK in early 1920's.

Rev Mark D. Purdom
Birth:
1859
Death:
1941
Burial:
McLain Cemetery
Muskogee
Muskogee County
Oklahoma

FWB minister and his son, Ulis C. Purdom (1906 - 1989) was also.

Inscription:
Asleep in Jesus

Ulis C. Purdom
Birth:
Jan. 8, 1906
Piette, Arkansas
Death:
Aug. 16, 1989
Quinton, Pittsburg County,
Oklahoma
Burial: McLain Cemetery
Muskogee, Muskogee County,
Oklahoma

He was an ordained FWB minister, and his name appears in old minutes, and in 1966, he was the District evangelist for Gaines Creek Association. His parents were M. D. Purdom (1859 - 1941) and Louisa Purdom (1865 - 1952) and his wife was Cora Brumley Purdom (1913 - 1978)

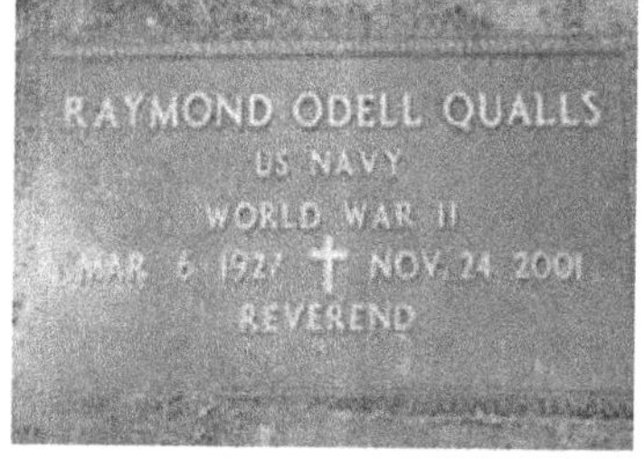

Raymond Odell Qualls
Birth:
Mar. 6, 1927
Mulberry, Crawford County,
Arkansas
Death:

Nov. 24, 2001
Fort Smith,
Sebastian County,
Arkansas
Burial:
Maple Cemetery
Maple,
Sequoyah County, okla

Funeral services for Rev. Raymond QUALLS, 74, of Muldrow, were held Wednesday, at 10 a.m. at the Eastside Freewill Baptist Church, with Revs. Wade Jernigan, Gilbert Pixley and Jerry Copeland officiating. His wife was Lona Mae Viles Qualls (1929 - 2011).

James W "Jim" Ragland
Birth:
Oct. 10, 1864
Tennessee
Death:
Oct. 23, 1950
Oklahoma
Burial:
Oakman Cemetery,
Oakman, Pontotoc County
Oklahoma

A Free Will Baptist pioneer minister, ordained in 1919, serving in the Center Association of churches (Pontotoc Co. OK) as its moderator in 1899. He held various offices of leadership through 1934.

Ellis F Reger
Birth:
Feb. 23, 1877
Death:
May 2, 1930
Burial:

Tecumseh Cemetery
Tecumseh
Pottawatomie County
Oklahoma

His spouse was Olive Arizona Smith Reger (1880 - 1957) and they had six Children: Rev. Luster A Reger (1900 - 1950); Herman True Reger (1906 - 1994); Edna B. Reger Leach (1914 - 2007); Clifford F Reger (1919 - 1991); Derril Lee Reger (1921 - 1921) and Corlene Olive Reger (1922 - 1938).

William Clay Richey
Birth:
Jan. 29, 1904
Aspermont,
Stonewall County, Texas
Death:
Sep. 3, 1961
Blanchard,
McClain County, Oklahoma
Burial:
Dibble Cemetery, Dibble,
McClain County, Oklahoma

He moved with his family from Texas to Oklahoma, attended schools and grew to manhood in around Grady and McClain counties, Oklahoma. He yielded his life to God's call to the gospel ministry in 1933 at once began "to preach Christ" in the local churches. He was ordained in the Free Will Baptist Church in 1933. He studied the scriptures assiduously, while gaining knowledge of parliamentary law, greatly aiding his denomination in its conference deliberations, he being selected to be the 'parliamentarian' for several sessions. He ably served the

Oklahoma. State Association of FWB as moderator for several years, and his name appears in their minutes in other positions where he served. He was a good speaker and preacher. He reasoned the scriptures and had a forceful delivery. He was esteemed among his peers. In 1959, he preached the funeral of his old mentor, Dr. I.W. Yandell, in Oklahoma City. He pastored churches at Dibble, Bryant, Springhill (at Lexington), and Pleasant Hill churches, and organized the First Church at Blanchard, before he died suddenly.

W. G. Ridge
Birth:
May 25, 1856
Death:
Apr. 3, 1937
Burial:
Laverty Cemetery, Chickasha,
Grady County, Oklahoma

Tombstone has his name as Rev. W.G. Ridge

Albert S. Roberts
Birth:
May 7, 1877
Death:
Mar. 22, 1937
Burial:
Palestine Cemetery
Russellville, Pittsburg County,
Oklahoma

He was the grandson of Olive Branch Roberts from North Carolina. Olive Branch had 16 children and one was named Pleasant, John Pleasant who was a N.C. state legislator for over 20 years. John Pleasant moved to Arkansas and had five children. His baby's name was Albert Slayton, born in 1879. He had six children and the youngest was Rev. William Thomas Roberts.

James M. Roberts
Birth:
Jul. 20, 1852
Death:
Dec. 26, 1940
Burial:
Garland Cemetery, Stigler,
Haskell County, Oklahoma

Elder Roberts was an early Oklahoma pioneer Free Will Baptist preacher from Arkansas. His own words from old letters and diaries best describe his life and labors. "In the year of 1884 I moved from Sebastian County, Arkansas to the Cherokee Nation near Weber Falls on the Arkansas River, rented a farm, and soon began preaching on Saturdays and Sundays in the little school houses here and there and underbrush arbors and shade trees. I had a wife and seven children at that time, for which I made a living on the farm, so it took a lot of my time. I had an appointment ten miles north of Weber's Falls near McClain at the old Buckhorn schoolhouse and other places too numerous to mention. In 1892 Brother O .J. Tailor (Taylor), a Free Will Baptist preacher from Texas, located near McClain and I soon formed his acquaintance, and we began preaching together. In the latter part of 1892, he and I organized the Concord Church at the old Buckhorn school house which was the first Free Will Baptist church organized in the Cherokee nation. Bro. Tailor and I worked together for six years and organized churches in many places." He wrote, "These were trying times. There was no money,

no roads, and no bridges." Elder Roberts made many of these long trips on foot while carrying his Bible and a change of clothing in a small satchel. Many times he waded the streams, even in winter. Sometimes he slept with his Bible for a pillow and his bed a pile of leaves or grass with the pale moon and the twinkling stars as a covering."The second church to be organized was the old 'Fields Chapel' Church Northeast of Porum, Oklahoma. It was then Star Villa, I.T. In 1885, another church was organized at old Cullachaha near Cameron in the Choctaw Nation, and Elder J. E. McGee began a work in that part of the country." A group of churches gathered near the old Scullvill Stant, in 1894 in the Choctaw part at a little school house known as Nubbin Ridge. There they were organized as the Territorial Association. But it was not perfected until Sept. 1894. Roberts was in the very formation of the Oklahoma FWB.

William Thomas Roberts
Birth:
Dec. 17, 1910
Mena,
Polk County, Arkansas
Death:
Mar. 29, 2000
Tulsa County, Oklahoma
Burial:
Floral Haven Memorial Gardens,
Broken Arrow,
Tulsa County, Oklahoma

Rev. Tommy Roberts was born to Rev. Albert Slayton Roberts and Nora Roberts. His father took his family from Arkansas to Oklahoma after their baby son, William Thomas was born.

Tommy resisted the call of God on his life, but at the age of 19 he accepted the Lord as Savior and the calling to preach God's Word. He married Lucy Marie Laughlin when he was 19 and she was 15. They had six children. When he passed away on March 29, 2000 he was probably the oldest FWB minister in Oklahoma at that time with 70 years of ministry and marriage.

He and his wife, Marie, pastored churches in Oklahoma, Kansas and California.

He "pastored" four churches at a time in the Stigler area. Some of them met in school houses with pot-bellied stoves. He didn't need a microphone or loud speaker because his voice carried strongly and he sang an impressive low bass.

Bro. Tommy was called to the New Home Free Will Baptist Church in Berryhill, Oklahoma in the 50's. He moved his family of six children and continued in the area of Tulsa, Oklahoma for many years. He also pastored Airport FWB Church, Cincinnati FWB Church, two FWB churches in Claremore. He began the church in Owasso FWB and was it's second pastor.

From Oklahoma he went to the Shawnee Mission FWB Church in Kansas City, Kansas. From there he went to California to pastor the Modesto FWB Church.

He was called to help struggling churches and with his wife, Marie, by his side with her great alto voice and gift for hospitality and evangelism, they left churches with increased attendance and sometimes with a remodeled church and church parsonage. A contractor by trade, he built churches, parsonages, dormitories, altars, benches and whole neighborhoods. Being his own boss, he took time off for all district and state and national meetings. He served on boards in whatever state they were in and he loved his denomination.

The couple supported FWB Christian education, whether it was in Nashville, Oklahoma or California. He enjoyed helping in camp ministries and improving camp ground properties.He was a great supporter of his local communities. Missions was a part of his message. "Either you go or you send," he preached. Missionaries, foreign and home, were always in their home and were supported by them.

He wore many hats throughout his life and ministry and has left his legacy. From his talent as a skilled workman, eight of his offspring have gone into the profession of construction or engineering. As a community spirit, eleven teachers from his family have participated in the public school and colleges. Others serve in the field of medicine, government, law enforcement, banking, chemistry, photography, transportation, business, and many other trades. As a man of God, thirty-three of his offspring have served in the ministry as preachers, deacons, youth ministers, gospel singers, and missionaries.

Nathaniel Burlington Sala
Birth:
Jun. 26, 1856
Indiana
Death:
Apr. 30, 1938
Fairland
Ottawa County
Oklahoma
Burial:
Hickory Grove Cemetery
Grove
Delaware County,
Oklahoma

He was an early minister in the Freewill Baptist church in MO, as old minutes state he preached in 1915 in Barton Co. at a state meeting. Nathaniel was married 5 times. He first married Delilah A. Milton in 1876, in Newton Co., Missouri. They had 3 children; Martha J.(Depriest) 1877-1899, Joseph William 1878-1963, and Samuel Edwin 1879-1963.Nathaniel, Delila, and their 3 children are listed in the 1880 Federal Census in Granby Township, Newton Co., MO. After Delilah's death, Nathaniel married Virginia M. Brazeal on October 7, 1882 in Neosho, Newton Co., MO. They had 2 children; Elmer Roy 1884-1928, and Effie Mae (Haworth) 1886-1944.After Virginia's death, Nathaniel married Salina E. Gallemore on July 22, 1888 in Coy, Newton Co., MO. They had 3 children; Minnie Margaret (Crosby) 1890-1947, Clarence Franklin 1893-1957,and Mamie Emaline (Darr) 1895-1986.After Salina's death he married Mary A. Brown on February 20, 1921 in Granby, Newton Co., MO., they had no children. After Mary's death he married Rosetta E. Bly on February 1930 in Webb City, Jasper Co., MO., they also had no children.

Rev Robert E Sessions
Birth
14 Jan 1850
Arkansas
Death
29 Nov 1918
Hitchita,
McIntosh County,
Oklahoma
Burial
Hitchita-Lackey Cemetery
Hitchita,
McIntosh County,
Oklahoma

Son of James Augustus Sessions and Lucinda Ivey; husband of Mary Zilpha Elizabeth "Silpha" Wammack married 12 Aug 1868 Scott County, Arkansas

A Free Will Baptist minister from Scott Co. AR, who was on ordaining council of Dr. I.W. Yandell in 1894. His name is in old church records.

Note: He was the greatgrandfather of Dari Goodfellow, Foreign Missions Dept.

John R. Shade
Birth
21 Nov 1938
Death
20 Apr 2009
Burial
Redbird Cemetery
Blackgum,
Sequoyah County,
Oklahoma

Carl David Shivers
Birth:
Sep. 14, 1925
Death:
Mar. 23, 2009
Burial:
Little Cemetery,
Little,
Seminole County,
Oklahoma

Carl served in the infantry of the U. S. Army during World War II from 1943-1946, achieving the rank of one of the youngest first sergeants. While in Germany he received many medals and commendations, including two bronze service stars. God called him into the ministry in August 1948 to preach the word of God for the Free Will Baptist denomination. Since that time he has pastored twelve churches which included: Paden, Vanzant, Prague, Sante Fe, Calvin, Stratford, Springhill, Gaar Corner, Mustang, campground, Cedar Grove, and Memorial of Sulphur. Helped organize and start three churches, Prague, Okemah, and Stroud. He has enjoyed preaching for Free Will Baptists and was a staunch believer in the Bible. Along with pastoring and preaching he was a farmer, rancher, oil field pumper, auctioneer, and real estate salesman. The ministry was always first in his life.

James T. Straight
Birth
1875
Death
1917
Burial
Dewey Cemetery
Dewey,
Washington County,
Oklahoma

Spanish-American War Veteran. 1900 Post Returns Presidio of San Francisco, National Archives

Corpl
Company A
37th Regiment
U.S. Infantry

Camey Alexander Sledge
Birth:
May 16, 1870
Toccopola,
Pontotoc County, Mississippi
Death:
Feb. 5, 1951
Valliant
McCurtain County, Oklahoma
Burial:
Felker
Free Will Baptist Church
Cemetery
Felker,
McCurtain County,
Oklahoma

Rev. C.A. Sledge's parents were Lemuel M. and Nancy Jane Terry Sledge, of Pontotoc Co. MS. On Sept. 14, 1892, in Pontotoc Co. MS, he married Miss Mary Susan DAVIS. It is unknown at this time when and where he was ordained a Free Will Baptist minister. They have an infant, born and died July 18, 1893, bur. MS, so it is easily assumed they came after this date but before 1904. They were found living in eastern Oklahoma, then Indian Territory. His name is in old church records showing that in 1904, he helped Rev. McGee form the Territorial Association of Free Will Baptists, to which Rev. Sledge belonged. This Association of early churches grew rapidly in the early 1900's, so that it was divided to further the progress; one was East Territorial and West Territorial, finally becoming Grand River. Rev. and Mrs. Sledge were early pioneers in all this work.

We must not demean life by standing in awe of death.

Rev Noah R. Smith
Birth
22 Mar 1897
Death
11 Mar 1982
Burial
Foster Cemetery
Foster,
Garvin County,
Oklahoma

Noah Smith married Miss Ora Nancy Neal on November 4, 1917.
Inscription
Smith
Noah R.
March 27, 1897

Apr 11, 1982
[with]
Ora Nancy
Nov 22, 1905
Feb 13, 1991
"Together we toil; Together we rest"

Ira W Smithey
Birth:
Oct. 22, 1896
Death:
Aug. 2, 1971
Burial:
Green Hill Cemetery,
Davis, Murray County,
Oklahoma,
Plot: Griffin Section,
Block North 5

Rev. Ira Smithey was the son of a pioneer Oklahoma preacher, Rev. J. W. Smithey. Ira worked bi-vocational, and while doing so, organized a church in Oklahoma City.

James William Smithey
Birth:
Jan. 9, 1865
Death:
May 15, 1944
Sulphur,
Murray County, Oklahoma
Burial:
Green Hill Cemetery, Davis,
Murray County, Oklahoma,
Plot: Old South, S5, row 14

Elder Smithey was ordained at Boyd schoolhouse near Bonham, TX. He came to Chickasaw Nation Territory in the early part of his ministry and began immediately to do evangelistic work throughout the old Chickasaw Nation and portions of the old Oklahoma Territory. In the 1915 Center Ass'n minutes, his name appears as having been elected to bring a message. We have no record of the number of conversions in his ministry nor the number of churches that he organized. We know that he was constantly engaged in evangelization of the old Chickasaw Nation and that a number of churches were organized as the direct result of his labors. Eld. Smithey possessed great power as an evangelist and his method of reasoning on the FWB doctrine was that he convinced ministers of other denominations to take membership in the church. He was a good organizer and did the more prominent work in the organization of the Oklahoma Association. His son, Ira J. Smithey, was also a minister.

Elder Aaron W Solomon
Birth:
Nov. 23, 1844
Death:
Jan. 6, 1920
Burial:
Lightning Ridge Cemetery,
Roff, Pontotoc County, Oklahoma
Aaron W. Solomon, was an ordained active minister of the Free Will Baptist church before statehood and after until his death.

Rev L E Staggs, Jr
Birth:
1921
Death:
1962
Burial:
Resthaven Gardens Cemetery
Oklahoma City
Cleveland County, Oklahoma
Plot: Sec. 11
Garden of North Chapel

Minister/pastor to several churches in Oklahoma. Had sons who were also minister.

James T. Staight
Birth:
1875
Death:
1917
Burial:
Dewey Cemetery
Dewey
Washington County Oklahoma
His name is listed as a minister in 1915 in Missouri State FWB meeting.
Spanish-American War Veteran.
1900 Post Returns Presidio of San Francisco, National Archives
Corpl Company A 37th Regiment U.S. Infantry

Harry E Staires
Birth:
Jun. 19, 1904
Thayer,
Oregon County, Missouri
Death:
Sep. 30, 1985
Drumright,
Creek County, Oklahoma
Burial:
Drumright North Cemetery,
Drumright,
Creek County, Oklahoma
The Rev. Staires served as pastor

of the Drumright Church a total of 21 years, serving for the first time in the 1930s during which time the church had a membership of over 400. He organized 12 new churches in Oklahoma including the Oilton Church, where he served as pastor, resigning in 1952. He assisted in organizing 25 other churches. Active in the Free Will Baptist administration, he served on the National Home Mission Board for 25 years, serving six of those years as chairman of the board. He was a moderator of the Oklahoma Association eight years and served six years on the Oklahoma Executive Board. In addition to Drumright and Oilton, he pastored churches in Tulsa, Duncan, Oklahoma City, Blackwell and Okmulgee.

Rev Troy Lecil Staires
Birth:
Aug. 17, 1930
Death:
Mar. 11, 2016
Burial:
Memorial Park Cemetery
Tulsa
Tulsa County
Oklahoma
Plot: Section 12, Lot 189, Space 3

Troy and his twin brother Roy were nephews of the Rev. Hary Staires. Troy served in the U.S. Navy. He answered the call to preach in 1958. He pastored the Cincinnati FWB curch for 7 years and then the Lewis Ave. FWB church for 25 years and the Broken Arrow First FWB church for 3 years.

Loys B Steele
Birth
11 Sep 1921
Death
3 Jul 2003
Burial
Blanchard Cemetery
Blanchard,
McClain County,
Oklahoma

Obit:
Loys B. (L.B.) Steele
Funeral services for Loys B. (L.B.) Steele, 81, of Blanchard were held at the Freewill Baptist Church in Blanchard with the Rev. J.R. Hall officiating.
He was born in Lexington, the son of Robert Dean and Alice
(Hughes) Steele. He married Eula Levally Sept. 15, 1940 in Maysville. Mr. Steele was ordained at the Spring Hill Church in May 1956 and spent his first year preaching all but two Sundays. In 1958 he was called to the Bridge Creek Free Will Baptist Church in Blanchard where he also worked for Asie Cottingham building and remodeling his rent houses.
In 1964 he pastored the Hawkins Free Will Baptist Church until he moved his family to Gypsum, Colo., to do mission work. In 1966 he was called to pastor the
Dibble Free Will Baptist Church. During this time he served as mayor of Blanchard for two years. In July 1970 he moved his family to Booneville, Ark., to serve in mission and the Antioch community near Booneville asked him to begin a church at that location. He served for six years and then was called to the Booneville Freewill Baptist Church. In September 1983 he moved back to Lexington, was then called back to Booneville Baptist Church where he served until 1993 and then moved to Blanchard to be close to their children.
---Purcell Democrat, July 7, 2003

Elmer F Steelman
Birth:
1918
Death:
1985
Burial:
Laflin Creek Cemetery, Alex, Grady County, Oklahoma

Jessey D. Stepp
Birth:
Jun. 10, 1915
Death:
Sep. 30, 1994
Burial:
Bixby Cemetery, Bixby, Tulsa County, Oklahoma

An ordained Free Will Baptist minister who pastored Bixby and other area churches for several years.

Albert Roma Stewart
Birth:
Oct. 16, 1927
Arkansas
Death:
Apr. 6, 1983
Burial:
Non Cemetery,
Non, Hughes County, Oklahoma

An ordained Free Will Baptist minister who first pastored in California and then in several churches in Oklahoma. He was a veteran of the Korean War.

J. B. Stone
Birth:
Feb. 6, 1878
Heber Springs, Cleburne County,
Arkansas
Death:
Mar. 13, 1934
Ada, Pontotoc County, Oklahoma
Burial:
Egypt Cemetery,
Ada, Pontotoc County, Oklahoma

Moved to Oklahoma and settled in Pontotoc County where he farmed and preached. He and his wife were long-time members of the Free Will Baptist Church.

James Gilbert Stone
Birth:
Jun. 16, 1875
Death:
Aug. 4, 1952
Burial:
Lightning Ridge Cemetery,
Ruff, Pontotoc County,
Oklahoma

I knew a man who once said, "Death smiles at us all; all a man can do is smile back."

Rev Luther D Stonecipher
Birth:
May 29, 1917
Garvin County
Oklahoma, USA
Death:
Oct. 10, 1992
Stratford
Garvin County Oklahoma
Burial:
McGee Cemetery
Stratford
Garvin County, Oklahoma

Free Will Baptist minister in the Ada, Pontotoc Co. OK area.

J W Strawn
Birth:
Jul. 24, 1823
Hawkins County,
Tennessee
Death:
Oct. 1, 1904
Beckham County,
Oklahoma
Burial:
Ural Cemetery
Beckham County,
Oklahoma

He was the son of John Strawn, of Tenn. He was married to Mary A. Jennings in 1847, and experienced religion two years later. He received license in 1881, ordination in 1883, from a council of Free Will Baptists from the Row Valley Q.M. Kansas, and had pastoral charge of the Bethsaida church.

Rev Loyd Summerhill
Birth
7 Jun 1923
Death
12 Apr 2003
Burial
Allison Cemetery
Sequoyah County,
Oklahoma,

Rev Loyd SUMMERHILL, 79, of Van Buren, Ark., formerly of Short, were held at the Vista Freewill

Baptist Church in Van Buren,. He was born June 7, 1923, in Short, to D.D. and Malinda SUMMERHILL. Survivors include his wife, Sue SUMMERHILL of the home; one daughter and son-in-law, Bonnie and her husband Jerry ; three sons and daughters-in-law, Paul and his wife Dellana, Kenneth and his wife Michelle and David and his wife Carolyn; 17 grandchildren; 11 great-grandchildren; five sisters, Letha, Quixie, Velma, Emma Lou and Verna Mae; one step-daughter and son-in-law, Leanne and her husband Thomas; and one step-son and daughter-in-law, Scott and his wife Kathy. He was preceded in death by his wife of 40 years, Hilma SUMMERHILL; his parents; two sisters, Ina SYROCK and his twin, Lois SUMMERHILL; and one brother, Fay SUMMERHILL.

Edward S. Sunday
Birth:
Jan. 1, 1912
Oklahoma
Death:
Mar. 7, 1966
Guymon,
Texas County, Oklahoma
Burial:
Stigler Cemetery,
Stigler, Haskell County, Oklahoma

His family was from the Cherokee Nation area of the Indian Territory. He was educated at Tahlequah and University of Tulsa, where he received a B.A. Degree. He was ordained a Free Will Baptist minister, and pastored churches in eastern Oklahoma at Checotah, Stigler, and others.

During early 1950's, he pastored at Healdton and Guymon, Oklahoma, where he died, from cancer. Rev. Sunday was a Cherokee Indian, and made his family proud. He was a soft-spoken person, and a very articulate and informed speaker. He was elected moderator of almost every association of churches where he pastored because he was a good parliamentarian and could move business along smoothly.

Rev Abram Talbert
Birth
21 Jul 1883
Arkansas, USA
Death
12 Oct 1963
Burial
Woodlawn Cemetery •
Claremore,
Rogers County,
Oklahoma, USA
Plot CP1-S.-A2.-14

Minister in the FWBapt. who labored in Okla. and California.

A Good-By; But Oh, It Is Not Forever

Rev James Luther Tatum
Birth
1856
Randolph County
Illinois
Death
29 Jul 1939
Durant,
Bryan County,
Oklahoma
Burial   Highland Cemetery
Durant,
Bryan County,
Oklahoma
Plot Drive 4, Section 4

Parents
William Barham Tatum
1820–1881
Emily Johnson Tatum
1823–1894
Spouse
Susan Emma Stephens Tatum*
1856–1947
Siblings
Caloway Constantine Tatum
 1847–1852
Thomas Morgan Tatum
 1849–1852
Franklin Clinton Tatum
1854–1859
William Johnson Tatum
1858–1861
Seth R Tatum
1861–1873
John Julian Tatum
1863–1931 (Early FWB Pastor and Leader in Texas)
Half Siblings
Phoebe Appy Tatum Townsend
1851–1940
Children
Julian Perl Tatum
1887–1933
William Roscoe Tatum
1893–1988
John Ralph Tatum
1896–1958

W. Bailey Thompson
Birth:
Nov. 7, 1931
Lexington, Oklahoma
Death:
Aug. 23, 2008
Burial:
Oakland Cemetery
Poteau,
Le Flore County, Oklahoma

He was born to the late Wooson and Trula (Johnson) Thompson. Rev. Thompson was called to preach at the age of 16 years and happily answered God's call on March 2, 1950. Rev. Thompson married Barbara Jean (Hickson) Thomspon. They welcomed to their lives, Jerry, Bob and Von Thompson. Rev. Thompson began pastoring the Freewill Baptist Church in Poteau, Oklahoma. He conducted over 350 revivals and served as Dean of Men at the Hillsdale Free Will Baptist College and as a moderator of the states of Oklahoma, Texas, and Arizona. His service was held at the Community Free Will Baptist Church in Pocola, Oklahoma. Rev. Bob Thompson, Rev. Cory Thompson and Rev. Keith Burden officiated the service.

Lewis Carlson Thronesbery
Birth
18 Mar 1888
Gatewood, Ripley County, Missouri

Death
22 Oct 1930
Oklahoma
Burial
Carney Cemetery
Carney,
Lincoln County,
Oklahoma

His father was also a FWB preacher and is buried in the Sutton FWB church cemetery in Pocahotas, Arkansas.

Rev James W Tignor
Birth:
Jan. 4, 1923
Oklahoma
Death:
Jun. 6, 1993
Oklahoma
Burial:
Ego-Coleman Cemetery
Coleman
Johnston County
Oklahoma

Rev. J.W. Tignor's name appeared in the 1962 Minutes of the OK State Association of Free Will Baptist. He was with the Folsom Church then. He was also a veteran of WW II.

Thomas Jefferson Townsend
Birth:
Jul. 4, 1856
Texas
Death:
Jan. 26, 1931
Wetumka,
Hughes County, Oklahoma
Burial:
Wetumka Cemetery,
Wetumka, Hughes County,
Oklahoma, Plot: Block 26

Rev. Townsend was a pioneer in spreading the gospel in the Indian Territory and later after it was called Oklahoma. His name is an honored name in the foundation of the Free Will Baptist work.

Rev Virgil Burl True
Birth:
Nov. 30, 1906
Arkansas
Death:
Sep. 12, 1989
Oklahoma
Burial:
Arlington Memory Gardens
Oklahoma City
Oklahoma County, Oklahoma

He was an ordained minister in the Free Will Baptist church. He and his wife, Wilma, had pastored churches in Arkansas, California and Oklahoma. After his health failed in his older years, he continued to assist his pastor in any way he could. He was faithful to attend district and state meetings of the church.

Melvin J. Tyson

Birth:
Oct. 11, 1932
Ramona
Washington County
Oklahoma
Death:
Dec. 19, 2014
Tulsa
Tulsa County
Oklahoma
Burial:
Morrison Cemetery
Morrison
Noble County,Oklahoma

An ordained Free Will Baptist minister. Faithful in every good work; hard worker, loving husband and father. Pastored and labored in churches for many years, and left a good legacy.

Larry Lee Tuttle

Birth:
Oct. 29, 1946
Broken Arrow
Tulsa County
Oklahoma
Death:
Dec. 26, 2015
Sapulpa
Creek County
Oklahoma

Burial:
Prairie Gardens Cemetery
Liberty
Tulsa County
Oklahoma

Larry Lee Tuttle, 69, of Sapulpa went to be with his Heavenly Father after a long and courageous battle with cancer. He was a graduate of Kellyville High School and held a Bachelor's degree from Oklahoma State University. Larry is survived by his wife Patricia (Stout) Tuttle. They met when they were 12 years old at Blue Bell Church and were married on August 13, 1965 at the same church. They celebrated their 50th wedding anniversary this year. Larry was a collector. He collected Briar Horses and Knives. He raised Yorkshire Pigs but raising Bassett Hounds was his favorite. His CB handle echoed that fondness as he was known as the "Long Eared Preacher Man." Larry also enjoyed playing the piano, singing and taking his travel trailer to Natural Falls State Park. Larry was retired from the Oklahoma Turnpike Authority where he worked 23 years.

Larry's true calling was serving the Lord and he did so by ministering for nearly 50 years. Larry served as the Pastor at Pretty Water Freewill Baptist Church for 26 years. Larry loved and cared dearly for his church family.

Funeral services were held at Pretty Water Free Will Baptist Church.

They rest from their labors

Rev Dale Wayne Underwood

Birth:
Oct. 11, 1932
Vian
Sequoyah County, Oklahoma
Death:
Jan. 3, 2016
Checotah
McIntosh County, Oklahoma
Burial:
Dawson cemetery
Checotah
McIntosh County, Oklahoma

Dale Wayne Underwood, 83-year-old Checotah, Okla., resident, in Checotah. He was born Tuesday, Oct. 11, 1932, to Cecil and Edna (Butler) Underwood in Vian. Dale grew up in Vian, where he attended school, graduated from Spiro High School and received his higher education from Northwestern College. He entered the Army on Thursday, Oct. 13, 1949, at 17, serving for 24 years. He married the love of his life, Nancy Welch and they were united in marriage Sunday, June 1, 1952, in Charleston. He worked full time for the National Guard as a recruiter administrator. Dale taught school in Missouri for four years and also began preaching. He was a Free Will Baptist Minister. Dale pastored in Missouri and Oklahoma more than 50 years. His first full-time position as a pastor was at Greenwood Free Will Baptist Church in Arkansas. He loved fishing, hunting, oil painting, woodworking and vegetable gardening. He was a member of Free Will Baptist Church in Checotah. Rev. Jackie Brown, the

Rev Roy R. Vanzant
Birth
7 Nov 1906
Death
19 Jul 1991
Burial
Little Cemetery
Little,
Seminole County, Oklahoma,

An ordained Free Will Baptist minister, his name appearing in roll of ministers in Oklahoma FWB State Association.

Rev Oma Anderson Viles, Sr
Birth
11 Jul 1929
Death
10 Apr 2009
Fort Smith,
Sebastian County,
Arkansas
Burial
Cottonwood Cemetery
Muldrow,
Sequoyah County, Oklahoma

The Rev. Oma Anderson Viles, 79,

Rev. Chris Brown and the Rev. Larry Montgomery officiated.

of Muldrow died in Fort Smith. He was a former pastor of Rose Hill Freewill Baptist Church and also had worked at Radiant Glass Company. Funeral at Fentress Mortuary Chapel. He is survived by his wife, Doletta; a daughter, Naomi Hyatt of Muldrow; a son, Oma Viles Jr. of Sacramento, Calif.; two sisters, Lona Qualls of Muldrow and Ona Seabolt of Roland.

James L Van Winkle
Birth:
Jun. 22, 1928
Death:
Mar. 10, 2000
Stillwater,
Payne County,
Oklahoma
Burial:
Highland Cemeter,
Pawnee,
Pawnee County,
Oklahoma,
Plot: Gate 6 East Section

He was bi-vocational minister pastoring seven churches in Oklahoma.
He was a SGT in the US ARMY serving in Korea. He was also commissioned to serve with the special services missile unit in Washington, D.C. and later served in Germany.
He taught auto body repair at the Tulsa Vo-Tech for 17 years until retiring.

Rev Carl Houston Waddle
Birth
23 Jun 1914
Cleveland County,
Oklahoma,
Death
6 Oct 1992
Oklahoma County,
Oklahoma
Burial
Resthaven Gardens Cemetery
Oklahoma City,
Cleveland County,
Oklahoma,

Parents
William Luther Waddle
1875–1956
Dollie Ophelia Baltimore Waddle
1879–1970
Spouse
Lola Oleta Greenwood Waddle
1921–2008

William Luther Waddle
Birth:
Jun. 5, 1875
Coryell County,
Texas
Death:
Nov. 6, 1956
Cleveland County, Oklahoma
Burial:
Lexington Cemetery
Lexington,
Cleveland County,
Oklahoma

Rev William Lee Wallace
Birth
19 Nov 1911
Death
8 Mar 1992
Burial
Fairview Cemetery
Tuttle,
Grady County,
Oklahoma

William Lee Wallace was born 11/19/1911, in Tulsa Co, OK, and passed away Sunday, 3/8/1992, in Oklahoma City. Mr Wallace lived most of his life in the Tuttle, Oklahoma City, & Davenport areas. He worked as a farmer & carpenter and a minister most of his life. He married Mary Alice Shahan 10/15/1932 in Creek Co, OK. Mr Wallace was a member of the Stroud Freewill Baptist church.

Lonnie E. Ward
Birth:
May 14, 1883
Texas
Death:
Apr. 7, 1958
Oklahoma
Burial:
Dibble Cemetery,
Dibble,
McClain County,
Oklahoma,
Plot: Sec 1, Row 7

An early FWB preacher. When he was ordained is unknown, but on his WWI Draft Registration on Sept. 1918, he stated his occupation as "minister." His ministry was long, and mostly confined to his home area in McClain and Garvin counties, where he preached and pastored churches with good success. His name appears in old church records as "delegate from Dibble to State Assn., 1935".

John H. West
Birth:
Nov. 24, 1901
Missouri
Death:
Apr., 1981
Tulsa,
Tulsa County, Oklahoma
Burial:
Rose Hill Memorial Park,
Tulsa, Tulsa County,
Oklahoma

At first he worked in the oil industry as a pumper. Sometime during this period he entered the ministry, and was ordained a Free Will Baptist minister, date is unknown, but before 1935, for his name appears in the records that year as one of the speakers at the State FWB Ass'n. He entered upon a long pastorate at the First FWB Church, Tulsa, where his ministry was blessed with success. He became known among his brethren as "Mr. Sunday School." His influence extended to young ministers whom he offered training and help to them. He was always active and working towards better education, and was involved in the establishment of the Hillsdale FWB College. The administration building now bears his name. He retired before his death and filled in for pastors and preached at meetings when called upon. He was a member of the national association Sunday school board and very instrumental in its progress.

William R West
Birth:
Apr. 14, 1857
Death:
Oct. 2, 1926
Oklahoma
Burial:
Vista Cemetery, Asher,,
Pottawatomie County,
Oklahoma

A Free Will Baptist minister who preached in the early territory churches.

James O. Williams
Birth:
Jul. 17, 1929
McCurtain, Haskell County,
Oklahoma
Death:
Aug. 6, 2012
Muskogee, Muskogee County,
Oklahoma
Burial:
Keota Cemetery, Keota,
Haskell County, Oklahoma

Bro James, as he was lovingly called, graduated from Keota Oklahoma in 1947 and enlisted in the US Navy in September 1947 and was discharged in 1951 as a Korean War Veteran Radioman reaching the grade of E-5 Petty Officer 2nd class. He spent all 4 years in San Diego, California where he sang with the Melodyaires Quartet for 2 years. He returned to Oklahoma in 1952 and entered Eastern A&M College in Wilburton graduating with an Associate Science degree. While there he organized and sang with a gospel quartet. The Lord called him into the ministry in 1960 and he was ordained as a Free Will Baptist minister in September 1961. Over the next 52 years he preached in churches all over Haskell County, Quinton and the Muskogee First Free Will Baptist Church for 10 years and 13 years at the Porum Free Will Baptist Church. He saw many people converted during his ministry. Next to his preaching, James loved gospel singing, playing the piano for over 60 years. He wrote several gospel songs and was published by Albert Brumley Music Company and Texas Legendary Music Company.

Muril Wilson
Birth:
Jun. 5, 1917
Death:
Oct. 18, 2002
Coalgate, Coal County,
Oklahoma
Burial:
Francis Cedar Grove Cemetery,
Francis,
Pontotoc County
Oklahoma

Ordained Free Will Baptist minister at Happyland Church, who also pastored other Oklahoma churches.

J Reford Wilson
Birth:
Apr. 3, 1924
Death:
Jan. 5, 1995
Burial:
Lexington Cemetery
Lexington Cleveland County
Oklahoma, Plot: E-R6-10

He was a visionary who pushed Free Will Baptist Foreign Missions in his leadership of 13 years. (1962-1975). The Oklahoma native's ministry spanned 50 years becoming active immediately after his conversion at age 16 in the Spring Hill Free Will Baptist Church in Lexington, Oklahoma. He was the agency's third director and during his tenure the number of adult foreign missionaries increased from 38 to 93. He was an conference speaker, journalist and administrator. He traveled extensively to the mission field to serve a missionary needs, consult the missionaries, attend strategy meetings with field counsels and speak at retreats around the world. In 1965 alone, he toured 13 countries in three months visiting major Free Will Baptist mission fields and doing initial work to open new fields. In 1979, in an article he wrote on world missions, he stated, " No church is properly functioning with real life unless the fire of missions is burning on its altar." He resigned in 1975 and returned to Oklahoma to teach four years Bible and Missions at Hillsdale Free Will Baptist College. In 1979, his final pastorate was at the Butterfield Free Will Baptist Church in Aurora, Illinois where he invested 11 years of his life with that congregation. In 1991, after retiring, he began serving again as Missions professor at Hillsdale College. He pastored six churches in four states: Oklahoma, Tennessee, Arkansas and Michigan. Three times, he was elected to three terms on the Foreign Missions Board. Four times, the Arkansas State Ass'n elected him as their moderator. He also served six years on the Board of Directors with the Evangelical Foreign Missions Association.

He also served as president of the Oklahoma FWB League Convention, conducted weekly radio broadcast as pastor in Pocahontas, Arkansas, and wrote curriculum for the Sunday School Department. He studied in several educational institutions: Oklahoma State University, Free Will Baptist Bible College, California Christian College, University of Tennessee and Southern Baptist Seminary.

Harry W Withers
Birth:
Unknown
Death:
Jul. 29, 2013
Burial:
Vernon Cemetery
Coweta
Wagoner County,
Oklahoma

An Oklahoma Free Will Baptist minister/pastor in the Tulsa area.

Billy Ray Wood
Birth:
Jul. 31, 1928, USA
Death:
May 30, 1989
Pottawatomie County
Oklahoma
Burial:
McGee Cemetery
Stratford
Garvin County
Oklahoma

His name appears in a Minister's list in 1982 Free Will Baptist State Association. At that time he was pastor of Pauls Valley church. He pastored other places also. Son of Louis and Lillie Mae Wood.

Frances M Wood
Birth:
Sep. 9, 1909
Arkansas
Death:
Feb. 12, 1996
Oklahoma County, Oklahoma
Burial:
Memorial Park Cemetery,
Ada,
Pontotoc County,
Oklahoma

He moved with his family to Oklahoma a few years after 1907 statehood. They lived and farmed around Stratford. F.M. was one of the younger of their children, Vard and Walter, also sons. Rev. F.M. was converted in a revival near Stratford, along with his brothers. He entered the ministry in the Free Will Baptist, and pastored churches in the Center Association and surrounding. He also was used as an evangelist. Preachers during these depressed, economic times were more than likely to farm or have other income to care for their family. Rev. F.M. worked some with the Rail Road. He and his wife had one daughter, the late Marie Wood, who married Rev. James Murray, who is a leader in the church. He was widowed at the time of his death and was living near his daughter, in OKC where he died. He was well-thought of, and was a good preacher.

He fulfilled righteousness

Weldon V. Wood
Birth:
Nov. 9, 1926
Oklahoma
Death:
Jun., 1967
Burial:
Memorial Park Cemetery,
Ada,
Pontotoc County,
Oklahoma

He was the son of Rev. Vard Wood. He grew up in Pontotoc Co. and was active in church activities from his youth. He married and raised three children, Jan Cason, (dec); Bruce Wood, and Tim Wood, a pastor in CA. He worked hard in the District and State Youth programs, which was called the "League" at that time. He was converted early in life. He was elected as State Clerk of the State Association of FWB, at age 25 yrs, and served for several years until his move to CA. He pastored Ada FWB church, and Capitol Hill in OKC, and probably others before these. He had a big smile, and very likeable personality. He was said to be "a rising star" when he was tragically killed in an auto accident on way from CA to OK, about 41 years of age.

William Vard Wood
Birth:
Mar. 5, 1890
Arkansas
Death:
Apr. 9, 1979
Pontotoc County,
Oklahoma
Burial:
Memorial Park Cemetery,
Ada,
Pontotoc County, Oklahoma

W. Vard Wood, was known in his adult years by the name "Vard". He was the son of James Perry Wood, and Melinda Elizabeth (McBee) Wood, of Arkansas, who moved to OK, early on and died near, or at Stratford. When he was ordained is unknown at this time, but he was converted in a large revival held in the late 1920's or early 1930's and entered the ministry soon afterward, and he served faithfully until his death. He was not college educated, but applied himself in study of the Bible, and other, learning where he found opportunity during those early times. He became one of the leaders in his Oklahoma Free Will Baptist church. He was used often in evangelistic meetings with great success. He was known to lead an exemplary life and his preaching was with power. He had a habit of quoting, verbatim, a verse of scripture, while gesturing as if he was reading it from his hand. His pleasant voice and kind-sounding speech made him immediately affable to meet, and converse with.

No known statistics of the number of revivals, converts and baptisms, he had, or the churches he pastored. But he had great success. He was loved and esteemed by all who knew him.

Rev Olen W Woodruff
Birth
9 Sep 1929
Death
27 Jul 1996
Burial
Sunny Lane Cemetery
Del City,
Oklahoma County,
Oklahoma,

An ordained Free Will Baptist minister, listed in roll of Okla. ministers in 1982 Minutes. Rest in peace.

Dr Isaac Wilson Yandell
Birth:
Jul. 16, 1876
Scott County,
Arkansas,
Death:
Dec. 19, 1959
Oklahoma City,
Oklahoma County,
Oklahoma,
Burial:
Lexington Cemetery,
Lexington,
Cleveland County,
Oklahoma,
Plot: SW-R4-41

He entered the gospel ministry at age 16, ordained in 1894, in Scott Co. Arkansas. He moved from Arkansas with his family before 1900, to Indian Territory (Okla.). He studied medicine at the Vance School in Northwest Arkansas and passed the Federal Medical Examination at McAlester and began helping the settlers with their medical needs. He also farmed as most old-time preachers did as they received

hardly any support from churches. He attended the Academy at Kully Chaha, an Indian School the government had set up, and took extended courses at various schools, working at any menial task to support his studies. Kully Chaha debating team would hold debates with the Presbyterian school team at Cameron, where he participated, and acquired a love of polemics. He studied law and parliamentary procedure.

His family moved into LeFlore Co., I.T. where his father died at age 49, and is buried in Royal Oak cemetery of that county.

He preached for the Free Will Baptist Church for 67 years, in Arkansas, Texas, California, and in Oklahoma. He was a leader in the organization of the Oklahoma. State Association of churches and served as its moderator. He served in many positions and offices of the FWB.

He served as president of the Old Southwestern Convention, before 1935, and offered advice and counsel towards forming the National body.

He was active and instrumental in organizing over fifty FWB churches. Many young ministers were under his tutelage.

During his time and era, the ministry demanded many sacrifices from which he did not draw back.

He was a great orator, preacher and debater, and as a speaker was always in demand wherever he went. He never ceased to study, even though he lost his eyesight several years before his death. He could recite many, many scriptures verbatim, and one time after he was blind, he counted 120 hymns of which he knew every stanza. He possessed an unusually keen and retentive mind and wisdom that had to 'be from above.' His wit and humor were enjoyed by all his friends and family alike wherever he went. He lived a life with many hardships, but he always saw a positive side and an uplifting attitude which served him well.

DeArthur Yandell
Birth:
Mar. 22, 1934
Alex, Grady County, Oklahoma
Death:
Sep. 1, 2009
Chickasha,
Grady County, Oklahoma
Burial:
Non Cemetery,
Non,
Hughes County,
Oklahoma

He was born to Dr. Isaac Wilson and Dovie Lee. DeArthur dedicated his life as a young man to serving the Lord and others with all his heart. He ministered for 58 years. DeArthur pastored churches in Oklahoma and California for many years, and the Chickasha Freewill Baptist from 1999 until he preached his last sermon on Easter Sunday 2009. DeArthur annually attended the Oklahoma State and National Associations of Freewill Baptist Churches, and the State Ministers Conference of Free Will Baptists, where he made many friends.

L D Yandell
Birth:
Jan. 5, 1923
Denison,
Grayson County,
Texas
Death:
Oct. 23, 2009
Oklahoma City,
Oklahoma County,
Oklahoma
Burial:
Lexington Cemetery,
Lexington,
Cleveland County, Oklahoma

He was preceded in death by his parents, Dr. Isaac Wilson and Dovie Lee Yandell. He was ordained in the Oklahoma District Association, and pastored Glendale FWB Church for over nine years. He was bi-vocational and preached and "filled in" when asked, after his pastorate. He also labored with his brother, Rev. DeArthur Yandell, in Trinity FWB Church in Oklahoma City. Only a robbery by two gunmen, with guns on him and his wife while made to lie on the floor, caused him to decide to retire from that occupation.

Strauther P. Yocham
Birth:
Jan. 24, 1909
Death:
Feb. 1, 1972
Burial:
Kellyville City Cemetery
Kellyville
Creek CountyOklahoma

His name appeared in a "Minister's Roll" in 1962 Minutes of State Association of Free Will Baptists, living at Sapulpa, OK, affiliated with Garden Heights church at that time.

Homer Lee Young
Birth:
Feb. 2, 1929
Death:
Oct. 10, 2007
Burial:
Little Cemetery,
Little
Seminole County, Oklahoma

He was a graduate of Connors State College, Oklahoma Bible College (Hillsdale) Tulsa Univ., where he studied theology. Ordained as a Free Will Baptist minister in 1952. He established and worked as pastor in several churches. First in Henryetta, then to Cushing, Stillwater, Tulsa, OKla. C,ity Moore, McAlester, El Reno, Wilburton, Wewoka, Chickasha. He also served as the Okla. Free Will Baptist State Exec. Sec. He was not only a minister, but a member of the State Minister's Quartet for forty years, which went everywhere singing in conventions, revivals and homecomings.

Waldo Young
Birth
30 Sep 1932
Econtuchka,

Pottawatomie County, Oklahoma
Death
8 Oct 2017
Oklahoma City,
Oklahoma County, Oklahoma
Burial
Little Cemetery Little,
Seminole County,
Oklahoma

Young, Waldo, 85, retired minister, died. Waldo Young was born the second of twin boys in Econtuchka Garden Grove community. He went to Prairie Dale School for six grades, then Centerview where he graduated in 1950.

Survived by his wife, JoAnn of nearly 66 years marriage, son, Richard Don Young (Brenda), daughters Sharon Beam (Edward) and Annette Strother (Robert), nine grandchildren, twenty great grandchildren. Also survived by his twin brother, John Young of Prague. Many nieces, nephews and extended family members.

Over a period of 60 years, he pastored twelve Free Will Baptist Church congregations. He loved being a pastor for 15 years at Spencer Road Free Will Baptist, almost 10 years at Northeast Free Will Baptist in Shawnee and Northwest Free Will Baptist in Oklahoma City, eight years at Bristow Free Will Baptist, plus some shorter pastorates in Oklahoma.

Bro. Young sang high tenor and played the piano for the Ministers Quartet for 43 years with his brother, Homer Young, friends Jack Richey and Delbert Akin. They ministered in at least 25 states with over 200 revival type meetings, and probably over 500 concerts.

Brother Young served in many denominational capacities. He was the clerk of the National Association of Free Will Baptist for 30 years. (1969-1999). He was also clerk of the State Association for 10 years. He preached at the Oklahoma State Association twice. He served on several boards and committees of the denomination from the local to national level.

The loves of his life were his wife.

He married JoAnn when they were nineteen and fifteen. They were truly best friends. He loved music. He could play any instrument with a keyboard. He played and sang with anyone who would play or sing with him. He sang with his brothers and mother when he was a child. His children were taught to play and sing when they could talk and walk. He played and sang the last time three weeks before his death at the nursing home where he lived the last few months of his life. Today he is singing with his mother, Brother Homer, and Delbert Akin, one of the members of the quartet who passed before him. Funeral Services at Sunny Lane Freewill Baptist Church, Del City.

Buford Francis Zinn
Birth:
Apr. 14, 1919
Porter
Wagoner County
Oklahoma
Death:
May 27, 1999
Sapulpa
Creek County
Oklahoma
Burial:
Green Hill Memorial Gardens
Cemetery
Sapulpa
Creek County
Oklahoma
Plot: Garden of Devotion, 121 D2

Buford lived most of his life in Creek County, Oklahoma. He was retired from Liberty Glass

Company. He was a member of Westside Free Will Baptist Church. Although he was an ordained minister, he never pastored a church. Buford liked to fish and visit with friends and family. He and Norma were married for over 50 years.

Everett Eugene Zoellers
Birth:
Nov. 1, 1927
Kansas City,
Jackson County, Missouri
Death:
Jan. 2, 2010
Dallas, Dallas County, Texas
Burial:
Hillcrest Memorial Park,
Ardmore, Carter County,
Oklahoma

Gene and Barbara (Thompson) were wed on November 12, 1945, in Ardmore, Okla. For most of his adulthood Gene was a minister. He pastored at Westside Free Will Baptist Church, Midland, Texas for several years. They then lived and ministered in Dallas.

Oregon

Rev Frank Fay Whitcomb
Birth:
Jul. 8, 1862
Hillsboro
Washington County, Oregon
Death:
Mar. 18, 1913
Portland
Multnomah County, Oregon
Burial:
Lincoln Memorial Park
Portland
Multnomah County, Oregon
Plot: Greenleaf Section

His Parents were Stephen Snyder Whitcomb (1824 - 1908) and Tabitha Bertha Whitlow Whitcomb (1838 - 1904).He was married to Grace Regina Steele Whitcomb (1863 - 1954)*
Note: He is a Twin to Belle Pearl Whitcomb.

He Is The Beginning And The End

Pennsylvania

R. E. Anderson
Birth:
1809
Norwich, Massachusetts
Death:
Feb. 27, 1888
Burial:
Bethel Cemetery, Franklin
Venango County, ennsylvania

The common school of his area formed the basis of his education. In 1848 he was ordained in the Wesleyan Methodists and afterwards joined the Free Baptists movement. He pastored in Pennsylvania as well as Conneaut and Chester, in Ohio. In his 50 years of service he baptized over 2000 people. When he was a Wesleyan Methodists he had served as the Pres. of the conference and afterwards as a Free Will Baptist was a delegate to the General Conference. He was also a delegate to the National Free-Soil Convention in 1852. In the contest against intemperance and slavery he has been a persistent worker.

Braziale Emerson Baker
Birth:
Jan. 11, 1830
Ohio
Death:
Jun. 8, 1919
Pennsylvania
Burial:
Venango Cemetery
Venango
Crawford County
Pennsylvania
Plot: 1 1/2; Sec 6

Rev Samuel W Barr

Birth:
Mar. 8, 1796
Dutchess County, New York
Death:
Jul. 25, 1878
Burial:
John Lyman Cemetery
Roulette
Potter County
Pennsylvania, Plot: R3l10

Son of John and Hannah C. Barr...Married (1) Sarah Edwards..8-10 Married(2) SusanT hompkins... Vet War of 1812.... Rev. Samuel Barr, a native of Coxsackie, NY., died at Roulette, PA. Jul 25 1878, age 82 years... He was converted about 27 years of age and soon began to preach, moving to PA. about 1843, he preached throughout Potter County, where he executed a wide influence and had many friends

Hiram Bacon

Birth:
Jul. 18, 1808
Death:
Nov. 12, 1886,
Burial:
Austinburg Pioneer Cemetery,
Austinburg,
Tioga County, Pennsylvania

Erastus Sterling Bumpus

Birth:
May 3, 1815
Death:
Jan. 23, 1880
Pennsylvania
Burial:
Plum Church Cemetery
Cooperstown, Venango
County, Pennsylvania

Bumpus was converted at the age of 14. In July 1837, he married Annette Shirley, and soon moved to Waterford, Pennsylvania, and then to Ohio, where he joined the Pierpoint church, and was ordained to the gospel ministry in the Free Will Baptist church, in the Ashtabula Quarterly Meeting. In 1853, he returned to Pennsylvania and ministered to the Big Bend, Croton, Plumb, Canal and other churches, remaining with the Cancul church nine years. He was a good man, generous and charitable. His preaching was plain, practical and earnest.

Rev Chauncy Burch

Birth: 1803
New York
Death: Mar. 21, 1878
Erie County
Pennsylvania
Burial:
North East Cemetery
North East
Erie County, Pennsylvania
Plot: Section F

He was born in Warren, N.Y., and converted at Westfield. Moving to North East PA, about 11848, he soon became pastor of the church, a relation which he sustained many years. He was ordained about 1856 (Freewill Baptist), and preached also a part of the time to the churches at Waterford, French Creek, and Greenfield.

Seldon Butler

Birth:
Jul. 15, 1806
Rochester,
Windsor County, Vermont
Death:
Oct. 19, 1888
Tioga County, Pennsylvania
Burial:
Butler Hill Cemetery,
Tioga County, Pennsylvania

Rev. Butler was licensed to preach in 1841, and ordained in February, 1843, in the Freewill Baptist Church. Rev. Wm. Mack and others served on his council. His ministry from the first was in one vicinity, commencing in the Bradford and Tioga Quarterly Meeting. He held revivals, baptized three hundred and fifty converts and organized six churches. He was active in his community and raised a large family while doing the work of a minister.

James Calder
Birth:
February 16, 1826
Harrisburg,
Pennsylvania
Death:
1893
Burial:
Harrisburg Cemetery
Harrisburg,Dauphin County,
Pennsylvania

He was married on December 25, 1850, to Ellen C. Winebrenner, eldest daugh-ter of Rev. John Winebrenner, the founder of Church of God.
She died in 1858 and he later married Elizabeth DD Murphy of Harrisburg.
His son Rev. William Calder was a missionary to Rangoon, Burma. His only daughter was the wife of Prof. J. W. Preston of Pennsylvania State college. He pursued his preparatory studies in Harrisburg and Bristol, Pennsylvania and Norwich, Vermont. He graduated from the Wesleyan University, Middletown, Connecticut on August 1, 1849. He was converted on February 11, 1837 and United with the Methodist Episcopal Church receiving license in 1847 and entering the Philadelphia conference. In October, 1850 he was appointed a missionary to China; and after receiving his ordination in December he sailed for China on March 1851. In November 1853, because of a change of belief as to baptism and church policy, he was baptized at Hong Kong, withdrew from the Methodist Episcopal Church and returned to America in 1854 and united with the Church of God.

He served as pastor of the church in Harrisburg until 1859 when he and a majority of the members organized the first Free Baptist Church of which he continued to pastor until 1869 when he became the Pres. of Hillsdale College, in Michigan and was the pastor of the church at that place. In 1871 he accepted the presidency of Pennsylvania State college where he remained until 1880. He then became pastor of the church at Harrisburg again. He was the editor of the *Church Advocate* from 1856-1858, and was principal of the Shippensburg Collegiate Institute, then professor of Belles-Letters in Penn-sylvania Female College and was a Trustee of Storer college from its organization.

Bela Cogswell
Birth:
Jan. 10, 1817
Death:
Dec. 2, 1900
Burial:
Cogswell Cemetery,
Silvara
Bradford County,
Pennsylvania

He started out his career in the ministry as a Methodist, but changed his viewpoint towards religion about 1850 when he became a Freewill Baptist, a group who stood up against Slavery. He was a founder of the Silvara Freewill Baptist church in 1856. He improved those which he had to the best advantage studying and reading as far as he could, until the people thought he was qualified to teach, when he taught several terms. Previous to 1837, before he was twenty years old, he was licensed to preach the gospel, and for more than forty years he has been engaged in the work of the ministry and preached to the same people.

He was one of the original members of the Free Will Baptist church on the Tuscarora, and was mainly instrumental in its organization, and in erecting the Pleasant Church edifice, which is used by the congregation. This church as a marble pulpit of unique construction, and on the marble tablets surrounding it are the names of the members, pastors, contributors, etc., a constant reminder of the worshipers of those who are affiliated with them in the ties of the spiritual brotherhood. Mr. Cogswell has been their first and last pastor. In addition to his duties as pastor, he has frequently had to perform the official duties of a citizen, having, besides other township offices, been justice of the peace fifteen years.

Asa Dodge
Birth:
1829
Death:
August 3, 1883
Burial:
Wellsboro Cemetery
Wellsboro
Tioga County, Pennsylvania
He commenced preaching in 1851, having been approved by the Ridgeway church, and received a Quarter Meeting license and in 1854 and was ordained by the Tioga County Quarterly Meeting in 1867. He did good work as an evangelist rather than as a pastor and at his death resolutions

appreciative of his character and youthfulness were passed by the Potter County and Tioga County Quarterly Meetings within the bounds of which his labors were chiefly spent. Had three bros. who were also FB ministers.

Calvin Dodge
Birth:
Oct. 12, 1814
Lisbon
Grafton County, New Hampshire
Death:
May 15, 1882
Cadis
Bradford County, Pennsylvania
Burial: Cadis Cemetery
Cadis,
Bradford County, Pennsylvania

Rev. Calvin Dodge was one of four brothers who were Free Baptist ministers: Gurley, Edward, and Asa Dodge, whose parents were Asa and Sarah DODGE.He married Charlotte Allen in 1844.He was licensed for the ministry at 25 yrs, and three years later was ordained by the Owego Quarterly Meeting at Dryden, N.Y., while engaged in a Revival with the Troy church. He held revivals after license at Cuba, Wirt, and Bolivar.He was a useful man. Died age 67 years.

Edward E Dodge
Birth:
1794
New Hampshire, USA
Death:
May 4, 1837
Cadis, Bradford County, Pennsylvania
Burial:
Cadis Cemetery
Cadis, Bradford County, Pennsylvania

Rev. Edward E. Dodge, brother of Rev. Asa Dodge, was converted in 1812, he was baptized by Rev. Joshua Quinby, and united with the Free Baptist church at Lisbon, N.H. He soon after began to conduct meetings. About 1819 he removed to Dryden N.Y., near the head of Lake Cayuga, and united heartily with Rev. John Gould, the only Free Baptist preacher in the great state, in breaking to the people the bread of life.In 1821, after two years of successful labor, he attended the Vermont Yearly Meeting held at Turnbridge, and was there ordained.He returned to labor with Gould and to organize churches at Berkshire, Candor, and Owego, and Choconut in Pennsylvania. On May 27, 1820, they met in conference and organized the Owego Quarterly Meeting, consisting then of an isolated band of one hundred and sixty brethren. He was untiring in his labors in the revival of 1825 in that region.

Elder Gurley Dodge
Birth:
Mar. 24, 1809
Death:
Nov. 17, 1835
Cadis
Bradford County
Pennsylvania
Burial:
Cadis Cemetery
Cadis
Bradford County
Pennsylvania

He was a Free Will Baptist minister, one of four brothers. His ministry only spanned about two yrs, but it was useful.

Siblings:
Edward E Dodge (1794 - 1837)
Gurley Dodge (1809 - 1835)
Calvin Dodge (1814 - 1882)

Rev William Ensign
Birth:
May 30, 1797
Massachusetts
Death:
May 30, 1870
Portage,Pennsylvania
Burial:
Portage Township Cemetery
Sizerville
Cameron County
Pennsylvania
William married Mary Stevens in Jan 1818 in Middlebury, Schohare County, New York. Mary was born on 15 Jul 1798 in Schenectady, New York. She died on 22 Apr 1860 in Portage, Pennsylvania.

Rev Nelson Fessenden
Birth:
1826
New York
Death:
Dec. 6, 1890
Little Meadows
Susquehanna County
Pennsylvania
Burial:
Little Meadows Cemetery
Little Meadows
Susquehanna County
Pennsylvania

Husband of Angeline D FESSENDEN, Rev. N. (a "Rev. Nelson Fessenden, Parents, John Fessenden, b. 1796, and Mary Barney, b. 1796; he mar. Mary Breed, Sep. 1846; next Angeline Smith; next Fairchild, bef 1895. It seems he was b. Penn. and died there.   He is on Findagrave: #
[There is a family, Henry Fessenden, from NY,   in Rock Co. Wis., with one son, Daniel N., is only one I can find and he died about 23 yrs.

Rev Joseph D Flannery
Birth:
Mar. 31, 1928
Scranton
Lackawanna County
Pennsylvania
Death:
Mar. 11, 2005
Pennsylvania
Burial:
Cathedral Cemetery
Scranton
Lackawanna County
Pennsylvania

An early minister/pastor in Flatt River FWB Church, MO. (before 1938).

Daniel Mcbride Graham
Birth:
Nov. 17, 1817
Huron County, Ohio
Death:
Dec. 21, 1888
Philadelphia
Philadelphia County,
Pennsylvania
Burial:
Mount Moriah Cemetery
Philadelphia
Philadelphia County,
Pennsylvania

His parents, reverent Lemuel L. And Hannah were of Scottish descent and gave their son religious instructions. He was baptized in the LaGrange County, Indiana in 1839 and entered the sophomore class of Oberlin college in the spring of 1841. He lived part of his time with Prof. Charles G. Finney, and the degree of Master of Arts was conferred in 1847. The degree of Dr. of Divinity was conferred by Bowdoin college in 1863. Graham received license from the Calhoun Quarterly Meeting in 1844, and was ordained by the same body three years later. He was president of Michigan Central college at Spring Arbor, Michigan, 1844-48. He then ministered to the church in Saco, Maine two years and that the New York City church for 11 years. Then at Portland, Maine and Chicago Illinois in the years that followed. In 1871 he became Pres. of Hillsdale College filling that position with credit for three years. For several years he was editor of the *Free Will Baptist Quarterly* also of the *Christian Freeman*. He was a frequent contributor to the columns of *The Morning Star*, *The Free Baptists,* and the *Religious Intelligencer* of New Brunswick. He held various positions on many of the denominational boards and aided in securing the cooperation of brothers in New Brunswick and Nova Scotia in foreign missionary work. And in 1860 served the denomination as delegate to the General Baptists of England. His later ministry was with the church at East Somerville, Massachusetts and churches in Philadelphia, Pennsylvania where his last pastorate was. His ministry was attended with divine blessings. His records show that he had more than 1000 converts and baptisms during his years of service

Since I accepted Christ, dying is all I've been living for!

Rev John H Green
Birth:
Nov. 10, 1823
Brandywine
New Castle County
Delaware
Death:
Jan. 11, 1909
Bradford County
Pennsylvania
Burial:
Jillson Cemetery
Warren Center
Bradford County,Pennsylvania

Rev. J. H. Green, experienced religion in 1842. He was ordained in 1872, by order of the Gibson Quarterly Meeting,(QM) at a session of the Susquehanna Yearly Meeting at West Lenox. His ministry was spent in the Gibson and Owego QMs, his labors blessed, expecially with the Warren and Windham churches, where he had his longest pastorates.

Oliver Clinton Hills

Birth:
June 8, 1824
Death:
1913
Roulette
Potter county, ennsylvania
Burial:
Wellsboro Cemetery
Wellsboro
Tioga County, Pennsylvania

He experienced the new birth in February, 1843 and was licensed to preach on December 23, 1854. He was ordained by a Council of the Spafford Quarterly Meeting on September 9, 1855. His early ministry was in the Spafford and Troy Quarterly Meetings. He ministered to churches in the New York and Pennsylvania Quarterly Meetings and had revivals each year of his ministry. He organized six churches and baptized 221 converts. He assisted in raising funds for building several meeting houses during, 1868-70, he engaged in church extension work under the direction of the Pennsylvania Missionary Society receiving cash and subscriptions for church buildings amounting to more than $9000. Twice to served as a delegate to the General Conference. He was in the ministry for many years, having been pastor of several churches in Tioga county and was for some time chaplain at the Tioga County Home. The funeral services were at the Free Baptist church on East avenue, Rev. A.C. Shaw, D.D. officiated.He was one of those plain unassuming preachers whose chief aim in life was that of doing good in a quiet, but effective manner, which gained for him many friends among those with whom he came in contact.

Daniel W. Hunt

Birth:
April 21, 1821
Otsego County, New York
Death:
Oct. 31
Knoxville, Pennsylvania
Burial:
Woodlawn Cemetery
Austinburg
Tioga County, Pennsylvania

He studied in the Deerfield, Pennsylvania school where he was brought to God in 1855. In the same year received license to preach. He was ordained on September 26, 1858 being connected with the Brookfield church of the Tuscarora Quarterly Meeting. Hunt, aged 81, died in Knoxville at the home of his son, Mr. John B. Hunt. When a youth he removed with his parents and their many children to Brookfield township, where he remained nearly 30 years and where his marriage to Miss Ann Wakley took place. After living in Troupsburg, N.Y., for a time they moved to Knoxville for the remainder of his life. When still a young man Mr. Hunt became a member of the Free Will Baptist Church, and for many years had been a licensed preacher in the denomination. His funeral service was largely attended and was held on Sunday afternoon, at the Free Will Baptist church in Austinburg, Brookfield township, where Mr. Hunt had been a member for nearly half a century.

John Welsley Ingerick

Birth:
Apr. 24, 1831
Rutland
Tioga County, Pennsylvania
Death:
Sep. 13, 1915
Wellsboro
Tioga County, Pennsylvania
Burial:
Wellsboro Cemetery
Wellsboro
Tioga County, Pennsylvania

He was licensed in the Tioga Quarterly Meeting, February, 1884 and did a good work in serving the outlying districts in the word of life. He served for 10 years as the quarterly meeting clerk.

Info: Wellsboro Gazette, September 14, 1950, page 3

Rev Smith Lent

Birth:

Aug. 27, 1808
Cortland
Cortland County, New York
Death:
Jun. 12, 1894
Rome
Bradford County, Pennsylvania
Burial:
Rome Cemetery
Rome
Bradford County, Pennsylvania

Went to PA in 1832, ordained by Eld. A. Dodge and others in 1840 at Rome. He was an early advocate of abolition and temperance. Of several children, three sons served in the army and one, Geo. A. was in the ministry. Rev. Smith Lent was the son of Joseph and Anna (Smith) Lent. Mary Anne (Miller) Lent was his 1st wife. They were married October 30, 1830 and she died September 5, 1879. Sarah "Sally" Russell Lent was his 2nd wife. They were married in 1880 and she died July 8, 1892.

Rev John B. Page
Birth:
Jul. 6, 1819
East Alton
Belknap County
New Hampshire
Death:
Feb. 7, 1899
Pennsylvania
Burial:
Platea Cemetery
Platea
Erie County
Pennsylvania

Rev. John B Page, the son of Rev. John and Susan (Clark) Page was married in Boston, MA to Miss Ruth R. Lombard. His early education was in the schools of Maine and New Hampshire, and removing to Boston he supplied the churches in Boston, S. Boston, Charlestown and Roxbury, while pursuing his studies.

In 1842 he moved to NY state and supplied various churches and assisted by Rev's H. Whitcher and G.H. Ball, he organized the Rome church. At a session of the whitestown Q.M., in 1846 he was ordained, and preached at Gilbert's Mills one year. During this time he preached at Phoenix, and organized the church there and became its pastor. In 1849 he moved to Lockport, Erie co. PA where he remained thirteen years preaching to the churches in Lockport, Wellsburg, Pageville and Pierpont. In 1861 he moved to Maumee City, OH, continuing to preach in the churches in that vicinity. In 1864 he was called to the pastorate of the church in Chicago. The building of a church edifice was begun, and it was dedicated free of debt Dec. 7, 1865. At noon of that day the church burned to the ground. The McHenry Q.M. was in session, and it was voted to rebuild. Bro. Page engaged in evangelistic work in the Q.M., but overwork brought on paralysis, and he had to cease work for the time being. In 1870 he accepted the pastorate of the church in New Lyme, OH, where he remained three years. From here went to Penn. and preached at Wellsburg, Greenwoood, Canal, in that state. His baptisms number over five hundred, and he has often held responsible positions in the denomination of the Free Will Baptists.

Chester Prince
Birth:
Jun., 1792
Dudley, Worcester County,
Massachusetts
Death:
May, 1867
Rome, Bradford County,
Pennsylvania
Burial:
Rome Cemetery
Rome, Bradford County,
Pennsylvania

He was converted at the age of sixteen, moved in 1815 to Bradford County, Pa., where he died. He joined the Rome church at an early day, being a pioneer, Died age 74y 11m.

Since I accepted Christ, dying is all I've been

living for!

Caleb S Rogers
Birth:
Mar. 14, 1791
Bennington County, Vermont
Death:
Aug. 15, 1879
Greenfield, Pennsylvania
Burial:
Lowville Cemetery
Wattsburg, Erie County,
Pennsylvania
Plot: Sect or Lot 7

His parents were Nehemiah and Lydia (Smith) Rogers, who moved to Luzerne Co. Pennsylvania, at an early day. He was converted in western New York when twenty-seven years of age under the labors of Rev. J. Parmenter, and licensed at the Bethany Quarterly Meeting on Jan 24, 1825. A year later he was ordained. He labored in Genesee and Livingston Counties until 1836, and at Freedom, N.Y., until 1841. Then he moved to Sparta, PA. in the Washington and French Creek Q.M's until his death. Here, though so aged, he had preached only the Sabbath before. He traveled extensively, and was well known and highly esteemed throughout this region. (This was found in the History of Genesee Co. online:"The Freewill Baptist church, organized in 1809, was the first

in town." (Bethany). Area where Rev. C.S. Smith was active in early times). He married Chloe Warriner, 13 April 1815, Bennington, NY. They had several children, When a very young man, he served in the Navy in the War of 1812.

Cary Rogers
Birth:
Aug. 22, 1815
Grafton, Rensselaer County,
New York
Death:
Aug. 30, 1894
Cranesville, Erie County,
Pennsylvania
Burial:
Hope Cemetery
Cranesville, Erie County,
Pennsylvania

Rogers, was an ordained Freewill Baptist minister.. His parents were Nathan and Sarah (Steward) Rogers, who were of English and Scotch descent. His wife was Mary Rogers, who he married on 1/17/1848. He was licensed in 1876 and ordained in 1878. He assumed the pastoral care of the Pageville, Pennsylvania, church in 1877 and continued his labors with them until 1887, when failing health caused him to resign his position as pastor.

Samuel Buck Seaman
Birth:
Aug. 4, 1810
Tioga County,
Pennsylvania
Death:
Mar. 3, 1854
Wilmore
Cambria County,
Pennsylvania
Burial:
Wilmore United Brethren
Church Cemetery

Wilmore
Cambria County,
Pennsylvania

He was engaged in ministerial labor several years have been be connected with the Jefferson church of the Cook's town quarterly meeting, Pennsylvania since his ordination about 1844.His wife was Anne Ashbaugh Seaman (1819 - 1899).

Nicholas J. Shirey
Birth:
Jul. 24, 1846
Death:
1931
Burial:
Barren Run Methodist
Cemetery
Smithton
Westmoreland County,
Pennsylvania

Rev. N.J. Shirey, was educated at Mt. Pleasant and at Edinboro' Normal School, PA, and received ordination Nov. 16, 1879, into the Freewill Baptist church. He has ministered to the Jenner and Dunnings Creek churches two years, to the Deanville and Oakland churches one year and is now [1889] with the Brookfield and Cameron, N,Y., churches. He has labored as an evangelist, and baptized ninety-one converts.In August 1884, he was married to Cora

E. Bailey.

Joshua G Shoemaker
Birth:
Oct. 7, 1830
Death:
Dec. 11, 1900
Burial:
Deanville Cemetery
Deanville
Armstrong County,
Pennsylvania

His father with the Rev. George Shoemaker, who was a founder of the Church of the Brethren in Christ. Brother Shoemaker became a Free Baptist in 1880 and was minister of the Deanville church. His early ministry was devoted to itinerant work with the Church Of Brethren In Christ. His son, M. N. Shoemaker was a student in the theological Department of Hillsdale College Michigan.On August 4, 1861, Joshua married Elizabeth Ann Myers 1839-1892 and to them seven children were born. Later he married Nancy J Miller but there were no children to this union.

John Corydon Steele
Birth:
Mar. 4, 1834
Boston
Erie County, New York
Death:
Jun. 3, 1910
Burial:Non-Cemetery Burial
Pennsylvania

He began the Lord's service in 1852 and received his license to preach in 1854. He was ordained by the Erie Quarterly Meeting in New York in 1862. The same year he was married to Caroline Griffith and they had two daughters. His ministry has been with the church at Attica, Warsaw, Chagrin Falls and Parma, Ohio. Most of his work was done in the state of New York organizing churches and laboring to build up the cause under the direction of the Home Mission Society. Besides revival meetings in all these places some of them were largely successful. He was very active not only in revivals and organizing churches but had great influence in the Western part of New York State. He was very prominent in the work of the Central Association and also served as a delegate to the General Conference.

Rev Willard Stickney
Birth:
Aug. 23, 1808
Bethel
Oxford County,Maine
Death:
Aug. 29, 1880
Rockdale Acres
Crawford County
Pennsylvania
Burial:
Miller Station Cemetery
Cambridge Springs
Crawford County
Pennsylvania

Rev. Willard Stickney, a native of Bethel, ME, united with others in forming the Durham church in 1827. His ministerial labors began in Franklin, VT in 1831, and he was ordained at Starksboro, Jan. 25, 1835.

For some time he labored as an evangelist in Vermont, New York, and Canada. His soul yearned for the perishing, and he labored earnestly to win them to Christ. He afterwards settled in Pennsylvania, gathered several churches [Wellsboro, in 1839, and was its first pastor] and remained in Penn. until the close of his life. He was a useful man, and many were sad at his death.

He was married to Clarissa Cummings and they had three daughters, Ina, Julia, and Sarah.

Dutton Stiles
Birth:
Apr. 6, 1818
New York
Death:
May 14, 1874
Wharton
Potter County,
Pennsylvania
Burial:
Rees Cemetery
Potter County,
Pennsylvania

He was a Free Baptist minister from NY, but moved to Potter Co. and worked in the Potter Co. Quarterly Meeting of which he was the clerk for 21 years. He was a zealous Christian worker and in connection with his ministerial labors, engaged in teaching several years. Son of Reuben Stiles and Phebe Dutton

Benjamin Towner
Birth:
July 8, 1803
Rome, Pa.
Death:
Apr. 2, 1866
Lawrence, Pa.
Burial:
Evergreen Cemetery
Tioga, Tioga County,
Pennsylvania

His early religious experiences were with the Methodists, but he did not agree with them and was told that he was a Free Baptist, the first he had ever heard of the denomination. He immediately sought them, and spent some years in the ministry. He was especially giftedin singing and aided much in revival services.

Henry H Van Amringe
Birth:
Jan. 13, 1796
Philadelphia, Pa.
Death:
May 24, 1862
Philadelphia, Philadelphia
County, Pennsylvania
Burial:
Laurel Hill Cemetery
Philadelphia, Philadelphia
County, Pennsylvania

He was graduated honorably by Columbia college, New York city, in 1815. Immediately after graduating he studied law, and in 1818 was admitted to practice in the Supreme Court of the State of New York. He subsequently settled at Westchester, Chester Co., Pa., and by his ability and integrity soon gained a distinguished position at the bar. During the administration of Gov. Shulze he was appointed by Attorney General Ellmacher his deputy for Chester County. This office he resigned in 1835. He became Recorder of Pittsburgh, Pa., in 1840, by appointment of the Governor. He resigned the Recordership in 1844, and, though he had a brilliant legal and political career open before him, he quit forever the practice of the bar to devote himself to the Chrisatian ministry. From this time forward he labored assiduously to disseminate the gospel. He itinerated through various parts of Pennsylvania, New York, Ohio, Illinois and Wisconsin, as an evangelist and a lecturer on such practical reforms as he deemed best calculated to secure to all free homes, personal liberty, education, and the perpetuity of our republican institutions. His influence had much to do with the passage of a homestead exemption law by Wisconsin, which still remains in force. He wrote much for the papers, many pamphlets on subjects of religion and reform, and several religious works.In 1854 he united with the F. W. Baptists, and became pastor of their church near Burlington, Wis.. His arduous labors shattered his constitution, and he was compelled at last to yield through physical exhaustion. He resigned the pastorship of the Freewill Baptist church at Prairie Centre, Illinois, in the latter part of 1859, and by invitation west to live in Philadelphia with his sister and her family, by whom he was attended with the most devoted and untiring affection till his death. Though he was afflicted with paralysis, which extended gradually over his body and affected at last even his speech, and, at times, with acute neuralgic and rheumatic pains, no impatient or complaining word ever escaped his lips. He seemed not to think of himself, but was the charm of the family from the uniform cheerfulness and sweetness of his temper, the inexhaustible fund of information which he was ever ready and pleased to impart, the tender interest he manifested in the welfare of all about him, and the noble Christian example his daily life afforded. His death was as calm as his hope was steadfast. As he approached his end, the paralysis in a great measure left him, and he slept himself away as gently as an infant. His friends scarecely knew that he had gone till his silent pulse informed them that his spirit rested in the bosom of his Father. After his death there were found among his private papers two of what he had terms *"Books of Remembrance."* In one of them was the following remarkable entry. "Faithfully did he keep the vows here made and most signally were his prayers answered." In the early part of the evening on which this entry was made he had recorded that he was reading Upham on Christian Perfection and in conformity with direction consecrated himself solemnly to God.

Rev Francis M. Watkins
Birth:
Jul. 18, 1857
Ohio
Death:
Aug. 17, 1927
Burial:
Nye Cemetery
Chauncey
Athens County, Ohio

WATKINS, Rev. F. M. (Francis M), 1857-1927 ,bio in Cyclopedia; Buried in Nye Cemetery, Chauncey, Athens Co. OH, Ordained Free Baptist minister; son of Wm. T. and Elmira L (Beaman) Watkins. He was ordained in Salem, Ind. Jan. 6, 1889 and pastored the church there, where he prospered in that work. (source: Cyclopedia of Free Baptist, pub. 1889).
Inscription:
PVT 119th INF. 50 DIV.
WORLD WAR I VETERAN

Rev George W Webb
Birth:
1808
Massachusetts,
Death:
Jun. 3, 1863
Pennsylvania
Burial:
Woodlawn Cemetery
Austinburg
Tioga CountyPennsylvania

An ordained Freewill Baptist minister who ministered in Penn.

David Winton
Birth:
Jan. 25, 1825
Centerville, Crawford County, Pennsylvania
Death:
Dec. 29, 1870
Pierpont, Ashtabula County, Ohio
Burial:
Hope Cemetery, Lundys Lane, Erie County, Pennsylvania

At the age of fifteen, he was converted and the next year commenced the work of an evangelist. He traveled in Crawford, Venango and Erie Counties. In April 1846, he became pastor of the Free Baptist Church of Wellsburg, and for six years labored incessantly, preaching in Lockport, Girard, Franklin and Pikeville. He spent three months in western New York. In August, 1854, he became pastor of the church in Jackson, Mich., and for several years he labored with the Jackson and Spring Arbor churches. He served three years as a chaplain and two years as general agent of the Michigan State Prison. In 1869, he returned to Pennsylvania, and the following February took up the work at Pierport, Ohio, where after a brief illness he died, Dec. 29th. Rev. Winton's gift was that of a revivalist. He was an able preacher. Temperance, education and freedom had in him a strong advocate.

Rhode Island

Thomas L. Angell
Birth:
Nov. 10, 1837
Greenville
Providence County
Rhode Island
Death:
1923
Burial:
Smith Lot
Smithfield
Providence County
Rhode Island

When 3 years old he began to attend the common school of Greenville, and continued in this school several years with the loss of only one term. December 1855, he went to Thetford, Vt., and remained two terms. The next two years he was at the Wesleyan Academy, Wilbraham, Mass., fitting for college. He entered Brown University in 1858, and graduated in 1862.

The following winter he taught the school in Greenville. In November, 1863, He entered the Theological School at E. Windsor, Conn. The next spring he taught school in Greenville again, and in the fall of 1864, became an assistant of Rev. B. F. Hayes in Lapham Institute. He was for three years Principal of that school, until the Summer of 1868 In January 1869, he entered upon the Professorship of Modern Languages in Bates College. After the close of the college year, he spent a year in Europe in study. In early years he had marked religious impressions through parental instruction and the powerful influence of the devout teacher of the Greenville school.He was baptized by Rev. James McKenzie. He preaches more or less along with his work in the college. His first sermon was preached in the F. B. Church of Harrison, Me., Jan. 5, 1873. On July 31, 1862, he married Miss Emily Brown of Providence, R. I. His only daughter, Miss F. Angell, entered Bates College in 1886.

Reuben Allen
Birth:
Sep. 4, 1793
Gilmanton
Belknap County
New Hampshire,
Death:
May 30, 1872
North Scituate,
Providence County
Rhode Island
Burial:
Smithville Cemetery
North Scituate
Providence County
Rhode Island

In October, 1811, while apprenticed to a blacksmith, he experienced a radical change of heart and at age 19, after a struggle back from death's door, he yielded his life to the Lord and began holding a revival meeting at Northfield, where 35 were converted. In 1818, he went to Vermont, where he preached at Wheelock and Cabot. He was ordained to the ministry; fifty persons were baptized and two churches organized. Early in 1820 he traveled and preached in Burlington, St. Albans and other towns in VT. In 1821, he visited Rhode Island, reaching Burrillville on horseback, Oct. 13, for the organization of the RI Quarterly Meeting. The next day he preached the sermon at the ordination of Daniel Green, the first Freewill Baptist ordination which took place in the state. His labors were prolific in Vermont and Rhode Island.

A Day of Victory

Alfred Williams Anthony
Birth:
Jan. 13, 1860
Death:
Jan. 20, 1939
Burial:
Swan Point Cemetery,
Providence,
Providence County,
Rhode Island

Anthony was born in Providence, Rhode Island on January 13, 1860 to Lewis Williams Anthony and Britannia Franklin (Waterman) Anthony. He was a descendant of Rhode Island founder, Roger Williams. Anthony graduated from Brown University in 1883 and Cobb Divinity School in 1885, which was then affiliated with Bates College. Anthony also received an A.M. degree from Brown in 1886.

In 1887, he was appointed to a professorship at Cobb Divinity School. When the Divinity School merged with the College religion department, he became a religion professor at Bates College serving from 1908 to 1911. Anthony was active in various Freewill Baptist institutions and served as President of the Board of Trustees of Storer College in West Virginia. He travelled to Africa and Asia as Secretary for the Free Will Baptist Home Missions Council. Anthony also as a Trustee for Bates College, Hillsdale College, and Brown University.

A Prof. at Bates College and the author of *An Introduction to the Life of Jesus* (1896) and *The Method of Jesus* (1899) and *Bates College and Its Background* (1936). He received an honorary D. D. from Bates in 1902, Brown in 1908, and an L.L.D. from Colby in 1914. He had a strong influence on the merger with the Northern Baptists.

Ammi Ruhamah Bradbury
Birth:
Dec. 3, 1810
Auburn, Maine
Death:
Sep. 3, 1899
Burial:
Swan Point Cemetery
Providence
Providence County
Rhode Island

He was son of Samuel and Jane Gurney Bradbury. He studed in the common school and began teaching at age seventeen; he fitted for college at Kent's Hill Academy, then at Hebron Academy, and graduated from Bowdoin College in 1837. He studied theology a year at Bangor and three years at Yale Theological Seminary. He was awakened in the spring of 1834 while at Bowdoin Collge through the Holy Spirit, through Rev. Thomas Upham, D.D., and led by his pious room-mate, Abion Andrews, since Governor of Mass. He was baptized by Rev. George Lamb and united with the Freewill Bapt church at Brunswick. He was licensed in 1836, and ordained at Bangor as pastor in 1838. He has held pastorates in Bangor, Limerick, ME; Chepachet, R.I., Springvale, and N. Berwick, ME; Portsmouth, Crown Point and Candia, NH; Biddeford, ME, Park St. Church, Providence, R.I., and Auburn R.I., He has seen converts baptized in every pastorate. He was a teacher of the Classics and afterward Principal at Parsonfield Seminary: he was associate principal at Smithville Seminary, was principal at Strafford Academy and associate pastor at the time with Rev. Enoch Place. He was Recording Sec'y of the FWB Educational Society 1852-57. He has been for six years associate editor of the *"Freewill Baptist,"* of New Berne, N.C. He published (1887) the "Transfiguration," Ten Commandments" and "Miracles of Christ."
Feb. 20, 1844, he was married to Caroline L.J. Johnson, and they had four children; three sons were graduates of Brown

University, Providence. William A. after studying one year in the Theological Seminary, suddenly died. Fred W. Bradbury, became a physician in Auburn, R.I., and Samuel J. a physician in NYC.

Jonathan McDuffee
Brewster
Birth:
Nov. 1, 1835
New Hampshire
Death:
Jun. 2, 1882
Rhode Island
Burial:
Pocasset Cemetery
Cranston
Providence County
Rhode Island
Plot: old-cem

Rev. Jonathan McDuffee, son of Daniel and Sarah (McDuffee) BREWSTER, was born in Alton, NH, While a child his parents moved to Wolfborough, an adjoining town, and occupied the farm of the Brewster ancestors. At the age of fourteen he united with the church there. He studied in the common schools and in the academy of the town. He pursued preparatory studies at New Hampton and graduated from Dartmouth College in 1860. He studied theology at New Hampton and at Andover, Mass. In May 1863, he became pastor at Springvale, ME, and was ordained Dec. of that year. In May, 1864, at the solicitation of William Burr, he became ass't editor of the "*Morning Star.*" At Burr's death he wrote and published his biography. For a short period (1869-70) he supplied the church in Fairport, NY, and in 1871, entered upon a pastorate of three and a half years at North Scituate, RI. There he served the town as superintendent of public schools. In March, 1875, he entered upon the pastorate with the Park Street church, Providence, which closed with his death, June 2, 1882.

His illness was brief but his work was thoroughly done. From 1872 to his death he was clerk of the R.I. Assn, and from 1875 he was a corporator of the Printing Establishment. He was one of the executive board of Foreign Missions and an original trustee of Storer College. He was author of "*The Free Baptists of Rhode Island and Vicinity,*" published in Centennial Minutes of the state for 1880: of "The Freewill Baptists and their Foreign Missionary Enterprise," both published in the Centennial Record (1880), which he edited.

He was a member at the time of his death of the executive committee of the R.I. Woman's Suffrage Association. In October. 1863, he married Miss Marilla Marks Towle, of North Danville, NH, who survives him.

A Freewill Bapt. minister, educator, publisher, and leader in the Randall FWB movement of that time. His name is on many publications.

Marilla Towle Marks
Brewster
Birth:
1838
N. Danville, NH
Death:
1897
Connecticut
Burial:
Pocasset Cemetery, Cranston
Providence County
Rhode Island
Plot: old-cem

Mrs. Marilla Marks BREWSTER, wife of Rev. J.M. Brewster, was born to Nicholas and Mary (Page) TOWLE, were of Scotch descent and bequeathed to their five children sound principles and a thirst for knowledge. From the "red school-house" she went for a few months to Kingfield Academy and at fifteen began to teach. Largely through her own earnings she graduated from New Hampton Institution in 1860. She was converted and baptized in 1853 by Rev. M.W. Burlingame and united with the church in her native place.

On her graduation she became preceptress of the academy at Waukegan, Ill. and the second year she assumed full charge of the institution. At another time, she also served as lady-principal of the academy at

East Greenwich, R.I.

She became the wife of Rev. J.M. Brewster 06 Oct. 1863, and was recognized as an untiring helper in the relation of pastor's wife for eighteen years.

Many positions of trust and responsibility have fallen to her. From its organization she has been a member of the executive board of the Woman's Missionary Society. The Missionary Helper, its organ, had its beginning largely in her faith, and for nine years she was its editor and publishing agent till ill-health compelled her to relinquish the task. *"Missionary Reminiscences,"* by Mrs. M.M.H. Hills, came into being through her influence. For three years she was President of the Woman's Educational and Industrial Union of Rhode Island, a member of the executive board of the Prisoners' Aid Society, and secretary of the Suffrage Association. She held responsible positions in the W.C.T.U. She was an original member of the Rhode Island Woman's Club, and is one of the two women who have been made honorary members. She was two years secretary of the Woman's Auxiliary of City Missions in Brooklyn, NY. In 1888 she was a delegate to the International Council of Women held in Washington, D.C., and the same year represented the Woman's Missionary Society of the denomination at the World's Conference of Foreign Missions held in London. She gave some time to the study of mission work in that city and traveled on the continent.

As a writer she wields an easy, graceful pen, as a lecturer she is interesting and instructive, as a Christian she is quick in her sympathies for the downtrodden and unfortunate and consecrated to a noble work to her Saviour,

---

Allen Brown

Birth:
Mar. 31, 1788
Providence,
Providence County,
Rhode Island
Death:
Nov. 6, 1860
Providence,
Providence County,
Rhode Island
Burial:
North Burial Ground,
Providence,
Providence County,
Rhode Island

He enjoyed the privileges of the best schools his city afforded. He united early with the First Congregational church under the care of Rev. Mr. Wilson. After serving an apprenticeship in the hardware store of Governor Jones, he went for a year in 1810, to Savannah, GA, and engaged in business for himself. He then established the business under the name of Dyer and Brown in Providence. Feeling a call to the ministry, he entered on a course of study in Philadelphia, and on graduating returned to Providence and took the pastoral charge of the Third Baptist church, then just organized. During the six years that followed he witnessed many conversions. His views were decidedly Arminian and he was ordained not without hesitation by the council. He was a member of the "Union Conference," with Zalmon Tobey, Henry Tatem, and Ray Potter, which ordained Martin Cheney, April, 24, 1825.

In 1827, at the expiration of his pastorate with the Third Baptist church, feeling he had no sympathy from the Baptist brethren, he joined the Olneyville, R.I., Freewill Baptist church under Rev. Martin Cheney, and also the Q.M.

During the next thirty years of his life he held no pastorate. He was bookkeeper in Merchants' Bank of Providence for twenty years. He then entered the counting-room of Dr. Samuel B. Tobey as confidential clerk.

On the opening of the Dexter Asylum, he became chaplain, preaching regularly to the unfortunate for more than twenty years till his last sickness laid him aside for over a year.

To the Freewill Baptist Foreign Mission Society he bequeathed the sum of five hundred dollars. For many years he was well known to the readers of *The Morning Star* by his contributions in poetry and prose over the signature "A.B." He is also profiled in the book, *"Memoirs of Eminent Preachers In The Freewill Baptist Denomination (1874)",* by Selah Hibbard Barrett of Rutland, Ohio.

Gideon A. Burgess

Birth:
May 29, 1854
Death:
Mar. 4, 1945
Burial:
North Burial Ground,
Providence,
Providence County,
Rhode Island

Burgess, Rev. Gideon A., son of Albert Williams and Mary B. (Williams) Burgess, was born in Providence, R. 1., May 29, 1854. He descended through both parents from Roger Williams, and by paternal descent from Rev. Samuel Winsor, father and son, who held the pastorate of the First Baptist church, Providence, 1732-71. He graduated from the Providence High School in 1874, Brown University in 1878, and Bates Theological Seminary in 1881. Converted Oct. 6, 1872, he was baptized by Rev. J. Mariner in January, 1873, uniting with the Greenwich Street church. Having been licensed by the Rhode Association in 1878, he was ordained at Greenville, R. I., as pastor of the First Smithfield church, Nov. 22, 1882, the Rev. J. Mariner preaching the sermon.

He has baptized 40, solemnized 37 marriages, and attended 111 funerals. He was Secretary of the Rhode Island Sunday-School Union from 1883, resigning the office to assume the pastorate of the First church in Minneapolis, Minn. , Jan. 1, 1889. He has been Corresponding Secretary of the Free Baptist Education Society since 1886. He was chosen state agent for the Church Extension fund, and a member of the Minnesota State Mission Board in 1889. He is one of the editors of the Free Baptist Cyclopcedia published in 1889. He married Jan. I, 1884, Miss Emma A., daughter of Simon S. Steere, of Greenville, R. I.

**And with unfaltering lip and heart,
I call the Saviour mine.**

Maxcy Whipple Burlingame
Birth:
May 5, 1805
Gloucester,R. I.
Death:
Mar. 4, 1879
Georgiaville, R. I.
Burial:
Winsor-Hunt Lot
Glocester, Providence County,
Rhode Island

He was the youngest of ten children of Stephen and Abigail Burlingame. His father was a farmer of respectable standing, and both his parents were Christians. He could not remember the time when he was not accustomed to pray. During his childhood he often wished he might participate in a revival of religion. At the age of nineteen he made a public profession, was baptized by Rev. Joseph White in September, 1825, and united with the church in Gloucester. He now became sensible that he must have experienced religion when but a child. The impressions in regard to preaching were renewed with increased power, and though his diffident and sensitive spirit sought to stifle them, at length an abiding and increasing sense of duty lead him to consecrate himself to the work of the ministry. He attended a grammar school for some time in Killingly, Conn., and afterward the Wilbraham Academy. At the latter place he had the society of a number who were preparing for the ministry. In May, 1828, he received license to preach from the Rhode Island Q. M. His family then moved to Deerfield, Pa., where he taught and preached. Conversions resulted, and a church was organized. He returned to Rhode Island in the spring of 1829 and preached through the summer to several churches. He was ordained at Chepachet. January 28, 1830, he was married to Miss Harriet Winsor, of Gloucester. Soon after, he began to preach at Chepacher and Blackstone, Mass:, regularly, and fifth Sundays at Burrillville for a time. He soon dropped the latter appointment. Revivals occurred at the othe places and considerable additions to the churches. In the summer and autumn of 1834 he preached a part of the time at Pautucket with success. In the following winter he took charge of a school in Georgiaville, which had been broken up. He succeeded in the school. A revival resulted from his labors which induced him to move there in the spring of 1835. A church was soon organized and during the two years that he was pastor about fifty persons were baptized, among them his wife. Two of the earlier members became ministers. He had continued to preach at Blackstone, Mass., a part of the time, and now, in 1837, moved there and devoted all his time to that interest.He labored there in all over sixteen years. About 550 persons were received into the church. After four years a new house of worship was built. He also preached occasionally at Saundersville, in Grafton, Mass., and was instrumental in the organization of a church there afterward the Farnumsville church. He left there in 1846. The next three years he preached at Greenville and then at Chepachet. After a short time at Gilford Village, N. H., he settled at New Market, N. H. Other pastorates were in Danville, N. H., and Topsham, Me. He preached also in North Berwick, New Gloucester and Cornish, Me., at West Scituate, R. I., and East Killingly, Conn. About nine years before his death he returned to Georgiaville. He served as pastor there four years, and preached also at Tiverton and Carolina Mills, R. I., and

Westford, Conn. He was more than fifty years in the ministry. At his death no Free Baptist minister in Rhode Island had performed more service than he. He promoted missions, education and reform. From 1844 to 1859 he was a corporator of the Printing Establishment. He was efficient in originating the Smithville Seminary. He was a member of several General Conferences. His usefulness was not from superior intellect or talent in preaching, though he was above the average, but from loyalty to Christ and sympathy for men. He was very sensitive, but as tender toward others as he would have others be to him. His overflowing sympathies were governed by discretion. Ten ministers participated in his memorial service at Georgiaville, and five others were present.

George H. Chappell
Birth:
Feb. 4, 1850
Death:
Aug. 8, 1930
Burial:
Oak Dell Cemetery
South Kingstown
Washington County
Rhode Island
Plot: Section E, Lot 132

Martin Cheney
Birth:
Aug. 29, 1792
Death:
Jan. 4, 1852
Burial:
Pocasset Cemetery, Cranston,
Providence County,
Rhode Island

He was born in Dover, Massachusetts. Ordained to Preach April 28, 1825. Was installed Pastor over the First Free Will Baptist Church in Olneyville (Providence, Rhode Island) on Nov. 7, 1828 and continued until his death Jan. 4, 1852.
He was a warm Personal Friend, a kind Husband, an affectionate Father, a strng advocate for Liberty and Humanity, and a faithful servent of God.His last words were "I have a hope that endureth to the end.

William Crookes
Birth:
1824
England
Death:
Jan. 18, 1893
Rhode Island
Burial:
North Burial Ground
Providence
Providence County,
Rhode Island

He was converted at age of 14 and was licensed to preach on January 29, 1863 and ordained on September 19, 1840 by Rev. J. A. Mckenzie, and George Wheeler and others. His pastorates were basically in the Rhode Island area where he witnessed extensive revivals under his labors from which he baptized about 100 converts. At Maple Root church he had 175 come forward during six weeks; and at West Greenwich he had about 40 and at Ash Mills 60. He had a circuit of four churches, one for each Sunday during the month during his profitable ministry.

David Culver
Birth:
Apr. 30, 1795
Death:
Jun. 10, 1866
Pontiac, R. I.
Burial:
Greenwood Cemetery
Coventry, Kent County,
Rhode Island

Fifty years of his life were spent in the ministry, mostly among the Methodists. After his union with the Free Baptists, he evinced strong sympathy with reforms, discretionin counsel, energy in work and faithfulness in pastoral duties.

Gilbert Bancroft Cutler
Birth:
May, 1848
East Machias
Washington County
Maine
Death:
1934
Rhode Island
Burial:
Greenville Cemetery
Smithfield
Providence County
Rhode Island

An ordained Free Will Baptist minister and pastor.

George T. Day
Birth:
Dec. 8, 1822
Day Center,
Saratoga County, New York
Death:
May 21, 1875
Providence,
Providence County,
Rhode Island
Burial:
Pocasset Cemetery, Cranston,
Providence County,
Rhode Island

He was baptized by Martin Cheney in May 1840 uniting with the church at Olneyville. Attended Smithfield Seminary in 1845 he entered the biblical school at Whitestown, New York. In 1850 he moved to Chester, Ohio to become principal at Geauga Seminary. In 1852 he became the successor of Martin Cheney as the Pastor of Olneyville Free Baptist Church 1852-1857. Pastor, Roger Williams Free Baptist Church 1857-1867. Editor, *The Morning Star* 1867-1875. Possessing great natural ability, broad culture, deep piety, commanding eloquence and thorough devotion to principle. He was a prominent denominational leader, a successful Christian worker and a valued personal friend. In 1876 the Biography of Dr. Day, was written by Rev. Wm. H. Bowen, D.D., printed by the Free Will Baptist Printing Establishment, Dover, New Hampshire. He was a convert of Rev. Martin Cheney, at Olneyville, and a life-long friend.

Wilbur Eugene Dennett
Birth:
Jun. 22, 1852
Buxton
York County, Maine
Death:
1938
Biddeford
York County, Maine
Burial:
Locust Grove Cemetery
Providence
Providence County,
Rhode Island

He was converted in boyhood and graduated from the scientific Department of the University of Wisconsin in 1879 and from the theological Department of Hillsdale College in 1883. License to preach was granted him in 1880 and on April 8, 1883 he was ordained to the ministry. His ministry has been with the churches at Cambridge Rome, Michigan and later in the state of New York where his labors were blessed immensely.

Edmund G. Eastman
Birth:
Feb. 16, 1846
Madison, New Hampshire
Death:
Jan. 21, 1908
Burial:
Pocasset Cemetery
Cranston
Providence County,
Rhode Island

He was converted in 1858, and licensed by the Exeter, Maine Quarterly Meeting in March, 1875, and ordained in March 1776. He pastored numerous churches in Maine and New Hampshire before becoming the pastor of the Warwick Central church in Rhode Island in 1884, where 49 united with the church. He served in the Civil War over two years and was overseer of the poor and first selectmen in Parkman, Maine.

Herbert Ruthwen Farnum
Birth:
Aug. 19, 1853
Death:
Dec. 13, 1901
Burial:
Swan Point Cemetery,
Providence,
Providence County,
Rhode Island

A noteworthy influence in the Rhode Island Freewill Baptist work.
He was superintendent of the Bernon Mills for many years, and has given his influence heartily for the church in all its lines of usefulness, and for the general good of the community. To his effort and care the continued exclusion of the liquor traffic from the village is largely due.

Caleb Greene
Birth:
August 31, 1803
West Greenwich, Rhode Island
Death:
Dec. 27, 1894
Rhode Island
Burial:
Greene-Waite Lot
West Greenwich
Kent County, Rhode Island

He was converted in March, 1823, license in 1838, and ordained June 18, 1840 as the pastor of the Warwick and East Greenrich church. In 1843 he organized a church at West Greenwich and was its pastor for seven years.

Rev Daniel Greene
Birth:
Aug. 4, 1797
Foster, R.I.
Death:
May 22, 1896
Burial:
Line Cemetery ,Foster
Providence County
Rhode Island

Rev. Daniel Greene, son of Job and Dorcas (Round) Greene, married Waity Stone, May 10, 1818. Converted in June 1824, he was ordained as a deacon Aug. 9, 1832, and was licensed Dec. 2, 1841. He was ordained June 4, 1846, by Rev's Daniel Williams, Charles Wade, and Reuben Allen. He organized and was pastor of churches in E. Putnam, Conn., So. Scituate, and South Foster, R.I. He assisted in revivals and baptized converts in Shady Oak and Foster, R.I., in Putnam, Killingly, and Sterling, Conn. He retired from active service at age 89.

Rev Jesse Hayes
Birth:
Jun. 2, 1797
New Gloucester
Cumberland County, Maine
Death:
May 11, 1865
North Scituate
Providence County
Rhode Island
Burial:
Riverside Cemetery
Lewiston
Androscoggin County, Maine

Rev. Jesse Hayes, was a younger brother of Rev. Robert Hayes, both Free Will Baptist ministers.

On reaching his majority he enjoyed his first opportunity for an unbroken term of school, The

money he could now earn at his trade he purposed to expend for education. He felt the need to preach at age nineteen, and needed to seek the qualifications

as an ambassodor of the gospel. But at the earnest entreaty of his parents, he returned to the care of his farm. In June 1828, he was married to Mary, daughter of Daniel Harmon, Esq., of Durham, Me. Being frequently encouraged by ministers to conduct religious meetings he at length did so, and in 1831 received license from the Methodist Conf., and preached in the vicinity til 1842 when he began to occasionally supply Free Baptist churches in the Cumberland Q.M.

Having united with the Poland and Danville church he became its pastor and was ordained there Mar. 14, 1844. After two years the failure of health left him an invalid for the rest of his life. He removed to Auburn, ME,

joining with his family the church in Lewiston. For three years he was treasurer of the county.

On the removal of his son, Rev. Benj. F. Hayes, to Olneywille, R.I. in 1859, he also took up his residence there: in 1863 he moved to North Scituate.

His character was one of rare simplicity and transparency. He was always a true helper of the pastor in the churches where he lived, with comforting words being

constant in his attendance at church.

Spouse: Mary Harmon Hayes (1802 - 1889). Children: Benjamin Francis Hayes (1830 - 1906).

George Ellison Hopkins
Birth:
Dec. 18, 1811
Foster, Rhode Island
Death:
May 21, 1890
Burial:
Acotes Hill Cemetery
Glocester
Providence County,
Rhode Island

He studied at Scituate Academy and Westfield (Conn) Academy. He was ordained in about 1837, and was pastor of Foster Free Will Baptist Church ten years, where membership tripled. He served as pastor at Chepachet, Westford, and East Putman churches.He was two years representative in the Legislature and had been superintendent of schools in Foster, Glouscester and Scituate. He also taught for many years. His seven children were all teachers, two sons having graduated from Brown University.

Ezekiel R. Littlefield

Birth: 1815
Rock Island, Rhode Island
Death:
1891
Burial:
John R. Dodge Cemetery
New Shoreham
Washington County,
Rhode Island

The Rev. Ezekiel Littlefield's gravestone is surprisingly small for a member of such a highly esteemed profession. Located in the NE quarter of the cemetery, its inscription simply reads "aged 76 years" His mother was the daughter of Rev. Enoch Rose, who was a devoted and acceptable Free Baptist minister who had been ordained in 1817. Ezekiel was converted in 1830 and was licensed in 1843 and later ordained in 1845 by Rev. J. A. Mackenzie, Silas Hall, a Calvinistic Baptists; and John Tillinghast, a six principle Baptist. Soon after his ordination, he lost nearly all of his left hand by the explosion of a blasting powder. Because of this he was only able to baptize two people, yet he held extensive revivals. He ministered the Second New Shoreham church and supplied some 20 years. In 1835 he married Lucretia, the, daughter of Capt. Robert C. Hodge.

James A. McKenzie

Birth:
Dec. 3, 1812
Newport, R. I.
Death:
Apr. 10, 1873
Tiverton, R. I.
Burial:
Pleasant View Cemetery
Tiverton, Newport County,
Rhode Island

He was decidedly unique in his religious experience and in other characteristics. His father was a Scotchman, and a ship captain. His mother was a native of Newport. At the age of twelve. he was returning from berrying, and coming through a swamp to a dry knoll, he knelt and prayed, "And," he said, "I beheld the glory of God; I felt changed; I was at one "with God." Knowing of no company of disciples nor of any social meetings, he began to gather the boys from their plays, "and then tell them what I knew of the Word and work of grace on the soul, and whereunto I saw it would lead. After awhile they became so taken with it that we found a place for our meetings. The first we had was a 10ft in the barn, and after that the best rooms in marry and good houses. But somehow or other, the best meetings we had were those in the barn chamber.

These boys eventually formed themselves into a sort of society, consisting of upwards of forty, and saved somewhat from their spending money every week for the benefit of the poor. The most of these boys became good and honorable men in the churches of Christ. Several became ministers of the gospel" He finally united with the First Baptist church in Newport and was encouraged to take part in the meetings,which he did very acceptably. After a lengthy examination of the Scriptures, he was not satisfied with the sprinkling he had received in infancy, and was immersed, March, 1828, at the age of fifteen,and united with the church. He was encouraged to preach by the church and became assistant to the aged pastor, the Rev. Mr. Eddy. A portion of the church began a new interest, which was afterwards known as the Fourth Baptist church. Mr. McKenzie was ordained August 12, 1830, in his eighteenth year, and became pastor of this church. Two years after, he joined the Rhode Island Q. M. of Free Baptists,and in 1838 the church also united with that Q. M. After this he was settled fora time in Portsmouth, N. H. He was seven years pastor of the Roger Williams church, Providence, R. I., during which time the church prospered greatly and many were added to its membership. He left there in 1847 to go to Tiverton, where he would receive half the salary, because he thought he could do more good there. In this and many other cases he was actuated to a considerable extent by what he termed" divine suggestions. He remained at Tiverton till 1853, when he became pastor at Greenville (First Smithfield). After three years here and three years in Providence with the Third church, he returned to Tiverton. He was original in his preaching and possessed some oddities both as a preacher and as a man. Once when he had preached in a Close Baptist church, a communion service was held from which he, of course, was left out. He rose in the pulpit, and looking down upon them, said with the simplicity of a child: "I'll tell my Father of you." He was remarkably gifted in prayer and greatly beloved.

Salome *Lincoln* Mowry
Birth:
Sep. 13, 1807
Raynham, Bristol County,
Massachusetts
Death: ,
Jul. 21, 1841
Warwick,
Kent County, Rhode Island
Burial:
Pleasant View Cemetery,
Tiverton, Newport County,
Rhode Island

An early female preacher. About 1823, she was baptized with nine others, by Rev. Ruben Allen, a Free Will Baptist minister, who was pastor of the church at Taunton, where she united at that time. Her mind was upon religious thoughts and she read her Bible faithfully. She somehow, felt a deeper duty to do more for God but wrestled with the question because she was a woman. This was very rare in that time for a woman to speak publicly. She however, thought if she didn't, she would not be obedient to God. She preached her first sermon, Oct. 17, 1827. However, she was never ordained by any church. But she became a voice for good. She behaved in a most appropriate manner and deportment throughout her life. She dressed suitably and had few gestures when speaking, but her deep toned and heavy voice commanded attention, and large audiences could hear her. Her sermons were of substance and many times there was no standing room when she preached. She was welcomed in most places by other clergy to a pulpit; the Reformed Methodist pastor, in the town where she lived, wrote a letter of commendation for her testifying to her character. On Dec. 2, 1835, she was married to Rev. Junia S. MOWRY, a Free Will Baptist minister. Her burial took place at mid-night, due to having to go by boat across the bay and the tide was not favorable. The delay because of winds caused them to not arrive until midnight at the place of burial. (From *"The Female Preacher, or Memoir of Salome Lincoln..."* by Almond H. Davis, 1843 Providence, R.I.)

The Dead
In
Christ
Will
Rise First.

Rev Gideon Noka
Birth:
Apr., 1841
South Kingstown
Washington County
Rhode Island
Death:
Feb. 13, 1902
South Kingstown
Washington County
Rhode Island
Burial:
Oak Dell Cemetery
South Kingstown
Washington County
Rhode Island
Plot: LOT D-101

Rev. Gideon Noka, son of John and Esther (Rodman) NOKA. He received limited education. He was converted in 1856. Licensed in 1868, he was ordained as an evangelist by the Second adventists. He has labored among the Adventists, Methodists and Free Baptists. He married Miss A.F. Perry in 1860, [Dec. 16, 1860], and has five children living.

William N. Patt
Birth:
November 17, 1808
Scituate, Rhode Island
Death:
Apr. 29, 1891
Burial:
Smithville Cemetery
North Scituate
Providence County,
Rhode Island

His father was a sea captain for over 20 years. William was the next to the youngest of nine children and received early Christian training from an earnest Christian mother. He went away to school in at the age of 16 and was qualified to teach. He also served an apprenticeship as a carpenter and a builder in Providence. He became a Christian on January 16, 1827 and thereafter his motto was, "Holiness Of Heart And Life." After years of thought and struggle, he began his ministry in 1842 was licensed to by the Rhode Island Quarterly Meeting. He preached in a number of churches in Rhode Island and in Maine. And after serving one of their churches in Rhode Island, he was ordained in 1847 by Reverend's M. W. Burlinggame, M. J. Steere and D. Williams and continued his pastorate for two years longer. He also preached in Connecticut. He labored with his hands for his daily support and has given of his earnings $1500 to the aid of the cause of Christ, besides traveling 100,000 miles mostly on foot to attend religious meetings, and preaching some 1200 times, attending 3000 conferences and prayer meetings. He was very earnest in temperance and anti-slavery support.

Benjamin D Peck
Birth:
Apr. 11, 1813
Bristol
Bristol County, Rhode Island
Death:
Jun. 11, 1896
Burial:
Oak Hill Cemetery
Woonsocket
Providence County,
Rhode Island
Plot: D 0035

Rev. B.D. Peck, was brought up by pious parents, especially his mother, who influenced his upbringing. He was baptized in a revival as a young man, and united with the Freewill Baptist church where he lived. He felt that he needed to do more and began to study for his life-work, at Belton Academy, for two years. He preached his first sermon Nov. 1838, and the next spring, began as successor of Rev. Martin J. Steere. In 1840, he received a call to the church in Grafton, MA, where he was ordained on June 4th of that year. Here he remained for six years as pastor, as the church grew. His next pastorate was Waterford, successor to Rev. Burlingame. He was nominated by the Free Soil Party as candidate for the Massachusetts Legislature and, receiving a large vote, was elected while still pastor of the church. At the close of the Legislative session in 1848, he

removed to Portland. Rev. Peck was prominent in the Temperance Movement in that state. He was an active member in the Temperance Watchman organization from Maine, and became editor of *"The Watchman"*, a FWB temperance paper, pub. at Portland. He did this while carrying on his pastoral labors. He served his denomination as member of several benevolent boards and societies, and was esteemed as a worthy man.
---info on his ministry taken from *"The Rhode Island Pulpit,"* pub. 1852, by Rev. A. D. Williams.

Benjamin Phelon
Birth:
Jun. 1, 1806,
Halifax, England.
Death:
Jul. 18, 1882
Providence
Providence County,
Rhode Island
Burial:
Major General George Sears
Greene Lot
Warwick, Kent County,
Rhode Island
Plot: 00050

His parents were Christians, and he had faithful Sabbath-school instruction.He was converted at sixteen and united with the General Baptist church at Haley Hill in his native town. He preached his first sermon in a private house in Halifax, Jan. 30, 1825. He preached two years with good acceptance and then entered the General Baptist Academy at Heptonstall Slock, under the charge of Rev. Richard Ingham. He supplied churches during the three years of this course and for three years afterwards. In the summer of 1834 he spent several months at Derbyshire studying under the direction of Rev. J. G. Pike and supplying pulpits of neighboring churches. In December of that year he came to America. A note from Mr. Sutton, who was then in this country, induced him to visit New England. By his advice, also, he went to Apponaug, R. I., where soon after a church was organized, with which he remained two years and a half.He preached in Boston, Mass, one year, Centredale, R. I., one year, again ·in Boston two years, in Nashua, N. H., one year, and then spent six years in Fall River, Mass., building up a new interest. By vigorous and ceaseless toil he succeeded. A church was formed, and eventually a meeting-house erected. In 1849 he returned to Apponaug and remained there more than twenty years,until failing health compelled him to resign. He spent the remainder of his days in Providence. A part of the time he was able to serve churches. Especially valuable was his work at Tiverton during the long sickness of their pastor, Rev. J. A. McKenzie. His classical

tastes he retained and in a measure gratified. He was an early and persistent abolitionist and teetotaler. He was a good man, an able and faithful minister, and universally respected.

Mowry Phillips
Birth:
Aug. 20, I820
Lancaster, N. Y.
Death:
Jul. 4, 1881
Gloucester, R. I.
Burial:
Oak Hill Cemetery
Woonsocket,
Providence County,
Rhode Island

His grandmother and mother lived at Pascoag, where they were baptized by John Colby. When fifteen years of age, his mother died at Marcellus, N. Y., where the family then resided. She was the only Christian in the family. Years after, he thus speaks concerning himself at that time: "At this time I was a wicked, prayer less boy, yet when the truth flashed upon me that my mother was no more, I rushed to a solitary place, threw myself upon my knees, and prayed as sincerely and earnestly as I ever did, that God would bless the stricken flock; and shelter those littleones left without a mother's care. However, this was the only vocal prayer which I offered for months, or even years. Soon after his father gave him his time. He worked in Manchester, N. Y. two years, in Marcellus one year, a few months in Michigan, and then attended school at Alexander Academy, New York. While there he was cheered

with the news that his father was converted. Returning home in the spring of 1841, he himself yielded to Christ, was baptized, and joined the M. E. church in Marcellus. He then studied at the Onondaga Academy. Moving to Rhode Island, he united with the Free Baptist church at Waterford. The following year he was licensed to preach. He was acting pastorof the Reformed Methodist church at Millville, Mass., two years. March 1, 1845, he was ordained at Pascoag by the Western Rhode Island Q. M. In April, 1846, he became pastor of the Georgiaville church. During this pastorate of eighteen years many were converted and the church edifice was built. He was next pastor of the Pascoag church ten years, during which time many were gathered into the church, and the church edifice was refitted and enlarged. On account of sickness, he moved to a farm in Gloucester. After years of rest he became pastor of the West Scituate church, six miles away, but did not change his residence.

He preached his last sermon in the fall of 1880, when hewas so feeble through consumption that he was obliged to sit during the discourse. He was a man of fervent piety and greatly beloved. A Freewill Baptist clergyman. He preached the funeral sermon of Rev. Reuben Allen, in 1872.

Stephen Phillips
Birth:
Oct. 6, 1833
Marcellus
Onondaga County, New York
Death:
May 13, 1904
Wisconsin
Burial:
Slatersville Cemetery
North Smithfield
Providence County, Rhode Island

Phillips, Rev. Stephen, brother of Rev. Mowry Phillips, was born in Marcellus, Onondaga County, N. Y., Oct. 6, 1833. He studied three years at Smithville Seminary under Hosea Quinby. Converted in 1847, he was licensed in 1859 by the Rhode Island Q. M., and was ordained in 1863, by the Western Rhode Island Ministers' Conference. He was pastor of the West Seituate church from 1862-70. In 1865-66 he baptized twenty as the result of revivals. From 1870-80 he was confined at home by sickness. In 1883 he entered pastorate at North Foster. He married, Oct. 24, 1855, Mary E. S. Brown, and May 27, 1858, Abby L. Paine. He had five children, four of whom were teachers.

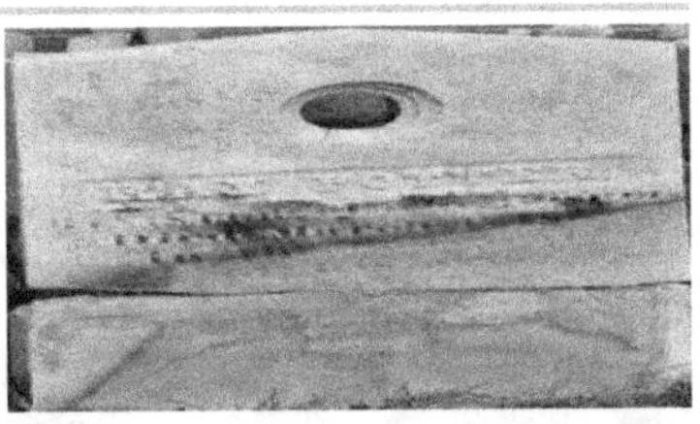

Ray Potter
Birth:
Jun. 22, 1795
Death:
Mar. 1, 1858
Providence County
Rhode Island
Burial:
Mineral Spring Cemetery
Pawtucket
Providence County
Rhode Island
Plot: Between Avenues F & G
and between Centre & Pine
Aves

He was the son of Andrew Potter and Nancy Remington Potter who are both buried in Knightsville Meeting House Cemetery, Cranston, RI
Ordained by the Six-Principle Baptists, pastored Pawtucket, later the Freewill Baptists, became clerk of the RI Quarterly Meeting; the church grew, but had some faction problems later. He separated from the QM in 1823, and in 1825, assisted in the ordination of Rev. Martin Cheney in a "Union Conference

Inscription:

Minister of the Gospel

in the 62d year
of his age

Rev John Pratt
Birth:
Aug. 5, 1807
Rhode Island
Death:
May 7, 1877
Newport, R.I.
Burial:
Common Burying Ground
Newport, Newport County
Rhode Island

Rev. John Pratts his father was a government officer. An ordained Freewill Bapt. minister, his name listed in Minutes of the church, in roll of those ministers who had died in 1877. He was 70 yrs.
He was converted in the autumn of 1827, in Newport, and the following spring was baptized with his father, James A. McKenzie and others. While preaching in Pawtuxet he was ordained Jan. 24, 1846, by Rev's Martin Cheney, J.A. McKenzie, and others. He afterwards held the following pastorates: Tiverton, Rehoboth, West Scituate, Gloucester and Jamestown, for seven years, till his death. While at Newport he was accustomed to worship with the Second Baptist church and felt especial interest in its prosperity. He was a strong advocate of reforms.
Just before the war he represented Newport in the General Assembly.

Amarancey Paine Sarle
Birth:
1812
Death:
1882
Burial:
Pocasset Cemetery
Cranston
Providence County,
Rhode Island
Dau. of Squire and Amy

(Hills) Paine. Married Orris Sarle, who only lived six yrs more. She was a lover of books, and charitable service. A member of the Freewill Baptist church, Olneyville, RI.

Benjamin A. Sherwood
Birth:
1843
Death:
1930
Burial:
Pocasset Cemetery
Cranston
Providence County,
Rhode Island

Graduated Bates Theological School, in 1875. An ordained Free Communion Baptist, and pastored Free Baptist churches in several states with good success.

Charles Shippee
Birth:
Mar. 6, 1809
East Greenwich, Rhode Island
Death:
Mar. 18, 1896
Burial:
Joseph Carpenter Lot
East Greenwich
Kent County, Rhode Island

He was converted in 1835 and ordained in 1852 by T. Tillinghast, J. Place, B. B. Cottrell, and P. Harrington. During his ministry he baptized over 150 converts in 1832 he was married to Jane Tarbox.

Daniel Angell Sweet
Birth:
1805
Death:
Jun. 28, 1861
Johnston, Rhode Island
Burial:
Rev. Daniel A Jenckes Lot
Johnston
Providence County,
Rhode Island

He began to preach about 1842 and was ordained by the Six Principle Baptist about 1845 but holding views on open communion differing with them, he with his church in 1856 united with the Free Baptist Quarterly Meeting. In 1858 he added 23 to his church by baptism. His funeral was preached by Rev. Rueben Allen.

Nathaniel Sweet
Birth:
1806
Death:
Nov. 13, 1873
Johnston, Rhode Island
Burial:
Sweet Lot
Johnston
Providence County, Rhode Island
He was a brother to the Rev. Daniel Sweet and served in the ministry nearly 50 years.

Martin J Steere
Birth:
Oct. 15, 1814
Providence
Providence County,
Rhode Island
Death:
Jan. 18, 1877
Athol
Worcester County,
Massachusetts
Burial:
North Burial Ground
Providence
Providence County,
Rhode Island

Rev. Martin Jenckes Steere, son of Stephen, a grandson of Elisha, was born in Smithfield. In 1834 he joined the Second Smithfield Free Baptist Church, at Georgiaville. He wished to prepare himself for the ministry, and with this end in view fitted for college at Fruit Hill Seminary, near Manton, R.I., but ill health obligded him to relinquish for a time his further course of study. However, in May 1837, he was ordained by the Rhode Island Conference, and the same year succeeded the Rev. M.W. Burlingame as pastor of the Georgiaville church, remaining until 1839. He then was appointed assistant editor of the "Morning Star," the organ of the denomination and editor of the Sunday-school paper. He then pastored the Apponaug church for three years, then went to North Scituate, where he labored for three years.He also spent one year at Waterford, Mass. He wrote and published at the request of the General Conf., a book entitled "The Friend of Chasity."After twenty years of active service in the ministry of the Free Baptist denomination, a change in his theological views led him, in April, 1859, into the Universalist Church. He pastored several church in Lawrence, W. Haverhill, MA, Lewiston, ME and Maridon, Conn, and Mechanics Falls, ME. His health suffered from the severities of his labors and the harshness of the climate and he was compelled to desist. He removed in June 1876, to Hardwich, MA, where he purchased a small estate, hoping still to preach and write for the press.He died from pneumonia at the house of his daughter, Mrs. Horace C. Smith, (Sarah Frances) Athol, MA while on a visit Jan. 18, 1877.

When we die, we will not die alone because we will be with Jesus forever.

Elder Abel Thornton
Birth:
Aug. 16, 1799
Death:
Oct. 14, 1827
Burial:
Robert Thornton Cemetery,
Johnston,
Providence County,
Rhode Island

In 1820 he was captivated by the earnest preaching of Ms. Clarissa H. Danforth and the Elder Joseph White of the Smithfield "Free Will" Baptist Church. Abel became increasingly active in this Christian society. He died of consumption October 14, 1827, while wandering around New England as an itinerant preacher, spreading the word of God to all who would listen. His "diary," *The Life of Elder Abel Thornton,* was printed in Providence by the Free Will Baptists in 1828.

Rev Ezra Tuttle
Birth:
Jul. 16, 1817
Death:
Jul. 7, 1888
Burial:
Pocasset Cemetery
Cranston
Providence County
Rhode Island

Ordained in 1846 and pastored in Mass., New Hampshire, Maine. He was a member off executive boards of Education, Home and Foreign Missionary Societies; many years clerk of the New Durham QM; town treasurer, Richland, Wis.

Charles Wade
Birth:
Jun. 27, 1790,
Glocester,
Providence County,
Rhode Island
Death:
Apr. 13, 1883, Norwich,
New London County,
Connecticut
Burial:
Swan Point Cemetery,
Providence
Providence County,
Rhode Island

He was converted through the faithfulness of an old friend, and was baptized and joined the Foster Free Will Baptist church in Nov. 1828, four months after its organization, Rev. Daniel Williams being pastor. He was ordained as deacon of this church Nov. 7, 1825, with Rev's Reuben Allen and Joseph White's assistance, he preached his first sermon, Feb. 12, 1826. In 1837 he returned to his farm and lived there for thirty-seven years. In 1841, he was ordained a Free Will Baptist minister, and before 1843, working with the church sixty-one converts had been baptized to the church. The Morning Star church was organized in 1846, and he was called as its first pastor. He continued with this church until his seventieth year, when he baptized some thirty-four converts and retired from active ministry. He took the church paper, "Morning Star" from the first, and was attached to his denomination and was a close student of God's word. He died in his 93rd year, April 13, 1883. His son, Almon Wade, has for many years been a prominent member of the Roger Williams church, Providence, R.I.

Rev Luke Waldron
Birth
Aug. 6, 1800
Rochester
Strafford County, New Hampshire

Death
Jan. 10, 1858
Newport
Newport County, Rhode Island
Burial:
North Burial Ground
Providence
Providence County,
Rhode Island, Plot: AA-675

He was ordained as a Free Will Baptists in 1837 and labored in Maine until 1840. He became a Methodist a few years before his death.

David Richards Whittemore

Birth:
Jul. 31, 1819
Salisbury, Merrimack County,
New Hampshire
Death:
Mar. 23, 1888
Providence,
Providence County,
Rhode Island
Burial:
Pocasset Cemetery, Cranston,
Providence County, Rhode
Island

As a student in Dracut Academy, and the publishing agent of "Zion's Banner," a weekly religious newspaper, he was especially active in religious work. Early in 1842 he removed to Rhode Island, and in October of that year was ordained as Free Will Baptist pastor of the church in North Providence. Rev. Martin Cheney and Rev. James A. McKenzie were members of the council. In 1846, he became pastor of the South church in Newport. Since 1849 he has resided in the western part of Providence. He has been deeply interested in organizing and perfecting the work of the association, and has aided many of its churches in securing supplies and settling

pastors. He long cherished the plan of securing the best possible historical and literary facilities for the denomination. Through his zeal the *"Free Baptist Cyclopeaedia"* was under-taken. For many years he was an active agent in the association for the *"Register"* and *"Morning Star."* He was an outspoken Abolitionist when it cost much to be outspoken; he was always an advocate of total abstinence and prohibition; for many years he has held office in the Rhode Island Peace Society. He has successfully prosecuted at the same time the insurance and other business. Incisiveness of intellect, correctness of judgment, and positiveness of opinion made him a wise counselor and bold leader.

Clarence O. Williams

Birth:
Nov. 10, 1859
Foster,
Providence County,
Rhode Island
Death:
Sep. 10, 1889
Burial:
Williams Lot, Foster,
Providence County,
Rhode Island

He prepared for college in the Grammar and High School, Providence, and graduated at Brown University in 1883. From 1883 to 1886. He was professor of Latin and metaphysics at New Hampton Institution in New Hampshire. In 1886-87 he attended Bates Theological School and taught mathematics in Nichols Latin School. At the same time he preached for the South Lewiston church. He was then elected to the chair of Latin in Hillsdale College, Michigan.

Henry Williams

Birth:
Feb. 10, 1823
Death:
Mar. 5, 1900
Burial:
Williams Lot,
Scituate,
Providence County,
Rhode Island

His father was a descendant of Roger Williams, and his mother a descendant of King Phillip. His parents and grandparents all died in triumphs of faith in Christ.

He was converted March 1849, and joined a Christian Union church at Rice City, Coventry, Rhode Island.

After preaching from place to place, he took a letter and joined the Six Principle Baptist church of Crompton.

After six months trial he was ordained March 17, 1874.

He afterwards joined the Free Baptist church in West Greenwich. Many have been converted under his labors.

Irving Winsor
Birth:
Nov. 20, 1859
Smithfield
Providence County, Rhode
Island
Death:
Jul. 29, 1933
Rhode Island
Burial:
Colonel Abraham Winsor Lot
Smithfield
Providence County, Rhode
Island

He studied at New Hampton College, NH, and graduated from Cobb Divinity School in 1889. He entered the ministry of the Freewill Baptist and was licensed in 1888. He preached at West Bethel and Winningham.

Joseph Winsor
Birth:
Oct. 4, 1714
Death:
Sep. 4, 1802
Burial:
Winsor Lot
Glocester,
Providence County,
Rhode Island

His parents were Samuel Winsor (1677 - 1758) and Marcy Harding Winsor (1683 - 1771) and his wife was Deborah Mathewson Winsor (1716 - 1785).

Death is the crown jewel for the Christian.

Samuel Winsor, II
Birth:
Nov. 18, 1677
Death:
Nov. 17, 1758
Burial:
North Burial Ground
Providence,
Providence County,
Rhode Island

Pastored the Roger Williams Bapt. Church in Providence. His parents were Samuel Winsor (1644 - 1705) and Mercy Williams (1640 - 1705) he was married to Mercy Harding on 7 Jan 1703

South Carolina

Rev Carroll G. Alexander
Birth:
1933
North Carolina
Death:
Dec. 28, 2013
South Carolina
Burial:
Greenlawn Memorial Park
Columbia
Richland County
South Carolina

Rev. Alexander was a son of the late Rev. D.W. and Margaret Alexander. He was a graduate of the Free Will Baptist College where he served as president of his senior class in 1954, and also Columbia Bible College where he received his master's degree. He was ordained into the Gospel Ministry at Winterville, N.C. in 1954, and then he pastored Westside Free Will Baptist Church, Johnsonville, S.C., Faith Free Will Baptist Church, Kinston, N.C., and Columbia Original

Free Will Baptist Church, Columbia, S.C.

Within the Free Will Baptist Denomination, he held many offices including: Free Will Baptist College Board of Trustees (Welch College), Clerk of South Carolina Conference, Moderator of SC State Association, Presbytery and Examining Board, and District Conference Home Mission Board. Married to his wife of 57 years,

Wilburn Beasley
Birth:
unknown
Marion County, Alabama
Death:
Mar. 19, 2002
Turbeville, Clarendon County,
South Carolina
Burial:
Horse Branch
Free Will Baptist Cemetery,
Turbeville,
Clarendon County,
South Carolina

He was a Free Will Baptist Minister having graduated from the Free Will Baptist Bible College in Nashville, Tennessee in 1954. Afterwards, he pastored the Beech Springs Free Will Baptist Church in Mississippi, the Glennville Free Will Baptist Church in Georgia, the Horse Branch Free Will Baptist Church, Turbeville, and High Hill Free Will Baptist

Church in Lake City, both in South Carolina. He was very active in the denomination on all levels and was a member of the Board of Retirement and Insurance for 12 years in Nashville, Tennessee.

Jimmie William Brown
Birth:
May 29, 1924
Chesterfield County
South Carolina
Death:
Mar. 1, 2002
Nashville, Tennessee
Burial:
Elmore Cemetery, Coward,
Florence County,
South Carolina

He was a veteran of World War II and the Korean War serving both in the United States Navy and the United States Marine Corps. He was also active in the United States Army reserves and National Guard spending a combined total of more than 20 years. He attended the Free Will Baptist Bible college from 1956 to 1960 and worked in campus maintenance during this time. Afterwards, he pastored churches in Brilliant Alabama; Townley, Alabama; and Hartselle, Alabama for about 10 years. Then, he served as house parents at Free Will Baptist Home for Children in Greenville, Tennessee and Virginia Baptist Children's Home in Salem, Virginia for a total of eight years. Upon his retirement in 1985 he returned to the Free Will Baptist Bible

College to do part-time maintenance for several additional years.

Joseph Lee Cagle
Birth:
Jul. 12, 1938
Johnsonville,
Florence County,
South Carolina
Death:
Feb. 13, 2011
Florence,
Florence County,
South Carolina
Burial:
New Prospect Free Will
Baptist Church,
Pamplico,Florence County,
South Carolina

Rev. Cagle was currently serving as Pastor at Little Bethel FWB Church. His other pastorates included New Prospect FWB Church, Mill Branch FWB Church, St. John FWB Church, and Hillside FWB Church. Under God's guidance and direction, he helped start the New Prospect Christian School. Rev. Cagle was a National Association of FWB General Board member.

Percy Rufus Coffey
Birth:
Nov. 15, 1926
Death:
Feb. 12, 2001
Massachusetts
Burial:
Bowman Memorial Cemetery,
Bowman,
Orangeburg County,
South Carolina

A pastor and denominational leader. His early pastorates were among the Southern Methodists before uniting with the Free Will Baptists in 1954 for whom he also pastored in South Carolina, Tennessee and Virginia. In 1962 he served five years as the Director of Missions Education for the Foreign Missions Department and thereafter was elected the Executive Secretary of the National Association of Free Will Baptists where he served until 1979 when he returned to the pastorate. He was a graduate of Bob Jones University and later studied at Vanderbilt University. His ministry spanned 54 years.

Robert Edwards
Birth:
1937
Death:
2000
Burial:
Clarendon Memorial Gardens
Manning
Clarendon County,South
Carolina

He was a well-known state and national minister and leader.

Webster Pressley Gause
Birth:
Jun. 5, 1863
Death:
Nov. 24, 1918
Burial:
High Hill Cemetery
Scranton
Florence County,South
Carolina

He was the son of William Nelson Gause (1834 - 1899) and Jane D. Gause (1831 - 1885) He was married Ellen Cornelia Evans Gause (1867 - 1942).

Norwood A. Gibson, Sr
Birth:
Mar. 5, 1928
Florence,
Florence County, South
Carolina
Death:
Apr. 22, 1999
Florence
County,SouthCarolina
Burial:
Florence Memorial Gardens,
Florence,
Florence County,

South Carolina
He was a Free Will Baptist pastor and Promotional Sec. for the South Carolina Association of Free Will Baptists. He led this Association to be one of the best giving Associations to missions and the national departments. He also served on the Foreign Mission Board of the national Association. He was also proud that he had served in the U.S. Army for his country.

Moab Hewitt
Birth:
1795
Death:
1863
Florence County, South
Carolina
Burial:
Lynch's Memorial
Gardens Cemetery,
Florence County, South
Carolina

A early South Carolina Free Will Baptist Minister.

Elijah Myers Hicks
Birth:
Jan. 15, 1853
Death:
Sep. 29, 1921
Burial:
Bethel Baptist Cemetery
Olanta
Florence County,South
Carolina

Plot: c117

He was the son of Elijah Hicks (1812 - 1881) and Francis R. Myers Hicks (1814 - 1878). He married Elizabeth Welsh Hicks (1854 - 1932).

Rev Louis Arlo Holliday, Sr
Birth:
Apr. 6, 1909
Death:
May 13, 1984
Burial:
Oak Grove Methodist
Cemetery
Manning
Clarendon County
South Carolina

Inscription:
"Beautiful Are The Feet Of Them That Preach The Gospel Of Peace"

Herman A. Hyman
Birth:
Aug. 5, 1938

Pamplico, Florence County
South Carolina
Death:
Jan. 3, 2007
Florence, Florence County,
South Carolina
Burial:
Mount Elon Freewill Baptist
Church Cemetery, Pamplico,
Florence County,
South Carolina

Free Will Baptist pastor and patriot. He was educated in the Florence school system, Florence. Darlington Technical College and after his call to the ministry, he was a student at Bethel Bible Institute. He founded the Immanuel Free Will Baptist church in Santee in 1986 and served as Orangeburg County Sheriff's Department as a chaplain from 1995-2006. He was pastor of the Immanuel Free Will Baptist Church for 19 1/2 years before going to Auburndale, Florida to pastor. Due to bad health he returned back to his home in Santee. He served in the United States Navy from 1958 through 1960.

Elison Pickett Kirby
Birth:
1883
Death:

1977
Burial:
New Town Cemetery
Clarendon County
South Carolina

He was in attendance in the 1936 Nat'l Association of FWB, registering as a minister.

The Rev. Kirby Services Set

CADES—The Rev. E. Pickett Kirby, 94, a retired Baptist minister and farmer, died Monday at a Florence nursing home after a long illness.

Funeral services will be Wednesday at 5 p.m. at New Town Freewill Baptist Church, with burial in the church cemetery, directed by Lake City Funeral Home.

He was born in Clarendon County, a son of the late Drewry and Julia Dubose Kirby. He was a member of the New Town Freewill Baptist Church and the South Carolina Freewill Baptist Conference, where he served as secretary and treasurer until his retirement. The Rev. Mr. Kirby was the oldest ordained Freewill Baptist Minister in South Carolina. He was the widower of Sue Estelle Kirby and of Mamie Sims Kirby, his second wife.

Surviving are two sons, the Rev. Eugene T. Kirby of Cades and Slyron J. Kirby of Timmonsville; three daughters, Mrs. Alberta Miles of Olanta, Mrs. Essie Teal of Lake City and Mrs. Jim (Ira) Snyder of Manning; a sister, Mrs. Maggie Mitchum of Columiba; 24 grandchildren and 42 great-grandchildren.

Memorials may be made to New Town Freewill Baptist Church.

Rev A. J. Lambert
Birth:
Jan. 24, 1909
Death:
Aug. 13, 2000
Burial:
Mt Pleasant Memorial Gardens
Mount Pleasant
Charleston County
South Carolina

A Free Will Baptist minister, named in FWB Nat'l Association committee to revise the Treatise in 1947.

Arthur F Lawter
Birth:
Jun. 24, 1904
Death:
Jan. 31, 1965
Lockhart,
Union County,
South Carolina
Burial:
Whitney Cemetery,
Spartanburg,
Spartanburg County,
South Carolina

Reverend Lawter was the pastor of Lockhart Free Will Baptist Church

Miller H Mellette
Birth:
Jul. 6, 1888
Death:
May 19, 1960
Burial:
Horse Branch Free Will Baptist Cemetery,
Turbeville, Clarendon County,
South Carolina

A Free Will Baptist minister. He was on the Executive Committee in 1936.

Rev John Beaty Moore
Birth:
May 1, 1847
Death:
Apr. 26, 1925
Burial:
Bethel Free Will Baptist Church Cemetery
Florence
Florence County
South Carolina

Rev Lewis Lee Moore
Birth:
Aug. 9, 1881
Williamsburg County
South Carolina
Death:
Aug. 7, 1949
Florence
Florence County
South Carolina
Burial:
Union Baptist Church Cemetery
Hannah
Florence County
South Carolina

A Free Will Baptist minister.
Son of Alec & Eliza Flowers Moore
Spouse:
Annie Eliza Thomas Moore (1892 - 1968)

Redding Floyd Moore
Birth:
Feb. 18, 1903
Death:
Aug. 7, 1981
Burial:
Carolina Memorial Park,
North Charleston,
Charleston County,
South Carolina

Samuel Moore
Birth: 1803
Death: 1878
Burial:
Lynch's Memorial Gardens Cemetery

Florence County
South Carolina

Rev. Samuel Moore is listed in the Minutes as an ordained minister in the organization of the South Carolina General Conference, which included thirteen churches organized in 1858, meeting at the Ebenezar Church in Williamsburg District.

Believe this Eld. Samuel Moore could be the son or Eld. Redding Moore, (1795-1849) who names a son, Samuel, in his 1849 Will, and he was supposed to have had a son, Samuel, who was a FWB minsiter.

Samuel M. Moore, Jr
Birth:
Mar. 25, 1912
Death:
Mar. 16, 1997
Burial:
Evergreen Cemetery, Chester, Chester County, South Carolina

Mancy C Noles
Birth:
Sep. 9, 1933
Death:
Sep. 6, 2002
Burial:
Evergreen Memorial Park
Sumter
Sumter County, South Carolina

Walker's Chapel FWB Church, Sumter was organized on April 21, 1974 by Rev. Mancy Noles with 12 charter members. Services were held for 2 years in a single wide mobile home put in front of a 4 room house (Whose rooms were used for Sunday School). In 1976 the building the Church now occupies was constructed on 2 lots of land donated by Rev. Noles. Later an addition was built onto the back of the church for Sunday School Rooms and rest rooms. Then, as the Church grew, a fellowship building was built behind the Church and eventually a drive thru covered walk way was added. The Fellowship Building also contained more rest rooms and the baptismal pool. And all the buildings and land are completely paid for. Brother Mancy was the Pastor of this church until his death on September 6th. He suffered a stroke in 1999 which affected his speech. More strokes eventually confined him to a wheel chair but he continued to faithfully do all he could in the Church.

James Benjamin Rice, Jr
Birth:
Feb. 27, 1928
Death:
Sep. 10, 1993
South Carolina
Burial:
Hillcrest Memorial Gardens, Greer, Spartanburg County, South Carolina

He was a Free Will Baptist pastor and denominational leader, serving in South Carolina and Georgia. He established the First Free Will Baptist Church in Greer, S.C., as a joint project with the Beavercreek Home Mission Board and the National Home Mission Board of the National Association of Free Will Baptists. Afterwards, he became the Superintendent of the Free Will Baptist Children's Home, where he served for 11 years prior to his death. He was a graduate of University of Georgia and a United States Navy veteran serving during World War II. Inscription: HA1 US Navy World War II

Evander S Robinson
Birth:
Oct. 26, 1860
Death:
Jan. 27, 1944
Burial:
Horse Branch Free Will Baptist Cemetery, Turbeville, Clarendon County, South Carolina

His funeral was conducted by two other early preachers: George C. Vause and M. H. Mellette.

Rev H Reedy Saverance
Birth:
Timmonsville
Florence County
South Carolina
Death:
Jun. 2, 2016
Pamplico
Florence County
South Carolina
Burial:
Bay Branch Cemetery
Timmonsville
Florence County
South Carolina

Rev. H. Reedy Saverance, 90, of Pamplico, SC went home to be with his Lord and Saviour after a brief illness.Rev. Saverance was son of the late Ellington Severance and Carrie Windham Severance. He was a graduate of the Free Will Baptist Bible College in Nashville, TN and a WWII veteran of the United States Navy. He served for over 60 years pastoring churches in Arkansas, Georgia, Florida and South Carolina and founded Cherryvale Free Will Baptist Church in Sumter. He was an avid volunteer for McLeod Regional Medical Center and received many awards for his civic service throughout his lifetime.

Rev Floyd W Seay, Sr
Birth:
1928
Death:
1983
Burial:
Sunset Memorial Park

Spartanburg
Spartanburg County
South Carolina,Plot: Section F

Rev Paul Jones Sheehan
Birth:
Apr. 3, 1908
Clifton
Spartanburg County
South Carolina
Death:
May 23, 1979
Florence
Florence County
South Carolina
Burial:
Greenlawn Memorial Gardens
Spartanburg
Spartanburg County
South Carolina

Served as Supt. of Children's Home in Turbeville, as well as other positions. Parents:
Joseph Ervin Sheehan (1873–1927)and Emma Frances Morris (1874–1937)

Stephen Elias Smith
Birth:
Sep. 27, 1849
Death:
Sep. 1, 1921
Burial:
Oak Ridge Memorial Cemetery
Williamsburg County,South Carolina

Early Minister.

Sam Richard Truett
Birth:
Sep. 24, 1945
Death:
Aug. 7, 2001
South Carolina
Burial:
Grove Hill Cemetery,
Darlington,
Darlington County,
South Carolina

He was a Free Will Baptist pastor for 33 years pastoring four churches in South Carolina and one in North Carolina. He was ordained to preach at age 23 in September of 1968.

He was an active denominational leader both in North and South Carolina and on a national level. He spoke twice at the national convention of Free Will Baptists. First in Louisville, Kentucky in 1981 and 1989 in Tampa, Florida. He was a skilled journalist and wrote Sunday school literature for Randall House Publications. He also served 15 years on the Board of Trustees at Free Will Baptist Bible College. He earned both a Bachelors and Masters Degree from Bob Jones University in Greenville, South Carolina. He had one son, Rev. Chris Truett who is a very versatile and talented Minister.

**Today is not a day of distress
But a day of delight.**

Jason B Turner

Birth:
Jul. 23, 1971
Death:
Apr. 5, 1998
Burial:
Oak Grove Methodist
Cemetery,
Manning,Clarendon County,
South Carolina

The Rev. Jason Turner

MANNING — The Rev. Jason Bennie Turner, 26, died Sunday, April 5, 1998, at his home in Manning. Born in Manning, he was a son of the Rev. I. Bennie Turner and Vivian White Turner.

He was a member of the Fellowship Free Will Baptist church where he served as youth and music minister. He was a dispatcher for the Clarendon County Sheriff's Department, attended Free Will Baptist College in Nashville, Tenn., was an ordained minister, a certified EMT, a volunteer fireman, a licensed chaplain for the Sheriff's Department and a baseball coach.

He is survived by his parents of Manning; one sister, Mrs. Alvin "Patara" Hyman of Manning; and two nephews.

Cornelius Acue Vause

Birth:
Sep. 1,1893
Death:
May 16, 1967
Burial:
Bethany Cemetery,
Florence County,
South Carolina

He was a very early South Carolina leader and preacher. He was a Veteran, WW I.

Rev George Cole Vause

Birth:
Jan. 11, 1877
Death:
Jul. 19, 1953
Burial:
Bethany Cemetery
Florence County
South Carolina

Early Free Will Baptist minister in South Carolina. His son Julius was also a leader in the FWB Movement.

Parents:
Julius E. Vause (1854 - 1934)
L Roxie Sims Vause (1859 - 1920)

Julius B Vause

Birth:
May 10, 1904
Death:
Feb. 3, 2001
Burial:
Bethany Cemetery,
Florence County,
South Carolina

Early South Carolina leader and organizer. He was honored by the South Carolina Conference Home Mission Board for 20 years of service. He was a pastor for more than 30 years, which included five years as Superintendent at the Free Will Baptist Children's Home.

Rev Thomas Arthur Williams

Birth:
Mar. 2, 1888
Death:
Dec. 30, 1960
Burial:
Williams Hill FWB Cemetery
Midway Crossroads
Georgetown County

South Carolina

An ordained FWB minister; his name was listed in old 1930's Minutes of the Eastern General Association of FWB.

Inscription:
I have fought a good fignt, I have finished my course, I have kept the faith II Tim 4:17
Father

Wright Wilson
Birth:
Mar. 17, 1811
Death:
Jan. 28, 1887
Clio, Marlboro County, South Carolina
Burial:
McLucas Cemetery, Clio, Marlboro County, South Carolina

He served Free Will Baptist long before the present national convention.

South Dakota

Timothy Edward Coats
Birth:　Apr. 24, 1953
Minnehaha County
South Dakota
Death:　Apr. 22, 2017
Pennington County
South Dakota
Burial:
Mountain View Cemetery
Rapid City
Pennington County
South Dakota

RAPID CITY | Timothy Edward Coats, 63, passed away was born to Harry and Ruth (Rudolph) Coats in Sioux Falls, SD. He was the second born son, having an older brother, who died in infancy. He then became the oldest of seven children. Tim graduated from Lincoln High School and joined the U.S. Navy in 1971. He served as a data systems technician for the next six years. While being stationed in California, Tim became a born again Christian. Upon receiving an honorable discharge in 1977, he decided to attend Free Will Baptist Bible College in Nashville, TN, to pursue a BA degree in Pastoral Administration. During his time at Bible College, he met his future wife, Kathy Jenkins from Norton, VA. They were married on Aug. 2, 1981.Tim and Kathy enjoyed a short mission's trip to the country of Panama with Steve and Judy Lytle. Tim was then employed by the Free Will Baptist Home Missions Department to establish a church in the surrounding area of Rapid City, SD. Harvest Time Free Will Baptist Church was founded in Box Elder. Here Tim would remain for the next thirty-three years. These years were blessed with five children and a number of secondary jobs. Tim served as the chaplain for Rapid City Regional Hospital, Hospice Chaplain, a driver for Croell Redi-Mix, a customer service representative for Ditech, and Combined Insurance.. Tim loved the beauty of the Black Hills and the abundant opportunities for hunting that could be enjoyed here. Unfortunately, he was involved in a hunting accident that would claim his life. Funeral services were at Calvary Baptist Church.. Published April 27, 2017Rapid City Journal RAPID CITY | A missing hunter was found dead from an apparent accidental shooting Sunday morning on Forest Service land.

Laban Clark Cobb
Birth:
Feb. 6, 1810
Buckland, Massachusetts
Death:
Jan. 30, 1885
Colman, South Dakota
Burial:
Union Cemetery
Flandreau, Moody County

South Dakota, Plot: 14-2-1

Rev. Cobb was born in Massachusetts, but early removed to Monroe County, New York where he was converted under the labors of Rev. Eli Hannibal. He was married on December 30, 1834 to the daughter of Rev. William Greenleaf, who was born in Columbus, New York on September 2, 1817. After their marriage they were active members of the church, together moved to Wisconsin in 1849 where they entered into a wider field of usefulness. They preached in new and destitute localities, and the spirit of God worked through them with great power. Both he and his wife, Minerva, were both licensed to preach at the Marquette Quarterly Meeting in Wisconsin about 1858 and In 1864 they went to Winona County, Minnesota where they labored in the Root River Quarterly Meeting and was ordained in 1868 in connection with the Root R

iver Quarterly Meeting in Minnesota. They continued many years to work with marked success. Later their health impaired and they moved in 1879 to Colman South Dakota. He was known to be a man of great power in prayer.

Minerva U. Cobb
Birth:
Sep. 2, 1818
Columbus, New York
Death:
Mar. 5, 1890
Colman, South Dakota
Burial:
Union Cemetery
Flandreau
Moody County, South Dakota
Plot: 14-2-2

She was the daughter of Rev. William Greenleaf, who was born in Columbus, New York on September 2, 1818. After her marriage to Laban Clark Cobb, they were active members of the church. Together they moved to Wisconsin in 1849 where they entered into a wider field of usefulness. They preached in new and destitute localities, and the spirit of God worked through them with great power. Both she and her husband, were both licensed to preach at the Marquette Quarterly Meeting in Wisconsin about 1858 and In 1864 they went to Winona County, Minnesota where they labored in the Root River Quarterly Meeting and was ordained in 1868 in connection with the Root River Quarterly Meeting in Minnesota. They continued many years to work with marked success. Later their health impaired and they moved in 1879 to Colman South Dakota.

John Gilbert Hull
Birth:
Nov. 5, 1822
Vermont
Death:
Feb. 29, 1884
Souix Falls,
South Dakota
Burial:
Mount Pleasant Cemetery
Sioux Falls, Minnehaha
County, South Dakota

He was converted at nineteen years and began to preach immediately. After a few months, he went to Biblical School at Whitestown, NY, where he remained a year. Then he pastored successively Phoenix, Amboy, Hastings, Parish and Union churches, NY. In 1855 he moved to Wisconsin and was active with churches in Rock and Dane Quarterly Meetings, living in Jefferson Co. Wisconsin. He was zealous for souls even to the end. His labors were made more efficient by the assistance rendered by his devoted wife, formerly Miss Lois A. Higbee, whom he married in 1846. Their son,, John J., b. 1847, also became a Free Baptist minister, later located in Wisconsin, and was very effective. He also went to Dakota when his father died where he gathered a church in Souix Falls.

Tennessee

James Richard Adams
Birth:
Unknown
Death:
Mar. 2, 2012
Antioch,
Davidson County, Tennessee
Burial:
Evergreen Cemetery,
Erwin, Unicoi County, Tennessee

Dr. Adams was born in Erwin, TN, and lived there until he moved to Nashville to attend Free Will Baptist Bible College. After graduating in 1966, Richard and his beloved wife Carolyn, moved to Kannapolis, NC, where he became the pastor of Ben Avenue Free Will Baptist and stayed until 1970. At that time, the couple, along with their two children moved to Elizabethton, Tennessee when "Preacher Adams" served as the much-loved pastor of East Side Free Will Baptist Church for twenty years. In January of 1990, the Adams' family moved to Nashville, TN, where Richard became the Director of Development with Free Will Baptist Home Missions North America. Over the next eighteen years, Richard directed the Church Extension Loan Fund which enabled church planters to buy land and build facilities all across North America. Richard worked the Build My Church Campaign raising millions of dollars for Home Missions. He and Carolyn traveled around the world to Canada, Mexico, the Virgin Islands, Puerto Rico, and the United States, representing the cause of Christ and Home Missions. In honor of Richard's tireless work for missions, the Free Will Baptist Home Missions Board named the million-dollar endowment of funds he raised in his name-the Richard and Carolyn Adams Endowment. Dr. Adams made a tremendous impact of the cause of Christ and for Free Will Baptists around the world. He will be sorely missed not only by family, but also by literally hundreds of friends across our nation.

Randall Adkins
Birth:
Apr. 15, 1805
Tennessee
Death:
Aug. 16, 1888
Tennessee
Burial:
Adkins Cemetery, Oak Grove,
Campbell County, Tennessee

Broken Headstone Looks like the death date on stone could read August 6, 1888 but others have August 16, 1888.

W. S. Adkins
Birth:
Unknown
Death:
Mar. 25, 1904
Burial:
Adkins Cemetery, Oak Grove,
Campbell County, Tennessee

Member of Church for 15 years) age 51 years.

J A Albright
Birth:
Jun. 21, 1840
Death:
Nov. 30, 1921
Burial:
Albright Cemetery
Dickson County, Tennessee
He was one of the early Free Will Baptist ministers and central Tennessee and was affiliated with the Ashland Quarterly Meeting.

Hildon Clarence Beasley
Birth:
May 15, 1916
Stewart County, Tennessee
Dec. 21, 2003 Erin,
Houston County, Tennessee
Burial:
McIntosh Cemetery,
Houston County, Tennessee

He was a Free Will Baptist Minister.

Charlie Bennett
Birth:
Unknown
Death:
May 22, 2011
Johnson City
Washington County Tennessee
Burial:
Roselawn Memorial Park,
Johnson City,
Washington County, Tennessee

He was 93 at the time of his passing. He was a member and pastor of the True Gospel Free Will Baptist Church for nearly 50 years.

To be absent in body is to be present with the Lord

G. W. Binkley
Birth:
Oct. 17, 1850
Tennessee
Death:
Mar. 21, 1903
Davidson County,
Tennessee
Burial:
Turrentine-Binkley Cemetery
Ashland City
Cheatham County,
Tennessee

George Washington Binkley was the son of Turner and Martha (Mayo) Binkley. On Nov. 17, 1870, Binkley married Florence Waggoner. In 1888 he was a member of the Ashland Quarterly Meeting in which he served as a Free Will Baptist minister.

James B Bloss
Birth:
1884
Death:
1959
Burial:
Polk MemorialGardens, Columbia, Maury County, Tennessee

Rev. J. O. Bloss, was a Free Will Baptist minister, affiliated and listed in the 1945 minutes of the National Ass'n.
In 1939, AL, he married Myrtle A (unk), and afterward they lived in Columbia, TN. where he was a pastor. He pastored in Tennessee and Alabama.
(WWI) Soldiers Grave Pearl Rivers. He was also a member of the Foreign Missions Board of the National Association.

To Die is the gain Him who gave life after death.

Rev Charles Dwight Bohanon
Birth:
Apr. 26, 1938
Death:
Jan. 9, 2015
Lancing, Tennessee
Burial:
Mount Hope Cemetery
Morgan County
Tennessee

His love for Christ lead him to be a Freewill Baptist Minister for over 40 years.
He was a loving husband to his wife Leila for 58 years, Loving father to 8 children, 19 grandchildren and 21 great-grandchildren. He was preceded in death by his parents, daughters, Marsha Lee, Mary Catherine, Son, and Charles Ricky
He is survived by his wife Leila Ellen Gallagher Bohanon, Daughters, Deborah (Rev. Henry) Miracle, Cynthia (Jon) Hankins, Kimberly Ellen (Gary) Crozier, Susan (John) Keathley, Son, Dwight (Michelle) Bohanon, 1 sister and 1 brother. Also surviving are a host of other family and friends. Rev. Henry Mircale, Rev. Joshua Crozier and Rev. Rick Taylor officiated.

Terry Lockert Boyd
Birth:
unknown
Death:
Jan. 26, 2005
Pleasant View, Cheatham County, Tennessee
Burial:
Pleasant View
Methodist Church Cemetery,
Pleasant View,
Cheatham County,
Tennessee

A Free Will Baptist minister and owner of the Boyd Funeral Home in Ashland, Tennessee. He was a member of the Good Springs Free Will Baptist Church in Pleasant View, Tennessee. A book, *In My Father's Words*, was written by his daughter Sheila Boyd Cook in 2015 as a tribute to her father.

Fred L Bradshaw
Birth:
May 8, 1909
Death:
Mar. 5, 1963
Burial:
Highland Cemetery,
Sparta,
White County, Tennessee,

Fred Arvel Brewer
Birth:
Jul. 18, 1942
Johnson County,Tennessee
Death:
Apr. 20, 2002
Sullivan County, Tennessee
Burial:
Rainbow Cemetery
Mountain City
Johnson County, Tennessee

He was a Freewill Baptist Minister for 31 years. He had pastored several churches in Johnson City, Washington County and Sullivan County. He sang with his family in churches all over North Carolina, Virginia and Tennessee.He was preceded in death by two brothers, Ernest Brewer and Rev. Bill Brewer.

William Lafayette Bright
Birth:
Jul. 4, 1883
Death:
Apr. 9, 1951
Burial:
Corinth Cemetery, Loudon,
Loudon County, Tennessee

Rev Cicero A Brooks
Birth:
Jul. 18, 1854
Tennessee
Death:
Mar. 29, 1892
Tennessee
Burial:
Meadow Branch Cemetery
Bean Station
Grainger County
Tennessee

Rev. Cicero A. Brooks, son of P. M. and Sarah E. (Garrison) Brooks, married Nannie Holt in 1878, and has five children.
He was converted in 1879, two years later he received license, and Sept. 9, 1882, he was ordained. He devoted his time to teaching and preaching until 1885, when he entered upon revival work among the Free Baptist churches of eastern Tennessee and western North Carolina, which he has since continued with success, and some 200 being converted. He was the pastor of the Clear Creek church of the Union Association, Tennessee.

Rev Harley Cletis Brown
Birth:
May 15, 1922
Death
Nov. 18, 2014
Knoxville
Knox County
Tennessee
Burial:
Sherwood Memorial Gardens
Alcoa
Blount County, Tennessee

Retired pastor Harley C. Brown (92) of Knoxville, TN went to be with the Lord Tuesday, November 18, 2014. During his thirty year ministry, he pastored churches in Tennessee as well as four other states. He had been a longtime member of Forest Grove Free Will Baptist Church in Knoxville at the time of his death.

Rev Greene Baker Brown
Birth:
Jan. 23, 1857
Tennessee
Death:
Apr. 4, 1932
Board Valley
White County
Tennessee
Burial:
Board Valley Cemetery
Sparta
White County, Tennessee
An ordained Free Will Baptist minister whose name is found in old church records. The Rev G B

"Dock" Brown, 78, pioneer Baptist minister, died at his Board Valley home after a lingering illness. Parents: Gideon Brown (1827 - 1880). Spouses: Lillie Clouse Brown (1883 - 1969) and Mary Vestina Stanley Brown (1858 - 1900).

Corp A H Burgess
Birth:
Apr. 17, 1844
Death:
May 14, 1922
Burial:
Liberty Freewill Baptist Church Cemetery,
Old Washington County,
Tennessee

He served in the 2nd NC Mounted Infantry Co E.

John Sankey Burgess
Birth:
Sep. 17, 1876
Tennessee
Death:
Jul. 3, 1952
Johnson City
Washington County
Tennessee
Burial:
Liberty Freewill Baptist Church Cemetery Old
Washington County
Tennessee

A minister whose name appeared in 1938 Tenn. State Free Will Baptist minutes..

Rev Elmer Richard Carter, Sr
Birth:
May 30, 1927
Bristol, Sullivan County
Tennessee
Death:
Mar. 7, 2016
Mountain Home
Washington County
Tennessee
Burial:
Happy Valley Memorial Park
Elizabethton
Carter County, Tennessee

Reverend Elmer R. Carter, age 88, of Elizabethton, went home to be with the Lord from the James H. Quillen VA Medical Center Hospital. Reverend Carter was the son of Elmer Gaylord Carter and Maude Overbay Carter Stout. In addition to his parents, he was preceded in death by a son, Elmer Richard Carter, Jr.; and a sister, Betty Barlow.

Reverend Carter was born in Bristol, Tennessee but had lived most of his life in Carter County. He was a United States Navy veteran, having served in World War II. He was a retired minister and had served over 50 years in various Free Will Baptist churches. He was a member of East Side Free Will Baptist church and a member of Appalachian Association of Free Will Baptist, which he helped organize. He had also served as chairman of the board of Free Will Baptist Family Ministries. He had a passion for lost souls and loved his family and his church families.

A service to honor the life of Reverend Elmer R. Carter was conducted in the Riverside Chapel of Tetrick Funeral Home, Elizabethton with his son, Rev. David Carter, officiating and Rev. Justin Deaton, assisting.

Herman Christian
Birth:
Apr. 6, 1928
Death:
Jun. 9, 2008
Burial:
Center hill Cemetery,
Warren County, Tennessee

The idea is to die young as late as possible.

Benjamin Clouse
Birth:
Aug. 2, 1824
Cedar Creek
White County
Tennessee
Death:
Dec. 31, 1896
Board Valley
White County
Tennessee
Burial:
Board Valley Cemetery
Sparta
White County
Tennessee

His name appears in list of pioneer Free Will Baptist ministers in Putnam Co. Siblings: Benjamin Clouse (1824 - 1896)- John Clouse (1827 - 1897)- Francis Marion Clouse (1828 - 1892)- Nancy Ann Clouse (1832 - 1869)- William Riley Clouse (1835 - 1888)- Thomas Jefferson Clouse

(1837 - 1895)- Elijah Crockett Clouse (1838 - 1908)- Charles Lee Clouse (1848 - 1917)- James Kelly Polk Clouse (1853 - 1921)- Simpson Clouse (1854 - 1913)- Andrew Jackson Clouse (1857 - 1913)- Dillard Martin Clouse (1866 - 1954)- Sarah Unicy *Clouse* Campbell (1869 - 1940).

Elder Thomas Jefferson Clouse, Sr

Birth:
Jan. 8, 1801
Washington County
Tennessee
Death:
Jul. 18, 1872
White County
Tennessee
Burial:
Thomas J. Clouse Cemetery
Monterey
Putnam County
Tennessee

Thomas's occupation was a Preacher for Free-Will Baptist Church

Thomas was struck by a falling tree while clearing land. It crushed his chest and caused him to get pneumonia. He died a couple of weeks later. He died three months after his daughter, Rachel, was born of Peggy Eller. He was 71 years old.

Thomas married three times during his lifetime having many children and grandchildren.

Thomas Jefferson Clouse

Birth:
Jan. 1, 1837
Cedar Creek
White County, Tennessee
Death:
Nov. 11, 1895
Putnam County, Tennessee
Burial:
Clouse Cemetery
Cookeville
Putnam County, Tennessee

Rev. T. J. Clouse, of Board Valley, died Monday night. He was taken violently ill Sunday and sank rapidly. Bro. Clouse was a most excellent gentleman and a good preacher. His presence will be greatly missed in his community. [Date 11/14/1895, Vol. IX, No. 3, Page 5]

The following church history was written by the late Judge Ernest Houston Boyd Sr. as part of a series of historical articles in the Putnam County Herald. It was published December 31,1953. The articles were compiled by Christine Spivey Jones into a book called Nuggets of Putnam County History.

The Free Union Baptist congregation is one of the oldest Baptist congregations in Putnam County. Its church building is located on the head of Martin's Creek, in the 18th District of Putnam County.

From 1865 until 1918 this was a Christian Baptist congregation, but since 1918 it has been affiliated with the Missionary Baptist denomination.

In the early history of the Free Union Church it was a large congregation, but on account of the building of other churches and the organization of new congregations in the section in which this church is located, its present membership is much smaller than it was in former years. This is also, partly due to deaths and removal from the community of a number of families active in this church in former years.

In its early history, when the congregation was a large one, the annual sessions of the Stone Christian Baptist Association were frequently held at this church.

The old minutes of that Association show that both the 1891 and 1892 annual sessions of that Association were held with the Free Union Church. It seldom happen in the history of that Association that a second annual session of the Association, in succession, was held at the same church.

Among the early pastors of this church were T. J. Clouse, J. L. Kinnaird, F. M. Flatt, Benjamin Clouse, W. B. Gentry and J. W. Stone.

Thomas was ordained to preach in White County, Tennessee when a young man, and his life was spent as a Baptist Minister. Then came the Civil War. He was strongly opposed to slavery and often preached openly against it. In late December 1862, Thomas was holding a revival on the Calfkiller River. He was in the pulpit when the Guerillas came into the church and took him. They took him to Murfreesboro, arriving there December 31, 1862 at the Battle of the Stones River. He somehow managed to escape and made his way to the Union forces where he joined them. He worked in the hospitals and served as Union

Army Chaplain throughout Kentucky and Ohio until the end of the war.

Inscription:
T.J. CLOUSE
BORN JAN 1, 1837
DIED NOV 11, 1895

Rev William Suttles Clouse
Birth:
Jan. 11, 1861
Board Valley
White County
Tennessee, USA
Death:
Dec. 9, 1943
Cookeville
Putnam County
Tennessee
Burial:
Cookeville City Cemetery
Cookeville
Putnam County, Tennessee

Rev. W.S. Clouse's name is listed in old Free Will Baptist minutes. He was in the Old Stone Association Minutes in 1879, when it convened in Cumberland Co., at Laurel Creek Church.

From the Book "*A Family History of Whitaker, Clours, Finley and Connected Families*" by Blanche Whitaker Jernigan: "William was a Baptist Minister like his father. He bought a tract of land on the Burgess Falls Road, which had been known as the Carmichael Farm in 1903. From J.V. Randolph he bought 27 acres, from J.M. Bray he bought 50 acres, and 20 acres from A.F. Massa all adjoining the Simp Officer line. He ran a grocery store there for many years. He later moved to Cookeville after he retired from the Ministry. He died in Cookeville on the 9th day of December 1943. William Suttle and his second wife Ann Eliza are buried at the Cookeville City Cemetery. His first wife is buried at the Broad Valley Cemetery in White County, Tennessee."

From the book *"A Book of Remembrance of The Clouse Family Descendants of George Clouse, 1"* Compiled and Edited by Prietta Clouse Franklin Rt. 2 Box 408 Cookeville, Tennessee 38501:

"STINGING SERMON

Mrs. Estalee Rippetoe Howard of Cookeville relates the story of an old time country revival that reminds us of the one up home in years gone by when wasps to all intent and purpose broke up the service.

Mrs. Howard tells about a revival at the old Post Oak Shade Free Will Baptist Church. The house had no underpinning, she says, and every Tom, Dick and Harry's hogs slept under the floor. Which meant that fleas were hopping all over the place. Old Brother Sut Clouse was the evangelist and he was one of the big gun preachers, as the saying is back then. He really preached hellfire and damnation. He called himself the "Devil Skinner".

He would preach loud and pop his fists every few minutes. He could really make you think about things. I sang with the alto group and our seat was right near the front. But it was pretty hard to sing, or listen to the Word of God with a flea crawling up and down your spine, stopping every now and then to take a fresh bite.

I don't suppose hogs sleep under many churches any more to create a flea menace. But wasps still prefer a church to any other place to build their nests."

Behold
He Lives!

Thomas Charles Cofer
Birth:
Aug. 19, 1836
Death:
Aug. 10, 1885
Tennessee
Burial:
Carney Cemetery # 1
Whites Creek,
Davidson County, Tennessee

Thomas C. Cofer organized the a Free Will Baptists church in 1880 at William T. Trotter's home. Trotter lived in a Civil War barracks on a dirt road, Buena Vista Pike. Pastor Cofer led in erecting a building at the corner of Buena Vista and Scott Street. He served as pastor of the church until his death in 1885.

The first Free Will Baptist church in Nashville, called the North Nashville Free Will Baptist Church, changed its name to honor the founder. That first building burned about ten years later and the city bought the lot for Buena Vista School on the street called Ninth Avenue North.

The church rebuilt on Arthur Avenue near what is now Garfield. In 1930 the congregation bought the brick building at 1600 Tenth Avenue North. The church built a parsonage there in 1952 for $8,000.

It was at this church that in 1935 the National Association of Free Will Baptists was formed through the efforts and leadership of the pastor of more than 40 years, John L Welch. Free Will Baptist Bible College in 2012 changed the name to Welch College in honor of him and his wife who had been a librarian and at the college for many years. He was also very influential in the early days of the college and very instrumental in it being in Nashville, Tennessee.

Cofer was married on May 14, 1857 to Florissa Moses who was born in 1836. Thomas was a Free Will Baptist preacher. They had the following children: William T.1858; James M. 1862; Sarah F. 1865; Johanna 1866; Charles M. 1869; David 1871; and Flora 1879.

Inscription:
Rev. T. C. Cofer
Born Aug. 19, 1836
Died Aug. 10, 1885
Blessed are the pure in heart for
they shall see God

Rev Frederick Cogswell
Birth:
Mar. 23, 1792
New Hampshire
Death:
Aug. 5, 1857
Memphis
Shelby County, Tennessee
Burial:
Elmwood Cemetery
Memphis
Shelby County, Tennessee
Plot: Lot 389, Chapel Hill

Frederick Cogswell, Free Baptist, son of Judge Thomas and Ruth (Badger) Cogswell, was born March 23, 1792. Labored in Barnstead, Allenstown, and other places in New Hampshire. In company with his cousin. Rev. Joseph Badger, and his brothers-in-law, Rev. John L. and Rev. Edward H. Peavy, he made preaching tours in the Southern and Western states, and became a well-known preacher. Spent his later years, till 1853, in Tamworth.

Residence, Memphis, Tenn., 1853-7. Died there, July, 1857.
Married Hannah Rogers, daughter of Col. Anthony and Elizabeth

Rev Charles Clifford Cooper
Birth:
Jun. 8, 1930
Rickman
Overton County
Tennessee
Death:
Apr. 6, 2016
Rickman
Overton County
Tennessee
Burial:
Okalona Cemetery
Okalona
Overton County
Tennessee

Rev. Charles Clifford Cooper, age 85, was born to the late George Cullum Cooper and Sarah Cooper Cooper.

Charles raised his family in Michigan and spent his adult life in the Ministry as a

Free Will Baptist pastor. He was co-founder of three churches in Michigan; the East Side Free Will Baptist Church in Detroit, Faith Free Will Baptist in Romeo and the Free Will Baptist Mission in Lewiston, as well as helping his son establish the One-Eleven Fellowship in Cookeville Tennessee. During his time as pastor Bro. Cooper served two churches; the West Side Free Will Baptist Church of Detroit for 10 years and the Troy Free Will Baptist Church for 35. Charles also served on the Executive

Committee of the National Association of Free Will Baptists, was the promotional director for the Michigan Association of Free Will Baptists, moderator of the Liberty Association of Free Will Baptists, and founder and editor of the Free Will Baptist monthly newspaper called the Menorah.

He enjoyed music and sang with the Tennessee Harmony Boys Trio for 10 years and the Straitway Trio for 14 years.

Bro. Cooper also had a radio ministry in Royal Oak, Michigan for 10 years. He enjoyed playing golf, and spending time with his grandchildren.

William Edward Coville, Sr
Birth:
Mar. 4, 1903
New York
Death:
Apr. 13, 1956
Madison
Davidson County
Tennessee
Burial:
Woodlawn Memorial Park and
Mausoleum
Nashville
Davidson County
Tennessee

William E. Colville, d. from a sudden heart attack at age 54 yrs. He was the son of William Patrick COLVILLE, b. NY, and Phoebe (Ducette) COLVILLE, NY.

He was in armed services in 1920-22. In Tennessee he met and married Irene J. POLSTON, dau of Fred and Fannie POLSTON, Nashville, TN.

Wm. E. and Irene J. began their family in Nashville, where he worked in civil service as a postal clerk for R.R.

They were involved with her family in the Tennessee Free Will Baptist church work, where her mother was organizing and beginning a woman's auxiliary for the greater body. William E. served as Assistant Treasurer of the Eastern General Ass'n of FWB, in 1937 when it convened in So.

Caroline, at Turbeville. They were living in Nashville, TN in the 1930.

Robert Barrett Crawford

Birth:
Jun. 21, 1913
Death:
Aug. 9, 2001
Burial:
Gibbs Cemetery, Ashland City,
Cheatham County, Tennessee

A minister, denominational leader and the first full-time Executive-Secretary of the National Association of Free Will Baptists. He was converted to Christ at age 12, ordained to preach age 21, and pastored churches in Alabama, Tennessee, North Carolina and Florida. He was the founding pastor of the Trinity Free Will Baptist Church in Greenville, North Carolina. He graduated from the University of Alabama and attended the Vanderbilt Divinity School. For 20 years he served in the Public Relations Department of Free Will Baptist Bible College in Nashville, Tennessee. He was active in ministry for 65 years and was one of the founders and shapers of the Free Will Baptist denomination.

Ronald Creech

Birth:
Unknown
Death:
Aug. 16, 2005
Burial:
Woodlawn Memorial Park,
Nashville,
Davidson County, Tennessee

A Free Will Baptist pastor, state Executive Secretary for the state of North Carolina Free Will Baptists. He retired from Free Will Baptist Bible College in Nashville Tennessee where he served as the Director Of Development.

Missionary Daniel Wickert Cronk

Birth:
February 28, 1923
Detroit Michigan
Death:
November 20, 1997
Nashville,
Davidson County, Tennessee
Burial:
Cremated

He graduated from Hazel Park High School, Detroit, Michigan; Free Will Baptist Bible College, Nashville, Tenn.; Columbia University, Columbia, South Carolina and Middle Tennessee State University, Tennessee. He was ordained to the gospel ministry in 1943 and served his denomination as a missionary to India for 25 years, a professor at Free Will Baptist Bible College for nine years and a member of the Board Of Foreign Missions for 15 years.

Missionary Trula *Gunter* Cronk

Birth:
Jun. 7, 1924
Greene County, Tennessee
Death:
Dec. 22, 2009,
Thailand
Burial:
Shelton Mission Cemetery,
Greystone,
Greene County, Tennessee

Mrs. Cronk grew up in the school years at Zion Mission, a circuit of schools and churches, which was started by the United Presbyterian missionaries from Pennsylvania.

She lived her teen years at Free Will Baptist Children's Home, located near Camp Creek School. Rev. I. L. and Mary Frances Stanley were very instrumental in her life. Later, the Rev. Paul and Nelle Woolsey would come to oversee the home and take Trula in as their own. She was the valedictorian of her graduating class at Camp Creek High School. With the love and support of "mom and dad" Woolsey, she was able to attend college and fulfill her calling to be a missionary to India. At the Free Will Baptist Bible College, in Nashville, where she would meet her future husband, Daniel Cronk, who was from Michigan. Together they went on to graduate from Columbia College in South Carolina. Trula also attended Peabody College. "They served the Lord as Free Will Baptist Pioneer Missionaries in India. The couple relocated to Nashville in 1972, where the Rev. Cronk was professor of the missions program at the Free Will Baptist Bible College and Mrs. Cronk taught school in 1994. The home in which she lived at the Free Will Baptist Children's Home was given the name 'The Trula Gunter Cronk Home for Children' in honor of her being the first resident there. *"Over Mountain or Plain or Sea"* was published in 2003 and is a two-part autobiography detailing parts of Mrs. Cronk's childhood and her many years as a missionary. "In 2004, Mrs. Cronk moved back to Greeneville. Although she had lived in the Himalayas, traveled the Nile at midnight, seen the Taj Mahal, Buckingham Palace, the Louvre in Paris, Pharook's Palace in Alexandria, walked the Sahara Desert, climbed the Leaning Tower of Pisa and Cheops Pyramid, vacationed on beautiful Dal Lake in Sri Nafar, sipped tea with movie stars, world statesmen, and Scottish tea planters, shared seats with Mother Teresa, hunted crocodiles, tigers and rode camels, visited Japan, China, Germany, Russia and traveled the world over, no place was ever as dear to her as Greene County. In November of 2006, she left the mountains of East Tennessee to live with her son, Randall, a resident of Thailand.

Rev James Milton Crowson
Birth:
Mar. 15, 1930
Toccopola
Pontotoc County
Mississippi
Death:
Jun. 6, 2016
Nashville
Davidson County
Tennessee
Burial:
Woodlawn Memorial Park and Mausoleum
Nashville
Davidson County
Tennessee

James Milton Crowson was born the son of James Homer Crowson and Pearl Westmoreland Crowson. On April 9, 1949, he married Martha Frederick, whose father Joe Cephas Frederick pastored the church the Crowson family had begun to attend. He died peacefully in his sleep on June 6, 2016, at the age of 86. A history buff, he would have appreciated the significance of passing away on the day of the WWII allied invasion of Normandy, known as D-¬Day.

In 1955 he moved his young family to Nashville, TN, where he began his B.A. program at Welch College (known then as Free Will Baptist Bible College). He managed to keep up a full academic load, and support a family, all while working as a tool and die maker, usually the night shift. Following graduation in 1960, he began studies for his M.A. at Bob Jones University. He completed his degree after having served as pastor to churches in South Carolina, Oak Ridge, Tennessee, and Russellville, Alabama. In 1968 he moved back to Nashville to join the faculty of Welch College. It was not,

however, his first experience as a Welch College instructor. In his senior year, he had been asked to step in temporarily to teach beginning Greek for the normal professor, Dr. Robert Picirilli, who was continuing his own studies at the time!

Later, he worked again as a tool and die maker, wallpaper tradesman, as well as a condo/apartment property manager.

Milton Crowson loved God, the Bible, his wife, his family, history, gardening, and fishing — and usually in that order, although history and fishing often tried to move higher up the list!.

Rev Matthew F Curtis
Birth:
Oct. 11, 1849
Caplin, Tennessee
Death:
Apr. 22, 1923
Dowelltown
DeKalb County, Tennessee
Burial:
Snow Hill Baptist Church Cemetery
Smithville
DeKalb County, Tennessee

He was converted in 1865 and two years later received license to preach from the Methodist Episcopal denomination. He was ordained in September, 1878, by the new union association and conducted several revival and organized four churches and was engaged in publishing the Christian Progress and was a manager for a company for printing religious tracts in 1889. He took a leading position in the New Union Conference.

Matthew first married Mary Elizabeth Johnson in 1867. After her death he married Louvisa Jane Vanderpool in 1880. After her death he married Lillie Scurlock in 1913.

Robert M Cutshall
Birth:
Aug. 23, 1912
Death:
Dec. 10, 1990
Burial:
Burnetts Chapel Cemetery,
Greene County, Tennessee

James Thomas Davis
Birth:
Unknown
Death:
Aug. 11, 2001
Burial:
Williamson Memorial Gardens,
Franklin,
Williamson County, Tennessee

Dr. Davis was a minister, church planter, pastor, professor and research scientist. He was a founder of a number of churches in central Tennessee and at his retirement was pastor emeritus of the Franklin Community Church. He had been a professor at Free Will Baptist Bible College and was a Bio-Chemist with the Vanderbilt University Medical School.

F. A. Dewitt
Birth:
Mar. 9, 1883
Death:
May 21, 1970
Burial:
McMinn Memory Gardens,
Athens,
McMinn County, Tennessee

Robert H Doan
Birth:
Mar. 25, 1907
Virginia
Death:
Nov. 9, 2001
Medina County, Ohio
Burial:
Morning View Cemetery
Bluff City
Sullivan County, Tennessee

Early Free Will Baptist pastor who served in West Virginia pastoring the Ansted Free Will Baptist Church in 1955-56. He also spent time in Ohio.

George D. Dunbar
Birth:
Aug. 13, 1889
Tennessee
Death:
Jun. 20, 1968
Washington County,
Tennessee
Burial:
Liberty Freewill Baptist Church
Cemetery,
Old Washington County
Tennessee

George Dobson Dunbar In June 1917, registered for WW I Draft. He was described as tall and of medium build, blue eyes and brown hair. He was a minister in the Free Will Baptist Church where he was ordained, and became a leader in the eastern Tennessee Free Will Baptist churches. He was Pastor, Evangelist and Exec. Sec'y of the Union FWB Assn., in Washington Co. in the 1940's. He was responsible for the preparation, arrangement and publication of *"God, A Hundred Years and A Free Will Baptist Family"* by Rev. Paul Woolsey, a FWB Missionary to India, a book which preserved many historical facts and accounts that could have been lost had it not been published.

Zadock D. Duncan
Birth:
Feb. 1, 1830
Death:
Feb. 1, 1921
Burial:
Hoodoo Cemetery
Hoodoo
Coffee County, Tennessee

He was a Free Will Baptist minister affiliated with the New Union Association which belong to the state of Tennessee. He served in the Military - Lt, Co., I, 34th TN Infantry, C.S.A

Kenneth Paul Eagleton
Birth:
Jul. 1, 1928
Death:
Aug. 26, 1999
Burial:
Middle Tennessee State Veterans Cemetery, Nashville, Davidson County, Tennessee, Plot: PP 02 15

Minister, missionary to Brazil for International Missions of the Free Will Baptist denomination. He was a graduate of Free Will Baptist Bible College in Nashville, Tennessee. He was a veteran of the United States Air Force and achieved the rank of staff Sgt. and served in Korea.

Missionary Marvis Eagleton
Birth:
Apr. 27, 1926
Death:
Feb. 21, 2003
Burial:
Middle Tennessee State Veterans Cemetery, Nashville, Davidson County, Tennessee, Plot: PP 02 15

She was a missionary to Brazil for the International Board of Foreign Missions for the Free Fill Baptist denomination. She was a graduate of Free Fill Baptist Bible College in Nashville, Tennessee.

William Donald Ellis
Birth:
2 Jan 1931
Montgomery County, Tennessee
Death:
1 Jan 2018
Fairfield, Freestone County, Texas
Burial:
Heads Free Will Baptist Church Cemetery Cedar Hill, Robertson County, Tennessee,

William Donald Ellis, 87, of Fairfield, TX formerly of Longview, TX, at his daughter's home in Fairfield. He was born, in Montgomery County, TN to the late William Robert and Alice Gertrude Gower Ellis. He graduated from Coopertown High School in Coopertown, TN with the class of 1949, and attended Freewill Baptist Bible College in Nashville, TN and served as a minister his entire life. He married Emma Elizabeth Johnson on Sept. 4, and she preceded him in death on Feb. 16, 2000. Mr. Ellis moved to Fairfield three years ago from Longview. He was a member of First Freewill Baptist Church in Carthage. Mr. Ellis was preceded in death by his parents; wife; brother, Bobby Ray Ellis; and son, Donald Jewel Ellis.
A funeral service, at Jimerson-Lipsey Funeral Home Chapel with Bro. Mike Fields and Bro. Shane King officiating.

Herman Hughes Ellis
Birth:
Jul. 2, 1934
Gause, Tennessee
Death:
Jul. 19, 2006
Cedar Hill, Tennessee
Burial:
Heads Free Will Baptist Church Cemetery, Cedar Hill, Robertson County, Tennessee

He was saved in July of 1960, and later attended the Free Will Baptist Bible College and ordained as a Minister of the gospel at Head's Free Will Baptist Church in 1961. He was a pastor in Michigan, Alabama and Tennessee and used as an evangelist across the entire nation.

George W. Farless
Birth:
Apr. 15, 1885
Death:
Apr. 24, 1968
Burial:
Gnat Hill Cemetery
Manchester
Coffee County, Tennessee

He was a minister in the New Union Association of Free Will Baptists.

Harrison William Farrell
Birth:
Jan. 15, 1848
Coffee County, Tennessee
Death:
Aug. 6, 1924
Warren County, Tennessee
Burial:
Hillsboro Cumberland Presbyterian Cemetery
Hillsboro
Coffee County, Tennessee

He was a minister that was affiliated with the new Union Association, which had been affiliated with the United Baptists, and the state of Tennessee

Winford R Floyd
Birth:
1932
Death:
1995
Burial:
Happy Valley Memorial Park, Elizabethton, Carter County, Tennessee, Plot: Mausoleum of Peace

He was a well-known Minister in eastern Tennessee and active in denominational leadership.

Joe T Fort
Birth:
Dec. 27, 1866
Death:
May 22, 1924
Burial:
Fort Family Cemetery, Clarksville, Montgomery County, Tennessee

Edward Johnson Fox
Birth:
23 Dec 1933
Tennessee
Death:

26 Nov 2017
Tennessee
Burial:
Greenbrier Cemetery
Franklin,
Williamson County,
Tennessee

He always had a smile on his face. He worked for his company, Fox Insurance Agency, and served his community for ovRead More er 30 years. He was extremely active in his community and enjoyed being the Pastor at Berean Freewill Baptist Church. He loved people and he was loved by everyone.

Estel M French
Birth:
Sep. 12, 1902
Death:
Apr. 21, 1978
Burial:
Mosheim Central Cemetery, Mosheim, Greene County, Tennessee

Jake Muriel French
Birth:
Dec. 7, 1901
Death:
Oct. 7, 1966
Burial:
Hickory Valley Cemetery
Unitia
Loudon County
Tennessee

Wooley's book mentions him at the FWB Home for children.

Malcolm Craig Fry
Birth:
Jun. 6, 1928
Detroit,
Wayne County, Michigan
Death:
Aug. 24, 2007
Locust Grove,
Mayes County,
Oklahoma
Burial:
Hermitage Memorial Gardens,
Old Hickory,
Davidson County,
Tennessee

He was a Free Will Baptist minister and a denominational leader. He was the National Church Training Service Director and Adult Curriculum Director at Randall House in Nashville Tennessee. He was an outstanding pianist and singer and made many recordings. He also served with the U.S. Army and was also a U.S. Air Force Veteran;

You Are Home At Last!

Willie M. "Bill" Gardner, Jr
Birth:
Unknown
Norfolk,
Norfolk City, Virginia
Death:
Jun. 15, 2001
Nashville,
Davidson County, Tennessee
Burial:
Woodlawn Memorial Park,
Nashville,
Davidson County, Tennessee

A well-known pastor, recording artist and denominational leader whose singing ability brought many pulpit opportunities. During his ministry, he pastored churches in four states; Tennessee, Indiana, Mississippi and Georgia. He attended Free Will Baptist Bible College, with later studies at North Carolina State University, and earned a Masters degree in music at Mississippi State University. He was known for his clear, high tenor voice singing frequently at many national conventions, state associations and Bible conferences. He was a member of the Music Commission and Media Commission. His last recording effort occurred during the production of *"He Keeps Me Singing"* video which featured 50 Free Will Baptist singers and musicians. He was a role model for many musicians and singers.

Benjamin F Garland
Birth:
1846
Death:
September 15, 1887
Burial:
Garland Cemetery
Carter County, Tennessee

He was a Free Will Baptist minister and died at age 35. The Headstones Provided for Union Soldiers.

Inscription:
Co L, 13th Tenn Cav.

Rev Vernon Hugo Gober
Birth: Jun. 7, 1938
Winston County
Alabama
Death: Jul. 28, 2004
Adamsville
McNairy County, Tennessee
Burial:
Milledgeville Cemetery
Milledgeville
McNairy County, Tennessee

REV. VERNON H. GOBER of Adamsville, 66, was born AL the son of Victor Hugo and Mattie Naomi Owen Gober. He was united in marriage to the former O. Ruthie Benson on Aug. 16, 1961. Rev. Gober was a Free Will Baptist minister for 40 years and a farmer. He pastored churches in Tennessee and Alabama. He was a member of Plummer's Chapel Free Will Baptist Church and served on the board of directors for the Free Will Baptist Family Ministries in Greeneville. He was a former member of Soil Conservation and McNairy Farmers CO-OP. He was a veteran of the United States Navy. Dr. James Kilgore, Dr. Charles Thigpen and Rev. James Carrington officiated.

H. Wilks Gower
Birth:
Aug. 3, 1842
Death:
Feb. 5, 1924
Burial:
Heads Free Will Baptist Church Cemetery, Cedar Hill
Robertson County, Tennessee

James W Gower
Birth:
Aug. 30, 1821
Robertson County, Tennessee
Death:
Jul. 29, 1886
Robertson County, Tennessee
Burial:
Heads Free Will Baptist Church Cemetery
,Cedar Hill,
Robertson County, Tennessee

Was a minister in the Free Will Baptist Church for 29 yr. (written on tombstone

Paul Frederick Hall
Birth:
Feb. 20, 1938
Durham, Durham County,
North Carolina
Death:
Nov. 5, 2008
Nashville,
Davidson County, Tennessee
Burial:
Spring Hill Cemetery, Nashville,
Davidson County, Tennessee

He graduated from Durham High School in 1956, That fall he entered FWBBC. After attending two years he married Ruthann Edwards from Illinois in August 1958. Fred was called as assistant pastor at Swannanoa FWB church. During that time their first child was born. The family returned to Nashville to continue his education. After another year of college, Fred was called to be minister of music and assistant pastor at Central FWB church in Royal Oak, Michigan.. After two years the desire to finish his education led Fred to resign and return to Nashville. Finally in 1964 he received his BA degree. Fred served churches in North Carolina, South Carolina, Tennessee, Illinois, Kentucky and Michigan during his years of ministry. Fred wrote Sunday School literature for Randall House Publications several years and served in several roles in the denomination. Many people knew him for his beautiful singing voice and while he loved to sing, his first love was preaching and teaching. In 1984 Fred earned

a Master of Arts Degree in Pastoral Studies from FWBBC. In 2000 he earned a second Master's degree from this Pensacola Christian Seminary in Bible Exposition.
He had started work on a doctor's degree from Pensacola Christian Seminary, but by this time his health was failing and was not able to attain that goal. He loved to study and maintained a 4.0 grade average in both of his masters programs. During his lifetime Fred had built up quite a library. When he passed away, his family gave it to Trinity FWB Church in Bowling Green, KY. The "Rev. Fred Hall Memorial Library" was established in his honor. They had celebrated their 50th wedding anniversary on August 17 of that year while he was in the hospital.

Charles Edgar Hampton
Birth:
Mar. 25, 1938
Blanchard,
McClain County,
Oklahoma
Death:
Mar. 5, 2007
Nashville,
Davidson County,
Tennessee
Burial:
Harpeth Hills Memory Gardens,

Nashville,
Davidson County,
Tennessee

Dr Hampton is an alumnus of Free Will Baptist Bible College, Oklahoma Baptist University, Oklahoma University, and the University of Texas. He also retired from the Free Will Baptist Bible College after 26 years. Funeral services was at the Free Will Baptist Bible College with Dr Paul Harrison officiating.

Ralph C. Hampton
Birth:
Dec. 13, 1934
Dibble, McClain County,
Oklahoma
Death:
Sep. 7, 2012
Nashville. Davidson County.
Tennessee
Burial:
Harpeth Hills Memory Gardens,
Nashville,
Davidson County, Tennessee

The Oklahoma native was converted at age 12 during a youth camp and ordained to preach in 1960. Hampton's ministry to the broader denomination included six pastorates in Tennessee and Missouri, articles for *Contact* and *ONE Magazine,* and curriculum writing for Randall House Publications. His signature leadership role came during a 15-year span when the National Association of Free Will Baptists elected him moderator nine times (1987-1996) and assistant

moderator six times (1981-1987). He moderated during several controversial and pivotal sessions, including the emotionally charged 1995 national convention. Ralph began his 50-year tenure at Welch College in 1958 at age 23. Like most young educators, he wore several hats, which meant that he taught 15 hours per semester, served as Christian Service Director, and was the dormitory supervisor. The son of a Free Will Baptist preacher and oldest of four brothers, he spent half a century changing the landscape of denominational education, preparing students for ministry in a world-wide community, and raising a family of three children with his wife Margaret—all three children graduated from Welch College. He pushed himself hard as an educator, earning five degrees —A.A. degree from East Contra Costa Junior College (1955), B.A. degree from Welch College (1958), M.A. degree from Winona Lake School of Theology (1961), M.Div. from Covenant Theological Seminary (1970), and the D.Min. (ABD) from Trinity Evangelical Divinity School. He was the former chairman of the Biblical and Ministry Studies Department at Welch College and a member of the college faculty for 50 years, died after a two-year battle with cancer.

R S Harris
Birth:
1870
Death:
1940
Burial:
Troy Cemetery
Troy
Obion County, Tennessee

He was a member of the Clinch River Association which was situated west of the John Wheeler Association in Virginia and Tennessee. And was one of the early ministers the Association.

Steven Robert Hasty
Birth:
Jun. 15, 1949
Death:
Apr. 21, 1998
Tennessee
Burial:
Greenbrier Cemetery,
Greenbrier
Robertson County, Tennessee
A Free Will Baptist pastor for 25 years serving five churches in Michigan, Tennessee, Florida and Georgia. He was a prolific writer and noted historian serving 10 years on the National Historical Commission. He launched *"The Time Machine"* for the Georgia FWB Historical Society and *"Resources for Free Will Baptist History"* for the national commission. He researched and wrote a 35 chapter historical novel about the denomination which was in its final stages when he died.

Wallace Ray Hayes
Birth:
Jun. 21, 1940
Tennessee
Death:
Sep. 24, 2015
Mount Juliet
Wilson County, Tennessee
Burial:
Greenwood Cemetery
Charlotte
Dickson County, Tennessee

Mr. Hayes was a Freewill Baptist Minister who has served in Davidson, Dickson, Humphreys, Stewart & Wilson counties. He was very devoted and worked very closely with the Cumberland Youth Camp for over 45 years.

George Head
Birth:
Mar. 14, 1794
Death:
Oct. 27, 1868
Burial:
Heads Free Will Baptist Church
Cemetery
Cedar Hill
Robertson County
Tennessee
A pioneer in the church work for Free Will Baptists in Tennessee. He was baptized by Rev. Robert Heaton, another early minister. He gave 1/2 acre for the cemetery.

Rev George R Head
Birth:
Aug. 4, 1834
Robertson Co Tennessee
Death:
Jul. 5, 1902
Burial:
Heads Free Will Baptist Church
Cemetery
Cedar Hill
Robertson County
Tennessee
Rev. George Richard HEAD, son of George and Elizabeth (Winters) HEAD, At the age of nineteen he was converted, and July 14, 1866, he received a license. The following year he was ordained [Free Will Baptist minister]. His ministry has been in the Cumberland Association, TN, in which he has occupied a prominent position. He was married to Joanna F. Moore, October 23, 1853."

Rev George Richard Head
Birth:
Apr. 6, 1857
Death:
Dec. 31, 1927
Burial:
Heads Free Will Baptist Church
Cemetery

Cedar Hill
Robertson County
Tennessee

Free Will Baptist minister in the latter 1800's until his death. Was married to Lavina Ann (Harris)...sometimes listed as Ann, or Anna Lavina. Children:Hubert Head (1888 - 1943), Ernest Head (1893 - 1982)

Rev Wiley H Head
Birth:
Jan. 27, 1818
Death:
Apr. 5, 1888
Burial:
Heads Free Will Baptist Church
Cemetery
Cedar Hill
Robertson County
Tennessee

Rev. W.H. Head, listed in FWBapt Cyclopedia as "prominent minister having died recently." [pub. 1889].He served among the Ashland Quarterly Meeting, TN.
He was an early Free Will Baptist minister in the Ashland Quarterly Meeting, whose name appears in a listing of churches and pastors: Good Spring; Heads; Bethlehem; Oakland; Charity; Mt. Zion; Shady Grove; Grange; Old Zion; Oaklawn and North Nashville. Rev. W. H. Head was a minister of one of those churches, maybe, more than one as the custom was in that early day. Parents: George Head (1794 - 1868) & Elizabeth Winters Head (1800 - 1856). Spouse: Angaline D Head (1858 - 1890). Sibling: George R Head (1834 - 1902).

William H. Head
Birth:
Mar. 31, 1839
Death:
Jul. 10, 1923
Burial:
Heads Free Will Baptist Church
Cemetery,
Cedar Hill,
Robertson County,
Tennessee

Herman Lawrence Hersey
Birth:
Jan. 1, 1926
Chicago,
Cook County, Illinois
Death:
Jan. 26, 2008
Jackson,
Madison County, Tennessee
Burial:
Highland Memorial Gardens
Jackson
Jackson County,
Tennessee

A Free Will Baptist minister, pastor and denominational executive. A minister of the gospel for 58 years serving churches in North Carolina and was the Director of the Board of Retirement and Insurance for the National Association Of Free Will Baptists. He was a graduate of Bob Jones University, Chicago Musical College and attended the St. Louis Institute of Music at George Washington University. He is remembered as an outstanding pianist.

William J. Hill
Birth:
Jan. 10, 1928
Death:
Aug. 17, 2001
Burial:
Green Acres Memorial Gardens,
Crossville,
Cumberland County, Tennessee

Hill was a Minister that span 50 years and was the college chaplain at Taylor University in Indiana. He spoke in many universities in the United States as well as abroad. He began his ministry in 1948 as Minister of the first Free Will Baptist Church in Myrtle, Missouri. Later he pastored churches in Tennessee and Michigan and later the Evangelical Mennonite church in Indiana and Ohio. He was a graduate of the Free Will Baptist Bible college in Nashville and did graduate work at the University of Detroit in Michigan and Anderson College in Indiana. And was author Of "Organizing The Free Will Baptist Sunday School" printed by Randall house publications.Two other brothers were also noted ministers, namely; Bob Hill and Dr. Don Hill.

Critt Holman
Birth:
Sep. 6, 1908
Death:
Sep. 27, 2002
Burial:
Stewart Cemetery,
Cookeville,
Putnam County, Tennessee

Nathan Honeycutt
Birth:
Jul. 20, 1824
Buncombe County,
North Carolina
Death:
1907
Burial:
Nathan Honeycutt Cemetery,
Tiger Valley,
Carter County, Tennessee
Nathan was an early Free Will Baptist minister and was noted in Paul H. Woolsey's *"My Woolsey Free Will Baptist Family"*, pub. 1949:"Reverends Nathan Honeycutt and "Bobby" Moore's labors were especially blessed in Carter County, Tennessee. Today (1949) there are more Free Will Baptist Churches in this than any other county in the state - some twenty, belonging to the Union and Toe River Associations. Brother Honeycutt was the first minister to enter the young association after its birth in 1850. Of all the other early leaders, Brother Honeycutt proved to be

the most earnest and efficient helper, outside the Union Association, in the planning and building of a denominational school. Soon after commencement of Free Will Baptist work in this vicinity Father Woolsey began correspondence with the General Conference of the North. It was Brother Honeycutt who stood with him for the unification of the work with the entire denomination. In those formative years many questions of policy, doctrine and rules had to be adopted."His ability and leadership was instrumental to the church's growth in that part of Tennessee.

Joseph Clarence Howington
Birth:
Aug. 27, 1889
Death:
Jul. 20, 1970
Burial:
Highland Cemetery
Elizabethton
Carter County, Tennessee

Mentioned in 1937 Minutes.

Inscription:
Sgt Co G 3 Infantry World War I

Jesse E Hudgens
Birth:
Dec. 5, 1862
Cheatham County, Tennessee
Death:
Aug. 17, 1952
Ashland City
Cheatham County, Tennessee
Burial:
Hudgens Cemetery
Cheatham County, Tennessee

He gave fifty years of ministry and service to the Free Will Baptist denomin-ation.

Richard M Johnson
Birth:
1851
Death:
1913
Burial:
Alder-Livesay Cemetery,
Kyles Ford,
Hancock County, Tennessee

Rev G. G. Joyner
Birth:
Jan. 17, 1880
Death:
Sep. 4, 1964
Burial:
Parsons Cemetery
Parsons
Decatur County
Tennessee

Ordained Free Will Baptist minister in Tenn.

Matthias Judd
Birth:
May 30, 1844
Putnam County
Tennessee
Death:
Feb. 2, 1925
Cookeville
Putnam County
Tennessee
Burial:
Judd Church Cemetery
Cookeville
Putnam County
Tennessee

Rev. Matthias Judd was the son of Rev. Nathaniel Judd, whose property the cemetery was on. He was affilated with the Free Will Baptist, and his name appears in a list of ordained ministers, in 1879 Conference Minutes. He served in 1st Tennessee Mounted Infantry Regiment USA Union Roster during the Civil War. Enlisted on Aug 20, 1864 and Mustered on Jan 7, 1865 in Company I as a Corporal. Promoted from Private Jan 7, 1865

1st Matthias married Mary Bullington 14 Jan 1864 in Cookeville, Putnam Co, TN. Mary was the daughter of George Washington Bullington and Malinda Grinder. Mary was born 7 April 1847 in Putnam Co, TN and died 26 Mar 1902 in Cookeville, Putnam Co, TN.

Matthias Judd and Mary Bullington had a son, Nathan Alpheus Judd born 11 May 1865 in Cookeville, TN and died 11 April 1940 in Lubbock Texas.

2nd Matthias married Mary Ellen Smith 12 Apr 1903 in Cookeville, Putnam Co, TN. Mary Ellen was born 27 Nov 1870 in Cumberland Co, Kentucky, and died 6 April 1937 in Putnam Co, TN.

Rev Nathaniel Jackson Judd, Sr
Birth:
Sep. 5, 1807
Adair County,Kentucky
Death:
Mar. 21, 1885
Cookeville
Putnam County,Tennessee
Burial:
Judd Church Cemetery
Cookeville
Putnam County,Tennessee

He was a minister/pastor in the Old Stone Association of Christian Baptist Church, org. 1835, which later united with the Free Will Baptist in Tenn. Rev. Nathaniel Judd is listed in the names of FWB ordained ministers in Minutes of Old Stone Ass'n, when convened at Laurel Creek church, Cumberland Co. TN, Fri. Oct. 3, 1879. There was also a Rev. M. Judd, in the same listing.
His grandfather was Rowland Judd {1720-1801} DAR Library # A063428
His parents were John Judd {1761-1765-1 Oct 1823 Adair Co KY} DAR Library # A208840 and Polly {b.1775-d.Sept 1839 Adair Ky}
A son of Rowland Judd was Robert Judd 1766-1847} he was married to Rachel Greer {b.1770} who was a daugther of Benjamin Greer and Nancy Wilkerson who was a daugther of Sarah Boone sister to the Frontiersman Daniel Boone.

Christ Has Led the Way

Paul Jackson Ketteman
Birth:
Jul. 24, 1924
Illinois
Death:
May 21, 1987
Nashville,
Davidson County,
Tennessee
Burial:
Harpeth Hills Memory Gardens,
Nashville,
Davidson County,
Tennessee

Paul J. Ketteman, was on the college's first graduating class in 1942. In May 1945, Paul graduated from the new school's two year program after working hard to pay for his education. He immediately enrolled in Columbia Bible College, Columbia, S. C. To finish his degree in 1947. Paul pastored first at Mt. Elon FWB Church, then at Edgemont FWB Church in Durham, North Carolina, then back to Mt. Elon (this time full-time), and later at First FWB Church, Columbus, Mississippi. He served four years as clerk of the National Association of Free Will Baptists and nine years on the Bible College Board Of Trustees. He worked for the college 25 years in fundraising and public relations. His wife, Mrs. Helen Ketteman, taught business 20 years at the college.
Paul was a native of Illinois and was raised in a minister's home. His life was totally dedicated to his Lord and the college that he represented. He began the annual Christmas fund drive that was given his name after his death. He understood better than most how costly it is to provide Christian education. The idea of challenging churches and individuals to operate the college for a day originated with the Paul J. Ketteman, long time public relations director at FWBBC.

Dewey R Kirk
Birth:
Jan. 18, 1937
Death:
Jun. 25, 1982
Burial:
Island Ford Cemetery,
Lake City,
Anderson County,Tennessee

Jesse Laws
Birth:
1889
Death:
1931
Burial:
Laws-Green Cemetery,
Cocke County,
Tennessee

William Wallace Lee
Birth:
Nov. 26, 1857
Hawkins County, Tennessee
Death:
Aug. 28, 1944
Sullivan County, Tennessee
Burial:
Collins - Gravelly Rd
Sullivan County, Tennessee

His name is in early FWB records.Pastored at the Morning Star Freewill Baptist Church Hawkins County, TN

James Willard McCarroll
Birth:
Aug. 12, 1935
Death:
Jan. 5, 2009
Joelton,
Davidson County,
Tennessee
Burial:
Joelton Hills Memory Gardens,
Joelton,
Davidson County, Tennessee

He was a Minister of the Gospel for over 45 years and pastored four churches; Harper Road Free Will Baptist Church, Mount Zion Free Will Baptist Church, First Free Will Baptist Church of McEwen and was currently serving the Olivet Free Will Baptist Church in Clarksville, all in Tennessee.

Henry Melvin
Birth:
Jul. 8, 1905
Death:
Jun., 1971
Nashville, Davidson County,
Tennessee
Burial:
Spring Hill Cemetery,
Nashville,
Davidson County, Tennessee

Brother Melvin was saved in a Methodist revival in Kynesville, Florida at the age of 17 and later surrendered to God's call to the ministry. He was ordained on October 3, 1925 in that city. In his early ministry. He pastored in Florida and Georgia. Prior to the formation of the National Association in 1935 brother Melvin attended the General Conference for the first time in 1927. This conference dates back to 1920. Melvin preached the opening sermon the very next year in 1928. He was a frequent program personality thereafter, including messages in 1928 and 1932. He was a leader in Christian Education illustrated by his service on the annual education committee in 1929 and in 1931. In 1929 he was elected General Secretary Of Young People Word for the General Conference. Many acknowledge that the most significant contribution to his denomination was his ministry to the youth--first with the League Board and later the Church Training Service Board. Altogether, he served 39 years with The League and CTS board. He was known for his energetic and visionary leadership which kept the youth board moving ahead for Christ. He showed his interest in mission's early serving on the annual missions committee of the convention in 1927 and again in 1932. The 1932 minutes show that his sermon was on "The Church" and he strongly emphasized the church's mission in bringing the world to Christ. In 1935, he was very instrumental in producing an atmosphere of optimism in the merger of the Western and Eastern conferences. Following the report of the committee, brother Melvin suggested that all stand and sing, *Blessed Be The Tie That Binds,* as a token of the reality of the coming tie. In the mid-30's brother Melvin pastored the Edgemont Free Will Baptist Church in Durham, North Carolina. It was here that a close relationship between he and Thomas and Mabel Willey came into existence and he introduced them to the Free Will Baptist Missions program where they later served under their auspices. At the Seventh Annual Session of the national association in Nashville, Tennessee in 1943, the Board Of Foreign Missions commended him for his involvement in the missions program by sponsoring a trip for him to Cuba in February, 1943, during which time he assisted Rev. and Mrs. Willey in the organization of the Cuban national convention.. In 1946 he was elected to the Free Will Baptists Bible College Board of Trustees. He was the college business manager the following year. Because of his strong musical talents he was selected to the 1964 music committee for the new Free Will Baptist hymn book. He was a well-respected pastor with at least 26 sons in the ministry during those pastorates.

His son, Dr. Billy Melvin, became the Executive-Secretary of the National Association of Free Will Baptists and later the Director of the National Association Of Evangelicals.

He Is The Beginning And The End

Trymon Messer
Birth:
Nov. 13, 1932
Pontotoc, Mississippi
Death:
Jan. 10, 2015
Nashville
Davidson County, Tennessee
Burial:
Middle Tennessee State Veterans
Cemetery
Nashville
Davidson County, Tennessee

The former U.S. Marine who brought home four medals from Korea began practicing what drill instructors taught him on Paris Island—leadership.

As Lay pastor for 11 years in Salina, Kansas, the congregation mushroomed to a record attendance of 859, completed three building programs, and helped start five Kansas churches. He chaired the Kansas Mission Board and was elected to Hillsdale FWB College's Board of Trustees. Wherever he went, people stepped up to follow his leadership. The National Association elected him to the Home Missions Board in 1973.

Twice named Layman of the Year—in 1964 by Hillsdale FWB College and in 1969 by Master's Men—Messer was sought by pastors nationwide to lead church-growth conferences.

When Trymon was 45 years old, the Home Missions Department named him associate director (1978), where his practical biblical knowledge and sense of humor made him one of the agency's top spokesmen. He was named general director in 1995 and completed 22 years with the department.

Trymon Messer lived by a simple philosophy: "I believe that if a man will claim God's promise, practice God's presence, and demonstrate God's power, he cannot fail."

LaVerne Dale Miley
Birth:
Sep. 9, 1928
Kirksville,
Adair County, Missouri
Death:
Mar. 15, 2005
Nashville,
Davidson County, Tennessee
Burial:
Woodlawn Memorial Park,
Nashville,
Davidson County, Tennessee

A Free Will Baptist minister, medical doctor, missionary, and college professor. He opened the medical work in the Ivory Coast, Africa, where he served as a medical missionary for 19 years. For many years he was a professor at the Free Will Baptist Bible College in Nashville, Tennessee and served as a medical consultant for Free Will Baptist International Missions. He also worked with the Navajo Indians in the western United States and served in the Men of Valor Prison Ministry and was a longtime member of Cofer's Chapel Free Will Baptist Church in Nashville, Tennessee.

William H Morelock
Birth:
1875
Death:
1956
Burial:
Beech Creek Missionary Baptist
Church Cemetery, Rogersville,
Hawkins County, Tennessee

Rev Joseph Wesley Moyers
Birth:
May 31, 1854
Death:
Oct. 13, 1934
Burial:
Cox Cemetery
Claiborne County
Tennessee

Rev. Joseph A. Moyers, was an ordained Free Will Baptist minister in the Stone Association, as shown in its Annual Minutes, Oct. 3, 1879, when meeting with the Laurel Creek church, Cumberland Co. TN:

"...On motion, and in pursuance of Section 9 of the Declaration of Rights, there were appointed as Presbyters, Elders T. J. Clouse, John Brewster, Joseph A. Moyers, G. L. Moyers and John Stowers for the next associational year. On motion, the ministers were appointed to attend the several churches as pastors..." [Then it gives names of several churches in the group.] Evidently, Rev. Moyers was a leader and esteemed minister who was given responsibilities they thought he would faithfully carry out. Nothing at this time is known regarding the year he was ordained. Husband of Elizabeth Jane Eastridge Moyers. Son of Abraham Wheeler Jefferson & Anna Goin Moyers

Howard T. Munsey
Birth:
Jun. 27, 1926
Death:
Aug. 14, 2009
Burial:
Jefferson Memorial Gardens Cemetery, Jefferson City, Jefferson County, Tennessee

He was the founding pastor of Peace Free Will Baptist Church in Morristown, delivered his first sermon in 1953 at Greenville First Free Will Baptist Church. He joined the U.S. Navy in 1942 and served during World War II and the Korean War, achieving the rank of petty officer first class. Rev. Munsey worked for Magnavox, built homes, and later part-owner of Hearthstone Log Homes in Dandridge during the 1970s and 1980s. During his lifetime, he organized two and pastored seven other Free Will Baptist churches. He had an effective revival and pulpit-supply ministry. Rev. Munsey served as the president, until his death, of Berea Ministries Inc., a mission organization he created in the 1950s to support the ministry of national pastors in Mexico. It was first chartered as the mission arm of a radio ministry called "Cross Beams Missions."

James Alan Munsey
Birth:
Aug. 10, 1950
Death:
Feb. 3, 2001
Texas
Burial:
Union Cemetery, Newport, Cocke County, Tennessee

Munsey built the Free Will Baptist Church in Weslaco, Texas, while he worked with Free Will Baptist churches in Mexico. He was very instrumental in building many churches in Mexico and organizing numerous ones. He also was instrumental in building a Free Will Baptist Institute for the training of Mexican pastors. He was the son of Howard Munsey.

James Harrison Oliver
Birth:
Apr. 6, 1882
Cadiz, Kentucky
Death:
Jun. 8, 1939
Burial:
Hays/Hayes Cemetery
Stewart County
Tennessee

Parents: William Harrison Oliver (1847 - 1929)- Susan Litchfield Oliver (1849 - 1931)
Spouse: Frances L Hembree Oliver (1884 - 1960)
Children: William Henry Oliver (1903 - 1991), James Herschel Oliver (1910 - 2007), Myrtle Oliver Stanley (1914 - 2005), Pearl Oliver Miller (1917 - 2007).

William Henry Oliver
Birth:
Nov. 4, 1903
Indian Mound
Stewart County, Tennessee
Death:
May 15, 1991
Nashville
Davidson County, Tennessee
Burial:
Forest Lawn Memorial Gardens
Goodlettsville
Davidson County, Tennessee

Rev. Dr. William Henry Oliver, a Free Will Baptist minister for 68 years, in Nashville. Hundreds attended his funeral May 18 at East High School where he served 18 years as principal (1939-1957).Rev. Oliver once said in an interview that he had three goals in mind when he started college--- to become a preacher, a teacher and a writer. He eventually accomplished all three. "I felt the Lord wanted me to be a preacher. I had to be a teacher, and I wanted to be a writer," he said. Mr. Oliver began teaching in Nashville city schools in 1930 at Hume Fogg HS. He taught algebra and English and coached the school's boxing and baseball teams, leading the baseball players to a city championship. He received his bachelor's degree from Vanderbilt University in 1926, and later received master's degrees in arts and education at George Peabody College. In 1957, the Nashville Board of education elected Mr. Oliver as city school superintendent. He retired in 1963 after the city and county government merged. He taught at Belmont College for the next seven years and then took a similar position at Free Will Baptist Bible College (1970-1977).He was ordained a minister in 1924 and later founded and became the first pastor of the East Nashville Free Will Baptist Church. He wrote literature and poetry including one well received poem titled At Twilight. In 1987 he was awarded an honorary Doctor of Literature Letters from Cumberland University. He was a member of the Kappa Alpha fraternity, Civitan, the Red Cross board, past president of the East Nashville YMCA and a past member of the Nashville Chamber of Commerce.

Rev Tim Anthony Osborn
Birth:
Jan. 22, 1964
Russellville
Franklin County, Alabama
Death:
May 17, 2014
Memphis
Shelby County,Tennessee
Burial:
Fayette County Memorial Park
Oakland
Fayette County, Tennessee

He received his education in the Alabama Public School System and was a graduate of the Baptist Bible College in Nashville, Tennessee. He was married *December 21, 1985 to the former* Robyn Barnes of Farmington, Missouri, who currently serves as a teacher at the Macon Road Baptist Church School.Pastor Osborn had been a minister for over 25 years and had formerly served pastorates in North Carolina and was involved in church missions in the Memphis area before serving in Fayette County. Anyone that knew Tim knew without question that his God and his family were his passions and his church family was an important part of his life. At the time of his death, Pastor Osborn served as the chaplain for the Macon Fire Department in Macon, Tennessee. The officiating ministers were David Crowe, Richard Atwood and Michael Gillock. Graveside Services

followed in the Fayette County Memorial Park Cemetery on Highway 64 with remarks given by Gwyn Pugh.

Hardy C Pace
Birth:
May 30, 1846
Death:
Oct. 16, 1928
Burial:
Taylor Cemetery
Stewart County, Tennessee

He served as a Free Will Baptist minister in the Ashland Quarterly Meeting in the late 1800s. He was married to   D Attie Wallace Pace (1847 - 1929)

Rev Billy Gene Outland
Birth:
Mar. 25, 1935
Kenly

Johnston County
North Carolina
Death:
Mar. 9, 2015
Nashville
Davidson County
Tennessee
Burial:
Harpeth Hills Memory Gardens
Nashville
Davidson County
Tennessee

Long-time Free Will Baptist pastor and denominational leader passed from this life at Saint Thomas Hospital in Nashville after years of declining health. His wife Peggy preceded him in death. He is survived by their daughter Angela (Mark) Trotter and a granddaughter Audrey Jordan (Blake). The Outland's last pastorate was the Hazel Dell Free Will Baptist Church in Sesser, Illinois. They moved back to Tennessee after retirement a few years ago. Before moving to Illinois, they served the Cofer's Chapel Free Will Baptist Church in Nashville.

No one can confidently say that he will still be living here tomorrow.

Jerry Franklin Presley
Birth:
Jan. 16, 1932
Death:
Sep. 28, 1993
Tennessee
Burial:
Sweetwater Valley Memorial
Park, Sweetwater,
Monroe County, Tennessee

He was a Free Will Baptist minister and pastor for 26 years in Tennessee and Illinois until poor health forced him to resign from full-time pastoral service. He held numerous denominational positions, including Promotional-Secretary for the Tennessee Union Association, Youth camp Director, and 10 years as clerk of the Union Ministerial Association. He taught school in four Tennessee counties. He served in Korea with the U.S. Army.

Fannie Lee Binkley Polston
Birth: 1881
Death:
Apr. 24, 1964
Nashville
Davidson County
Tennessee
Burial:
Spring Hill Cemetery
Nashville
Davidson County
Tennessee
Plot: Sect G

Daughter of Henry J. and Rhoda (Sanders) Binkley
Married Frederick Polston in 1903

One daughter, Irene, born to this union
Employed as a pantry maid in a hotel before marrying Fred.

Mrs. Polston⁶⁴ Dies at 82

Mrs. Fannie Lee Polston, 82, of 513 Woodland St., one of the founders of Nashville Free Will Bible College, died yesterday morning in Miller's Hospital after a heart attack.

Services will be at 10 a.m. Sunday at East Nashville Free Will Baptist Church. The Rev. J. L. Welch, the Rev. Henry Melvin and Dr. L. C. Johnson will officiate. Burial will be in Spring Hill Cemetery.

The body is at Cosmopolitan Funeral Home.

A NATIVE of Ashland City, she was a daughter of Henry J. and Rhoda Sanders Binkley. She attended Cheatham County public schools and was married in 1902 to Fred Polston. He died in 1933.

Mrs. Polston organized the West Nashville Free Will Baptist Church in 1924 and was a charter member. She was the current president of the Nashville Women's Christian Temperance Union and had been a member of the board of Eureka College in Ayden, N.C.

Mrs. Polston was one of the founders of the Nashville Free Will Baptist Bible College in 1942 and continued to take an active part in the college up to the time of her death.

Mrs. Polston also was instrumental in the founding of Free Will Baptist Children's Home in Greenville, Tenn.

Survivors are a daughter, Mrs. Irene Coville, Morehead City, N.C.; a sister, Mrs. J. W. Maxey, Ashland City; three grandchildren, Mrs. Eve Griffin, Nashville, Mrs. Frances Walder, Morehead City and William Coville, Akron, Ohio, and four great-grandchildren.

Twenty-one year old Cleo (Dalton) Pursell, ordained by the West Fork District Association in 1939.

Tennessee State University and Luther Rice Seminary.

Cleo Pursell
Birth:
Feb. 16, 1918
Fort Worth,
Tarrant County,
Texas
Death:
Dec. 17, 2009
Nashville,
Davidson County
, Tennessee
Burial:
Woodlawn Memorial Park and
Mausoleum, Nashville,
Davidson County,
Tennessee

She became the first full-time Executive Sec. of the Women's National Auxiliary Convention and led the organization for 22 years (1963-1985). The headquarters of this woman's organization is located in Nashville, Tennessee and is part of the National Association of Free Will Baptists. The ministry flourished under her capable leadership and eventually she led the membership to an all-time high. She was a prolific writer of books and pamphlets as well as writing a regular feature for *Contact* Magazine called "Words for Women". She will be remembered for her far-reaching vision and constant leadership. She was 91 at her passing. She was an ordained minister and outlived her minister husband, Rev. Paul Purcell, who is buried in Oklahoma.

Roger C Reeds
Birth:
Sep. 16, 1928
Saint Louis,
St. Louis City,
Missouri
Death:
May 2, 2007
Joelton,
Davidson County,
Tennessee
Burial:
Joelton Hills Memory Gardens,
Joelton,
Davidson County, Tennessee

A Free Will Baptist pastor, author, and denominational leader. Converted in November 9, 1947 and called to preach the next year. He pastored churches in Missouri, North Carolina, and Tennessee. He was the founding Director of Randall House Publications, in Nashville, Tennessee, where he served 31 years, and was on the committee of founders of Donelson Christian Academy. He held degrees from Free Will Baptist Bible College, Middle

Norman Howard Richards
Birth:
Sep. 30, 1938
White County, Arkansas
Death:
Aug. 22, 2013
Nashville
Davidson County, Tennessee
Burial:
Mount Olivet Cemetery
Nashville
Davidson County, Tennessee

Norman age 74, of Nashville, passed away at the Vanderbilt Medical Center. He faithfully loved and served the Lord as a Missionary in Africa and as a Minister, presently with The Donelson Fellowship Church. He was preceded in death by his parents; 2 brothers and 1 sister. Rev. Richards is survived by his loving wife of 50 years, Bessie Richards; sons, Gene Richards (Patti), and Randal Richards (Patty); 4 grandchildren, Wesley, Julia, Olivia, and David; 2 brothers, Wayne Richards (Patsy) and

Claude Presnell (Juanita); and 3 sisters, Mildred Sowell, Juanita Dickson (Ray), and Madie Walker (Don). Funeral services were conducted at the church with the Rev. Robert Morgan officiating. A private family graveside service was conducted in the Mount Olivet Cemetery.

Charles Raymond Riggs
Birth:
Oct. 15, 1915
Randolph County, Arkansas
Death:
Apr. 13, 2009
Burial:
Crest Lawn Cemetery,
Cookeville,
Putnam County, Tennessee

In November of 1934, he was married to Velma Staten and she passed away two months later. He then was united in marriage to Winona Mae Gates on October 25, 1936. She preceded him in death in March 1999.

Then he married Burnice Davis on July 22, 1999, in Cookeville, Tennessee. Brother Riggs was in his early ministry a school teacher, and as a minister known for his singing. He became an outstanding pastor and minister in the Detroit area. Under his leadership as the first Director Of Foreign Missions for the National Association of Free Will Baptist the organization grew. He is remembered as an early statesman for the denomination and has left a legacy of having many sons and grandchildren as ministers within the denomination.

Carol A. Waring Robirds
Birth:
Mar. 8, 1938
California
Death:
Mar. 30, 2010
Brentwood,
Davidson County,
Tennessee
Burial:
Woodlawn Memorial Park and
Mausoleum,Nashville,
Davidson County,Tennessee

Carol and her husband, Don, served as FWB missionaries in Brazil from 1964 to 1971, when Don was asked to join the office staff in Nashville as Dir. of Communications. Carol served as his assistant for several years.

Willie B Rodgers
Birth:
Jun. 14, 1918
Putnam County, Tennessee
Death:
Feb. 7, 2005
Cookeville
Putnam County, Tennessee
Burial:
Rodgers Cemetery
Baxter
Putnam County, Tennessee

Rev. Willie B. Rodgers passed away at his home. He was 86 years of age, and a native of Putnam Co. TN. Bro. Rodgers had a very fruitful ministry in South and North Carolina, and Tennessee. Most of his ministery was in Tenn. Churches he pastored: Antioch; Lily's Chapel; Duncan's Chapel; Manchester First; Trinity (Nashville); Taylor's Providence; Post Oak Shade; Algood First; United Hensley's Chapel; Taylor's Seminary; Cedar Hill; and Community Church.Rev. Jack Taylor conducted his service. He commented that he had many times sought good counsel from Bro. Rodgers. He was a devoted Bible student. He lived what he preached and was a great influence to many people. He married Velma Ramsey Rodgers.

Inscription:
Married April 28, 1950;
PFC US Army WWII

Rev John Russell
Birth:
Jan. 15, 1814
Death:
Jan. 26, 1905
Tennessee
Burial:
Sims Cemetery
Sevier County
Tennessee

His name and dates are listed in Free Baptist Cyclopedia, for TN, with other ministers serving in NE TN in the 1887 roster.

Melvin R Sanford
Birth:
Jan. 31, 1920
Death:
Oct. 17, 1993
Burial:
Fairview Free Will Baptist Church Cemetery
Anderson County, Tennessee

He ministered for over 54 years and started several churches in West Virginia pastoring numerous churches there. He also pastored churches in Ohio and Florida. He was known for his revivals some of which went as much as six weeks or more.He saw a great number of converts during his ministry. He was married to Helen L Sanford (1925 - 1998)

Inscription:
Married June 23, 1943

Ernest Sawyer
Birth:
Unknown
Death:
Aug. 2, 2012
Del Rio, Cocke County, Tennessee
Burial:
Fugate Free Will Baptist Church Cemetery,
Del Rio, Cocke County, Tennessee

He pastored the Fugate Free Will Baptist church near Del Rio for 29 years.

Billie J Lay Sexton
Birth:
Feb. 13, 1934
Coxton, Kentucky
Death:
Dec. 20, 2015
Burial:
Happy Valley Memorial Park
Elizabethton
Carter County
Tennessee

She attended Virgie, Kentucky High School and Free Will Baptist Bible College, Nashville, Tennessee. She married Don Sexton, the love of her life, on December 23, 1950. Billie was a stay-at-home mom until Don became a minister and she became a dedicated pastor's wife, including learning to play the piano. Don and Billie pastored the Roan Street Free Will Baptist Church in the early 1960s in Elizabethton. They started the First Free Will Baptist Church in Chattanooga, Tennessee, and Billie started working as a dental assistant to supplement the family income, while still very actively serving as a pastor's wife.

In 1972, at the ages of 42 & 38, Don & Billie answered the Lord's call and went to Switzerland to language school to learn French so they could start a Free Will Baptist Church in France. They first served the church in Nantes, France, then started a church in St. Nazaire, France. In 1979, when Don's health began to fail due to Parkinson's disease, they returned to the United States. Don & Billie worked tirelessly all across the country to raise money in support of foreign missions, which led to the creation of the annual Don & Billie Sexton Walk-A-Thon.

A Celebration of Life Service was held at Tetrick Funeral & Cremation Services, Johnson City with Wesley Simons officiating.

Donald Ray Sexton
Birth:
July 9, 1930
Kentucky
Death:
1997
Tennessee
Burial:
Happy Valley Memorial Park
Elizabethton
Carter County, Tennessee
Plot: Mausoleum of Peace

Sexton was licensed of preach in 1950 and ordained in 1951. He was a native of Jenkins, Kentucky. He graduated from Free Will Baptist Bible College in 1960 and attended language school in Switzerland and France. He served as Tennessee's first state missionary in 1963 and moderated the Tennessee State Association between 1967-71. He pastored six churches, four in Tennessee and two in Kentucky. He and his wife Billie were missionaries to France beginning in 1971 and served until 1979 when Don was diagnosed with Parkinson's disease. During his ministry in France, Sexton started the First Free Will Baptist Church in in Nantes. He was elected the Field Director in 1976. After he returned to the states, Sexton was asked by the Foreign Mission Board to promote foreign missions in the United States. For the next 13 years he traveled, informed and motivated Free Will Baptist about foreign missions. He resigned in 1990 due to his health problems. From his efforts the Don and Billi Sexton walk-a-thon became one of the most successful efforts in the denomination raising nearly 1,000,000 for missionary support.

About Dying, Living Isn't Going To Be Much Fun.

Robert Logan Shockey
Birth:
Sep. 16, 1927
Clay City,
Powell County, Kentucky
Death:
Mar. 7, 2008
Chapmansboro,
Cheatham County, Tennessee
Burial:
Bet
Ashland City,
Cheatham County, Tennessee

He was called to preach in 1955 and ordained to preach in 1956.His education consisted of Bible Diploma/Free Will Baptist Bible College in Nashville, Tennessee, in 1958. His pastorates included Raccoon Free Will Baptist Church in Greenup, Kentucky. From 1954-55; Bethlehem Free Will Baptist Church in Ashland City, Tennessee. From 1955-1957; Donelson Free Will Baptist Church in Nashville, Tennessee. from 1957-1959; Second Free Will Baptist Church in Ashland, Kentucky, from 1959-68 and 1973-74; Dothan Free Will Baptist Church in Dothan, Alabama from 1971 to 1973; Heritage Temple Free Will Baptist Church in Ashland, Kentucky from 1978-1984; Portland Free Will Baptist Church in Portland, Tennessee. in 2004. Denominational positions included: Moderator: Kentucky State Association of Free Will Baptists from 1959-1966; Moderator: Blue Grass Conference/Kentucky; Pastor of the Year Kentucky 1964; President: Bethel Bible Institute Paintsville, Kentucky from 1982-1984. Home Missions Department from 1961-1978; Member: Home Missions Board (1961-1966); Promotional Secretary (1967-1971); General Director (1972-1978) (includes Director of Evangelism and Director of Military Chaplains); Free Will Baptist Bible College 1984-1995; Campus Pastor, Christian Service Director, Ministerial Fellowship Director, Director of Student Support. National Radio Speaker Radio & TV Commission, Victorious Faith Program. Evangelist 1954-2008; United States/Canada/Mexico/ Virgin Islands. His publications included Let's Go Fishing (pamphlet); How to Call a Pastor (pamphlet); Five Smooth Stones (pamphlet); The Teacher (pamphlet); Bus Ministry (pamphlet); How to Go Soul winning (pamphlet). Tracts include Gods Simple Plan of Salvation; Tip; Now That You Are Saved; Keys to a New Life. Other accomplishments include: United States Navy, Psychiatric Nurse, Served two enlistments.

Rolla Darrell Smith
Birth:
Dec. 29, 1920
Norwood, Wright County,
Missouri
Death:
Mar. 15, 2013
Nashville, Davidson County,
Tennessee
Burial:
Hermitage Memorial Gardens
Old Hickory, Davidson County,
Tennessee

He pastored at Hazel Creek Free Will Baptist (FWB) Church (MO), Fellowship FWB Church (Flat River, MO), Donelson FWB Church (Nashville), First FWB Church

(Savannah, GA) and Grant Avenue FWB Church (Springfield, MO). He was a man of ordinary means yet rich in what matters most...love for God, love for family and love for friends. He was the General Director at FWB International Missions Department from 1960-1962 and 1975-1986 and Missions Instructor at Welch College from 1987-1989. Honorary Pallbearers were missionaries and staff members from the FWB International Missions Department and members of the Harvesters Sunday School Class at Cross Timbers FWB Church. A life celebration service was held at Harpeth Hills Funeral Home with Dr. Paul Harrison officiating.

Sam Peyton Stewart
Birth:
Jan. 18, 1857
Death:
Jun. 3, 1910
Burial:
Stewart Cemetery, Cookeville,
Putnam County, Tennessee

Rev. S. P. Stewart died at his home in the Seventh district. The news writer extends his sympathy to the bereaved family and friends. He was a Free-will Baptist minister. History of Putnam Co. TN Cane Creek Free Will Baptist membership roll shows Rev. Sam Peyton Stewart was a member there when he died in 1910. Samuel P. Stewart was the son of Jesse Peyton Stewart and Arminty Dorman Ray.

Rev Joseph Winfield Stone
Birth:
Aug. 30, 1869
Death:
Jan. 12, 1949
Burial:
Judd Church Cemetery
Cookeville
Putnam County
Tennessee

The Rev. J. W. Stone, 79, of Bloomington Springs, died suddenly of a heart attack Wednesday afternoon, 4½ miles west of Lebanon, while en route home from Nashville.
Rev. J. H. Roberson and the Rev. Oliver Lane officiated. The Rev. Stone was one of the oldest Baptist ministers of the Stone Association as well as this part of the State. He had been very active in the work of the Association having served as Moderator on many occasions and held a record of attending 50 consecutive annual meetings of the Association. He served, as pastor, practically every rural church in the Stone Association. He was ordained as a minister in 1896. However, he told his relatives only that he had preached for two years before he was ordained. Rev. J.W. Stone's name is in a list of ministers of the Old Stone Association, which later united with the Free Will Baptist.

Rev John William Stowers
Birth:
Feb. 22, 1849
Loudon County
Tennessee
Death:
Mar. 25, 1932
Fentress County
Tennessee
Burial:
Springs Chapel Cemetery
Banner Springs
Fentress County
Tennessee

Minister in the Old Stone Association of Free Will Baptist, shown in Minutes in their 1879 session, with Laurel Creek Church, Cumberland Co. Tenn. He was married three times. Following are the Spouses:
Catherine Burton (1863 -1920), Jensy Emeline Brown Stowers (1851 - 1910), Matilda May Atkinson Stowers (1878 -1916).

Missionary
Virginia Dawn Sweeney
Birth:
October 3,, 1958
Stacy, North Carolina
Death:
January 5, 2016
Nashville, Tennessee
Burial:
Cremated

Virginia Dawn Sweeney, age 57 of Nashville, TN was born to Rev. Quincy Winston and Fannie Jewel Addington Sweeney. She served in France and had to return because of failing health. Afterwards she worked in the Crisis Center for Family Ministries in Greenville, Tennessee. Ms. Sweeney was a graduate of Free Will Baptist Bible College.
She was preceded in death by her parents and is survived by her brother, Winston Larry Sweeney.

William Horace Teague
Birth:
Aug. 2, 1918
Death:
Nov. 1, 2000
Burial:
Union Cemetery, Newport
Cocke County, Tennessee

He was called to preach in 1943 and was ordained in 1947 by Tennessee's union Association. He began passing immediately at Johnson's Chapel Free Will Baptist Church. He was a Free Will Baptist minister for 53 years and pastored a church is in his home state of Tennessee and for five years a church in Michigan. He then returned to Newport, Tennessee where he continued his ministry. He served as the moderator of the Tennessee state Association. He was a dedicated man who slap was fully yielded to Christ and he sacrificed for the ministry and suffered in order to preach the gospel. He had two sons that likewise became ministers Rev. Harold Teague of Beckville, Texas and Jim Teague of Chuckey, Tennessee

Elbert Worth Tippett
Birth:
Dec. 19, 1940
Portsmouth,
Portsmouth City,
Virginia
Jan. 5, 2011
Nashville,
Davidson County,
Tennessee
Burial:
Harpeth Hills Memory Gardens,
Nashville,
Davidson County,
Tennessee

Bert Tippett was the long-time voice of Free Will Baptist Bible College as he headed the media office for numerous years. He was a great preacher, gentleman and a person of sterling character.

Ray Carroll Turnage
Birth:
May 8, 1931
Lenoir County
North Carolina
Death:
Jun. 14, 2017
Oklahoma
Burial:
Oak Grove Freewill Baptist
Church Cemetery
Tusculum
Greene County
Tennessee

Ray Carroll Turnage was born to Roy Edward and Helen Onita (Abbott) Turnage. Ray was a graduate of Free Will Baptist Bible College in Nashville, TN and went on the get his M.E. from Middle TN State University in Murfreesboro, TN. He worked as a Superintendent at Free Will Baptist Home for Children in Greeneville, TN and retired from Greene County Schools. On August 23, 1953, Ray married Lissie (Chaudoin) Turnage, and together they shared 63 years of love, life, family, and friends. Ray was a member of the Heritage Baptist

Church in Johnson City, TN, the Ruritan Club, an FFA Honorary Chapter Farmer and was presented the 1965 Free Will Baptist Layman of the Year award. Ray is survived by his wife, Lissie; daughters, Vicki Toombs of Edmond, OK and Renee Brogan of Loganville, GA; grandchildren; Beau Toombs of Chicago, IL, Amy Brogan of Cincinnati, OH, and David Brogan of Kennesaw, GA; sister, Nellie Turnage of West Columbia, SC; and sons-in-law, Larry Toombs of Edmond, OK.

Note: He was cremated and his remains are buried in the plot with his son Daniel in the same cemetery.

Rev Wendell Trussell
Birth:
Unknown
Death:
Oct. 6, 2014
Nashville
Davidson County, Tennessee
Burial:
Blantons Chapel Cemetery
Manchester
Coffee County, Tennessee

He served as pastor of the Faith Free Will Baptist Church in Manchester, Tennessee, where he served as pastor for thirty-one years. He had pastored Loyal Chapel in Columbia, Tennessee, the New Salem FWB church in Colquitt, Georgia and the Pelham FWB church, Pelham, Tennessee.

Rev Greg Tyson
Birth:
Mar. 18, 1959
Saint Louis
St. Louis City, Missouri
Death:
Aug. 3, 2014
Indian Mound
Stewart County, Tennessee
Burial:
Dunbar Chapel Cemetery
Stewart County, Tennessee

Rev. Greg Tyson, age 55 of Indian Mound, TN, went to be with the Lord on Sunday, August 3, 2014 at his residence.

Funeral services were held at Dunbar Chapel Freewill Baptist Church with Rev. Maxie Milliken and Rev. James Black officiating. He was born March 18, 1959 in St. Louis, MO son of James Noel and Ocie Milliken Tyson. Mr. Tyson received a bachelor's degree from Welch's Bible College, minister for over 27 years at Dunbar Chapel Freewill Baptist Church, had ministered at Brandon's Chapel Freewill Baptist Church and was safety coordinator of Nashville Wire.

As the image on the seal is stamped upon the wax, so the thoughts of the heart are printed upon the actions.

R. Eugene Waddell
Birth:
1935
Death:
Oct. 21, 2007
Burial:
Harpeth Hills
Memory Gardens, Nashville,,
Davidson County, Tennessee

He served with distinction churches in South Carolina, Virginia, and North Carolina before becoming pastor of Cofer's Chapel FWB Church in Nashville, Tennessee, a position he held from 1964 - 1981. He joined FWB International Missions where he was the Associate Director and then Director, until he retired in 1998. As the Director of International **Missions, Mr. Waddell traveled to more than 40 countries,** ministering to both the unchurched and the churched, and to the missionaries who called him their pastor. During his tenure the Mission began ministering in Russia, Mongolia, China, and Central Asia. Under his leadership contact with Cuba was reinstated, 64 missionaries were appointed, overseas church attendance almost doubled, and the TEAM summer missions program for high school students was initiated. In addition to his time as general Director, Waddell served as Associate Director for five years (1981-1986) and completed over 20 years (1959-1981) as an active member of the Board of Free Will Baptist Foreign Missions.

Following his December 31, 1998, retirement, he served as Minister of Care and, more recently, Pastor Emeritus at Cofer's Chapel FWB Church in Nashville, Tennessee. Waddell leaves behind an impressive legacy of faith, love, and resilience, passion for reaching unreached peoples, integrity, compassion, mediation, vision and servanthood. Mr. Waddell earned a B.A. from FWBBC in Nashville and a M.A. from Columbia (SC) International University.

Clarence Wayne Wagner
Birth:
Jan. 22, 1936
Stigler
Haskell County, Oklahoma
Death:
May 9, 2014
Nolensville
Williamson County, Tennessee
Burial:
Nolensville Cemetery Nolensville
Williamson County
Tennessee

Reverend Clarence "Wayne" Wagner was the son of Clarence Wagner and Katie (--) Wagner. He was married about 1958 to Maxine -- . Wayne was a Free Will Baptist pastor and had preached for 55-plus years and his last position was with Heads Free Will Baptist Church in Cedar Hill, Tennessee. A resident of Nolensville, Wayne was 78 years old when he passed away.

John L. Welch
Birth:
Unknown
Death:
Jul. 24, 1988
Nashville,
Davidson County, Tennessee
Burial:
Spring Hill Cemetery,
Nashville,
Davidson County, Tennessee

He had early influence in both conferences of the East and West, and had much to do in bringing them together as a denomination in 1935. The meeting was held at the Cofer's Chapel Free Will Baptist Church where he pastored. Reverend Welch was the first moderator of the National Association of Free Will Baptists in 1935. He also had influence in the beginning the Free Will Baptist Bible College to Nashville, Tennessee., and served 12 years as a member of the college's Board of Trustees, and pastored Cofer's Chapel Free Will Baptist Church in Nashville 53 years.

Mrs. Mary Welch served faithfully as a secretary at the college, spent nearly 60 years as a pastor's wife, and was a leader in the women's movement. For the past five decades, there has been a building on campus named in honor of John and Mary Welch — the historic Welch Library. He was 94-years-old at the time of his death. Free Will Baptist Bible College in 2012 renamed the school Welch College in their honor.

WELCH, Rev. John L— Sunday morning July 24, 1983 at a local infirmary. Age 94 years. Survived by daughter, Mrs. William M. (Jean) Henderson, Joplin, Mo.; daughter-in-law, Mrs. Bessie Welch Smalley; four grandchildren; eleven great grandchildren. His remains are at the Eastland Chapel, 904 Gallatin Road. The remains will lie in state at the Cofer's Chapel Free Will Baptist Church, 4300 Clarksville Highway Tuesday afternoon from 1 until time of services at 2 p.m. with the Pastor Billy Gene Outland, Dr. Robert E. Picirrille, Rev. R. Eugene Waddell, Rev. Henry Oliver, and Dr. D. Michael Henderson officiating. Interment Spring Hill Cemetery. Honorary Pallbearers: Ministers of Cumberland Association, Free Will Baptist Headquarters, and Free Will Baptist Bible College. Active: Bill Smith, Jimmie Carter, Seybert Basford, Jack Trotter, Jack Nicholson, John Boyte, Willie Owen, Jarman Goodman, and Webb Cofer. IN LIEU OF FLOWERS, MAKE CONTRIBUTIONS TO COFER'S CHAPEL FREE WILL BAPTIST CHURCH OR TO THE FREE WILL BAPTIST BIBLE COLLEGE. ROESCH PATTON DORRIS & CHARLTON, Eastland Chapel, 904 Gallatin Road, 244-6480

Rev Jerry Wayne Whitworth
Birth:
Jun. 2, 1951
Springfield
Robertson County, Tennessee
Death:
Apr. 12, 2005
Nashville
Davidson County, Tennessee,
Burial:
Heads Free Will Baptist Church
Cemetery
Cedar Hill
Robertson County, Tennessee

The Rev. Whitworth was owner of Old Stuff Antiques and a member of Pardue Memorial Free Will Baptist Church. He was a minister at Christian Home Free Will Baptist Church in Blountstown, FL, Second Free Will Baptist Church in Ashland City, KY, and director of Cumberland Camp in Clarksville, TN. He was a member of the Montgomery County Historical Society, the Middle Tennessee Genealogical Society, and a charter member of the Cheatham County Art Guild.

Funeral services were held at Heads Free Will Baptist Church in Cedar Hill, TN, with Brothers Len Scott and David Williford officiating.

Juna J Wilkerson
Birth:
Jun. 2, 1910
Death:
Dec. 19, 1994
Burial:
Carters Chapel Cemetery,
Greene County,
Tennessee

All say, "How hard it is that we have to die" - a strange complaint to come from the mouths of people who have had to live.

Dr Jack L Williams
Birth:
1942
West Carroll Parish
Louisiana
Death:
Apr. 29, 2016
Antioch
Davidson County
Tennessee,
Burial:
Cremated

Dr. Jack Williams, former editor of Contact magazine, died Friday, April 29, 2016, at age 73. Jack had struggled to regain his health since November 2012, when a massive stroke left him partially paralyzed. Jack was born in 1942 on a sharecropper's cotton farm in West Carroll Parish, Louisiana. He was saved in 1958 at age 16 at nearby Sardis Free Will Baptist Church. Eight months later he accepted God's call to preach. When the Sardis Church offered him a pastorate shortly thereafter, the 17-year-old high school senior accepted, and using a borrowed Bible, began his nearly 60-year ministry.

After graduating from high school, Jack attended Free Will Baptist Bible College, graduating in 1966 with Bachelor of Arts and Bachelor of Theology degrees. More importantly, he met and married Janis Wilcox, "prettiest girl in West Virginia," as he called her. He continued his education at Sacramento Baptist Theological Seminary, completing a M.A. in 1973 and a Ph.D. from Louisiana Baptist University in 1976.

From 1959-1969, Jack pastored churches in Louisiana, Tennessee, and Arkansas, before accepting a position as academic dean at California Christian College, where he remained for eight years. Then, in 1977, Jack began what became his life's work as editor of Contact magazine and executive assistant for the Free Will Baptist Executive Office. In addition to editing the magazine, the role included oversight of day-to-day operations and the planning of the annual convention.

Jack quickly earned a reputation for excellence and professionalism, both in the convention planning community and in the publishing world. He was named Meeting Planner of the Year by the Association for Convention Operations in 1995 and received the President's Award from the Religious Conference Management Association in 2001.

He was known for witty writing, journalistic objectivity, and constant encouragement and development of new writers. His strong journalistic ethics are evident in the words of his final Contact magazine editorial: "Those who wield the journalistic sword must be careful where they lay the edge of the blade lest they harm the innocent while probing for truth." His writing and work as editor earned 13 awards from the Evangelical Press Association and helped launch a fleet of new Free Will Baptist writers.

In 2005, after Contact magazine ceased publication, Jack accepted a position as director of publications for Welch College, where he remained until his retirement in 2014. Provost Greg Ketteman reflected on Jack's time at the school: "He arrived on campus early each day and maintained an open-door office policy welcoming students, faculty, staff, and visitors. He did an excellent job preparing news releases, editing publications, and fulfilling other duties as communications director."

Throughout his life and ministry, Jack remained fully dedicated to the work of Free Will Baptists. In addition to a number of local and regional positions, he served as assistant moderator of the California State Association (1971-1977), member of the national Sunday School Board (1975-1977), and chairman of the Free Will Baptist Press Association (1978-1991). Another notable denominational work was with the Free Will Baptist Historical Commission, where he served from 1977 until his passing.

Robert E. Picirilli recalls his long-time friend: "Jack was one of the good guys, a personal friend whom I admired. Nobody loved the Free Will Baptist denomination and its ministries any better. He was a gifted speaker and writer, spoke positively about others, and believed in building up rather than tearing down. We'll remember him most for his long stint as editor of Contact, and I for the many years we worked together on the FWB Historical Commission. We will miss him."

Executive Secretary Keith Burden noted, "Jack Williams was an encourager, a cheerleader. He may have been short in stature, but he cast a long shadow across our denomination. I'm a better leader and writer because of Brother Jack."

Perhaps the best way to remember Jack is to recall his own words, penned in an editorial for Contact magazine: "The point of all this is that the work of God goes on when the people of God die. Abraham dies—Isaac steps up. Moses dies—Joshua leads Israel across Jordan. Stephen dies in the last verse of Acts 7. Acts 8 opens with God's hand already on a young man named Saul of Tarsus. The work of God never stops. The people of God wipe away the tears, strap on their spurs, and keep looking up...I like the way God writes obituaries for His people. They all end, not with a period, but with a comma."

Jack is survived by Janis Wilcox Williams, his wife of 53 years; daughter, Dr. Rebecca Deel and husband Recardo; son, Brad Williams and wife, Tina; grandchildren, Austin Deel, Andrew Deel, Kristen Williams and Kullen Williams; sister, Carol Mariche; and brother, Jerry Williams. He was preceded in death by a grandson, Kyler Williams.

Funeral services was held Wednesday, May 4, 2016, 7:00 p.m., Woodbine Funeral Home, His grandson, Becky's son, Andrew Deel, gave the eulogy and then he read the obituary which he said Jack wrote a few years back. Jack's pastor, Steve Marcum of the FWB church in LaVergne, TN brought the message.

Homer Emerson Willis
Birth:
May 8, 1924
Clintwood,
Dickenson County, Virginia
Death:
Feb. 17, 2005
Nashville,
Davidson County, Tennessee
Burial:
Woodlawn Memorial Park,
Nashville,

Davidson County, Tennessee
A Free Will Baptist pastor, evangelist and denominational leader. He was converted to Christ at age 15 and ordained to the ministry at age 18. He graduated from Free Will Baptist Bible College in Nashville, Tennessee in 1946 and also Trinity College. He pastored churches in Michigan, Tennessee, Kentucky and North Carolina. He was General Director of the National Home Mission Board of Free Will Baptists from 1956 until 1973. During his tenure the department planted churches in 33 states and he opened the work in Canada, the Virgin Islands, Puerto Rico, and extended the work in several states of Mexico. He was founder and editor of *Mission Grams*, the Director Of Evangelism, founder of the Church Loan Fund Program and the Director of the Chaplain's Ministry. He preached in all 50 states and Canada, Mexico, Puerto Rico, the Virgin Islands, Germany, Israel and Egypt. His ministry took him to every continent except Australia. He was an honorary life member of the Gideon's, a past Lieutenant Governor of Kiwanis International, an organization that he had served for 50 years. He was a member of the Who's Who in Tennessee.

Rev Caleb Winters
Birth:
1760
Death:
Feb. 18, 1843
Adams
Robertson County, Tennessee
Burial:
Heads Free Will Baptist Church
Cemetery
Cedar Hill
Robertson County, Tennessee

Rev. Caleb Winters is said to have been a charter member of Heads FWB Church, in 1840. His dau., Elizabeth, married Rev. Geo. Head, (1760-1843) who donated the land for Heads church and cemetery on of Moses Winters and Elizabeth Head.

Large monument in cemetery lists

children and spouses. Occupation was Baptist Minister. He was one of the first settlers in this part of Tennessee. Came to TN with his father in 1779. Father of 21 children total. Four born after he turned 75.

About 1781 Caleb settled on a farm in Robertson County. It is said that he subsisted entirely upon meat during the first season. From *"Goodspeed's History of Robertson County, TN"*
About 1781 Caleb Winters settled on the farm now owned by Hon. G. A. Washington. It is said that he, like Kilgore, subsisted entirely upon meat during the first season. Caleb Winters was a pioneer Baptist Preacher. He came with the first settlers in 1779, he lived in a cave on Caleb's Creek the first year, and was a citizen of Robertson County for over 60 years. Parents: Moses Winters (1732 - 1798) & Elizabeth Head Crain Winters (1737 - 1815). Spouses: Mary Duncan Winters (___ - 1852) & Sarah Harris Winters (1765 - 1826).

Rev Clayton Ballard Wolfenbarger
Birth:
Oct. 23, 1904
Bryson Mountain
Claiborne County, Tennessee
Death:
Oct. 19, 1946
Fonde
Bell County, Kentucky
Burial:
Cedar Grove Cemetery
Cedar Grove
Knox County, Tennessee

Clayton Ballard Wolfenbarger, 42 of Fonde, KY, was a minister of the gospel. He was married to Mrs. Lula Mitchell Wolfenbarger, of Fonde, KY; The funeral service,was in the Free Will Baptist Church in Fonde, KY, with the Rev. Billie Moyers and Rev. Ben Bowman officiating.

Paul H. Woolsey
Birth:
Nov. 23, 1908
Death:
Jun. 19, 1989
Burial:
Burial:
Harris Memorial Cemetery
Greene County
Tennessee

Rev. and Mrs. Paul Woolsey were tremendously interested in the educational system of the county in East Tennessee. Woolsey served on the Greene County Board of Education for six years, two of which he was chairman of the

board and one year due to the sickness of the superintendent, most of the work of that office fell to him. When he accepted the call to the mission field, he and Mrs. Woolsey were teaching in the elementary school of Cedar Creek, formerly the Cedar Creek Presbyterian Academy.
Rev. and Mrs. Woolsey worked in the local church and continued their visits in the interests of the entire work of the denomination during the year and a half that they were in the community. They not only supported the school in every possible way, but contributed liberally to their equipment fund for India.
They left America from New York City April 10, 1947, and arrived in Bombay Monday on May 5. They proceeded to Kotagiri, Nilgiris, South India and joined Miss Barnard in her labors there during the hot season. In the month of July they entered the Language School at Landour, Mussoorie, in the United Provinces of North India, preparatory to the opening of a new work in North India. Turbulent India, about to gain her complete independence, is a long way from the peaceful home where the family had dwelt since the days of the independence of the United States. Much of the history of the Woolsey family can be found in the book he wrote entitled, *"God, A Hundred Years and a Free Will Baptist Family."*

William B. Woolsey
Birth:
May 19, 1821
Greene County, North Carolina
Death:
Feb. 10, 1905
North Carolina
Burial:
Harrison Cemetery, Greystone,
Greene County,
Tennessee

He was converted at the age of 21 yrs and joined the Nebo Baptist Church. He soon felt his calling to further endeavors and began to preach, being licensed in 1843. However, his strong views on Arminism vs Calvinism, saw a break and along with two other older talented ministers, Moses Peterson and John Wheeler, they withdrew and formed the Toe River Association of Free Will Baptists with six churches, scattered between the mountains. William Bonaparte was elected clerk and remained so for eighteen years. By 1854, they had twelve ministers and more churches. He, though not afforded a formal education, began at once to study, buy Bible helps, and classics, as he could, and soon rose to a place of leadership among the people. He knew the value of education, sought it himself, and promoted it for others. He was self-educated and had a wise head about him. He, and others, established the Woolsey College, going far and near to try to secure funds or support, to build it, which they did, so that the youth could attend school and have some training after the devastation suffered by the Civil War. He organized Horse Creek Church in 1849; assisted in organizing Dry Fork FWB; and Nebo. He lived an active life in the ministry, and raised a large family who followed his footsteps. ("My Free Will Baptist Woolsey Family", by Rev. Paul H. Woolsey, pub 1949" a great-grandson.)

Texas

Rev. Gladys E. Beam
Birth:
Oct. 16, 1904
Death:
Jan. 14, 1996
Burial:
Edom Cemetery
Edom
Van Zandt County
Texas

She was the wife of　Grady W. Beam (1904 - 1932).

Hubert Ray Berry, Jr
Birth:
Nov. 10, 1943
Houston,
Harris County,Texas
Death: Jun. 9, 2014
Hoover,
Shelby County,
Alabama
Burial:
Neeley Cemetery
Pone, Rusk County,Texas

H. Ray Berry, Jr. of Hoover, AL, was born to the late Rev. H. Ray, Sr. and Asa Hillin Berry. Ray graduated from Bryan High School in 1960 and Old Dominion University in 1973. He pastored several churches and founded Christian Deaf Fellowship. He was a source of joy and encouragement to everyone he met.

Hubert Ray Berry, Sr
Birth:
May 26, 1912
Death:
Burial:
Jul. 2, 1999
Neeley Cemetery
Pone, Rusk County, Texas,
Plot: R 1 F 4

Well Known Texas pastor and church builder. His son: Hubert Ray Berry (1943 - 2014) is buried in Texas and a daughter is married to FWB pastor Dale Burden.

A J Birdwell
Birth:
Apr. 14, 1881
Death:
Oct. 17, 1932
Burial:
Myrtle Springs Cemetery
Myrtle Springs
Van Zandt County
Texas

Earley Texas misister.
Father's Name: W E Birdwell
Mother's Name: Alice Flanigan

Joseph Leeford Bounds
Birth: 1887
Death: 1940
Burial:
Oak Hill Cemetery
Edgewood
Van Zandt County
Texas, USA

Spouse: Helen Brown Bounds
(1896 - 1943)*
Children: Leeford   Gayther
Bounds (1918 - 1978)*

Lewis K Brashier
Birth:
Sep. 26, 1905
Death:
Feb. 13, 1990

Burial:
Stewart Cemetery
Henderson
Rusk County
Texas,
Parents: James Plinie Brashier
(1873 - 1928)-   Lillie Curry
Brashier (1873 - 1951)
Spouse: Clover Brashier
(1909 - 1980)
Children: James   Lewis
Brashier (1926 - 2001)
Siblings: Coey Lee Brashier
(1893 - 1949)-   Lucile Brashier
Jacks (1897 - 1988)-   Wilburn
Arling Brashier (1902 - 1956)-
Lizzie Mae Brashier Harrison
(1905 - 1988)-   Lewis K Brashier
(1905 - 1990)

John Andrews Brooks
Birth:
Jun. 6, 1893
Death:
Feb. 24, 1973
Clay County,
Texas
Burial:
Pleasant Valley Cemetery
Buffalo Springs
Texas

Brooks was born on June 9, 1893, in Gravette, Arkansas. He migrated to Texas with his family and in 1912 he married Edith Covington, sister of Rev. Tiff Covington. John and Edith had ten children. John was ordained to the gospel ministry on August 14, 1917, by the West Fork District Association of Free Will Baptists. In the 1920's he attended one semester at Decatur Baptist College in Decatur, Texas.

John Brooks had a long and distinguished ministry. He pastored about a dozen churches, all of them in the West Fork Association. He founded the First Free Will Baptist Church of Wichita Falls, Texas, in 1952. Preaching revival meetings took him to Oklahoma and New Mexico occasionally.

During the many years of his ministry he worked at manual labor to support himself and his large family, and never pastored a church full-time. Early in his ministry he moved his family to West Texas to work in the cotton fields which seemed to extend to the horizon. In the late 1930's John and his brother-in-law, Tiff Covington, held a six weeks long revival meeting in a brush arbor at Buffalo Springs, Texas. At the end of the revival they baptized one hundred twenty converts in a stock tank. In other states a stock tank would be called a pond. During World War II there were not enough Free Will Baptist preachers for all of the small, rural churches to each have a pastor. During this time he pastored four churches at once, preaching at each of them one Sunday per month. He was widely admired as being an effective preacher and he was called upon frequently to speak at district and state meetings in Texas. He retired from active ministry at the age of seventy-six. He passed away on February 24, 1973. His beloved wife Edith passed away on September 22, 1985, at the age of ninety-five

William Thomas Franklin "Tom" Clement
Birth:
Mar. 12, 1869
Death:
Jun. 10, 1947
Burial:
Greenleaf Cemetery
Brownwood, Brown County, Texas,

Parents: Peter Richard Clement (1840 - 1914) Wife: Sarah Isabell Reed(Read) Clement (1848 1891) Children: Thomas Ezra Clement (1893 - 1894)

John David Cole
Birth: Nov. 26, 1867
Parker County
Texas, USA
Death: Nov. 27, 1935

Millsap
Parker County
Texas, USA
Burial:
Cole Cemetery
Garner
Parker County
Texas, USA

Son of George W. and Elizabeth Boatman Cole. Married Margaret "Maggie" Lena Millsap June 17, 1888 in Parker Co., TX. Father of Lottie, Eula, Jackie, and Martin Leonodus Cole.

Rev J G Cole
Birth: Jun. 19, 1866
Death: Jun. 4, 1917
Burial:
Balch-Senterwood Cemetery
Alvarado
Johnson County
Texas

Jasper Wilburn Cook
Birth:
May 28, 1915
Death:
Feb. 23, 2007
Burial:
Oakwood Cemetery
Cisco, Eastland County, Texas
Plot: Block 247, Lot 5, Space 5

Jasper Wilburn Cook, 91, of Cisco, Texas. Jasper attended five colleges and universities. From a comedian in Vaudeville he became a successful pastor. His preaching, music and singing, as well as his poetry, reveal his love for mankind and his desire to help his fellow man. He had a zest for life and will be sadly missed.

H, Zirl Cox
Birth:
November 30, 1919
Antelope, Texas
Death:
1993
Duncanville,
Dallas County, Texas
Burial:
Vashti Cemetery,Vashti,
Clay County, Texas

Harry Zirl Cox was born to Robert Ebbie and Margaret Sue (Blackmon) Cox. He was licensed to the gospel ministry in 1941. He earned a Bachelor's degree in Bible from Dallas Baptist College and in 1953 he earned a Master of Theology degree from Bible Baptist Seminary. He served in the United States Army during World War II as a medic and chaplain's assistant from 1943 to 1945. During the last year of the war he served in Germany as the Allied Army closed in on Berlin and destroyed Hitler's plans for a thousand year empire. H. Z., as he was commonly known, married Artelle Barnette and they had three children: Robert, Michael, and Cynthia Ann. His first pastorate was the New Salem Free

Will Baptist Church, just south of Decatur, Texas, which he pastored from 1945 to 1947. In September of 1947 he became pastor of the First Free Will Baptist Church of Dallas, Texas, and embarked on a long and productive ministry which would make him well known, not only in Texas, but in the denomination at large. He became a full-time pastor in 1954 and continued as pastor of the First Free Will Baptist Church in Dallas until his retirement in November of 1986, thirty nine years. The church changed locations and built new facilities on several occasions due to the steady growth of the church. His final move was to the Dallas suburb of Duncanville, at which time the church became the First Free Will Baptist Church of Duncanville. Brother Cox was a skilled businessman and located the church on prime, highly visible property in a rapidly growing community. The church building is beautiful and expansive.

Brother Cox served as moderator of the West Fork District Association for a number of years, as he did for the Texas State Association of Free Will Baptists. He served a term on the National Home Missions Church-Extension Board, and was very active in home missions in Texas, on both a district and state level. His business acumen was utilized in numerous projects in the state. He had a knack for getting things done. He represented Texas as a delegate to the meeting in Nashville, Tennessee, when delegates from each state association met to hammer out a workable agreement on the question of the state of the backslider. The statement upon which they agreed was inserted as an appendix into the *Free Will Baptist Treatise* in July of 1969.

One of his loves was the West Fork Youth Camp. He worked in the camp faithfully every year until his health no longer pemitted it. He served in many capacities at the camp, but he perhaps is best known for taking the campers on a morning hike and devotion time. The conference room in the Barber Center at Hillsdale Free Will Baptist College in Moore, Oklahoma, is named the H. Z. Cox Conference Room because of his support of the college.

Rev Tiff Covington
Birth:
Aug. 25, 1895
Panola, Kentucky
Death:
Nov. 3, 1984
Burial:
Buffalo Springs Cemetery
Buffalo Springs (Clay County)
Clay County, Texas

Anderson Tifton "Tiff" Covington was born to Milton Conner and Charlotte Covington. The Covington family, parents and ten children,migrated to Clay County, Texas, arriving in Henrietta by train on September 3, 1908. Tiff was thirteen years old at the time. They settled in the Buffalo Springs community. In August of 1916 Tiff was converted at a revival meeting being conducted in the Pleasant Valley community by Rev. J. W. Shults, and was baptized in a nearby stock tank. He married the daughter of Rev. Shults, Carrye Dell, on July 29, 1917. Carrye was always called Carrye D to distinguish her from Tiff's sister Carrye. Their first home was a ten by twelve foot tent, with a dirt floor. It was furnished with a bed, cook stove, cabinet, and a trunk.

From this marriage came four children: Granvel, Marverene, Wilburn Conner, and Ramona.

In 1918 Tiff was drafted and reported to Henrietta to be inducted into the army. The head of the draft board told him, "Tiff, you're not going because you are needed more at home." His father was an invalid by this time. The head of the draft board took Tiff to Dallas that day and got him released from his military obligation.

Though he only had a seventh grade education, Tiff answered the call to the ministry and was licensed to preach in 1928. Shortly thereafter he became the pastor of the New Salem Free Will Baptist Church in Decatur, Texas. He was also called to be the pastor of the Pleasant Valley Will Baptist Church, south of Buffalo Springs. He was ordained by the West Fork District Association in 1932, at the Silver Creek Free Will Baptist Church near Azle. In 1936 the Pleasant Valley church relocated and changed its name to the Pleasant Mound Free Will Baptist Church, widely known as The Rock Church. For several years Tiff pastored both the New Salem and the Pleasant Mound churches, preaching at New Salem once a month.

During the early years of his ministry he worked as a carpenter and farmer to support his family, because the churches could not pay him a livable salary. Tiff and Ruel Conner organized the First Free Will Baptist Church in Bowie, Texas, and Tiff pastored it for seven years. Carrye D had a series of strokes and became bedridden. Tiff moved to Wichita Falls so she could be near the doctors. He became the pastor of the First Free Will Baptist Church in Wichita Falls, pastoring it for nine and a half years. Carrye D passed away on February 12, 1962. Tiff then married Ethel Inman on January 1, 1963.

In 1967 Tiff once again became pastor of the Pleasant Mound Free Will Baptist Church at Buffalo Springs and pastored there until

May 1, 1980.

Over the years Tiff became a legend in North Central Texas, not so much because of his pastoring, but because of the funerals he conducted. He had a gift for it. He spoke with such compassion, empathy, and sweetness that people far and wide wanted Tiff Covington to preach their funerals. During his lifetime he conducted well over three thousand funerals. He preached some very productive revival meetings. One such meeting was begun by Rev. M. L. Sutton at Buffalo Springs, who preached for two weeks, morning and evening. Then Tiff and a Methodist minister continued it, taking turn's morning and night. Tiff finished the meeting, which altogether lasted for thirty-one days. There were eighty-two conversions and rededications.

Another revival meeting in Buffalo Springs was conducted by Tiff and his brother-in-law, Rev. John A. Brooks. After the six weeks revival they baptized one hundred twenty converts in a stock tank.

Tiff was a popular preacher and spoke many times at quarterly meetings and state association meetings. He pastored a total of fifty-two years, all of them in the West Fork District Association.

Rev. Jasper Creamer
Birth:
Jul. 24, 1852
Georgia
Death:
Dec. 21, 1925
Plainview
Hale County
Texas
Burial:
Indian Creek Cemetery
Comanche
Comanche County
Texas

The Creamers lived in Alabama until October, 1869, when they moved to Texas. After living one year on the Brazos River, they moved to Comanche County, where they farmed and were proprietors of a store in the Creamer Community. They traveled extensively to preach at many churches. The December 7, 1923, Comanche Chief Newspaper carried a front page announcement of Jasper's death, in which it stated: "A minister of the gospel of the Freewill Baptist persuasion, for more than fifty years he had carried the story of Jesus through the pioneer country. Traveling horseback, in a buggy, and often on foot, he was faithful in the discharge of his duty....Earth has one pure spirit less, heaven one pure soul more."

Wm. H. Davidson
Birth:
1859
Death:
1943
Burial:
Restland Memorial Park
Dallas
Dallas County
Texas
Plot: Section H

Rev. Z B Dally
Birth:
Mar. 12, 1870
Death:
Mar. 24, 1958
Burial:
Algoma Cemetery
South and North
Marshall
Harrison County
Texas
Plot: Section:
Center Circle

He who has gone, so we but cherish his memory, abides with us, more potent, nay, more present than the living man.

Kirby Chapman
Birth:
Jul. 23, 1896
Death:
Sep. 22, 1973
Burial:
Leagueville Cemetery
Leagueville
Henderson County
Texas, USA
Plot: Row 17 # 37

He was pastor of the Bryan First FWB in 1919-1920.

Rev William H "Bill" Denmon
Birth:
Jul. 23, 1860
Texas

Death:
Sep. 28, 1923
Burial:
Denman Cemetery
Jasper County
Texas

From the Southeast Texas Freewill Baptist Association minutes at Friendship Church, Jasper County, Texas on Thursday night before the second Sunday in October 1923.

It has pleased an All-Wise Creator to remove from out midst Bro. W. H. Denmon, who was a minister of the Gospel from the 13th day of October, 1905 until his death, who departed this life September 28th, 1923.

Bro. Denman leaves a wife and seven children, with a host of friends to mourn their loss. But we trust that our loss is his eternal gain.
Rev. Wm. Henry Denmon attended the SoWest Coop. Association in 1910, in TX, and gave his residence as "Buma." He listed his occ. as 'farmer' on most censuses, as that was the means of their support; preaching/ministering was a "calling" and not counted on census.

William D Denman
Birth: Mar. 17, 1906
Death: Mar. 19, 1966
Burial:
Antioch Cemetery
Buna
Jasper County
Texas

Parents: Amon and Nancy Denman

Joseph S. Dillard
Birth: Jun. 20, 1856
Alabama
Death: Apr. 5, 1932
Alabama City
Etowah County
Alabama
Burial:
Waxahachie City Cemetery
Waxahachie
Ellis County, Texas

Rev. J. S. Dillard was living in Ellis Co 1910 census with his wife & children, and his widowed son-in-law's Buse family. His name was listed in the 1912 Minutes in a roll of ministers and he listed Italy, Ellis Co.

Daniel W Diserens
Birth:
Sep. 1, 1894
Death:
Mar. 10, 1979
Burial:
Masonic Cemetery
Gatesville
Coryell County
Texas

Parents:
John William Diserens (1872 - 1971)
Mary E Shehorn Diserens (1872 - 1906)
Spouse:
Minnie M Diserens (1895 - 1971)

Rev Devan Judson Dollar
Birth:
Mar. 2, 1854
Alabama
Death:
Nov. 7, 1931
Rusk County
Texas
Burial:
Mount Hope Cemetery
Joinerville
Rusk County
Texas

Parents: John A Dollar & Martha Ann Nutt Dollar. A minister in the New Hope Association of Free Will Baptists, in 1899 in Arkansas.

Spouse:
Amanda Melvina Alford Dollar (1854 - 1924)*

James Hill Dowell
Birth:
Jan. 28, 1882
Willowhole, Madison County, Texas
Death:
Mar. 29, 1953
Kerrville
Kerr County
Texas
Burial:
Willowhole Cemetery
North Zulch
Madison County, Texas

James Hill Dowell was married to Miss Nancy Batson in 1901. He united with the Baptist Church early in life and was ordained as minister of the gospel by Free Will Baptist Church in 1911. He spent 22 years in pastoring churches. Services were conducted by Rev. J. D. Walker assisted by Rev. A. R. Housewright and Rev. McDonald of North Zulch. Married Nanie Batson 17 Nov 1901 in Madison Co., TX

Robert Burnett Easley
Birth:
Sep. 1, 1850
War Eagle
Benton County, Arkansas
Death:
Dec. 26, 1940
Vandyke
Comanche County, Texas
Burial:
Zion Hill Cemetery
Comanche
Comanche County, Texas

He was the second son of Burnett M. and Orpha Dorinda (Garrett) Easley. He married Mary Ann McGuire on January 22, 1870, in Benton County, Arkansas. The following year, 1871, he migrated to Comanche County, Texas. He founded the Easley's Chapel Free Will Baptist Church, just north of Comanche, Texas, when he was thirty-six years old. The church was founded in his pasture, across a creek, upon a hill, south of his home, under an old fashioned brush arbor.

The congregation met in several different places at first. In the 1870's, when Comanche County was pretty much on the western edge of the Texas frontier, with bands of Comanches still roaming free in West Texas, people came from far and near to attend Easley's Chapel, especially for revival meetings and singings.

Then, in 1889, they built a church building. The lumber for the building was hauled from Dublin, Texas, by team and wagon. The church was constructed by Rev. Easley, the deacons, and church members.

In 1935 three acres of land were purchased from Mrs. J. E. Gartman, where the church is presently located. Pastor Easley said, "We will call this place Gartman's View." That's why some call the church Easley's Chapel and others call it Gartman's View.

Rev. Easley was the father of eleven children: John M., Zora, Thomas, Orpha D., Dicie, Simon Peter, Deffa, Robert Burnett, Jr., Phillip Jeff, William Paul, and Luke Ellery Easley. Many of his descendants still live in the Comanche-DeLeon area. The Easley Chapel Church continues its ministry well into the twenty-first century.

Rev. R. B. Easley, as he was known, was one of the true pioneers of the Free Will Baptist work in Texas. As other Free Will Baptist churches were started nearby, Easley's Chapel became a member of the West Texas Free Will Baptist Association, which was organized in 1891. Later the Easley's Chapel Church joined the West Fork Association, of which it is still a member. In 1910 or 11, while attending a Free Will Baptist convention near Tecumseh, Oklahoma, Rev. Easley met a young, licensed woman preacher by the name of Miss Elizabeth Lawless, whom he brought to Comanche to pastor the Easley

Chapel Church until the spring of 1911. That young woman would later become well known as Rev. Mrs. Lizzie McAdams. Pastor Easley was a mentor and an encouragement to other young preachers, as well. His name is still spoken with veneration and admiration in the area where he lived and ministered.

Rev John A Edmonson
Birth:
Jul. 25, 1865
Death:
Jul. 10, 1940
Burial:
Eastview Memorial Park
Vernon
Wilbarger County
Texas,
Plot: 12-8-5

His name was in a minister's roll in Minutes of the Southwest Cooperative Association of Free Will Baptists in 1910. Spouse: Ella Mosely Edmonson (1867 - 1938)

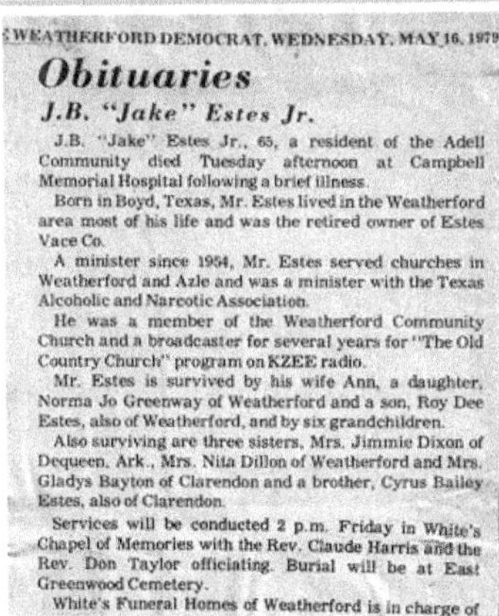
WEATHERFORD DEMOCRAT, WEDNESDAY, MAY 16, 1979

Obituaries
J.B. "Jake" Estes Jr.

J.B. "Jake" Estes Jr., 65, a resident of the Adell Community died Tuesday afternoon at Campbell Memorial Hospital following a brief illness.

Born in Boyd, Texas, Mr. Estes lived in the Weatherford area most of his life and was the retired owner of Estes Vace Co.

A minister since 1954, Mr. Estes served churches in Weatherford and Azle and was a minister with the Texas Alcoholic and Narcotic Association.

He was a member of the Weatherford Community Church and a broadcaster for several years for "The Old Country Church" program on KZEE radio.

Mr. Estes is survived by his wife Ann, a daughter, Norma Jo Greenway of Weatherford and a son, Roy Dee Estes, also of Weatherford, and by six grandchildren.

Also surviving are three sisters, Mrs. Jimmie Dixon of Dequeen, Ark., Mrs. Nita Dillon of Weatherford and Mrs. Gladys Bayton of Clarendon and a brother, Cyrus Bailey Estes, also of Clarendon.

Services will be conducted 2 p.m. Friday in White's Chapel of Memories with the Rev. Claude Harris and the Rev. Don Taylor officiating. Burial will be at East Greenwood Cemetery.

White's Funeral Homes of Weatherford is in charge of arrangements.

James Bailey Estes, Jr
Birth: Mar. 13, 1914
Texas,
Death: May 15, 1979
Weatherford
Parker County
Texas,
Burial:
East Greenwood Cemetery
Weatherford
Parker County,Texas

Parents: James Bailey Estes (1885 - 1965)- Margaret Lelia Cross Estes (1889 - 1971)
Spouse:-   Annie Marie Hardin Estes (1917 - 1999)

Clifford Mabry Fain
Birth:
Dec. 14, 1879
Death:
Dec. 14, 1967
Burial:
Prairie View Cemetery
Aransas Pass
San Patricio County
Texas

Clifford M. Fain

Clifford M. Fain, 88, of 3050 Sunnybrook, died at 3:45 a.m. today in a local nursing home after a long illness.

A resident of Ingleside from 1929 to 1964, Fain was retired from Humble Oil and Refining Co. He moved to Corpus Christi three years ago.

Funeral services will be at 2 p.m. tomorrow at the First Baptist Church in Ingleside with the Rev. W. A. Butler, a retired minister, officiating. Burial will be in Prairie View Cemetery in Aransas Pass under direction of Cage-Mills Funeral Home here.

Surviving are four sons, L. R. Fain of Corpus Christi, W. T. Fain of LaPorte, T. A. Fain of Baytown and W. L. Fain of Pampa; 11 grandchildren, and nine great-grandchildren.

s/o Thomas Fain.   Spouse:
Eula Eugenia Smith Fain (1883 - 1961)*

Johnny Lee Fears
Birth:
Aug. 1, 1906
Death:
Dec. 7, 1975
Burial:
Neeley Cemetery
Pone
Rusk County
Texas, USA
Plot: R 5 B3

Retired minister in the Free Will Bapt churches in his area.

Spouse: Lou Mary Weems Fears (1916 - 2009)
Children: Gwindolyn Rae Fears Chapman (1929 - 2015)- Dan Gregory Fears (1939 - 1991)- Betsy Dean Fears (1940 - 1940)

A. F. Ferguson

Birth:
Nov. 8, 1909
Memphis,
Shelby County, Tennessee
Death:
Apr. 18, 2008
Georgetown,
Williamson County, Texas
Burial:
Tyler Memorial Park & Cemetery,
Tyler, Smith County, Texas

Allie Fennel Record Ferguson was born in Memphis, Tennessee, on November 8, 1909.

When he was yet a boy his father moved the family by train to Alvarado, Texas. After World War I the family moved to Berryvillle, Arkansas. There Allie attended a school named Hide Out. Allie became a Christian at the age of sixteen, while they still lived in Arkansas. The family made several moves and then ended up at Sherman, Texas.

Jessie Zeona Van was born near Gainesville, Texas, on September 17, 1912. She became a Christian in June of 1925. A new family moved to the community and all of the teenage girls were in a buzz about the handsome new boy. It had been Jessie's prayer for some time that she would marry a preacher and be a preacher's wife. Word got around that the good looking young man was going to be a preacher. It was almost too much to believe that this fellow would become her husband. She almost dismissed the idea. She thought he didn't know she existed. Unknown to her he was praying about who would be his life's partner. In church their eyes met and there was an instant attraction. Her beautiful eyes and sweet smile kept drawing his eyes to hers. She Couldn't keep her eyes off him. Eighteen months later they went to Durant, Oklahoma, and were married on Sunday afternoon, November 29, 1931. In time Allie and Jessie had two children, Norman and Glenna.

During the Great Depression of the 1930's work was hard to find for an unskilled laborer.

He tried in Oklahoma, Missouri, and Arkansas. Allie and Jessie moved to Fort Worth where Allie found a job with Justin Boot and Shoe Manufacturers. The day he went to work he had one dime in his pocket. He worked a fifty-four hour week for a salary of $9.00. With his paycheck he had to support seven mouths, because Allie and Jessie lived with his mother and siblings.

Allie and Jessie attended the First Free Will Baptist Church, then the Trinity Free Will Baptist Church, both pastored by Rev. M. L. Sutton, who became their mentor. In 1931 Allie was licensed to the gospel ministry by the West Fork District Association and then ordained in August of 1933. His peers were men such as Tiff Covington, Ruel E. Conner, and Bill McPhail. H. Z. Cox and Clarence Hearron were two of his younger peers. Jessie also answered the call to preach and she was licensed by the West Fork on September 1, 1934. She was ordained to the gospel ministry on January 27, 1946.

His first pastorate was the New Hope Free Will Baptist Church in Parker County. Over the next half century Allie pastored sixteen churches in Texas, California, Oklahoma, and Mississippi, always willing to go wherever God in His providence took him and Jessie. While pastoring the Shafter Church in California Allie served on the Board of Trustees of California Christian College.

Allie and Jessie started the Bible Free Will Baptist Church in Odessa, Texas, which he pastored for eight years. At the peak of their ministry in Odessa the church attendance ran in the 60's and 70's.

During his ministry in Weatherford, Texas, the house was full, with a great many young people attending.

Jessie never pastored, but did preach. Her work was mostly assisting Allie in his ministry and raising a family. She was a leader in the Woman's Auxiliary work in Texas.

During more than sixty years in the gospel ministry Allie pastored 16 churches. He and Jessie were always active in the district and state work, especially in Texas. He preached on many occasions at district and state meetings, and very often was part of a spontaneously formed quartet which provided special music for the meetings. He and H. Z. Cox were two of the men who helped organize and have the first summer youth camp in the West Fork District Association.

On the occasion of Allie's 93rd birthday,

Dr. Jack Williams, editor of Contact Magazine, wrote:
Thank God for the A. F. Ferguson's
Who broke the ground...
Laid the foundation...
Planted the crop...
worked in the shadows...
and let guys like me stand on their shoulders.

Rev. Mrs. Jessie Ferguson

Jessie passed away on March 24, 1993. Allie's home going occurred on April 18, 2008.

Allie and Jessie are buried in the Tyler Memorial Cemetery in Tyler, Texas. Graveside services for the Rev. A.F. Ferguson, 98, Georgetown, were held with the Rev. James Walker officiating. He was born to the late Thomas and Jeannie Ferguson. He pastored 16 churches and started two over a period of 60 years in Texas, Oklahoma, Mississippi and California. He was a member of Lake Hills Freewill Baptist Church of Cedar Park, and a junior founder of Justin Boot Co. in Fort Worth. He was preceded in death by his wife of 62 years, Jessie Ferguson. Published in the *Tyler Morning Telegraph* on 4/21/2008.

Lewis Franklin Fitzgerald
Birth:
May 22, 1893
Johnson County
Texas, USA
Death:
Sep. 20, 1955
Vernon
Wilbarger County
Texas, USA
Burial:
Eastview Memorial Park
Vernon
Wilbarger County
Texas

He was an early minister in the area. His name appears in a conference of Free Will Baptists, Southwestern Cooperative Association, in 1912, with residence Tama, Coryell Co. TX. Son of John Fitsgerald and Lorenda (Baker) Fitzgerald. Spouse: Allie Shepherd, Mar. 1914, Wilbarger Co. TX.

James Alexander Ford
Birth:
Jul. 14, 1842
Death:
Oct. 24, 1912
Burial:
Pleasant Grove Cemetery #01
Decatur,
Wise County,
Texas

Rev Josephus Wesley Ford
Birth:
Jan. 31, 1848
Death:
Jul. 19, 1898
Burial:
Pleasant Grove Cemetery #01
Decatur
Wise County, Texas

Rev. Josephus Wesley Ford and Markley Stanford "Sandy" Ford married sisters, Eliza Ann Young and Lurana Elizabeth "Luraney" Young. And their brother, Rev. William Henry Ford, Sr., married the aunt, Elizabeth E. "Bet" Young, of these Young sisters. In the McDonald County records, page 633, dated August 15, 1880: *"This certifies that the bearer, J. W. Ford, of the County of McDonald and State of Missouri a regular member of the Free Will Baptist Church in said county has this day been publicly set apart to the work of the gospel ministry by prayer and laying on of hands according to the usage of the Freewill Baptist Denomination and is hereby authorized to preach the Gospel and administer its ordinances whenever God in his providence may call him."* Rev L H Robertson, ordaining M H Ford, council This August the 15th 1880. Filed and recorded May 4 1887. John Black, clerk *"Goodspeed's 1888 History of McDonald & Newton Counties* shows the Free-Will Baptist Church of Gooden Hollow as organized in September, 1886, at the Wilson Mill, with J.W. Ford as moderator. The membership in March, 1888 was nineteen, with Rev. J. W. Ford, preacher. The Western Mount Zion quarterly meeting convened July 8, 1887 with the Pleasant Hill Free-Will Baptist Church, on White Rock Prairie, with a delegation from eight churches, and seven ministers. Rev. J. W. Ford officiated as moderator. Free-will Baptist Churches were located at Oak Grove, Pleasant Hill, Hopewell, Gooden Springs, Wire Springs, Sulphur Springs, McDonald County Church, Antioch Church, & Shiloh Church. Rev. Josephus Wesley Ford was one of the organizers of the New Salem Free Will Baptist Church on 4 Apr 1893 at the old Perrin School House near Decatur, Wise County, Texas. According to family history from the family of his son 'Pate' Ford, he died at the 'dinner on the grounds' after running a 'foot race' and taking a big bite of fresh honey. From Josephus's son Roy's daughter, Goldie Mae Wood in Dodge City, Kansas a partial copy of his obituary: (the first part was missing-)............in the beautiful home of the soul. To the bereaved family and church' the beautiful sentiments of the poem comes as a welcome greeting in his hour and we too will" Judge not the Lord by feeble sense. But trust him for his grace, behind a frowning providence He shows a shining face." A Freewill Baptist himself,

Bro. Ford came from a race of Freewills and Methodists and his warm friendship came from the fact that he recognized God's children in all churches. He was born in Washington County, Arkansas, in 1848. He has been in the ministry 18 years; was married in 1871 to Miss Eliza Ann Young, and to them were born 13 children, 12 of whom are now living and 5 of whom are now trying to meet their father in that happy land. It is hard to realize that our (at this place the newspaper clipping had deteriorated) _ _ _ _ _ r (father?), our friend, and our pastor beyond is in an unknown land. To all our inquiries the still small voice replies, do your duty to God to yourself and to your fellowman and leave the rest to Him who doeth all things well. He is gone from among us and a grateful church mourns his loss and honors his memory. The church tenders its heartfelt sympathy to her whose sorrow is the deepest and to the bereaved family. We gently fold the drapery of his couch about him and lay him down to sleep where immortals and forget-me-nots will bloom over his grave. We try to bow with resignation to the summons that called him away. And we leave him with the angels who will stand by his tomb and keep watch over his slumbers; and we invoke Him who is above all angels principalities and powers, to care for her whom his dispensation has left widowed and alone in the world. The life boat soon is coming by the eye of faith I see. As she sweeps through the waters to rescue you and me. She will land us safely in the port with the friends we love so dear. Get ready cries the captain. Oh look! She is almost here.John T. Sanford, Josephus Wesley Ford was also a member of the Masonic Lodge in Wise County, Texas, and after his death, his widow was heard to say she could not have raised her family without the help of the Masons. They wrote: In Memorium: Whereas it has pleased the All wise and Supreme Ruler of the Universe to call from our midst our beloved brother Rev. J. W. Ford who departed this life July 18, 1898. Again the Golden Chain has been broken and we bow submitting to his will believing that our loss is his gain and that our worthy brother has been called to refreshment in that Celestial Lodge above where the Supreme Architect presides. Therefore be it resolved that Azle Lodge #60l A.F. and A. M. Azle Texas has lost a zealous member, his church a faithful worker, his family a loving husband, and kind father, and the community a good man, and neighbor. Resolved that these resolutions be spread upon our minutes, and copies be furnished the widow of our deceased brother, and the Decatur and Fort Worth papers for publication. Gladden Lovell, J. W. Walker, Com.J. Frank Snodgrass.- Larry Carpenter

Rev Markley Stanford Ford
Birth:
Mar. 25, 1852
Newton County
Missouri
Death:
Feb. 12, 1917
Wise County
Texas
Burial:
Fairview Cemetery

Midland
Midland County
Texas

Rev. Markley Stanford "Sandy" Ford and Rev. Josephus Wesley Ford married sisters, Lurana Elizabeth "Luraney" Young and Eliza Ann Young and their brother Rev. William Henry Ford, Sr., married the aunt, Elizabeth "Bet" Young, of these sisters.

For those who love history, there were often family members who told the stories that lay behind the photographs, and family.

Sandy Ford is No More

Markley S. Ford, a citizen of Decatur since 1893, died at his home Monday morning in North Decatur. He was 85 years old. The burial took place at the Fairview cemetery, south of town, the services being conducted by Rev. Moreland. A number of friends and relatives attended the funeral. "Sandy" as he was known to all our people, will be missed. He was a good man; honest as the day was long, and true as steel to his God. Fate had been unkind to this man: he strived and battled against adversity; he contested the cruel advances of poverty for many long years, and, although a mere shadow of a physical man, he fought heroically. Through it all he smiled and battled the best he could, feeling assured that the rest coming after the storm on this earth would last for countless ages. "Sandy" Ford's spirit went home to his God; he stood the acid test, a test that has made multiplied millions lose hope and grope in the gloom of despair, and his reward has come. Men more brilliant than he have shuffled off this mortal coil; kings of fi...

Tommie Franklin
Birth:
Feb. 19, 1896
Bryan
Brazos County, Texas
Death:
Aug. 7, 1977
Bryan
Brazos County, Texas

Burial:
Bryan City Cemetery
Bryan
Brazos County, Texas
Block 6, Lot 25, Space 1.

Tommie Franklin was born in Brazos County, Texas, in 1897. Some of the earliest Free Will Baptist churches in Texas were in that area of Central Texas. On one rainy Sunday morning when Lizzie McAdams was a guest preacher at the First Free Will Baptist Church in Bryan,

Tommie met her for the first time. The young Miss Franklin confided in Lizzie that she had been called to preach, but felt that ministry was closed to her. Over lunch the two women had a heart to heart talk about the possibility of Miss Franklin entering the ministry. The next day Tommie joined Lizzie in Mexia, Texas, and went with her to Tecumseh, Oklahoma, where Lizzie dropped her off to attend Tecumseh College, a Free Will Baptist school, for Bible training. When the summer break came Tommie went to North Carolina and became a member of Lizzie's evangelistic team. She would be a member of that team, on and off, for several years.

Tommie (Pictured top left with Ava Walker and Rev's Hiram and Lizzie McAdams) pastored several churches during her ministry: one in Washington, North Carolina, the First Free Will Baptist Church of Denison, Texas, the First Free Will Baptist Church in Bryan, Texas, a Free Will Baptist church near Henderson, Texas, and the

Parkview Free Will Baptist Church in Desloge, Missouri.

Tommie was of a sweet disposition and gentle smile and was committed to the Lord all of her life. She was listed as one of the ordained ministers in the Central Texas District Association until her death, but in those latter years was not active in the ministry as the idea of women preachers was falling into disfavor, even though Free Will Baptists had a long heritage of them dating back to 1790.

Her simple, flat, marble headstone reads only "Tommie Franklin 1897-1977." Tommie's funeral was conducted by Dr. Eugene Richards.

Zachary T Fuller

Birth:
1848
Death:
1929
Burial:
North Belton Cemetery
Belton
Bell County
Texas
Plot: 569 Old Section

He was in the roll of ministers in 1912 at the session of the Southwestern Co-op Association of Free Will Baptists. His D/C states he was a minister, and it gave the title "Rev." in front of his name.

James C. Gartman

Birth:
Dec. 27, 1885
Youngsport
Bell County
Texas, USA
Death:
Mar. 31, 1952
Burial:
Sharp Cemetery
Killeen
Bell County
Texas

He was a young lad when his father died; his mother carried on, as censuses show. A strong family.
Parents:
Thomas Bartholomew Gartman (1819 - 1899)
Mary Frances Sowel Gartman (1861 - 1941)

Spouse:
Emma G. Gartman (1895 - 1978)

Rev Thomas E. Glaze
Birth:
Nov. 15, 1858
Limestone County
Alabama, USA
Death:
Oct. 31, 1929
Burial:
Abilene Municipal Cemetery
Abilene
Taylor County
Texas, USA
Plot: Masonic 3/7/10

An early Free Will Bapt. minister in Texas, his name appearing in Minutes of the Southwestern Cooperative Association of FWB in 1912. He listed his residence as Haskell, TX
Spouse:
Mary Virginia Biles Glaze (1865 - 1929)*
Children:
George Edwin Glaze (1888 - 1960)*
Henry B Glaze (1892 - 1928)*
Nora Zula Glaze Shelton (1893 - 1959)*

Barney A Grant
Birth:
Apr. 28, 1902
Death:
Dec. 26, 1997
Burial:
Lakewood Memorial Park
Henderson
Rusk County, Texas

Rev John E Graham
Birth:
Jan. 3, 1866
Coryell County
Texas
Death:
Dec. 23, 1948
Gatesville
Coryell County
Texas
Burial:
Restland Cemetery
Gatesville
Coryell County
Texas

Rev. John E. Graham, born in the Harmony Community, was a son of Curtis Beason Graham and Elizabeth Jane Thornton Graham. Rev. John E. Graham married Nancy Elizabeth "Betty" Brookshire. They had four children.

Rev Walton Graham
Birth:
Aug. 28, 1868
Texas, USA
Death:
Feb. 7, 1941
Rylie
Dallas County
Texas, USA
Burial:
Kleberg Cemetery
Kleberg
Dallas County
Texas, USA
Siblings:
Harrison M Graham (1862 - 1936)*
John E. Graham (1866 - 1948)*
Walton Graham (1868 - 1941)
Sarah Emaline Graham Nunn (1871 - 1950)*
Malisia Elizabeth Graham Wright (1878 - 1954)**
Ella Virginia Graham Wilson (1881 - 1959)**
Curtis Beason Graham (1882 - 1965)**
Isaac E Graham (1884 - 1972)**
Julia Lee Graham Norman (1886 - 1969)**
Nancy Graham Wilson Howard (1887 - 1980)**

Clyde Forrest Goen

Birth:
Apr. 26, 1893
Death:
Feb. 9, 1985
Burial:
Bright Light Cemetery
Bryan, Brazos County,Texas
Parents: William R. Goen (1858 - 1926) Nancy A. Pate Goen (1863 - 1952) Spouse: Grace M. Goen (1894 - 1990) Siblings: Amzia Goen (1881 - 1883) Icy Goen (1890 - 1950) Clyde Forrest Goen (1893 - 1985)
Preston S. Goen (1895 - 1981)
Inscription:
U.S. Navy WWI

Dolphus Crawford Hargrove

Birth:
Nov. 5, 1868
Hopkins County, Texas
Death:
Sep. 8, 1946
Navasota
Grimes County, Texas
Burial:
Zion Methodist Cemetery
Iola
Grimes County, Texas

HARGROVE was born to James William Hargrove and Dorinda E. Couch. Dolphus was first married on 27 Nov 1889 to Anna Ophelia Gressett in Grimes County, Texas, and they had FOUR His first wife passed away on 16 December 1899.

Dolphus second marriage was on 11 January 1905 to Anna Artelia Young in Grimes County, Texas. Dolphus passed at Brazos Valley Hospital in Navesota.

The Central Texas District Association, formed in 1906, sent Rev. John Swanwick and Rev. D. C. Hargrover as delegates to the Southwestern Convention in 1908.

Hubert Haskel Haston

Birth:
Mar. 4, 1898
Oklahoma, USA
Death:
Mar. 22, 1981
Paducah
Cottle County
Texas, USA
Burial:
Garden of Memories Cemetery
Paducah, Cottle County, Texas

Spouse: Eunice Naomi Burleson Haston (1899 – 1974), Children: David Elmer Haston (1921 – 1944), Clark W. Haston (1927 – 2014), Rachel Ann Haston Cole (1938 – 2013).

W D Haston

Birth:
May 10, 1860
Death:
Jun. 4, 1929
Burial:
Buck Creek Cemetery,
Paducah, Cottle County, Texas

At about 30 years of age, he entered the ministry and affiliated with the Free Will Baptists. He married Sallie McLemore, 16 Sept. 1880, Yell Co. AR. He and Sallie later moved to Texas and continued in work and raising a large family.

A short notice/bio of his death appeared in the Free Will Baptist paper, *"The Gem"* July 1929 issue, in Missouri, where Eld. J. A. Edmondson, wrote that he was called to conduct his fellow minister's funeral in Paducah, TX. He stated Eld. W.D. Haston "had for over 40 years, preached all over and organized churches."

For those who love history, there were often family members who told the stories that lay behind the photographs, and family.

Everett D. Hellard
Birth:
Sep. 29, 1923
Death:
Feb. 11, 2007
Texas
Burial:
Garden Park Cemetery,
Conroe,
Montgomery County, Texas

He pastored churches in many areas for the Free Will Baptist and was a leader at all levels. His beautiful tenor voice caused him to have many invitations to sing at many of the conventions. *Ship Ahoy* was always asked as the song for him to sing.

Alvin Floyd Halbrook
Birth:
May 27, 1914
Womack, Missouri
Death:
Jul. 23, 2000
Bryan
Brazos County, Texas
Burial:
Bryan City Cemetery
Bryan
Brazos County, Texas

He began pastoring even before he was licensed to preach. He pastored the Richwoods Free Will Baptist Church and others from 1933 to 1939. He was licensed to preach on July 31, 1936, by the St. Francois County Quarterly Conference of Free Will Baptists. He was ordained by them in 1938. One of the names on his ordination certificate is illegible, but the names of the other people who signed it are Elder James F. Miller, of Flat River, and Elder Tommie Franklin of Desloge. Alvin realized the need for specific training for the ministry and enrolled at Free Will Baptist Bible College, and began classes in 1944. There he met Miss Ida Frances Tinnin of North Carolina. While in Nashville he served as interim pastor of the East Nashville Free Will Baptist Church, one of the denomination's foremost churches in the 1930's and 40's.

Alvin finished his schooling at the Bible College and graduated, in 1945, as did his future wife, the aforementioned Miss Ida Frances Tinnin. Alvin and Ida were married on July 7, 1945, in Durham, North Carolina.

In August of 1945 Alvin Ida moved to Texas. For the next several years he pastored several Texas churches on a rotating basis. These included the North Zulch Free Will Baptist Church, the Evergreen Free Will Baptist Church, the Blue Lake Free Will Baptist Church, and the Bright Light Free Will Baptist Church. In 1947 Bright Light built a parsonage so the Halbrooks could live and serve near the church, and they moved there. He continued to preach on Saturday and Sunday afternoons at churches which did not have a pastor for almost all of his time at Bright Light.

Alvin never pastored a church full-time, always having to work at a secular job to support his family. During his tenure at Bright Light he worked in the library at Texas A&M University.

He was graduated from A&M in 1955. He wrote his thesis on rural churches.

He was a studious sort of person, and that's what enabled him to be a teaching pastor. He loved to study God's Word and memorize Scripture. Even in his older years he studied and read continually. The Lord was both his passion and his hobby. He loved people, too. It was his practice to carry a little notepad in his pocket and whenever he met people, he would write their names in it so he could remember them and pray for them.

Alvin held a number of positions in the Central Texas District Association: assistant clerk, ordaining council, credentials committee, foreign missions board, and moderator. Her served for several years as clerk of the Texas State Association of Free Will Baptists, beginning in 1950, served on the Superannuation Board and served on the Texas Foreign Missions Board.

He retired from Bright Light in 1968. He then worked at the Bryan Municipal Golf Course. During his retirement years he pastored the North Zulch Free Will Baptist Church, though he continued working at a secular job.

Alvin passed away on July 23, 2000. Ida then passed away on April 5, 2006.

Julia Keener Harper
Birth:
Jul. 7, 1873
Death:
Jan. 6, 1944
Burial:
Grace Hill Cemetery
Longview
Gregg County, Texas

Julia Keener was born July 7, 1873, to Nancy Matilda Brown and Jesse A. Keener of North Carolina. She married William M. Harper (1871-1956) and they had 7 children, including Ira Harper, who was also a Free Will Baptist minister in East Texas. The minutes of the four-teenth annual session of the Texas Free Will Baptist Convention, which met at the Woodlawn Church in McClelland, County, August 28-31, 1928, has a partial list of the ministers in the association. Listed as one of the ministers of the association is Mrs. Julia Harper, Route 2, Marshall, Texas. She is also listed in the 1929 minutes as living at Route 2, Marshall. Daughter of Jesse Keener and Nancy Matilda Brown (Madison, NC)

Rev J C Harvey
Birth:
Sep. 2, 1855
Death:
Jun., 1932
Burial:
Rosemound Cemetery
Waco
McLennan County
Texas
Plot: Section O 49

Rev Robert Elias Helms
Birth:
Nov., 1854
Tennessee
Death:
Jan. 20, 1930
Wichita County
Texas
Burial:
Riverside Cemetery
Wichita Falls
Wichita County
Texas
Plot: Block C, lot 3, sp 5

Parents: John F. Helms (1820 - 1897). Spouse: Amy Frances Coleman Helms (1859 - 1947)
Children:
John Critton Helms (1876 - 1959)*
Annie Elizabeth Helms Joyner (1879 - 1955)*
William Jennings Helms (1888 - 1964)*
Robert D Helms (1895 - 1974)*

Rev Lemuel Herrin
Birth:
1787
Death:
Aug. 25, 1852
Burial:
Old Macedonia Cemetery
Holland Quarters
Panola County
Texas
Spouse: Mary Hendon Herrin (1787 - ___)
Children: Elizabeth Herrin Scruggs (1820 - 1870)- Karenhappuck Herrin Winder (1826 - 1892)- Lorenzo Herrin (1835 - ___)*

Rev William Jackson Higgins
Birth: Feb. 2, 1862
Prentiss County
Mississippi, USA
Death: Aug. 4, 1944
Stephenville
Erath County
Texas
Burial:
West End Cemetery
Stephenville
Erath County
Texas

He was born in Prentice Co., MS, and died in Stephenville, Erath Co., TX. He married Sarah Paralee

Harty on 12 September 1880, in Young Co., TX.

Family links:
  Parents:
    David Matthew Higgins (1842 - 1913)
    Margaret Lavinia Clement Higgins (1842 - 1897)

  Spouse:
    Sarah Paralee Harty Higgins (1860 - 1939)

  Children:
    William Matthew Higgins (1883 - 1916)*
    Infant Higgins (1885 - 1885)*
    Albert Higgins (1885 - 1885)*
    Sarah Lavinia Higgins Callaway (1886 - 1957)*
    James Dennis Higgins (1889 - 1956)*
    Ottie T Higgins (1896 - 1980)*
    Austin Higgins (1899 - 1964)*
    Abel Dalton Higgins (1905 - 1988)

William Matthew Higgins
Birth:
May 3, 1883
Young County
Texas
Death:
Apr. 8, 1916
Floyd County
Texas
Burial:
Lakeview Cemetery
Floyd County
Texas

Parents:
  William Jackson Higgins (1862 - 1944)
  Sarah Paralee Harty Higgins (1860 - 1939)

Rev J. C. Hodges
Birth: Mar. 15, 1860
Death: Dec. 20, 1944
Burial:
Greenwood Memorial Park and Mausoleum
Fort Worth
Tarrant County
Texas, USA

John Burton Holmes
Birth:
1850
Death:
1925
Burial:
Bethel Methodist Church Cemetery
Parker County
Texas

Rev J B Hooser
Birth: 1857
Death: 1922
Burial:
Girard Cemetery
Girard
Kent County
Texas

Children:
  Eugene G. Hooser (1891 - 1976)*
  Joseph Fletcher Hooser (1895 - 1965)*

Egbert Statewright Jameson
Birth:
Oct. 16, 1878
Rusk County,
Texas
Death:
Feb. 25, 1950
Henderson,
Rusk County,
Texas
Burial:
Tatum Cemetery
Tatum,, Rusk County;Texas

Egbert Statewright Jameson was the son of D. R. Jameson of Alabama & Mary Irwin of Texas. His occupation was a Minister.
Rev. Jameson became a minister (from his obit) about 1905, and presumably ordained about that time. He was affiliated with the Free Will Baptist, and in the 1915 Convention of the Southwestern Convention, held at Stratford, OK (Garvin Co. OK) was the elected President of that Convention. This Convention was formulated about 1901 of Missouri, Oklahoma and Texas churches that had not merged in the northeastern Randall FWB movement with the Northern Baptists in 1911.
He was also a school teacher in Rusk Co. TX.
--taken from book by Rev. G.W. Million, pub. 1958, "A History of Free Will Baptists."

Rev D. R. Jimmerson
Birth:
May 14, 1853
Death:
Jul. 4, 1934
Burial:
Crow Cemetery
Henderson
Rusk County
Texas, USA

Minister of the Free Will Baptist church, b. AL. His name is in the Minutes of the Southwestern Cooperative Association of FWB in 1910.

Spouse:
Mary Irwin Jimmerson (1855 - 1916)*

Children:
Romalus Jimmerson (1880 - 1946)*
James M Jimmerson (1882 - 1939)*
Nannie Jimmerson Tipps (1884 - 1942)*
Emma Jimmerson Gibson (1888 - 1976)*
Minnie L Jimerson (1892 - 1935)*
Angus Jimmerson (1895 - 1918)* Alvin R. Jimmerson (1900 - 1991)*

Minnie L Jimmerson
Birth:
Jul. 27, 1892
Death:
Feb. 26, 1935
Burial:
Crow Cemetery
Henderson,
Rusk County, Texas

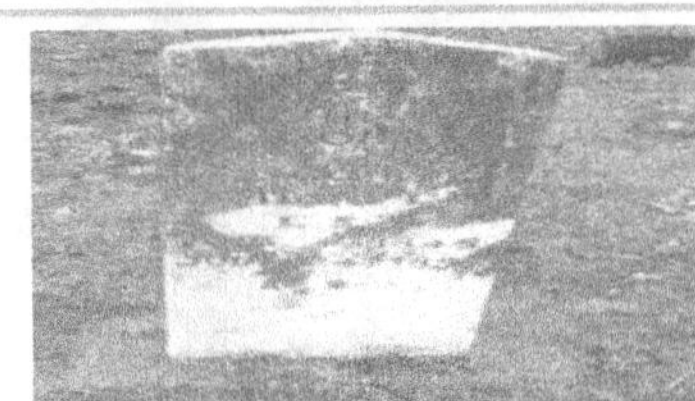

J. W. Johnson
Birth:
Aug. 4, 1845
Death:
Jul. 24, 1899
Burial:
King Cemetery
Henderson County, Texas

In 1888 he was one of the ministers in the Denton Creek Association of Free Will Baptist which is located northwest of Dallas.
Inscription:
Co K3 Texas Cav C.S.A.

Billy Marion Jones
Birth:
Feb. 3, 1937
Houston Harris County Texas
Dec. 19, 2011
Fort Smith
Sebastian County, Arkansas
Burial:
Steep Hollow Cemetery,
Bryan,Brazos County, Texas

Bill was a minister, pastor, missionary to Ivory Coast for 10 years, editor of *"Heartbeat"* a missions magazine in Nashville, TN, President of Hillsdale Free Will Baptist College in Moore, OK for 8 years, Director of Oklahoma Missions for 2 years, served on the Foreign Mission Board for 26 years, professor of Theology at the college, Senior Adult pastor Poteau FWB Church.

Rev J. E. Jones
Birth:
Jul. 4, 1809
Death:
Dec. 20, 1876
Burial:
Rutland Cemetery
Douglassville
Cass County,Texas

Inscription:
Born in Abbeville Dist. S. C.
Died in Atlanta, Texas

Rev Mrs Amanda Jane Crouse Kester
Birth:
Jan. 20, 1891
Miami
Ottawa County
Oklahoma
Death:
Apr. 5, 1957
Henderson
Rusk County
Texas
Burial:
Lakewood Memorial Park
Henderson
Rusk County, Texas

Daughter of Henry Crouse and Emma Majors, both born Oklahoma.She was a housewife, 66 years old, widowed, and a resident of Henderson for the past 3 years. Informant was Mrs. Eva Dobson; burial was April 7, 1957. Pearson Funeral Home was in charge of arrangements.
(Texas death certificate# 22146)
Spouse: Charles Joseph Kester (1880 - 1946)

Inscription:
Mother
Have Faith In God

Joshua Timothy "Tim" Lee
Birth:
May 6, 1859
Decatur County
Georgia,
Death:
Apr. 16, 1931
Kirbyville
Jasper County
Texas
Burial:
Kirbyville City Cemetery
Kirbyville

Jasper County, Texas
Husband of Emily Ann Westbrook Lee. Father of 12 children, all of Kirbyville,TX. Son of Elias M.C.Lee and Dorcus Morgan Lee, Georgia.

Rev Jay Truron Lee
Birth:
Feb. 2, 1912
Death:
Jan. 22, 1982
Burial:
Gann Cemetery
Lufkin
Angelina County, Texas

Spouse: Wruble Wilson Lee (1920 - 2011)

J W Loftis
Birth:
Nov. 8, 1869
Death:
Jan. 8, 1906
Burial:
Jacksonville City Cemetery
Jacksonville
Cherokee County, Texas

He was one that the earlier pastors in the Brazos Quarterly Meeting which was started in 1887.

James Pierce "Jim" Lunsford
Birth:
1834
Tennessee
Death:
Nov. 27, 1918
Burial:
Old Prospect Cemetery
Mount Enterprise
Rusk County
Texas

James Pierce Lunsford was born to Aris and Mary Lunsford, who had come from South Carolina. James married Sarah Ann Walters of Georgia, in Chattahoochee County, Georgia, on June 27, 1855. James and Sarah Ann moved to Covington County, Alabama, about 1862.
James was a Confederate soldier in the American Civil War, serving between 1862 and 1865. He served in the First Alabama Heavy Artillery Battalion, Company D, and fought in the Battle of Mobile Bay and the Battle of Spanish Fort. The Battle of Spanish Fort took place from March 27 to April 8, 1865 in Baldwin County, Alabama, as part of the Mobile Campaign of the Western Theater of the war. He was wounded, captured, and then released at the end of the war.
His family came to Texas in a wagon train after the Civil War, about 1876, and settled in Cherokee County. Later they lived in Rusk County where he started the Old Prospect and Mount Union Free Will Baptist churches.
When James founded the Old

Prospect Church in Rusk County 1887, it was started in a building shared with the Methodists. The original building still stands beside the newer Baptist church next to it. There is a petrified wood marker by it.

James and Sarah Ann raised eleven children, two of them being born in Texas. Sarah Ann, died in 1908. Both are buried in the Old Prospect Cemetery. His grave spot in the cemetery is unknown, but many other relatives are buried there, presumably beside him.

Isaac Martin
Birth:
Dec. 31, 1812
Death:
Nov. 2, 1888
Burial:
Alto City Cemetery
Alto
Cherokee County
Texas

He was one of the early ministers in Chattahoochee Association in Georgia and is recorded in the 1842 minutes. He married Mary Polly Truitt on June 6, 1834 in Jasper County, Georgia. She died in 1890 in Cherokee County, TX; Reverend and Mrs. Martin had eleven children. His parents were James Martin (1788 – 1869) and Hester Bogan Martin (1789 – 1867) who is buried in Georgia and was the parents of four preachers one of which started the Martin Association in the state of Georgia. Isaac is a brother to Samuel C. Martin listed below along with Rev. George W. Martin buried in Georgia and Rev. Robert Martin buried in Louisiana.

Rev John Andrew Martin
Birth:
Feb. 16, 1852
Death:
Apr. 5, 1932
Burial:
Mann Cemetery
Colmesneil
Tyler County
Texas, USA

Parents:
　Wiley Martin (1829 - 1882)
　Mary Ann Sears Martin (1832 - 1910)
　Spouse:
　Elizabeth Enloe Martin (1854 - 1898)*
　Children:
　Arminta Martin Walker (1891 - 1954)*
　Siblings:
　John Andrew Martin (1852 - 1932)
　Mary Elizabeth Martin Mann (1855 - 1938)*
　Nannie E Martin (1860 - 1911)*
　Eliza Martin Kirkland (1860 - 1888)*

Inscription:
A faithful soldier of the cross

Robert Martin
Birth:
Aug. 24, 1856
Death:
Jun. 23, 1871
Burial:

Steep Hollow Cemetery
Bryan
Brazos County
Texas
Plot: Section 2, Space 281

An early minister in Texas Parents: Samuel Crawford Martin (1825 - 1903) Sarah Ann Cheshire Martin (1824 - 1901)

Elder Samuel Crawford Martin
Birth:
Jan. 20, 1825
Alabama
Death:
Dec. 23, 1903
Steep Hollow
Brazos County, Texas
Burial:
Steep Hollow Cemetery
Bryan
Brazos County, Texas
Plot: Section 2, Space 278

Transcription of Obituary from The Bryan Eagle, Thursday, 24 Dec. 1903. REV. S. C. MARTIN DEAD. Venerable Pioneer Baptist Preacher Gone to his Reward. Brazos county mourns the loss of one of her oldest, noblest and best citizens, and the holidays have been darkened in homes throughout the length and breadth of the county, where his name was a household word, by the death of Rev. S. C. Martin at his home in the Steep Hollow community on Wednesday morning, December 23, 1903, at 8:30 o'clock. Rev. Martin, infirm with the weight and labors of 79 years, has been in failing health for some time and ill for several weeks, so that his death was not unexpected. Nevertheless, it was a sad blow to the family and host of friends when the news came from the darkened chamber that his noble spirit had taken its flight. Rev. Martin was a native of Alabama and came to Texas before the civil war, locating in Tyler County. He moved to Brazos County more than thirty years ago and has since resided in the Steep Hollow community. For more than half a century he preached the gospel and his labors were graciously blessed in the salvation of soul. Not only did he serve as pastor of nearly every Baptist church in Brazos County, but though out his life he did much successful revival work. He was sincere, earnest, uncompromising, unselfish and consecrated. He labored as faithfully without reward as when his labors were abundantly rewarded. In deed his best service was given to the Master with numerically weak and struggling churches, and it may be truly said that he gave his life to the gospel, the church and humanity. His brother was the founder of the Martin Association in the state of Georgia and had three other brothers who were Free Will Baptist preachers. His ancestry has roots in South Carolina with one of them buried in the Horse Branch Free Will Baptist Cemetery. I am strongly assuming that he was also a Free Will Baptist preacher even though I have not been able to find verification of that in the state of Texas.

Elizabeth R McAdams
Birth:
Oct. 1, 1884
Luverne,
Alabama
Death:
Sep. 1, 1964
Burial:
Falba Cemetery,
Huntsville,
Walker County,
Texas

At 13 she recalls she wanted to be a missionary. At 25 she felt that God was calling her to preach. She was licensed to preach in October, 1910. In 1911 she married Rev. Hiram McAdams and they established themselves as an evangelistic team in North Carolina, Missouri, Texas, Oklahoma, Arkansas etc. Elizabeth became known as Lizzie, or Sister Lizzie, realized her teenage dream of being a missionary when she, her husband, and 6 year old Naomi Rebecca went to Barbados, British West Indies, in 1918 as missionaries. They spent a short time on the island and then returned to the States as evangelists. Back in the States Mrs. McAdams worked hard at trying to bring Free Will Baptist in the West and East together. At the meeting in Cofer's Chapel in 1935, she stood and made the motion that East and West unite as the National Association of Free Will Baptists, and without a reading of the committee's report on the

Treatise, the motion passed and the National Association became a reality. At her death at the age of 80, she had spent 54 years in the ministry. In her book, *Rolling Stones,* she summed up her ministry: "We have preached in 17 states, have held about 300 revivals with about 10,000 professions of faith in the Lord Jesus, organized 11 churches and numerous Auxiliaries and Leagues in different states. During this period of time, spent four years as home missionaries. She also wrote *My Experiences, Six Gospel Sermons, Rolling Stones, Go Tell that Fox, Getting a Shave in the Devil's Barbershop, My Trip to the West India Islands,* and *Woman's Bible Right to Preach the Gospel.* She was also a member of the national home mission board in the early years of the denomination. She was active in travielng among our churches. She was an evangelist, a promotional Secretary for various departments, and was pastor of a number of churches.

Hiram Mullens McAdams
Birth:
Jun. 18, 1879,
Walker County, Texas,
May 24, 1964
Huntsville,
Walker County, Texas,
Burial:
Falba Cemetery, Huntsville,
Walker County, Texas

McAdams married Elizabeth Rachel Lawlis, in 1911.They had a daughter, Naomi R., in 1913, born in Texas. Rev. Hiram and his wife, Rev. "Lizzie" as she was affectionately called, were ordained as ministers in the 1920's in the Free Will Baptist Church. They were co-pastors, and an evangelistic team holding large revivals in North Carolina, Texas, Alabama, Oklahoma, Missouri, and Nebraska. They organized churches and promoted Tecumseh College in Oklahoma, and was active in church missions throughout. In 1918, they acquired passports and went to Barbados, West Indies, as missionaries for a short time, before they returned to become very involved in mission work in the states. His wife wrote several books, some of which described their work. They were respected and held in esteem by those who knew them, and in memory by those who read and know of their labors. It is noteworthy that Rev. "Lizzy" outlived her husband only three months and 8 days.

Elder Thomas J McBride
Birth:
1851
Death:
1913
Burial:
Bright Star Cemetery
Wills Point
Van Zandt County
Texas

An ordained Free Will Baptist minister, his name appearing in roll of ministers in 1910 Minutes of Southwest Cooperative Association of FWB, including states of Missouri, Oklahoma and Texas.
Spouse:
Minerva A Kinard McBride (1859 - 1904)
Children:
Mittie C McBride Furrh (1884 - 1970)*
Ella Mable McBride Rusk (1889 - 1959)*
Henry George McBride (1891 - 1976)*

Rev Thaddeus James McBride
Birth:
Feb. 13, 1909
Tuttle
Grady County
Oklahoma
Death:
Mar. 23, 1986
Paige
Bastrop County
Texas
Burial:
McBride Family Cemetery
Paige
Bastrop County
Texas, USA
Plot: Private Land

Married Martha Reed in Mena, Arkansas on March 26, 1937. Parents: Hiram Young McBride (1857 - 1937)-Lovica Colbert McBride (1868 - 1963)

John Henry Measures
Birth:
Oct. 27, 1901
Texas
Death:
Jun. 26, 1978
Parker County
Texas
Burial:
Memory Gardens of the Valley
Weatherford
Parker County,Texas

Spouse: Carrie Leona Measures (1904 - 1994).

Schooley Lemmon Morris
Birth:
April 5, 1856
Zanesville
Morgan County, Ohio
Death:
May 19, 1922
Ashley
Washington County, Illinois
Burial:
Unknown
Ashley, Washington County,
Illinois

Schooley Lemmon (or Lemon) Morris was born to David and Rachel Ann (James) Morris. In the 1880 census he was listed as a photographer. Later references list him as a Free Will Baptist minister. Morris began to make his mark on Free Will Baptists when he became the editor and publisher of *the Free Will Baptist News,* which he published in Weatherford, Texas, as early as 1910. He also pastored the First Free Will Baptist Church in Weatherford. He was a friend and mentor to the younger Lizzie McAdams, who often referred to him as "father Morris." In 1912 he was an agent for the Southwestern Freewill Baptist General Convention. At the 1912 convention he gave a talk on The Free Will Baptist News.

He continued publishing the News for several years. In 1916 Free Will Baptists in Texas, Oklahoma, and Missouri organized the Cooperative General Association of Free Will Baptists at a meeting at the Philadelphia Church, near Pattonsburg, Missouri. Morris was present and was chosen to preach during one of the evening services. The moderator appointed him to be on a committee to devise reporting forms for the association. Morris also preached at a called session of the association on December 26, 1917, at the Northview Church near Tecumseh, Oklahoma.

The Cooperative General Association at its organizational session voted to purchase the *Free Will Baptist News* from Morris and to name him the editor and publisher. They paid him $350.00 for the News and $913.00 for the printing equipment and other assets, and voted to change the name of the News to the *New Morning Star*. It was printed in Weatherford, Texas, for about a year.

In 1919 Samra Smith, a native of North Carolina, merged his publication, the *Biblical Beacon,* with the Star and became co-editor with Morris. At about the same time Rev. W. C. Austin merged his paper, the *Gospel Pruning Hook*, with the Star, thus three papers became one, with a much larger circulation. At first the Star was published twice a month, then weekly for a time, and then back to twice a month.

The Cooperative General Association opened Tecumseh College on September 2, 1917.

The *New Morning Star* was moved from Weatherford, Texas, to Tecumseh, Oklahoma. The latest printing equipment was purchased for the Star, such as Linotype, a larger cylinder press, a large job press, a motorized paper cutter, and a mailer. Morris made the move with the Star, and became the first pastor of the Tecumseh College Church, which had been organized earlier in the year. Morris and his wife, Grace I. Morris, were also on the faculty of Tecumseh College. Their salaries were $70.00 per year for each of them.

Morris was widowed twice in his lifetime. In the 1880 census his wife was listed as Josephine Morris, and they had a three month old son, Corral (or Carlos) W. Morris. On March 4, 1891 he married Belle Adams. In the 1900 census he is listed as having three children: Corral W. age 20; Hallie, E., age 17; and Nellie, age 13. After her death he married Grace Irene Topping on March 24, 1901, in Ashley, Illinois.

Rev. S. L. Morris passed away at the age of 66. In November of 1924 his widow, Grace I. Morris, became the president of Tecumseh College

---

Rev Thomas Henry Newsom
Birth:
Aug. 9, 1876
Death:
Jul. 24, 1944
Burial:
Springtown Cemetery
Springtown
Parker County, Texas

Early leader in Texas Freewill Baptist, as chairman, of a committee, in 1929, resisted association with the larger northern group of Baptists, other than in Christian fellowship. (See Hist. of FWB State Associations)
Son of John Randolph Newsom and Mary Dixon, married Mattie Elizabeth Young. Son of John Rabdolph Newsom and Mary Dixon, married Mattie Elizabeth Young (1879 - 1970).
Children: Mary Ruth Newsom Martin (1907 - 1987), Mattie Jewell Newsom (1911 - 2005), Joseph Edward Newsom (1913 - 1992).

Oliver Roy Norie, Jr
Birth:
Jul. 24, 1923
Death:
Jul. 19, 1998
Burial:
Crestview Memorial Park,
Wichita Falls,
Wichita County, Texas

Most of his life and ministry was invested in Texas Free Will Baptist churches. In his early years he traveled the state promoting home and foreign missions and gave every month to missions work in Texas. At the time of his death he was the pastor of the new Salem Free Will Baptist Church.

Dr J. D. O'Donnell
Birth:
Apr. 5, 1929
Alabama
Death:
Nov. 29, 2014
Arizona
Burial:
Non-Cemetery Burial
Texas

He was born into a family that gave him a solid foundation in life. He attended Bob Jones University and graduated in 3 years. He came home to Steele, Alabama and was the principal of the Chandler Mountain School for a year. He then went to his first full time pastorate in Columbus, Mississippi. He would go from there to attend the New Orleans Baptist Seminary and would earn his THD. He taught at Welch College in Nashville, Tennessee. He would go from there to be the president of Hillsdale College in Moore, Oklahoma. He would serve as the moderator of the Free Will Baptist denomination for several years. He worked at the Randall House Publications. He would pastor FWB churches in Tennessee, Missouri, and Texas. He would also pastor several Methodist churches in Texas. He retired for the final time from pastoring churches at the age of 78. He is survived by his sons, Dan and Darryl.

JD was a man who loved God, his family and people. He wrote several books for Free Will Baptists including The Deacon Handbook, Faith For Today, Church History and Free Will Baptist Doctrine. He was an educator who had the knack of building a house when he wanted to. His kindness and gentle spirit was the highlight of knowing him. He always had the other person in mind. He had an impact on those who were his students.

Earth has lost a great man, but heaven is enriched with his presence!

Judson B Palmer
Birth:
April 25, 1851
Orangeville, Ohio
Death:
1937
Burial:
Galveston Memorial Park
Hitchcock
Galveston County, Texas
Plot: Section B

He attended Hillsdale College in Michigan where he assisted in teaching and graduated from the theological department. He was ordained in May, 1873 with Reverent's A. A. Smith, A. H. Chase and other serving on the Council. He served as a teacher in the Cairo mission for two years and as a state missionary. His pastorates consisted in churches in Michigan, Wisconsin, and Iowa. He was engaged in many revivals where the presence of the spirit was manifest and he baptized over 150 converts. He became the general secretary of the YMCA a Galveston, Texas where he died.

Rev James Luther Payne
Birth:
Dec. 21, 1881
Texas
Death:
Feb. 4, 1965
Houston
Harris County
Texas
Burial:
Forest Park Cemetery
Houston
Harris County
Texas

CASWELL AND SARAH EMLEY (ORRELL) PURSELLEY

Rev Caswell Purselley
Birth:
Nov. 29, 1845
Roane County
Tennessee, USA
Death:
Dec. 17, 1916
Mambrino
Hood County
Texas, USA
Burial:
Nubbin Ridge Cemetery
Mambrino
Hood County, Texas

Married to: Sarah Emily Orrell, on 25 Feb 1866, Zion Hill, Carroll Co, Arkansas
See deed 1849 Hiwasse Dist. Farmer, Preacher (Primitive Baptist). A Descendant who wrote for Hood Co., Tx Genealogical Society, says he was a Freewill Baptist.

Civil War Confederate Arkansas Infantry Caswell Age 16, Capt. Evans' Co., Regiment, McBride's Brigade, AR Infantry. Roll dated at Camp Bragg, AR Feb 15, 1862 to July 31, 1862. Enlisted at Carrollton, by Capt. Evans for 1 year. PVT.

Parents:

James Alpha Purselley (1819 - 1907)

Martha Caroline Osbourne Purselley (1822 - 1870)

Rev James Eldridge Raney
Birth:
Apr. 15, 1861
Allen County, Kentucky
Death:
Jun. 8, 1933
Fall Creek, Hood County,Texas
Burial:
Fall Creek Cemetery
Fall Creek, Hood County,Texas

Rev W B Rhea
Birth:
Feb. 4, 1855
Death:
Jun. 20, 1929
Burial:
Cedar Creek Cemetery
Red River County, Texas

James O. Riggs
Birth:
Mar. 17, 1872
Death:
Mar. 28, 1954
Burial:
South Park Cemetery
Pearland
Brazoria County, Texas

Spouse:
Gertrude B. Riggs (1887 - 1975)*
Children:
Lida Riggs (1908 - 1953)

Rev R A Roberts
Birth:
Nov. 12, 1865
Death:
Nov. 20, 1930
Burial:
Fall Creek Cemetery
Fall Creek
Hood County, Texas

James Edward Rogers
Birth:
Mar. 11, 1868
Texas
Death:
Oct. 11, 1966
Ennis
Ellis County
Texas
Burial:
Ennis Memorial Cemetery
Ennis
Ellis County, Texas

Son of Austin Rogers and Jane Hooks. Spouse: Sallie Lee Rogers (1876 - 1925) Widowed minister died at 903 S. Preston Street with cerebral hemorrhaging

Information provided by Louis Gipson; James R. Jeter MD Source: Texas Death Certificate #65261

Marshall I Sanford
Birth: Nov. 17, 1867
Winn Parish
Louisiana, USA
Death: Feb. 26, 1940
Dallas
Dallas County
Texas, USA
Burial:
Western Heights Cemetery
Dallas
Dallas County
Texas, USA

Father: William Sanford b NC; mth: Sarah Foster, b NC. wid, age 72 yrs. Ret'd from Nursery Business.
Spouse: Fannie Carter-b. TX
Children:
Sarah Sanford Davidson (1896 - 1926)*
Lee Roy Sanford (1902 - 1974)*
Berta Mae Sanford McCloskey (1905 - 1972)*

Rev James F Scott
Birth:
Feb. 12, 1869
Tennessee, USA
Death:
Jul. 27, 1943
Wichita Falls
Wichita County
Texas, USA
Burial:

Ringgold Cemetery
Ringgold
Montague County
Texas, USA

He was a retired Free Will Baptist minister in the early work in Texas. He attended as a minister, the Southwestern Cooperative Association of FWB in 1912. He was b. Crossville, TN. (see TX Dth cert.)

Father: Henry Taylor Scott
Mother: Zillie Lary
 Spouse:
 Martha Ellen Whitaker Scott (1868 - 1947)

Rev Thomas A Searcy
Birth:
Nov., 1866
Texas
Death:
1933
Texas
Burial:
Willowhole Cemetery
North Zulch
Madison County, Texas

He was pastor of the First FWB church in Bryan, Texas during the years 1907-1909. He and his wife were also charter members of this church which was organized in 1894 with 14 members.

Robert Edward Lee Sheffield
Birth:
1911
Death:
1984

Burial:
Friendship Cemetery
Kirbyville
Jasper County, Texas

From "The Burial Locations of Free Will Baptist Ministers." DOB/DOD from SSDI and TX Dth Records. He was listed as a son of John B. and Hazel Sheffield, in both 1920-1930 TX Jasper & Walker Co.'s Census'.
U.S. Army Veteran of WW II.

Rev J M Smith
Birth:
Dec. 4, 1846
Death:
Aug. 25, 1935
Burial:
Mount Zion Cemetery
Shelby County,Texas

Rev T W Smith
Birth:
May 27, 1881
Death:
Oct. 14, 1954
Burial:
New Prospect Cemetery
New Prospect, Rusk County, Texas
A Free Will Bapt. minister in early TX church work.
Inscription:"Father"

Rev J W Shults
Birth:
Mar. 11, 1853
Death:
Apr. 3, 1926
Burial:
Buffalo Springs Cemetery
Buffalo Springs
Clay County, Texas

Joseph Wilburn Shults was born in Missouri to W. C. and Melinda Shults, who had migrated west from Kentucky. In the 1860 census, when J. W. was 7, the family was living in Spring Creek Township, Dent County, in South Central Missouri. J. W. married Comilla Frances Bowles (1859-1935), but little else is known about her except that she was born in Texas in June of 1859. In 1900 J. W. and his family were living in Denton County, Texas, on a rented farm with seven children. Their daughter Carrye Dell had been born in Indian Territory in 1894.
In late December of 1913 Shults moved his family to Post Oak, Texas. Less than five months later, on May 1, 1914, he organized the Pleasant Valley Free Will Baptist Church, three miles north of Post Oak and three miles south of Buffalo Springs in Clay County, Texas. The church services were held in the Pleasant Valley School, which was a one room schoolhouse and pastored the church from 1914 to 1919, and again from 1921 to 1924. The church would go on to become one of the better known Free Will Baptist churches in Texas.
Joseph and "Fannie" had seven children: George L., Maggie B., Effie B., John P., Carrye Dell, Clyde A, and William P. Carrye Dell married Rev. Tiff Covington who twice pastored the church Brother Shults had started (1928-1949; 1967-1980). Tiff had been converted at the Pleasant Valley Church when Brother Shults was preaching a revival in August of 1916. Tiff would go on to become a legend in North Central Texas. In 1936 the Pleasant Valley Church built a new sanctuary one mile north of Pleasant Valley. The new

church was on higher ground than at its previous location in the valley and its name was changed to the Pleasant Mound Free Will Baptist Church, affectionately known in the community as the Rock Church, because it was constructed of local field stones. He and Fannie are buried in the Buffalo Springs Cemetery in Texas.

Clarice Lucinda Gressett Snook
Birth:
Aug. 7, 1877
Louisiana, USA
Death:
Sep. 7, 1933
Houston
Harris County
Texas
Burial:
Concord Cemetery
Iola
,Grimes County,
Texas

Lucy Gressett is listed in the 1909 and 1911 Free Will Baptist Registers as being a member of the Spring Hill Free Will Baptist Church, the Plainview Quarterly Meeting, and the Southwestern Free Will Baptist General Convention. She was residing in Iola at the time. Spouse:Ruben Snook (1874 - 1959)

Nicholas Burkhardt Stanley
Birth:
Mar. 7, 1858
Howard County
Missouri, USA
Death:
May 16, 1941
Floydada
Floyd County
Texas, USA
Burial:
Floydada Cemetery
Floydada
Floyd County
Texas, USA
Plot: North, Section 2, Row 1, Space 23

Father: Tom Stanley
Mother: Paulina Huffman
  Spouse:
  Catherine Ellen Manning Stanley (1865 - 1937)*

Newton Willis Stout
Birth:
Jan. 7, 1895
Normangee
Leon County
Texas, USA
Death:
Nov. 19, 1984
Harris County

Texas, USA
Burial:
Glenwood Cemetery
Houston
Harris County
Texas, USA
Plot: Section I, Lot 119

Son of Delano Stout and Frances "Fannie" Davies.
  FW Bapt.Minister in Texas.
  Spouse:
  Myrtle Monroe Williams Stout (1901 - 1973)
  Children:
  Harold N. Stout (1925 - 1944)*

Angus McAllister Stewart
Birth:
Aug. 25, 1853
Death:
Sep. 17, 1913
Burial:
Odd Fellows Cemetery
Carthage
Panola County,Texas

In 1878 a number of churches in Panola County entered into an organization which became known as the Texas Association. He was very instrumental in to organize associations as well as local churches.

He and his wife we among the 14 charter members of the Bryan First FWB church and its first pastor.

During his ministry the church began to grow and he owned and operated The Bryan Academic and Collegiate Institute, which was a grade school. This school filled a unique place in the early history of Bryan and the church.

Lula & Thomas Strain

Thomas Albert Strain, Jr
Birth:
Nov. 25, 1885
Death:
Nov. 16, 1971
Seadrift
Calhoun County
Texas, USA
Burial:
Seadrift Cemetery
Seadrift
Calhoun County,Texas
Plot: A-222-5

WEDDED 65 YEARS

Spouse:
Lula Mae Bone Strain (1888 - 1977)

Children:
Lillian Irene Strain Borowski-Forney (1909 - 1998)*
Clora Estelle Strain Apostalo (1911 - 1963)*
William Allen Strain (1914 - 1985)*
Ida Mae Strain Smith (1916 - 2008)*
Jossie Marie Strain Borowski (1919 - 1981)*
Delonia Vandella Strain Kimbrell (1921 - 2013)*
Olin B. Strain (1922 - 1945)*

John Swanwick
Birth:
Jun. 13, 1870
Bradley
Kankakee County
Illinois
Death:
Aug. 2, 1941
Houston
Harris County
Texas
Burial:
Bryan City Cemetery
Bryan (Brazos County)
Brazos County
Texas
Plot: Block 4 Lot 95/C

Parents: Curtis Conn Swanwick (1831 - 1874) Louise Ann Garner Swanwick (1838 - 1913)

Early Texas minister.

Milton L Sutton
Birth:
Jan. 25, 1899
Louisiana
Death:
Nov. 1, 1980
Wichita Falls,
Wichita County,
Texas
Burial:
Buffalo Springs Cemetery,
Buffalo Springs,
Clay County, Texas

He was an ordained pastor and leader in the Texas church. He pastored at Ft. Worth for years and was a popular and able leader in Texas and the national.

Rev Isaac G. Swearingen

Birth:
Jan. 14, 1854
Death:
Jan. 3, 1919
Burial:
Swearingen Cemetery
Warren
Tyler County
Texas

Rev John Julian Tatum

Birth:
May 22, 1863
Steeleville
Randolph County, Illinois
Death:
Mar. 10, 1931
Bryan
Brazos County, Texas
Burial:
Bryan City Cemetery
Bryan
Brazos County, Texas

He received his theological education at Hillsdale College in Michigan. He was ordained in 1889 in his home church in Steeleville. On June 22, 1886, he married Hettie K. Mason in Pinkneyville, Illinois. Together Rev. and Mrs. Tatum served churches in Illinois, Indiana, and Iowa, until they accepted the call to the Bryan Free Will Baptist Church in 1905, a church he pastored three times, 1905-07, 1910-13, 1918-19. In 1914 he served as agent, promotional man, of the Southwestern Convention of Freewill Baptists and General Conference of Free Baptists, though his salary was paid exclusively by the General Conference. At the first annual session of the Texas State Association of Free Will Baptists, held October 8-9, 1915, at Bradley, Texas, Rev. Tatum was appointed by moderator E. L. Hill to serve on a committee to draft the first by-laws and constitution for the state association. He served on the committee with Rev. W. E. Dearmore and Rev. Charles C. Wheeler, two other men of able leadership capacity. Over the years he served on numerous committees and boards, displaying considerable literary skills and organizational abilities, reflecting the excellent training he had received at Hillsdale College in Michigan. From 1918 on the Tatum family lived in Bryan until their deaths. The Bryan area was astronghold for Free Will Baptists in the first half of the twentieth century.

As Field Secretary of the Southwest for the Free Will Baptist denomination, serving Texas, Oklahoma, Arkansas, Missouri, Kansas, and Nebraska.

Old church history says, "Rev. J. J. Tatum, was elected president in 1912, of the Southwestern Freewill Baptist General Convention which included Okla., Missouri, as well as Texas. He was closly allied with the northern FWB.

Obediah J. Taylor

Birth:
Feb. 14, 1851
Anderson County,
South Carolina
Death:
Feb. 14, 1939
Smith County, Texas,
Burial:
Hopewell Cemetery,
Swan, Smith County, Texas

His father died in 1864, in Franklin, Tennessee, Civil War, which left his mother a widow. She died about 1880 when they were in Mountain Home, Logan Co. Arkansas. After this is when he probably migrated to Indian Territory in eastern Oklahoma, for they were in the Chickasaw Nation census of 1900, Township 6, with six children. *First Hundred Years of Oklahoma Free Will Baptist,* pub. 2009, states that in Rev. J.M. Robert's diary, "O.J. Tailor (sic), was in Indian Territory in 1894, and preached with Rev. J. M. Roberts. In meeting minutes of Sept. 1, 1894, organization of churches in Indian Territory, 'Rev. O. J. Taylor, was elected ass't moderator' of their group. Where he was ordained and where his ministry took him is not known. It's possible he was ordained in Arkansas after they moved there. His occupation was always listed as "farmer" as most of the old pioneer ministers were, as they received precious little money for their ministerial labor.

Harold R Teague
Birth:
Nov. 30, 1937
Newport
Cocke County, Tennessee
Death:
Jan. 2, 2012
Burial:
Rusk County Memorial Gardens
Henderson
Rusk County, Texas

He attended Free Will Baptist Bible College in Nashville, Tennessee. He was a pastor and began his career preaching in Springfield, Tennessee in 1959. He then pastored Harris Memorial Freewill Baptist Church in Greeneville, Tennessee, First Freewill Baptist Church in Henderson, Texas, Longview Freewill Baptist Mission in Longview, Texas, Union Arbor Freewill Baptist in Beckville, Texas and returned again to First Free Will Baptist Church in Henderson where he retired in July 2007. Throughout his career, he held many positions of leadership in the Free Will Baptist Denomination at the district, state, and national level. He was honored as Who's Who in American Religion and touched many lives throughout his ministry career. He also worked for many years on the campuses of the schools for Pine Tree ISD. He was a member of the Lion's Club of Henderson, Texas. He was an incredible husband, father, grandfather, friend and pastor, but most of all he was a devoted follower of Jesus Christ.

Nor pain, nor death can enter there.

Charles B. Thompson
Birth:
Mar. 17, 1890
Death:
Sep. 2, 1977
Burial:
Bryan City Cemetery
Bryan
Brazos County, Texas
Plot: Block 21

PVT US Army World War II.
Spouse: Annie Lawless Thompson (1897 – 1988).

Rev Elbert J. Vaughn
Birth:
Apr. 8, 1889
Death:
Nov. 23, 1974
Burial:
Bright Light Cemetery
Bryan (Brazos County)
Brazos County, Texas

Elihu Nelson Waldrep
Birth:
Apr. 1, 1859
Moscow
Polk County
Texas, USA
Death:
Oct. 11, 1930
Texas, USA
Burial:
Midtown Cemetery
Saratoga
Hardin County,Texas, USA

Parents:
Searce D Waldrep (1821 - 1880)
Spouse:
Emily Jane Cliburn Waldrep (1862 - 1930)*
Children:
Mattie Virginia Waldrep Williams (1882 - 1964)*
Robert S Waldrep (1884 - 1942)*
Leonard L Waldrop (1887 - 1973)*
Alfred Carson Waldrep (1889 - 1971)*
Maggie Waldrep Beal (1892 - 1961)*
Hattie Rebecca Waldrep Creel (1903 - 1979)*
Siblings:
Laura Ann Waldrep Newton (1847 - 1934)*
John Henry Waldrep (1847 - 1915)*
Elihu Nelson Waldrep (1859 - 1930)
Tamsy Waldrep Crews (1860 - 1946)*

Rev James Milton Walker
Birth:
Aug. 10, 1861
Johnson County, Texas
Death:
Mar. 8, 1942
Weatherford
Parker County, Texas
Burial:
East Greenwood Cemetery
Weatherford
Parker County, Texas

He married Sarah Jane Brown on August 14, 1878. Sarah was born in Weatherford, Texas, August 2, 1861. James and Sarah had seven children, four sons and three daughters. Sarah passed away on March 9, 1907. In addition to being a Free Will Baptist minister, James owned and operated a café in Weatherford.

After Sarah's death James married Verda E. Smith, who had been born on August 19, 1893, Grimes County, Texas, and who was thirty-two years younger than he. James and Verda had three children: Fritz Morris, 1913; Mattie Elizabeth, 1914; and Jimmie Sue, 1925.

James pastored the First Free Will Baptist Church in Weatherford twice, from 1902 to 1904, and from October 1915 to December of 1918. Verda pastored it from August of 1940 to September of 1942. She assisted him while he pastored the New Hope Free Will Baptist Church in Parker County, Texas, and did the same while he pastored a church in Adams, Nebraska, near Lincoln. They worked together in a number of ministry efforts. They were elected as evangelists by the Southwestern Free Will Baptist Convention in 1914. Using a large tent owned by the convention, they preached evangelistic meetings far and wide, much the same way Lizzie McAdams used a tent for her campaigns, many of which resulted in the establishment of Free Will Baptist churches. James and Verda both worked with Rev. S. L. Morris, publisher and editor of the *Free Will Baptist News* and then *The New Morning Star,* both published in Weatherford, until *The New Morning Star* was moved to Tecumseh, Oklahoma, circa 1916. They worked together in preaching revival meetings in Free Will Baptist churches, as well.

As of 2014 James and Verda still have descendants who are active in the First Free Will Baptist Church in Weatherford. One of them, Deacon Morris Brandon, a grandson, was named after Rev. S. L. Morris, who was so helpful to young ministers, such as Verda Smith Walker, Lizzie Lawless McAdams, and countless others.

Verda Walker
Birth:
Aug. 19, 1893
Death:
Apr. 8, 1968
Burial:
East Greenwood Cemetery
Weatherford
Parker County, Texas

Verda was ordained to the gospel ministry at the New Hope Free Will Baptist Church on March 31, 1912, by the West Fork District Association. Among the men who signed her ordination certificate were Rev. James Milton Walker, who would later become her husband, and Rev. S. L. Morris.

It was Verda Smith Walker who performed the wedding ceremony for Rev. Lizzie Lawless and Rev. H. M. McAdams. Verda and Lizzie McAdams were close friends until Lizzie passed away in 1964.

James passed away on March 8, 1942 and Verda joined him on April 8, 1968. They are buried beside each other in the East Greenwood Cemetery in Weatherford, Parker County, Texas.

C. C. Wheeler
Birth:
Jan. 28, 1886
Death:
Jan. 14, 1918
Burial:
Bryan City Cemetery
Bryan (Brazos County)
Brazos County
Texas
Plot: Block 5 Lot 09/J

He received his theological training at Westminister College in Tehuascana, Texas. He served the Bryan First FWB church from 1913-15 and again from 1917-1918. He also held pastorates at Geneva, and Sutton, Nebraska, and in North Zulch, Kurren, Wellborn, Cross, Bright Light and Keith, Texas.

Being an educated man, Wheeler was appointed to a committee to draft the first constitution of the Texas State Association at its initial session in 1915 at Bradley, Texas. He served along with Rev. J. J. Tatum and Rev. W. E. Dearmore, two other men of unusual abilities.

Brother Wheeler married Maude Ellie Wheeler (1887-1963) and they had six children: Ruby, Ewell, Charles, Imaree, Mohnike, and Florence.

Wheeler's ministry was brought to an early end when he died in a train wreck on January 14, 1918, at the age of 31 years. Rev. J. J. Tatum signed his death certificate.

Rev Charles Booth Whiteley
Birth:
Apr. 26, 1800
Virginia
Death:
Apr. 27, 1875
Bell County, Texas
Burial:
Resthaven Cemetery
Belton, Bell County, Texas

Charles Booth Whitely, was the son of Joseph and Sarah (Stapleton) Whitely. Charles had two brothers, (among others), Samuel and Isaac Whitely, who all left Virginia, travelled through Tennessee, and on to Northwestern Arkansas, into Marion, then Madison Co. Charles B. was a United Baptist minister, and was the first of the brothers to settle in the newly opened Arkansas territory, and soon after his arrival, he established the Union United Baptist Church in Marion Co. at least by 1838. Goodspeed, in his History of Northwestern AR, mentions these brothers and their missionary work. These United Baptists were no strangers to the Separatist or Free Will history in Kentucky, but were a part of it.

C.B. Whitely and others left Middle Tennessee about 1835, along with the Isaac Boren, and Joel Plumley, for a a new beginning in Arkansas after a break with the Primitive Baptists over foreordination and free salvation issues. He along with the Plumley family and others organized a United church in the Plumley home in July 1838. Other churches were soon organized and the Union Association of United Baptist was formerly organized. (This info from old Association Minutes). This Union Ass'n was closely associated with the FreeWill Baptist throughout the ninetenth century. The Ass'n reported to the New England General Conference as early as 1883. (From William F. Davidson's History of FWB, 1727-1984, pub. 1985, Randall House Publications). Rev. Charles B. and wife Sarah, were still in Carroll, at Prairie in 1860, (info below says they removed to Texas in 1861 or

1862)-- and certainly before 1870 he was in Bell Co. TX census. He wrote to his 'beloved daughters' in 1866, from Texas, saying his goodbyes, as he had typhoid fever and it looked to him as though he would not recover. He did get medical treatment, and at the end of the letter, it stated that he thought he would recover. And he did.

Jasper Charles Withers, Sr
Birth:
Jan. 21, 1854
Indiana
Death:
Aug. 24, 1911
Comanche
Comanche County, Texas
Burial:
Oakwood Cemetery
Comanche
Comanche County, Texas

Richard V Whitaker
Birth:
Sep. 12, 1866
Death:
Sep. 16, 1944
Burial:
Mount Olivet Cemetery
Fort Worth
Tarrant County
Texas, USA
Plot: Plaza Garden

Rev Wendell Keith Woody
Birth:
Aug. 26, 1940
Mountain Home, Ark.,
Death:
Jul. 20, 2016
Texas
Burial:
Peaceful Gardens Memorial Park
Woodrow
Lubbock County, Texas
Wendell Keith was born to Arthur and Lyddie Woody. He married Neva Mowery on Dec. 24, 1959, in Levelland, Texas.
Keith Woody served as the pastor of eight different churches over the span of four decades in the ministry. He was a national leader in the Free Will Baptist Denomination. He was a loving husband, father, and grandfather.

There's nothing certain in a man's life except this:

That he must lose it.

Utah

Eugene Zephaniah Whitman
Birth:
Dec. 6, 1850
Woodstock
Oxford County, Maine
Death:
Dec. 4, 1930
Bountiful
Davis County, Utah
Burial:
Bountiful Memorial Park
Bountiful
Davis County, Utah

He was the son of Zephaniah Benson Whitman and Eliza Chase. On October 20, 1873 he was converted. He was a student at Kent's Hill Academy and was licensed as a Methodist April 7, 1875 and held three pastorates enjoying one revival in which 25 were baptized. On December 29, 1883, he was licensed by the Free Baptists and was ordained at the Waterville and Sydney churches, March 27, 1884. He entered of 1889 in the Cobb Divinity School at the same time serving the church at West Bowdoin. In 1888, he took the pastoral care of the Sabattus where a revival of 38 were added to the church.

Vermont

Mason Hezekiah Abbey
Birth:
Aug. 9, 1821 Westminster,
Windham County, Vermont
Death:
Jan. 8, 1895
Newport,
Orleans County, Vermont
Burial:
Sutton Village Cemetery,
Sutton,
Caledonia County, Vermont

He was educated at Clinton Seminary and entered the Free Baptist, holding pastorates at Harrisburg, Attica, Varysburgh, Warsaw, Philadelphia and Lowville, N. Y. In 1864 he served three months as missionary among the freedmen around Norfolk, Va. He was for fifteen years in evangelistic work. In 1884, he became pastor at Allegheny, Pa., where he remained for ten years, going from there to West Charleston, Vt.

"I See Heaven Open And Jesus On The Right Hand Of God."

Fernald Spokesfield Avery
Birth:
1835
Death:
Oct. 13, 1866
Corinth Corners
Orange County
Vermont
Burial:
Meadow Meeting House
Cemetery
Corinth Center
Orange County
Vermont

Parents: Elias Jones Avery (1809 - 1895) and Mary Sargent Woodman Avery (1805 - 1885). Children: Luthera Martin Avery (1835 - 1872)*

Shubel Boston
Birth:
1790
Death:
Dec. 23, 1841
Burial:
South Wheelock Cemetery
Wheelock
Caledonia County, Vermont

In 1826 he was ordained and became an itinerant preacher of the Parsonsfield Quarterly Meeting, Maine. In 1833 he moved to Wheelock Quarterly Meeting, in Vermont where he had a long and useful ministry until his death. He was pastor at St. Johnsbury from 1835 to 1839 and afterwards resided at Sheffied.

Joseph Bruce
Birth:
December 31, 1821
Springfield, Vermont
Death:
Dec. 16, 1860
Vermont
Burial:
Lower Branch Cemetery
Braintree
Orange County, Vermont

He was the grandson of a Calvinistic Baptist preacher. He moved with his father in 1822 to Schoon, Essex County, New York. He felt God was calling him as early as eight years of age but yielded finally in 1838 uniting with the Methodists. He was licensed in that body the year of his conversion, and he saw 15 converted in Chester and 30 in Horicon. His license was renewed in 1840 and, till 1858, he continued to preach in different circuits in Vermont but became dissatisfied with this form of church and government, and their policy on the question of slavery. He joined the Free Baptists in 1857 and in June 1858 was ordained. During 1858 he preached over 300 sermons going from place to place on foot. About this time he moved to Boldon. In the spring of 1859 he served the church at South Bolton and organized a church at Trout Lake. In the fall of that year his labors at Ford Ann were blessed with a revival. He continued to preach with a failing health till October 14 in 1860 when he preached his last sermon in Middlesex, Vermont. He died in his 40th year after having a ministry of Twenty-two years.

Rev Abel Bugbee
Birth:
1777
Burke
Caledonia County
Vermont
Death:
Jul. 24, 1861
Burial:
Burke Meeting House Cemetery
Burke Hollow
Caledonia County
Vermont

An ordained Freewill Baptist minister/pastor, b. 1777, in New England.

Inscription:
age 84 son of Ebenezer

Bugbee, Rev. Abel, died in Burke, Vt., July 24, 1861, aged eighty-four years. He was born in 1777, and converted at the age of fifteen. He commenced a settlement in Burke in 1802. He began to preach about 1811, and in 1818 was ordained. He led an itinerant ministry for thirty years, visiting the neighboring towns. During the last eighteen years of his life, he attended on the ministry of others, preaching but little himself. The doctrine which he had believed and preached, sustained him richly in death.

John F. Buzzell
Birth:
1836
Northfield, Vermont
Death:
1900
Burial:
Waitsfield Village Cemetery
Waitsfield
Washington County, Vermont

His father was Eli Buzzell and his mother was the daughter of Elder Aaron Buzzell. He became a Christian in 1859 and on January 1 of that year he was married to Martha meal. They had 10 children altogether. He was ordained by the Huntington Quarterly Meeting the limits of which he labored during his ministry. He was the superintendent of schools for 12 years.

Elder Daniel Chappel
Birth:
Jun. 12, 1757
New London
New London County
Connecticut
Death:
May 10, 1837
Sutton
Caledonia County
Vermont
Burial:
Sutton Village Cemetery
Sutton
Caledonia County
Vermont

He was ordained in 180_, and labored in the Freewill Baptist church.

Benjamin Chatterton
Birth:
1781
Acworth,
Sullivan County, New Hampshire
Death:
Jun. 11, 1855,
Middlesex,
Washington County, Vermont
Burial:
Chatterton Cemetery,
Middlesex,
Washington County, Vermont

Elder Benjamin Chatterton was a founder of the Freewill Baptist Church in Middlesex, Vt, now the Shady Rill Baptist Church. The cemetery is a small private cemetery up on McCullough Road, known as East Hill Road in the 19th century. Ben was active on the local school board and town committee's during his life in Middlesex. A biography on him can be found in *Hemenway's Gazetteer* of Washington County.

Rev Eli Clark
Birth:
Jan. 8, 1808
Strafford
Orange County
Vermont
Death:
Feb. 1, 1893
Burial:
Evergreen Cemetery
South Strafford
Orange County
Vermont

"Rev. Eli Clark, was the son of Jeremiah and Polly (Joy) Clark.
He married March 14, 1837 to Sophronia Tyler, and Dec. 12, 1843, to Mary Hackett, and has four children, one of whom is Rev. L.G. Clark.
He was licensed by the church in August 1829, and ordained Jan. 23, 1836, at Turnbridge. For three years was pastor of the Stowe and Waterbury church; for the next three years he accepted the appointment to travel in the Huntington Q.M. He then settled at Strafford where he lived.
In 1875 he was chosen to represent his town for two years in the Vermont Legislature.
He has married nearly three hundred couples, and attended over six hundred funerals."

Rev Lucian G Clark
Birth:
Jan., 1841
Thetford
Orange County
Vermont
Death:
Aug. 9, 1918
Burial:
Evergreen Cemetery
South Strafford
Orange County
Vermont

He was the son of Rev. Eli and Sophronia (Tyler) Clark.
He attended Green Mountain Seminary, but unable to hear instruction but in one ear due to hearing loss suffered in the War, he was advised to leave school, and enter upon the work.
He was licensed in 1874, and ordained in 1876. He was a member of the General Conference of Freewill Baptist in 1880.
He married Eunice G. Wells in 1865, who died in 1873. In 1875 he married Miss Sarah Swift. He had one child, born in 1867.

J. B. Collins
Birth:
1821
Death:
Mar. 21, 1883
Underhill
Chittenden County
Vermont
Burial:
Underhill Flats Cemetery
Underhill
Chittenden County, Vermont

Ordained Freewill Baptist minister in the 1800's. Died at age 62. Son of Samuel and Jane Collins. He was converted when eighteen years of age, and united with the church in Morristown, commencing to preaching about four years later. After a season at Clinton, NY, he settled in Franklin in 1845, and was ordained in 1847. He preached afterward in Morristown, also at Keeneville, Philadelphia, Depauville and Dickinson Centre, in St. Lawrence Yearly Meeting, which he represented in the General Conference of 1877, and in 1880 returned to Vermont, taking charge of the Underhill and Cambridge churches until failing health compelled him to rest.

Rev Rufus W Collins
Birth:
Sep. 4, 1832
Plainfield
Sullivan County
New Hampshire
Death:
Jan., 1934
Massachusetts, USA
Burial:
Riverbank Cemetery
Stowe
Lamoille County
Vermont

Rev. Refus W. Collins, son of Asa and Sally (Brown) Collins, was converted in November 1868, and licensed in October 1870. In March 1875, he was ordained by a council from the Enosbury Q.M. the sermon was preached by Rev. J.W. Burgin.

Rev. Collins has been pastor three years at Franklin and Enosburg Falls, VT; three years at Bolton, P.Q. where in 1878, a meeting house was built; one year in Hartley; five years in Est Albany, VT, where in 1883, a meeting house was built. Seventy-nine have been baptized.
December 20, 1855, he married Rhoda Douglas. Made it to 101 years, and used it wisely.

Joshua Coffrin
Birth:
Feb. 20, 1816
Waterbury, Vermont
Death:
Oct. 28, 1891
Burial:
Hope Cemetery
Waterbury
Washington County, Vermont

He was converted on January 1837 and was licensed to preach on November 18, 1843. He was ordained in Morristown by the Huntington Quarterly Meeting. He became pastor of the Franklin church where he was for 25 years and preached at other notable churches in the area for years. He was known for his many revivals and had baptized over 200 during a series of time he organized two churches.

David Cross
Birth:
1786
Wilmot, N.H,
Death:
Jun. 22, 1870
Newark,Vt.

Burial:
Sutton Village Cemetery
Sutton, Caledonia County,
Vermont

Cross died age 84 years and 6 months. He was occupied with farming until he settled in life for himself. After his marriage and when about thirty years of age he was converted and soon began the work of the ministry. Many were converted under his preaching, several who became earnest ministers. After preaching about ten years in several places in New Hampshire with good success, he settled at Sutton, Vt., where he lived and preached more or less for forty years. He always owned a farm from which he largely obtained his support.

Amos Davis
Birth:
Sep. 26, 179
Bakersfield
Franklin County, Vermont
Death:
1841
Bakersfield, Vermont
Burial:
Maple Grove Cemetery
Bakersfield
Franklin County, Vermont

He experienced religion early in life among the Methodists and united with the Free Will Baptist Church in Fairfield in the earliest history of the Enosburg Q.M. He was ordained at South Fairfield and rendered effectual service in building up the quarterly meeting.

Frank E Davison
Birth:
1853
Death:
1932
Burial:
South Hero Cemetery
South Hero
Grand Isle County, Vermont

Minister/pastor in several states for the Free Baptist; then later with the Congregational Church.

Lewis Dexter
Birth:
1824
West Topsham
Orange County, Vermont
Death:
1921
Burial:
West Topsham Cemetery
West Topsham
Orange County, Vermont,

Rev. Lewis Dexter was the son of Parker and Betsey (King) Dexter, of Topsham, VT. His parents were members of the West Topsham church. He became a Christian at ten. July, 1864, he enlisted in Co. H., Ninth Regiment, Vermont Volunteers, and served in the army till the war closed. He graduated at New Hampton Institution (NH) in 1869, and from Bates Theological School (Lewiston, ME) in 1872. In July he was ordained by Prof. J. Fullonton and others, and settled at Sabattusville, where he had already preached a year. He was licensed by the Corinth, Vermont quarterly meeting, in 1870. Soon after his ordination, Oct 17, he married Miss Clara Evans. During his three years at Sabattusville he baptized thirty and received forty-five into the church. From Oct. 1, 1874-June 1, 1878, he was pastor at Georgiaville, R.I., and added fifty-seven to the church. He was then called to the Greenwich Street church, Providence, where he lifted an oppressive church debt of over $8,000.

He baptized eleven and received twenty-one into the church during two years. From Sept. 1, 1880, to March 1, 1887, he was pastor of the church at Blackstone, Massachusetts where he baptized twenty-nine and added fifty to the church. The vestry of the church was remodeled. March 1, 1887, he accepted a call to the Doughty Falls church, North Berwick, Maine. He has succeeded in developing a deep interest in Sunday-school, missionary and temperance work. The Sunday-school normal instruction he introduced at Ocean Park (ME). He was clerk of the Ministers' Conference of the Rhode Island Association ten years. At the General Conference in 1880 he was delegate from Rhode Island."

If You Spend All Your Time Worrying About Dying, Living Isn't Going To Be Much Fun.

Rev Robert Dickey
Birth:
Jun. 26, 1778
Francestown
Hillsborough County
New Hampshire
Death:
Nov. 4, 1864
East Corinth
Orange County
Vermont
Burial:
East Corinth Cemetery (Old)
East Corinth
Orange County
Vermont

Was an early Free Bapt. minister in VT, helping to establish the first church of its kind in VT. Randall & Buzzell visited the church several times. He had a useful ministry, being ordained in 1814, but at last joined the Shakers.

Orange Dyke
Birth:
Jul. 8, 1799
Huntington, Chittenden
County, Vermont
Death:
Aug. 19, 1875
Westford
Chittenden County, Vermont
Burial:
Maplewood Cemetery
Huntington
Chittenden County, Vermont

Rev. Orange Dike, was born on 8 Jul 1799, and Huntington, Chittendon, Vt. To Jonathan Dike (II) (1751-1826) and Abigail Brown Dike (1757-1840), he married first on 19 Mar 1818 to Lois Mix and second he married on 23 Jun 1841 to Lois Randall Pine. Excerpts from *History of Chittenden County, Vermont With Illustrations and Biographical Sketches of Some of Its Prominent Men and Pioneers."* The first house built expressly for purposes of worship was erected at the north village in 1836 by the Methodists and Freewill Baptists. Another smaller house was built at the south village in 1841, and was owned chiefly by Calvinistic Baptists. Nearly all the denominations have at one time or another sustained services in Huntington, though the only regular organization now acting in town is the Freewill Baptist. The first preacher of this persuasion in town was Elder Charles Bowles, colored, who came here in the summer of 1817, and at various times has been succeeded by the following preachers: Benajah Maynard, Josiah Wetherbee, Orange Dike. The first post-office opened in town was established near the commencement of the century, at the house of Jabez FARGO, who was postmaster. As it did not quite pay expenses it was soon discontinued, and no other took its place until 1828, when Amos DIKE received the appointment and opened an office at the south village. In 1829, on application to the general department, it was transferred to the north village and Alexander Ferguson was appointed. Since then the postmasters at the north village (Huntington), have been as follows: 1829 to 1841 inclusive, Alexander Ferguson; 1842, Cyrus Johns; [April 2 1842-] 1843 To 1845, Orange Dike; 1846-47, ..."_The Freewill Baptist Quarterly._ Volume VI._ Dover: Freewill Baptisti Printing Establishment. Wm. Burr, Pinter, MDCCCLVIII, Page 83.

Rev Nelson Harvey Farr
Birth:
Jan. 10, 1834
Enosburg, VT
Death:
Feb. 15, 1913 Burial:
East Randolph Cemetery
East Randolph
Orange County
Vermont

Licensed 1862, and Ordained Nov. 23, 1863, by Rev's A.H. Chase and J.S. Manning; preached in PA, OH, Mich, RI, and in 1888 became pastor of Turnbridge, VT. He mar. Matilda Patterson, Apr. 30, 1862, and they have 2 daughters. Father: Samuel Bennett Farr & Mother: Wealthy Clarinda (Hazelton) Farr. Enlisted and mustered in on April 24, 1861 to Co. C, 9th IN Inf. Mustered out July 29, 1861 at Indianapolis, IN

Edward Fay
Birth:
May 6, 1783
Buckland, Franklin County,
Massachusetts
Death:
Feb. 7, 1860
Jericho,
Chittenden County, Vermont
Burial:
Jericho Center Cemetery,
Jericho,
Chittenden County, Vermont

He began preaching about forty years of age (abt 1823) and was ordaind in 1826, by the Free Will Baptist church. He was pastor of the church in Underhill, VT for thirteen years; then he returned to his former charge and retained it until his death. He preached much to the destitute churches of the Enosburg Quarterly Meeting.

John Forrest
Birth:
Apr. 18, 1831
Sutton, Vermont
Death:
Jan. 20, 1912
Burial:
South Barton-Willoughby
Cemetery
Barton
Orleans County,Vermont

He was converted to the age of 12, in 1843, and licensed by the Methodists as a local preacher in 1880. He united with the Free Baptists in 1884, and was ordained by them May 13 following at South Barton. The church was built up under his faithful labors.

Rev Ezra Butler Fuller
Birth:
Jul. 27, 1822
Stowe
Lamoille County
Vermont
Death:
Apr. 30, 1899
Brattleboro
Windham County
Vermont
Burial:
Waterbury Center Cemetery (Old)
Waterbury Center
Washington County
Vermont

Fuller, Rev. Ezra B., son of Joseph and Polly (Town) Fuller, was converted in 1837, licensed in 1843, and ordained in 1846 by the Huntington Q. M., in which, except six years, his ministry has been spent. He was pastor at Stowe. He organized a church at Middlesex, and was its pastor. He became pastor at Warren and Waterbury. He lost his health in overwork as financial agent for the Green Mountain Seminary at its erection. Before this, he had been called to preach a dedication sermon at the consecration of a church at Dickinson Centre, N. Y. In the revival which followed he baptized fifty souls. He settled with this church for six years, and about as many more were baptized. with health regained, he returned to Vermont and labored in revivals at Ellensburg, Burke, Fort Jackson, and Parishville. He was for ten years settled at Huntington, and had a branch interest at Jonesville, which he formally organized. In 1887 he became pastor at Waterbury Centre. He was delegate to General Conference in October, 1859, and in August, 1880. He represented Waterbury in the State Legislature in 1867-68. For five years he has been superintendent of schools in Huntington. In 1844 he married Mahala D. Carlton, of Brookfield, who died in 1849. In 1852 he married Lucy A. Minott, of Middlesex.

John Garfield
Birth:
April 15, 1801
Barre, Vt.
Death:
Jan. 8, 1878
West Wheelock, Vt.
Burial:
West Wheelock Cemetery
Wheelock, Caledonia County,
Vermont

When quite young, his parents moved to Glover. When about seventeen he was converted under the labors of Elder Fisk and joined the M. E. church. His unwillingness to preach caused him to backslide. He was awakened about six years afterward, and preached with the Methodists about twenty years. In Stannard, in 1841, his labors resulted in a great revival. September 11, a Free Baptist church was organized and he was ordained as pastor. He held the office fourteen years. The last seven years his health was poor. When unable to speak aloud, he would whisper words of comfort to the little band that gathered in his home for prayer and conference.

Rev Orange Green
Birth:
Sep., 1804
Death
May 27, 1839
Danby
Rutland County
Vermont
Burial:
Scottsville Cemetery
Danby
Rutland County
Vermont

An ordained Freewill Bapt. minister who died too young. He was baptized on June 28, 1835 and ordained in June 1836, after which he began to hold religious services in the vicinity of his home.

Inscription:
REV. ORANGE GREEN
DIED
May 27, 1839,
AE. 34 Yrs. 8 Mo.

Rev George Hackett
Birth: 1781
Death: Aug. 17, 1846
Tunbridge
Orange County
Vermont
Burial:
East Hill Cemetery
Brookfield
Orange County
Vermont

A faithful and committeed minister/pastor of the Freewill Bapt. church. His parents were Daniel and Hanna (Colby) HACKETT. He was married to Sally Adams, of Turnbridge. At twenty years of age he experience religion and united with the Turnbridge Free Will Baptist Church, of which he remained a worthy member until his death. In 1816 he was ordained. He labored mostly in the vicinity of his home, becoming the pastor after the organizer, Rev. Nathaniel King, left.

In 1819, in company with Rev's Nathaniel King and Ziba Woodworth, he crossed the Green Mountains and organized the Huntington Quarterly Meeting. In October, 1828, he entertained at Turnbridge the first session of the General Conference. He bore his long illness with fortitude and in confidence entered into rest.

From History of Turnbridge, VT

:"...When Daniel HACKETT came to Tunbridge he settled on East hill, on what is now called the old HACKETT farm. The soil was productive, and, being an energetic, hard-working man, he was quite successful. In a short time others had taken up and improved land in this part of the town, and, feeling the need of Christian worship, a church was erected called the "red meeting-house." A society was organized by Elder RANDALL, called the "Freewill Baptist Church," and the meetings were attended by all the settlers and great interest manifested. Eld. Nathaniel KING was the first settled minister, and he served without pay. After Elder KING removed from town Rev. George HACKETT, son of Daniel, became the settled minister, and remained in charge most of the time until his death, working on his farm during the week and preaching the gospel on the Sabbath "without money and without price." He was quite successful financially, and reared a large family of children who became scattered throughout the country.

Elder William Herrick
Birth:
Mar. 6, 1810
Vermont
Death:
May 19, 1838
Vermont
Burial:
South Woodbury Cemetery
Woodbury
Washington County
Vermont

William was ordained July 4, 1836, and died at his father's residence aged 28 yrs. He was fitted as a teacher, but consumption prevented his prosecuting the vocation as well as that of preaching, though he preached some in Vermont, New Hampshire and Maine. He was agent for a short time for Parsonsfield Seminary, Maine. He died age 28 yrs.

Peleg Hicks, Sr
Birth:
1738
Rehoboth
Bristol County,
Massachusetts
Death:
1826
Burke Hollow
Caledonia County, Vermont

Burial:
Burke Green Cemetery
Burke
Caledonia County, Vermont

He was a Baptist minister with two churches that united with the Wheellock, Vermont, and Quarterly Meeting on August 29, 1802. He was ordained about 179-.

Mark Hill
Birth:
May 22, 1796
Buxton, Me.
Death:
Nov. 3, 1866
Sutton, Vt.
Burial:
Sutton Village Cemetery
Sutton, Caledonia County, Vermont

Son of Nathaniel and Martha Crockett Hill was the youngest of thirteen children, all of whom he survived. Converted in the fall of 1817 he was baptized by Rev. Clement Phinney, and feeling called to the ministry he spent two years in preparatory studies at an academy. In 1820 and 1821 he was principally engaged in teaching. The next year he went to Rhode Island to confer concerning his call to the ministry with Rev. J. White, and soon found his place on the walls of Zion. He preached in Maine, and emigrated to Vermont.In 1825 he bought a farm in Lyndon of Rev. Joseph Quinby, on which he worked, teaching winters and preaching with Quinby and others. In 1827 he married Arvilla Ruggles, of Lyndon, and the same year united with the church there, being chosen its clerk. At the time of his marriage, of the three hundred dollars he possessed two hundred dollars had been loaned to the Free Baptist. Printing Establishment in Limerick. In 1833 he moved to a farm in

Sutton. In 1834 he was ordained in Lyndon. He preached chiefly in Sutton, Sheffield, Wheelock, Lyndon, and South Bartol, and saw many conversions. For twenty-five years he was clerk of the Wheelock O. M. He acquired a competence, and gave liberally for education and missions, generously remembering them in his will. His last public utterances were at an anti-slavery meeting.

Paul Holbrook
Birth:
Unknown
Death:
Dec. 3, 1821
Burial:
Tinkham Cemetery
East Montpelier
Washington County, Vermont
He was ordained in 1805 and died after a ministry of only about 20 years in Vermont.

Elder Calvin Huntley
Birth:
Aug. 11, 1780
Marlow
Cheshire County
New Hampshire
Death:
Aug. 13, 1856
Duxbury
Washington CountyVermont
Burial:
Duxbury Corner Cemetery
Duxbury
Washington County
Vermont

Rev. Calvin HUNTLEY, son of Isaiah, was married Elizabeth MILLER, November 4, 1804, and removed to Duxbury [VT] soon after, settling first on Ward's hill, and subsequently on the farm now owned by Martin L. HENRY. He was a Freewill Baptist preacher, and, as near as can be ascertained, the first settled minister in Duxbury. Elder HUNTLEY possessed rare and

excellent qualities of "head and heart," and left a fragrant memory.

Isaac Hyatt
Birth:
February 22, 1837
Quebec, Canada
Death:
1910
Vermont
Burial:
Riverside Cemetery
Swanton
Franklin County, Vermont

His father died when he was five years of age leaving the mother with two children. He went to live with Jacob Hyatt, his grandfather, and had an early had a thirst for knowledge. He graduated from the Biblical School at New Hampton in 1862. He was pastor in Tunbridge, Vermont and Rochester, New Hampshire where a church was organized and a house of worship built. After which he pastored in Pawtucket, Rhode Island where 37 additions were made. Then he returned back to Vermont subsequently pastoring in the Rhode Island, Maine, and New York.

Daniel W. Jackson
Birth:
Mar. 25, 1839
Starksboro,
Addison County, Vermont
Death:
Jan. 27, 1860
Burial:
Starksboro Village Cemetery,

Starksboro,
Addison County, Vermont

In 1855 he was converted, and a few months later was baptized. In 1856, feeling a call to preach, he consulted with Rev. Mark Atwood, and passed the winter in southern Starksborough, preaching and teaching school. In Sept. 1857, he was licensed by the Huntington Q.M. He spent the year in over a dozen places in Vermont and Canada, and had revivals in Huntington Gore, VT, and in Farnham, P.Q. In March, 1858, he went to the Biblical School in New Hampton, N.H., preaching in the vicinity. In the fall he visited Putnam, NY and returning to Vermont in January, he began traveling as an evangelist in the Huntington Q.M. He was ordained Feb. 13, 1859, by the Q.M. at West Berlin. In May, his health improving, he returned to the New Hampton Biblical School.

Joseph W Jackson
Birth:
1839
Richland
Kalamazoo County, Michigan
Death:
Sep. 13, 1865
Hinesburg
Chittenden County, Vermont
Burial:
Rhode Island Corners Cemetery
Hinesburg,
Chittenden County,
Vermont

He was born in Richland, Kalamazoo County, Mich., and moved with his father to Starksborough, Vt., at the age of ten. Brought up in a Christian home, he found Christ at seventeen and soon joined the church. He began, after hesitation, his ministry in 1861. At the September session of the Huntington Q. M. he was licensed, and in the spring of 1862 he settled with the Middlesex church. The coming summer he preached half of the time in Lincoln, where a church was organized and a house of worship built. The following December he was ordained as pastor of this church. In April, 1863, he gave half of his time to the Starksborough church, and continued pastor of both churches till his death.

Thomas M. Jackson
Birth:
April 24, 1801
Eaton, N. H
Death:
Sep. 27, 1828
Burial:
Sutton Village Cemetery
Sutton
Caledonia County
Vermont

At the age of eight he became deeply interested in the story of Jesus while reading the 'New Testament through at the wish of an aunt. When ten John Colby preached in Eaton and a deep impression was made upon his young heart.
He was converted Dec. 13, 1818, and was baptized on the 30th by Elder JonathanWoodman, uniting with the church at Eaton. He continued to teach and to study till October, 1822, when he went forth to an itinerant ministry, visiting Whitefield, Lisbon, Bethlehem and Laudaff, and seeing souls converted.

He continued to preach in New Hampshire and Vermont till he was ordained at Sutton, Vt., Oct. 31, 1824. He was in his twenty-fourth year, and he traveled incessantly with success.
Dec. 20, 1825, he married Matilda Perkins in Cabot, Vt. He was settled for brief periods at Sandwich Centre, N. H., and Sheffield. Vt. In Danville he organized a church. He began to sink with consumption.
He visited Daniel, his brother, at Ossipee, N. H.; together they went to Eaton. They preached and worshiped together, and finally Thomas went home to die. At the Q.M. at Sutton he preached his last sermon in August.
Sermons were preached to his memory at the General Conference held in Sandwich, Vt., in the following October.
He was sweet spirited and greatly beloved. His brother, Rev. Daniel Jackson, had a useful ministry; another brother, Rev. William C. Jackson, graduated from Dartmouth College in 1831, and became a Congregational missionary under the American Board, to Turkey.

Alanson Kilburn
Birth:
1786
Litchfield, Connecticut
Death:
Oct. 28, 1855
Vermont
Burial:
Enosburgh Center Cemetery
Enosburg Center
Franklin County, Vermont

When he was two years of age, his father in family moved to Castleton, Vermont. At 18 he went to New Haven, Vermont where he remained about three years. During this period he was converted and joined the Methodist Church where he became a class leader. After which, he moved to Dunham, Quebec, where he united with the Wesley Methodist and continued as class leader and received a license to exhort. He labored there are under the direction of English missionaries until 1825, when he joined the Free Baptist Church in farnham, Quebec. On April 9, 1826, he was ordained by a Council of the Enosburg Quarterly Meeting. Here he labored for five more years until his death came from Palsy which greatly impaired his speech.

George King
Birth:
Dec. 16, 1815
Orange County, Vermont
Death:
Nov. 1, 1872
Sutton
Caledonia County, Vermont
Burial:
Sutton Village Cemetery
Sutton,Caledonia County,
Vermont

When about twelve years of age, he was converted and united with the church in Topsham, Vt. He was licensed in 1850, and ordained at Goshen Gore, Oct. I, 1856, at the age of forty. He preached as an evangelist in Eden, Craftsbury, Albany and many other towns. In some places he witnessed many conversions. His last pastorate was at South Wheelock. He purchased a farm in Sutton, on which he lived the remainder of his life. He still preached occasionally in destitute places. He saw all of his large family of children converted before his death, and gave liberally for the support of the benevolent causes of the denomination.he He was the son of George and Mehitable Noyes King. He married 1st Diana Darling on Oct.13,1811 in Corinth,Vt.and 2nd Rebekah Burbank on Sep.29,1845 in Washington,Vt.

Nathaniel King
Birth:
Apr. 4, 1767
Hampstead,
Rockingham County,
New Hampshire
Death:
Oct. 18, 1852
Northfield,
Washington County, Vermont
Burial:
Mount Hope Cemetery,
Northfield,
Washington County, Vermont

As a early Father of the Denomination, history states he moved with his father at the age of eight to Sutton, NH, where he resided till he was twenty-one. He then visited Turnbridge, VT and purchased a tract of land which he soon began to improve. In 1794, he married Miss Lydia Noyes, and for fifty-eight years. Early in 1799, Daniel Batchelder and Nathaniel Brown held meetings in Turnbridge, and in the revival which followed Nathaniel King was converted March 31, 1799. A church was soon after organized. At Bro. King's house the persecuted Free Baptist preachers found a refuge and home. He himself soon began to conduct meetings. July 1, 1804, he was ordained in the Turnbridge church by Rev's. John and Aaron Buzzell, and Pelatiah Tingley. He was active in meetings and revivals and saw many people added. His labors were not confined to his own parish. For forty-two years he served the Turnbridge church, for seven, the Randolph church and for fourteen the Northfield. He held offices of trust and confidence. For thirteen years he

represented Turnbridge in the Legislature of the state. In 1811 he visited, in company with Rev. John Buzzell, churches in central Vermont. The same year he added thirty-two to his church. That year his Y.M., appointed him to collect funds for the poor. In 1819, he with two others crossed the Green Mountains, and organized the Huntington Q.M. In 1821, he was elected president of the Vermont Charitable Society at its organization. Benevolence was a leading trait of his character. He gave $100 for endowment of Biblical School at Whitestown, NY; $150 for the Bible cause; $350 for Missions and other benevolent purposes. He was interested in the anti-slavery movement. He was moderator of the second General Conference. Near the end of his life he repeatedly assured his friends that the doctrine he had preached for more than half a century sustained him in the time of trial.

Samuel Lord
Birth:
1780
Barnstead, New Hampshire
Death:
Dec. 27, 1849
Waterbury, Vermont
Burial:
Waterbury Center Cemetery
Old Waterbury Center
Washington County, Vermont

He accepts religion when but 10 years of age and entered the ministry in his 19th year. He was ordained in Maine in 1801 and the same year moved to Vermont and was among the earliest founders of the denomination in that state. He was active in organizing many churches and in the saving of souls.

John Moxley
Birth:
Unknown
Death:
Sep. 7, 1884, USA
Burial:
Hutchinson Cemetery
East Orange
Orange County, Vermont

As a young man he felt call to the ministry but did not accept that call. He served his town as Selectman, Justice Of The Peace, and a representative to the legislature. At the age of 55 years great sorrowed over the death of his two children led him to consecrate himself to the ministry. He was ordained at the session of the Strafford Quarterly Meeting on June 24, 1871. He later served many churches in that region. He also worked successfully with the Y.M.C.A. He was also clerk of the Stafford Quarterly Meeting for 15 years and was a delegate from Vermont yearly meeting to the Gen. Conference in Fairport, New York.

Jonathan Nelson
Birth:
1777
Barnstead, New Hampshire
Death:
Nov. 26, 1843
Burial:
Old Wheelock Village Cemetery
Wheelock
Caledonia County, Vermont

At the age of twenty-five married there Miss Betsey Collins. He did much hard work on a farm and reared a family of nine children, yet he found time to do public service for the Lord's people. Converted at the age of twenty-eight, he was baptized and joined the Methodists, by whom he was licensed to preach. He settled in Wheelock, Vermont, and was ordained by the Freewill Baptist Wheelock Quarterly Meeting in 1819. He served for years the churches of that section. In the great revival of 1823 he baptized sixty or seventy. In 1841, he went into Lower Canada, where he was stricken with fever, and lived long enough to send for his wife and two sons.He died in his 67th year, and was carried to Wheelock for funeral services and burial. He possessed sound judgment, was well versed in the Scriptures, and was hospitable and benevolent.

Live every day so as not to be afraid of tomorrow

J. M. Nelson
Birth:
Feb. 20, 1822
Hardwick,
Vermont
Death:
Jul. 29, 1895

He was a student at Peachham Academy. Converted in 1854, he received his license by the Wheelock quarterly Meeting two years later and in 1861 was ordained by the Enosburgh Quarterly Meeting. His ministry was basically within Vermont.

David Norris
Birth:
Unknown
North Danville, Vermont
Death:
Nov. 21, 1839
Burial:
Stanton Cemetery
North Danville
Caledonia County, Vermont

He was aged 71 at his death and for 47 years had been a Christian and Free Will Baptist Minister.

Inscription:
age 71 yrs
He was the son of Samuel Norris
1734-1816 and Huldah Bartlett

John Calvin Osgood
Birth:
Feb. 14, 1841
East Randolph
Orange County, Vermont
Death:
Jul. 14, 1907
Burial:
East Randolph Cemetery
East Randolph
Orange County, Vermont

He was the son of Dea. William and Almira (Dibbell) Osgood.He served in the military from Vermont in the Civil War.He married Miss Mary G. Flanders, July 15, 1868, and had one son living, Ernest Erle Osgood, who became a clergyman, and is buried in Virginia.He was an ordained Freewill Baptist clergyman. He became a Christian when about nineteen years of age. He received his preparatory education at New Hampton Institution, and graduated from the Theological School in 1868. He was licensed by the Strafford Quarterly Meeting, while a student, and was ordained at Gilmanton Iron Works, N.H., in the fall of 1868, by Rev's E.P. Ladd, A.D. Smith, J.M. Durgin, and others. He was pastor at Gilmanton Iron Works, Natick, Mass, Contoocook and Pittsfield, N.H., South Strafford, VT, Springvale, ME, and in 1887 pastor of the church at South Berwick, ME. He has had success and conversions in his pastorates, and has baptized about sixty converts.

Benjamin Page
Birth:
Jun. 9, 1780
Death:
Nov. 9, 1869
Burial:
Pleasant View Cemetery
Ludlow
Windsor County,
Vermont

He was ordained in 1803 in Vermont. For some years he worked with the Hardwick Quarterly Meeting and his ministry prospered. Becoming alienated from his brethren, he confessed that for three years did not feel right, nor added a single member to his church. From general loving treatment he felt better.

He joined the Christian order later, but at the January quarterly meeting in 1823 he returned making a confession for an satisfactory. Then preached to a deeply interested people a sermon that was full of power.

Charles Sumner Perkins
Birth:
October 25, 1836
Walden
Caledonia County, Vermont
Death:
Aug. 3, 1909
Walden
Caledonia County, Vermont
Burial:
South Walden Cemetery
South Walden
Caledonia County, Vermont

He prepared for college at the Lewiston Falls Academy, in Auburn; graduating from Bowdoin college in 1860 and from Bangor Theological Seminary in 1864. He became a Christian in 1857 was licensed by the Bowdoin Quarterly Meeting in 1863 and ordained by a Council of the same body on October 6, 1864. After his graduation from the theological Seminary he supplied the Free Baptist Church in New York City for one year, then in 1865-66 he supplied the Roger Williams church, Providence, Rhode Island in the absence of Dr. George Day. During the year his labors were rewarded with nearly 100 conversion. Afterwards, he became pastor of the Park Street church, Providence for six years the church and led it to reorganize, its location change from N. Main St. and the present location on Park Street. After pastoring in Rhode Island, he spent time in Portland Maine and then Boston, Massachusetts. He then became pastor of eight church in Lyndon Ctr., Vermont where he baptized over 200 people. He held numerous denominational positions. He was the record and corresponding secretary of the Foreign Mission Society, member of the foreign mission and home mission boards, on the executive committee of these and the education society, overseer of Bates College and member of four Gen. Conferences. He married on November 30, 1864 to Mary Murray of Brunswick, Maine.

You Are Home At Last!

Daniel Quimby
Birth:
Dec. 26, 1773
Weare,Hillsborough County
New Hampshire
Death:
Nov. 29, 1850
Lyndon, Caledonia County
Vermont
Burial:
Lyndon Center Cemetery
Lyndon, Caledonia County
Vermont

A document (deed) of land sold to Daniel Quimby on February 1, 1815 for $440 which was the middle third (110 acres) of the original tract of land bought by Jeremiah Olney, Lot #62, in Lyndon, in the County of Caledonia in the State of Vermont. The location of this piece of property was not in town but north of the village near Burke. According to a researcher from Lyndonville, VT, "an old book in Sutton, VT mentions the ordination of Brother Daniel Quimby as an Evangelist. Joshua Quimby gave the charge on September 16, 1819. Several books mention his name as a pastor, minister, leader in the FWB Randall movement. He was an esteemed man and loved.
Rev. Daniel died in Lyndon 29 November 1850 (says the Free Baptist Cyclopedia, p. 550); "Rev. Jonathan Woodman preached his funeral sermon."

Fernando Randall

Birth:
1831
Death:
Mar. 22, 1880
Bulwer,
Québec,
Canada
Burial:
Lyndon Center Cemetery
Lyndon
Caledonia County,
Vermont

He was converted and baptized while in the Army and for over year he was a chaplain. After being in business for a time. He answered the call to the ministry, and was ordained by a Council at the Wheelock Quarterly Meeting on February 17, 1870 at Newark. He was a member of the Lyndon Vermont church and labored with good success. In June, 1878, he went to Bulwer and built up a strong and thriving church and brought in valuable members. He was greatly beloved.Note: *He was a captain in Co. G 7th Vt. Vol.

Rev John Mooney Russell

Birth:
May 15, 1800
Woodstock
Grafton County
New Hampshire, USA
Death:
May 4, 1874
Concord
Essex County
Vermont
Burial:
Overlook Cemetery
East Concord
Essex County
Vermont

He preached most of the time until his death. He was a man of God and an earnest worker in God's service. The sick and the poor had his sympathy and help.
John Mooney Russell was the son of Joseph & Mary (Robbins) Russell and the husband of Sally Foss. They married in Peeling (Woodstock) New Hampshire on May 21, 1818

Rev Rufus J. Russell

Birth:
Dec. 3, 1835
Franklin County
Vermont
Death:
1920
Burial:
Sanborn Cemetery
East Hardwick
Caledonia County
Vermont

Licensed to preach Sept. 29, 1877, and ordained June 23, 1881. He entered upon his first pastorate at South Wheelock, where in five years a house of worship built. He married March 30, 1859, Miss Lettie E. Brill. Rufus is the son of Mitchell Russell & Cynthia Orcutt. He studied in the common schools and was licensed to preach Sept. 29, 1877, and ordained June 23, 1881. He entered upon his first pastorate at South Wheelock, VT, where in five years the church was quickened and a house of worship built.

Ophir Shipman

Birth:
Jan. 25, 1801
Washington
Orange County, Vermont
Death:
Oct. 10, 1874
West Topsham
Orange County, Vermont
Burial:
West Topsham Cemetery
West Topsham
Orange County, Vermont

Rev. Ophir Shipman, died at age 73 years. He was converted in 1829, was baptized by Rev. Timothy Mores, and united with the church in Northfield. After three years the church called a council which ordained him June 10, 1832. He continued pastor of this church seven years. He has since had pastorates at West Topsham, West Fairlee, Williamstown, and Middlesex. He also labored as an evangelist in different parts of the state. A few years before his death he moved to West Topsham in failing health, and purchased a home.

S. W. Stiles

Birth:
Sept. 26,1827
Danville, Vt
Death:
Aug. 26, 1877
Newport Centre, Vt.
Burial:
Pine Grove Cemetery
Newport, Orleans County,
Vermont

S. W. was a brother of Rev. Horace Stiles, At the age of sixteen he became a Christian and felt called to preach when twenty-one. Ten years later he began his ministry, giving a part of his property for the Master's use, as a thank offering. His first efforts at Hyde Park in December, 1845, resulted in many conversions. The next month he was licensed by the 327isconsi Q. M. He was ordained the following June. He served the churches in Newark, South Barton, Glover Centre and Sheffield. At Newton Centre he toiled hard, and a house of worship was built. He was taken with hemorrhage of the lungs, but kept at work and concealed his suffering still two weeks before his death. He was a sympathetic and faithful pastor.

Joshua Tucker
Birth:
Jun. 20, 1800
Leicester, Worcester County, Massachusetts
Death:
Aug. 7, 1877
Lincoln, Addison County,Vermont
Burial:
Green Mount Cemetery Starksboro, Addison County,Vermont

Tucker died at aged 77 years.He was converted in 1829, baptized by Rev. Stephen Leavitt, and united with the church in Washington, Vt. He soon began to preach, and was ordained in Williamstown in 1835 as pastor of the church there. He held this pastorate most of the time for ten years, during which more than fifty were added to the church. After 1845 he lived and preached most of the time within the limits of the Huntington Q. M. He was pastor at Starksboro' and other places. He was successful as an evangelist and was highly esteemed by all who knew him.

Jonathan Woodman
Birth:
Mar. 27, 1798
Wheelock,
Caledonia County, Vermont
Death:
Jan. 18, 1888
North Tewksbury,
Middlesex County,
Massachusetts
Burial:
Sutton Village Cemetery,
Sutton,
Caledonia County, Vermont

A Noted Free Will Baptist Minister. At age 17, he was in "trials of his mind regarding his duty to preach" when he met Daniel Quimby, who gave him relief, and Jonathan began a lifetime of useful labors. He was soon after licensed by the Sutton Free Will Baptist Church. In summer of 1816, he crossed NH on foot to attend the meeting of the NH Yearly Meeting at Parsonfield, ME. He offered to care for the horses at the meeting, and was admitted for entertainment to the house of Eld. John Buzzell. Multitudes assembled which the meeting house could not hold. Finally Sunday came, Eld. John Buzzell arose, but after a few words he confessed, "Brethren, I have not got the word; if anyone has it, let him stand forth." Immediately the Vermont boy, trembling by the pulpit stairs, and the burden of God upon his soul, arose to his feet and began to deliver his message. Then Eld. Buzzell said, "Hold on lad!" rising in his pulpit. "Brethren, shove some planks out of the window and give the boy a chance." They removed one of the side windows, made him a platform where he could stand and preach to the throng outside as well as the multitude within the house. His text, "the spirit of the Lord is upon me, because He hath anointed me to preach good tidings unto the meek." He poured forth his message; strong men wept, sinners trembled, and confessed, and there was not a day like that in the history of that church. And when in after time, candidates for

baptism were examined, more than a hundred dated their conviction for sin and beginning of a life of consecration from the sermon of that day. Jonathan Woodman was ordained in 1818 at age twenty, as pastor of the Effingham, N.H. church. In 1825, he was one of the nine who perfected plans and bore the financial responsibility for the publication of *"The Morning Star."* He suggested the name for the paper and rode forty miles through the mud to purchase the paper for the first issue. For two years he was one of the proprietors of the Printing Establishment, for seven years a trustee, and for 31 years a corporator. He became the first president of the Anti-Slavery Society in 1843. For two terms he sat in the Vermont Legislature. In 1828 he was chaplain to that body. In 1848, he was chosen by the FWB Gen. Conference to be a delegate along with another minister, to England's General Baptist Conference, and while away kept a diary of his travels, which diary is now in Bates College Edmund Muskie Archives and Special Collections, Lewiston, ME., He was a powerful and acceptable preacher, especially gifted in prayer, mighty in the Scriptures, a man of blameless life, a Christian eminently spiritual and cheerful. The whole denomination looked up to him with reverence.

Rev Ziba Woodworth
Birth:
Apr. 24, 1763
Norwich
New London County
Connecticut
Death:

Nov. 27, 1826
Burial:
Green Mount Cemetery
Montpelier
Washington County
Vermont

Elder Ziba Woodworth was the pastor of the Free Will Baptist Church in Montpelier

Inscription:
Elder Ziba Woodworth
Pastor Of The Free Will Bap
Tist Church In Montpelier
Died Nov. 27, 1826 In
The 64 Year Of His Age

The Saint Is Escorted To Better A Land

Virginia

Hobert Monroe Addington

Birth:
Apr. 11, 1919
Wise,
Wise County,
Virginia
Death:
Oct. 6, 2008
Wise,
Wise County,
Virginia
Burial:
Wise Cemetery,
Wise,
Wise County,
Virginia

Rev. Hobert Monroe Addington lived to the age of 89. He was a member of the Esserville Freewill Baptist Church, a pastor for several Freewill Baptist churches in the area, a member of the UMWA and was an employee of Old Ben Coal Co. for over 33 years.

Howard T Bostic

Birth:
May 31, 1905
Swords Creek,
Russell County, Virginia
Death:
Jul. 4, 1987
Swords Creek,
Russell County,Virginia
Burial:
Bostic Call Cemetery,
Swords Creek
,Russell County, Virginia

Rev James A. Boatright

Birth:
Mar. 30, 1891
Scott County
Virginia
Death:
Dec. 31, 1982
Burial:
Carter Cemetery
Scott County
Virginia

WW I Veteran, and a minister in the Free Will Baptist church.

Robert Franklin Breeden

Birth:
April 8, 1927
Buena Vista Rockbridge County
Virginia
Death:
January 13, 2016
Buena Vista Rockbridge County
Virginia
Burial:
Green Hill Cemetery
Buena Vista City
Virginia

Rev. Robert F. Breeden, 88, passed at home on Wednesday, in the town of his birth, Buena Vista, Virginia. Known to many as "Bob" and "Pastor Breeden", he was a retired ordained minister. He was a veteran of World War II and the Korean Conflict and served his country in the Navy, Marine Corps, and Army. He retired from the US Army in 1968 at the rank of Major. He pastored Free Will Baptist churches in North Carolina, New Hampshire, Maine, Tennessee, Wisconsin, Maryland and Virginia. He was married to Zalene Boone Lloyd on November 27, 1954 in her hometown of Durham, North Carolina. She died in December of 2004, a few weeks after celebrating their 50th wedding anniversary. Bob and Zalene adopted four children between 1956 and 1967.

Rev. Breeden is preceded in death by his parents, James Franklin & Carrie White (Sprouse) Breeden; seven brothers and sisters; his wife, Zalene Lloyd; and his son, Kenneth Wayne Breeden. He is survived by younger brother Edward Lyle Breeden; his son Wade Franklin (Terri), a daughter Rebecca (Breeden) Wentworth (Randal), his son Jonathan Russell Breeden; and seven grandchildren, Lance, Shannon, Brent, Dane, Hunter, Randal and Quent; and two great-grandchildren, Jenson and Madalyn.

The funeral was at the Bolling Grose & Lotts Funeral Home located at 2160 East Midland Trail in Buena Vista, Virginia at 11:00 am. The Rev. Stanley Waddell, pastor of Woodland Heights FWB Church of Martinsville officiating.

Missionary Zalene Lloyd Breeden
Birth:
Jun. 22, 1916
Durham, Durham County,
North Carolina
Death:
Dec. 14, 2004
Buena Vista, Rockbridge County,
Virginia
Burial: Green Hill Cemetery,
Buena Vista,
Rockbridge County, Virginia

At the age of 32, and single, she boarded with Dan and Trula Cronk on August 8, 1948 for India assigned by the Free Will Baptists missionary board to work with Laura Belle Barnard who had been in India several years. Midway through her term she resigned as a Free Will Baptist missionary and to work for Dr. Graham's homes in Kalimpong, West Bengal, situated in the Himalayan foothills in Northeast India. On her return back to the United States another classmate Marie Hanna and her husband were beginning their service in India.

On November 27, 1954, she married Robert F. Breeden, to whom she would become a devoted wife, mother, homemaker and pastor's wife. Afterwards, serving as a home missionary and pastor's wife in North Carolina, New Jersey, Alaska, New Hampshire, Maine, Wisconsin, Tennessee and Virginia. They celebrated their 50th wedding anniversary on November 27, 2004.

She was a graduate of Free Will Baptist Bible college in Nashville, Tennessee and Nyack college, Nyack, New York.

Gird Ashby Cave
Birth:
Mar. 16, 1884
Madison County
Virginia
Death:
Jul. 10, 1972
Burial:
Victory Baptist Church Cemetery
Comertown
Page County, Virginia

Rev. Gird Ashby Cave, 88, of Comertown died at home after a lingering illness. He had been a frequent patient in Harrisonburg and Luray hospitals. Mr. Cave was a preacher at Comertown's Independent Church and a country store merchant 35 years in Comertown. He was well-known throughout the county as a preacher, frequently heard on local radio stations and conducting street corner services in Luray. He was a son of the late John Isaac and Mary Katherine Offenbacker Cave. His wife the former Dorothy Ann Thomas. The couple celebrated their 67th wedding 330 isconsin 330 y Dec 26.

John A Cave
Birth:
1812
Death:
Nov., 1899
Burial:
Calvin H Cave Cemetery
Mauck
Page County, Virginia

He was an early minister in Virginia. His Wife was Mary Ann Phillips Cave who he married on August 31, 1835 in Virginia.

Waymond Larson Cave, Sr
Birth:
Aug. 4, 1933
Death:
Jan. 24, 1994
Burial:
Victory Baptist Church Cemetery
Comertown
Page County, Virginia

Rev. Cave died at age 60. He was pastor of the Comertown FWB Church in Shenandoah. He was ordained in Nov. 1, 1969. He was the co-founder of the Comertown church where he pastored for 25 years until his health failed. He played the guitar and sang gospel songs with his father and much of his encouragement came from his grandfather, Rev. G.A. Cave who gave the property for the church and who preached for 67 years before his death. His parents were Ralph William Cave and Elsie Lillian Breeden Cave.

John Colby
Birth:
Dec. 10, 1787
Death:
Nov. 30, 1817
Burial:
Saint Paul's Episcopal Churchyard, Norfolk, Norfolk City, Virginia

At age 30 Years he died while on a long preaching trip to Ohio and was on his way back home to Vermont. He died in Norfork, Va. Is in buried in a quaint gravesite near the Episcopal Church. His ministry, while short, touched many lives and many came to Christ a list of ministers accepted the call to preach became of him. A memorial to him is in the Sutton Village cemetery at Sutton, Vermont. He was a very talented rising star and mourned by his denomination when he died. A autobiography of his life was written and published by Free Will Baptists.

Albert Dingus
Birth:
Mar. 3, 1945
Death:
Feb. 25, 2008
Burial:
Laurel Grove Cemetery, Norton, Wise County, Virginia

He bgan preaching in October 1927 with Ben and Wade Powers at the FWB church on Mudtown Hill in Jenkins, Kentucky. He was ordained on April 21, 1928. He and 8 other believers organized the Burdine Free Will Baptist Church in Jenkins. For over 56 years he was the faithful and loving pastor of that church. His ledger contained more than a 1000 names of those he baptized, married and held funeral. In 1936 he was instrumental in organizing the Letcher County Conference of FWB which united with the John Thomas Association. More that 50 men surrendered to preach under his ministry. At a Bible Conference held at FWBBC in Nashville, Tenn. In 1982, he was asked to stand and was acknowledged as one of the outstanding pastors among Free Will Baptists.

Robert Aston Dingus
Birth:
Jul. 13, 1883
Virginia
Death:
Feb. 21, 1951
Virginia
Burial:
Sabras Chapel Cemetery,
Dungannon,
Scott County, Virginia
World War I Draft

Harley Graham Dye, Sr
Birth:
Sep. 30, 1903
Swords Creek
Russell County, Virginia
Death:
Oct. 25, 1993
Oak Ridge
Anderson County, Tennessee
Burial:
Greenhills Memory Gardens
Claypool Hill
Tazewell County, Virginia

He was a FWB preacher for 45 years conducting revivals and pastor numerous churches in the John-Thomas Association. He served on the New Durm Ordaining Council was a member and Honorary Pastor of the East Lebanon FWB church.

James Edward Dye
Birth:
Jun. 16, 1921
Drill
Russell County, Virginia
Death:
Nov. 5, 2011

Oakwood
Buchanan County, Virginia
Burial:
Haywood Wilson Cemetery
Swords Creek
Russell County, Virginia

Rev. James Edward Dye, age , 90, spent his early life in Drill, moving to Buchanan County in 1940. A United States Army veteran, serving serving in Europe during World War II. A retired coal miner, And a member of UMWA Local 2372 in Jewell Valley. He was a member of Guiding Light Free Will Baptist Church and had been a minister for over 60 years In the John-Thomas Association. Military honors were conducted by VFW Post 9864 of Lebanon, Virginia.

Finas "Bud" Arlin Hill
Birth:
Nov. 22, 1936
Death:
Aug. 10, 2002
Burial:
Hill Family Cemetery
Haysi
Dickenson County, Virginia

He was a minister in the Dickenson County Conference Of the John-Thomas Association, for 22 years. He was a member of Splashdam Freewill Baptist Church in Haysi and Pastor of Phillips Chapel freewill Baptist Church in West Dante.He worked for Chevrolet's Warren, Mich., plant for 14 years, a member of UAW Local No. 909. He worked for Island Creek Coal Comoany's No. 1 mine for 19 years and was a member of UMWA Local No. 1509.

Joseph Edgar Holden
Birth:
Jan. 1, 1869
Death:
Oct. 26, 1927
Burial:
Mayo Baptist Church Cemetery
Spencer
Henry County, Virginia

He was a member of the John Wheeler Association which helped its seventh anniversary on September 1, 1887 this Association had churches or were located in the extreme northwest part of North Carolina and the northeast part of Tennessee, with his territory extending northward even into Virginia. Rev. Holden was a member of this large body of Free Will Baptists.

Kyle Wilson Hubbard
Birth:
1902
Death:
March 4, 1990
Bristol, Virginia
Burial:
Russell Memorial Cemetery
Lebanon
Russell County, Virginia

He was a faithful member of the Tunnel Hlll Free Will Baptist Church where he was ordained into the ministry in The John-Thomas Association, November, 1940 at this church and at the time of his death was the pastor emeritus.

Monroe Hubbard
Birth:
Dec. 4, 1883
Death:
Apr. 10, 1977
Burial:
Dewey Memorial Cemetery,
Wise County, Virginia

Ezra Johnson
Birth:
Feb. 19, 1916
Dickenson County, Virginia
Death:
Dec. 19, 1986
Burial:
Dewey Memorial Cemetery
Wise County, Virginia

He was a Free Will Baptist Preacher For Almost 50 Years And He Loved To sing and taught sing and to anyone who wanted to learn. He taught all of his children to sing and he baptized and married six of them.

Emmett J Kilgore, Jr
Birth:
Aug. 8, 1914
Death:
Nov. 12, 2001
Burial:
Greenwood Memorial Gardens,
Coeburn, Wise County, Virginia

Harold Kilgore
Birth:
Feb. 13, 1931
Death:
Dec. 4, 1999
Wise,
Wise County, Virginia
Burial:
Wise Cemetery, Wise
Wise County, Virginia

He was a bi-vocational Free Will Baptist minister and was a book keeper for a large mining concern. His two sons also became FWB ministers as well.

James Patton Lambert
Birth:
Oct. 25, 1904
Death:
Mar. 11, 1983
Abingdon
Washington County, Virginia
Burial:
Sullivan Cemetery
Bee, Dickenson County, Virginia

He was a FWB and a member of the John-Thomas Association

William Henry Large
Birth:
Dec. 30, 1861
Hawkins County, Tennessee
Death:
Sep. 10, 1951
Blountville,
Sullivan County, Tennessee
Burial:
Johnson Cemetery,
Washington County, Virginia

S. M. McFall, Sr
Birth:
Jan. 30, 1887
Death:
Jan. 8, 1977
Burial:
Kilgore Cemetery,
Banner, Wise County, Virginia
Ordained a Freewill Baptist Minister, in Nov 1910 by Elders W. R. Stallard, Cain Counts, and John Pennel.

Vester McKinney
Birth:
Nov. 15, 1901
Death:
Mar. 21, 1989
Tazewell County, Virginia
Burial:
Ramsey Cemetery
Clinchco
Dickenson County, Virginia

He was a former employee of the WM Ritter lumber company, a retired coal miner, a minister of the Free Will Baptist denomination for 45 years In the John-Thomas Association, and a United States Army veteran.

Ersel McPeek
Birth:
Oct. 17, 1908
Death:
Sep. 18, 1994
Burial:
Dewey Memorial Cemetery
Wise County, Virginia

He was a member of the John-Thomas Assn. and a FWB preacher.

STORE UP YOUR TREASURES IN HEAVEN

Daniel James Merkh, Sr
Birth:
1928
Death:
Apr. 12, 2002
Burial:
Holly Lawn Cemetery,
Suffolk, Suffolk City,
Virginia

He was a student at the Free Will Baptist Bible college in Nashville, Tennessee and after his graduation he and his wife, Margaret, were commissioned in 1957 as missionaries. Rev. Merkh and family spent one year in Lausanne, Switzerland to learn the French language, four years in the Ivory Coast of West Africa and nine and a half years in France as missionaries. After these times of service they retired from foreign mission service in 1975. He was both a teacher and church planter on the mission field Rev. Merkh, a native of Camden, N.J., also served as a pastor in Tennessee, South Carolina and Virginia for 20 years and lastly serving the First Free Will Baptist Church in, Richmond, Virginia where he retired. He was a member of Ryanwood Free Will Baptist Church, Vero Beach, Florida. and a veteran of the U.S. Marines during World War II.

Missionary Margaret Lucille
Johnson **Merkh**
Birth:
Jan. 29, 1930
Death:
Feb. 21, 2012
Burial:
Holly Lawn Cemetery
Suffolk Suffolk City,
Virginia,

She was predeceased by her husband of 54 years, Rev. Daniel James Merkh, Sr. Rev. Merkh, Margaret, and family spent one year in Lausanne, Switzerland to learn the French language, four years in the Ivory Coast of West Africa, and nine and half years in France as missionaries. After returning to the United States, Margaret later went on to work and retired as an executive secretary for Dominion Power. She was a member of the Free Will Baptist Church in Carrollton, Virginia.

Ben Powers
Birth:
Unknown
Death:
1983
Virginia
Burial:
Temple Hill Memorial Park
Castlewood
Russell County,
Virginia

His lineage was from a circuit riding Methodist preacher background. He helped organize 23 Free Will Baptist Churches in the 1940's in Wise County, Va. And portions of Kentucky. He and his brother Wade Powers were used in numerous revivals in surrounding counties. They would stay with people in the community for two to three weeks at a time, from house to house, and then preach revivals during the evening hours. They would receive poundings of food items as honorariums.

David D. Powers, Sr
Birth:
Jul. 17, 1920
Death:
Sep. 3, 1993
Burial:
Laurel Grove Cemetery,
Norton, Wise County, Virginia

Inscription: PFC US Army World War II

R Harlis Powers
Birth:
Jun. 26, 1855
Scott County, Virginia
Death:
Jan. 14, 1922
Wise County, Virginia
Burial:
Round Top Cemetery,
Wise, Wise County, Virginia

Rev Rueben H Powers
Birth:
Jun. 26, 1855
Scott County
Virginia
Death:
Jan. 14, 1922
Wise County
Virginia
Burial:
Round Top Cemetery
Wise

Wise County
Virginia

A Free Will Baptist minister in Wise Co. Virginia. Son of George and Katherine Kennedy Powers

---

Wade H Powers, Sr
Birth:
1894
Death:
1970
Burial:
Perry Cemetery,
Wise, Wise County, Virginia

He and his brother Ben Powers were used in numerous revivals in surrounding counties. He preached as far as Louisa, Kentucky. They would stay with people in the community for two to three weeks at a time, from house to house and then preach revivals during the evening hours.

Eli E. Reedy
Birth:
1879
Death:
1950
Burial:

Clinch Valley Memorial Cemetery
and Mausoleum,
Richlands,
Tazewell County, Virginia

Howard Reynolds
Birth:
Mar. 29, 1925
Russell County, Virginia
Death:
Dec. 19, 2007
Lebanon
Russell County, Virginia
Burial:
Reynolds Family Cemetery
Honaker
Russell County, Virginia

Reynolds, 82,of Honaker, was a lifelong resident of Russell County, and a member and pastor of Tunnell Hill Freewill Baptist Church for 14 years in the John-Thomas Association.

George Wythe Salyers
Birth:
Aug. 1, 1918
Death:
Jan. 4, 1986
Burial:
Rugsby Church Cemetery
Dickenson County,
Virginia

He was a member of the Rachel Chapel Free Will Baptist Church and a minister for 25 years. He served on the ordaining Council for 15 years and served as pastor of the Yates Chapel church for 24 years. He was a veteran of World War II having served in the United States Army.

Glen W Stevens
Birth:
May 7, 1917
Virginia
Death:
May 21, 1988
Virginia
Burial:
Bowen Cemetery
Russell County, Virginia

He was a retired coal miner and a member of the Mt. View Freewill Baptist church on Combs Ridge. He was a Free Will Baptist minister With the John-Thomas Association.

Roy C. Vanover
Birth:
Dec. 5, 1918
Death:
Mar. 25, 2003
Burial:
Powell Valley Memorial Gardens
Big Stone Gap
Wise County, Virginia

He was called to preach in September 24, 1968 and was ordained on October 25, 1969. He served as pastor of the Pyles Memorial, Ferbie Chapel, and Lone Pine Chapel Of the John-Thomas Association. He was very active in many of the churches throughout the area in his preaching, singing and praying. He was a member of the Lone Pine Chapel. In his early years he sang with the Friendly Four Quartet. He was a member of that Dickenson County conference and was a member of this ordaining Council. He served on the Board of Directors also for Camp Jacob. He worked in the coal mines for 39 years and was a member of the UWMA union. He retired from Bethlehem Steel at the age of 55.

Ralph Edward Vicars
Birth:
unknown
Death:
Mar. 29, 2009
Norton, Wise County, Virginia
Burial:
Wise Cemetery
Wise, Wise County, Virginia

He was the pastor of the Burdine Free Will Baptist church.

Ralph Lee Weaver
Birth:
Nov. 10, 1915
Kannapolis
Cabarrus County, North Carolina
Death:
Oct. 21, 1992
Durham
Durham County, North Carolina
Burial:
Roselawn Burial Park
Martinsville
Martinsville, Virginia
Plot: 16-245

Rev. Ralph Lee Weaver, 76-year-old pastor of Woodland Heights Free Will Baptist Church, Martinsville, VA, since 1948, died from complications of bypass heart surgery in Duke University Hospital, Durham, NC. He preached his last sermon Sunday morning, Sept. 27th, after suffering chest pains all night. Weaver was the son of Ira Samuel and Margaret Ada (Bullard) Weaver, one of several children. Rev. Weaver served as moderator of the Maryland Association, and was a life member o f the Martinsville/Henry Co. Rescue Squad where he served as as chaplain. His long ministry at Woodland Heights began in 1948, with 12 members where he built the membership until the congregation outgrew their facility and purchased land in 1956 and began a building program in 1959, on the present location.Rev. Weaver was graduated from Martinsville Bible College and attended Patrick Henry Community College.

Harry Paul Whitaker
Birth:
Jul. 27, 1922
Bostic
Rutherford County, North Carolina
Death:
Mar. 29, 1994
Russell County, Virginia
Burial:
Temple Hill Memorial Park
Castlewood
Russell County, Virginia

He entered the ministry in 1955 and was ordained as a Free Will Baptist minister In the John Thomas Association on November 30, 1957. He dedicated 40 years serving the Straight Hollow Free Will Baptist where he pastored for 22 years.

You Are Home At Last!

Washington

Charles Henry Alborn
Birth:
Jul. 14, 1870
Blue Earth, MN
Death:
Feb. 27, 1936
Burial:
Sumner Cemetery
Sumner, Pierce County,
Washington

He accepted the Lord Jesus Christ in a little Methodist church in 1887. Taught his first school 1890-1891 in the Stormy Creek School, Eagle Bend, Minnesota. He also preached his first sermon at that school. He taught at Spruce Hill school 1891-1892 also near Eagle Bend, Minnesota. Charles Married Clara Kyes at Eagle Bend, Minnesota November 26, 1892. Charles, with a man named Joe Carter built a United Brethren Church in Eagle Bend, Minnesota and he was licensed to preach after the church was organized. Charles and Clara lived in a little log house he built in Eagle Bend. They lived in that house until they moved to Wood Lake, Minnesota in the summer of 1893. Then they moved back to Eagle Bend in the same fall for school again.

Here is where their first child was born (Everett Robert) on September 2, 1893. For the next school year he taught the Kohlhouse School near Bertha, Minnesota in Todd County 1893-1894. He taught summer school in the Carter district 1894 then taught in the same school 1895-1896. Lizzie Rebecca was born November 7, 1895 in Eagle Bend. He taught in the Coon school house 1896-97. Their 3rd child Jay Dewey was born on March 12, 1898. Their fourth child, Gladys Ellen was orn October 7, 1899 and she died October 14, 1900. They moved to Gray Eagle, Minnesota where he also taught school there in 1901 and 1902. Evan William was born here July 7, 1901. From here they moved to Hewitt, Minnesota and he taught school there and also pastored a United Brethren church in Wrightstown a few miles out of Hewitt 1902-03. Philip William was born in Hewitt, MN on June 13, 1903. Floyd Wayne was also born in Hewitt March 26, 1905. In June 1905, they moved to Glenville, MN and he pastored a United Bretheren Church June 1905 and this is where on September 4, 1906 Lila Ruth was born. In October 1906 they moved to Myrtle, MN to pastor a United Brethren Church until the autumn of 1908 when they moved to London, MN where he built and pastored the United Brethren Church until the autumn of 1909. They then moved back to Glenville, MN where Nettie May was born September 29, 1909. They moved in June of 1910 to Winneconnie, WI and until the spring of 1911 he pastored the Free Will Baptist Church there. They moved to Wyocena, WI where Edith

Adell was born June 4, 1911. He pastored the Baptist Church of Wyocena until 1913 when he started to pastor the Hillsdale, WI church. Around this time he served a church out in West Dallas, driving a team out from Wyocena for a little time. Having moved to Barron, WI, From the fall of 1921 until the fall of 1922 Charles pastored the Colville, WA Baptist church. June 1932. He moved to Sumner, WA to pastor the Sumner Baptist church until his death.

Lewis Woodbury Gowen
Birth:
Apr. 15, 1850
Sanford, York County, Maine
Death:
Jun. 9, 1935
Waitsburg,
Walla, Walla County,
Washington
Burial:
IOOF Cemetery, Waitsburg,
Walla Walla County,
Washington,
Plot: Block 32B; Lot 3; Space 5

On 1 June 1873 he entered the ministry and 3 June 1876 was ordained a minister of the Free Baptist denomination at Ossipee in Carroll County, New Hampshire. In 1881 he graduated from the theological department of Bates College at Lewiston, Androscoggin

County, Maine. He preached at Effingham in New Hampshire; Parsonsfield, Milo, and LaGrange in Maine; Cape Sable Island in Nova Scotia; and Evansville in Wisconsin. Sometime after 1883 Lewis brought his family west in a wagon train, driving a 'hack' [a short bed wagon with a rounded canvas dome top]. On a good day they traveled 20 miles, driving from sun-up to sun-down. About 1885 he accepted a call to the Baptist Church at Alexandria in Nebraska. While serving as Pastor of at Boise, Idaho he helped raise funds to build a church. The name 'Reverend L. W. Gowen' is printed in one of the stained glass windows. After holding a number of pastorates in the east and middle west, he accepted a call to the First Baptist Church at Boise, Idaho in 1888; afterwards serving in Pullman, Caldwell, Emmett, and, Weiser. Because of failing eyesight he gave up the active ministry in 1898 when he and Mrs. Gowen began work as colporters for the American Baptist Publication Society serving in Southern Idaho and Western Oregon. For over 13 years they covered this territory distributing Bibles and religious literature, organizing churches and Sunday Schools in neglected districts. In 1911 they retired because of Mr. Gowen's eyesight and moved to Waitsburg. He was totally blind for the last ten years of his life but learned to read with two sets of raised print systems and spent the last years of his life with his Bible.

Inscription:
'Rev.' LEWIS W. GOWEN
April 15, 1850 – June 9, 1935
'Minister of the gospel'

Rev Angus Matheson
Birth: Jul. 26, 1871
Ontario, Canada
Death: Dec. 28, 1947
Washington
Burial:
Washington Memorial Park
SeaTac
King County
Washington

Parents: Neil Matheson, b. Canada, English, and Mary M. McDonald, b. Canada, English Children: Gerald   Allan Matheson, 1941-2011, Idaho; (dth   record).   Mildred (Matheson) Stone, b. Port Arthur, Ontario, Canada 1904-? and, m. 03 Nov. 1923, to John N. Stone, in Pontiac. (Mich mar records).

Samuel Rodney Manning
Birth: Mar. 1, 1838
New York
Death: Jan. 25, 1923
Wenatchee
Chelan County
Washington
Burial:
Wenatchee City Cemetery
Wenatchee
Chelan County
Washington

Age at Death 84 years 8 months 25 days Estimated Birth Year 1839 Father's Name William R. Manning   Mother's   Name Harriett Adams MANNING, Rev. S.R. (Samuel Rodman) 1838, NY; d. 1923, Wash. state. He and his wife, Carrie B. (Dunten)   Manning   (1837-1916) are bur. in Wenatchee City Cemetery. Her bio states "...they were pioneer Christian workers in Gleason, WI. "

Benjamin F Paul
Birth:
Jul. 27, 1867
North Norwich, New York
Death:
Jan. 23, 1924
Burial:
Parkland Evangelical Lutheran Cemetery
Tacoma
Pierce County, Washington

He studied that the Cortland Normal School, New York and was converted in April, 1885, and was licensed to preach by the   McDonough   Quarterly Meeting the following June. He attended Hillsdale College in Michigan for two terms, and assisted   in   a   revival   at Globleville, Michigan and was employed as the evangelist by the Wisconsin Yearly Meeting. In May 1886, he entered the pastorate of the church at Warren, Illinois and received his   ordination   at   Wayne, Wisconsin   the   following month.

Rev A W Paul
Birth:
Aug. 9, 1839
Death:
Aug. 1, 1933
Burial:
Parkland Lutheran Cemetery
Tacoma
Pierce County
Washington

Ordained Free Baptist minister/pastor from NY to Wisconsin, and to Washington. Had a son, Benj. F. Paul who was also a FB minister.

The will of the One who understands

West Virginia

Rev Caudle Adkins, Jr
Birth:
Jun. 17, 1927
Dehue
Logan County, West Virginia
Death:
Jun. 26, 2014
Huntington
Cabell County, West Virginia
Burial:
Spring Hill Cemetery
Huntington
Cabell County, West Virginia

Rev. Adkins was a son of the late Caudle Adkins Sr., and Victoria Pack Adkins. Caudle was a U.S. Navy veteran of World War II and was retired from INCO. His life was devoted to his family and his ministry. For more than 65 years, he faithfully served his Lord, serving as pastor of several churches in West Virginia and Ohio and he traveled hundreds of thousands of miles sharing the Good News of Jesus Christ in Revival meetings from Michigan to Florida. For the last 35 years, he has hosted "The Lighthouse" Radio Ministry on WEMM FM 107 in Huntington. He was a founding member of Central Free Will Baptist Church in Huntington and at the time of his death, was the longest tenured ordained minister in the West Virginia Free Will Baptist Association. In recent years, he faithfully attended Westmoreland Baptist and First Altizer Free Will Baptist Churches. Caudle was raised as a child of the Great Depression. He worked hard to provide for his family and he often did unheralded charitable acts for others. Our comfort is in knowing the truth of the statement that closed each of his radio broadcasts for the past 35 years. "Remember, Christians will never see each other for the last time."
Caudle was also a veteran of the U S Navy and served in World War II. Military graveside rites from a local Honor Guard commemorated his service. His son Dr. C.J. Adkins officiated his services.

Andrew J Adkins
Birth:
May 25, 1887
Death:
Mar. 2, 1964
Burial:
White Chapel Memorial Gardens
Barboursville
Cabell County, West Virginia
Plot: T V Lot 111D SP 3

He was one of the early for pastors of the Union Free Will Baptist Church, Griffinsville, West Virginia which was founded in 1897 making it one of the oldest Free Will Baptist Church in West Virginia.

Dallas Carlton Adkins
Birth:
Jun. 6, 1924
Key rock,
West Virginia
Death:
Aug. 20, 1992
Beckley,
West Virginia
Burial:
Blue Ridge Memorial Gardens,
Prosperity,
Raleigh County,
West Virginia

Rev. Adkins was a 40-year resident of Pierpoint, a member of the Beckley Conference of Freewill Baptist Church, where he pastored for 24 years. He pastored Camp Creek Freewill Baptist Church, Ghent Freewill Baptist Church, Ury Freewill Baptist Church and Midway Freewill Baptist Church, Christiansburg, VA.

Rev. Adkins was a World War II Army veteran, chaplain and member of the Varney Cline American Legion Post No. 133 of Pineville and was second lieutenant in the Civil Air Patrol, serving as cadet leader teaching moral education. He was a member of the West Virginia Assn. Of Retired School Employees. Military graveside rites were conducted by the Varney Cline American Legion Post No. 133 of Pineville.

Roy W. Adkins
Birth:
Unknown
West Virginia
Death:
Jan. 25, 2013
Logan County,
West Virginia
Burial:
Highland Memory Gardens
Cemetery
Pecks Mill,
Logan County,
West Virginia

Roy was born in Putnam, West Virginia and at his death at 80 lived in Whitman.

He was a U.S.Army veteran, a member of the Monahill Free Will Baptist Church, and a retired salesman and Wisconsin.

Arnold J. Barker
Birth:
Nov. 12, 1909
Death:
1974
Burial:
Barker Cemetery
Ashford
Boone County, West Virginia

Rev. Ernold Barker and Paul Barker were early ministers of the Emmons Free Will Baptist Church in West Virginia.

Paul Barker
Birth:
Jul. 7, 1895
Death:
Apr. 7, 1979
Burial:
Barker Cemetery
Ashford
Boone County,West Virginia

Rev. Ernold Barker and Paul Barker were early ministers of the Emmons Free Will Baptist Church in West Virginia.

William Robert Bennett
Birth:
Aug. 7, 1954
Raleigh County
West Virginia
Death:
Nov. 10, 2015
Burial:
Blue Ridge Memorial Gardens
Prosperity
Raleigh County
West Virginia

Born in Beckley, WV, he was a son of the late William Carl and Bernice Irene Suttle Bennett. On February 7, 1975, he married the former Carol Jean Clay of Mount Hope.

Bill encouraged and ministered to individuals and families for over 21 years. He faithfully served as pastor at Ghent Free Will Baptist, Kilsyth Free Will Baptist, and Skelton Free Will Baptist where he was most recently a member.

By trade, Bill was an electrician working in the coal mine industry for 36 years. Upon retiring from Mankin Equipment in 2014, he served as a school bus driver for Raleigh County Schools.

Services was at Skelton Freewill Baptist Church in Skelton with Jeff Bennett and Rev. David Brooks officiating.

Blessed Are The Feet Of Them Who Publish The Good News.

Rev Bennie Blankenship
Birth:
Oct. 26, 1956
Death:
Sep. 4, 2010
Kistler
Logan County, West Virginia
Burial:
Forest Lawn Cemetery
Pecks Mill
Logan County, West Virginia

Rev. Bennie Blankenship, 53, of Kistler went home to be with the Lord surrounded by family and friends at his residence.Bennie was a coal miner for 34 years. He enjoyed golfing, hunting and preaching the Word of God. He announced his calling to preach on June 9, 2002, and began by preaching his first sermon on June 16, 2002. Bennie became the pastor of the Greenbranch Freewill Baptist on April 20, 2005. He loved his church and all those who entered.

Nathan Cook Brackett
Birth:
Jul. 28, 1826
Phillips Corner
Somerset County, Maine
Death:
Jul. 20, 1910
Burial:
Harpers Cemetery
Harpers Ferry, Jefferson
County, West Virginia

Founder of Storer College, Nathan Cook Brackett (July 28, 1836-July 20, 1910) was born in Phillips, Maine. He was a minister of the Free Will Baptist Church. Graduating from Dartmouth College in 1864, he joined the U.S. Christian Commission and was stationed in the Shenandoah Valley to assist both Union and Confederate soldiers and freed slaves. After the war, Brackett served his church's mission to educate freed slaves by supervising 25 young female teachers from the North, scattered in Free Will Baptist schools throughout the valley from Harpers Ferry and Martinsburg to Lynchburg, Virginia. He proposed that his church's best service would be to equip blacks to teach other blacks, rather than relying only on missionary teachers from New England. The church leaders embraced the idea and raised the necessary funding to establish Storer College at Harpers Ferry. The college opened in October 1867, with

Brackett as its first president. Brackett retired from Storer's presidency in 1897, although he continued as treasurer until his death. Brackett was respected by blacks and whites alike. He served on the Harpers Ferry Town Council and was for two years the superintendent of free schools there. He was a regent of the Bluefield Colored Institute (now Bluefield State College) for eight years, four as president of the board. He received the degree of Doctor of Philosophy from Bates College, Lewiston, Maine, at its Commencement in June, and 1883.he purchased a summer residence in Phillips, Maine, his

native town, and bought the local paper, The Phillips Phonograph. His religious preferences are Free-Will Baptist; in politics, he is a Republican. He was married October 16, 1865, to Miss Louise Wood, of Lewiston, Maine. Source: "Memorialia of the Class of '64 in Dartmouth College" complied by John C. Webster, Shepard Johnston, Printers, 1884, Chicago.

Thomas Preston Bell

Birth:
Mar. 22, 1889
Logan County, Kentucky
Death:
Oct. 19, 1928
Williamson, Mingo County,
West Virginia
Burial:
Milton Cemetery, Milton
Cabell County, West Virginia

Arthur C. Berry

Birth:
1887
Death:
1963
Burial:
Richwood Cemetery,
Richwood, Nicholas County,
West Virginia

Orvil Clinton Berry

Birth:
May 23, 1902
West Virginia
Death:
Dec. 5, 1980
Kanawha County,
West Virginia

He was on the Brotherhood Conference council that met to organize the Springdale Free Will Baptist Church, Hurricane, West Virginia on July 24, 1955. His parents were David Franklin Berry (1864 – 1943) and Sarah Ann Woodard Berry (1870 – 1967) His wife was Sena May Berry (1904 – 1984).

Ernest F Bias

Birth:
1906
Death:
1986

Burial:
Enon Cemetery, Salt Rock
,Cabell County,
West Virginia

Reverend Ernest Franklin Bias was the son of Evermont V. Ellender Rose (Hoskinson) BIAS.

Harry Herbert Booth
Birth:
Mar. 6, 1929
Stagle,
West Virginia
Death:
Mar. 25, 2012
Charleston,
West Virginia
Burial:
Highland Memory Gardens
Cemetery
Pecks Mill
Logan County,
West Virginia

He was a son of the late John and Rebecca Clay Booth. Harry enjoyed fishing, hunting, telling jokes, family functions, attending church, visiting the nursing home, cooking, canning, gardening, woodworking and reading the Bible, but more than anything he enjoyed witnessing for the Lord. Harry served as the Chaplain for the VFW, was a veteran of the US Army serving in the Korean War and retired from the coal mines. He was also in the nursing home ministry at Boone Nursing Home and a member of the Monclo Freewill Baptist Church.

Floyd Brown
Birth:
Oct. 24, 1834
Boone County, West Virginia
Death:
Dec. 6, 1923
Burial:
Coon Cemetery
Boone County, West Virginia

He and his wife had 13 children. His conversion took place in 1867 and he was licensed to preach in 18 seven day. He pastored several churches in West Virginia

Noah Estil Buckner
Birth:
Mar. 24, 1921
Morehead
Rowan County, Kentucky
Death:
Jul., 1979
Princeton
Mercer County, West Virginia
Burial:
Roselawn Memorial Gardens
Princeton
Mercer County, West Virginia

He was the first pastor of the Lashmeet Free Will Baptist Church. Records show that he was on the ordaining Council that ordained Rev. Jeff Dishner who later became the pastor of the Lashmeet Free Will Baptist Church, Princeton, West Virginia.

George Joseph Burns
Birth:
Jan. 30, 1933
Pleasants County, W.Va.
Death:
Sept. 9, 2008
St. Marys, W.Va..
Maple Lane Masonic Cemetery
Hebron, W.Va
He was a son of the late Charles Francis and Agnes Cecelia Nichols Burns. George was a 1951 graduate of St.Marys High School, a U. S. Navy veteran and had retired from the Pleasants County School System. He was a full-time minister at Beech Run Freewill Baptist Church. Services were Maple Lane Freewill Baptist Church, Hebron, W.Va., with the Rev. Bud Corbin officiating. He was a member of the Beech Run FWB Church, the Upper Ohio Valley Conference of FWB, and the WV State Association of FWB.

Wilson C Cadle
Birth:
1866
Death:
1945
Burial:
Jordan Harper Cemetery,
Walton,
Roane County, West Virginia

Earl David Campbell
Birth:
Jun. 17, 1948
Earling
Logan County, West Virginia
Death:
Oct. 28, 2015
Logan
Logan County, West Virginia
Burial:
Forest Lawn Cemetery
Pecks Mill
Logan County, West Virginia

Rev. Earl David Campbell, 67, of Accoville, went to Heaven leaving from Logan Regional Medical Center after an apparent heart attack.

He was born the son of Barbara Ann Jeffries Campbell of Accoville and the late Rev. Clarence Robert Campbell.

Earl David was the pastor of the Landville Freewill Baptist Church for the last 29 years. He was a coal miner for 25 years who retired from Amherst Coal Company and was a member of the UMWA local 5850. He enjoyed hunting, fishing, and ginsenging. Earl David loved working for the Lord, his church family, and lending a helping hand to all in need. Funeral services was at the Landville Freewill Baptist Church with Rev. Joe Lane and Brother Russell Nelson officiating.

Fermon C Calhoun
Birth:
Jun. 6, 1912
Newland, very County,
North Carolina
Death
Oct. 17, 1973
Raleigh County, West Virginia
Burial:
Blue Ridge Memorial Gardens,
Prosperity,
Raleigh County, West Virginia

He was a retired miner, a member of the UMWA and had pastored the Bethel Freewill Baptist Church for 10 years, prior to his retirement.

William Fleetwood Chapman
Birth:
Dec. 19, 1918
West Virginia
Death:
Aug. 19, 2002
Elkview
Kanawha County, West Virginia
Burial:
Elk Hills Memorial Park
Big Chimney
Kanawha County,
West Virginia

He was the son of George W and Verna Chapman He was elected pastor in 1954 and served until January 1963 the Loudendale Free Will Baptist Church near Charleston, West Virgini. Several successful revivals were held while Rev. Chapman was pastor and many of the present members of the church United with the church at that time.
Inscription:
PVT US ARMY WORLD WAR II

Carter Clark
Birth:
1872
Death:
Oct. 6, 1941
Burial:
Comer Cemetery
Loudendale
Kanawha County,
West Virginia

He was one of the leaders in getting the Little Harts Creek Free Will Baptist Church started along with Rev. John George and Rev. Willis Comer. An interesting note:' I'm the daughter of Nellie Clark Workman and she always told me stories about poppy Clark taking her with him to church. She said he would hold her hand and sit her up front so he could keep an eye on her while he preached. My mom loved her poppy.'

Arthur J. Collins
Birth:
Aug. 9, 1925
Death:
May 7, 1982
Burial:
Grandview Cemetery,
Grandview,
Raleigh County, West Virginia

For death is no more than a turning of us over from time to eternity.

William Cecil Combs
Birth:
Feb. 19, 1912
Honaker, Russell County,
Virginia
Death:
Nov. 14, 2003
Sophia,
Raleigh County, West Virginia
Burial:
Blue Ridge Memorial Gardens,
Prosperity,
Raleigh County,
West Virginia

Cecil Combs was a native of southwest Virginia. His father was a farmer, and his mother a homemaker who was active in founding Sunday Schools in the rural area in which they lived. Cecil loved nature and was an avid hunter. He spent countless hours in the woods and farm country learning much about animals, plants, and trees. He was preceded in death by his parents Cecil married Norma Elizabeth Ball in 1932 in Lebanon, Virginia. They moved to West Virginia in 1934, where their fifteen children were born and where they raised fourteen children to adulthood. The Combs lived in West Virginia until 1964 when they moved to central Florida with the intention of establishing a Free Will Baptist Church. During his ministry Bro. Combs pastored churches in Georgia, Florida, and West Virginia. Although an humble man, he emerged as a leader early in his ministry. Bro. Combs helped to lead Free Will Baptists in West Virginia to organize the State Association of Free Will Baptists. A CPA, he was elected Clerk, and served both the W Va. State Association and the Beckley Conference as moderator numerous times. Cecil Combs was a minister during the days when few Free Will Baptist Churches had full-time pastors. A builder by trade, he left a physical legacy as well as a spiritual one. He built hundreds of homes in Raleigh County, WV. In every church he pastored, he used his building skills to construct, remodel, or build additions to the churches, educational units, parsonages and youth camps. Bro. Combs and his son Billy helped construct the large Vehicle Assembly Building which houses rockets at the Kennedy Space Center on Merritt Island. This close proximity to Cocoa Beach brought a burden upon his heart for the town, leading him to establish the Cocoa Free Will Baptist Church, where he pastored for five years. He led in the building of the church facility at the Cocoa Church; youth camps both in West Virginia and Bonifay, Florida; gymnasium and classroom building in Sophia, Wva.; and additions to the parsonages at Piney Grove Church in Chipley, Florida, and in Sophia, W Va. He led the construction project for the West Virginia Cottage at the Free Will Baptist Children's Home in Greenville, Tennessee during his ministry in the 1950s. During his years in central Florida, Bro. Combs assisted in organizing Free Will Baptist churches in nearby Vero Beach and Titusville, organized the Indian River Association, which he served as moderator. He also served as the moderator of the Florida State Association and published the Free Will Baptist State Paper both in Florida and West Virginia. Bro. Combs was preceded in death by his wife Norma of 58 years. Several of their descendants are in ministry. Among them are sons Bob Combs, Wva. Pastor and a former Georgia pastor; Jim Combs, missionary to Brazil; sons-in-law Ed Cook, Kentucky pastor; Jim Puckett, Oklahoma pastor; grandsons Randy Puckett, Home Missionary in Texas; and John Hornsby, chaplain for the H. B. Zachry Company in San Antonio, Texas. The Lord blessed Bro. Combs with a sharp mind and the ability to recite a great body of scripture by heart. He was well-known for his Biblical knowledge, and especially of eschatology. Although retired after fifty years in the ministry, Bro. Combs continued to serve, conducting a weekly service at Heartland Nursing Home, and filling the pulpit at Sophia in the absence of his pastor.

Freedom Prospers When Religion Is Vibrant And The Rule Of Law Under God Is Acknowledged

Willis C Comer
Birth:
1867
Death:
1942
Burial:
Comer Cemetery
Loudendale
Kanawha County,

West Virginia

He was the first they had pastored the Little Harts Free Will Baptist Church and did so a number of times preceding his death. His wife was Lucinda Clark Comer (1869 – 1958).

Carl Joseph Cooper
Birth:
Death:
Feb. 9, 2011
Milton, WV.
Burial:
Forest Memorial Park,
Milton, WV.

Pastor Carl Joseph Cooper, age 78, of Milton, WV, beloved husband of Nelma Young Cooper, and faithful servant of the Lord Jesus Christ. After beginning his preaching ministry in December of 1964, Pastor Cooper served faithfully through evangelistic work, Pastor of several churches, active involvement in local, State, and the National Association of Free Will Baptists. Pastor Cooper served as a Home missionary to Wheeling, WV. He authored a book entitled Two Covenants and taught numerous Bible studi 391's es, many of them on the subject of The Wilderness Tabernacle using a scale model

that he constructed. In addition to his life in ministry, Pastor Cooper was a builder by trade and former owner of White Oak Lumber Company. Pastor Cooper was preceded in death by his parents, Pastor J.W. Cooper and Ada Leslie Nugen Cooper, and his brother Pastor Lloyd Cooper. He is survived by his faithful and loving wife of 59 years, Nelma Young Cooper, brother, Ezra Cooper, sister, Lorene Rooper, sons, Wesley Edward Cooper (Debbie), Pastor Daniel Joseph Cooper (Sandie), Paul Keith Cooper (Sandra), and daughter, Julie Cooper McCoy (Pastor Dale), seven wonderful grandchildren, and two very special great-grandchildren. Pastor Cooper was extremely proud that all his children and their families are faithfully serving the Christ he so loved and proclaimed.

Rev George H Cooper
Birth:
Aug. 24, 1866
Death:
Mar. 21, 1947
Burial:
Spring Hill Cemetery
Charleston
Kanawha County
West Virginia

Rev. George H. Cooper was a Free Will Baptist minister, whose name appeared in early records after 1900. A meeting of the General Cooperative Association met in 1918, at Paintsville, KY, and the Minutes of that meeting showed his name in the list. Don't know date of his ordination, but usually, those who attended back then were leading men who were active in the work of the ministry and the church.

James Wesley "J.W." Cooper

Birth:
Jan. 19, 1908
Death:
Jan. 7, 2002
Burial:
Forest Memorial Park
Milton
Cabell County, West Virginia

The Rev. James Wesley "J.W." Cooper, 93, of Milton widower of Ada Nugen Cooper, died Monday, January 7, 2002 in Teays Valley Nursing and Rehabilitation Center. He was a coal miner, carpenter, building contractor and pastor. Survivors include two sons, the Rev. Carl J. Cooper of Milton and W. Ezra Cooper of Hurricane; and one daughter, Lorene Rooper of Barboursville.

Roy Lee Cox

Birth:
April 8, 1933
Gillespie,
Ritchie County, W.Va.
Death:
June 20, 2009
Marietta, Ohio
Burial:
Maple Lane Masonic Cemetery
Hebron, Pleasants County, W.Va.

A son of the late Jacob and Nina Coss Cox. Roy was a graduate of St. Marys High School with the class of 1951 and was retired from the Pleasants County School System as a maintenance supervisor. He was known to his many friends as the "fix-it-man." He loved gospel music and singing in church, as well as being a member of the singing group "The Relative Quartet." He was the founder, member, and the retired pastor of the Beech Run Freewill Baptist Church at Arvilla, 231 231 W.Va. He was a member of the Beech Run FWB Church, the Upper Ohio Valley Conference of FWB, and the WV State Association of FWB A Celebration of Roy's life and ministry was held at the Beech Run Freewill Baptist Church at Arvilla, WV with Pastor Robert Cornell and the Rev. Rex Cox officiating.

Moss A Craddock

Birth:
May 5, 1907
Hewett
Boone County, West Virginia
Death:
Aug. 23, 1993
Burial:
Forest Lawn Cemetery
Pecks Mill
Logan County, West Virginia

Well-known Free Will Baptist preacher and pastor. He helped to organize the Chapman Memorial Free Will Baptist Church, Harts, West Virginia, along with Oliver Privett, Wayne Damron, J. A. Rakes.

Wayne Damron

Birth:
Unknown
West Virginia
Death:
Apr. 21, 1978
Logan County, West Virginia
Burial:
Forest Lawn Cemetery,
Pecks Mill,
Logan County, West Virginia

Well respected minister for Free Will Baptists in West Virginia. His last pastorate was at the Trinity FWB church in Henlawson.

Rev Floyd M. Dove

Birth:
Jul. 23, 1926
Kermit
Mingo County, West Virginia
Death:
May 9, 2015
Petersburg
Grant County, West Virginia
Burial:
Lahmansville Cemetery
Lahmansville
Grant County, West Virginia

Rev. Dove served in the United States Army during World War

II.In 1964 he was ordained a Free Will Baptist minister.

He pastored the Dumpling Run Community Church. He was a life member of the Nolan Free Will Baptist Church in Nolan, WV.

He was a retired Industrial Electrician teacher for the Grant County Board of Education.

Funeral service was at the Schaeffer Funeral Home Chapel with Rev. Ray Taylor and Rev. Edwin Hughes officiating.

Owen R Estep
Birth:
January 10, 1854
Boone County, West Virginia
Death:
Dec. 4, 1909
West Virginia
Burial:
Estep Cemetery
Ameagle
Raleigh County, West Virginia

He was ordained in March, 1884, by the Kanawha Quarter Meeting and since that time is been engaged continually in revival in organizing work. He organized over 15 churches and now is pastor of the Liberty, New Salem, Jarrett's Valley and Fifteen mile churches. His labors were largely among a poor people but few will it the R could do the work so efficiently with so little pay for his labors and travels.

Arthur G. Frye
Birth:
Feb. 2, 1923
Lincoln County, West Virginia
Death:
Aug. 10, 1991
West Virginia
Burial:
Franklin Cemetery
Branchland, Lincoln County,
West Virginia

He was a member of Chapman Memorial Church, previous West Virginia Promotional Director. He was retired from Columia Gas. He served as a Free Will Baptist minister for 43 years.

John E Garrido
Birth:
Jan. 27, 1934
Death:
Unknown
Burial:
Docks Creek Cemetery
Kenova
Wayne County, West Virginia

He was the first pastor of the Good Shepherd Free Will Baptist Church in Huntington, West Virginia which was organized on March 19, 1966.Note: A date of death is NOT listed on this marker

Rev Fred Almon Giles
Birth:
Unknown
West Virginia
Death:
Mar. 12, 2014
West Virginia
Burial:
Graceland Memorial Park
South Charleston
Kanawha County,
West Virginia

Pastor Fred Almon Giles, Sr., 87, left on this journey to be in the presence of the Lord at Hubbard Hospice House, Charleston, WV.

He lived his life within a mile and a half of where he was born. He worked as a clerk for FMC Corp, South Charleston. His life's commitment was to the churches where he pastored for 66 years in Boone, Kanawha and Lincoln Counties, and to the communities of Emmons and Dartmont.

Celebration of Life and service was at Hopewell Baptist Church, Rt. 119 and Brounland Road, Alum Creek, with his family officiating.

For death is no more than a turning of us over from time to eternity.

Alfred Joseph Gorgia
Birth:
Jun. 5, 1924
Kings County (Brooklyn)
New York
Death:
Apr. 22, 2016
Culloden
Cabell County
West Virginia
Burial:
Highland Memory Gardens
Chapmanville
Logan County
West Virginia

ALFRED JOSEPH GORGIA, 91, of Milton, W.Va., was welcomed into his heavenly home for which he had long desired at Cabell Health Care Center, Culloden, W.Va. He has "fought the good fight, he has finished the course, he has kept the faith," 2 Timothy 4:7, "absent from the body, present with the Lord" 2 Corinthians 5:8. He was born June 5, 1924, in Brooklyn, New York, the son of the late Oreste and Carmela Gorgia. In addition to his parents, he was preceded in death by his first wife, Rita Dale Vance Gorgia; his second wife, Kathleen Talbert Gorgia. He was an ordained minister of the Free Will Baptist Denomination, preaching and singing for many years in Logan and Cabell counties. He lived all of his married life and raised his children in Man and Logan, W.Va., working for Amherst Coal Company as store manager and timekeeper. He also worked and retired from Logan General Hospital in transportation. He is a veteran of WWII serving in the U.S. Navy. Funeral services conducted at Susannah Missionary Baptist Church, Fudges Creek Road, Ona, W.Va., with Rev. Tracy Call officiating.

Ottis Hensley
Birth:
Unknown
Death:
Oct. 4, 1993
Charleston
Kanawha County,
West Virginia
Burial:
Blue Ridge Memorial Gardens
Prosperity
Raleigh County,
West Virginia

Hensley was returning home from a preaching appointment when he stopped and fell down a steep embankment breaking his neck in the fall. He was the West Virginia Promotional Director, editor of the Messenger, and manager of the state book store. He was also in his fourth year as pastor of the Kilsyth FWB church. He was previously chairman of the State Home Mission board and served on the Steering Committee in 1991 when the West Virginia association hosted the National Association in Charleston. He was a graduate OF Bethany Bible College in Bethany, Alabama. He was 51 at the time of his death and has been a minister 23 years.

John M. Henson
Birth:
Feb. 22, 1898
Mercers Bottom,
Mason County, West Virginia
Death:
May 17, 1984
West Virginia,
Burial:
Valley View Memorial Park,
Hurricane,
Putnam County, West Virginia

He was definitely one of the pioneer Free Will Baptist preachers in the tri-state area of West Virginia, Kentucky, and Ohio. He was a friend to all pastors and ministers keeping the Free Will Baptist doctrine known where ever he preached. He knew ministers far and wide and did his portion of revivals where ever he could. And in his day he had to travel anyway possible. Before he passed into eternity wrote his life's story in his book *"My Journey with Jesus"* filled with hundreds of names of people he baptized and preachers with whom he fraternalized. Rev. Hansen was a veteran of World War I serving in Company B 52nd infantry. He served in England, France, and Germany. He joined the Free Will Baptist denomination on December 28, 1928.

John Hockenberry
Birth:
1921
Death:
1985
Burial:
Forest Memorial Park
Milton Cabell County
West Virginia,

Hockenberry was a very respected Minister in West Virginia. He died in the pulpit while preaching at the Prince of Peace Free Will Baptist Church in Huntington, West Va. Where he was pastor for many years. He served in the United States Navy during World War II.

C.C. Lett
Birth:
1888
Death:
1971
Burial:
Woodmere, Memorial Park,
Huntington,
Cabell County, West Virginia

Leslie Allen Lilly, Sr
Birth:
Aug. 30, 1898
Camp Creek community
Mercer County, West Virginia
Death:
Sep., 1976
Camp Creek community
Mercer County, West Virginia
Burial:
Roselawn Memorial Gardens
Princeton
Mercer County, West Virginia

Father: John Wallace Lilly and his Mother was: Mary Ellen Epling He joins the ranks of many whose last name is Lilly who were Free Will Baptist preachers. He spent the majority of his life in the Camp Creek area of West Virginia and ministered basically in that area.

Andrew Jackson

Linville
Birth:
Dec. 20, 1843
Kanawha County, West Virginia
Death:
Apr. 21, 1920
Charleston
Kanawha County, West Virginia
Burial:
Spring Hill Cemetery
Charleston
Kanawha County, West Virginia

He served as a federal soldier during the rebellion, and married Nancy Stowers in 4 Oct 1865. They had eight children. He was ordained among the free salvation Baptists in 17 scratch that 1875 and became a free Baptist minister in 1885. Most of his ministry was in the first Kanawha quarterly meeting where he engaged in revival work in which he had been very successful.

Frank Lovejoy
Birth:
Mar. 17, 1895
Death:

Dec. 9, 1950
Burial:
Lovejoy Cemetery, Palermo,
Lincoln County, West Virginia

The Rev. Lovejoy was a veteran attached to the 128th division in World War I during which he was wounded. He was a member of the Freewill Baptist Church.

Homer Lane Mayhew
Birth:
Dec. 18, 1948
Logan
West Virginia
Death:
May 14, 2014
Burial:
Mountain View Memory
Gardens
Maher
Mingo County
West Virginia

Homer Lane Mayhew, 65, of Ragland, went home to be with the Lord while surrounded by his family at his home.
He was a son of the late John David and Elva Merle Pauley Mayhew. Homer was a Seaman 3rd. Class E4 Petty Officer in the U.S. Navy having served in Vietnam. He served on the USS Okinawa and the USS Thuban from 1965 to 1967. He was honored with Military Rites by the DAV Chapter 141 Belfry, Ky. An ordained minister for more than 36 years, Homer loved to preach God's word. He was a member of the Laurel Creek Freewill Baptist Church. Along with serving God for many years he was also pastor of many churches throughout that time.
Services were held at Chafin Funeral Home with Rev. Daniel Lane Mayhew and Rev. Eugene Marcum officiating. Published in Williamson Daily News from May 15 to May 16, 2014

Albert Meade
Birth:
Apr. 14, 1888
Wayne County,
West Virginia
Death:
Apr. 15, 1943
Logan County,
West Virginia
Burial:
Pack Cemetery
Atenville
Lincoln County,
West Virginia

He was the founder of the Little Harts Freewill Baptist Church, Little Harts Creek Road, Harts (Atenville), Lincoln County, WV, and was from Wayne County, WV

Tillman Clayton Morgan

Birth:
Aug. 13, 1909
Lewis County,
West Virginia
Death:
1988
West Virginia
Burial:
Woodmere Memorial Park
Huntington
Cabell County,
West Virginia

He was the son John Dallas Morgan and Bertha May (Walker). He began his ministry with Free Will Baptist in the fall of 1945 and continued preaching until his death in 1988. He served the brotherhood conference as clerk for several years. He was also clerk and Treas. Of the West Virginia state Association. During these years he pastored several churches in West Virginia. He served for two terms as mayor of the town of Nettie and he traveled thousands of miles among his churches while living in Huntington.

Alexander Hatch Morrell
Birth:
Oct. 10, 1818
Berwick
York County, Maine
Death:

Dec. 25, 1885
Irvington
Essex County, New Jersey
Burial:
Harpers Cemetery
Harpers Ferry
Jefferson County, West
Virginia

Alexander Hatch "Alex" Morrell was the son of Josiah Morrell, Jr and Sarah Quint his wife, who for many years were members of the Society of Friends. At 18 years of age he united with the Free Will Baptist Church in Litchfield, Maine. He served as a book salesman in Kentucky. He was ordained at Phillips, Maine in 1850. His work there and surrounding towns continued until 1861. His pastorates in Maine were very successful until in 1867 the Home Mission Board asked him to work in the Shenandoah Mission and there after became the soliciting agent for Storer College. He is known for being an ideal pastor and had a clear and forcible voice and a good sermonizer. On 8 Jun 1845 in Hall County, Maine, Alex married Eliza "Lizzie" Seavey of Georgetown, Sagadahoc County, Maine. He was an ordained Freewill Baptist minister, who felt a mission to help educate freed slaves, and began a very useful work at Storer College, in Harper's Ferry, Jefferson County, West Virginia. He retired and died in New Jersey, but his body was taken to Harper's Ferry where he is buried.

James Edwards Mounts
Birth:
Nov. 12, 1934
Ranger, Lincoln County,
West Virginia
Death:
Apr. 20, 2011
Ranger, Lincoln County,
West Virginia
Burial:
Frye-Nelson Cemetery,
Ranger, Lincoln County,
West Virginia

Rev. Mounts was a tipple mechanic for Pittston Coal Group at Loredo, and he was the pastor of the East Fork Freewill Baptist Church of Ranger for 40 years.

Sam Mullins
Birth:
Jul. 3, 1877

Virginia
Death:
May 30, 1956
West Hamlin
Lincoln County, West Virginia
Burial:
Lucas, Harts
Lincoln County, West Virginia
Helped to organize the new Zion Free Will Baptist Church between 1910 and 1915 along with H. H. Daniels which is near Logan, West Virginia.

Rev Timothy Murphy
Birth:
1840
Death:
Nov. 21, 1920
Burial:
Spring Hill Cemetery
Charleston
Kanawha County
West Virginia

REV. TIMOTHY MURPHY, aged 80 years died early Sunday morning at the home of Mrs. John Lambert, Ruffner hollow, of cancer of the stomach, from which he had suffered for the past few months.

Rev. Mr. Murphy had been a minister for the past 40 years and was a well-known minister in this section at one time and was well known to all the elderly people of this community and was a member of the Grand Army of the Republic, having been a soldier in the Union army during the civil war.

Source: The Charleston Daily Mail Newspaper - Charleston, Kanawha Co., West Virginia - Monday, November 22, 1920

An ordained Free Will Baptist minister, represented for WV in the dedication of Tecumseh FWB College, OK, in 1917, with a leading role.

Rev John Curtin Newcomer
Birth:
1863
Death:
1937
Burial:
Harpers Cemetery
Harpers Ferry
Jefferson County
West Virginia

Active minister, missionary and teacher at Storer College.
His wife was the dauther of Nathan Brackett the founder of the school for the Freemen after the civil war.

His wife was Celeste Brackett Newcomer (1871 - 1951) and to them was born a son Daniel Brackett Newcomer (___ - 1918)*

Eldon M. Pauley
Birth:
Jan. 22, 1877
Death:
May 23, 1943
Burial:
Indian Mills Cemetery,
Indian Mills,
Summers County, West
Virginia

George Pauley
Birth:
unknown
Death:
May 23, 1974
West Virginia
Burial:
Blue Ridge Memorial Gardens,
Prosperity,

Raleigh County,
West Virginia

The service for Rev. Pauly was in the Bradley Free Will Baptist Church. This information came from the Beckley Post Herald on May 26, 1974.

Rev John James Perry
Birth:
Unknown
Orange County,
Virginia
Death: 1884
Salt Rock
Cabell County,
West Virginia
Burial:
Benjamin Perry Cemetery

Salt Rock
Cabell County, West Virginia

Early minister representing in the FWB Register. Confederate veteran USA Civil War.

James Albert Rakes
Birth:
Jun. 11, 1897
Lincoln County, West Virginia
Death:
Jan. 22, 1960
ManLogan County, West
Virginia
Burial:
Forest Lawn Cemetery

Pecks Mill
Logan County, West Virginia
He was the son of Amos Rakes who was born on Oct 1873 in Lincoln County, WV. And his mother was Nancy M. Vance born Apr 1879 in Lincoln County, WV.   And who died on 18 Jul 1930 in Lincoln County, WV. He helped to organize the Chapman Memorial Free Will Baptist Church in harts, West Virginia, along with Oliver Privett, Moss Craddock, and Wayne Damron.

Stephen Columbus Rigg
Birth:
Oct. 1, 1858
Fayette County West Virginia
Death:
Feb. 7, 1947
Powellton
Fayette County West Virginia
Burial:
Alderson Cemetery
Alderson
Greenbrier County
West Virginia
An ordained Free Baptist minister who ministered to the churches of Kanawha Quarterly Meeting, W.VA.

Paul J. Scarbro
Birth:
Feb. 22, 1921

Rock Creek, West Virginia
Death:
Nov. 7, 2008
Beckley, Raleigh County,
West Virginia
Burial:
Blue Ridge Memorial Gardens,
Prosperity, Raleigh County,
West Virginia

He was of the Free Will Baptist faith and was a minister and pastor for over 50 years. Among the churches he pastored were Packsville Baptist, Shumate Branch, Coal City Free Will Baptist, Price Hill Free Will Baptist, and North Sand Branch Baptist.

Henry W. Scott
Birth: 1888
Death:
Apr. 11, 1975
Charleston,
Kanawha County,
West Virginia
Burial:
Sunset Memorial Park,
South Charleston,
Kanawha County,
West Virginia

The Rev. Henry W. Scott was a retired Freewill Baptist minister after 45 years of service.

James Harold Shafer
Birth:
Unknown
Death:
Jun. 14, 2011
Elkview,
Kanawha County,West
Virginia
Burial:
Elk Hills Memorial Park,
Big Chimney,Kanawha County,
West Virginia

He retired from Union Carbide with 34 years of service and was a minister throughout his life. He was a member of Meadowbrook FWB church and the Kanawha Free Will Baptist Conference. He pastored several FWB churches in West Virginia.

Abram Clark Shaver
Birth:
Jul. 21, 1842
Scalia County, Ohio
Death:
Oct. 13, 1923
Kanawha County, West
Virginia
Burial:
IOOF Cemetery
East Bank
Kanawha County,
West Virginia

He was converted in 1860 and baptized by Rev. Thomas E. Peden. After serving in the army, he settled in West Virginia and married in 1869 Miss M. Baker. For some years he was manager of a large mercantile establishment. His faithfulness and influence aided materially in establishing the cause of Free Will Baptists in the Kanawha Valley. Where he served the Lord with great interest in his church and vicinity.

Sherman Sizemore
Birth:
Jul. 4, 1918
Death:
Oct. 13, 1985

Burial:
Grandview Memorial Park
Dunbar
Kanawha County, West
Virginia

One of the pastors and the early members of the Herndon Free Will Baptist Church, Herndon, West Virginia. His wife was Olivia Mae Selbe Sizemore (1920 – 2006)

Rev Alvin Snuffer
Birth:
Jul. 7, 1932
Beckley
Raleigh County West Virginia
Death:
Aug. 30, 2015
Charleston
Kanawha County West

Virginia
Burial:
Blue Ridge Memorial Gardens
Prosperity
Raleigh County, West Virginia

Snuffer was a Korean Conflict Veteran serving in the US Army. He ministered 45 years in the Free Will Baptist church in WV, Ohio, Georgia, and Alabama. His last years of ministry was with the Terry Christian Church. Rev. Lynn Halstead officiated his burial.

Rev James Edward Stanley
Birth:
Oct. 7, 1923
Johnson City
Washington County,
Tennessee
Death:
Feb. 22, 2015
Crab Orchard
Raleigh County, West Virginia
Burial:
Blue Ridge Memorial Gardens
Prosperity
Raleigh County, West Virginia

Jim was the son of Nelson Cox Stanley and his wife Nellie Alice Doan Stanley. The family moved to Fitzpatrick in Raleigh County, WV when Jim was one. He served in the US Navy during WWII.
Jim worked for Appalachian Power Company before taking a job with a coal company at Milburn. Jim was a member of the UMWA and later retired from Stotesbury coal mine. He played baseball on the Milburn coal company's team and was such a good pitcher that he was scouted by the Chicago Cubs as a potential professional player. Jim also worked for Carolina Supermarket, was a carpenter and electrician. He also built homes in the Raleigh County area for many years.
Jim served as Deacon and Choir Director at Crab Orchard Brethren Church. He was a member of the Christian Harmoneers and other gospel singing groups. He had a music program on Beckley radio station WWNR with his family and taught Shaped Note Music Schools throughout WV and other states.
He was ordained as a minister of the gospel in the 1960s and served as Pastor of the Sprague Freewill Baptist Church for 13 years. He also Pastored the Bradley Freewill Baptist Church and the House of Prayer Freewill Baptist Church in Crab Orchard. Rev. Stanley performed many weddings and funerals as part of his ministry, but his life's goal was serving Christ and leading others to Christ and through the waters of Baptism.
A celebration of Jim's at Blue Ridge Funeral Home in Beckley with Rev. Eric Murphy and longtime friend Rev. John Hart officiating..

Roy Lee Stanley
Birth:
Nov. 16, 1943
Death:
Jan. 15, 2011
Burial:
Independence Cemetery,
Sandyville,
Jackson County, West Virginia

He was an ordained minister serving many congregations throughout the region prior to his retirement. He was also a proud veteran of the United States Air Force.

Gaylord M. Shrewsbury
Birth:
Jul. 19, 1940
Death:
Aug. 3, 2000
Burial:
Shrewsbury Cemetery, Beeson
Beeson
Mercer County, West Virginia

He was pastor for 18 years the Old State Road Free Will Baptist Church in Beeson, West Virginia.
Inscription:
He Fought A Good Fight.
He Kept The Faith.
Military Marker:
EN 2 U. S. Navy
July 19, 1940 – Aug. 3, 2000

John H. Surratt
Birth:
Jan. 2
0, 1847
Fayette County, Virginia
Death:
May 9, 1933
Burial:
Alexander Cantley Cemetery
Rock Creek
Raleigh County,
West Virginia

He married Jannette Cantley in 1868 and with his wife joined the Free Baptists in 1884. The same year he received license to preach and own June 13, 1886 he was ordained. His labors were as an evangelist in the Raleigh Quarterly Meeting of which he was the clerk.

Rev Thomas Harvey Terry
Birth:
Aug. 9, 1940
Huntington, WV
Death:
Mar. 14, 2015
Burial:
Dolen Family Cemetery
Cabell County
West Virginia

Rev. Thomas Harvey Terry, 74, of Barboursville, WV, fell asleep at the Emogene Dolin Jones Hospice House due to an extended illness. He was son of the late Alex Hartsel and Dorothy Lorena Sydenstricker Terry.

Rev. Terry was pastor of Park Circle Free Will Baptist Church in Kenova, WV since 1971 where he was recently honored as Pastor Emeritus. He never gave up preaching or teaching his Sunday school class. He was a tremendous supporter of the Ladies Auxiliary and their goal to build a fellowship hall. Throughout his ministry, he and his wife led hundreds to the Lord and mentored many young preachers. He was a member of the Brotherhood and Good Will Conferences. Rev. Terry was a skilled musician and lead singer of his family's Southern Gospel Group, The Terry Family. He was inspired to write the song, Won't You Take a Look with me at Calvary which has blessed many through the years. In addition to pastoring, he was an evangelist. He held many revivals preaching and singing with his family through West Virginia, Kentucky, Ohio and Florida. Rev. Terry also hosted the WEMM Christian radio broadcasts Let's Look to Calvary and An Evening with the Terry Family. An avid reader, he wore out countless Bibles and two Kindles by burning out the page turner button. Rev. Terry was a retired Carmen for CSX Railway and the financial secretary and assistant local chairman for the B.R.C. union local 455.

Funeral service was at Park Circle Freewill Baptist Church, Kenova, WV with Pastor Rev. Randy Jeffers, Assistant Pastor, Rev. Bill Napier, Rev. John Terry and Rev. David Dolen officiating.

Rev Jeff Thomas
Birth:
Dec. 8, 1860
Mineral County
West Virginia
Death:
Oct. 7, 1946
Kanawha County
West Virginia
Burial:
Graceland Memorial Park
South Charleston
Kanawha County
West Virginia

Rev. Jeff Thomas was the son of William Thomas and Sarah (Good) Thomas. He was an ordained Free Will Baptist minister who was active in his ministry, his name appearing in old Cooperative General Association Minutes, when it convened in 1918 in Paintsville, KY.

Inscription:
FREE WILL BAPTIST

William Travis
Birth:
May 30, 1923
Ceredo, WV
Death:
November 9, 1994
Burial:
Docks Creek Cemetery,
Kenova, Wayne County,
West Virginia

He served in the U.S. Navy during WWII. Transferred to the U.S. Army after the war, hoping to make a career of the military. He was saved in 1952, kneeling at a tree stump in the woods in Texas where he was working for the Texas State Prison system as a building superintendent. He loved working their annual rodeos. He discharged from the Army after becoming a Christian and answered the call to preach soon thereafter. He was ordained in 1953 and began preaching as a "fill-in" preacher in various towns in Texas. He once held a 6-week revival in China Grove, Texas, under a thatch roofed structure and was paid with vegetables from the people's gardens. For several months, he drove 100 miles each way to fill in at a part-time church which only met every other week. In 1955, he felt the call to the mission field and went to the Bible College for a year studying missions. Then, in 1956, he took his family to Pinar del Rio, Cuba to work at Los Cedros del Libano (Cedar of Lebanon) Bible Institute with Mom and Pop Willey and fill-in for missionaries who were on leave of absence. They filed for permanent residence papers so they could stay and work as full-time missionaries, but were refused after Batista lost the war to Castro. There were many times, the Institute's bus was stopped, torn apart and searched by Communist soldiers. Daddy joined the other men from the Seminary to help the people in neighborhood villages that were burned at night by Castro's army. It was there we saw first-hand the work of Satan as his demons possessed people who would run wildly on the Seminary grounds, then saw the miraculous work of our Savior as he healed those people following times of severe stress and mighty prayers. He was forced to leave the island after being there only 6 months. He moved to Ft. Lauderdale to fill in at the FWB church, and later was called to his first full-time pastorate. Later a small group began meeting in a childcare facility in nearby Deerfield Beach, and the church grew from there. Deerfield Free Will Baptist church was built and today supports a school with grades K4-12. He was bi-vocational while pastoring there. After 7 years in Florida moved Jasper, Alabama in 1963 where he pastored the First FWB Church in Jasper for about 7 years. Then he answered to call to Thomaston, Georgia. The church in Thomaston was built from two used Army barracks that were bought and brought to the church property. He was in Thomaston till around 1980-1981, then moved to Hazelhurst, Georgia and pastored there about 3 years; and his final pastorate was in Millen, Georgia, where he passed away in 1995.

Roy Alex Tyree
Birth:
Mar. 19, 1917
Beckley
Raleigh County, West Virginia
Death:
Apr. 16, 2007
Beckley,
Raleigh County, West Virginia,
Burial:
Blue Ridge Memorial Gardens,
Prosperity,
Raleigh County, West Virginia

Mr. Tyree was a retired miner and a member of UMWA District 17, and a retired Free Will Baptist minister with more than 50 years of service, having officiated a host of weddings and funerals. During his ministry, he pastored: Terry Community Church, Weirwood Community Church, Willis Branch Community Church, Naomi Free Will Baptist Church, Fairdale Free Will Baptist Church, Maple Fork Community Church (three times), Rock Lick Community Church, Oak Grove Baptist Church at Backus Mountain, Layland Community Church, Zickafoose Memorial Church at Landisburg, Charmco Free Will Baptist Church, North Baptist Church at Sand Branch and the Spruce Tabernacle. Rev. Tyree was also on WOAY Radio for 23 years and was on WOAY-TV for 2 ½ years.

Dell Upton
Birth:
Aug. 2, 1854
Leon, Mason County,
West Virginia
Death:
Jul. 15, 1942
Mason County, West Virginia
Burial:
Wolfe Valley Cemetery,
Leon, Mason County,
West Virginia

Rev. Upton was a leader in the Free Will Baptist church of which he ministered until his death. His name is found in many records, one, in which he was pastor of Cofer's Chapel FWB Church, Nashville, TN in the early decade of 1900's: "Coming as pastor in 1907 was Dr. Dell Upton from Leon, West Virginia. Perhaps only in heaven will he know that he gave Cofer's Chapel a start in directions which continue to this day. December 17, 1907, he gathered a group of women in his home and organized what they called 'The Ladies' Aid Society.' In the organization were such women as Fanny Polston, Mrs. Ed Parker, and a teenager, then known as Annie Weaver (later Mrs. Mary Ann Welch, affectionately known as Miss Mary.)"(Taken from Dr. Mary Ruth Wisehart's *History of Cofer's Chapel,* 2008 Homecoming History of church.). Dr. Upton envisioned a FWB college in Nashville in 1907, and obtained a charter, but for whatever reason, it did not materialize at that time. He was awarded the Doctor of Divinity degree for his work and leadership abilities. He was one of the ministers who opposed the merger of FWB with the Northern Baptists in 1911.

Carl Wesley Vallance
Birth:
Mar. 18, 1918
Holden,
Logan County, West Virginia
Death;
May 27, 2006
Huntington,
Cabell County, West Virginia
Burial:
White Chapel
Memorial Gardens,
Barboursville,
Cabell County, West Virginia

He was graduated from Kitt's Hill High School, Ohio, in 1936, with highest-grade honors in his class. For many years Carl was bi-vocational, working full time as a master carpenter in the Huntington area, building, selling and remodeling homes. His greatest joy in woodworking was cabinet construction. He also served as a church pastor for over 68 years of active ministry. Carl considered the most important happening in his young life occurred May 10, 1938, when he asked Jesus Christ to forgive his sins, and was saved. He immediately began to preach, was licensed and ordained in the West Virginia Yearly Meeting of Free Will Baptists, which later became a part of the National Association of Free Will Baptists and was faithful in his service to God for all his life. More than 20 men accepted the call to preach through his ministry. His work included numberless revivals from Canada to Florida. His spiritual impact on West Virginia, the United States and worldwide, will continue through the many lives he touched with the message of the Gospel. He always promoted Bible education, missions and the denominational ministries of Free Will Baptists. His first pastorates included these churches in Logan County, WV: Holden No. 7 and No. 8 Community Church, Holden No. 22 Community Church, Pine Creek Church at Omar, and Monaville Community Church, which through his leadership became Monaville Free Will Baptist Church. While there, he once preached to over 3,000 in an open-air service without aid of voice amplification. He was noted for the loudness of his voice, his knowledge of the scripture, his authority in the pulpit and his abiding concern for the spiritual needs of the people as he preached. In October 1950 the family moved to Huntington, in Cabell County, W.Va., when he accepted the pastorate of Thomas Memorial FWB Church. He served there for 26 years, until 1976. In those years the church enjoyed growth to over 500 in attendance, and underwent several expansions of the property. Pastor Vallance and his wife hosted 15 trips to Israel, beginning in Christmas of 1969. They introduced hundreds to the awesome experience of walking in the footsteps of Jesus in the Holy Land. He became founding pastor of Central FWB in Huntington in 1976, where he ministered until retirement in 1994. During his pastorate the church purchased property at 6th Ave and 5th Street. He was overseer of construction of the new worship center in 1980, using plans drawn by his son, Robert, a civil engineer. With Carl's leadership the church purchased four plots of property to provide growth opportunity for the church. In the service of his denomination, Carl began his ministry in the Yearly Meeting of Free Will Baptists in West Virginia. He was in attendance at the organizational meeting of the Wva. Free Will Baptist State Association, and was a pioneer in this ministry. He served in such positions as Moderator, Parliamentarian, and Foreign Missions Board member. He was elected as the General Board member, making him the representative of the Wva. State ministry to the National Association. He began attending the National Association of FWB in 1947, and only missed three meetings. He served as Executive Committee member on the national level, helping to oversee the ministry operations of the National Executive Office, and plan programs for annual National Conventions.

Preston Vance
Birth:
Apr. 4, 1919
Beauty, Fayette County,
West Virginia
Death:
May 6, 2012
Logan, Logan County,
West Virginia
Burial:
Forest Lawn Cemetery,
Pecks Mill,
Logan County, West Virginia

A well-known area minister, Vance, 93, of Chauncey, died at Logan Regional Medical Center. He was a son of the late Everest and Audrey Sullies Vance. Rev. Vance was a retired coal miner, a member of the UMWA, a former employee of the Wva. Coal and Coke Company and a veteran of the U.S. Army where he served as Staff Sergeant of the 94th Infantry Division during World War II. Rev. Vance was the founder of the Beth Haven Christian School at Omar. He was a minister for 53 years. During this time, he was pastor of the Mt. Calvary Freewill Baptist Church at Atenville for 12 years and pastor of the Walnut Grove Freewill Baptist Church at Chauncey for 23 years. He was also a member of the New Life Freewill Baptist Church at Rossmore and a member of the Huff Creek Freewill Baptist Conference.

Robert Lee Vance
Birth:
Jan. 19, 1910
West Virginia
Death:
Dec. 28, 1985
Ferrellsburg, Lincoln County,
West Virginia
Burial:
Robert Velva Vance Farm
(Little Harts Creek) Harts,
Lincoln County
West Virginia

He was pastor of the Little Harts Freewill Baptist Church, Little Harts Creek Road, Harts, WV, and was retired from the West Virginia Dept. of Highways.

Ward Vance
Birth:
Apr. 1, 1943
Harts, Lincoln County
West Virginia
Death:
Sep. 2, 2009
Logan, Logan County,
West Virginia
Burial:
Forest Lawn Cemetery,
Pecks Mill,
Logan County, West Virginia

Pastor of the Little Harts Freewill Baptist Church, Harts, WV. He pastored "officially" for 24 years and was a member for about 45 years. He was an Assistant Pastor to his father for many years prior his pastoring. He served as a deacon for nine years helping his father with pastoral duties. He loved the Church greatly. He worked at Sunset Furniture in Huntington, WV, in the mid-1960s, Vance's Amco at Atenville, Wva., as a mechanic, and served as a State Inspector for the State of West Virginia. He later started his own business, Ward's Workshop, as a building contractor until he got hurt in 1986. He was a member of the United States Chamber of Commerce.

Chester C. Wainwright
Birth:
1847
Jefferson County, West Virginia
Death:
Aug. 13, 1902
Charles Town
Jefferson County, West Virginia
Burial:
Fairview Cemetery
Gibsontown
Jefferson County, West Virginia

He married Lizzie Dunlap on December 27, 1877. He was ordained about 1875, pastoring of the churches at Charlestown and Shepherdstown. He was a student at Storer College, Harpers Ferry, West Virginia, about 1876-78, and ministered the Charlestown church to which more than 100 have been added by baptism.

Rev Norwood M Webb
Birth:
Feb. 26, 1935
Winifrede
Kanawha County
West Virginia
Death:
Oct. 17, 2014
West Virginia
Burial:
Kanawha Valley Memorial Gardens
Glasgow
Kanawha County
West Virginia

Rev. Norwood M. Webb, 79, of Chelyan, went to be with the Lord after a short illness. His final days were spent lovingly surrounded by family and friends.

He was born to parents, Melvin and Nancy Webb. He served two tours in the U.S. Army and spent the majority of his life serving God. He was the clerk for the Freewill Baptist State Association for 38 years and Kanawha conference. He served as the pastor at Cabin Creek Carbon Freewill Baptist for many years. He was also a member of the UMWA.

Norwood is survived by his wife of 54 years, Opal Webb; son, Timothy Webb and wife, Barbara Webb, of Atlanta, Ga.; son, Ricky Webb and wife, Patricia Franklin Webb, of Detroit, Mich.; son, Danny Webb of Chelyan; son, Brian Webb and companion, Patricia McCown, of Winifrede.
Funeral service with Rev. Rick Holstein and Dan Kelly officiating.

Earl Austin Whitmore
Birth:
Dec. 25, 1917

Death:
Jun. 16, 1996
Cabell County,
West Virginia
Burial:
Greenbottom Cemetery
Green Bottom
Cabell County,
West Virginia

One of the former pastors of the Good Shepherd Free Will Baptist Church, Huntington, West Virginia.

Samuel Franklin Wills
Birth:
Mar. 3, 1855
Raleigh County, West Virginia
Death:
Mar. 26, 1936
Burial:
Barker Cemetery
Ashford
Boone County,
West Virginia

In 1875, he married Paulina Webb and was ordained at December 6, 1886. His pastorates was with the New Hope and Rock Creek churches in West Virginia.

His mother was Lucia Ann Wills. He was an ordained Free Will Baptist minister for many years, his name appearing in a list of ministers in Minutes of Cooperative General Association, in 1918, when convened in Paintsville, KY.

Omer L. Williams
Birth:
Aug. 18, 1913
Death:
Jun. 18, 1976
Burial:
Sunset Memorial Park
Beckley
Raleigh County, West Virginia
Plot: Locustvale Section

He founded the Shelton Free Will Baptist Church in Shelton, West Virginia and served as its pastor from 1958 until 1963.

Shelia G. Williams
Birth:
Jul. 14, 1937
Long Branch
Fayette County, West Virginia
Death:
Feb. 14, 2015
Harper
Raleigh County, West Virginia
Burial:
Dock Lively Cemetery
Long Branch
Fayette County, West Virginia

She was the daughter of the late Arthur (Clate) and Junie (Rene) Saye Williams.

A graduate from Pax High School in 1955, Shelia went on to graduate from the Free Will Baptist Bible College in Nashville, TN in 1968 and was also a graduate of language school in Texas in 1970 having studied Spanish.

Ms. Williams left the United States in 1970 to work on the South American mission field in Quito, Ecuador. She spent 13 years overseas teaching adults and children about the Lord - starting several churches.

Shelia gave her heart to the Lord at a very young age. She was a member of the Bradley Free Will Baptist Church where she taught Sunday school and was a leader in the youth groups. She taught Vacation Bible School at several local churches; was a member of Women Active for Christ at Bradley and also involved with the jail house ministry.

Returning home to help care for her parents, she went back to school and graduated from Concord College with a Bachelor of Science in Education in 1986. She went on to teach Special Needs Children in Fayette County for many years as well as teaching Adult Spanish night classes at the Fayette Vo-Tech. Always the student Shelia continued her education while working and received a Master's degree from the College of Graduate Studies at Institute in 1990. She retired from the WV education system.

We all have the same body, the same human flesh, and therefore we will all die.

Wisconsin

George C Alborn
Birth:
1877
Death:
1956
Burial:
Wauwatosa Cemetery
Wauwatosa,
Milwaukee County,
Wisconsin

Rev. Alborn, a graduate of Hillside College, a Free Baptist institution and the first college in Michigan to organize under the general college law in 1853, was a prolific and scholarly writer, publishing a novel (*Ish Kerioth, 1904*), A history (*History of the First Baptist Church if Bricelin, Minnesota, 1933*) and *a collection of poetry (Rhythms of Life), 1941,*

He served as pastor of the Burnett church (Dodge County) from 1899 to 1901, the Fairwater (Fond du Lac County) and Grand Prairie (Green Lake County) churches from 1902 to 1905, the Greenbush church (Sheboygan County) from 1906 to 1907, the Allenville church (Winnebago County) from

1908 to 1909, and the Oak Center and Oakfield churches (Fond du Lac County) in 1911. Following the dissolution of the Wisconsin Freewill Baptist church, he also served other congregations including the Underwood Memorial church in Wauwatosa.

Rev. Alborn also served as secretary of the Home Mission Board of the Wisconsin Freewill church and was instrumental in promoting the merger of the Freewill church with the general Baptist church, as reported in the May, 2007, newsletter of the historical society:

The topic of reunion remained relatively quiet until 1904, when it was raised again during Yearly Meetings in Wisconsin, Minnesota and Maine in the belief that the Baptist church had grown closer to the theological positions of the Freewill church.

Among other initiatives, Rev. George C. Alborn, pastor of the Fairwater congregation, advanced a resolution at the Wisconsin Yearly Meeting calling for a merger of the two denominations. In response, the national General Conference created a committee to study the issue.

In accordance with an act passed by the 1913 legislature authorizing the change, the trustees of the Wisconsin

Yearly Meeting of Freewill Baptists, in session at Fairwater, Wis., September 23, voted to dissolve the corporation. The resolution filed with the secretary of state provides that all property coming to the corporation shall inure to the benefit of the Wisconsin Baptist state convention, and that the affairs of the corporation shall be wound up. Rev. P. Kisner is president and Rev. George C. Alborn secretary of the convention. (September 30, 1913, Janesville Daily Gazette)

Rev Abiezer "Bizer" Bridges
Birth:
Feb. 5, 1786
Penobscot
Hancock County
Maine, USA
Death:
Mar. 22, 1883
Monticello, Wis
Burial:
Zwingli Cemetery
Monticello
Green County
Wisconsin

Rev. Abiezer Bridges, closed his earthly pilgrimage at aged 79 years. He was converted and commenced preaching on South Fox Island, Maine, where his labors were blessed. He was at this time connected with the Congregationalists. Being a Free Baptist in sentiment, he went to Lincolnville, where he was baptized, and ordained in 1821. He preached in various places with success, organizing churches at Long Island, Hope, and China, and baptizing during his ministry more than 1,000 converts. Without especial training for the work, his good common sense, and his happy faculty of expressing his ideas clearly and easily with his love of singing, gave him a large measure of success.

Jesse Burnham
Birth:
May 16, 1778 Lee,
Strafford County,
New Hampshire
Death:
Dec. 5, 1869
Janesville,
Rock County, Wisconsin
Burial:
Mount Pleasant Cemetery,
Rock County,
Wisconsin

He moved to Sebec, Maine, in 1806, and began to preach there with success. Jointly with Rev. Mr. Sealels and Rev. Mr. Libby organized a church there. Baptized many hundreds in the region where now are the towns of Atkinson, Charlestown, Garland, Corinth, Dexter, Exeter, Bradford, Dover, Foxcroft, Sebec, Brownsville, Milo, Medford and other places and gathered them into the Sebec Quarter Meeting. He was ordained in 1808 in New Hampshire, and He moved to Maxfield, ME, 1815, and Howland, ME, 1818. Organized a church there. Afterward, organized churches at Passadumkeng, ME, another at Lincoln, and Lowell, ME. In 1840 he moved to Janesville, Wisconsin, being the second Free Will Baptist minister in WI, after Rev. Mr. Cheney, together, organized the First QM in Wisconsin. He organized Prairie du Sac church in 1841. He assisted in organizing the Honey Creek Q.M. and was also in the Yearly Meeting. He did good service as a pioneer preacher on the prairies of Wisconsin and northern Illinois. He labored many years and died in his 86th year, preaching till within four weeks of his death.

Richard M Cary
Birth:
Dec. 10, 1794
Williamsburg,
Hampshire County,
Massachusetts
Death:
Oct. 16, 1868
Rock County, Wisconsin
Burial:
North Johnstown Cemetery,
Milton,
Rock County, Wisconsin

In 1806, when still a young boy his family moved to western New York, which was rugged and wild with no neighbor south or west, for 40 miles. He had limited opportunity for education or religious training, but by untiring effort he began to study and received a common English education. No minister was near when needed for a funeral, so his father often said the words of comfort; this the father did for Richard's brother, Calvin, who was killed at Buffalo, NY in War of 1812. His brother's death affected Richard deeply. In 1814, a Freewill Baptist missionary, the Rev. Jeremiah Folsom, visited this newly settled country, and he embraced the earliest opportunity of hearing the stranger. In Sept. 1816, he was baptized with seven others and organized with them into a Freewill Baptist Church. He felt impressed with a duty to preach. On Oct. 3, 1816, Erie Co. NY, he delivered his first sermon. He was ordained in June 1820 to the ministry. He began to hold meetings and baptize a number of converts. In Nov. he organized a church, and pastored the church for a portion of the time for the next twenty years. In Aug. 1821 he assisted in the organization of the Holland Purchase Yearly Meeting, which included all twenty-seven churches. At this time, he became acquainted with David Marks, a lad of 15 years, who was out on his first preaching tour. They together, at Eden, had a large number they organized into a church. He continued in ministry until 1842 when he moved out West, to Johnstown, Wis. Where he soon organized a church. He took a leading part in planting other churches and in organizing the Wisconsin Y.M. He also pastored two years in Cherry Valley, IL in the 1850's. Elder Cary was a man of unbiased judgment and earnest convictions, with more dignity than is usual, tall, slender, and of a very fine and graceful figure. He was prematurely gray from ill health. His preaching was Biblical and impressive. He and his wife were companions for more than half a century. Their son, Roswell, educated at Hillsdale College, was a pre-eminent member of the Tennessee bar, but died suddenly in Feb. 1868.

Of their seven children who survived at his death, Benjamin, who died earlier, had served as a member of the Wisconsin Legislature, and for six years as Treasurer of Rock County. His own words, "...about five hundred have received baptism at my hands."

He planted twelve churches and assisted in several others. He assisted in ordaining about twenty ministers and preached about six hundred funeral sermons. The denomination lost one of its early pillars, and the church one of its wisest counselors.

Rufus Ellis Cheney
Birth:
May 4, 1780
Hillsborough County,
New Hampshire
Death:
Aug. 30, 1869
New Berlin,
Waukesha County, Wisconsin
Burial:
Sunnyside Cemetery,
New Berlin,
Waukesha County, Wisconsin

Cheney was born in Antrim, New Hampshire. He began to preach about twenty-three years of age, and was ordained in 1810. After residing for a time in Vermont, near St. Johnsbury, he moved to Attica, New York, where, with the assistance of Rev. N. Brown, he was instrumental in gathering a church. During his three years at that place it increased to 120 members. In 1817 he settled in Porter, Ohio, and organized a small church,

which soon numbered more than 100. (This church still exists and the pastor is the moderator of the Ohio State Association and active in the national convention.) In his labors the Little Scioto Quarterly Meeting had its origin. Returning to New York, he ministered to the Attica church several years, and built there a house of worship. In 1837 he settled in Wisconsin, where he organized the New Berlin church in 1840, and the Honey Creek church in 1841,- the first churches gathered in the state. He was the father of the Honey Creek Quarterly Meeting, and, with Cary and others, took an important part in building up the Wisconsin Yearly Meeting. He enjoyed the confidence of all who knew him.

Don't worry about tomorrow because God has already taken care of it.

Joseph Clough

Birth:
Oct. 9, 1813
Gilmanton, Belknap County,
New Hampshire
Death:
Dec. 12, 1894
Burnett, Dodge County,
Wisconsin
Burial:
Hyland Prairie Cemetery
Oak Grove, Dodge County,
Wisconsin

He was an ordained Freewill Baptist minister, and settled in 1848 on a farm in Burnett, (Dodge Co) Wis., where he died. He united with the Rolling Prairie church at its organization; received license to preach in August, 1854, and was ordained by the Waupun Quarterly Meeting, in February, 1858. He was at different time's pastor of some of the churches in the vicinity, and was respected by all.

Good-by; but oh, it is not forever

Rev Ruel Cooley

Birth:
Apr. 19, 1819
New York
Death:
Apr. 13, 1885
Johnstown
Rock County
Wisconsin
Burial:
North Johnstown Cemetery
Milton
Rock County, Wisconsin

He graduated from Oberlin College, Ohio, in 1846. Rev. Cooley was an ordained Freewill Baptist minister and pastor. He had also served as missionary to India before his health forced him from the field. He was involved in preaching and organizing churches in the western states, and was about to go to Kenesaw, NE, when he took ill and died.

It was a great loss to the fledging church movement there as he was an able minister and esteemed by all who knew him.

Abner Coombs

Birth:
Dec. 1, 1794
Brunswick, Cumberland
County, Maine
Death:
Mar. 15, 1880
Honey Creek, Walworth
County, Wisconsin
Burial:
Honey Creek Cemetery
Honey Creek,
Walworth County, Wisconsin
Plot: Block 3 Lot 2

He was converted when twenty-two years of age and married to Annstrus Melcher two years later. His ordination by the Sebec, Quarterly Meeting took place Sept. 22, 1830. Residing at Foxcroft, he organized a church there and at Sangerfield, and assisted in gathering several others. Removing to Wisconsin in 1842, he soon united with the Honey Creek church, and remained in it until his death. He was pastor of that church seven years, also for a time at Pike Grove and Wheatland, Sharon and other places also enjoyed his labors. He baptized 178 converts, was thoroughly evangelical and never swerved from the plain precepts of the Bible.

Albion P. Coombs

Birth:
1829
Death:
Sep. 22, 1899
Burial:
Oakwood Cemetery
Waterford
Racine County
Wisconsin
Plot: Section 51

A Freewill Baptist minister who did good work lbion Paris

Coombs was the son of Rev. Abner and Annstrus (Melcher) COOMBS. He was married to Harriet White 5 Oct 1848. His father and mother were living in their HH in their late years.

Isaac G Davis
Birth:
Mar. 18, 1819
Canada
Death:
Dec. 23, 1862
Fayette, Lafayette County, Wisconsin
Burial:
Fayette Cemetery
Fayette, Lafayette County, Wisconsin,

His parents were Silas L. Davis and Phoebe (Bennett) DAVIS. His family had moved to Vermont and his brother, Rev. Jairus E. Davis was in a protracted meeting when Isaac G. declared that from 'from that moment on he was for the Lord.' He began to feel it his duty to preach, and in 1838, he began holding meetings and studying with reference to the great work. His efforts were favorably looked on and the Huntington Quarterly Meeting of Freewill Baptist, gave him license in June 1839 to preach. He was ordained the next year on the 26th of Sept. 1840. He was accepted by the Missions Board as a foreign missionary, but it was finally concluded that his health would not endure the climate of India. However, his heart was always enlisted in the cause of Missions, and he gave of his scanty means, as well as his life going and preaching, to help. While attending Biblical School at Lowell, he labored with the church in Roxbury, MA, which was greatly increased in strength and numbers. In Aug. 8, 1843, he was married to Almira Bullock, in Lowell, Mass. They spent one year in Portsmouth, NH, then two years of faithful service to Deerfield, NH. A trip to Nova Scotia and New Brunswick was made where his labors were successful. After a three-month supply of the desk at Lawrence, he removed West. For several years, with the exception of a year or two spent in Elgin, Ill., most of his time was given to missionary labors in Boon and McHenry Quarterly Meetings and in other parts of Illinois and Wisconsin. In 1855, he took the pastoral care of the FWB Church in Fayette, WI, where (with exception of one year in Warren, Ill) he continued faithfully until his death. He enjoyed the confidence of his congregation. In Dec. 1862, he served as moderator in Quarterly Meeting, apparently in good health; was immediately taken ill, and died in eleven days. Prof. Ransom Dunn, whom he had selected, addressed a large and deeply-affected audience upon the occasion, from II Corinthians 4:17-18. His life and example were unusually blameless. His friends were many; his enemies, none. He left the inestimable treasure of a good example to the world. He left four brothers,-- Mr. Silas A. Davis, the Yearly Meeting Clerk; Deacon W. Bennet Davis, and Revs. Jairus E. and Kinsman R. Davis. Also, three or four sisters, and an aged father, who, for more than fifty years, has been a faithful member of the Freewill Baptist Denomination. His own family consisted of a daughter and three sons, the oldest of whom went in the army, and the youngest–a child two years old–to heaven, having departed two days in advance of his father. He was aged 43 years. Source: Info is from an old book, "Memoirs of Eminent Preachers in the Freewill Baptist Denomination (1874)," by Selah Hibbard Barrett. (Copyright is public domain). Also, a short bio confirms relationships to his minister brothers, etc, in *"Cyclopedia of Free Baptist,"* pub. 1889, by Burgess and Ward as well as a short bio of Isaac G. Family.

Samuel Drown
Birth:
Mar. 10, 1796
Sheffield,
Caledonia County, Vermont
Death:
Sep. 9, 1884
Beaver Dam,
Dodge County, Wisconsin
Burial:
Oakwood Cemetery,

Beaver Dam, Dodge County, Wisconsin, Plot: Sec 1b

He was ordained a Free Will Baptist minister in 1831 in New Hampshire, and labored for a time in the Wheelock Quarterly Meeting, and also, in New Hampshire, where he was a member of the Legislature three years. In 1845. He moved to Dodge Co., Wisconsin, and obtained land, and continued to reside at Beaver Dam until his death. He was treasurer of Dodge Co. in 1847, and connected with the Jefferson QM of FW Baptists, being widely known and respected.

It is knowing that God WILL!

Benjamin Garret Fowler
Birth:
1774
Death:
Dec. 12, 1848
Burial:
Union Cemetery
Brothertown, Calumet County, Wisconsin

Fowler, a native of Mohegan, Conn., and one of the Brothertown Indians, was ordained in New York in 1819, and died in Manchester, Wis., Dec. 12, 1848, aged 73 years. "This may certify that Benjamin Fowler is acknowledged as a public administrator in the Free-Will Baptist connection.- Done by order of the Union Yearly Meeting Council at Sherbum, June 14, 1845. Samuel Nichols, Yearly Meeting Clerk."
He was much loved as a good citizen and philanthropist and was respected as a faithful minister. In his advanced years he supplied the Manchester church, preaching his last sermon December 2. He was marshal of the town for several years, and a peacemaker from 1808 to 1811. In religious affairs he was a leader, and ministered as an elder of the Freewill Baptist order. He removed to Wisconsin with his family, and aged 74. His gravestone bears the tribute: 'He spoke the language of his Master, 'little children, love one another',

Josiah Fowler
Birth:
Jul. 29, 1794
Thetford,
Orange County, Vermont
Death:
Dec. 29, 1864
Wyocena,
Columbia County, Wisconsin
Burial:
Wyocena Cemetery,
Wyocena,
Columbia County,
Wisconsin

His father was a native of England, a cooper by trade and lived in humble circumstances, which compelled the children early to form habits of industry. Rev. Fowler at 13 years of age, gave himself to God; he became connected with the Free Baptists when twenty-one, and while teaching in Camillon, New York, preached his first sermon in his schoolhouse. He received license in Apr 1816, and ordination Aug. 20, 1819, Rev's N. Brown, N. Ketchum and N. Hinckley serving on the council. He had great success as an evangelist and in surrounding towns he baptized multiplied converts which enabled him to organize churches. Out of the many converts, nine became ministers. In 1836, Rev. Fowler became a member of the Ohio and Pennsylvania Y.M., and was active in the work, serving as pastor at Mecca, Ohio. Wellsburgh and Big Bend, Pennsylvania, health permitted. A few months before his death he sought relief in a change of climate, but without avail, and died in Wyocena, Wisconsin. Rev. Fowler was esteemed as one of the church's ablest ministers. He had strong religious sensibilities, and was greatly blessed of God in his chosen line of work. Two of his sons served as officers in the Civil War; one became an attorney and one professor of mathematics in Hillsdale College.

Rev Joseph Benjamin Gidney
Birth:
Apr., 1847,
Canada
Death: 1933
Wisconsin
Burial:

Milton Cemetery
Milton
Rock County, Wisconsin

Spouse: Annie E Gidney
(1852 - 1914)

Emeline *Wade* Griffin
Birth:
Mar. 29, 1817
Ontario, Canada
Death:
Sep. 1, 1906
Hortonville,
Outagamie County, Wisconsin
Burial:
Allenville Cemetery, Allenville,
Winnebago County, Wisconsin
Married Jacob Griffin 06 Oct. 1836, in Canada. Her husband was a minister, who went from Canada to United States and back, finally to Wisconsin, where they for 35 years together had been successful in their preaching and church endeavors. She, successfully preached alongside her husband, as per written records. Their work resulted in much good. She died at age 89.

Jacob Griffin
Birth:
Nov. 5, 1815
Lincoln County, Ontario,
Canada
Death:
Jan. 26, 1901
Hortonville,
Outagamie County, Wisconsin
Burial:
Allenville Cemetery, Allenville,
Winnebago County, Wisconsin

His parents held loyalist sentiments and went to Canada to escape. It was mostly an untamed area, and Jacob did not have many educational opportunities, but at age 16 years, he heard Rev's David Marks and Obadiah Jenkins preach. After the meeting he joined the Free Will Baptist Church there. He began to preach in 1843, and ordained in Canada in 1844. At once he began in evangelizing and organizing churches. On 06 Oct. 1836, he married Emeline WADE, and shortly thereafter, they migrated to Illinois. He was useful there in that state, but moved back to Canada in 1852, remaining until 1867, when he accepted a call to Winnebago and Vineland churches in Wisconsin. He was abundant in his labors, pastoring and evangelizing in the region. Over 700 were baptized by him. He was a sympathetic friend, a true minister, who sought neither wealth nor the praise of men. His wife Emeline survived him; two sons, Rev. Z.F. Griffin of Keuka College, New York, who for ten years was a missionary in India; Norvell W. Griffin, a farmer in Oklahoma. A short funeral service was held at his home, then his body was carried by train to the Free Baptist Church, in Allenville, where the Rev. J. M. Kayser, long-time friend, and fellow churchman, officiated at his service.(more information can be found on the Wisconsin Free Will Baptist Historical Society web site, History of Nebraska, Vol 3, by Julius S. Morton).

Rev William B Hamlin
Birth:
1816
Vermont
Death:
Aug. 6, 1874
Burial:
Evergreen Cemetery
Oconto
Oconto County
Wisconsin

Nathaniel Harvey
Birth:
Jan. 9, 1788
New Hampshire
Death:
Jun. 4, 1870
Fulton, Rock County,
Wisconsin
Burial:
Mount Pleasant Cemetery
Janesville, Rock County,
Wisconsin

Harvey was born in Nottingham, N. H., and was converted in early life under the labors of Elder Benjamin Randall. He began to preach when eighteen years of age, and was ordained in 1812, when he settled at Atkinson, Maine, Where he remained pastor about thirty years. In 1844 he moved to Fulton, Wisconsin, where he remained until about four years before his death, at Evansville. While in Wisconsin, Brother Harvey was connected with the Calvinistic Baptists.

Herman Jenkins
Birth:
1785
Massachusetts
Death:
Jul. 23, 1855
Heart Prairie
Walworth County
Wisconsin
Burial:
Millard Cemetery
Millard
Walworth County
Wisconsin
Plot: Sec. A, Row 4

He was converted in a revival immediately following the organization of the Bethany, NY, church in 1809, about twenty-four years of age. The second session of the Bethany Free Will Baptist Quarterly Meeting (Q.M.) was held at his house in Batavia in May 1813, and he was ordained Aug. 20, 1814. He remained connected with the Bethany church until 1840, when he went to Ashtabula Co. Ohio, and in 1843, he settled in Wisconsin. His death occurred at his house on Heart Prairie, Wis., July 23, 1855.His education was limited, but his acquaintance with human nature and experimental religion, and his great familiarity with the Bible enabled him to labor with great success. The venerable Nathaniel Brown being also with the Bethany church, Bro. Jenkins was permitted to labor much abroad.

His firm health permitted him to indulge his ardent zeal. He was at Boston, NY, in 1817; at Middlebury, NY in 1824, and saw here and elsewhere the abundant blessing of God. He made an exploring tour into Canada in 1822, assisting Elder Banghart at Dunwich, and another tour in 1828, gathering the church in Southwold. He was especially successful at Trumbull and Hart's Grove, OH. Having preached at Penfield, NY in 1830, a revival began, which was continued by others and over fifty persons dated their conviction to his sermons. Few men on the Western frontier have done more efficient service.

He Is The Beginning And The End

William W Joy
Birth:
Mar. 29, 1831
New York, USA
Death:
Oct. 17, 1906
Wisconsin
Burial:
Mound Cemetery
Racine
Racine County
Wisconsin

William W. Joy, age 30, was a student of Hillsdale College, Hillsdale, Mich, in 1860 Census. He living in Household of College Prof. Henry S. Whipple, 46y, b. VT, and wife, Elizabeth, 45y, b. MA.
A Whipple dau, Roseann, 19, and Marion Packard (female) 18, b NH as well as W.W. JOY, 30, b NY were all college students.
He was mar. To Ruhama Lefler, and they had at least one child, May Joy. Mar. Jerome Spencer, 26 June 1907, Racine, WI.
In 1855 Renselaer Co. NY census Wm. W.'s parents were shown as Martin Joy, age 83y of Renselear Co. NY and Polly Joy, 74ys.
(See Ruhama Joy's memorial for her obit).

J. M. Kayser
Birth:
Mar. 19, 1831
Columbiana County, Ohio
Death:
Dec. 21, 1913
Seattle,
King County, Washington

Burial:
Allenville Cemetery, Allenville,
Winnebago County, Wisconsin

He was ordained a Free Will Baptist minister, in Athens, Ohio Quarterly Meeting in 1862. He had been licensed by same, on Nov. 23, 1861. During his first two years of ministry, he traveled as evangelist with the Rev's I. Z Haning and B. V. Tewksbury. He prepared in the Atwood, Ohio Institute for one year, then finishing with the University of Ohio for three years. His pastorates included: Albany, Ohio; Liberty, Illinois; Gobleville and Waverly, Michigan; and Winneconie, Wisconsin, where his labors were blessed. He has filled the Chair of Mathematics at Atwood Institute for three years; was a delegate to the General Conference, was president of the Wisconsin Home Mission Board. He also served in Nebraska Free Will Baptist churches doing mission work and helping there, before going to Wisconsin, where he spent 36 years of his ministry. He was used in many funerals and weddings as he ministered in Wisconsin.

Rev Leman W Lee
Birth:
Aug. 3, 1784
Vermont
Death:
Feb. 15, 1875
Winnebago County
Wisconsin
Burial:
Allenville Cemetery
Allenville
Winnebago County
Wisconsin
Plot: Section A, Row 3

Rev. Lemon W. LEE, a native of Vermont, was licensed to preach in 1820 and ordained in Boston, N.Y., Nov. 12, 1831. He labored several years in western New York and saw much good.
After a season in Illinois, he went, some twenty years before his death, to Wisconsin, laboring for a time at Winneconne, and later residing at Winnebago, where he died, aged 90 years.
His last sermon was preached the June preceding his death. He was a true, devoted minister.

Greenly Mevis

Birth: Aug. 6, 1818
New York
Death: Aug. 21, 1894
Waukesha
Waukesha County
Wisconsin
Burial:
Prairie Home Cemetery
Waukesha
Waukesha County
Wisconsin
Plot: Sec N, Blk 50, Lot 1, Sp 1

Greenly Mevis wrote many religious pamphlets.
Family links:
Parents:
Hannah Blanchard Mevis (1782 - 1867)

Spouses:
Orinda H Mevis (1831 - 1898)
Caroline Janes Mevis (1823 - 1887)*

William Mitchell

Birth:
Mar. 5, 1821
Death:
Jan. 8, 1904
Burial:
Union Cemetery
Hortonville, Outagamie County, Wisconsin

Rev. William Mitchell was born at New Portland, Maine and married to R.C. Staples in 1847. Twenty-seven years later [1874] he was married again to B.L. Raymond. He was converted in 1840, and ordained in 1844. His ministry of more than forty years has been spent mostly in Wisconsin with the Fairwater, Harrisville, Rosen- dale, Eldorado, Greenbush, South Prairie, Winnebago, Vinland, Hortonville and Dale churches. The church at Hortonville, where he served as pastor at intervals, in all amounting to more than twenty years.

Elder David Moon

Birth:
Jan. 19, 1803
Herkimer County
New York
Death:
Dec. 8, 1877
Dodge County
Wisconsin
Burial:
Kekoskee Cemetery
Kekoskee
Dodge County, Wisconsin

Son of Benajah and Sarah Gould Silver Moon. David and Catherine's children: Priscilla (Fleming), Emma (Crane), Owen S., Esther Catherine (Roby), William, Henry, Prudence, Clarissa (Clark), Albert, Charles, David Jr., and Tryphena.
The 1860 census enumerates him as a farmer.
The 1870 census enumerates him as a clergyman.
--From the 110th anniversary booklet of the Russia (NY) Union church:
-David, born Jan. 19, 1803; died Dec. 8, 1877, in Williamstown, Dodge County, Wis.; married, 1st, Catherine Rhodes, born Nov. 30, 1802, the daughter of Richard and Effy (Clapper) Rhodes; 2nd, Martha Kinney of Mohawk, N.Y.; 3rd, Maranda Nobles. David Moon was a Baptist clergyman and served the Russia Church, 1847 to 1848. Elder David Moon, as he was called, went to California alone, stayed four years and returned with a bag of gold which he sold for $1200. He then went to Wisconsin and purchased a farm. He lived at Kekoskee, Wis., and later Williamstown, Wis.
Alvin Moon (1807 - 1893)*
Roxana Moon Plumb (1811 - 1846)*

Inscription:
In the circle at top: Absent Not Dead/ Christ Is My Hope. The bottom inscription-very worn- I think the second line starts with "Was" and ends with "death", the third line seems to be "have laid his body in this grave" and the last line" His Soul Has Gone to Rest".

Rev Joseph Baker Morford

Birth:
Nov., 1795
Death:
May, 1855
Burial:
Pierceville Cemetery
Sun Prairie
Dane County, Wisconsin

Early FW Baptist preacher in Wisconsin.

Augustus Phillips

Birth:
Mar. 27, 1825
Marcellus,
New York
Death:
Apr. 30, 1907
Eau Claire, Wisconsin
Burial:
South Lawrence Cemetery
De Pere,
Brown County,
Wisconsin

The first two decades of Wrightstown's Freewill Baptist congregation are in- exorably tied to the career of Augustus Phillips, one of northeastern Wisconsin's most remarkable religious figures in the second half of the nineteenth century. Three of Phillips' five brothers became Freewill Baptist ministers serving congreg- ations in New England. Phillips apparently received no formal education.

He left home at the age of eleven and went to Ohio, then back to New York, and then to Rhode Island, working as a farm laborer and woolen goods manufacturer. In 1846 he married Minerva Greene, and in 1851 the couple moved to Wisconsin, where he purchased 160 acres of land in an unincorporated settle- ment known as Sniderville, approximately 2 miles northwest of the village of Wrightstown. This farm, later expanded with the purchase of additional acreage, was the family's home for the next 54 years. In September 1864 Phillips enlisted in Company E of Wisconsin's 42nd Infantry Regiment; he was mustered out in June 1865, after distinguished service, with the rank of corporal. Phillips' religious activities began soon after he arrived in Wisconsin.

He served as a lay preacher beginning in the mid-1850s at the "earnest request" of his neighbors, preaching to Methodist congregations, a practice he may have continued for ten years. He was ordained a Freewill Baptist minister in 1866.

On January 6, 1866, Phillips and fourteen men and women met and organized Wrights- town's Freewill Baptist congregation. Two years later they acquired land and began constructing their church in the village. Within a few years, some of the original members organized separate Freewill Baptist congregations at Sniderville and at Greenleaf, another unincorporated settlement approximately four miles east of Wrightstown. Phillips is credited with establishing all three of these congregations, and he served

all three as pastor until 1885. In that year he withdrew from the pastorates of Wrightstown and Greenleaf but continued as pastor at Sniderville, finally retiring from that pulpit in 1905.

Phillips was known for leading successful revivals throughout his pastorate. In September 1876 a revival began in Wrightstown "which bids fair to be equal to the one recently held over at Greenleaf, where between 40 and 50 conversions.

In addition to preaching in the three churches at Wrightstown, Greenleaf, and Sniderville, Phillips also exchanged pulpits with other Freewill Baptist ministers throughout the region, including Kaukauna, Oshkosh, Shiocton, and Hortonville, preaching to the latter congregation every other week "for quite a long time. Phillips and lay members of the Wrightstown church also attended Quarterly Meetings of the Waupun District at various communities throughout northeastern Wisconsin. In October 1905 Phillips preached his farewell sermon to the Sniderville Baptist congregation; Baptists from Wrightstown, Kaukauna, Appleton "and other places" attended. Phillips died in Eau Claire. His body was returned to northeastern Wisconsin by train, his funeral "very largely attended, people from Menasha, Greenleaf, Kaukauna, Wrightstown and De Pere being present." Phillips was buried in the Sniderville Baptist cemetery. Phillips' wife Minerva died on January 6, 1913, and is buried next to him in the Sniderville cemetery-the South Lawrence Cemetery.

Mowry Phillips
Birth:
Mar. 16, 1857
Death:
Jan. 27, 1942
Burial:
South Lawrence Cemetery
De Pere, Brown County,
Wisconsin

Parents: Augustus Phillips (1825 – 1907) Minerva A. Greene Phillips (1825 – 1913)

Rev Mary Pitcher
Birth:
May 2, 1887
Death: unknown
Burial:
Colby Cemetery, Colby
Clark County, Wisconsin

PITCHER, Rev. Mrs. Mary; (May or may not be, but she was a minister in Wis);Bur. beside husband, Benj. Pitcher; Pitcher, Mary (1832 - 1887), Taylor County, Wisconsin Biographical, History & Ancestry RecordsPitcher, Mary (1832 - 1887), Taylor County, Wisconsin Biographical, History & Ancestry Records Pitcher, Mary (1832 - 1887), Taylor County, Wisconsin Biographical Records

---

James Raymar Pope
Birth:
May 13, 1819
Windsor
Hartford County, Connecticut
Death:
Jun. 8, 1897
Clinton,Rock County, isconsin
Burial:
Clinton Cemetery
Clinton,Rock County,
Wisconsin

Rev. James Raymar Pope 9th child of Dr. Samuel Pope and Freelove Waterman Pope of Union, Broome Co., NY., and Freelove Pope of Janesville, Rock Co., WI.At the age of 5 years his father Samuel Pope, was a prominent physician, moved to Broome Co., NY. At the age of fifteen James' father died, leaving a family of nine children, of which he was the seventh son. In 1839 Mr. Pope

came to Wisconsin probably with mother and brother Cyrus Waterman Pope, settling in Rock County, near Janesville where other brother Virgil Pope resided Section 14, Janesville. At the age of twenty-two he began the study of law, but was converted a year later and joined the Free Will Baptist Church. He abandon the bar and took the pulpit, and began preparation for the same at once. In June 1848 Bro. Pope was ordained to the gospel ministry and in 12 June 1851 in Harmony, Rock Co., WI., was united in marriage to Justina V. Miller a daughter of Cornelius Miller and wife Selinda Smith Miller.In 1889 he was pastor of Longbranch Free Will Baptist Church, located 6 miles southeast of Tecumseh, Johnson Co., Nebraska.

W. A. Potter
Birth:
Jan. 23, 1820

Bennington, Vermont
Death:
Jul. 23, 1880
Monticello, Wisconsin
Burial:
Zwingli Cemetery
Monticello
Green County, Wisconsin

Rev Oscar J Shannon
Birth:
Aug. 5, 1842
Vermont
Death:
Apr. 9, 1878
Kansas
Burial:
Burnett Corners Cemetery
Burnett
Dodge County, Wisconsin

SHANNON, Rev. Oscar J), mar. 7 July 1870 to Gertrude Mary Lockwood, Dodge Co. Wis; Fth/Mth: John A Shannon and Maryette/Margarette (?)
Inscription:
Age 35y 8m 4d

Robert Davenport Sparks
Birth: Feb. 8, 1827
Summit
Schoharie County
New York
Death: Jan. 7, 1913
Waushara County
Wisconsin
Burial:
Plainfield Cemetery
Plainfield
Waushara County
Wisconsin
Plot: Row 1, Lot 25,

SPARKS, Rev. R. D (Robt. Davenport), 1827-1913, Bur. Plainfield Cem.,Plainfield, Waushara Co. Wis. His memorial/stone has "Rev" and Kevin Sparks is the contributor.
Robert Davenport Sparks is my 4th great Uncle.   Yes he was a Free Baptist Minister.   He retired in 1907.   I have virtual cemeteries on my profile listing some of the marriages he performed.

A. B. Taylor
Birth:
Unknown
Southwold, Ontario, Canada
Death:
Jan. 28, 1876
Burial:
Rienzi Cemetery,
Fond du Lac,
Fond du Lac County,
Wisconsin

Rev. Taylor, when nineteen years of age, became a follower of the Saviour, and soon after began preaching. During his labors in Canada he was permitted to see the results of his efforts, and conversions among those with whom he toiled were of frequent occurrence. But as a sense of the paramount importance of the work in which he was engaged came to be fully recognized by him, he felt the need of greater educational advantages than he had yet enjoyed accordingly and soon after entered the Theological department of Hillsdale College. During the time he spent here he was continually at work for the Master, usually preaching three times upon the Sabbath. Revivals seemed to be a natural outgrowth of his labors, and he was permitted to be largely instrumental in the organizing of two or more churches in southern Michigan. So zealously did he labor that it was said of him by one of the teachers, "He has done a lifework before his graduation. "Completing his studies in June, 1873, he received a call to the pastorate of the Free Baptist church in Fond du Lac, and soon after entered upon his work. There he continued to labor until a few weeks before his death.

Death Opens The Door For The Soul To Take Its Flight.

George A. Taylor
Birth:
Nov. 13, 1842
Huntington
Huntington County, Indiana
Death:
Jun. 29, 1913
Los Angeles
Los Angeles County, California
Burial:
Greenwood Cemetery
Dallas
Barron County, Wisconsin

He died at the Pacific Branch, National Home for Disabled Veteran Soldiers, Los Angeles

County, California, aged 70 years, 7 months and 16 days, where he had been admitted November 7, 1912. His remains were shipped to Dallas, Barron County, Wisconsin, and buried there beside the remains of his wife Nancy in Greenwood Cemetery.On November 24, 1859, George was united in marriage to Nancy Alvise Rogers, by Reverend G. Dissmore, at Lindina, Juneau County, Wisconsin. Nancy was born August 17, 1838, in Indiana. She died December 29, 1905, aged 67 years, 4 months and 12 days, and was buried in the Taylor family plot in Greenwood Cemetery. They were the parents of nine children. George was a Civil War veteran who enlisted March 10, 1865, at St. Paul, Minnesota, to serve one year as a Private in the 1st Minnesota Infantry, and was mustered into Federal service with Company C the next day at the same location. At that time he received 1/3 of his $100.00 enlistment bounty and was listed as a 22 year and 3 month old, 5'8" tall farmer, with brown hair, brown eyes and a fair complexion, born in Huntington, Indiana, and from Mapleton, Cottonwood Township, Brown County, Minnesota. On March 5, 1865, his name was on a roll of men at the Draft Rendezvouz at Ft. Snelling, St. Paul, Minnesota. On July 14, 1865, George was discharged with Company C, at Jeffersonville, Indiana. His original discharge is in his pension file at the National Archives. On their muster out roll it was noted that he was due 1/3 of his enlistment bounty less $6.00 for arms retained.After his discharge,

George returned to Minnesota. He was ordained by the Blue Earth Valley Quarter Meeting in Minnesota, June 13, 1869. He assisted in the organization of the Medo, Minnesota and Dallas, Wisconsin churches and was formerly clerk of the Blue Earth Valley Quarterly Meeting. He was also the first clerk of the Minnesota Southern Yearly Meeting, was a clerk of the St. Croix Quarter Meeting, and was a member of the Minnesota yearly Meeting Home Mission Board. As a citizen he held the office of accessor, town clerk, chairman of the Board Of Supervisors, Justice of the Peace, member of the school board.

He resided there until 1870, when he moved to Mauston, Juneau County, Wisconsin. In 1871, he moved to Colby, Clark County, Wisconsin, and in 1875, to Huntington, Huntington County, Indiana, returning the same year to Mauston. In 1876, he moved to Dallas, Barron County, Wisconsin. He farmed near Dallas and Hillsdale, in that county, and nearby Ridgeland, Dunn County, Wisconsin, until 1908, when he moved to Cauldwell, Idaho. In 1912 he moved to Los Angeles County, California.

Rev George W. Town
Birth: 1810
Vermont
Death: 1894
Burial:
Oak Center Cemetery
Oak Center
Fond du Lac County
Wisconsin

His memorial already had "Rev" on it.   He mar. Sophia

Jane (Blackwood), and they had at least nine or ten children.   I've found several and sent links. to the parents. He was bn.   VT, and was in Clinton Co. NY in 1850, with five kids before ending up in Wisconsin.   He had a son, George W. but I have not found anything of him being a minister.   He mar.   Marcia (Mary) Kising in Wis, 09 July 1874.

Clyde Wayne Tripp
Birth: Apr. 10, 1898
Sparta
Monroe County
Wisconsin
Death: Jan. 7, 1988
New Richmond
St. Croix County
Wisconsin
Burial:
Calvary Cemetery
Deer Park
St. Croix County
Wisconsin

Husband of Eve Bader Tripp and father of Robert, Raymond and Lois. Kind and gentle man. Raised a wonderful family and was a devoted and loving husband.
Rev. C. W. (Clyde Wayne); b. 10 April 1898; d. 07 Jan 1988, St. Croix, Wis;
Family links:
  Parents:
    John N Tripp (1857 - 1933)
    Caroline Eleanor Kinney Tripp (1860 - 1911)

Orin Haines True
Birth:
May 30, 1831
Moultonborough,
Carroll County,
New Hampshire
Death:
Nov. 27, 1913
Burial:
Maple Hill Cemetery
Evansville,
Rock County,
Wisconsin
Plot: Original Block 1, Lot 135

His parents, Asa W. and Rebecca (Haines) TRUE, gave him early instruction in religion and he was converted when about five years of age. He graduated from the literary department of the New Hampton Institution in 1858, and subsequently from the theological.
He married Miss Sarah L. Bean, of Candia, NH, on Aug. 22, 1860 and after her death, fourteen years later, he married Mrs. E. H. Hudson, of Johnstown, Wis. His ordination took place June 20, 1861, his subsequent ministry being with the churches at Lisbon and W. Lebanon, ME, N. Scituate, R.I., Nekimi, Rosendale, Fond du Lac, Evansville, Oakland, York Prairie, Monticello, Scott,

Marcellon and Winneconne, Wisconsin. Much of the time his pastoral care has been bestowed upon two of these churches simultaneously. Revivals have attended his ministry, and the churches have been strengthened.

Amos Tyler
Birth:
Apr. 11, 1802
Piermont, N. H.
Death:
Aug. 13, 1876
Big Spring, Wis.
Burial:
Big Spring Cemetery
Big Spring, Adams County,
Wisconsin

Tyler died at age 74 years. His early ministry as a licentiate was with the Methodists. In 1834 he moved to Hatley, Québec, Canada, where he united with the Free Baptists, and was ordained Oct. 2I, 1836. Here he preached in various

townships until 1855, when his health became impaired and he moved to Newport, Wis. With returning health he again engaged in ministerial work, gathered the Big Spring and Kilbourn City church, and engaged in many revivals in the Sauk County Q. M. He was eminently social, very helpful in prayer and exhortation, and benevolent in his gifts, especially to the needy interestnear his home. His daughter is Mrs. Rev. W. E. Dennett.

Rev Simmons E Very
Birth:
Jun. 16, 1847
New York
Death:
Jul., 1925
Oshkosh
Winnebago County
Wisconsin
Burial:
Riverside Cemetery
Oshkosh
Winnebago County
Wisconsin

He married Viola Eliza Bowen, dau of Elias Bowen and Lucinda (Clark) Bowen, 06 July 1873, Ellicott, Chautauqua Co. NY.He was enum. in 1860, 1870, & 1880 censuses, E. Otto, Cattaraugus Co., NY. In 1900, he was in Illinois. Sometime between 1900-1920, He moved to Wisconsin. The Oshkosh, Wis, City Directories, 1822-1995, shows "Residence: 'Rev. Simmons E. Very, Clergyman.'"
He and Viola had five children, and an obit is included in the memorial of daughter, Letha (Very) Corbett, who d. in 1927. From State records found on Family Tree(s):Marriage: Viola

Eliza Bowen, 06 JUL 1873 in Ellicott, Chautauqua Co., NY
Children:
Mary Very b: 30 APR 1884 in NY
Charles L. Very b: 18 NOV 1886 in NY
John Wesley Very b: 23 MAR 1891 in PA
Bertha C. Very b: 14 APR 1876 in NY
Myrtle E. Very b: 23 JAN 1879 in NY
Letha Very b: 14 JUN 1881 in NY

J. J. Wakefield
Birth:
Sep. 15, 1821
Death:
Jul. 28, 1865
Burial:
Beaver Dam City Cemetery
Beaver Dam, Dodge County,
Wisconsin
Plot: L-29

Wakefield was a native of Cornish, Me., died at age 33 years. Such was the type of his piety that the church urged upon him a license to preach, and he was ordained May 30, 1853, at Neenah, Wisconsin. He preached to destitute churches for a time and in 1854 became pastor of the Berlin and Fairwater churches. After four years he settled with the Johnstown church; but in 1860 he moved his family to La Crosse and traveled for his health, yet continued to work for the Master. His gifts were admirably adapted to winning souls, and his early death was widely lamented. Recorded in the *Morning Star* on September 6, 1865.

Comfort Babcock Waller
Birth:
Jul. 24, 1813
Washington County,
New York
Death:
Feb. 23, 1891
Fond du Lac County,
Wisconsin
Burial:
Oak Center Cemetery,
Fond du Lac County,
Wisconsin

He became a minister just prior to his marriage. And was among the first to pioneer Freewill Baptist work in Wisconsin. He married Nancy Batchelder in 1832 in New York. They moved to Ohio where he was involved in the ministry until 1842 when he removed to Trenton, Washington County, Wisconsin. A little later he moved back and forth serving both the Trenton Freewill Church and one in Scott, Scheboygen County, Wisconsin. Grieved by the loss of his son, David (Co. D 12th Wisconsin Infantry) a prisoner in Andersonville, he decided that a change was in order, so he moved to Fond du Lac County. He did continue to preach and gave his last sermon in the Boltonville Freewill Baptist Church in the fall of 1890.

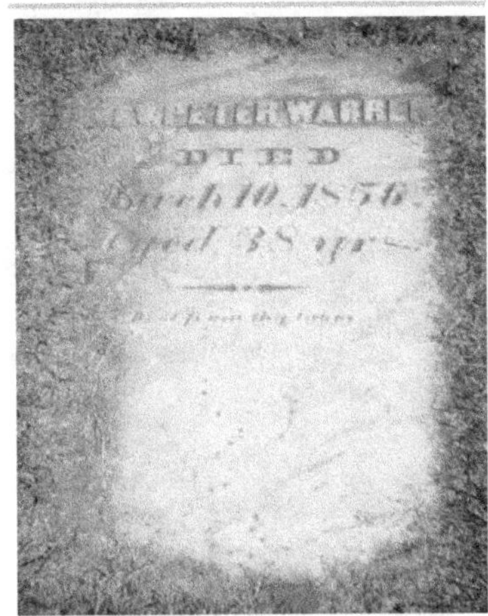

Peter Warren
Birth:
Jan., 1818
Maine
Death:
Mar. 10, 1856
Burial:
Woodland Cemetery
Kohler
Sheboygan County,
Wisconsin

Rev. Peter Warren, was converted at the age of sixteen and soon began preparation for the ministry. He graduated at Redfield, Maine, and was in the Biblical School 1843-45. He sought improved health in the West, where he taught schoolHe was ordained by the Fond du Lac Quarterly Meeting, Wisconsin, June 6, 1852. The next August he became pastor of the Boston, New York, church and later of the Attica church. But health failing, he returned to Greenbush, Wis., where he died in the 39th year of his age.He possessed a mind of high order and was an able minister. Inscription:Aged 38 years.

William Warner
Birth:
October 25, 1796
England
Death:
Dec. 3, 1885
Wisconsin
Burial:
Oaks Cemetery
Valton Sauk County, Wisconsin

He fought in the British ranks at the battle of Waterloo. After coming to America he enlisted in the Army of Jesus Christ in 1820 and soon received license to preach. His early labors were in Quebec, Canada and his ordination being received at Hadley, Quebec, Canada on January 17, 1837. Continuing in the Canadian Province most of the time until about 1848 when he moved to Enfield, New Hampshire and labored there and in the vicinity of a number of years. He then moved to New Hampton and while there gave a very able lecture on the Battle of Waterloo. About 1864 he moved to Clementsville21, Wisconsin uniting with the Vineland church.

Rev Francis M. Washburn
Birth:
Aug., 1845
Montgomery County
Indiana
Death:
Dec. 2, 1919
Stanislaus County
California
Burial:
Maple Hill Cemetery
Evansville
Rock County
Wisconsin
Plot: Original Block 2, Lot 19

Rev. F. M. Washburn became connected with the Sauk County Quarterly Meeting (QM), Wisconsin, as early as 1879. He soon became pastor of the Evansville and Oregon churches of the Rock and Dane Q.M., and about 1884 of the Mt. Pleasant church of the Honey Creek QM. His labors in Wisconsin have been highly esteemed. He served for some time as treasurer of the Mission Board, and was a delegate to the General Conference in 1886. In 1888 he took charge of the important church at San Francisco, CA
Rev. F.M. Washburn, was a Free Will Baptist clergyman, before he became a Methodist, pastoring churches in Wisconsin.

The northern Freewill Baptists merged their churches with the Northern Baptists, or, now, American Baptists, in 1911. Many of the Free Baptist ministers then went to the Methodists, rather than the Northern Baptists.

Hiram Watrus
Birth:
Jan. 26, 1815
Williamson
Wayne County,
New York
Death:
Jan. 25, 1874
Boscobel
Grant County,
Wisconsin
Burial:
Boscobel Cemetery
Boscobel
Grant County,
Wisconsin

He was converted in 1833, while living in Geneva, Ohio, and ordained in 1861. While at Scott, Wis. He engaged actively in the work of the ministry in Crawford and Grant Counties, residing ten years at Marion and in 1873 went to Boscobel, where he hired a house of worship and soon organized a church. He was rich in all the Christian graces, and his death was felt to be a great loss.

Rev Emmonds H. Webster
Birth:
Aug. 8, 1830
Onondaga County
New York
Death:
Apr. 28, 1896
Plymouth
Sheboygan County
Wisconsin
Burial:
Union Cemetery
Plymouth
Sheboygan County
Wisconsin

Plymouth Review
Wednesday April 29, 1896
REV E.H. WEBSTER DEAD
He Had Been a Plymouth Resident for the Past Three Years. Was a Baptist Minister and About Ten Years of His Life Were Devoted to Church Work – He Was a Soldier of the Rebellion, Having Served His Country From '61 to '65 – H.P. Davidson Post G.A.R. to Take Charge of the Funeral.
The death of Rev. Emmonds H. Webster occurred about 9:15 o'clock last evening at his home on South street where he had resided the past three years. He had been in ill health for a number of years and for the past two or three months was confined to his bed a greater share of the time. Although a resident of Plymouth but a comparatively short time he was well known, having resided in the county for a least thirty years, and in his death the city loses one of its most highly respected citizens.
On December 25th, 1857, he was married to Miss Lucy A. Stewart at Sheboygan Falls, and she survives him, besides whom there are four children, Miss Clara Webster, at home, Mrs. O.W. Williams of Ashland, Wis., Clinton of Kaukauna and Lee at home, also an only sister, Mrs. Hiram Ashcraft of Sheboygan Falls.
For four years Mr. Webster served as a soldier in the rebellion, having entered the service Sept. 25, 1861, as a member of Company B., 8th Wisconsin Regiment, and was discharged in 1865. At the close of the war he returned to Greenbush. In 1860 he was ordained a minister of the Baptist church and two years later removed to Boltonville, Washington county, where he continued to preach until 1893. Then account of failing health he was obliged to give up the work, and came to Plymouth where he has since made it his home. Being a member of the H.P. Davidson Post, G.A.R., that order will have charge of the funeral which will be held at one o'clock Thursday afternoon. Rev. Wellman of Greenbush will conduct the services and interment will be made in the city cemetery.

Zere Lysander Wellman
Birth:
Nov. 9, 1835
Otsego County
New York
Death:
Dec. 14, 1908
Dane County
Wisconsin
Burial:
Riverside Cemetery
Stoughton
Dane County
Wisconsin

Son of Buri and Samantha (Sharp) Wellman, husband of Susie Tibbits and father of Edward, Samantha, Ada and Grace.

VETERAN CLERGYMAN
GOES TO HIS REWARD

Mr. Wellman's death occurred in M.V. Gunsolus' house on W. Main street, where he and his wife were residing for the winter in order to enable their daughter, Grace, to attend the high school. He was down town Saturday, and was in his usual health until about 8 o'clock in the evening when as before stated, he was taken with a chill.
Funeral services were conducted by Rev. T. B. Hughes at the First Baptist church, Decedent was a native of Otsego County, N.Y., where he was born Nov. 9th, 1835, thus being just past seventy-three years of age. During the Civil war he served three years with the 37th N.Y. Volunteers, and in

1868 came to this locality where he was married two years later to Miss Susan Tibbit. For three years and a half he was pastor of the Star church in Rutland, and afterwards held the pastorate of a Free Baptist church at Greenbush in Sheboygan county, for a period of eight years. He has not now been actively engaged in preaching for many years, residing on his little tract of land a mile south of the Star church.

Rev John Westlake
Birth:
Jan. 5, 1840
Hartland
Devon, England
Death:
Feb. 27, 1902
Winnebago County
Wisconsin
Burial:
Greenbush Cemetery
Greenbush
Sheboygan County
Wisconsin

Born in England, Rev. John Westlake, was the son of Robert and Elizabeth (Hartop) WESTLAKE.

He immigrated to U.S. in 1853. He married Harriet L. (Gibson), dau of Daniel and Dolly Gibson,

in Wisconsin, Nov. 01, 1861. His parents lived in Marquette as did Harriett.

Early Freewill Bapt. minister in Wisconsin. Soon after in 1861, he received ordination from the Wolf River Freewill Bapt. Quarterly Meeting and had charge of Harrisville, Greenbury and Raymond Wis. churches. He also held the office of town treasurer.

Jacob Wescher
Birth:
Ger.
Apr. 20, 1847
Death:
Mar. 15, 1904
Burial:
Forest Home Cemetery
Marinette
Marinette County
Wisconsin

His wife was Louise J (Hesse) Wescher, b. Ger, 1858, d. Aug. 1922, and her stone on other side of his obelisk one

Rev Lovell Wheeler
Birth:
Apr. 24, 1800
Newport
Sullivan County
New Hampshire
Death:
Apr. 26, 1888
Oshkosh
Winnebago County
Wisconsin
Burial:
Ellenwood Cemetery
Oshkosh
Winnebago County
Wisconsin
Plot: Sec F Row 7

A faithful minister in the Freewill Baptist church from Newport, N.H. Son of Abel and Prudence(Warren) WHEELER, both of NH. His education was obtained in the academy of his native town, and he was ordained by the ministers of the Weare Quarterly Meeting in August, 1831. His ministry was spent in New Hampshire, Vermont, Minnesota and Wisconsin. Several churches were gathered through his labors. They had at least one son, Darius G. Wheeler, b. NH, and mar. Levina Jane Dunn, of Spring Grove, WI, on July 03, 1887, at Albany, Green Co. WI. She was the dau of Wm. Brown, and Lucy (Smily) Brown.

Rev Warren Whiting
Birth:
Oct. 2, 1816
Douglas
Worcester County
Massachusetts
Death:
Jan. 2, 1897
Waupun
Fond du Lac County
Wisconsin
Burial:
Wedges Prairie Cemetery
Waupun
Fond du Lac County
Wisconsin

Warren Whiting was the son of Amos and Alcy (Chase) Whiting. After leaving his parents' home in Mass., he immigrated to Wisconsin, in 1846, first settling in Rock County. He removed to Fond du Lac County a few months later where he engaged in farming, eventually amassing 600 acres of land which he farmed and managed.

At the age of 26, Warren Whiting entered the ministry of the Free-will Baptist Church, and after preaching for a short time was ordained. He continued his ministry for 35 years, but, because of ill health, was forced to lay aside his ministerial duties.

Ministers Who Passed after the layout was prepared for publishing.

Rev Mark E. Leonard
Birth
2 Jan 1958
Dayton, Montgomery County, Ohio
Death
2 Mar 2018
Burial
Mossy Grove Cemetery
Florence County, South Carolina

Reverend Mark E. Leonard, 60, husband of Myra Matthews Leonard, died Friday, March 2, 2018, at home after an illness. Reverend Leonard was born on January 2, 1958, in Dayton, Ohio, son of Dellene Meek Leonard and the late Albert E. Leonard. He was a graduate of Park Hills High School in Fairborn, Ohio and Welch College in Nashville, Tennessee. Reverend Leonard was a retired Free Will Baptist Minister, who had served a number of churches in Ohio and South Carolina for over 40 years. He and his wife enjoyed music and served many years in youth ministry.

Billy Melvin
Death:
Florida
Creamated

The National Association of Evangelicals (NAE) celebrates the life and ministry of Billy Melvin, who died February 1, 2018, at age 88. Melvin served as the NAE executive director for 28 years, retiring in 1995.

"Billy Melvin led and loved the National Association of Evangelicals during the rapid expansion of evangelicalism in America," said Leith Anderson, NAE president. "He blessed and encouraged me as the once youngest member of the NAE board, in our travel together across developing countries of Africa, and more recently as a supporter of the NAE after his retirement."

Melvin joined the NAE as executive director in 1967 after serving as executive secretary of the National

Association of Free Will Baptists for eight years. Prior to his post at the denomination's headquarters, he pastored several Free Will Baptist churches and served as a chaplain in the Civil Air Patrol.

While Melvin was NAE executive director, the organization expanded on several fronts, including the 1979 construction of the Evangelical Center, which sought to support the local church's mission of preaching and teaching the gospel, in Wheaton, Illinois; the expansion of the Office of Public Affairs in Washington, D.C.; and a concerted effort to enlist new denominations in the NAE. During Melvin's tenure, Presidents Ronald Reagan and George H. W. Bush spoke to NAE audiences, and the NAE celebrated several legislative victories. Melvin sought to elevate the status and role of denominations in the NAE. Between 1981 and 1990, 15 denominations joined the NAE.

Harold Smith, president and CEO of Christianity Today, served as the NAE director of information and editor of United Evangelical Action magazine while Melvin was executive director. Smith said, "Billy helped the then fresh-out-of-school young man see and more fully engage the 'big tent' of evangelicalism. He modeled for me the movement's language of gospel conviction lived out in Christ-centered love. And with all that, God used him to set me on an unlikely course that would eventually lead me to Christianity Today. Thank you, Billy. And to God be the glory!" Melvin authored "Randall

House Minister's Manual" and numerous articles directed to pastors. His service to the evangelical community was recognized by several organizations. He received honorary doctorate degrees from Azusa Pacific University (1968), Taylor University (1984) and Huntington College (1995), and was awarded the Legion of Honor from Taylor University in 1993. He also served on the board of the American Bible Society for many years.

Melvin studied theology at the Free Will Baptist Bible College (now Welch College), completed his undergraduate education at Taylor University, attended Asbury Theological Seminary, and completed his M.Div. at Union Theological Seminary.

Melvin is survived by his two children, eight grandchildren and three great-grandchildren. He is reunited with his wife and ministry partner of 65 years, Marcia Darlene (Eby), who went to be with the Lord on August 19, 2017.

Andrew Workman
Pioneer Evangelist in Ohio

Indes of Ministers by state and page location

Surname	Given	Page
Baker	George W.	90
Baker	Braziale E.	208
Ball	George	6
Ball	Clifford H.	91
Ball	Mance	91
Ballard	Jerald P.	37
Ballard	Loy Everett	38
Ballard	John Henry	38
Ballard	Willis W.	39
Ballard	John H.	154
Ballwin	Starks W.	153
Banks	Jerry Cleo	153
Bare	Vernie	91
Barfield	J. M.	39
Barker	Arnold	340
Barker	Paul	341
Barnes	John	154
Barnhardt	Larry	154
Barnhart	Peter	91
Barnhill	Alford	154
Barr	Samuel	208
Barrett	Selah	91
Barrett	Selah H.	92
Barrow	Jesse P.	39
Barrow	Nigel Bruce	40
Barton	Pleasant	154
Bates	Laban Eli	6
Bates	Daniel E.	92
Bates	Samuel D.	92
Beam	Gladys	281
Beaman	Thomas E.	40
Bean	John E.	155
Bean	Leonard	155
Beasley	Wilburn	237
Beasley	Hilton C.	247
Beebe	Velorus	7
Beebe	Warner	93
Beene	Dalton	155
Bell	Thomas P.	342
Bennett	Jesse R.	40
Bennett	Charlie	247
Bennett	William R.	341
Benson	Eugene	155
Berry	H.R. Sr	282
Berry	Arthur C.	342
Berry	Orvil C	342
Berry, Jr.	Hubert R	282
Bess	Ransom	155
Bevan	Paskel D	155
Bias	Ernest F.	342
Bingham	Justus	7
Bingham	Roy M	156
Bingham	W. M.	156
Binkley	G. W.	247
Bird	Ben	93
Birdwell	A. J.	282
Bissette	Edward	40
Blackburn	Peyton	93
Blair	James A	93
Blair	Joe	156
Blake	Orvil	94
Blalock	J. A.	40
Blankenship	Bennie	341
Bliven	Elijah	7
Bloss	James B.	247
Blount, Sr.	John L	94
Boatright	James	329
Bohanon	Charles	247
Bookout	Addie Fay	157
Booth	Marvin	94
Booth	Harry	343
Bostic	Howard T.	329
Boston	Shubel	315
Bounds	Joseph L.	282
Bowen	Clarence F.	41
Bowles	Charles	7
Bowman	Charles R.	94
Boyd	James D	95
Boyd	Terry	248
Boykin	William	41
Brackett	Daniel	95
Brackett	Nathan C	343
Bradbury	Ammi R	220
Bradshaw	Fred L.	248
Brandon	Kenneth	156
Brashier	Lewis K.	282
Bratcher	William	157
Braxton	Levi	41
Breeden	Zalene L	329
Breeden	Robert F.	330
Brewer	Fred Arvel	248
Brewster	Marilla	222
Brewster	Jonathan M.	221
Bridges	Abiezer	362
Bright	William L	248
Bristol	Ernest E.	157
Brodeoux	Andrew J.	41
Brooks	Hiram	95
Brooks	Homer S.	96
Brooks	Cicero	248
Brooks	John Andrew	282
Brown	Daniel	8
Brown	Nathaniel	8
Brown	Charles	42
Brown	Noah D.	42
Brown	Morgan H.	96
Brown	Elias	96
Brown	Joseph	156
Brown	Allen	222
Brown	Jimmy W	237
Brown	Greene B	249
Brown	Harley C	249
Brown	Floyd	343
Bruce	Joseph	315
Buckelew	Edna Hunt	159
Buckner	Noah Estil	343
Bugbee	Abel	315
Bullard	Seldon D.	42
Bullard, SR	Johnny	157
Bullock	Adam	8
Bumpus	Erastus	209
Bundy	Benjamin	8
Burch	Chauncy	209
Burch, Jr	Tommy L	42
Burgess	William	158
Burgess	Gideon A.	223

Dally	Z. B.	286
Dalton	Marvin P.	163
Dame	Stephen A	164
Dame	William D	164
Damron	Wayne	347
Daniels	Amos	11
Daniels	John	100
Darst	Budd L.	100
Darte	Freeman	11
Davenport	Frank	46
Davidison	William R.	286
Davidson	James R.	47
Davidson	George	164
Davis	James E.	47
Davis	Herbert C.	100
Davis	John M	100
Davis	James T	255
Davis	Amos	318
Davis	Isaac	365
Davison	Frank	318
Day	Ira	11
Day	George T.	225
Dean	Zebulon	11
Deans	Benjamin	47
Dearmore	William E	164
Deaton	Austin	165
Decker	Jacob	12
Delawter	Alfred F	101
Delling	Manoah	12
Denman	William D.	286
Denman	William H.	286
Dennett	Wilbur	226
Denny	Oscar	12
DePriest	Roy T	101
Deweese	Levi	48
Dewitt	F. A.	255
Dexter	Lewis	318
Dickey	Robert	319
Dilda	Sigbee B.	48
Dillard	James	287
Dimm	Thomas	101
Dingus	Albert	331
Dingus	Robert A	332
Diserens	Daniel	287
Dixon	Burrell	49
Dixon	Othel T	165
Dixon	Thomas H.	165
Doan	Robert H.	255
Dodge	Amasa	12
Dodge	Asa	12
Dodge	Eusebius	102
Dodge	Asa	210
Dodge	Calvin	211
Dodge	Edward	211
Dodge	Gurley	211
Dollar	John J.	287
Dove	Floyd	347
Dowell	James Hill	287
Drown	Samuel	366
Dudley	Cyrus	102
Dudley	David	103
Dudley	Moses	103
Dudley	Thomas	103
Dudley	Jerry D.	165
Dunbar	George D.	256
Duncan	Zadock D.	256
Duniphin	D. B.	165
Durham	Robert J.	49
Durkee	Jacob	13
Dutton	Charles T	103
Dutton	Jimmy R.	104
Dye	James E	332
Dye, JR	James	166
Dye, Sr.	Harley G	332
Dyke	Orange	319
Eagleton	Marvis	56
Eagleton	Kenneth P	256
Easley	Robert B	287
Eason	Nason Earl	49
Eastman	Edmund	226
Edmonson	John	288
Edwards	Lewis W	166
Edwards	Robert	238
Elliot	george	13
Ellis	Donald	104
Ellis	Herman H	257
Ellis	William D.	256
Elswick	John	105
Elswick	John W	105
England	Quentin	105
Ennis	Lonne R.,	50
Ensign	William	212
Epperson	Arlie Barton	167
Estep	Floyd E.	105
Estep	Owen	348
Estes, JR	John B.	288
Evans	Sylvester	13
Evans	James A.	50
Evans	Calvin	105
Evans	Fred C.	106
Everett	W. B.	51
Everton	James W.	51
Fain	Clifford	288
Fairchild	Vernal Lee	106
Fairfield	Edmund B	106
Farless	George W.	257
Farley	John	13
Farmer	Danny	167
Farnum	Herbert R	226
Farr	Nelson H	319
Farrell	George	51
Farrell	Zalph	51
Farrell	Harrison W	257
Fassio	Cecil R.	167
Fay	Edward	320
Fears	Jimmy Lee	288
Fellabaum	Ward	168
Fergueson	James A	168
Ferguson	Jessie	290
Ferguson	A. F.	289
Ferrall	William M.	51
Fessenden	Nelson	212
Fields	William G.	168
Fife	Raymond L	107
Fincher	Sadie E.	169
Fitzgerald	Lewis	290

Flannery	Joseph	212
Floyd	John Eugene	51
Floyd	Winford R.	257
Fonville	Frederick A.	52
Ford	James A	290
Ford	Josephus W	290
Ford	Markley S	291
Forrest	John	320
Fort	Joe T.	257
Fowler	Benjamin	366
Fowler	Josiah	367
Fox	Jesse A	169
Fox	Edward J.	257
Franklin	Anthony	107
Franklin	James A	169
Franklin	Tommie	292
Freeman	Hershey	107
Freeman, Jr	Claud	169
French	Estel M.	258
French	Jake M.	258
Frisbee	Kenneth	108
Fry	Malcolm C	258
Frye	Arthur G.	348
Fulcher, Jr.	William M.	52
Fuller	William	14
Fuller	Zachary	293
Fuller	Ezra B	320
Fullerton, Sr	Isaac	108
Fulton	William J.	109
Fulton	Samuel	108
Gage	Howard J	169
Gage	Jake W.	170
Gallant	Richard H	170
Ganey	Houston O.	53
Gardner	James S.	14
Gardner	Levi	14
Gardner	Squire	14
Gardner, Jr	Willie M.	258
Garfield	John	320
Garland	Benjamin	259
Garrido	John E.	348
Garris	Owen	53
Gartman	James	293
Gaskins	Raymond A.	53
Gause	Webster P	238
Gibson, Sr	Norwood A.	238
Gidney	Joseph B.	367
Giles	Fred Almon	348
Gillett	Truman	14
Gilman	Hiram	15
Glaze	Thomas	293
Glenn	Earl	54
Gober	Vernon H	259
Goen	Clyde F	294
Goff	Henry	53
Gorgia	Alfred J.	348
Gould	Delbert G	110
Gould	Olen	111
Gow	Cornelia	109
Gow	David W.	109
Gow	Ruda	110
Gowen	Lewis W	337
Gower	H. Wilkes	259
Gower	James W.	259
Graham	Daniel M.	212
Graham	Walter	294
Graham	John	293
Grant	Barney A.	94
Green	Louis H.	54
Green	Millard	109
Green	John	213
Green	Orange	321
Greene	David	15
Greene	Caleb	227
Greene	Daniel	227
Greeson	Shelby V	170
Griffin	Susan C	16
Griffin	Zibina	16
Griffin	Emmaline	367
Griffin	Jacob	368
Griffin Sr	Jesse C.	54
Griffiths	Ansel	15
Gumm	Alva	170
Hackett	George	321
Halbrook	Alvin Floyd	295
Hale	Johnie Eli	171
Hale	Ernie	171
Hales	Milford	54
Hall	James	55
Hall	James M.	111
Hall	John R.	171
Hall	Lonnie	171
Hall	Paul F	259
Hall Jr	John	55
Hallenbeck	Joseph	17
Hallock	C. E.	16
Hamar	Clyde	171
Hamlin	William	368
Hampton	Charles E	260
Hampton	Ralph C.	260
Hampton, Sr	Ralph C	172
Haning	Ira Z.	111
Hanks, Jr	George W	172
Hannibal	Ely	16
Hansley	David Wells	55
Hanson	Luther	17
Hargrove	Dolphus C	294
Harness	Joseph F	111
Harrell	Bobby E.	56
Harris	William	56
Harris	R. S.	260
Harris	Lemuel	297
Harris, Sr	Charlie J.	56
Harrison	Thaddeus F.	56
Harrison	Ernest	172
Harvery	Nathaniel	369
Harvey	J. C.	296
Haston	Hubert H	294
Haston	W. D.	295
Hasty	Stephen R	261
Hathaway	Edward D.	57
Hawkins	Henry Lee	112
Hayes	David A.	112
Hayes	Jesse	227
Hayes	Wallace R	261

Head	George	261	Hoag	Isaac	18	Inman	Cyrus	115
Head	George R.	261	Hockenberry	John	350	Isham	George M.	175
Head	George R	261	Hodge	Ephriam	18	Jackson	Chester	19
Head	Wiley	262	Hogue	Herbert C	174	Jackson	Daniel	19
Head	William H.	262	Holbrook	Paul	322	Jackson	Nelson	20
Hearn	Rufus	57	Holden	Joseph E	332	Jackson	Billy Gray	60
Hearod	Arty	172	Holliday	Louis	239	Jackson	Robert C	60
Hearron	J. Author	173	Hollifield, Sr.	Milton A.	58	Jackson	Roy H.	60
Hearron	William H.	173	Holman	Critt	263	Jackson	Daniel W.	322
Heath	Jeremiah	57	Holmes	John	297	Jackson	Joseph	323
Hecox	Luther	112	Holt	George	18	Jackson	Thomas M.	323
Hellard	Everett D.	295	Holt	Clint H.	60	Jameson	Egbert S.	298
Hemmerly	Abraham	112	Homes	G. W.	58	Jarrett	Clarence A	176
Henderson	James	173	Honeycutt	Nathan	263	Jasper	Creamer	285
Hensley	Ottis	349	Hooper	William	114	Jeffrey	John	115
Henson	Herbert	112	Hooser	J. B.	297	Jenkins	Calvin	20
Henson	Jess	173	Hopkins	George	228	Jenkins	Herman	369
Henson	John M.	349	Howell	Curtis	59	Jenson	Earl	176
Herrick	William	321	Howell	Danny H.	59	Jernigan	Hannibal	61
Hersey	Herman L	262	Howell	W. M.	59	Jernigan	Isaac	61
Hewitt	Moab	239	Howes	Solomon	18	Jernigan	Walter L.	61
Hickman	Barb E.	173	Howington	Joseph	263	Jernigan	Wade T.	176
Hicks	Elijah M	239	Hoyt	Jonathan	114	Jimmerson	Minnie L.	298
Hicks	Peleg	321	Hubbard	Kyle Wilson	332	Johnson	M. L.	61
Hidde	Robert D	174	Hubbard	Monroe	333	Johnson	Richard M.	263
Hidde	Robert L.	174	Huckeby	Henry S	174	Johnson	J. W.	298
Higgins	Kendal	113	Hudgens	Jesse	263	Johnson	Ezra	333
Higgins J.	William	297	Huling	Daniel	19	Jones	James R.	62
Higgins M.	William	297	Huling	James	174	Jones	Calvin	61
Hill	Isaac	17	Hull	John G	246	Jones	Scott	177
Hill	John David	58	Humphreys	Sardine	114	Jones	William C	177
Hill	Horace	113	Hunsucker	Retes	175	Jones	Billy M	299
Hill	William J.	262	Hunt	Robert	19	Jordon	Daniel A	62
Hill	Mark	322	Hunt	Marion	175	Joy	William	369
Hill	Finas Arlin	332	Hunt	Daniel	213	Joyner	Alan C	62
Hills	James W.	17	Huntley	Calvin	322	Joyner	George	62
Hills	Clinton	213	Husketh	Eugene	60	Joyner	Grover	62
Hills	Samuel F	349	Hyatt	Isaac	322	Joyner	G.G.	263
Hisey	Jacob	113	Hyman	Herman A.	239	Judd	George E	177
Hisey	John	113	Ide	Rogers	19	Judd	Mathias	264
Hix	Donald	113	Iker	Phillip	175	Judd	Nathaniel	264
Hoag	Charles	17	Ingerick	John W.	214	Kayser	J. M.	370

Keith	Charles E.	62
Kellet	Myrl	177
Kemper	John R	115
Kennedy	Robert	63
Kennedy	Richard P.	178
Kennedy, Sr	Rashie	63
Kester	Amanda	299
Ketcham	Nathaniel	20
Ketchum	Bob L.	178
Ketchum	William O.	178
Ketteman	Paul J.	264
Kilbourn	Marcus	115
Kilburn	Alanson	323
Kilgore	Harold	333
Kilgore, Jr	Emmett J.	333
Kimble	Howard	116
Kimbrough	John D	178
King	George	324
King	Nathaniel	324
Kirby	B. T.	177
Kirby	Elison	239
Kirk	Dewey R.	265
Kittle	Jobe	116
Knapp	George	20
Krum	Stephen	21
Lambert	A. J.	240
Lambert	James P	333
Lancaster	Needham	63
Lane	Richard G.	179
Langdon	James	64
Langworthy	John	21
Large	William H	333
Lawrence	George W.	116
Laws	Jesse	265
Lawter	Arthur F.	240
Layne	Jimmy	179
Lee	Lunda	64
Lee	Harry	179
Lee	John Alvin	179
Lee	William W	265
Lee	Joshua T	299
Lee	Jay	299
Lee	Leman	370
Lent	Smith	214
Lett	C.C.	350
Letts	James	21
Lewis	Claudis	117
Lighthall	W. A.	21
Lilley, Sr.	Leslie Allen	350
Lindsey	William E.	356
Linville	Andrew J	350
Littlefield	Ezekiel	228
Littlejohn	James	117
Lofts	J. W.	299
Long	Edgar	117
Loomos	Arron	21
Lord	Samuel	324
Loring	Horatio	21
Losee	Arad	22
Lovejoy	Frank	350
Loveless	John	22
Lucas	John W.	64
Lucas	Malachi D	64
Lucas	Patrick T	64
Lundsford	James P	300
Lunsford	John W.	180
Lupton	Alice V	64
Lupton	William H	65
Lykins	Charles	117
Lynch	John T.	180
Lyon	Daniel	22
Lyons	Bobby J.	117
Mack	Enoch	22
Mack	William	23
Mankster	David T.	180
Mann	Marvin K	180
Manning	Samuel	338
Marcum	Herman	118
Markin	Marvin D	118
Marks	Thomas	65
Marks	David	117
Marmon	Amos	118
Martin	William R	65
Martin	James W.	119
Martin	Eugene	119
Martin	Moses W	119
Martin	Isaac	300
Martin	Samuel C	301
Martin	Robert	300
Martin	John A.	300
Masters	Chester V.	119
Masters	Virgil Q.	120
Matheson	Angus	338
Matthews	Thomas H	66
May	Isaac	120
May	Lovell	120
Mayfield	Leona M	181
Mayhew	Homer	350
Maynard	Authur	121
Maynard	Robert L	121
Maynard	Lester J	181
McAdams	Elizabeth	301
McAdams	Hiram M	302
McAffrey	Alvis Lee	181
McAlister	Lonnie E.	182
McBride	Thomas	302
McBride	Thaddeus	302
McCage	Furman A	182
MccAlvain	Robert	182
McCarroll	James W	265
McCarty	Billy O.	121
McCarty	William	122
McCarty	Sturgell	121
McCowan	Elmer D	265
McCowan	George W.	265
McDaniel	Alva	122
McFall, Sr.	S. M.	333
McGee	Joshua E.	183
McGehee	Dottis	183
McGuire	Milliard	182
McKee	Martin	183
McKeel	Richard	69
McKenzie	Cecil E.	183
McKenzie	James	228
McKinney	Vester	333
McKoon	Benjamin	23

Surname	Given	Page	Surname	Given	Page	Surname	Given	Page
McKoon	Daniel W.	23	Morgan	J.C.	185	Noka	Gideon	230
McKoon	Newton	24	Morgan	Tillman C.	351	Noles	Mancy C.	241
McMillen	Raymond	182	Morrell	Alexander	351	Norie, Jr	Oliver Roy	304
McPeek	Ersel	334	Morris	Edward C.	67	Norris	David	325
Meade	Robert Lee	122	Morris	Kevin W	124	Nutting	William	25
Meade	Albert	351	Morris	E. E.	185	O'Donnell	Dennis H.	187
Meadows	Reford	122	Morris	Schooley L	304	O'Donnell	Emris Allen	187
Measures	John Henry	302	Morris Jr	J. R.	68	O'Donnell	J. D.	304
Mellette	Milton H.	240	Morse	Horace	123	Oiler	George S.	127
Melvin	Henry	265	Moses	William	124	Oliver	William H	268
Merkh	Margaret L	334	Moulton	Albanus A	124	Oliver	James H	267
Merkh	Daniel J	334	Moulton	Albanus K.	125	Osborn	Tim A	268
Messer	Trymon	266	Mounts	James E.	352	Osgood	John C	325
Metcalf	John	184	Mowry	Salome L	229	Outland	Billy Gene	269
Mevis	Greenly	370	Moxley	John	325	Outlaw	Addie H.	69
Milam	Russell	122	Moye	James C.	68	Overman	C. H.	69
Miley	Laverne D	266	Moyers	Joseph W	267	Owens	Harold	127
Miller	Bert	122	Mullendore	W.E.	185	Pace	Hardy C.	269
Miller	Troy	123	Mullins	Sam	352	Packard	Isaac	127
Milner	Carrol B.	184	Muncy	Carl	125	Page	John	214
Miner	Melville	24	Munkus	B. C.	185	Page	Benjamin	326
Mintz	Harry	66	Munsey	Howard T.	267	Palmer	Judson B.	304
Mitchell	William	370	Munsey	James Alan	267	Pannell	James M	187
Monk	William M	66	Murphy	Timothy	352	Parker	Thomas	25
Moon	David	371	Murray	James	186	Parker	Washington	26
Moore	Alfred	66	Music, Sr	James R.	126	Parker	Henry	70
Moore	J. W.	66	Myers	Clifford C.	186	Parker	Joseph	70
Moore	J. H.	67	Myers	Clifford G.	186	Parker	Joseph	70
Moore	James	67	Naves	William	126	Parker	Seth	128
Moore	John	67	Nelson	Homer	126	Parker	Daniel	187
Moore	Thomas	67	Nelson	J. M.	325	Pate	Bryant	70
Moore	Gerald G.	123	Nelson	Jonathan	325	Pate	Thomas	71
Moore	Milo	123	Nesbitt	Robert	24	Pate	Isaac N	188
Moore	Tommy	123	Newby	John C	187	Patrick	Christopher	71
Moore	Allen A	184	Newcomer	John	352	Patt	William	230
Moore	John B.	240	Newell	Samuel	24	Paul	Hiram G	72
Moore	Redding F	241	Newell	Samuel	29	Paul	A. W.	337
Moore	Samuel	241	Newman	Clarence	126	Paul	Benjamin	338
Moore	Louis L.	201	Newsom	Thomas H	303	Pauley	Eldon M.	353
Moore, Jr.	Samuel M.	241	Nichols	Asahel	25	Pauley	George	353
Morelock	William H.	267	Nicholson	John	25	Payne	Donald	188
Morford	Joseph B	371	Nobles	Walter	69	Payne	James L	305

Peck	Benjamin	230	Prescott	Matthew C	73	Rickard, Sr.	Roy Lee	76
Peden	Thomas E.	71	Presley	Jerry F	269	Riddlebarger	Milford W	132
Perkins	Charles S	326	Preston	Levi	27	Ridge	W. G.	191
Perry	James J	128	Price	Cecil W	130	Rigg	Stephen	353
Perry	Berton	188	Priest	Johnny H.	189	Riggs	Charles R	271
Perry	John J	353	Prince	Chester	215	Riggs	James	305
Peterson	Moses W.	72	Proctor	J. R.	189	Risner	Russell H.	132
Pettyjohn	George	188	Pruitt	Susie A	189	Rivenbark, Jr.	Fred A.	76
Phelon	Benjamin	231	Pults	Eli	189	Roberts	Moses	76
Phillip	Edgar T.	72	Purcell	Cleo	270	Roberts	Albert	191
Phillips	Mowry	231	Purdom	Ulis	190	Roberts	James M.	191
Phillips	Stephen	232	Purdom	Mark	190	Roberts	William T	192
Phillips	Talmadge	269	Purselley	Caswell	305	Roberts	R. A.	305
Phillips	Augustus	371	Putnam	Charles	27	Robinson	Evander S.	242
Phillips	Mowry	372	Qualls	Raymond	190	Robirds	Carol	271
Phinney	A. P.	26	Quimby	Daniel	326	Roby	James	132
Pierce	Cedric	72	Rackliff	Benjamin	87	Rodgers	Willie B.	272
Pierce	Asa	128	Radford	Francis	73	Roel	Edison M.	28
Pimlott	Edwin	128	Ragland	James W.	190	Rogers	Caleb	215
Pinson	Lester C.	5	Rakes	James A	353	Rogers	Cary	215
Pinyan	Pauline	72	Randall	Pemberton	130	Rogers	James E	305
Pipkin	Isaac H.	69	Randall	Fernando	327	Rollin	D. M. L.	28
Pitcher	Mary	372	Raney	James E	305	Rood	Farrell	132
Pittman	Robert F.	73	Rankin	Earl	131	Rose	Oscar	76
Pitts	Bill E.	129	Raper	William B	74	Rose	Kenneth	132
Pollard	Arnold	129	Ratliff	Archie W	74	Ross	David Valoy	28
Pollock	James	129	Reed	Thomas	27	Ross	David V.	133
Polston	Fannie	269	Reeds	Roger C.	270	Rouse	John	77
Pope	James R	373	Reedy	Eli E.	335	Rowland	Benjamin	28
Porter	R. P.	129	Reese	John R	131	Ruffin	Joseph	77
Potter	Ray	232	Reger	Ellis F.	190	Russell	John	272
Potter	W. A.	373	Renfrow	Willie	74	Russell	John R.	327
Powers	Raymond S.	129	Reynolds	William W	75	Russell	Rufus	327
Powers	Ben	334	Reynolds	Howard	335	Sala	Nathaniel	192
Powers	R. Harlis	335	Rhea	W. B.	305	Salmon	Joseph	77
Powers	Ruben H.	335	Rice	Mary Ellen	75	Salyers	George W	335
Powers, Sr.	David D.	334	Rice	Gabriel P	75	Sanford	Melvin R.	272
Powers, Sr.	Wade H.	335	Rice	David	131	Sanford	Marshall	306
Poynor	David L	189	Rice, Jr	James B	241	Sarle	Amarancy	233
Pratt	Thomas	26	Richards	Norman H	271	Saverance	H. Reedy	242
Pratt	Thomas	26	Richardson	Richard	28	Sawyer	John E.	77
Pratt	John	233	Richey	William C	191	Sawyer	William R	77

Surname	First Name	Page
Sawyer	Ernest	272
Scalf	Spartan	78
Scarboro	Paul J.	353
Schnell	Samuel S.	133
Scobey	George	29
Scott	Adam	78
Scott	James	306
Scott	Henry W.	353
Seaman	Samuel B	216
Searcy	Thomas A.	306
Searl	Miranda	133
Seay	Floyd	242
See	Jacob	133
Seitz	Isaac	133
Sessions	Robert	193
Sexton	Billy lay	272
Sexton	Donald	273
Shade	John R.	193
Shafer	James H	354
Shannon	Louis	134
Shannon	Oscar	373
Sharp	James	29
Shaver	Abram C	354
Sheehan	Paul J	242
Sheffield	Robert L	306
Sheppard	William J.	134
Sherwood	Benjamin	233
Shipman	Ophir	327
Shippee	Charles H	233
Shiry	Nicolas	216
Shivers	Carl D	193
Shockey	Robert L	273
Shoemaker	Joshua G.	216
Shonkwiler	Jacob	134
Shonkwiler	James A.	135
Shrewsbury	Gaylord M.	365
Shults	J. W.	307
Simpkins	Warren	134
Siver	George	29
Sizemore	Carl R.	135
Sizemore	Jesse	134
Sizemore	Sherman	354
Sledge	Camey A	194
Sluder	Ervin	78
Smith	Samra	79
Smith	Denver E	135
Smith	Troy	135
Smith	Noah	194
Smith	Stephen E	242
Smith	Rolla D	274
Smith	J. M.	306
Smith	T. W.	306
Smithey	Ira W.	194
Smithey	James W	194
Snook	Clarice	307
Snuffer	Alvin	354
Solomon	Aaron W.	195
Southwick	George B.	30
Sowards	Ted B.	135
Sparks	Crate D.	136
Sparks	Delmar C.	136
Sparks	Robert D.	374
Spears	David L	79
Spencer	R. B.	79
Stafford	David R	80
Staggs	L. E.	192
Staires	Harry E.	195
Staires	Troy	195
Stallard	Carlee	78
Stancil	Thomas	80
Stanley	Chester V.	80
Stanley	Nicholas	307
Stanley	James	355
Stanley	Roy Lee	355
Stanley	George E.	355
Stanwick	John	308
Stearns	Asa	136
Stedman	Eli	137
Steele	Loys	196
Steele	John C	216
Steelman	Elmer F.	196
Steere	Cyrus	30
Steere	Martin	234
Stepp	Jessey D.	196
Stepps	James D	80
Stevens	Thomas A.	30
Stevens	Glen W.	336
Stewart	Albert R	196
Stewart	Sam P	274
Stewart	Angus M	308
Stickney	Willard	217
Stiles	Dutton	217
Stiles	S. W.	327
Stone	Anna M.	30
Stone	Hertis	137
Stone	J. B.	196
Stone	James Gilbert	197
Stone	Joseph W.	274
Stonecipher	Luther	192
Stout	Newton	307
Stowers	John W	275
Straight	Freeborn	30
Straight	James	194
Strain, Jr	Thomas	305
Strawn	J. W.	197
Strickland	James	80
Styron, Jr.	Simon H.	81
Summerhill	Loyd	197
Sunday	Edward S.	197
Surratt	John	355
Sutton	J. A.	137
Sutton	Milton L.	310
Swaim	Lawson	273
Swearington	Isaac	310
Sweeney	Virginia D	275
Sweet	Daniel A	233
Sweet	Nathaniel	233
Talbert	Abram	198
Tallman	Ezra	31
Tanner	Brighton N.	138
Tatum	James L.	198
Tatum	John Julian	310
Taylor	William	32
Taylor	Paul	138
Taylor	Obediah J.	311
Taylor	A. B.	374

Surname	Given	Page
Taylor	George A.	374
Teague	William H	275
Teague	Harold R.	311
Teets	Merlin E	138
Terry	Thomas	55
Terry, Jr.	Thomas O.	81
Thacker	James	139
Thomas	Jeff	356
Thompson	John	81
Thompson	Robert B.	140
Thompson	Bailey	198
Thompson	Charles	311
Thompson, Jr	Clyde	140
Thornsbery	Lewis C.	198
Thornton	Abel	234
Tignor	James	199
Tippett	Benjamin	81
Tippett	Elbert W	275
Titus	Samuel	140
Toler	Duffy	81
Totman	Alpheus M	81
Town	George W.	375
Towner	Benjamin	217
Townsend	Thomas J	199
Townsend	Thomas	155
Travis	William	356
Tripp	Herbert	81
Tripp	Clyde W.	375
Trout	Miles Lee	140
Truett	Sam R.	242
Trussell	Wendell	276
Trusty	Alvin	141
Tucker	Joshua	328
Tufts	Francis	144
Tufts	John	144
Tufts	Benjamin	143
Turnage	James	82
Turnage	Ray	276
Turner	Jason B.	243
Tuttle	Larry Lee	199
Tuttle	Ezra	234
Twining	Charles	141

Surname	Given	Page
Twining	F. A.	142
Twining	William	142
Tyler	Amos	376
Tyree	Roy Alex	357
Tyson	A. A.	82
Tyson	Melvin	199
Tyson	Greg	276
Underwood	Dale W	200
Underwood	Dale	200
Upton	Dell	357
Utley	A. B.	82
Utley	Jacob	82
Vail	Charles L.	32
Vallance	Carl W	358
Van Tuyl	William	32
Van Winkle	James L.	201
VanAmburgh	Freeman	32
VanAmringe	Henry H.	217
Vance	Preston	359
Vance	Robert Lee	359
Vance	Ward	359
Vanhoose	Clyde M.	144
Vanover	Clovis	144
Vanover	Roy C.	336
Vanzant	Roy	200
Vaughn	Elbert J.	311
Vause	Jesse	83
Vause	Cornelius	243
Vause	Julius B.	244
Vause	George C.	242
Very	Simmons	375
Vicars	Ralph	336
Viles, Sr	Oma	200
Waddell	R. Eugene	277
Waddle	William	201
Waddle	Carl	201
Waddle	William L.	201
Wade	Charles	234
Wagner	Clarence	277
Wainwright	Chester C.	359
Wait	Alverdo	32
Wakefield	J. J.	376

Surname	Given	Page
Waldron	Orrin	32
Waldron	Luke	235
Waldrop	Elihu W.	312
Walker	Kenneth	145
Walker	Verda	312
Walker	James M	311
Wallace	William	201
Waller	Comfort B	377
Ward	Lonnie E	202
Warner	William	377
Warren	Peter	377
Washburn	Francis	378
Watkins	Francis M.	145
Watkins	Francis	218
Watrus	Hiram	378
Way	Russell	33
Weaver	Ralph Lee	336
Webb	Charles	145
Webb	Eugene	145
Webb	Harrison	146
Webb	George W.	218
Webb	M.	360
Webster	Emmons	378
Weed	Simeon J.	146
Welch	John W.	277
Wellman	Zere	379
Wells	Alonzo	83
Wescher	Jacob	380
West	Robert	83
West	John H.	202
West	William R.	202
West	Pamela S	83
Westlake	John	379
Wetherington	Luke	84
Whaley	Lee	84
Wheeler	John	84
Wheeler	John	146
Wheeler	Charlie C.	313
Wheeler	Lovell	380
Whitader	Richard	314
Whitaker	Harry Paul	336
Whitcher	Hiram	33

Whitcomb	Frank Fay	208		Wing	Amos	35		Zinn	Buford	207
White	Billy Joe	146		Winsor	Joseph	236		Zoellers	Everett E	207
Whiteley	Charles B	313		Winsor II	Samuel	236		TRUE	Virgil	199
Whitfield	William	33		Winters	Caleb	280		TRUE	Orin Haines	375
Whiting	Warren	380		Winton	David	218				
Whitley	Jonas	84		Wireman	Joe M.	148				
Whitman	Eugene Z	314		Wireman	Lesle	148				
Whitmore	Earl Austin	360		Withers	Harry W.	203				
Whittemore	Edwin E.	34		Withers	J. C.	314				
Whittemore	David R	235		Wolfenbarger	Floyd	148				
Whittler	Philander	146		Wolfenbarger	Clayton	280				
Whitworth	Jerry W	278		Wood	Joseph	35				
Widdig	David	147		Wood	Frances M.	204				
Wiggs	Nestus D.	85		Wood	Weldon V.	204				
Wiggs	Phillip	84		Wood	William V	204				
Wight	Philip	34		Wood	Billy Ray	206				
Wilburn	Marion	147		Woodard	Marcellus	86				
Wilcox	John	34		Woodman	Jonathan	328				
Wilcox	John	34		Woodmansee	Ray	35				
Wilder	Alvin	147		Woodruff	Olen	205				
Wiley	Charlie	147		Woodworth	Dyer	35				
Wilkerson	Junis J.	278		Woodworth	Ziba	328				
Wilkins	Noah	34		Woody	T. E.	86				
Willey	Emma R	85		Woody	Wendell K	314				
William	Omer	361		Woolsey	Paul H.	280				
Williams	Allen	147		Woolsey	William B.	281				
Williams	Paul E	147		Wooten	James	86				
Williams	James O.	202		Workman	Andrew	148				
Williams	Clarence	35		Wyatt	Samuel	150				
Williams	Henry	236		Wyatt	Nathaniel	149				
Williams	Thomas A.	244		Wynn	John	150				
Williams	Jack L.	278		Yandell	Isaac W	205				
Williams	Sheila	361		Yandell	Dearthur	205				
Willis	Homer E	279		Yandell	L. D.	206				
Wills	Samuel F	360		Yeley	Bessie N.	150				
Wilson	Joseph	35		Yeley	Gilbert L	150				
Wilson	Zadie Volena	85		Yeley	John Sowers	151				
Wilson	J. Reford	203		Yockan	Strauther	207				
Wilson	Muril	203		Young	William W.	35				
Wilson	Wright	244		Young	Homer Lee	206				
Windham	Daniel A.	85		Young	Waldo	206				
Windsor	Irving	236		Zell	Benjamin F	151				